AF605863

MEDIEVAL EAST CENTRAL AND EASTERN EUROPE

Medieval East Central *and* Eastern Europe

FLORIN CURTA *and*
SÉBASTIEN ROSSIGNOL

UNIVERSITY OF TORONTO PRESS
Toronto Buffalo London

Toronto Buffalo London
utppublishing.com
Printed in Canada

ISBN 978-1-4875-6625-8 (cloth)
ISBN 978-1-4875-6626-5 (paper)
ISBN 978-1-4875-6629-6 (EPUB)
ISBN 978-1-4875-6627-2 (PDF)

Library and Archives Canada Cataloguing in Publication

Title: Medieval East Central and Eastern Europe / Florin Curta and Sébastien Rossignol.
Names: Curta, Florin, author | Rossignol, Sébastien, author
Description: Includes bibliographical references and index.
Identifiers: Canadiana (print) 20250147394 | Canadiana (ebook) 20250147459 | ISBN 9781487566258 (cloth) | ISBN 9781487566265 (paper) | ISBN 9781487566296 (EPUB) | ISBN 9781487566272 (PDF)
Subjects: LCSH: Europe, Eastern – History. | LCSH: Europe, Central – History.
Classification: LCC DJK38 .C87 2025 | DDC 947 – dc23

Cover design: Heng Wee Tan
Cover image: The "White Angel," detail of the scene of the Myrrh-Bearing Women at the tomb of Christ, fresco on the southern wall of the Church of the Savior in the Mileševa Monastery (Serbia)

We welcome comments and suggestions regarding any aspect of our publications – please feel free to contact us at news@utorontopress.com or visit us at utppublishing.com.

Every effort has been made to contact copyright holders; in the event of an error or omission, please notify the publisher.

We wish to acknowledge the land on which the University of Toronto Press operates. This land is the traditional territory of the Wendat, the Anishnaabeg, the Haudenosaunee, the Métis, and the Mississaugas of the Credit First Nation.

University of Toronto Press acknowledges the financial support of the Government of Canada and the Ontario Arts Council, an agency of the Government of Ontario, for its publishing activities.

CONTENTS

Part 4: Early Medieval Peripheries

Part 5: Societies and Cultures in the Early Middle Ages

Part 6: Religion in the Early Middle Ages

Part 7: Literacy and Art in the Early Middle Ages

Part 8: The High Middle Ages

MAPS

PLATES

TABLES

INSERTS

INTRODUCTION

"Paradox" is a word that might come to mind when learning about East Central or Eastern Europe. In the Middle Ages these regions were much closer, in a variety of ways, to the West than either Byzantium or the Caliphate, yet these parts of Europe are now far less present in Anglophone scholarship and university teaching than either one of those two civilizations. Remarkably stable states were organized in East Central and Eastern Europe that played a key role in the medieval history of Europe as a whole. Despite its importance, that part of Europe is perceived as peripheral to the history of the continent, for example as the target of conquest and colonization by West Europeans. In fact, even though Europe is increasingly defined as a meeting point of Christian, Muslim, and Jewish cultures, the coexistence in the eastern parts of the continent of Judaism, Christianity, and Islam – in far more spectacular ways than perhaps anywhere else in the world – is often forgotten. In the age of global history, some argue that no special study of those regions is necessary and that it suffices simply to integrate them into the global history of the Middle Ages. So far, however, that approach has shown its limitations: it distills the specific history of those regions to a simple solution that makes them appear as an appendix to that of Western Europe. The current scholarly interest in East Central and Eastern Europe, outside of the regions themselves, tends to focus on the nineteenth and twentieth centuries, the period of nationalism. Often forgotten is that the symbols and myths of all nationalisms in those regions are of medieval origin or refer in one way or another to the Middle Ages. Misperceptions and stereotypes abound, particularly in the English-speaking world, and they are not just a matter of Cold War legacy. Medieval East Central and Eastern Europe deserve better. Over the last few decades, several historians have indeed recognized the importance of integrating the eastern part of the European continent into surveys of the Middle Ages. Unfortunately, their valuable efforts have been stymied by the lack of accessible overviews and insightful introductions. As a result, despite their good will, few have paid attention to East Central Europe and Eastern Europe, their specific features, problems of chronology, and historiography.

As an idea, "Eastern Europe" is the product of the Enlightenment, a way to prove the superiority of Western Europe over other parts of the continent. The underlying, yet unwarranted assumption is that, lagging behind Western Europe, the eastern lands lacked any history worth studying. That is why for a very long while there was no interest in the history of the region, particularly that of the Middle Ages. In fact, a concern with the history of the eastern half of Europe as a whole (as opposed to that of any given country in the region) appeared only during the first half of the twentieth century. Polish historians were the pioneers in that respect, and the most prominent of them was Oskar Halecki (1891–1973). A refugee in the United States during World War II, he first defined East Central Europe as the part of the European continent which during the Middle Ages was located between the Holy Roman Empire and Kievan Rus'. Excluding Russia was probably a reaction to the political divisions of the early Cold War period. However, those divisions are also responsible for the narrow meaning of "Eastern Europe" – the territories of present-day Belarus, Ukraine, and (European) Russia. Romanian historians pioneered the study of Southeastern Europe, a phrase first introduced in the late nineteenth century to refer to the entire region between the Carpathian Mountains, the Dniester River, and the Aegean, Black, and Adriatic seas. Nicolae Iorga (1871–1940) established in 1913 an institute of Southeast European studies in Bucharest and in 1922 launched the first periodical entirely dedicated to them. After World War II, Eastern Europe regained the meaning it had earlier, defined in opposition to the West, this time because of the political and economic circumstances of the Yalta and Potsdam agreements of 1945. The Cold War did not invent Eastern Europe but solidified its understanding as the "other Europe." Despite the eastward extension of the European Union at the beginning of the twenty-first century, the idea of a West-East division of the continent has not entirely disappeared.

In this book, we use "Eastern Europe," "Northeastern Europe," "Southeastern Europe," and "(East) Central Europe" in a purely geographic sense (that is, to make sense of the vastness and diversity of the area covered), and in no way as political divisions or in opposition to a presumably essentialized Western Europe. From a strictly geographical point of view, the eastern half of Europe is the vast area of the European continent situated between 36 and 70 degrees north latitude (roughly between the Arctic Circle and Greece) and from 12 to 60 degrees east longitude (from the Czech lands to the Ural Mountains). East Central Europe is between 12 and 35 degrees east, while in the narrow sense mentioned above Eastern Europe represents the part between 35 and 60 degrees east. The western part of the area covered in this book could then be subdivided latitudinally at 45 degrees north to distinguish Southeastern Europe located to the south from that parallel. Northeastern Europe refers to the lands of the eastern Baltic, including the modern states of Estonia, Latvia, and Lithuania, and the former country of Prussia. The land mass demarcated in such a manner represents two thirds of the entire European continent and has a remarkably varied geographical frame (see map 0.1).

A basic understanding of geography is essential for a consideration of the medieval history of East Central and Eastern Europe. The most important feature of the western part of that area (East Central and Southeastern Europe) is the most complicated system of mountain ranges of Europe. In that system, the Carpathians form a loop on the eastern side of the river Danube, sweeping in a southeast direction towards that river's delta. The lands inside the semicircle of the mountains form the Carpathian Basin, divided into three unequal parts by the rivers Danube and Tisza flowing on a north-south direction. Transylvania is the eastern part of the Carpathian Basin. To the south from the Carpathian Basin, no less than four chains of mountains run radially from the center of the Balkan Peninsula – the Dinaric Alps to the northwest (towards the Carpathian Basin), the Pindus to the south, the Rhodope to the southeast, and the Balkans (Stara Planina) to the east. The latter are separated from the Southern Carpathians (also known as Transylvanian Alps) by the fertile plain of the Lower Danube. Two lower ranges of mountains run in a northwestern direction from the westernmost end of the Carpathians – the Bohemian Forest and the Sudeten, with the Moravian Heights between them. Between those mountains and the Carpathians to the south, as well as the Baltic Sea to the north, East Central Europe

Map 0.1. Principal geographic features mentioned in the book: 1 – Apuseni Mountains; 2 – Black Sea; 3 – Bohemian Forest; 4 – Carpathian Mountains; 5 – Central Russian Uplands; 6 – Danube River; 7 – Dinaric Alps; 8 – Dnieper River; 9 – Don River; 10 – Mezen River; 11 – Moravian Heights; 12 – Niemen (Nemunas) River; 13 – Northern Dvina River; 14 – Northern European Plain; 15 – Pechora River; 16 – Pindus Mountains; 17 – Plain of Hungary (Alföld); 18 – Rhodope Mountains; 19 – Stara Planina Mountains; 20 – Sudeten Mountains; 21 – Tisza River; 22 – Ural Mountains; 23 – Ural River; 24 – Valdai Hills; 25 – Vistula River; 26 – Volga River; 27 – Volga Heights; 28 – Western Dvina (Daugava) River. Additional features: A – Alps; Az – Sea of Azov; B – Baltic Sea; Ba – Barents Sea; C – Caucasus Mountains; Ca – Caspian Sea; W – White Sea.

consists of a vast lowland corridor – the North European Plain, which extends eastwards all the way to the Ural Mountains. Another lowland corridor extends on a west-east direction from the Danube to the Aral Sea, and beyond. Those were the steppe lands of Eastern Europe, located to the north of the Black and Caspian seas and divided by several major rivers, the most important of which, from west to east, are the Dnieper, the Don, the Volga, and the Ural. Some parts of that region (the so-called Caspian Depression) are below sea level, with marshlands and patches of semi-arid desert. The Central Russian Uplands and the Volga Heights are the only elevations of Eastern Europe between the North European Plain and the steppe lands to the south. Because of them, several rivers flow through the North European Plain and into the neighboring seas. The most important are the Vistula, the Niemen (Nemunas), the Daugava or Western Dvina (emptying into the Baltic Sea), the Northern Dvina, the Mezen (emptying into the White Sea), and the Pechora (emptying into the Barents Sea).

The arrangement of the geographic features described above is rarely employed in historical works. Both historians and archaeologists prefer to use biogeographical, band-like units: the steppe belt (the westernmost segment of the Great Steppe of Eurasia) is between

200 and 600 miles (322 to 966 kilometers) wide; the forest-steppe belt immediately to the north; and the forest belt, a very broad, wooded band extending to the north all the way to Finland and the White Sea, into the taiga. There are only a few lines of communication between those three belts, the most important of which is the Volga, the longest river of Europe that springs in the Valdai Hills, on the northern edge of the Central Russian Uplands, and flows into the Caspian Sea through a very large delta (which was much smaller in the Middle Ages than it is now). Because the Dnieper and the Daugava also rise from the northern sector of the central Russian Uplands, the three rivers played a major role as axes of communication, trade, and political centralization in the Middle Ages.

Much of what is known about the history of East Central and Eastern Europe (broadly defined) during the Early Middle Ages (understood here as the period from ca. 500 to ca. 1000 CE) comes from sources written outside the region, and only later by authors from the region. The information derives from Byzantine chronicles, those written in the Holy Roman Empire, in Armenia, and in Georgia, from Carolingian annals and Icelandic sagas, as well as works of geography written in Arabic. Besides narrative sources, a great deal of information may be gleaned from law codes, charters, acts of church councils, inscriptions, and letters written inside and outside the region at various moments during the Middle Ages. For the earliest segment of the medieval history of East Central and Eastern Europe, the only "native" sources are archaeological. Archaeology plays a key role for the later periods as well, along with art history.

The earliest narrative sources appeared in the twelfth century, the first being the *Primary Chronicle* of Rus' (also known as *Tale of Bygone Years*, previously – albeit erroneously – as *Chronicle of Nestor*), compiled by several authors, the last of whom finished writing in ca. 1113. The *Deeds of the Princes of the Poles* was written by an anonymous author (known as Gallus Anonymus) at the Cracow court of Bolesław III Wrymouth (1102–38). Cosmas of Prague finished his *Chronicle of the Czechs* shortly before his death in 1125. The earliest surviving historical writing in Hungary is the *Deeds of the Hungarians*, written around 1200 by a former member of King Béla III's chancery.

Of considerable importance for the economic history of the eastern half of Europe are coins – Roman, Byzantine, Islamic, and Western – that have been found in abundance in the region. The earliest "native" coins were struck in Bohemia for Duke Boleslav I in the 960s, followed by those struck for Vladimir of Kiev in the late tenth century, as well as those minted in Hungary and Poland for King Stephen I (997–1038) and for Duke Bolesław Chrobry (992–1025), respectively. Coins are important also for the images and the titles of rulers, offering unique glimpses into various modes of power representation. Similar to the coins are the lead seals. Because they bear the names and sometimes the rank and office of their owners, seals are extremely valuable for the reconstruction of the administrative structures of the state or the church. Seals of wax were employed for charters in Bohemia, Poland, and Hungary during the High and Late Middle Ages (understood here as the periods of the eleventh to thirteenth and of the fourteenth and fifteenth centuries, respectively).

There is no dearth of source material for studying the Middle Ages in East Central and Eastern Europe. While making extensive use of a great variety of sources, this book seeks to understand the history of that part of Europe in its own right, looking at societies that were remarkably similar to those in Western Europe, but also strikingly different. The goal of this book is not to create a dichotomy between East and West. On the contrary, this is an introduction to the incredible diversity of the historical developments in regions of Europe that deserve more attention.

PART 1

From Late Antiquity to the Early Middle Ages

1

THE BALKANS AND THE CRIMEA: ROMANS IN EASTERN EUROPE

***Keywords in this chapter*:** Late Roman Empire, forts, trade, cities

The Roman perspective on Eastern Europe was essentially peninsular. The Istrian Peninsula as well as the central and southern parts of the Balkan Peninsula were conquered in the second century BCE, with the other parts becoming provinces of the Roman Empire by the late first century CE. While garrisons were established in the main cities during the second century CE, a provincial administration in the Crimean Peninsula did not appear until 500 CE. The Roman provinces in the Balkan Peninsula were grouped into three prefectures, with the northwest included in Italia, the center in Illyricum, and the eastern parts in Oriens (see map 1.1). It is along the boundary between Italia and Illyricum that the administration split in 395 between the West Roman and the East Roman Empire.

The Roman presence in Southeastern Europe and the Black Sea region was well established and recognizable by 500 in the fabric of the cities, in institutions, and especially in the presence of the army. The layout of such cities as Dyrrachion (now Durrës, in Albania), Thessalonica (now Thessaloniki, in Greece), or Chersonesus (near Sevastopol, in the Crimea) remained intact and, in some cases, survived well into the Middle Ages, for those cities were never abandoned. In many other cases, particularly in the northern and central parts of the Balkan Peninsula, cities contracted or regrouped around fortified enclosures, sometimes located on the highest elevation possible. Instead of civilian, public buildings, the skyline of those cities was now dominated by churches, some of them quite large. Even in cities such as Iustiniana Prima (most likely Caričin Grad, in central Serbia) or Zikideva (Veliko Tărnovo, in Bulgaria), which were new, sixth-century foundations, the most important buildings were large, episcopal churches. In Chersonesus, a city which witnessed a building boom, no less than ten churches came into existence in the sixth and early seventh centuries.

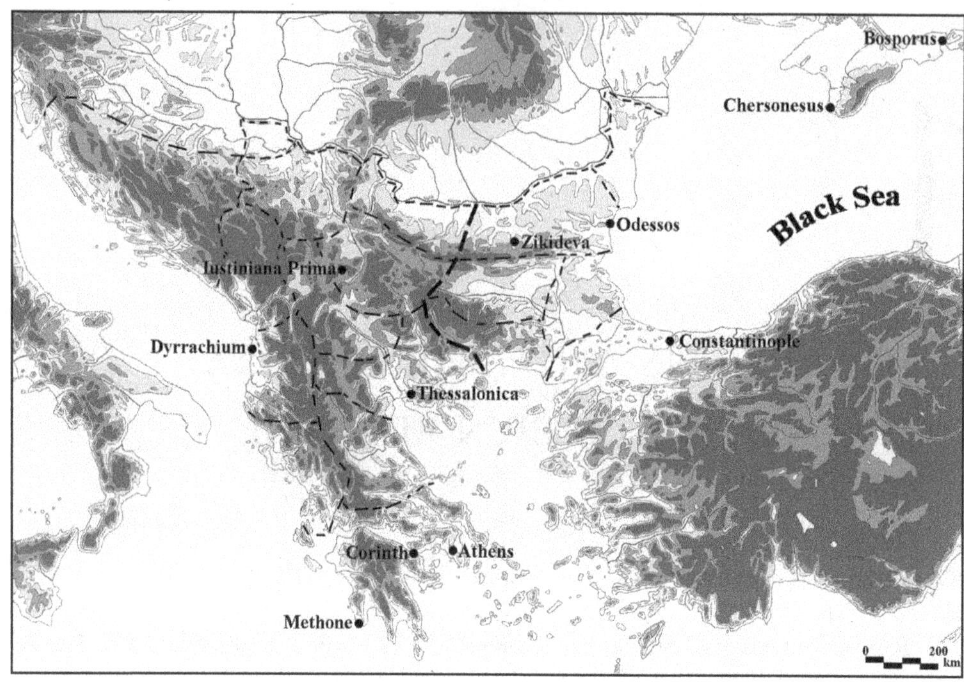

Map 1.1. The Roman world in the Balkan Peninsula and in the Crimea, ca. 500. The thick line shows diocesan boundaries (Thrace to the east, and Moesia to the west), while thin lines are provincial boundaries. The thick line also marks the boundary between the prefectures of Illyricum and Oriens, with the westernmost province shown on the map belonging to the prefecture of Italia.

Urban settlements in the sixth-century Balkans were heavily fortified with massive walls, horseshoe-shaped towers, and double enclosures. According to Procopius of Caesarea, who wrote his *Buildings* in the mid-sixth century to celebrate the building achievements of Emperor Justinian (527–65), there were more than 600 forts in the Balkans, eight times more than in the entire Asian part of the Empire. Inscriptions from Greece and Albania reveal that Justinian's architect Victorinus was responsible for the implementation of this grandiose program of fortification. The project, or at least its most important part, was probably completed in some twenty years between the early 530s and the early 550s. Most forts had at least one church, which was sometimes built against the walls or blocked the main entrance into the fort. Forts in the central region of the peninsula were quite large and were occupied permanently. Along the river Danube and in the immediate hinterland, relatively smaller forts were built. Erecting so many forts was clearly a response to the constant threat that the Balkan provinces of the Empire faced in the sixth century from the lands across the Danube: first the Antes in 518 and 533–45; the Bulgars in 519, 529–30, 535, and 539; then the "Huns" (a generic name early Byzantine sources employed for steppe nomads) in 528, 539, 544, and 550–52; followed by the Sclavenes in 545, 548, 549, and 550–51. The strategic response to the many raids of all those groups was to put the entire population in the Balkans behind the walls of fortified settlements, sieges of which were both time-consuming and beyond the military capabilities of most marauders. In addition, the armies that the empire deployed against the attackers began to adopt similar tactics, relying more on cavalry troops for increased mobility. However, such measures were predicated upon the idea that the provinces, in which the population withdrew behind fortifications, could not support themselves and had no economic basis for the maintenance of the many troops coming to their rescue. Consequently, a new administrative unit was introduced in 536, called *quaestura exercitus*, which combined rich, overseas provinces (islands in the Aegean Sea, western Anatolia, and Cyprus) with the northernmost provinces in the Balkan Peninsula (Moesia inferior and Scythia minor), all ruled from Odessos (present-day Varna, in Bulgaria) by a prefect. The rationale behind this administrative change was to secure the efficient defense of the Danube frontier both militarily and financially. The main responsibility of the prefect was to distribute taxes collected overseas to the troops stationed in the two Balkan provinces, either in cash (to pay the soldiers) or, more often, in kind (primarily food). This new arrangement was thus meant to alleviate a conspicuous problem of the sixth-century Balkan provinces of the Empire – the absence of any large-scale cultivation of crops necessary to feed the local population.

The archaeological (finds of agricultural tools), paleobotanical (seeds of plants, particularly cereals), and zooarchaeological (bones of domestic animals) evidence shows clearly that neither large estates nor smallholdings were in existence in the central and northern Balkans at that time. In the absence of any archaeological evidence of open settlements (non-fortified villages) with exclusively agricultural functions, how was food procured for the population of cities and forts? At least the soldiers in the Roman troops stationed in the northern Balkans had to rely on the state-run distribution of food through the *quaestura exercitus*, as well as food supplies captured from the enemy (the Sclavenes living north of the Danube) and hunting. Even the urban population relied on local resources, especially cattle, sheep, and goats for meat and dairy products, as well as on small-scale cultivation of crops on plots inside or outside city walls.

Nonetheless, there is also evidence of prosperity in Greece, on the northern and eastern Adriatic coast, as well as in the Crimea. Istria was the corn basket of the Ostrogothic kingdom in Italy, while the agricultural surplus of Greece was exported elsewhere in the empire. In 533, when moving against the Ostrogoths in Italy, in order to prevent heavy losses among his troops inflicted by food poisoning from the rotten bread they had taken with them from Constantinople, the general Belisarius ordered the sequester of all the bread available in southwestern Greece around the city of Methone. In 575, Emperor Tiberius II exempted the cities of Chersonesus and Bosporus (now Kerch, in eastern Crimea) from deliveries of food supplies to the fleet. Unlike the Balkans, there is clear archaeological evidence of rural, open settlements in the Crimea, as well as of agricultural production.

The primary source of prosperity in the Crimea, however, was not agriculture, but the fishing industry, which relied on the biannual migration of large shoals of anchovies to the northern coasts of the Black Sea and the Sea of Azov, where the rivers Dnieper and Don brought fresh water to the sea. The main products of that industry were salted fish and fish sauce (*garum*), both produced in very large quantities, as illustrated by the discovery of fish-salting vats. This production was geared towards trade and sent primarily to

Constantinople, where the demand must have been very high. In 655, in one of his letters sent from exile, Pope Martin I (649–55) mentioned salt in the context of ships from Constantinople coming into the harbor of Chersonesus with cargoes of grain. The ships that carried the grain to Crimea most likely returned with cargoes of salt, salted fish, and *garum*. The importance of trade is illustrated also by the fact that throughout the sixth century, as well as later, Chersonesus had a currency of its own, which was most likely meant to meet the demands of the market economy in the city. Similarly, the mint in Thessalonica struck coins in a local system of denominations, mostly for low-value transactions on the local markets. This system vanished rapidly after 562, when the imperial government gave the mint in Thessalonica the task of supplying the eastern provinces with one specific denomination, which was accepted and used on most markets across the empire.

By contrast, with no large-scale cultivation of crops, marketplaces, or a diversified monetary mass, the world of the northern Balkans was one of strongholds maintained and supported by the state. With no peasants in the neighboring villages, the soldiers with their wives and children who lived in forts had to make do with the public dole. That is why after ca. 620, when most troops were withdrawn from the Balkans to face the Persian threat on the eastern front, the Roman world in the northern and central Balkans ceased to exist. The withdrawal of the army coincides in time with the definite cessation of the distribution of grain supplies from Egypt and other rich provinces overseas, which were now occupied by the Persians. Without the state-run distribution of food supplies, there was no reason or incentive for any Roman presence to remain in the region. The Arab conquest of Syria (637) and subsequent developments prevented the return of the troops to the Balkans. The Roman world in Eastern Europe was now restricted to the coastal areas around Thessalonica, Corinth, and Athens, in addition to Istria, the eastern coast of the Adriatic Sea, and the western coast of the Black Sea (see map 1.2). The interior of the Balkan Peninsula experienced a demographic collapse. There are no archaeological sites in the central part of the Balkans that could be dated to the seventh century. However, a number of cemeteries in northern Albania signal the existence and continuity of a population that was both Christian and sufficiently prosperous to build new churches in such mountain towns as Komani or Lezhë (see plate 1.1). Those communities had few, if any, commercial ties with the eastern Mediterranean, or even with the Adriatic region. Coin finds in the seventh century are restricted to Dobrudja (the area between the Black Sea and the Lower Danube, now in Romania), as well as a few cities in Greece (Thessalonica, Corinth, and Athens).

However, the seventh century did not coincide with any decline in the trade activity in the Crimea. During that century, Sogdian merchants from Central Asia established Sogdaia (now Sudak) on the southeastern coast of the peninsula, while Phanagoria (on the eastern shore of Taman Bay) began to grow into a major trade center opened to the world of the steppe to the north. The lucrative commerce taking place in the city of Chersonesus attracted the attention of the imperial government, as indicated by finds of seals belonging to officials in charge of taxing the trade (*kommerkiarioi*). During the seventh century, the northern coast of the Black Sea played a key role in provisioning Constantinople and its

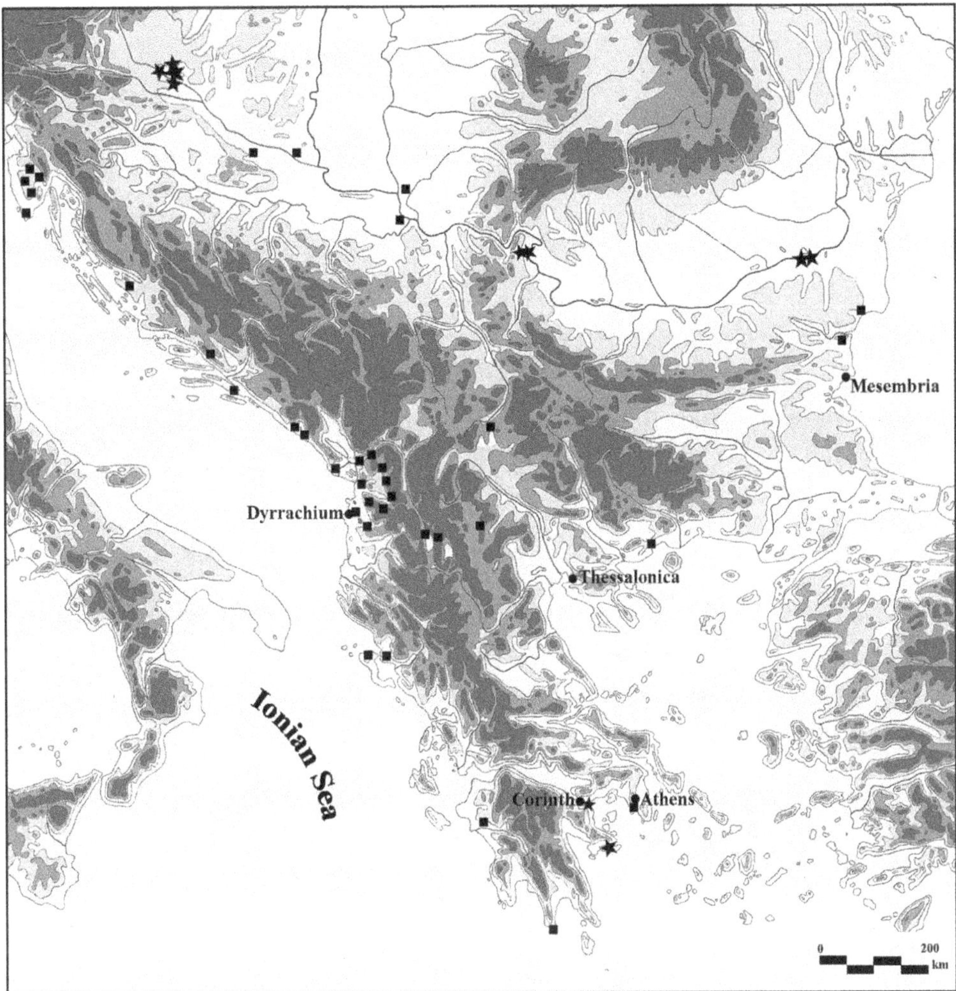

Map 1.2. The Balkans in the seventh century, with the Adriatic Sea to the west and the Black Sea to the east. The map shows cities that were still inhabited, settlements (stars), and cemeteries or isolated graves (square) that have been dated to the seventh century. The cluster of cemeteries in the upper left corner of the map is in Istria, the peninsula on the northern coast of the Adriatic Sea.

hinterland with grain. After the fall of Egypt, first to the Persians (in 618), then to the Arabs (in 642), Crimea became one of the key granaries of the empire.

FURTHER READING

Bowden, William. *Epirus Vetus: The Archaeology of a Late Antique Province*. London: Duckworth, 2003.

Gândilă, Andrei. *Cultural Encounters on Byzantium's Northern Frontier, c. AD 500–700: Coins, Artifacts and History*. Cambridge: Cambridge University Press, 2018.

Plate 1.1. The fortified town of Lezhë (Albania). Wikimedia Commons, the free media repository.

Karaiskaj, Gjerak. *The Fortifications of Butrint*. London: Butrint Foundation, 2009.

Nasrallah, Laura, Charalambos Bakirtzis, and Steven J. Friesen, eds. *From Roman to Early Christian Thessalonikē: Studies in Religion and Archaeology*. Cambridge, MA: Harvard University Press, 2010.

Poulter, Andrew G., ed. *The Transition to Late Antiquity on the Danube and Beyond*. Proceedings of the British Academy 141. Oxford: Oxford University Press, 2007.

Sarantis, Alexander. *Justinian's Balkan Wars: Campaigning, Diplomacy and Development in Illyricum, Thrace, and the Northern World AD 527–65*. Prenton: Francis Cairns, 2016.

Terry, Ann Bennett, and Henry Maguire. *Dynamic Splendor: The Wall Mosaics in the Cathedral of Euphrasius in Poreč*. University Park: Pennsylvania State University Press, 2007.

Vagalinski, Liudmil, Nikolai Sharankov, and Sergei Torbatov, eds. *The Lower Danube Roman Limes (1st–6th c. AD)*. Sofia: National Archaeological Institute and Museum, 2012.

2

SLAVS AND AVARS: MIGRATIONS AND RAIDS

Keywords in this chapter: Slavs, agriculture, Avars, horsemen

The large number of forts and military sites in the Balkan Peninsula is a reminder that surprise attacks were a great concern of sixth-century imperial politics in that region. There is hardly any year within the first half of that century without a mention of raids by people whom the early Byzantine authors, writing as they did in the tradition of classical historiography, regarded as barbarians, without much concern for accurate or objective ethnographic description.[1] During the first decades of the century, most raids are attributed to the "Huns," a generic term used for nomadic horsemen. Before 540, most raids targeted the eastern provinces in the Balkans, especially Thrace and Moesia inferior, an indication that they must have originated in the steppe lands north of the Black Sea. Marauding expeditions were the work of one or several chieftains working together, such as those intercepted, defeated, and killed in 539 after devastating Scythia minor and Moesia inferior. It is the frightful havoc among the inhabitants of the Balkan provinces caused by that particular raid that prompted Justinian to accelerate his project of fortifying the Balkans and the Danube frontier on a scale without any precedent (see chapter 1).

Elsewhere, the emperor chose a different strategy. Ever since the Gepids – a group that had been little known until then – occupied Sirmium (now Sremska Mitrovica in northern Serbia) during the Gothic war in Italy, they had become the second most important problem in the northern Balkans after the "Huns," with whom they formed an alliance in 535 to raid Moesia. The Gepids were led by petty kings who ruled over most of the eastern part of the Carpathian Basin in what are now eastern Hungary, northern Serbia, and western Romania. Despite their raiding deep into the Balkans, the Gepids were theoretically clients of the Roman emperor, from whom they received annual subsidies. At the beginning of

1 Florin Curta, ed., "Procopius on the Slavs," in *Medieval Eastern Europe, 500–1300: A Reader* (Toronto: University of Toronto Press, 2024), 3–4.

INSERT 2.1. SCLAVENE, SLAV, SLAVIC – A HISTORY OF WORDS

The English word "Slavs" derives from the Latin word *Sclavi*, itself derived from the Greek word *Sklavoi*. However, the latter is only the "abbreviated" form of the name *Sklavenoi*, which appears in the earliest sources dated immediately after the middle of the sixth century. The "long" form of the name is the Greek version of a word that in Slavic must have been *Slovene*. If so, then the consonant *k/c* that appears in the Greek and Latin names is an addition made by speakers of the two languages (Greek and Latin), who could not properly pronounce *sl-* at the beginning of the word.

What did the name *Slovene* mean? Some believe that the name derives from *slovo*, "word." The *Sclavenes* were therefore "speakers of the same language," as opposed to *Nemtsy*, which is what speakers of Slavic called Germans in the Middle Ages (*Nemtsy* derives from the Slavic word for "dumb"). Others maintain that the name *Slovene* derives from *slava*, "glory." The Slavs were therefore brave, glory-seeking warriors. None of those theories can be accepted, the former because *Nemtsy* is recorded in much later sources, and the latter because of sound differences. Moreover, the ending *-ene* in the name *Slovene* appears in tribal names such as *Moravane*, *Timochane*, and *Stodorane*, which derive from place names (in the first two cases, the names of the rivers Morava and Timok). If so, the Sclavenes were people living in a particular place, although it is not at all clear what or where Slova may have been.

his reign, Justinian renewed the alliance with the Gepids, but when they refused to leave Sirmium, the emperor attacked them in 538, without much success. Justinian then turned to another group, the Lombards, to whom he now paid the subsidies previously reserved for the Gepids. The emperor used the Lombards against the Gepids, who were defeated by an allied Lombard-Roman force in 547 and, again, in 551 or 552 by the Lombards alone.

Meanwhile, the main problem of imperial policy on the Danube frontier was that created by yet another group, the Sclavenes (see insert 2.1). Relying primarily on the linguistic evidence of the (modern) Slavic languages, historians of an earlier generation believed that the homeland of the Slavs (whom they equated to the Sclavenes mentioned in the sources) was in the swampy area of the river Pripet, near the present-day Ukrainian-Belarusian border. From there, they presumably migrated to the Danube region, where Procopius located them, because of the harsh climatic conditions of the north. From their homeland, the Slavs were believed to have migrated not only to the Balkan Peninsula but also to the west, into Poland and Germany, as well as to the northeast, into Russia. Since no sixth-century source mentions any migration of the Slavs, historians have turned to archaeological sources, particularly to pottery, to track the Slavic ethnicity and migration. However, the Slavic "homeland," at least for the sixth-century authors who wrote about the Slavs, was north of the Lower Danube, not in the Belarusian-Ukrainian borderlands. To be sure, the raids of the Sclavenes in the 540s and 550s, some reaching as far south as Thessalonica and Dyrrachion, were particularly devastating. However, after each one of them, the Slavic marauders returned "home," which is specifically said to be located just north of the river Danube.

Many of the approximately one hundred settlement sites excavated in Romania, Moldova, and Ukraine and dated to the sixth and seventh centuries are located on the lowest river terraces, often on rich soils good for agriculture. Each one of them is no larger than about five acres (about two hectares), with between ten and fifteen houses per habitation phase. This suggests that none of those settlements was occupied for a period of time longer than a couple of generations. Each one of them was abandoned when new settlements were established nearby. The cause of this settlement shift was an itinerant form of agriculture, in which arable lands were left to lie fallow for a varying number of years, sometimes for a period sufficient for old fields to turn back to waste land. There is abundant archaeological evidence of tools and implements – plowshares, sickles, scythes, and bill-knives. The small size of the plowshares suggests that the tilled fields were relatively small, and perhaps located next to settlements (see plate 2.1). The importance of agriculture in this society is reflected in a comment by the author of the *Strategikon* (a military treatise written ca. 600), who knew that the Sclavenes possessed an abundance of all sorts of livestock and produce, "especially common millet and Italian millet."

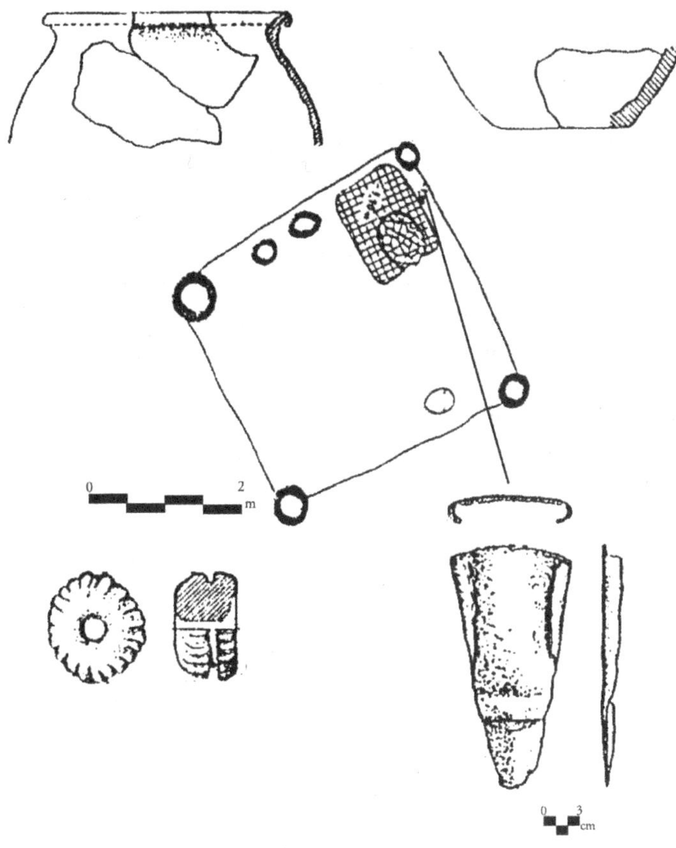

Plate 2.1. Gropşani (Romania), house 17, plan with associated artifacts (wheel-made pottery, spindle whorl, and plowshare). Drawing by Florin Curta.

Houses in settlements discovered in the lands where the sources locate the Slavs were typically buildings with floors sunken (dug) into the ground for insulation. None of them is larger than necessary to accommodate about five individuals, the minimal family. Much of what has been found inside each house was by the oven, either of stone or of clay, built in one of the corners. By far the most common category of artifacts found on those settlement sites is pottery, both hand- and wheel-made, often fired within one and the same kiln. Sometimes, ceramic assemblages included fragments of clay pans used for baking flat loaves of bread. Metal artifacts typically include knives, flint steels, buckles, sixth-century coins, and fibulae (dress pins). The latter were certainly of local production, as demonstrated by finds of molds for casting, which often took place within one and the same house. However, there is also evidence of ironworking, primarily in the form of smelting furnaces made of stone, sand, and clay. Although found within the same settlements as other, regular sunken-floored houses, those furnaces were located in separate quarters. They were most likely operated by craftspeople who must have been a group of specialists under the protection and working upon the commission of the leaders of local communities.

While no names of chiefs or even warlords are known from Procopius of Caesarea, the Slavic raids of the 570s and 580s involved large numbers of warriors, often under the

INSERT 2.2. KHAGAN AND KHAN – POWER IN THE WORLD OF THE NOMADS

According to Theophylact Simocatta, the Avars designated their leaders "with the appellation of khagan."[2] The word (sometimes spelled *qagan*) is of Turkic origin, but of uncertain meaning. In the eastern half of Europe, it first appears with the Avars. The khagan was more than a chieftain, for his power was imperial in nature. He ruled more over people than over territory. A commander in war, first and foremost, he was also in direct connection to the divine. The latter attribute is clearly attested for the Khazars, who believed in the sacred person of the khagan. The title was so strongly tied to supreme leadership in the case of the Avars that, to outsiders, it became a personal name. The title of khan may have been used by at least some Bulgar rulers. One of them, Omurtag, called himself *kana sybigi* in inscriptions written in Greek. Unlike the khagan of the Avars, he was very concerned with territory and the boundaries of his authority, not just with ruling over people. The Cumans also had khans, but their power was very different from that of the Bulgars. In the Cuman world, a khan was the chief of a tribal union, but there was no paramount khan ruling over all tribal unions. That position came into being only with the Mongols, most prominently with Genghis Khan, whose power was indeed more imperial than that of all the khagans of earlier times.

leadership of chiefs known by name. For example, a certain Ardagastus led a raid in 585 that reached the outskirts of Constantinople. Seven years later, he was targeted for elimination, during the campaign that Emperor Maurice (585–602) launched into the Sclavene territories north of the Danube frontier, in an attempt to put a stop to the devastations of the Sclavene warriors in the Balkans. The accumulation of wealth must have already been advanced by that time, because in 578 the leader (khagan) of the Avars demanded tribute from the lands north of the Lower Danube (see insert 2.2). He knew that the Slavs were quite wealthy, for they had successfully raided the Roman Empire without themselves having been raided by anyone.

The Avars played a key role in early Slavic history. In 582, the Avars conquered Sirmium after a long, drawn-out siege. To keep the Roman armies busy elsewhere, they had encouraged the Sclavenes to invade Thrace and Thessaly in 581. Slavic warriors also operated on the western border of the territory under Avar control. In 610, Istria, which was still under Byzantine rule, was raided by both Slavs and Avars. According to Theophylact Simocatta, who wrote during the reign of Emperor Heraclius (610–41), the name of the Avars was a misnomer. They were not true but rather "Pseudo-Avars," a group of fugitive "Scythians," who had taken over the awe-inspiring name in replacement of their original names, Var and Chunni.[3] The European Avars are believed to be remnants of the Juan-Juan

2 Curta, ed., "Theophylact Simocatta on the Origin of the Avars," in *Medieval Eastern Europe*, 5.

3 Curta, ed., "Origin of the Avars," in *Medieval Eastern Europe*, 5.

(Rouran) mentioned in Chinese annals. While there is no way to verify that assumption, the DNA analysis of skeletal remains from seventh-century cemeteries in Hungary has indeed confirmed that at least some members of the Avar elite came from Inner Asia. New burial customs and artifact types (the most important of which are stirrups), for which there is no analogy anywhere in Europe, have been associated with the immigration of the Avars. When the Avars moved to the Carpathian Basin, after defeating the Gepids together with their Lombard allies, they were a larger and more diversified population, as many other groups in the steppe lands had decided to join them. After their defeat, many Gepids continued to live under Avar rule, as did groups of Late Antique population in Pannonia (western Hungary), who maintained relations with and imitated fashions of the Merovingian Franks. There were also many Bulgars and Slavs in the Carpathian Basin now ruled by the Avars. In addition, the Avars exercised some degree of control over the Slavs who lived outside the territory under their direct rule, although not always successfully.[4]

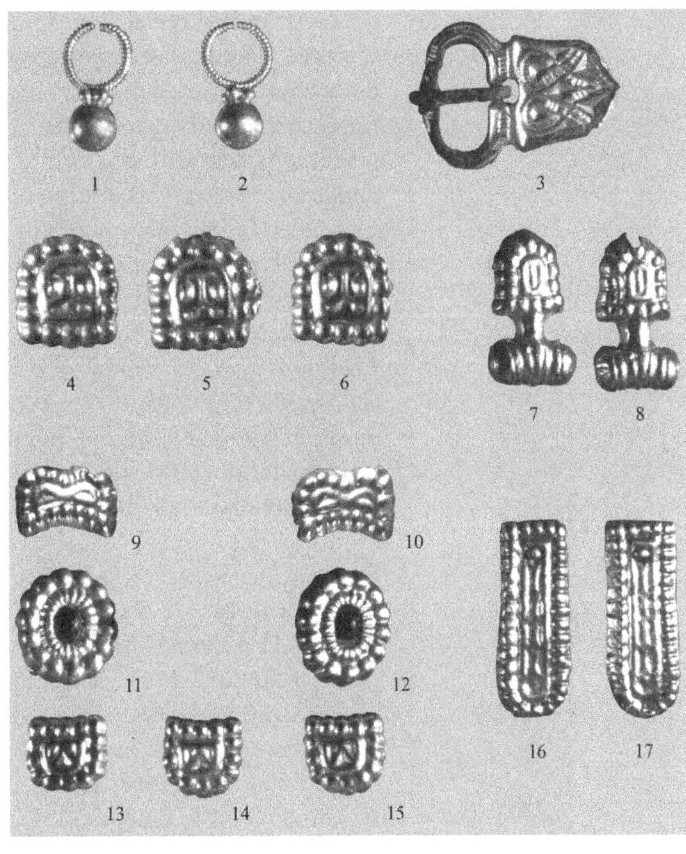

Plate 2.2. Gold earrings and belt fittings from the Avar age, male grave in Petőfiszállás (Hungary). Photo by Béla Kiss.

Under their khagan named Bayan, the Avars constantly raided the Balkan provinces of the empire, as far as Constantinople and Greece. They managed to capture some of the key fortifications in the Roman system of defense and extorted enormous amounts of imperial gold nominally paid as stipends. Through a combination of deceit and threats they obtained an ever-higher rate of annual stipends, which grew from almost 900 to over 1,600 pounds of pure gold. Gold coins were most likely melted down to provide raw material for gold dress accessories, which were found in great quantities in early Avar graves (see plate 2.2). Avar society was highly stratified, as indicated by written sources referring to *archontes* ("leaders") and *logades* ("captains"). In the early seventh century, small family groups occupied the valleys of some of the tributaries of the Tisza or the Danube and moved also in the vicinity of Lake Balaton. They made extensive use of natural resources for their predominantly pastoral economy. Villages inside the Avar territory are mentioned in the written sources, and some have been explored archaeologically. The standard house in each one of them is the sunken-floored building with a stone oven in the corner. The inhabitants of those settlements cultivated crops – common wheat, barley, and proso millet. There is evidence of

4 Curta, ed., "Avars and Slavs," in *Medieval Eastern Europe*, 6–8.

large settlements specializing in iron smelting and weaving dated to the seventh and eighth centuries. Craftsmen enjoyed great social prestige in Avar society, which may explain the occasional deposition of weapons, helmets, and even horses in their graves, which in that respect are directly comparable to those of the elite. In imitation of the early Byzantine practice, the belt with multiple straps decorated with metal plates was a symbol of social rank. Social status was displayed through the jewelry with which Avars were buried; the especially rich grave goods of young women might express the high status that was attributed to women at the age of marriage.

During the 580s and early 590s, as the imperial armies were busy on the eastern frontier against the Persians, the troops remaining in the Balkans were no match for the Avars. Their heavy cavalry was made up of warriors clad in armor and trained to employ the bow and arrows, the sword, and the lance. That versatility was greatly enhanced using stirrups. Sirmium fell in 582, while Singidunum (now Belgrade, in Serbia) was twice conquered and plundered. In 585, the Avars sacked a great number of forts along the Danube frontier, from Bononia (Vidin, in northwestern Bulgaria) to Tropaeum Traiani (Adamclisi, in southeastern Romania). The war continued the next year, when the Avars inflicted several demoralizing defeats on the imperial armies. An army said to have been 100,000 Sclavenes and other barbarians obeying the command of the khagan appeared suddenly under the walls of Thessalonica on September 22, 586. The city withstood the attack, but in 592 the Avars invaded the Black Sea coastal region and in just a few days reached the outskirts of Constantinople. Beginning with the mid-590s, therefore, Emperor Maurice turned against the Avars. Roman troops crossed the Danube and defeated a much superior force in a series of encounters, killing almost the entire Avar army and the khagan's four sons at its head. By 602, the success of the Roman army had begun to take its toll on the prestige of the Avar ruler and the stability of the regime. However, the events leading to the beginning of Emperor Heraclius's reign, especially his withdrawal of the Balkan troops, ca. 620, allowed the Avars a comeback and a wider range of control in the Balkans. In 623, they ambushed the emperor himself in the vicinity of Constantinople and got hold of the imperial treasury. To appease the enemy, Heraclius agreed to pay the Avars 200,000 gold coins annually and gave his own son as hostage. Nonetheless, in 626, the Avars put Constantinople under siege. They were not able to establish effective cooperation with the Persian army on the other side of the Straits, and the seaborne attack of the Slavs under Avar command was repelled by the superior force of the Byzantine fleet. The military failure quickly turned into disaster. Conflicts between the Slavs and the Avars seem to have followed the siege, and the subsequent decades witnessed some of the worst political and, possibly, social convulsions in the history of the Avars. The civil war broke out in 631 or 632, opposing the Avars to the Bulgar "party." Meanwhile, the Wends – according to a Frankish chronicler, sons of Slavic mothers and Avar fathers – rose in rebellion against the Avars and elected a certain Samo as their king. He is said to have ruled over the independent Wends for thirty-five years (see chapter 6).[5]

5 Curta, ed., "Slavs, Avars and Franks," in *Medieval Eastern Europe*, 8–11.

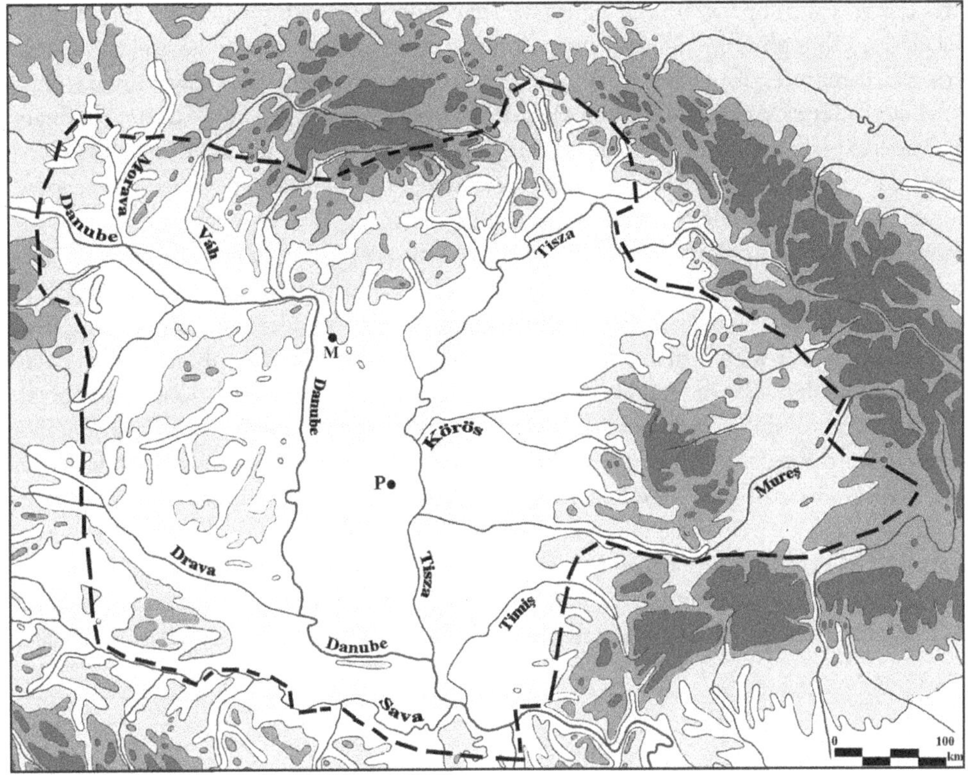

Map 2.1. The approximate extent of Avar power in the Carpathian Basin during the eighth century. The map shows the Carpathian Mountains forming a semicircle, and the Apuseni Mountains in its middle (west of the Mureş River). The location of two archaeological sites mentioned in the text is indicated – Maglód (M) and Petőfiszállás (P). The region of Vienna is in the upper left corner of the map, next to the confluence of the Danube and the Morava.

No names of khagans are known for the next 150 years of Avar history, but despite the turmoil of the civil war, the political center was still located between the Middle Danube and the Middle Tisza in what is now central Hungary. That is where the richest graves of the Avar age have been found. During the remaining part of the seventh century, several military innovations became apparent, especially the adoption of single-edged sabers. The military posturing so visible in burial assemblages is probably a reflection of Avar belligerence, which is responsible for the expansion of the area controlled by the Avars into southern Slovakia and the region of Austria around present-day Vienna (see map 2.1). After 700, very few written sources mention the Avars. Archaeology is therefore the only major source of information for the last century of Avar history. Between ca. 680 and ca. 820, major cultural changes are visible in material culture, one of the most important being the adoption of cast belt sets, which were available in greater numbers and variety than before. If elites are visible in the archaeological record, it is not because of an abundance of goods made of precious metals, as was the case earlier. Most open settlements have large cemeteries nearby, a clear indication of a growing population. The hallmark of the long-term occupation of such sites is the well, a settlement feature most typical for this late period. Those were communities dedicated to agriculture, with little, if any, mobility. The organization of most craft activities was restricted to the household. Some smelting sites continued to operate in the eighth century, but on a much smaller size than earlier. Similarly, although a few eighth-century kilns are known, they seem to have been used for firing all categories of pottery. Changes in pottery production reflect new culinary practices, with clay cauldrons now employed for cooking over an open fire. The new culinary practices explain some of the changes taking place in burial customs as well. Most graves, especially of men (their skeletons having been sexed through anthropological methods), contain remains of domestic animals, especially poultry, while eggshells appear in female and child burials. Similarly, the symbolism of sickles deposited in graves points to agricultural production. While the overall number of weapons deposited in graves declined, a greater number of weapons were found with skeletons of older men. Weapons appear in graves together with ornamented belts, an indication that their symbolism was related not just to age but to social status as well. Weapons were also deposited along with horses, although the number of graves with horses but without weapons increased considerably throughout the second half of the eighth century. The number of graves with weapons and horses is particularly large in cemeteries excavated in southwestern Slovakia and in neighboring eastern Austria. This was a region of special status on the border of the Avar territory, perhaps a "militarized frontier." From that region, Avar mores and fashions spread farther to the west and to the north, into those areas of East Central Europe in which Avar symbols of social rank, especially belt sets, seem to have been particularly popular.

FURTHER READING

Bálint, Csanád. *The Avars, Byzantium and Italy: A Study in Chorology and Cultural History*. Varia Archaeologica Hungarica 31. Budapest: Institute of Archaeology, Research Centre for the Humanities, Hungarian Academy of Sciences, 2019.

Barford, Paul M. *The Early Slavs: Culture and Society in Early Medieval Eastern Europe*. London: British Museum, 2001.

Bollók, Ádám. *A Century of Gold: The Rise and Glory of the Avar Khaganate in the Carpathian Basin*. Budapest: Research Centre for the Humanities, Institute of Archaeology, 2021.

Curta, Florin. *The Making of the Slavs: History and Archaeology of the Lower Danube Region, c. 500–700*. Cambridge Studies in Medieval Life and Thought 52. Cambridge: Cambridge University Press, 2001.

Curta, Florin. *Slavs in the Making: History, Linguistics, and Archaeology in Eastern Europe (ca. 500–ca. 700)*. London: Routledge, 2021.

Dulinicz, Marek, and Sławomir Moździoch, eds. *The Early Slavic Settlement in Central Europe in the Light of New Dating Evidence*. Interdisciplinary Medieval Studies 3. Wrocław: Institute of Archaeology and Ethnology of the Polish Academy of Sciences, 2013.

Hurbanič, Martin. *The Avar Siege of Constantinople in 626: History and Legend*. Cham: Palgrave Macmillan, 2019.

Kardaras, Georgios. *Byzantium and the Avars, 6th–9th Century AD: Political, Diplomatic and Cultural Relations*. East Central and Eastern Europe in the Middle Ages, 450–1450, 51. Leiden: Brill, 2018.

Pohl, Walter. *The Avars: A Steppe Empire in Central Europe, 567–822*. Ithaca: Cornell University Press, 2018.

Živković, Tibor. *Forging Unity: The South Slavs Between East and West: 550–1150*. Belgrade: Institute of History, 2008.

3

SERBS, CROATS, BULGARS: MORE MIGRATIONS, REAL AND IMAGINED

Keywords in this chapter: Bulgars, Croats, Serbs, migration, warrior graves

Historians writing about the Balkan Peninsula in the Early Middle Ages have long relied on the accounts of the migration of Croats and Serbs given in *On the Administration of the Empire*, a work commissioned and supervised in the mid-tenth century by the Byzantine emperor Constantine VII Porphyrogenitus. The accounts appear in a series of chapters (29 to 36) written in 948 or 949, except for a later interpolation of chapter 30, which was most likely composed by another author after Emperor Constantine's death in 959.

According to chapter 30, the Croats used to live "beyond Bavaria, where the Belocroats are now" (see plate 3.1). Led by five brothers and two sisters, they moved to Dalmatia, where they defeated and expelled the Avars who had taken possession of that land. A different story of Croat migration appears in chapter 31 of *On the Administration of the Empire*. To be sure, they are still described as descendants of the "unbaptized Croats, also called 'white,'" and as coming from the lands beyond Hungary "and next to Francia." However, the Croats are now said to have arrived in Dalmatia "to claim the protection of the emperor of the Romans [i.e., the Byzantine emperor] Heraclius." It was by command of that emperor that the Croats attacked the Avars, defeated them, and expelled them from Dalmatia. By his mandate, "they settled down in that same country." Furthermore, the emperor brought priests from Rome and baptized the Croats under Prince Porgas.[1] The mention of Heraclius suggests a date for those events between 610 and 641, possibly before the siege of Constantinople in 626. However, Heraclius bringing about the conversion of the Croats is likely the invention of the Byzantine author. The point of the story in

1 Florin Curta, ed., "Emperor Constantine Porphyrogenitus on the Migration of the Croats," in *Medieval Eastern Europe, 500–1300: A Reader* (Toronto: University of Toronto Press, 2024), 18.

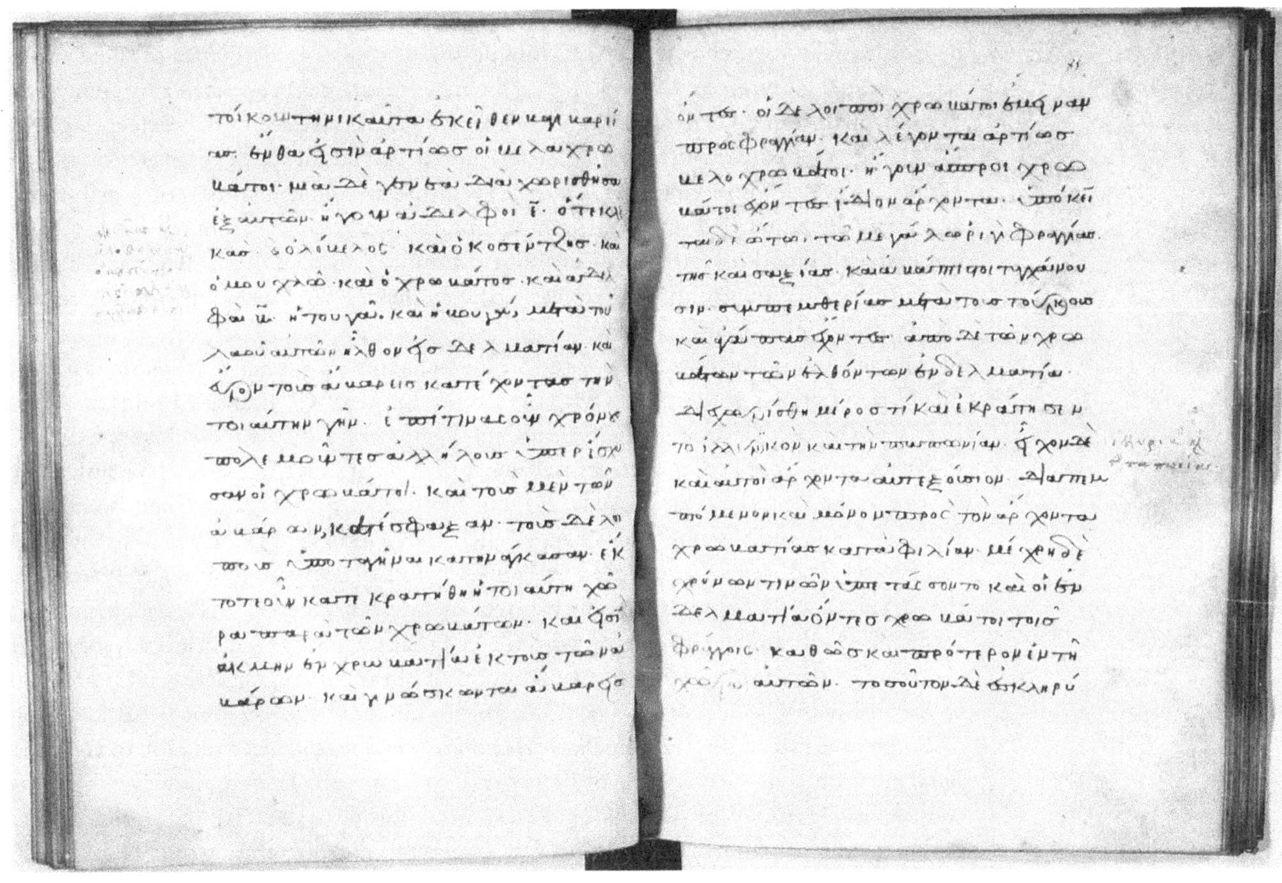

Plate 3.1. The beginning of the account of the Croat migration in chapter 30 of *On the Administration of the Empire*. Twelfth-century manuscript, now in the Bibliothèque Nationale in Paris, ms. Grec 2009, f. 91r.

chapter 31 is that ever since Porgas, the princes of the Croats were expected to submit to the Byzantine emperor.

The mention in chapter 30 of the Franks who subjected the Croats points on the other hand to a later date for the events, namely the late eighth or early ninth century, the time of the Frankish encroachment into Southeastern Europe (see chapter 7). Both chapters 30 and 31 of *On the Administration of the Empire* place the homeland of the Croats next to the Frankish Empire, but also near Bavaria, beyond Hungary. In both chapters, Croats still living in that homeland during Emperor Constantine's lifetime are called "white." "White" Croatia is mentioned by several other independent sources, but none of them can be dated earlier than the mid-ninth century.

Archaeology, on the other hand, suggests that no new population came to Dalmatia in the early seventh century. On the contrary, the region seems to have experienced a dramatic population decline during the first half of the seventh century, with only coastal towns surviving. The earliest burial assemblages that have been attributed to the Croats cannot be dated before the year 700. The sudden appearance of inhumation cemeteries with weapon burials and other cultural elements has been interpreted as an entirely new phenomenon, with no links to the previous period. Since the earliest phase of those cemeteries is dated between ca. 800 and ca. 850, the new culture has been taken as an indication of a late migration, like that mentioned in chapter 30. At stake seems to be the movement of small groups of warriors, perhaps at the initiative and under the supervision of the Franks. However, most elements of the new culture are in fact symbols of social status, and many are either of Frankish origin or imitations of artifacts from the core areas of the Frankish kingdom (later the Carolingian Empire). Instead of a sudden appearance of a new population group, the archaeological evidence therefore points to the rise of a clearly differentiated elite.

The account of the migration of the Serbs in chapter 32 of *On the Administration of the Empire* poses similar problems. As with the Croats, Emperor Constantine brings the Serbs from lands situated beyond Hungary, with the White Croats as neighbors. Like the Croats, the Serbs are said to have come to the Balkans at the invitation of Emperor Heraclius. They moved to the hinterland of Thessaloniki, but then decided to return to their homeland. Upon reaching the Danube, they changed their mind and asked Heraclius to grant them some other land. They were settled on lands previously devastated by Avars. Much like the Croats, the Serbs were supposedly baptized by priests brought from Rome by Emperor Heraclius. Such similarities – along with the fact that such migrations are a stereotype of early medieval narratives – suggest that the account of the Serbian migration is the creation of the author of *On the Administration of the Empire*, and not based on some tribal tradition.

Some have placed the Serbs in *On the Administration of the Empire* in relation to Dervan's *Surbi* mentioned in the chronicle of Fredegar (see chapter 6).[2] There is, however, no indication of a migration from the lands in East Central Europe to the territory of present-day Serbia (or the neighboring regions). A few cemeteries dated to the late eighth and early ninth centuries are known from northern and northwestern Bosnia, the region in which the early ninth-century Frankish annals place the Serbs. However, unlike contemporaneous burial assemblages in Croatia, there are no weapons in any of those cemeteries that could be associated with the representation of male status, although sharp gender differences are marked by means of a greater number and variety of grave goods, primarily dress accessories, found in female graves. In other words, the Serbs were also an elite, although represented by means different from those of the Croats.

There are similar problems with the migration of the Bulgars. The account of that migration may be found in the works of Theophanes Confessor and Patriarch Nicephorus I. While the former finished his *Chronographia* in 813 or 814, the latter wrote the *Short History* in or shortly after 828. Both works are more than a century later than the events in the story. Both authors place those events within the reign of Byzantine emperor Constantine IV (668–85). The migration is directly associated by both authors with the defeat that that emperor suffered at the hands of the Bulgars in the lands north of the Danube

2 Curta, ed., "Slavs, Avars and Franks," in *Medieval Eastern Europe*, 10.

delta. The leader of the victorious Bulgars was Asparukh, one of the five sons of Kubrat, who is said to have ruled over Great Bulgaria and the Onogundurs. Theophanes describes Great Bulgaria as stretching from the Sea of Azov to the river Kouphis, "where the *xyston*, the Bulgarian fish, is caught."[3] Since that river has been identified with the Kuban, most historians have placed Great Bulgaria in the steppe lands to the east of the Sea of Azov.

Kubrat advised his sons to stick together. However, they separated after his death, and each moved in a different direction. Batbaian, the eldest, followed his father's advice and remained in the ancestral lands. The second son, Kotragos, moved across the river Don and settled with his people next to Batbaian. The fourth son crossed the Danube and settled in Pannonia, under the rule of the Avars, while the fifth son went to Pentapolis near Ravenna and submitted to the Christians there. Asparukh was the third son, and he crossed the Dnieper and the Dniester with his people, before settling in the lands between the rivers Danube and Onglos, for he "thought the location secure and invincible from all sides, for it was marshy ahead and surrounded by rivers in other directions."[4] The chronology of Asparukh's arrival is still under debate, but it is likely that he was already on the Onglos by 670. At any rate, it is there that Emperor Constantine IV attacked the Bulgars in the summer of 680. The expedition was in retaliation for the Bulgar raids into the regions of the eastern Balkans, along the western coast of the Black Sea. During the expedition, the Byzantine fleet blocked the segment of the Danube between the Danube delta and the mouth of the Prut River. However, the campaign went awry when the emperor, "suffering severely from gout, had to withdraw to Mesembria" (now Nesebăr, on the Black Sea coast in Bulgaria), together with his retinue and a part of his fleet.[5] A rumor spread that the emperor was fleeing, and in the debacle, the Bulgars crossed the Danube and "came to Varna near Odyssos and its hinterland." Two Slavic groups, the so-called Seven Tribes and the Severeis, were forced into submission and the Bulgars resettled them as border guards, respectively, in the west against the Avars and on the southern frontier against the Byzantines.[6]

This account inspires trust, especially since it is confirmed by independent sources. For example, the Armenian *Geography* attributed to Movses Xorenac'i, but most probably written by Ananias of Širak in the seventh century, reports that Asparukh, son of Kubrat, settled on the island of Peuke (Danube delta). Moreover, in later centuries the Bulgar elite maintained a strong sense of its historical past, and a few texts show that migration was part of that collective memory.

The archaeological evidence, however, is at variance with the relative clarity of the written sources. A power center existed, apparently, in the lands north of the Crimea, on both sides of the Middle and Lower Dnieper River, as indicated by several exceptionally rich burials, all dated to the seventh century. Besides weapons, exquisite dress accessories,

3 Curta, ed., "Theophanes on the Bulgar Migration," in *Medieval Eastern Europe*, 15.
4 Curta, ed., "Theophanes on the Bulgar Migration," in *Medieval Eastern Europe*, 15.
5 Curta, ed., "Theophanes on the Bulgar Migration," in *Medieval Eastern Europe*, 16.
6 Curta, ed., "Theophanes on the Bulgar Migration," in *Medieval Eastern Europe*, 16.

Plate 3.2. The early eighth-century grave of a Bulgar warrior discovered in Kabiiuk, near Shumen (Bulgaria). Photo by Stanimir Stoychev.

and Byzantine and Sassanian silverware, one of those burials produced three golden finger-rings with monograms deciphered as referring to a certain *patrikios* named Koubratos. If those were the burials of the Bulgar aristocracy before Asparukh's migration to the Balkans, no such assemblages are known from Bulgaria. Nor are there any finds in that country that could be compared to the material culture reflected in those rich burials. The migration of Asparukh and his Bulgars is utterly invisible in the archaeological record. It is not known where the first generation of Bulgars in Bulgaria lived or where they buried their dead. Only three graves of warriors can so far be dated to the years shortly after the year 700 (see plate 3.2). The belt sets with which those men were buried have no analogies in the steppe lands north of the Black Sea. Nothing is known about the residences or burial sites of the first rulers of Bulgaria – Asparukh and his successors.

FURTHER READING

Curta, Florin, ed. *The Other Europe in the Middle Ages: Avars, Bulgars, Khazars and Cumans*. East Central and Eastern Europe in the Middle Ages, 450–1450, 2. Leiden: Brill, 2008.

Doncheva-Petkova, Liudmila, Csilla Balogh, and Attila Türk, eds. *Avars, Bulgars, and Magyars on the Middle and Lower Danube*. Sofia: Archaeolingua, 2014.

Dzino, Danijel. *Becoming Slav, Becoming Croat: Identity Transformation in Post-Roman and Early Medieval Dalmatia*. East Central and Eastern Europe in the Middle Ages, 450–1450, 12. Leiden: Brill, 2010.

Dzino, Daniel, Ante Milošević, and Trpimir Vedriš, eds. *Migration, Integration, and Connectivity on the Southeastern Frontier of the Carolingian Empire*. East Central and Eastern Europe in the Middle Ages, 450–1450, 50. Leiden: Brill, 2018.

Evans, Huw M. A. *The Early Medieval Archaeology of Croatia AD 600–900*. BAR International Series 539. Oxford: BAR, 1989.

Kasparova, K. V., Zlata A. L'vova, Boris I. Marshak, Irina V. Sokolova, Mark B. Shchukin, Vera N. Zalesskaia, and Irina P. Zaseckaia. *Treasures of Khan Kubrat: Culture of Bulgars, Khazars, Slavs*. Sofia: Centre for Publicity and Print at the Committee for Culture, 1989.

4

THE BALTIC REGION: DEMOGRAPHIC COLLAPSE AND CONTINUITY

Keywords in this chapter: gold hoards, silver jewelry, Aestii, Vidivarii

According to Procopius of Caesarea, who wrote in the mid-sixth century, when a group of barbarians decided to leave the Middle Danube region for the very end of the world, they crossed a great swathe of land that was completely deserted before reaching the Ocean which, according to ancient beliefs, surrounded the earth. In the early sixth century, Cassiodorus, secretary to Theoderic the Great, penned a thank-you letter on behalf of the king of the Ostrogoths. In this letter, which was meant to accompany a return gift, Theoderic acknowledged the receipt of a shipment of amber, which had arrived with envoys from the Aestii, otherwise known from the earlier Roman literature. However, it is likely that the letters in Cassiodorus's collection titled *Variae* (Various Letters) were more for literary entertainment than actual documents from the royal archive. At any rate, the letter of Theoderic the Great mentions the description of amber given by Cornelius Tacitus in his *Germania*, a work written in the year 98, which the presumed recipients of the letter could not have known, much less read. Baltic amber, the "northern gold," traveled to the southern parts of Europe, to Italy, to the Carpathian Basin, to Crimea, and even to the Caucasus region during the sixth and early seventh centuries, largely as part of an inter-elite exchange system. Amber beads and, occasionally, raw amber have been found in large quantities in cemeteries excavated in Hungary, but in much smaller numbers in the Baltic region, particularly in Lithuania and northeastern Poland. A direct contact between Ostrogothic Italy and the Baltic region is attested by numerous hoards of fifth- and early sixth-century Roman gold coins, found in western Pomerania, especially around the delta of the river Vistula. Those coins probably represent payments for warriors in the Ostrogothic armies that returned to their homeland – either Pomerania or, more likely, the islands of Öland and Gotland in the Baltic Sea – at the end of their military service. The hoard found at Karsibór on the northern shore of the Szczecin Lagoon (northwestern

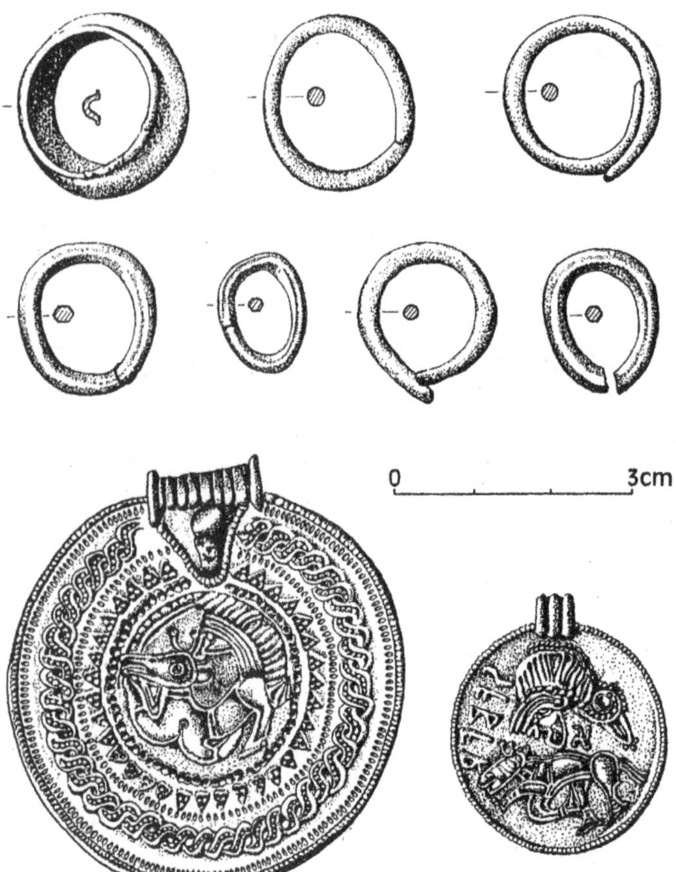

Poland) contains coins struck with the same die as others discovered on the island of Gotland.

The Aestii are also mentioned in *Getica*, a work that Jordanes wrote in the mid-sixth century, supposedly based on the now-lost *Gothic History* of Cassiodorus. In the geographical and ethnographic introduction of his work, Jordanes describes the shore of the Ocean and the people living there. Among them are the Aestii, said to be very peaceful, and their neighbors, the Vidivarii, a people allegedly made up of various tribes who inhabited the delta of the river Vistula. The precision of the location (Jordanes knew that the delta had three branches) seems to show clear knowledge of the abodes of the Vidivarii, who are otherwise not mentioned in any other source. Archaeology confirms the presence of a warlike population on the eastern shore of the Vistula Lagoon. The cremation cemeteries discovered in the region of the present-day city of Elbląg (Poland) have been attributed to immigrants from the lands farther to the northeast (the Sambian Peninsula in what is now the Kaliningrad region of Russia).

To the west of the river Vistula, however, the lands now in Poland witnessed a severe depopulation after the mid-fifth century. The only finds are those between the rivers Oder and Vistula, the region of Pomerania. Besides gold coins, hoards found in this region include golden torcs, finger-rings, and bracteates (thin gold pendants with depictions of Scandinavian gods) (see plate 4.1). Such artifacts are typical for fifth- and sixth-century Denmark and southern Sweden, which strongly suggests the presence of Scandinavians on the southern shore of the Baltic Sea. In addition to hoards, the region has also produced cemeteries, with both cremations and inhumations, for which the closest analogies are on the island of Bornholm in the Baltic Sea. Since no settlements are known from the area, it is quite possible that, whoever the Scandinavians were who came to northern Poland in the sixth century, they were only visiting, with no intention to remain in Pomerania. A few settlements dated to that century are known from the lands in western Poland along the middle course of the Oder River and consist of sunken-floored buildings. More settlements appeared shortly after 600 in southeastern Poland. The quern stones (for manual mills) and cereal seeds found in many of them show that those people practiced agriculture. They may have been immigrants from the neighboring lands now in western Ukraine, where such finds are also well known. Historians and archaeologists regard them as the earliest Slavic-speaking

Plate 4.1. Rings and bracteates from the hoard discovered in the nineteenth century in Wapno, near Bydgoszcz (Poland). Drawing by Joanna Sawicka.

population in Poland, which later spread to Silesia and other parts of the country. Northern Poland, especially Pomerania, does not seem to have experienced repopulation before ca. 700 (see chapter 6).

To the east of the lower course of the Vistula and along the southeastern shore of the Baltic Sea, there are signs of demographic stability and even growth. Those are the lands now divided between (northeastern) Poland, the Russian enclave (the region of Kaliningrad), and the three Baltic states of Lithuania, Latvia, and Estonia. In Late Antiquity and the Early Middle Ages the inhabitants of this region are believed to have spoken Baltic languages related to modern Lithuanian and Latvian. Several small settlements are known from this area, and finds of sickles, quern stones, and underground silos bespeak the agricultural occupations of their inhabitants. Sickles and mattocks have also been found in female graves, while scythes were associated with weapons in male burials. Some have interpreted that contrast as women being involved in the cultivation of crops (mattocks for breaking the soil, and sickles for harvesting), while men, particularly those whose military status was marked in death by the deposition of weapons, were in charge of livestock (scythes being used for cutting grass to make hay). However, agricultural tools appear also in hoards, along with torcs (neck rings), bracelets, and weapons. In other words, such tools may have been symbols of social status, much like burials with horses, which indicate the ability of only a few members of society to raise and control livestock.

In northern Estonia, both lavishly furnished burials (many of which included weapons) and the deposition of hoards of silver ornaments, often in ritually significant locations (such as bogs), signal the rise of new social elites. The same region also produced evidence of intensified agricultural production. The preferred method of farming was slash-and-burn agriculture, in which forested land was clear cut, with the remaining foliage being burned. The predominant crop on the newly opened fields was rye. Since this does not coincide with any significant increase of population, the introduction of rye cultivation is regarded as a strategy to maintain control over a relatively small population within an increasingly stratified society. Moreover, there is some evidence of long-distance contacts with elites elsewhere. For example, in large cemeteries in the Sambian Peninsula, several artifacts, primarily ornaments for horse tack and for the saddle, are decorated with the so-called Germanic Animal Style I, which played an active role in creating a shared elite identity in contemporaneous Scandinavia and western Europe, where it was displayed especially on female dress accessories. In northern and northeastern Estonia, a few richly furnished graves dated to the early sixth century illustrate the display of social prestige. This is a completely novel phenomenon for a region in which social differences were not marked in material culture at any point during the previous 300 years. Since some of those graves contained weapons, the rise to prominence of local chieftains may well have involved violence.

Similarly, exceptionally rich burials under barrows (burial mounds) appear in eastern Lithuania at about the same time; they may have been the resting places of local "dukes." To judge by the number of richly furnished burials, there were fewer members of the elite around the year 500, which strongly suggests that power was concentrated in the hands of a few. At the same time, burials of young males became considerably richer than those of older males, an indication of profound social change. Older males, who had meanwhile lost their warrior status, were somewhat closer to females in their position in society. This phenomenon was accompanied by a substantial number of people buried with no grave goods whatsoever. However, the status of women remained stable in relation to age and seems to have been less affected by the social transformations taking place in local communities. In northern Lithuania and southern Latvia, gender distinctions were clearly marked in cemeteries, with males being buried in the opposite direction from females. This change coincided in time with the standardization of grave good sets and the salient marking of warrior status in the burial ritual. Male status was connected directly to military activity and the social notions surrounding it, as demonstrated by the deposition of a long battle knife, along with two or three spears, in each grave. The unusual number of daggers of the same type found in male graves in central Lithuania points to the formation of local retinues of "professional" warriors.

It is possible that the Vidivarii mentioned by Jordanes emerged as a local elite in the lands to the east of the Vistula delta under conditions very similar to those revealed by the analysis of the archaeological record in Lithuania and Estonia.

FURTHER READING

Bertašius, Mindaugas, ed. *Transformatio Mundi: The Transition from the Late Migration Period to the Early Viking Age in the East Baltic.* Kaunas: Kaunas University of Technology, Department of Philosophy and Cultural Science, 2006.

Bliujienė, Audronė. *Northern Gold: Amber in Lithuania (c. 100 to c. 1200).* East Central and Eastern Europe in the Middle Ages, 450–1450, 18. Leiden: Brill, 2011.

Bursche, Aleksander, John Hines, and Anna Zapolska, eds. *The Migration Period between the Oder and the Vistula.* East Central and Eastern Europe in the Middle Ages, 450–1450, 59. Leiden: Brill, 2020.

Kontny, Bartosz, Jerzy Okulicz-Kozaryn, and Mirosław Pietrzak. *Nowinka, Site I: The Cemetery from the Late Migration Period in Northern Poland.* Gdańsk: Muzeum Archeologiczne, 2011.

Rudnicki, Mirosław. *The Olsztyn Group in the Early Medieval Archaeology of the Baltic Region: The Cemetery at Leleszki.* East Central and Eastern Europe in the Middle Ages, 450–1450, 52. Leiden: Brill, 2018.

Tvauri, Andres. *The Migration Period, Pre-Viking Age, and Viking Age in Estonia.* Tartu: Tartu University Press, 2012.

PART 2

Early Polities and Peoples

5

KHAZARIA

Keywords in this chapter: Khazars, Arabs, burial mounds, sabers, dirhams

The seventh-century Armenian *Geography* mentioned in chapter 3 is also the first source to mention a new group of nomads that appeared in the steppe lands of Eastern Europe in the Early Middle Ages. The Khazars emerged to fill the vacuum of power created ca. 660 by the dissolution of earlier nomadic confederations. Their khaganate came into being at the same time as the rise of the Arab Caliphate and its expansion into the Black Sea and Caspian Sea regions, following the conquest of Sassanian Persia. In its golden age, the Khazar khaganate was the largest political entity established by nomads in Eastern Europe during the Early Middle Ages and one of the most stable state formations in Eurasia. The core of Khazaria stretched from the Donets to the Volga on the west-east axis, and from the middle course of the river Don to the foothills of the Caucasus Mountains in a north-south direction (see map 5.1).

The first clash between the Khazars and the Arabs took place in 652, when the general Abd ar-Rahman ibn Rabiyah crossed the Caucasus Mountains and put the town of Balanjar (of unknown location) under siege, before being defeated and killed by the Khazars. Over the next decades, the Caucasus range became a buffer zone between the Arabs and the Khazars. Meanwhile, the latter made their presence felt in the Crimea, although Cherson (the medieval name of ancient Chersonesus) remained in Byzantine hands. While banished to the Crimea in 695, the former Byzantine emperor Justinian II married a sister of the khagan of the Khazars (none of whom is known by name). At the request of the new emperor in Constantinople, Tiberius III Apsimar (698–705), the khagan ordered two of his deputies to eliminate his brother-in-law. One of the two deputies was the Khazar "governor" of the Crimea, the other was the military commander (probably of the Khazar garrison) in Bosporus. However, Justinian managed to kill the would-be assassins, after which he sailed to the western coast of the Black Sea, where he persuaded the Bulgar ruler Tervel to help him recuperate the throne in Constantinople (see chapter 8). During his second reign (705–11), relations with the Khazars turned sour. In 710, the garrison in

Map 5.1. The approximate extent of Khazaria in Eastern Europe, ca. 900. The location of the following sites is indicated: B – Bosporus; Ba – Balanjar (probable); Ch – Cherson; I – Itil (probable); M – Maiackoe; S – Saltovo; Sa – Sarkel. The mountains in the lower left corner of the map are the Carpathians, those on the bottom – the Caucasus, and those on the right – the Urals.

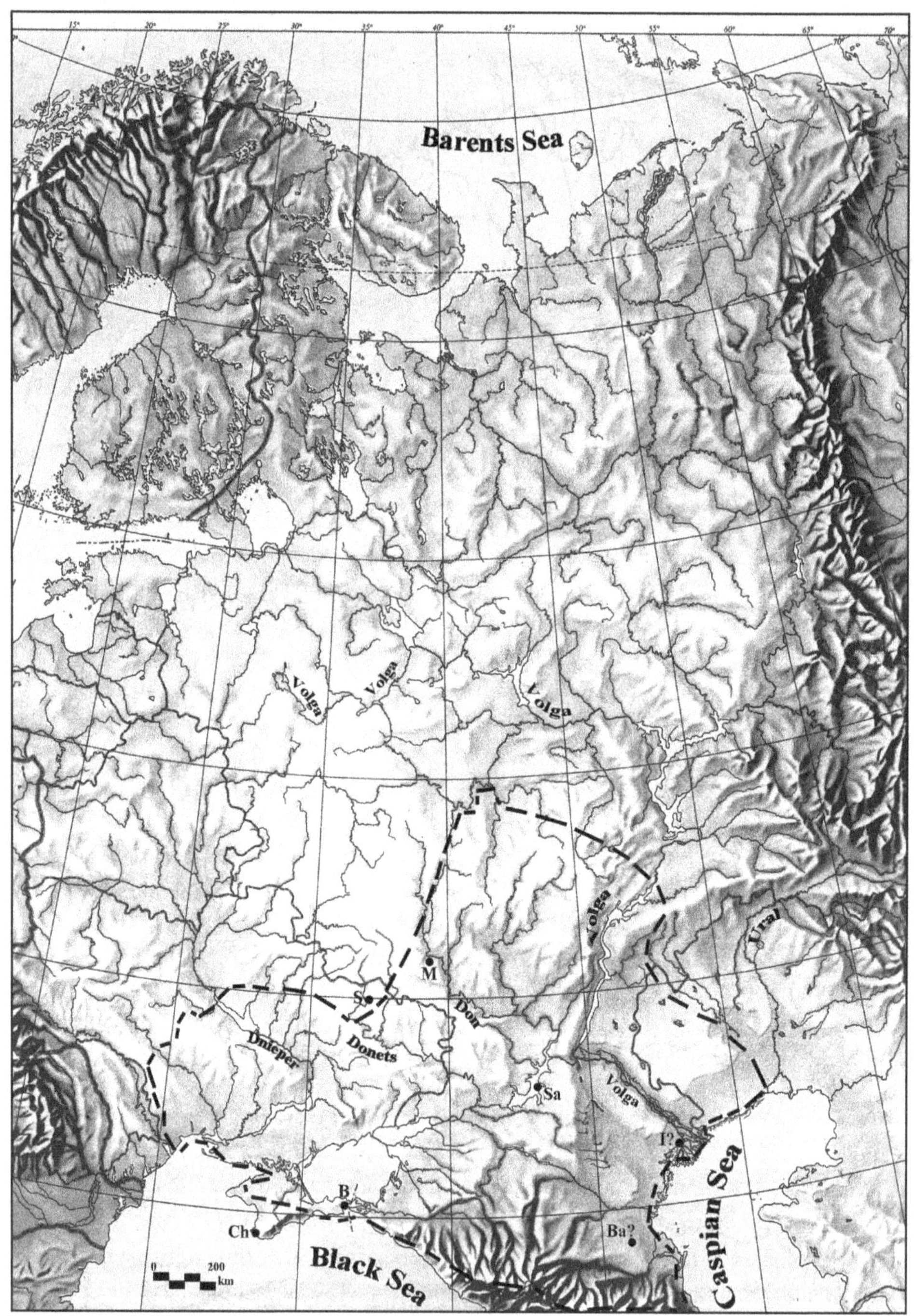

Cherson rebelled against the emperor, having the support of the khagan. Justinian sent a sizeable fleet to reclaim the city, but the fleet was wrecked by storm on its way to Cherson. The emperor dispatched an embassy to negotiate with the Khazars, but the Chersonites killed the envoy and then proclaimed an emperor of their own. Another naval expedition sent against the usurper failed to dislodge the Khazars from Cherson, and the imperial troops sided with the usurper. Justinian was eventually captured and executed, and the new emperor paid no further attention to the Khazars in the Crimea.

Meanwhile, the Arab pressure increased in the Caucasus region. In 713 or 714, the Arab general Maslama ibn Abd al-Malik crossed the mountains and took Darband (present-day Derbent, in Dagestan), before raiding deep into Khazar territory. He had to withdraw when the Khazar army approached. In 722, a Khazar raid led by the son of the khagan was stopped and crushed by al-Jarrah b. Abdallah al-Hakami, the governor of Armenia and Azerbaijan. It may well have been at this point that the decision was taken to move the political center of Khazaria to the lower reaches of the river Volga. In 730, a large Khazar army invaded Azerbaijan and reached as far as northern Iraq. The Khazars defeated and killed al-Hakami at Ardabil (in northwestern Iran), taking and sacking the city. The victory of the Khazars brought them to the attention of the Byzantines. In 732, the year in which Maslama crossed the Caucasus against the Khazars, the Byzantine emperor Constantine V (son and co-ruler of Leo III, 717–41) married Tzitzak, the daughter of the khagan. Baptized under the name Irene, she would become the mother of Emperor Leo IV, nicknamed "the Khazar." Five years later, the new governor of Armenia and Azerbaijan, Marwan ibn Muhammad (the future caliph Marwan II, 744–50), took a large army across the Caucasus Mountains and raided deep into Khazaria. He obtained a major victory against the Khazars and forced the khagan and his retinue to convert to Islam. Although Khazaria was now formally subordinated to the caliph, the khagan renounced Islam as soon as Marwan withdrew. Following the assassination of Marwan in 750, all conflict with the Khazars ceased, and they seem to have returned to their traditional alliance with the Byzantines.

To judge from the archaeological evidence, by 750 the center of power was in the northeastern region of the Black Sea and the lands around the Sea of Azov. Byzantine coins and metal artifacts found in graves from that region bespeak contact with the empire but also help date those graves to the first third of the eighth century. Some of the richest burial assemblages in the East European steppe lands, those are inhumations with niches along the long sides of the pit, in which the head and the legs of a horse are typically deposited next to the human skeleton. A different kind of burial in that same region is represented by graves under barrows surrounded by square or oval ditches. Those were monuments erected for the Khazar elite and they typically cover inhumation pits with tunnel-shaped shafts that contain the entire skeleton of a horse buried with stirrups, bridle bit, and reins. About a quarter of the barrows have no graves underneath and must have been commemorative monuments (cenotaphs), perhaps for members of the elite who had died elsewhere. Indeed, the barrows with square or oval ditches have been dated between 720 and 760, that is, during the political turmoil caused by the wars with the Arabs and leading to the military disaster of 737. Those monuments were therefore a desperate attempt at reaffirming power at a time when it was contested.

However, the Arab-Khazar wars had even deeper implications. Archaeology suggests that refugees from the North Caucasus region moved after ca. 730 into the steppe lands along the Lower Don, as well as across that river to the northwest, in the valley of the Donets. The northern and northeastern region of the Sea of Azov thus became densely populated, with many open settlements and forts. Burial customs in the region rapidly changed after ca. 730. Family tombs in catacombs with multiple skeletons appear around that date, imitating burial chambers in the lands at the foot of the Caucasus Mountains. Equally new are cremation burials, the closest parallels to which are again in the North Caucasus region. The northern and northeastern region of the Sea of Azov is the area in which the first relatively large cemeteries appear that have been attributed to the Saltovo-Mayaki culture of the "classical" Khazar age. The culture is named after two key sites – the catacomb cemetery in Saltovo (now Verkhniy Saltiv, in Ukraine) and the fort in Maiackoe (near Voronezh, in Russia). Between 750 and 950, this culture spread throughout the whole territory of Khazaria, and even beyond it. Some forts, especially those along the river Oskol, have earthen ramparts; others have stone walls. The former were probably built by clan-based communities, while the latter were most likely elements in a line of defense organized by the central authority of Khazaria. The direct source of inspiration for the forts with stone walls was the Byzantine military architecture. The best example of that is Sarkel, a fortress built by a team of Byzantine engineers at some point during the reign of Emperor Theophilus (829–42), most likely against the Magyars or the Rus' on the opposite side of the river Don.

The economy of Khazaria was a complex combination of pastoralism, agriculture, and trade. While some Arab sources mention cows, sheep, and slaves coming from the country of the Khazars, others refer to farms around Itil (the capital city, location unknown). Other sources describe the Khazar elite following what may be called a nomadic cycle – spending the winter months in Itil, leaving in spring, and making the rounds of the khaganate until the onset of the following winter. This suggests that nomadism was not an economic strategy, but a mark of social distinction. Agriculture appears in three distinct regions of Khazaria. In eastern Crimea, there is abundant evidence of crop cultivation, particularly of wheat, rye, barley, and millet. In addition, agricultural implements, especially plowshares and hoes, are prominent among settlement finds, along with querns. The same is true for the forest-steppe zone along the Donets River. The analysis of charred seeds found in that region revealed a similar profile, but with different proportions. Two-field rotation (for which see chapter 31) appears to have been associated with dry farming in the Donets region, while irrigation is implied by Arabic sources reporting on the hinterland of Itil. Large numbers of animal bones have been found on sites in the Donets region. Faunal assemblages allow both the identification of species (predominantly long-horned cattle, followed by sheep and goats) and the understanding of economic strategies applied to animal breeding. By contrast, predominantly pastoralist communities were clustered in the steppe lands between the Lower Don and the Lower Dnieper rivers.

INSERT 5.1. UMAYYADS AND ABBASIDS – THE DYNASTIES OF THE CALIPHATE

The rise of Islam coincides with the organization of a state ruled by "successors" (the word in Arabic is *halifa*, from which the English word "caliph" derives) of Muhammad. The first four caliphs were in one way or another related to Muhammad. However, after the assassination of Ali in 661, the governor of Syria, a man named Muawiya, became caliph, even though he was not related to Muhammad, whom he had in fact initially opposed. Muawiya was a member of Banu Umayya, the leading clan of the Quraysh tribe in Mecca (of which Muhammad himself was a member). The Umayyads were therefore the first dynasty of the Caliphate, for Muawiya designated as successor his son, Yazid I, whose own son, Muawiya II, became the third Umayyad caliph (683–84). The Umayyads made the title of caliph hereditary and turned the Caliphate into the largest empire of its age, extending from the Atlantic Ocean to the Indus River. However, Marwan II, the last Umayyad caliph, was overthrown in 750 by a revolt led by the Abbasids (named after al Abbas, an uncle of Muhammad, whom they claimed as ancestor). The rebels were members of the Hashim clan, a rival of the Banu Umayya, and were based in the northeastern, Iranian part of the Caliphate. With the proclamation of Abu al-Abbas al-Saffah as caliph in 750, a new dynasty came to power, which would last until the end of the Caliphate (namely, until the conquest of Baghdad by the Mongols in 1258). The Abbasid Caliphate witnessed the golden age of Islam but also the first signs of political fragmentation, particularly the rise of the Fatimid Caliphate in Egypt and the Umayyad Caliphate in the Iberian Peninsula.

Bloomery furnaces in the Don region are not unlike those found on contemporary Avar sites in Hungary. Blacksmithing is well documented archaeologically, both in Crimea and in the Donets region. Metallographic analyses of tools and weapons found on Saltovo-Mayaki sites indicate that local smiths employed a variety of sophisticated techniques for different qualities of tools with sharp edges. This is also true for Khazar-age sabers, the first such weapons in the medieval steppe lands. The social stratification visible in the number and quality of grave goods, as well as in differences in burial customs, is not matched by information from the written sources. All that is known from the Arab sources is that by 800 the Khazar society was ruled by a khagan, who was a nominal king, since real power was in the hands of his military commander, the beg.

During the seventh and first half of the eighth centuries, merchants from Central Asia, particularly from Sogdia (in present-day Kyrgyzstan), moved along trade routes that crossed Khazaria, to reach the northern shore of the Black Sea. The situation changed dramatically when the Khazar-Arab wars came to an end in the mid-eighth century. The new Abbasid dynasty in the Caliphate was interested in opening trade routes across the Caucasus Mountains, along which only armies had previously moved (see insert 5.1). Silver coins (dirhams) struck in the Caliphate (as well as in distant parts of the Muslim world, such as northern Africa and Spain) began to enter Eastern Europe via Khazaria, but by the 880s this flow of Muslim silver stopped (see insert 5.2). Shortly after that,

INSERT 5.2. DIRHAMS – THE SILVER COINAGE OF EAST CENTRAL AND EASTERN EUROPE IN THE EARLY MIDDLE AGES

The Arabic word *dirham* derives from the Greek word for silver coin (*drachm*), which was taken by Persians, and from them (after defeat of the Sassanians at al-Qadisiyyah in 636) by Arabs as well. While coins minted in the Umayyad Caliphate before 697 imitated the Byzantine coinage, things radically changed with the monetary reform of Caliph ʿAbd al-Malik (685–705). Dirhams were aniconic coins, in that they had no images, only Quranic verses and religious phrases in addition to the name of the caliph, the mint, and the date (according to the Hijra calendar). The reform of ʿAbd al-Malik was a reaction to changes in the Byzantine gold coinage. Under the first reign of Justinian II (685–95), a new gold coin was introduced, which had on one side the portrait of the emperor and on the other a larger image of Christ Pantokrator ("All-Mighty"). The new coins angered Muslims who reject any depiction of the divine. Although in Islam Jesus is recognized only as a prophet (and not as the Son of God), the image on the Byzantine gold coins prompted the reform of the Muslim coinage. The first changes targeted the gold coins (dinars), but the reform of ʿAbd al-Malik effectively replaced the dinar with the dirham. The dirham became the standard circulation coin of the Abbasid Caliphate, the economy of which boomed shortly after 800. The high value of the coin was backed by the high concentration of silver in it, and because of that the coin was appreciated both within and outside the Caliphate. Although Byzantine coins appear there as well, the sheer quantity of dirhams found especially in hoards discovered in Russia, Ukraine, Belarus, Estonia, Latvia, Lithuania, and Poland indicates that the dirham was the main silver coinage in East Central and Eastern Europe during the Early Middle Ages.

Muslim merchants discovered another source of, and route to, dirhams in large quantities, namely the Samanid amirate of Central Asia. The flow of the dirhams struck in Samanid mints reached Eastern Europe ca. 900 via the steppe lands between the Caspian and the Aral Sea (Kara Kum and the Ustyurt Plateau), then along the Middle Volga region. The new commercial route effectively bypassed Khazaria, which had dramatic economic and political consequences. Not being able to trade in Khazaria anymore, the Rus' (for whom see chapter 11) wanted simply to cross its territory in order to raid the Muslim lands on the southern shore of the Caspian Sea. Greatly weakened, Khazaria was destroyed when Sviatoslav, prince of Kiev, attacked and sacked Sarkel and Itil in 965.

FURTHER READING

Curta, Florin, ed. *The Other Europe in the Middle Ages: Avars, Bulgars, Khazars, and Cumans*. East Central and Eastern Europe in the Middle Ages, 450–1450, 2. Leiden: Brill, 2008.

Golb, Norman, and Omeljan Pritsak. *Khazarian Hebrew Documents of the Tenth Century*. Ithaca: Cornell University Press, 1982.

Golden, Peter B. *Khazar Studies: An Historico-Philological Inquiry into the Origins of the Khazars*. Budapest: Akadémiai kiadó, 1980.

Golden, Peter B., Haggai Ben-Shammai, and András Róna-Tas, eds. *The World of the Khazars: New Perspectives. Selected Papers from the Jerusalem 1999 International Khazar Colloquium Hosted by the Ben Zvi Institute*. Handbook of Oriental Studies, Central Asia 17. Leiden: Brill, 2007.

Koloda, Vladimir V., and Sergei A. Gorbanenko. *Agriculture in the Forest-Steppe Region of Khazaria*. East Central and Eastern Europe in the Middle Ages, 450–1450, 66. Leiden: Brill, 2020.

Zhivkov, Boris. *Khazaria in the Ninth and Tenth Centuries*. East Central and Eastern Europe in the Middle Ages, 450–1450, 30. Leiden: Brill, 2015.

6

THE WESTERN SLAVS

Keywords in this chapter: Wends, Franks, Abodrites, ringforts, Sorbs

Whereas in the East the Roman world pursued its existence in the form of the Byzantine Empire, in the West the Roman provinces transformed during the fifth and sixth centuries into barbarian kingdoms. The largest of them, that of the Franks, was governed by Merovingian kings until the mid-eighth century. Starting in the late sixth century, Frankish authors located the Avars, whom they identified with the "Huns" previously known from fifth-century sources, on the eastern frontier of their kingdom (see chapter 2). In the following century, they also mentioned another group known to East Roman ethnographers of Late Antiquity: the Slavs. How Slavic peoples managed to appear in Central Europe is a complicated question to which researchers have sought to provide answers using the tools of history, linguistics, and archaeology. That those whom Frankish authors labelled as "Slavs" spoke Slavic is attested only in later times. Archaeology cannot tell anything about the languages spoken in the region in this early period but unveils cultural changes that happened there between the sixth and the eighth centuries.

Characteristic features of the material culture generally associated with the early Slavs include simple, handmade pottery, square sunken-floored huts with an oven in a corner, and cremation burials. To refer to all those characteristics together, archaeologists have coined the term "Prague-Korchak culture," which applies to sites in Bohemia, Moravia, southern Poland, and Ukraine. Such sites are dated shortly after the year 600 and are believed to represent a population that merged with the remnants of the Germanic peoples living in those same regions in Late Antiquity. The extent to which material culture was shaped by internal social transformations, an influx of "Slavic" migrants, or a combination of both is the subject of ongoing debates. Another group, known as the "Sukow-Dziedzice culture," appears in the north, between Mecklenburg in Germany and Mazovia in Poland, and features aboveground log houses and pit cremation burials, sometimes with mounds. This group developed in the late seventh to early eighth centuries and is believed to be a variant of the culture identified as "early Slavic" to the south. This suggests that during that time, a material culture and the lifestyle associated with it expanded to the north into territories that had been largely abandoned by the Germanic peoples of Antiquity during the sixth century. The lifestyle of these likely ancestors of those later identified as Slavs was characterized by a subsistence economy, a low level of social differentiation, and small local communities.

Contacts between Franks and Slavs are recorded in the chronicle of the so-called Fredegar, who, writing around 660, narrated a conflict between the Merovingian king Dagobert and a man named Samo. Samo was a Frankish merchant who, in 623/624, ventured into the land of the "Slavs called Wends" (see chapter 2).[1] The Wends had been paying tribute to the Avars and fighting in their army, but the ruling-class Avar men were coercing Wendish women into sexual relationships. The Wends rebelled against their Avar lords and chose Samo to be their "king." They successfully repelled the Avars, who were busy fighting the Byzantines on the eastern front, when trouble with the Franks emerged. Dagobert, upset at an attack on merchants perpetrated by the Wends, launched a war against them with the support of Lombards from Italy. Samo received support from the Sorbs and their duke Dervan and was again victorious.

The *Chronicle* of Fredegar is, unfortunately, the only contemporary source to mention the "kingdom" of Samo; its location remains unknown. It might have been somewhere in the border regions of Austria, the Czech Republic, and Slovakia. Although Samo is said to have had many children from his twelve Wendish wives and to have reigned for thirty-five years, little appears to have survived from his "kingdom" after his death. Be that as it may, the episode attests that by the seventh century, the Franks were aware of a new population on their eastern frontier whom they named Slavs or Wends, the latter name probably derived from that of the ancient Venedi.

Slavs made occasional appearances in Frankish hagiographical texts of the seventh and eighth centuries. The *Life of Saint Columbanus*, written around 640 in Bobbio, Italy, recounts how the Irish missionary in the Frankish lands considered preaching to the Slavs before giving up his plan. According to the unknown author of a *vita* written in the early eighth century, one of Columbanus's disciples named Amandus, bishop of Maastricht, unsuccessfully attempted to preach to the pagan Slavs. The monk Sturm, who established the Fulda Abbey, is also said to have encountered Slavs and to have abandoned any idea of converting them.

In Francia, the Merovingians were succeeded by rulers of the Carolingian family. One of them, Charlemagne, united the Frankish realm and conquered the Lombard kingdom in Italy. Ruling over the largest territory in Europe since Antiquity, he was crowned (western) Roman emperor in Rome in 800. Charlemagne waged many wars; among them were those against the Avars (see chapters 2 and 7) and the Saxons, a Germanic people who lived on the eastern border of the Frankish kingdom, from the Ems River to the Elbe and from the

1 Florin Curta, ed., "Slavs, Avars, and Franks," in *Medieval Eastern Europe, 500–1300: A Reader* (Toronto: University of Toronto Press, 2024), 9.

North Sea to the Harz Mountains. The Saxon wars that raged between 772 and 804 were a drawn-out conflict involving large-scale massacres (for example, 4,500 Saxons are said to have been executed at Verden in 782), forced relocation of populations, and the threat of the death penalty for those who rejected the tenets of Christian religious practices. Even the monk Alcuin, Charlemagne's main adviser, complained of the brutality of the means utilized to achieve conversions. Once the wars were over, however, a network of bishoprics and monasteries was established.

Regular conflicts on the Slavic frontier began as soon as the Saxon wars were coming to an end and are mentioned in Frankish annals throughout the ninth century. The policies of the Carolingian rulers towards the Slavs were nonetheless very different from those towards the Saxons. The Carolingians did not intend to conquer and to integrate, let alone to convert the Slavic peoples on the other side of the Elbe. They rather limited themselves to forcing them to pay tribute, occasionally taking hostages, and sending punitive expeditions when they refused to abide. The capitulary of Thionville issued by Charlemagne in 805 also testifies to attempts at controlling trade on the Elbe frontier by restricting it to a few trading posts – Bardowick, Magdeburg, and Schezla (probably near Höhbeck, in Lower Saxony) – and preventing the sale of certain items, particularly weapons, to the Slavs (see map 6.1). At the same time, small groups of Slavs moved into Bavaria and Thuringia, settled there, and became integrated into the local economy, even as far from the Elbe as the area around the modern city of Würzburg – the "Main and Rednitz Wends." Altogether, the Carolingians were concerned mostly with securing stability on the eastern border.

Change is visible throughout the eighth century in the society of the Slavs east of the Elbe. The first Slavic chieftain mentioned by name in the lands east of the Carolingians was Dragovit. In 789, together with Saxon, Sorb, and Abodrite auxiliary troops, Charlemagne crossed the Elbe and moved against Dragovit into the Peene area of present-day northeastern Germany. Dragovit was besieged in his stronghold; he surrendered, gave hostages, and agreed to pay tribute. The earliest fortifications, known as the Feldberg forts, were built in the hinterland of what is now eastern and northern Germany in the mid- to late eighth century. Built with earth-and-timber ramparts, the forts took advantage of the topography to maximize protection. Extending often between 200 and 350 m in diameter, those strongholds were densely occupied and populated.

Intensified Carolingian aggression against the Slavs after 800 triggered accelerated societal developments. The military and political challenge required leadership and resulted in more complex social relations. For example, the Slavic tribe of the Linons lived in open, dispersed settlements on the shores of the lower Elbe in the late eighth century. The Franks began attacking them in the early ninth century to impose tribute and built an elevated hillfort in a symbolic position on the western side of the Elbe at Höhbeck (halfway between the modern cities of Hamburg and Berlin). In response, the Linons erected earth-and-timber strongholds on the other side, at Lenzersilge and Lenzen-Neuehaus, which, although smaller than those of the earlier period, were in the tradition of the Feldberg forts. The need to defend and protect themselves, and possibly to have a territorial organization required for the payment of a regular tribute, fostered more stable societal

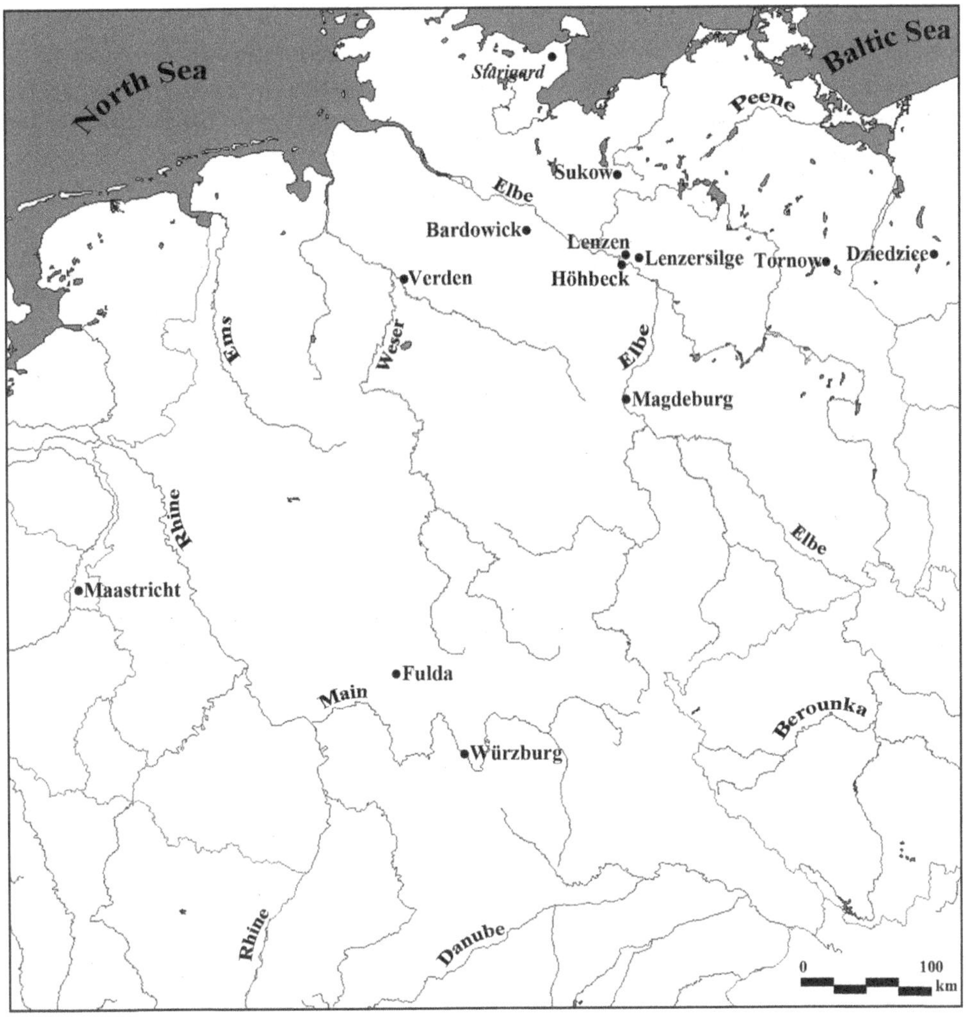

Map 6.1. The lands of the northwestern Slavs between the seventh and the ninth centuries.

structures. Throughout the ninth century, Slavic groups in the Elbe area appeared under their own specific ("tribal") names, such as the Smeldingi, the Siusli, the Bethenzi, and many others. All were in tributary relationships to the Franks that were similar to that of the Linons.

However, growing social differentiation evolved in various circumstances. In some regions of the West Slavic world where no major military conflict was expected, strongholds were built as symbols of emerging elites competing with one another. In the mid- to late ninth century, a new type of stronghold rapidly gained in popularity. Ringforts of the Tornow type were smaller, circular lowland fortifications of between 60 and 90 m in diameter. Those were typically seats of power, with local elites – probably no more than a family, in each case – imposing their authority over the immediate hinterland. The multiplication of such ringforts in various regions of present-day Germany and Poland testifies to a period of political fragmentation and localized authority, for example in Lower Lusatia or northern Mazovia. Local chieftains profited when economic conditions improved, especially when trade networks reached the regions in the interior. Larger fortresses began to be built in the ninth, but especially in the tenth, century as residences of powerful rulers, particularly in the lands of the Abodrites. The "Old Fortress" known as Starigard in Slavic and Oldenburg in German (now Oldenburg in Holstein, near Kiel) is the best example of that new form of power representation.

Among the first Slavic territories to be integrated into the East Frankish realm were those of the Sorbs in the Saale area, to the east of Thuringia. "Kings" of the Sorbs who, like other Slavic tribes, paid tribute to Frankish rulers, appear in the sources throughout the ninth century. In the mid-ninth century, the border zone around the Saale River was known as the "Sorb frontier" (*limes Sorabicus*) and was ruled by the Carolingian margrave Thakulf, whom the *Annals of Fulda* describe as being knowledgeable in the "laws and customs of the Slavic people."

FURTHER READING

Biermann, Felix. "North-Western Slavic Strongholds of the 8th–10th Centuries AD." In *Fortified Settlements in Early Medieval Europe: Defended Communities of the 8th–10th Centuries*, edited by Neil Christie and Hajnalka Herold, 159–76. Oxford: Oxbow, 2016.

Biermann, Felix. "The Small Early Medieval Lowland Ringforts in Northern Masovia and Their Counterparts in the Northern West-Slavic Territories." In *Grody średniowiecznego Mazowsza: Księga poświęcona pamięci Marka Dulinicza*, edited by Małgorzata Krasna-Korycińska and Magdalena Żurek, 39–49. Archaeologica Hereditas 4. Warsaw: Wydawnictwo Fundacji Archeologicznej, 2015.

Brather, Sebastian. "The Archaeology of the Northwestern Slavs (Seventh to Ninth Centuries)." *East Central Europe* 31, no. 1 (2004): 77–97.

Curta, Florin. "Slavs in Fredegar and Paul the Deacon: Medieval 'Gens' or 'Scourge of God'?" *Early Medieval Europe* 6, no. 2 (1997): 141–67.

Curta, Florin. *Slavs in the Making: History, Linguistics, and Archaeology in Eastern Europe (ca. 500–ca. 700)*. London: Routledge, 2021.

Mühle, Eduard. *Slavs in the Middle Ages between Idea and Reality*. East Central and Eastern Europe in the Middle Ages, 450–1450, 89. Leiden: Brill, 2023.

Schneeweiß, Jens, and Thomas Schatz. "The Impact of Landscape Change on the Significance of Political Centres along the Lower Elbe River in the 10th Century A.D." *Quaternary International* 324 (2014): 20–33.

7

GREAT MORAVIA

Keywords in this chapter: Eastland, Moravians, stronghold, papacy, Magyars

To Notker the Stammerer, a monk from the abbey of St. Gall in what is now Switzerland, who wrote a century after the events of the Frankish expeditions to the Carpathian Basin in the late eighth century, the Avars (whom he anachronistically called "Huns") were tadpoles not worth any serious war. By contrast, to Einhard, who wrote a biography of Charlemagne a few years after the emperor's death in 814, the war with the Avars was the greatest of all that Charlemagne had waged, second only to that against the Saxons (see chapter 6). In the 770s, the Avars were allies of all the enemies of Charlemagne, including the Lombards and the Bavarians. At his deposition in 788, Tassilo III, the duke of Bavaria, was accused of conniving with the Avars against the Franks. In that year, the Avars raided northern Italy, as far as Verona. Accused of "mischief," they were themselves attacked by the Franks, not because of being nomad (they had long become sedentary) or pagan, but for the sole purpose of expanding the frontiers of the Frankish kingdom (soon to be empire) to the east. Soon after the demise of the Avar polity, the lands conquered by the Franks were divided into two new administrative units, one of which was the prefecture of the East (which included the Avar lands west of the Middle Danube) and Carantania. Frankish sources ceased to refer to Avars as an ethnic group; instead, the lands formerly inhabited by Avars now appeared as populated by Slavs.

In 828, the prefecture of the East was incorporated into the Bavarian Eastland, headed by a Frankish nobleman named Ratpot. Five years later, he received a refugee from the lands north of the Danube. Named Pribina, the man seeking asylum in the Bavarian Eastland was apparently married to a woman of a Bavarian noble family, the Wilhelminer; he had been expelled from his stronghold in Nitra (now in Slovakia) by his western neighbor, a Moravian named Mojmir. Ratpot decided to send Pribina, together with his son Kocel, to Louis the German, who at that time ruled over Bavaria and who ordered the baptism of the two refugees. Soon, Pribina came into conflict with Ratpot and fled to Bulgaria. He later returned and took refuge with the count of Carniola, Salacho, who mediated his reconciliation with Ratpot. Shortly after that, between 838 and 847, Louis the German (now king of East Francia) granted to Pribina a large area at the western end of Lake Balaton, expanding into what is now western and southwestern Hungary. Pribina ruled from a stronghold placed in the middle of the marshy lands at the mouth of the river Zala, called Mosapurc (now Zalavár, in Hungary). He brought with him an important churchman in the person of Bishop Oswald, a suffragan of the archbishop of Salzburg. The Mosapurc stronghold thus became a bishopric, the easternmost in the entire East Frankish kingdom. Three churches were built in Mosapurc, all known from archaeological excavations. That dedicated to St. John was most likely the episcopal church (cathedral), judging by the fact that it had an episcopal palace next to it. Pribina's private chapel was dedicated to the Virgin Mary, while a three-aisled basilica with glass windows was dedicated to St. Hadrian. During the conflict between Louis the German and Louis's son Carloman, Pribina was killed in 861 by Moravians. Pribina's son Kocel celebrated Christmas in Mosapurc in 865 together with the archbishop of Salzburg. A decade later, however, Kocel disappeared from the written sources, perhaps in the circumstances surrounding the rise to power of Carloman's illegitimate son, Arnulf of Carinthia (king of East Francia between 887 and 899). Mosapurc became one of Arnulf's residences, as he issued charters from that place dated to 888, 889, and the 890s. In some of those charters, Mosapurc is even described as "royal town." The presence of Arnulf in Mosapurc was caused by his war against the Moravians, for which he allied himself with a new group of nomads from the east, the Magyars.

Who were the Moravians? Archaeologists have long recognized a dramatic change in burial customs around the year 800 in the region of the Morava River north of the Danube (in what is now the eastern part of the Czech Republic) (see map 7.1). The reason for ninth-century Moravia to be called "great" is simply that in the terminology employed in one of the sources pertaining to its existence, the treatise *On the Administration of the Empire* commissioned in the mid-tenth century by Emperor Constantine VII Porphyrogenitus, various territories are called "great" or "small" (or "lesser") depending upon their proximity to the Byzantine Empire (see insert 7.1). Great Moravia was thus farther away from the Byzantine territory than Moravia in the Balkans (along another river called Morava, which now flows through Serbia). Because of that, the location of Moravia has been disputed for some time in scholarship but is now generally believed to have been in the eastern part of the Czech Republic (the province named Moravia) and southwestern Slovakia. All cremations disappeared from that region, perhaps because of the adoption of Christian burial customs. The representation of status through furnished burial, however, continued well into the ninth century. For example, men were buried with spurs and weapons (battle axes, so-called "winged" lance heads, and especially swords with high-quality steel blades of Frankish production). Despite Charlemagne's capitulary of Thionville (805), which prohibited the trade with weapons with Avars and Slavs, Frankish swords clearly reached Moravia in considerable numbers. At the same time, the military posturing of the elites in Moravia is indicated, among other things, by large strongholds that emerged along the river Morava and its tributaries. The most impressive fortifications are at Mikulčice and Pohansko (Czech Republic), as well as at Pobedim and Bojná (Slovakia), all of which were

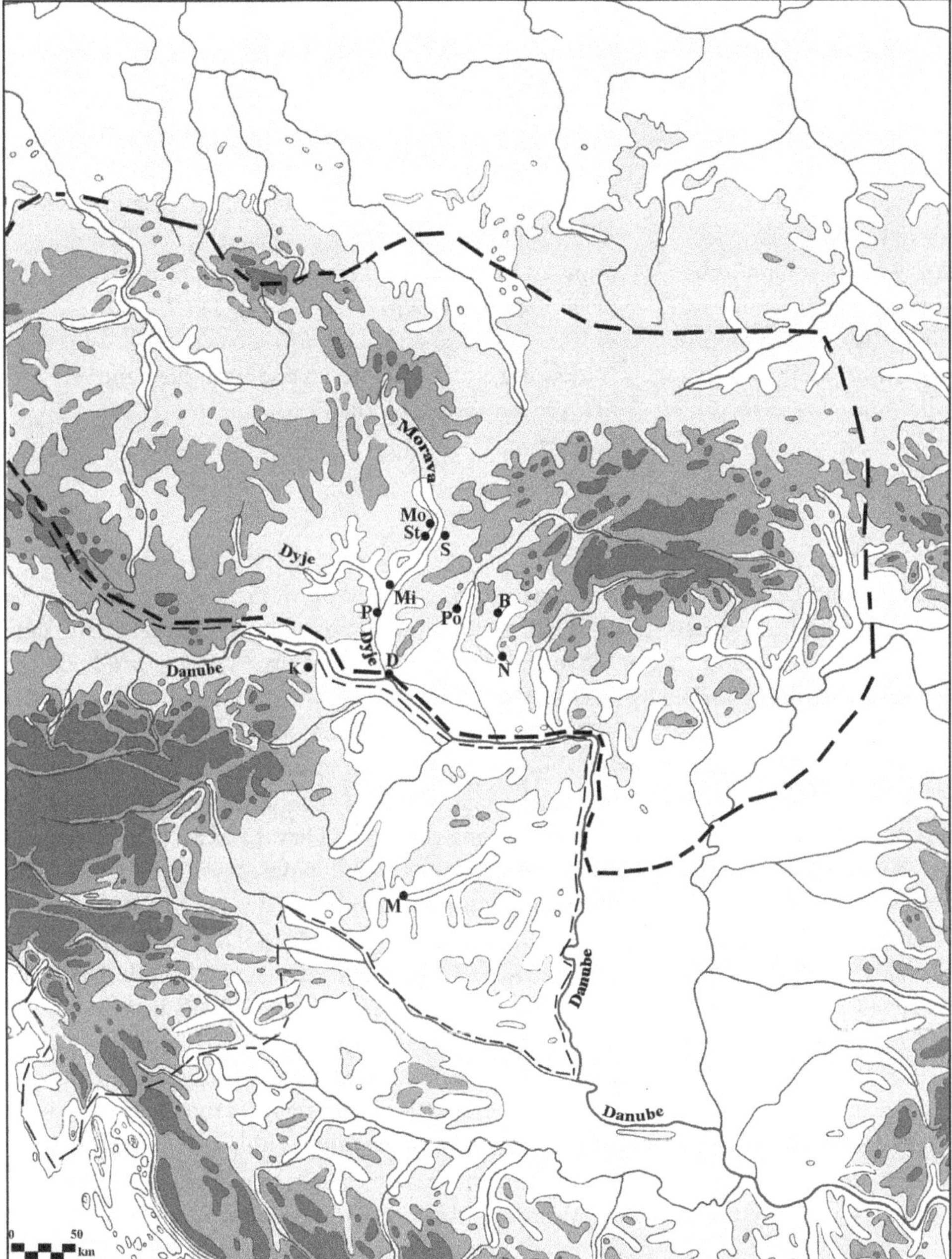

Map 7.1. The Middle Danube region in the ninth century, with the approximate extent of Great Moravia (thick lines) and of the Bavarian Eastland (thin lines). The location of the following sites is indicated: B – Bojná; D – Dowina; K – Kaumburg; M – Mosapurc; Mi – Mikulčice; Mo – Modrá; N – Nitra; P – Pohansko; Po – Pobedim; S – Sady; St – Staré Město. The mountains on the left side of the map are the Eastern Alps, those at the bottom are the Dinaric Alps, those at the top the Western Carpathians, and those at the right the Apuseni.

built in the late ninth century. The Moravians (called *Marvani* in the Frankish annals) first appeared at the imperial court in Frankfurt in 822, alongside envoys from other Slavic groups on the eastern frontier of the empire. The term "Moravians" probably designated, at least initially, the aristocracy of the Slavs living beyond the Danube. Missions from both

INSERT 7.1. THE BYZANTINE, OR EAST ROMAN, EMPIRE

The Roman Empire did not cease to exist when the western emperor, Romulus Augustulus, was deposed in 476: there was still an emperor who resided in Constantinople (today Istanbul). In fact, he was ruling over the eastern, primarily Greek-speaking, part of the empire, while the kingdoms of Western Europe were gradually drifting away from his authority. The phrase "Byzantine Empire" was coined by modern historians to designate the polity that, in the Middle Ages, was in direct continuity with the eastern Roman Empire of Late Antiquity. While Byzantine society and culture changed and evolved over the course of the Middle Ages, Byzantines continued to see themselves as Romans. Rival empires emerged in the Balkans when Bulgarian and, later, Serbian rulers adopted imperial titles and thus competed for political hegemony (see chapters 17 and 45). The Byzantine Empire was weakened by various crises in the later Middle Ages and came to an end with the conquest of Constantinople by the Ottomans in 1453 (see chapter 52).

Salzburg and Passau had already targeted those Slavs, with Moravia soon becoming the object of dispute between the powerful archbishop of Salzburg, Adalram (821–36), and Bishop Reginhar of Passau (818–38) over the borders of their respective dioceses. Louis the German settled the dispute by placing Moravia within the jurisdiction of Passau. A later source even claims that Reginhar baptized the Moravians in 831. According to another source, Archbishop Adalram of Salzburg consecrated a church in Nitra, at that time still under the rule of Pribina. In Moravia, churches appeared at about that same time in Sady and Modrá. Mojmir ruled over the lands along the Dyje (Thaya) and Svrtaka rivers, and he was probably already Christian. His successors, whom the sources sometimes call dukes and other times kings, were all members of the same family – a dynasty. They ruled over the territory on both sides of the river Morava, in what are now Moravia and southwestern Slovakia. The exclusive and never disputed role of the dynasty seems to have derived from its sacred legitimacy established at the time of the conversion to Christianity.

Louis the German attacked Moravia in 846; he defeated and killed Mojmir. The latter's nephew, Rastislav, took over, as he seems to have been until then a hostage at Louis's court. However, Rastislav gave shelter to several Frankish rebels as well as to Czech princes, so Louis decided to replace him. The Frankish expedition of 855 failed to conquer what the sources describe as Rastislav's impressive fortress, most likely one of the strongholds in Moravia (either Mikulčice or Staré Město). According to the *Annals of Fulda*, Louis "would rather leave alone for the time being an enemy who had fortified himself behind strong ramparts than risk [inflicting] losses on his troops in a dangerous battle."[1] In retaliation

1 Florin Curta, ed., "The Annals of Fulda on Moravia," in *Medieval Eastern Europe, 500–1300: A Reader* (Toronto: University of Toronto Press, 2024), p. 23.

INSERT 7.2. THE EAST FRANKISH KINGDOM – A BRIEF HISTORY

The division of the Carolingian Empire through the Treaty of Verdun (843) left the eastern parts to Charlemagne's grandson, Louis (nicknamed "the German" in the eighteenth century, to distinguish him from his father of the same name, Louis the Pious). Louis had until then been duke of Bavaria, but the treaty added Thuringia, Saxony, and Franconia to his domain. Later, he also added Lotharingia. Confronted by the armed rebellion of his three sons, Louis divided the kingdom among them before his death in 876. His second son, Louis the Younger, became king, succeeded by the third son, Charles the Fat, who managed to reunite briefly all three components of Charlemagne's empire under one ruler. Facing a rebellion of his nephew, Duke Arnulf of Carinthia (southern Austria), Charles was deposed. Arnulf became king in 887, then emperor after conquering Italy in 895. Arnulf's successor, Louis the Child, was crowned in 900, but power during his reign was controlled entirely by noblemen and bishops. Louis died in 911 at the age of eighteen, and he had no heirs. With him, the Carolingian line ended in East Francia. The noblemen elected Conrad, duke of Franconia, as the next king, but during his short reign the internal political crisis continued. At his death in 918, Conrad designated Henry I (nicknamed "the Fowler") as his successor. Henry's power was initially contested by the Bavarians, but he managed to obtain the recognition of his royal power by all territorial princes. At Henry's death in 936, his son Otto I (hence the name "Ottonian" for the dynasty) was elected king of the East Frankish kingdom. When Otto was proclaimed emperor in Rome in 962, the East Frankish kingdom became the core part of the Holy Roman Empire. The German rulers who held the imperial title continued to call themselves "kings of the Franks." They were first called "kings of the Teutons" (kings of the Germans) derisively in papal sources of the eleventh century that were hostile to them.

for the attack, Rastislav crossed the Danube and raided the Frankish lands. Three years later, in 858, Carloman (Louis's son) campaigned against Moravia as well, but in 861, Louis agreed to a peace with Rastislav, to prevent his alliance with Carloman (who had meanwhile rebelled against his father) (see insert 7.2). Taking advantage of the war between father and son, Rastislav occupied Lower Pannonia, after defeating and killing Pribina.

One year later, Rastislav sent an embassy to Constantinople to request a bishop, as well as a vernacular language of worship, both indicating that he wanted to distance himself and Moravia from the ecclesiastical influence of Passau and of the Frankish church in general. Emperor Michael III (842–67) responded to the Moravian embassy by sending two brothers from Thessaloniki named Constantine and Methodius. Although neither of them was bishop, they had apparently started to devise a special script (the Glagolitic alphabet) to render the sounds of a language (now known as Old Church Slavonic) into which they translated several liturgical texts, including the Gospels, the Acts of the Apostles, and the Psalms. Their intention seems to have been less to preach than to create a Moravian church in which the liturgy was to be neither in Latin nor Greek, but in Old Church Slavonic (see chapter 12).

There was no Frankish reaction to those developments, even though the Thessalonican brothers encountered a serious opposition from the Bavarian churchmen who resented the influence of the newcomers and their use of the new liturgy in Old Church Slavonic, a language that they did not know but which was apparently understood by Rastislav's subjects. When Louis the German attacked Moravia again in 864, he did so in retaliation for Rastislav's alliance with Carloman. The Franks besieged a fortress named Dowina (most likely Devín, near Bratislava), and Rastislav surrendered, giving up Lower Pannonia (where Kocel was installed at this point) and turning over hostages. Louis and Carloman, meanwhile reconciled, attacked Moravia again in 869, defeating Rastislav but failing to take Rastislav's seat of power. At the time, Rastislav seems to have shared power with his nephew Svatopluk, who had his own autonomous domain within Moravia, probably centered upon Staré Město. Svatopluk entered secret negotiations with Carloman and caught and delivered his uncle, Rastislav, to the Franks. Carloman began the occupation of Moravia, placed under the rule of two Frankish counts, William II and Engilschalk, the sons of Count William I of Traungau. Carloman ordered the arrest of Svatopluk, whom he believed to have joined the rebellion of Carloman's brother Charles III and of Louis the Younger. However, in Moravia, a new ruler was appointed in the person of a former priest named Sclagamar, who attacked the two Frankish counts without success. Carloman decided to send another Frankish army, at the head of which he placed Svatopluk after releasing him. Svatopluk managed to take Sclagamar's stronghold but immediately after that joined the Moravians, with whom he massacred the Frankish troops and killed the two counts. Renouncing his allegiance to Carloman, he rallied a Moravian force and raided Bavaria.

Carloman's response did not come before May 872, when he was unable to take any of Svatopluk's very well fortified strongholds. Moreover, the Moravian ruler crushed the Frankish forces and reversed the military and political situation. By 873, the Franks were on defense, so one year later, Louis the German was forced to recognize through the peace of Forchheim both Svatopluk's strong position and his undisputed rule over a vast territory in Central Europe. Moreover, in 880, Pope John VIII (872–82) issued a bull titled *Industriae tuae*, which placed Moravia under papal protection, bestowing upon Svatopluk the title of "sacred son of St. Peter" (which was otherwise used only for emperors crowned by the pope). The same bull confirmed Methodius (whose brother, Constantine, died in Rome in 869, after taking the monastic name of Cyril) as archbishop of Moravia. However, Svatopluk turned against his archbishop, who had to go to Rome to defend himself against accusations made by the Frankish clergy. At Methodius's death in 885, Pope Stephen V (885–91) forbade the use of the Slavonic liturgy. In Moravia, Svatopluk ordered the arrest of Methodius's disciples, but some of them managed to flee to Bulgaria, where they would play a major role in the organization of the church (see chapter 13). Furthermore, Svatopluk got involved in the internal strife of the (East) Frankish kingdom and invaded and ravaged Pannonia twice. Charles the Fat recognized his power at a meeting in Kaumburg near Tulln (884), and after the peace of 885, Arnulf recognized Svatopluk's power over Bohemia as well. Nonetheless, the conflict reignited a few years later, when

Arnulf invaded Moravia with the assistance of the Magyars, the new horsemen from the East European steppe lands.

Svatopluk died in 894 and Moravia was divided between his three sons, with the eldest, Mojmir II, recognized as grand prince, and the second son, Svatopluk II, ruling in Nitra. The two brothers went to war against each other in 898, while Arnulf campaigned against (all) Moravians. However, at Arnulf's death in 899, Mojmir II occupied the Eastern March, the Frankish territory south of the river Danube. A Bavarian expedition failed to dislodge him in 900, but by then Moravia was raided by the Magyars. When the Magyars inflicted a crushing defeat on the Bavarians at Bratislava (July 4, 907), the fate of Moravia was sealed as well. Moravia and the Moravians disappeared from the radar of the written sources, and historians and archaeologists alike believe that the polity collapsed as a result of the Magyar raids.

FURTHER READING

Betti, Maddalena. *The Making of Christian Moravia (858–882): Papal Power and Political Reality*. East Central and Eastern Europe in the Middle Ages, 450–1450, 24. Leiden: Brill, 2013.

Galuška, Luděk. *Great Moravia*. Moravian Museum Discovery Series, 4. Brno: Moravské Zemské Muzeum, 1991.

Kouřil, Pavel, ed. *Great Moravia and the Beginnings of Christianity*. Brno: Institute of Archaeology of the Academy of Sciences of the Czech Republic, 2015.

Macháček, Jiří, and Martin Wihoda, eds. *The Fall of Great Moravia: Who Was Buried in Grave H153 at Pohansko Near Břeclav?* East Central and Eastern Europe in the Middle Ages, 450–1450, 54. Leiden: Brill, 2019.

Poláček, Lumír, ed. *Great Moravian Elites from Mikulčice*. Brno: Institute of Archaeology, 2020.

Poláček, Lumír. *The Mikulčice-Valy Stronghold and Great Moravia*. Brno: Czech Academy of Sciences, Institute of Archaeology, 2018.

8

EARLY MEDIEVAL BULGARIA

***Keywords in this chapter*: inscriptions, Bulgars, frontiers**

The Bulgars who defeated the Byzantine army led by Emperor Constantine IV and crossed the Danube in 680 (see chapter 3) settled in what are now Dobrudja (the southeastern region of Romania between the Black Sea and the Lower Danube) and the northeastern part of Bulgaria. Historians have long regarded those events as the beginning of the state known in the Early Middle Ages as Bulgaria, with the capital at Pliska (see map 8.1). However, there is no archaeological evidence of the first generation of Bulgars in Bulgaria, and at Pliska no structure known so far could be dated with any degree of certainty before the late eighth century.

Asparukh's successor, Tervel (ca. 700–21), formed an alliance with the Byzantine emperor Justinian II (685–95 and 705–11) to help him regain his throne in Constantinople. According to much later Byzantine sources, in 705 Tervel received from Justinian the "imperial mantle" and the title of Caesar, which made him in principle the heir of Emperor Justinian. Tervel commemorated his achievements through a life-sized image of himself on horseback, which was carved into a cliff at Madara (northeastern Bulgaria) (see plate 8.1). The Madara Horseman, as the relief is called, is accompanied by an inscription in Greek that mentions the assistance that Tervel had given to Emperor Justinian.

Under Emperor Theodosius III (715–17), a peace treaty was concluded in 716, which, while establishing the boundaries between Bulgaria and the Byzantine Empire, also regulated the growing trade between the two countries. Throughout the first half of the eighth century, relations between Bulgaria and Byzantium were peaceful, even cooperative. For example, during the siege of Constantinople by the Arab general Maslama, the Bulgars offered military assistance to Leo III and made an important contribution to the subsequent defeat and humiliation of the Arabs. Tervel's successor, Kormesios (721–38), is mentioned in a second inscription next to the Madara Horseman.

Peaceful relations ended in 755, when Emperor Constantine V (741–75) began fortifying several towns in Thrace. He also moved into those towns Syrian and Armenian prisoners

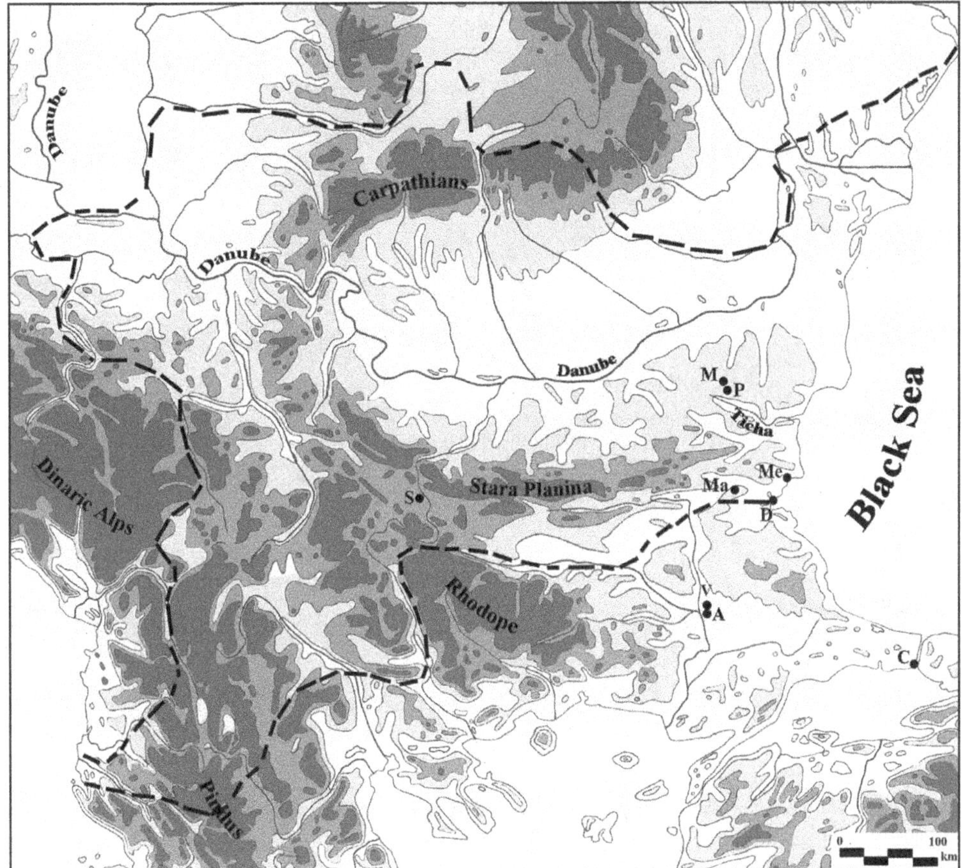

Map 8.1. The Balkan Peninsula in the eighth and ninth centuries, with the approximate extent of Bulgaria. South of the boundaries indicated on the map are the territories controlled by the Byzantine Empire. Dobrudja is between the Lower Danube and the Black Sea, and Thrace is between the Stara Planina and the Rhodope Mountains. The location of the following sites is indicated: A – Adrianople; C – Constantinople; D – Debeltos; M – Madara: Ma – Markellai; Me – Mesembria; P – Pliska; S –Serdica; V – Versinikia.

of war from the eastern frontier of the empire. New bishoprics were established in the new towns, a sign that the settlement was meant to be permanent, the launchpad of a campaign to annihilate and occupy Bulgaria. The Bulgars, correctly assessing the situation, demanded remunerative compensation for what they saw as a breach of the treaty of 716. When Constantine dismissed the charges, the Bulgars raided as far as the Long Walls near Constantinople.

Over the following sixteen years (760–75), Emperor Constantine V waged continuous war against Bulgaria, winning a series of major victories, which threw Bulgaria into a prolonged period of instability. The first Byzantine invasion was both on land and by sea (with a fleet of 500 ships). The land troops obtained a major victory at Markellai (near Karnobat, in southeastern Bulgaria), while the fleet entered the Danube via the river's delta and set fire to the Bulgar lands. The Bulgars sued for peace and agreed to give young sons of aristocratic families as hostages. Those whom the sources call "Bulgars" (most likely the same aristocrats) rose in rebellion two years later and killed all members of the ruling

Plate 8.1. The Madara Horseman. Wikimedia Commons, the free media repository.

dynasty, choosing as new ruler a young man named Telec. A new Byzantine invasion followed, both by land and by sea. The land troops obtained another victory on June 30, 763, against Telec and his Slavic allies, capturing many aristocrats, who were later slaughtered outside the Golden Gate of Constantinople. Telec himself fell victim to his former supporters, who replaced him with a new ruler named Sivin (Sabinos). Sivin sued for peace, but because of the opposition of the Bulgar aristocrats, who wanted war and revenge, he eventually fled to Mesembria (Nesebăr, on the Black Sea coast) and from there to Constantinople. The emperor then sent special troops to extract Sivin's kinsmen and wife from Bulgaria and bring them safely to Constantinople. Another ruler, Paganos (767–68), both by land and by sea pleaded for peace in the company of a group of aristocrats, called *boïlades* in the Byzantine sources and "boyars" in later, native sources of Bulgaria and Rus'. Paganos was reacting to a third very successful expedition against Bulgaria, in which the Byzantines coming on ships entered the Danube and attacked from the north, burning many villages in the region. Meanwhile, another Byzantine army attacked from the south, setting fire to many aristocratic courts ("palaces") along the river Ticha. Two more campaigns that Emperor Constantine mounted in 766 and 774 were dead from the start, as the fleets transporting them to Bulgaria were shipwrecked in the Black Sea. A third expedition with 2,000 ships entered the Danube in 774, but the new Bulgar ruler, Telerig (768–77), quickly offered peace. He later faked an attempt to defect to Byzantium, like Sivin before him, only to obtain the names of the Byzantine agents in Bulgaria, all of whom were promptly put to death. On his way on another expedition to Bulgaria, Emperor Constantine died in 775, and Telerig sought refuge, this time for real, with the new emperor, Leo IV "the Khazar." Under Kardam (777–803), small skirmishes took place, along with pitched battles, one of which took place at Markellai.

Despite the devastation brought by the Byzantine-Bulgar wars, judging from the number of cemeteries excavated by archaeologists both north and south of the river Danube and dated to the second half of the eighth century, at the earliest, the population of (northern) Bulgaria increased substantially within the first century of Bulgaria. However, nothing is known about the "courts" of the aristocrats that are mentioned in the written sources. In Pliska, the only building that may be dated to the late eighth or early ninth century is a circular structure known as the Large Yurt, apparently a timber imitation of the ceremonial hall in the imperial palace of Constantinople.

Kardam's son and successor, Krum (803–14), faced a revival of the Byzantine ambitions to annihilate Bulgaria. The expedition mounted by Emperor Nicephorus I (802–11) in 807 did not go beyond Adrianople (modern Edirne, in the European part of Turkey). One year later, Bulgar troops fell upon the Byzantine army stationed in the valley of the river Struma and seized its pay chest with over 1,100 pounds of gold. Krum attacked Serdica (modern Sofia) in 809, after Nicephorus had fortified and garrisoned the stronghold. Several disgruntled officers are known to have deserted to the Bulgar side from the Byzantine army. Moreover, when moving again against the Bulgars, Emperor Nicephorus faced a revolt of his troops. Nonetheless, after long preparations, he finally invaded Bulgaria in 811, crossing the mountains in the direction of Pliska.

Krum sued for peace, but Nicephorus was bent on finishing Bulgaria. He arrived at Pliska without encountering any resistance. Krum abandoned the site, without even taking his treasure or evacuating civilians, whom the Byzantines massacred indiscriminately, along with their animals. Nicephorus burned Pliska to the ground. Meanwhile, Krum closed all the mountain passes, thus cutting the retreat of the Byzantines. On July 25, 811, when crossing the mountains on its way back to Constantinople, the Byzantine army was ambushed and utterly defeated. Emperor Nicephorus was killed in battle, and many generals and high-ranking officers died as well. The new emperor, Michael I (811–13), rejected Krum's offer of peace, so the Bulgars took Debeltos (now Develt, near the Bay of Burgas), a key fort on the frontier. They took all its inhabitants, including its bishop, to the interior of Bulgaria. Upon learning the news, most towns in Thrace were promptly abandoned by their population. Capitalizing on the terror he had instilled in the Byzantine population of Thrace, Krum sent to Constantinople an envoy to ask for a renewal of the treaty of 716 but added new stipulations regarding the return of the defectors and the monitoring of spies disguised as merchants. The offer was rejected, so the Bulgars took Mesembria, the largest trade center in the region. In June 813, in an undecisive battle at Versinikia, on the right bank of the river Tundzha, near the present-day Bulgarian-Turkish border, Krum used troops under the command of Byzantine defectors, whose names appear in a contemporary inscription in Greek describing the organization of the Bulgar army.

Following the battle, Bulgar troops put Adrianople under siege, and Krum moved on to Constantinople. The new emperor, Leo V (813–20), unsuccessfully attempted to ambush and kill Krum, which only led to a thorough devastation of the suburbs of the Byzantine capital by the Bulgars. Krum returned to Adrianople and took the city, throwing the local bishop to the ground and stepping on his neck in a symbolic gesture of humiliation that imitated a Byzantine ritual called *calcatio*. All inhabitants of Adrianopole were then moved to the lands north of the Danube in what is now southern Romania. Krum was preparing a new siege of Constantinople when he died in 814.

Krum was succeeded by two men who ruled briefly, Dukum and Ditzevg. The latter launched a large-scale persecution of Christians, of whom there seems to have been many in Bulgaria. He ordered the execution of the bishops of Adrianople and Debeltos, but also of one of the Byzantine generals who had defected to Krum. The persecution continued under Krum's son, Omurtag (814–31). Relations with Byzantium improved after Leo V forced Omurtag to agree to a thirty-year peace. The treaty defined the frontier, which ran through Thrace from Burgas to the river Marica. Later, Omurtag ordered the building of a dike along that frontier, now known as the Erkesiia. An exchange of prisoners was implemented, with high-ranking officers for the Byzantine army returned for ransom and commoners "man for man." Krum's request of 813 regarding the defectors was also included in the peace of 816. It is not known whether the treaty obligated Omurtag to provide military assistance, but in 822 he intervened in the civil war in Byzantium, defeating, capturing, and executing Thomas the Slav. Omurtag was confronted with turbulence in the steppe lands to the northwest of the Black Sea and opened a new front in the northwestern Balkans against the Franks. He first requested a delimitation of the frontier through an embassy that showed up in Francia in 824. A second embassy demanded the rectification of the frontier but, like the first, returned home without any answer. A third embassy from Omurtag threatened war if his demands were not met immediately. Louis the Pious ordered troops to be gathered at the eastern frontier, but in 827 a Bulgar expeditionary corps entered the river Drava on boats, attacking the Slavs in Pannonia, who were clients of the Frankish Empire. The Bulgars replaced local chieftains with their own governors, possibly in anticipation of Bulgar occupation. Two years later, a second expedition set fire to Frankish estates along the Drava. Relations between the Bulgars and the Franks remained tense until 832, when envoys from Omurtag's son, Malamir, came to Louis bringing gifts and a message of peace.

Omurtag's reign coincides with the first major building program in Bulgaria. The exact chronology of the buildings in the Inner Town at Pliska is still a matter of debate, but the first walls made of stone were erected there in the ninth century (see chapter 31). Omurtag's palace came into being to the east of the Large Yurt. It had a secret underground passageway, which linked the palace to a private residence to the north. Inside, archaeologists discovered much pottery of fine quality, especially double-handled jugs and flagons, most likely containing wine or other precious liquids. Omurtag added his own inscription to those placed around the Madara Horseman by Tervel and Kormesis. In his inscriptions, of which many are known, Omurtag called himself "ruler from God" and *kana sybigi*, a title believed to be the Bulgar equivalent of "khan" or "emperor." Several other inscriptions of his reign mention high-ranking military commanders, such as the *kavkhan* and the *ichirgu boila*, as well as the distinction between *boilades*, *bagaines* (apparently aristocrats of lower rank), and commoners. Bulgar society seems to have been highly stratified in the ninth century.

Malamir was the youngest of Omurtag's sons, and he came to power after executing his older brother, Enravotas, for having been a Christian (832). He ruled together with an official of the highest rank, the *kavkhan* Isbul, who repelled a Byzantine attack after the expiration of the thirty-year peace in 836. At his death in that year, Malamir was succeeded by his nephew Presian (836–52), who offered military assistance to Emperor Theophilus (829–42). He nonetheless faced a crisis in the lands north of the river Danube, where those forcefully moved into the region under Krum rose in rebellion and called for Byzantine help. The emperor sent a fleet on the Danube, and the Bulgars, unable to stop them, called the Magyars from the steppe lands to assist them in attacking the rebels. Neither the Magyars nor the Bulgars could stop the return of the rebels to Constantinople on Byzantine ships. Presian also contacted Louis the German in 845 to demand a renewal of peaceful relations. Boris, another nephew of Malamir, succeeded Presian at his death in 852. Boris dispatched another embassy to Louis the German, but one year later he accepted bribes from Charles the Bald to attack Louis. No Bulgar attack on Eastern Francia is known. Instead, Boris attacked Croatia, with which Bulgaria now had a common border somewhere in the central Balkans on the territory of present-day Serbia, but without success. He also campaigned without much success against a prince of the Serbs named Mutimir. Together with his brothers Strojmir and Gojnik, Mutimir was able to defeat the Bulgars and to capture Boris's son Vladimir and twelve boyars. Boris had to plead for peace and exchanged gifts with the Serbs.

FURTHER READING

Dobrev, Petăr. *Universum Protobulgaricum I: Inscriptions and Alphabet of the Protobulgarians*. Vienna: MOSAIC, 1996.

Hupchick, Dennis P. *The Bulgarian-Byzantine Wars for Early Medieval Balkan Hegemony: Silver-Lined Skulls and Blinded Armies*. Cham: Palgrave Macmillan, 2017.

Minaeva, Oksana. *From Paganism to Christianity: Formation of Medieval Bulgarian Art*. Frankfurt a.M.: Peter Lang, 1996.

Petkov, Kiril. *The Voices of Medieval Bulgaria, Seventh-Fifteenth Century: The Records of a Bygone Culture*. East Central and Eastern Europe in the Middle Ages, 450–1450, 5. Leiden: Brill, 2008.

Sophoulis, Panos. *Byzantium and Bulgaria, 775–831*. East Central and Eastern Europe in the Middle Ages, 450–1450, 16. Leiden: Brill, 2012.

9

THE VOLGA BULGHARS

Keywords in this chapter: fur trade, trade posts, Islam, caravanserai

According to the Byzantine chronicler Theophanes Confessor, who wrote in the early ninth century, while one of Kubrat's sons named Asparukh moved west towards the Dnieper and the Dniester at his father's death (ca. 660), another son named Kotragos "crossed the Don River and settled across from the first" son, Batbaian, who remained in the ancestral lands ruled by his father (see chapters 3 and 8).[1] If one can trust the semi-legendary account in Theophanes Confessor, this was a group of Bulgars who, after crossing the Don River, moved to the Middle Volga, away from the Khazars who had meanwhile occupied the lands between the Lower Volga and the Don. However, the archaeological evidence from the region around the confluence of the Volga and Kama rivers in the region of present-day Kazan' (the capital of the Republic of Tatarstan, in Russia) does not support the idea of an immigration taking place during the last third of the seventh century. On the contrary, burials of warriors under barrows, which could be attributed to the Bulghars (the name given to the Turkic-speaking Bulgars in the region, to distinguish them from the Bulgars in the Balkans), are dated only to the eighth century.[2] Next to nothing is known from the written sources about the history of this region in the eighth and ninth centuries, but large cemeteries with inhumations have been found, which produced evidence of material culture not unlike that of Khazaria (see map 9.1).

At Tankeevka (halfway between Kazan' and Ul'ianovsk, on the left bank of the Volga), a cemetery with over one thousand graves, a material culture like that of Khazaria is combined with elements of the burial customs typical for the Finno-Ugrian populations of

1 Florin Curta, ed., "Theophanes on the Bulgar Migration," in *Medieval Eastern Europe, 500–1300: A Reader* (Toronto: University of Toronto Press, 2024), 15.

2 In order to distinguish between Bulgars in the northern Balkans and those in Eastern Europe, and to avoid confusion, historians often spell the name of the latter differently – Bulghars (instead of Bulgars).

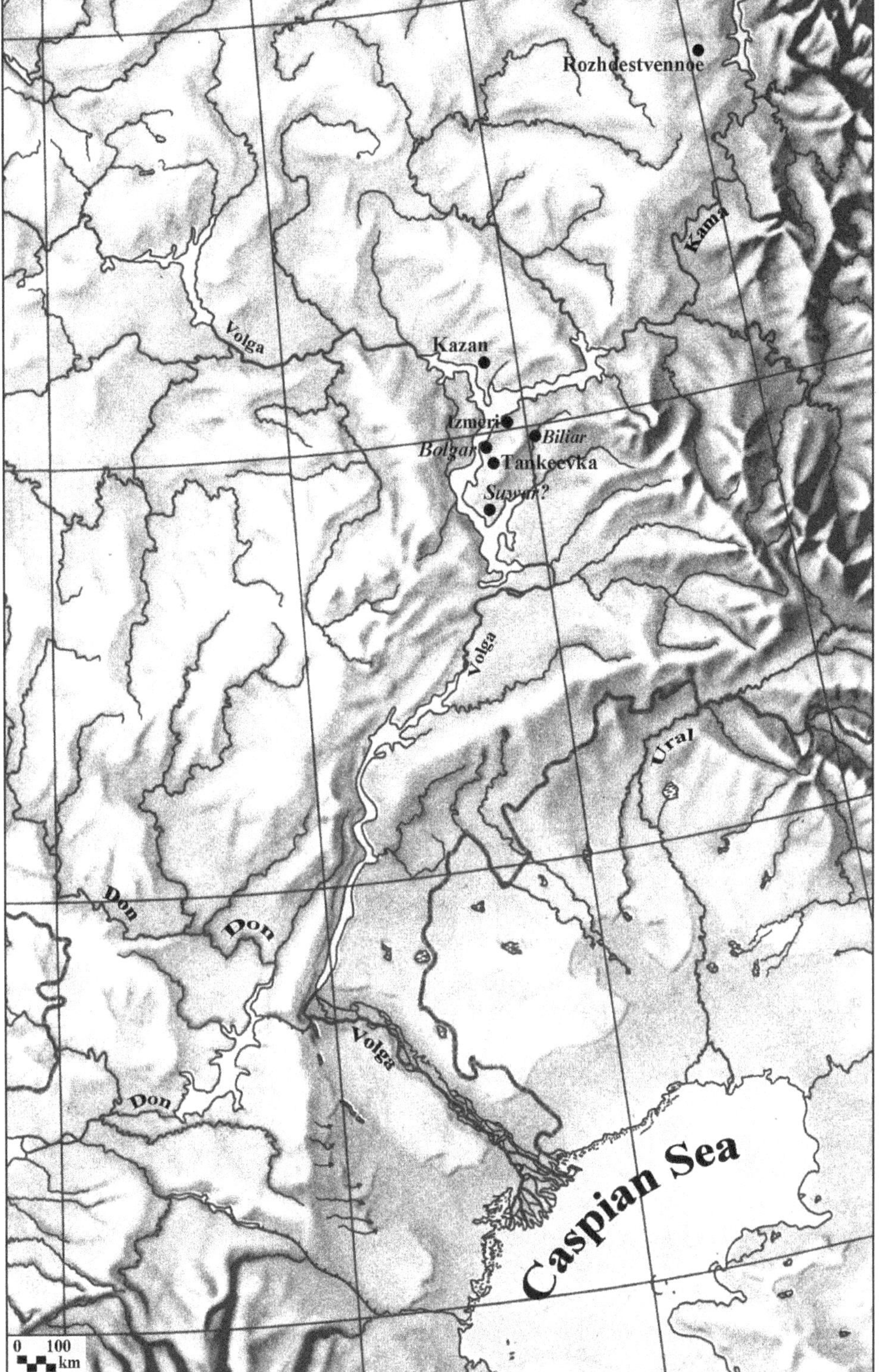

Map 9.1. Volga Bulgharia in the tenth century. Medieval place names are in italics. Itil, the capital of Khazaria, was most likely located in the delta of the river Volga, on the northern shore of the Caspian Sea.

the lands farther to the north, in the forest and forest-steppe zones along the Kama and the Upper Volga. It is in fact quite possible that in the ninth century the Bulghars already exercised political control over those Finno-Ugrian populations inhabiting the lands from which furs came. At any rate, they took advantage of the reorientation of the trade routes ca. 900, away from the Caspian Sea and the Lower Volga and towards the middle course of that river, as the connection to Central Asia was made through the steppe lands between the Caspian and Aral seas. At that time, however, the Bulghars must have themselves been subjects to the Khazars, since they were paying tribute in the form of sables (pelts of a species of marten from the forest belt) from every house of their realm. In addition to giving his daughter in marriage to the khagan of the Khazars (who reputedly had twenty-five wives), the ruler of the Bulghars also had to give as hostage his son, who apparently grew up at the Khazar court in Itil. However, there is no evidence of any garrisons or other form of military presence of the Khazars in Volga Bulgharia.

During the first half of the tenth century, Bulgharia on the Volga grew enormously rich because of the trade with Central Asia, the largest commercial network in the whole of East Central and Eastern Europe. In fact, Bulgharia served as a "silver bridge" between Scandinavia and Central Asia, as an estimated 125 million silver coins struck in the Muslim world entered Eastern Europe through Volga Bulgharia in the direction of Scandinavia. Only a few of those coins were retained locally, primarily those deposited in hoards, all of which are dated between 900 and 1000. However, rulers of Volga Bulgharia struck imitations of silver coins from Central Asia (dirhams), on which they inscribed their own names, otherwise not mentioned in any written sources. There were several mints in operation in Bulgharia during the first half of the tenth century. The earliest coins that were struck in Suwar (with unknown location, but perhaps in the region of Ul'ianovsk) were in the name of a ruler named Talib ibn Ahmad in 949/50. A few decades earlier, in the 920s and 930s, another ruler named Almysh, as well as his son Michael ibn Jafar, struck coins in Bolgar (near present-day Bolgary, in the Republic of Tatarstan). The largest number of Bulghar coins were struck in the 970s in the name of Mumin ibn Hasan and Mumin ibn Ahmad. These coins appear in hoards found at a considerable distance from Bulgharia, in northern and northwestern Russia, in Ukraine, Estonia, Poland, Finland, Sweden, and even Denmark. They testify to the extraordinary growth of the trade mediated by Volga Bulgharia, in which Vikings were involved (see chapter 12). There is plenty of evidence of Scandinavian goods in Bulgharia, and their presence cannot be explained without reference to trade. Furs were one of the main commodities involved in this long-distance trade system. The Bulghars (but not the Vikings) established trade centers in the fur-producing regions to the north. This was the region with the largest number of animals of the genus *Martes* (including marten and sable), but precious furs came to Volga Bulgharia from as far as western Siberia. This explains the presence in northern Russia of wheel-made pottery produced in the urban centers of Bulgharia, as well as in the valley of the river Kama. However, at least some of the wheel-made pots may have also been produced locally, for example in Rozhdestvennoe, a trade post established by Volga Bulghars on the river Obva in what is now the Perm region of Russia, next to the Ural Mountains.

Long-term excavations in Bolgar have revealed that the tenth-century fortification enclosing an area of about 22 acres was served by a few satellite settlements in the hinterland, all of which produced food for the elite and the merchants in Bolgar. The conclusion that Bolgar was involved in international trade results from the great number of glass beads found on the site, many produced in Syria and Egypt, as well as the sphero-conical vessels (some stamped) which may have transported mercury, a key ingredient in goldsmithing. Another urban center of Bulgharia was Biliar (near Biliarsk, in the Republic of Tatarstan), where archaeological excavations revealed a mosque built in the tenth century, as well as a large quantity of ceramic remains, mostly vessels produced in Central Asia, including the so-called Glazed White Ware with Arabic (Kufic) inscriptions. However, the most impressive discovery made in Biliar is a building of clay and stone – a combination of warehouse, kitchen, dining hall, central underground heating facility, numerous wells, and a little mosque – which has been interpreted as a caravanserai, a roadside inn for merchants entering the city. In Kazan', a fortified settlement built in the tenth century, excavations have produced spindle whorls made of a pink slate quarried in Ovruch (near the present-day Belarus-Ukrainian border, to the northeast from Kiev), several hundred miles away from Bulgharia. The coins discovered in Kazan' include a rare denier struck for the Czech duke Wenceslas, as well as another denier minted in Regensburg for Conrad I, king of the Eastern Franks (911–18). Trade centers with no fortifications also appeared on the banks of the river Volga. For example, at Izmeri, a site to the northeast from Bolgar, archaeologists discovered many coins, commercial balances, and weights, the latter being subdivisions of the Iraqi pound of 409.512 grams which served for the striking of coins. The most spectacular find from Izmeri is a bone mount with an inscription in Arabic on two rows, which reads, "Blessings. In the name of the merciful and gracious Allah."

The existence of trading centers such as Izmeri suggests that local markets had a great role in the organization of long-distance trade. That goods were manufactured locally, some of them out of imported materials (e.g., beads made from pre-manufactured rods of imported glass) further indicates that the Bulghars participated in the international trade on their own and did not simply take advantage of their geo-strategical position on the Middle Volga (as the Khazars did in relation to the lower course of that river). Moreover, it is unlikely that any merchants from Central Asia ventured into the fur-producing regions on the Kama River or in western Siberia. Instead, Bulghar merchants, either from Bulgharia or from one of the trade posts established in the northern lands, procured the pelts directly from local communities through exchanges that appear to have taken place at the trade posts or, perhaps, on native sites. They then brought the pelts to the markets in Bulgharia and sold them to Muslim merchants coming from the south.

The scale of the trade was so great that a drastic reorganization of the agricultural production was necessary to meet the food demands of both traders and the administrative personnel (in charge of taxing the booming trade) in the forts. Bulgharia is in the *chernozem* belt of Eurasia, a region so called because the "black earth" (which is what *chernozem* means in Russian) makes it one of the most agriculturally fertile lands of the world (to this day, this region is the granary of Russia). The Volga Bulghars are mentioned as agriculturists in the earliest sources, and they cultivated a variety of crops, from wheat and emmer to rye and oats.

The prosperity allowed the Bulghars to support a relatively large infrastructure for the trade. Commercial contacts with Central Asia also brought an interest in Islam, the religion of most merchants that came to visit the markets in Bolgar, Biliar, and Kazan'. The existence of mosques inside the commercial quarters and even the caravanserai of Biliar suggests that exposure to Muslim religious practices was a function of the ever-increasing volume of trade. It has been suggested that Islam provided the ideology necessary for some chieftains to assert control over the others. There are in fact three different tribes of Bulghars mentioned in the sources – the Bulghars, the Askal, and the Suwar. Only the former accepted Islam around 900 CE, with their ruler, Almysh, claiming that as a humble servant of the most powerful caliph, he had the right and duty to punish all the other chieftains if they disobeyed his orders. In 920, Almysh sent an embassy to Caliph al-Muqtadir (908–32) in Baghdad, asking him to "to send someone, who could teach him religion, who would have knowledge of the shariah [Islamic law], who could build a mosque for him and a *minbar* [pulpit in the mosque from which the sermon or *hutba* is delivered], so that he [Almysh] could carry the mission of conversion for him [i.e., al-Muqtadir's name] throughout his entire land and in all parts of his realm. Furthermore, he beseeched him [the caliph] to build [for him] a fort, in which he could defend himself against hostile kings."[3] The caliph responded by sending as his envoy a learned man named Ahmad ibn Fadlan. His account of the trip to Volga Bulgharia is the main source of the conversion of the Bulghars to Islam (see chapter 15).

FURTHER READING

Curta, Florin. "Markets in Tenth-Century Al-Andalus and Volga Bulghāria: Contrasting Views of Trade in Muslim Europe." *Al-Masaq* 25, no. 3 (2013): 305–30.

Kovalev, Roman K. "What Do 'Official' Volga Bulġār Coins Suggest about the Political History of the Middle Volga Region during the Second Half of the 10th Century?" In *Central Eurasia in the Middle Ages: Studies in Honour of Peter B. Golden*, edited by István Zimonyi and Osman Karatay, 193–210. Turcologica 104. Wiesbaden: Harrassowitz Verlag, 2016.

Noonan, Thomas S. "Volga Bulghāria's Tenth-Century Trade with Samanid Central Asia." *Archivum Eurasiae Medii Aevi* 11 (2000): 140–218.

Rudenko, Konstantin A. *Archaeology of Volga Bulgaria in the 10th–Early 13th Centuries*. East Central and Eastern Europe in the Middle Ages, 450–1450, 90. Leiden: Brill, 2023.

3 Curta, ed., "The Conversion of the Volga Bulghars to Islam," in *Medieval Eastern Europe*, 40.

Shopov, Petăr. "Commercial Relations in the Viking Age between Scandinavian Towns and the Ancient State of Volga Bulgharia." In *Vikingite – moreplavateli, otkrivateli, săzdateli. Material ot mezhunarodna konferenciia, provedena v Sofiiskiia universitet "Sv. Kliment Okhridski" (15–17 mai 2000)*, edited by Elizariia Ruskova, 120–30. Sofia: Universitetsko izdatelstvo "Sv. Kliment Okhridski," 2001.

Zimonyi, István. *Origins of the Volga Bulghars*. Studia Uralo-Altaica 32. Szeged: Universitas Szegediensis de Attila József nominata, 1990.

10

MEDIEVAL NOMADS: PECHENEGS, OGHUZ, AND CUMANS

Keywords in this chapter: nomadic pastoralism, tents, chieftain burial

The collapse of the Khazar khaganate in the tenth century (see chapter 5) triggered new and dramatic movements of population in the steppe lands of Eastern Europe. The first to move were the Pechenegs. Their appearance in the steppe lands on both sides of the Lower Volga is linked to another nomadic group named the Oghuz (Ghuzz or Uzes). The latter were driven in the mid-eighth century by yet other groups from northwest Mongolia and moved into Turkestan (the region of modern Uzbekistan around Tashkent). By the early tenth century, however, ibn Fadlan, on his way to the Volga Bulghars, saw them somewhere beyond the Ustyurt plateau between the western shore of the Aral Sea and the northeastern shore of the Caspian Sea, in what is now southwestern Kazakhstan. They had "houses made of wool" and their chieftain was "called *yabghu*; this is the word for ruler, and the one who rules over a tribe has that title."[1] However, there was no central authority in the land of the Oghuz. This may explain the conflict between different tribes or clans, the most famous of which was the separation, shortly before the year 1000, of a tribe under a chieftain named Seljuk (see insert 10.1).

The other Oghuz moved about the same time into the Kalmyk steppe between the Volga, Don, and Manych rivers. They thus became neighbors of the Pechenegs, whose name in Turkic means "brothers-in-law." The Oghuz pushed the Pechenegs north of the Caspian Sea in what is now northern Kazakhstan. This is how the Pechenegs came to the northern frontier of the Khazar khaganate. Islamic sources incorporated into the works of later authors mention regular raids on both sides of that frontier – Khazars against Pechenegs, and Pechenegs against Khazars. By 830, however, the Khazars allied themselves

1 Florin Curta, ed., "Ibn Fadlan on the Oghuz," in *Medieval Eastern Europe, 500–1300: A Reader* (Toronto: University of Toronto Press, 2024), 51.

INSERT 10.1. THE SELJUKS – BETTER KNOWN RELATIVES OF THE OGHUZ

The name of the Seljuks comes from Seljuk, a warlord who had a falling out with the *yabghu*, the supreme chieftain of the Oghuz. In the tenth century, the Oghuz controlled the steppe lands on both sides of the Aral Sea in what is now southwestern Kazakhstan. The main reason for internecine tribal conflicts at the time was religion. Seljuk was in fact among the early converts to Islam, ca. 985. His descendants fled from the region of the Aral Sea and in the 1030s moved into Khorasan (a region now divided between Turkmenistan and northeastern Iran). They defeated the powerful Ghaznavid emir Masud I (1030–41), which turned them into a formidable force of the eleventh-century Middle East. In 1055, the Seljuk warlord Tughril entered Baghdad in response to a call from the Abbasid caliph. Under Alp Arslan (1063–73) and Malikshah (1073–92), the Seljuks created a vast empire centered upon Iran that stretched from Anatolia to China. Alp Arslan obtained a major victory against the Byzantines at Manzikert (1071), while Malikshah and his vizier Nizam al-Mulk organized the empire on a solid religious basis. Despite ruling from Iran, the Seljuks were Sunni Muslims and they established a network of madrasas (Islamic colleges) for the training of administrative personnel and religious scholars. However, the Seljuks replaced the Arabic language with literary Persian, which became the language of instruction. After 1092, the empire began to disintegrate. One of the most important successor states was the Sultanate of Rum, so called because it was created in those territories taken from the Byzantines (or Romans) after Manzikert. It is against the Seljuks of that sultanate that the crusaders fought in the late eleventh century. The sultanate of Rum was obliterated by the Mongols in the thirteenth century. Families of Seljuk warlords also controlled Syria, but they were wiped out by the Mongols as well. By 1260, there was no Seljuk rule anywhere in the Middle East.

with the Oghuz. Unable to defend themselves, the Pechenegs crossed the Volga and the Don rivers and invaded the grazing fields of the Magyars, who lived by the "Sea of Rum," as Muslim sources called the Black Sea (referring to the Roman capital, Constantinople).[2] During the last decade of the ninth century, they destroyed the Magyar encampments and forced them to leave the steppe lands north of the Black Sea, cross the Carpathian Mountains, and move into the Middle Danube region (see chapter 18).

Over the following two centuries, the Pechenegs dominated the steppe corridor between the Don and the Danube rivers. *On the Administration of the Empire*, a work commissioned and supervised by Emperor Constantine VII Porphyrogenitus in the mid-tenth century, mentions the Pechenegs in relation to five rivers flowing through their territory, two of which are the Prut and the Siret, emptying into the Lower Danube right before the delta. The axis of the Pecheneg land was the river Dnieper, which played a key role in their seasonal migration together with their herds of animals, from the grazing fields

2 Curta, ed., "Ibn Rusta on the Magyars," in *Medieval Eastern Europe*, 47.

in the north to the lowlands by the sea. The Pecheneg economy was predominantly pastoralist. Settlements of agriculturists, however, are known from the westernmost region under Pecheneg rule, for example at Şendreni (near Galaţi, Romania). The Pechenegs were involved in trade, especially with hides. They also organized raids into neighboring sedentary societies, especially Rus' and Byzantium, with the goal of taking captives, whom they later sold as slaves.

There were eight districts in the land of the Pechenegs, four on each side of the river Dnieper. The Pechenegs in three of those districts were ranked higher than the rest and called *kangar* ("of noble birth"). Each district was further subdivided into five sections, with a "lesser prince" as its head. The system of inheritance was based on the principle of seniority, with cousins favored over sons. However, there was no well-structured or hierarchically organized polity, nothing like a state. Instead, by the eleventh century, the number of tribes, each with its own head, increased, and so did the competition between chieftains. The Byzantine chronicler John Skylitzes, who wrote in the late eleventh century, counted thirteen tribes, "all of which have the same name in common, but each tribe has its own proper name inherited from its own ancestor and chieftain."[3]

The first Pecheneg raid against Kiev known from the sources was in 915. By that time, the Pechenegs controlled the entire corridor of the steppe and could effectively interfere with the lucrative Rus' trade with Byzantium. They typically intercepted Rus' convoys in the region of the rapids on the Lower Dnieper (south from the present-day city of Dnipro, in Ukraine). In fact, upon returning from Bulgaria in 972, Sviatoslav, the prince of Kiev, was ambushed at the rapids and killed by the Pechenegs. To counter the danger, the Rus' allied themselves with the nomadic enemies of their enemies – the Oghuz. During the last decade of the tenth century, Sviatoslav's son Vladimir began building fortifications on the southern frontier of Rus' and recruited the Oghuz (known as "Black Hoods" in the Rus' chronicles) for their garrisons. In a battle just outside Kiev, Vladimir's son, Iaroslav the Wise, crushed the Pechenegs in 1036 and thus put an end to their raids against Rus'. The Cathedral of St. Sophia in Kiev was erected to commemorate that victory.

Increasing pressure from the Rus' and their Oghuz allies pushed the Pechenegs into the steppe lands north of the Black Sea closer to the frontier of the Byzantine Empire. During the first half of the eleventh century, Pecheneg marauders crossed the Danube numerous times and raided deep into the interior of the Balkan provinces. In 1046, defeated in a bid for power against a powerful chieftain named Tyrach, a "lesser prince" named Kegen fled with his men across the Danube into the neighboring Byzantine province. He converted to Christianity and was given a title and the supreme command of the troops in the Byzantine defense system on the Danube.[4] Two years later, a large-scale invasion of Tyrach's Pechenegs resulted from internecine strife, as well as the pressure of the Oghuz. The latter invaded the Byzantine Balkans in 1064 but were decimated by plague. Meanwhile, the

3 Curta, ed., "John Skylitzes on the Pechenegs," in *Medieval Eastern Europe*, 52.

4 Curta, ed., "John Skylitzes on the Pechenegs," in *Medieval Eastern Europe*, 53.

Pechenegs, who had moved in great numbers to the Balkans, remained a major problem for the region until they were crushed at the battle of Levunion (1091) by Emperor Alexius I Comnenus and his Cuman allies. After that, the Pechenegs appear only sporadically in the sources, with their last raid mentioned in 1122.

Plate 10.1. The burial of a Cuman chieftain on the bank of the river Chynhul. Photo by Yuri Rassamakin.

Of all nomadic groups, the Cumans had the longest and greatest influence upon the history not only of East Central and Eastern Europe, but of the medieval world in general. They gave a king to Hungary (Ladislas IV "the Cuman," 1272–90, son of a Cuman princess named Elizabeth; see chapter 42), an emperor to Bulgaria (George Terter, 1280–92), and one of the most famous sultans of the Mamluk dynasty of Egypt (Baybars, 1260–77). Known as *Polovtsy* in the Rus' chronicles and *Kipchak* to the Mongols, the Cumans made their appearance on the left bank of the Dnieper in the mid-eleventh century. They took advantage of the failure of the Oghuz invasion into the Balkans and extended their power to the Danube. Several Cuman tribes now controlled the vast steppe corridor. In the early twelfth century, the center of power was to the west of the river Dnieper. Two chieftains from those lands, Boniak and Tugorkan, helped Emperor Alexius I in the battle of Levunion. Boniak also attacked and raided Hungary, being defeated by King Ladislas before defeating King Coloman. Unlike the Pechenegs and the Oghuz, the Cumans had a much more stratified society, with lords and nobles. Just how rich any of them could be is well illustrated by the grave of a chieftain, buried under a large barrow on the right bank of the Chynhul River near Zamozhne (in the steppe lands north of the Sea of Azov). The burial assemblage contained a remarkable array of artifacts of Syrian, Rus', Byzantine, and even West European origin, including such exotica as imported silks, Byzantine amphorae, an enamel cup, a Syrian stone-paste drug jar, silver belt sets with damascened ornaments, and a bronze cover cup from the Rhine-Meuse region (see plate 10.1).

Around 1200, the federation of Cuman tribes turned into a more centralized polity under a chieftain named Konchek, who allied himself with the Rus' princes of Chernigov against those of Kiev and Suzdal'. Meanwhile, the Cumans became key allies of the Vlach rebels in the northern Balkans, who were responsible for the rise of the Second Bulgarian Empire (see chapter 45). They were the main cavalry force in the army with which Johannitsa Kaloyan won a major victory against the crusaders at Adrianople in 1205. To one of the chroniclers of the Fourth Crusade, they were "savage people, who neither plow nor sow, who dwell neither in huts nor in houses, but in a sort of felt houses, which they carry around with them, and they eat milk, cheese and meat."[5] Wagons, in which the Cumans carried their felt houses, are known from both written and archaeological sources. However, other sources refer to Cuman strongholds and towns, three of which are known by name – Sharukan, Sugrov, and Balin. The role of those towns as centers of power results from the fact that at least two of them are named after Cuman chieftains.

Shortly after their participation in the battle of Adrianople, the Cuman control over the steppe lands in Eastern Europe was broken. In the aftermath of their victory on the banks of the river Kalka (1223) over the Cuman-Rus' coalition, the Mongols established a long-term domination of the steppe corridor now known as *Desht-i-Kipchak* ("the Cuman steppe"). Only fifteen years later, Kuthen, a Cuman chieftain who had escaped from the massacre, fled to Hungary, where other Cuman groups had meanwhile sought asylum. Most Cumans, however, remained in the East European steppe lands and, after the Mongol invasion, became the majority population in the Golden Horde (see chapter 46).

FURTHER READING

Golden, Peter B. "The Shaping of the Cuman-Qïpčaqs and Their World." In *Il Codice Cumanico e il suo mondo: Atti del Colloquio internazionale, Venezia, 6–7 dicembre 2002*, edited by Felicitas Schmieder and Peter Schreiner, 245–77. Rome: Edizioni di storia e letteratura, 2005.

Nikolov, Aleksandăr. "'Ethnos skythikos': The Uzes in the Balkans (Facts and Interpretations)." In *The Steppe Lands and the World beyond Them: Studies in Honor of Victor Spinei on His 70th Birthday*, edited by Florin Curta and Bogdan-Petru Maleon, 235–47. Iași: Editura Universității "Alexandru Ioan Cuza," 2013.

Ostrowski, Donald. "The Rare and Excellent History of Konchak: A Polovtsian Chieftain." In *Portraits of Medieval Eastern Europe, 900–1400*, edited by Donald Ostrowski and Christian Raffensperger, 61–67. London: Routledge, 2017.

Paroń, Aleksander. *The Pechenegs: Nomads in the Political and Cultural Landscape of Medieval Europe*. East Central and Eastern Europe in the Middle Ages, 450–1450, 74. Leiden: Brill, 2021.

Spinei, Victor. *The Great Migrations in the East and Southeast of Europe from the Ninth to the Thirteenth Century*. Amsterdam: Adolf M. Hakkert, 2006.

5 Curta, ed., "Robert the Clari on the Cumans," in *Medieval Eastern Europe*, 54.

11

THE EARLY RUS'

Keywords in this chapter: Vikings, trade, towns, conversion, Christianity

The first mention of the Rus' appears in the *Annals of St. Bertin* under the year 839, when a group of mysterious people called "Rhos" arrived at the court of Emperor Louis the Pious in Ingelheim. Their leader was called a khagan, a title used for rulers of steppe peoples, such as the Avars who had been defeated by Charlemagne, Louis's father, or the Khazars who dominated the steppes at the time of this encounter (see chapters 2 and 5, and insert 2.2). Returning from Constantinople, they asked permission to travel through the Frankish kingdom on their way home. Louis's courtiers were confused about the exact identity of those visitors. Investigating the matter, they figured out that those who called themselves *Rhos* were in fact *Sueones*, a name used at that time for people living in what is now eastern Sweden.

The connection to Scandinavia was not accidental. In fact, the very name of Rus' was also given to Scandinavian adventurers, mostly from Sweden, who travelled to Byzantium through the river routes of Eastern Europe (see chapter 33). A fleet of Rus' pillaged the surroundings of Constantinople around 860; the Rus' were mentioned in Byzantine sources as warriors and merchants, and their leader was named the "khagan of the Northmen" in 871. The *Primary Chronicle* (otherwise known as the *Tale of Bygone Years*) compiled by monks in Kiev, the last of whom wrote in the early twelfth century, recounts the role of the Scandinavians in the early period of political formation. According to that narrative, people from the land of Novgorod who had been tributaries to Scandinavians known as Varangians sent out a delegation to them in 862, asking for someone to bring order and stability to their country. Three brothers accepted the invitation; after the death of his younger siblings, Riurik ended up ruling alone as *kniaz'*, a Slavonic title that is usually translated as "prince" but in fact means "king." As the chronicler put it, the inhabitants of Novgorod had all "descended from the Varangian race, but aforetime they were Slavs."[1]

1 Florin Curta, ed., "Varangians in Rus'," in *Medieval Eastern Europe, 500–1300: A Reader* (Toronto: University of Toronto Press, 2024), 68.

The names of Riurik and his son Oleg are clearly of Norse origins (Hrorikr and Helgi, respectively). The Rus' of the area of the Volkhov River (the hinterland of Novgorod) expanded to the south and in the late ninth century were established in Kiev, on the middle course of the river Dnieper, encroaching into the Khazar Empire (see map 11.1). The exact role of these Scandinavian newcomers in creating political structures has long been the subject of much speculation and nationalistic disputes. There is no doubt, however, that the Riurikids who reigned for centuries over the lands of Rus' were of Scandinavian heritage. The most probable explanation is that the Scandinavian adventurers first imposed the payment of tribute on the local populations and then gradually established more complex political structures.

In any case, the upper class at the Riurikid court of the earlier period appears to have had a mixed culture influenced by the Norse, the Eastern Slavs, and the steppe peoples. The early Rus' were pagans. Amulets representing Thor's hammer, such as found in Sweden, have been discovered on many archaeological sites such as the barrow cemetery in Gnezdovo, near Smolensk: they indicate worship of Norse gods long after the move to Eastern Europe. Moreover, Byzantine sources that mention interactions between Byzantines and the Rus' recount that the latter made oaths on the names of such deities as Perun and Veles, the former being a common god of people around the Baltic Sea – Norse, Slavs, and Balts. The mixed heritage of the early Rus' is attested by inscriptions that are sometimes in runes and other times in Cyrillic. The rulers' court long remained bilingual as new waves of newcomers kept arriving from Scandinavia. Rus' chroniclers made a distinction between the Rus', who in the twelfth century were people from distant Norse heritage but spoke Slavic, and Varangians, who were more recent immigrants from Scandinavia. Moreover, the use of the title khagan in Frankish and Byzantine sources of the ninth century suggests a political culture inspired by nomads in the steppe lands. The Khazars, whose empire dominated trade in the steppe world between Europe and Byzantium, provided an inspiring model for the early rulers of Rus'.

The mixed culture of the Rus' in the late ninth and tenth centuries found expression in dress accessories. Oval brooches of Scandinavian type worn by women were common in Rus' graves. Men, on the other hand, wore caftans with bronze buttons, following a fashion popular among the Khazars and Volga Bulghars. Female fashion in early Novgorod was shaped by eclectic influences from Slavic, Scandinavian, Finno-Ugrian, and Baltic traditions. Dress accessories included chains with jingling pendants and paired pins as pectoral ornaments, which were typical for the Finno-Ugrian populations of the northern part of Eastern Europe; bird- or horse-shaped pendants, as well as bracelets of Baltic-Finnish tradition; and temple rings characteristic of the female dress in regions farther to the south that were populated by Slavs. Typically Scandinavian artifacts such as oval brooches were rare in early Novgorod, which suggests a higher level of acculturation of settlers with Norse heritage than on other sites of early Rus'.

The early Rus' were involved in long-distance trade – especially with furs and slaves sold in Byzantium – as attested by numerous finds of Samanid coins throughout Eastern Europe and by early urban centers such as Staraia Ladoga (see chapters 32 and 33). Rus'

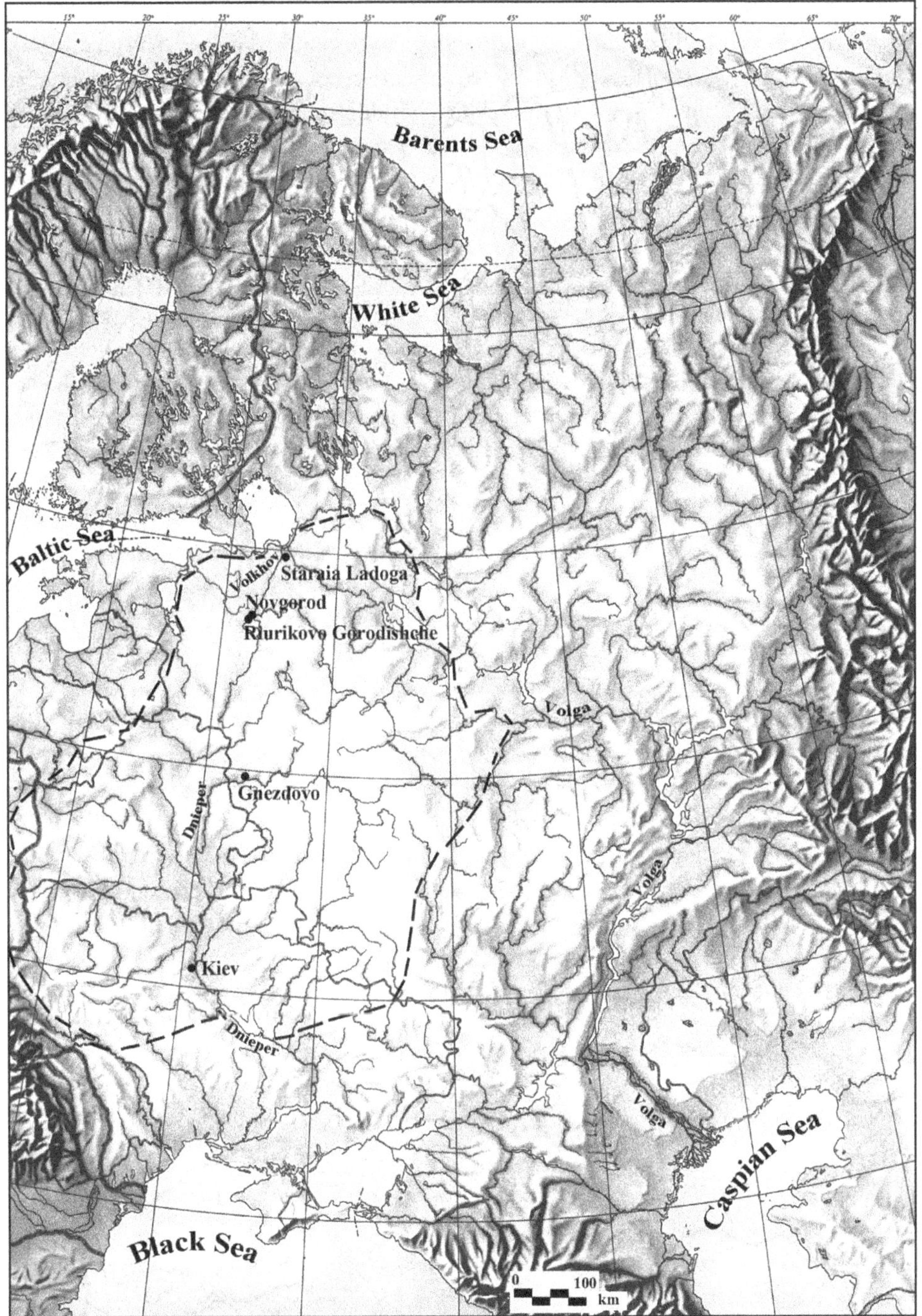

Map 11.1. The approximate extent of early Rus', ca. 1000. Shown in the lower left corner are the Carpathian Mountains, while the range on the right is the Ural Mountains.

merchants travelling to Byzantium entertained connections with the Volga Bulghars; early on they established commercial relationships with the Byzantines that were sealed through various treaties, such as those of 907 and 911 recorded in the *Primary Chronicle*. According to the treaty of 944, Rus' merchants coming to Constantinople had to carry certificates issued by their ruler in Kiev and enter the city of Constantinople without weapons but were entitled to an allowance provided by the Byzantine government for the duration of their sojourn.[2]

Prince Igor, who is mentioned in the text of the treaty of 944, began to rule in 940. By that time, the main center of power in the lands of Rus' had moved from Staraia Ladoga and Riurikovo Gorodishche, near Novgorod, to Kiev on the Dnieper River, which flows into the Black Sea. This reflected the reorientation of Rus' trade towards Byzantium. In 941, Igor launched an attack on Constantinople that brought him little success; the renewed treaty of 944 did not bring significant changes to the Byzantine–Rus' relations. One year later, Igor was killed when trying to exact tribute from the Derevlians, a tribe inhabiting the lands to the northwest of Kiev.

Igor was succeeded by his widow, Olga (the Slavic form of a Norse name, Helga). She ruled over Kiev single-handedly as regent for her young son, Sviatoslav, until he came of age around 964. Olga was a significantly more successful and respected ruler than Igor had been. The *Primary Chronicle* recounts how she began by avenging the murder of her husband: she slaughtered Derevlian envoys and sent a punitive expedition to their land. As a ruler, she traveled around the country to collect tribute and dispense justice; she reformed the tax collection system to secure more regular payments; and she established trading posts and hunting preserves. More peaceful relations with the Byzantine authorities resumed. Olga traveled to Constantinople in person – a visit mentioned in Byzantine sources – most likely in 957; the occasion may have been yet another renewal of the commercial treaty. She arrived at the imperial court with a group of Rus' princesses and women from her entourage along with a delegation of Rus' merchants and was very well received, for she was allowed to sit at the imperial dining table and was given great honors. Byzantine sources call her *archontissa* ("female ruler") and *hēgemōn* ("leader, commander"). Such a reception, highly unusual for a ruler of a barbarian, pagan people from the distant north, was directly linked to Olga's decision to be baptized (see chapter 16).

FURTHER READING

Androshchuk, Fedir O. *Vikings in the East: Essays on Contacts along the Road to Byzantium (800–1100)*. Studia Byzantina Uppsaliensia 14. Uppsala: Uppsala Universitet, 2013.

Franklin, Simon, and Jonathan Shepard. *The Emergence of Rus 750–1200*. Longman History of Russia. London: Longman, 1996.

2 Curta, ed., "A Trade Agreement between the Rus' and Byzantium," in *Medieval Eastern Europe*, 73.

Katona, Csete. *Vikings of the Steppe: Scandinavians, Rus', and the Turkic World (c. 750–1050)*. New York: Routledge, 2022.

Murasheva, Veronika V., and Ol'ga V. Orfinskaia. "Tenth-Century 'Idol' from Chorna Mohyla." In *A Viking Century: Chernihiv Area from 900 to 1000 AD*, edited by Stepan Stepanenko, 153–72. Hlib Ivakin Memorial Series. Paris: ACHCByz, 2022.

Pokrovskaya, Lyubov V. "Female Costume from Early Novgorod and Its Ethno-cultural Background: An Essay on Reconstruction." In *Vers l'Orient et vers l'Occident: Regards croisés sur les dynamiques et les transferts culturels des Vikings à la Rous ancienne*, edited by Pierre Bauduin and Alexander E. Musin, 101–12. Caen: Presses universitaires de Caen, 2014.

Raffensperger, Christian. *The Kingdom of Rus'*. Past Imperfect. Kalamazoo/Bradford: Arc Humanities Press, 2017.

PART 3

Conversions and New Polities

12

CONVERSION TO CHRISTIANITY: MORAVIA

Keywords in this chapter: mission, Glagolitic script, Old Church Slavonic

One of the immediate consequences of the Frankish encroachment into East Central Europe (see chapter 7) was that Moravia and parts of what is now southwestern Slovakia became the target for missions from neighboring bishoprics. Credit for the baptism of Mojmir I, ca. 820, is usually given to Bishop Reginhar of Passau. At some point before 829, a church in Nitra was consecrated by Archbishop Adalram of Salzburg. The conflict between the archbishop and his suffragan in Passau was aggravated when Mojmir defeated and expelled Pribina. As a result of Louis the German's arbitration (see chapter 7), Moravia fell under the influence of Passau, and by the mid-ninth century Christianity was implemented in many strongholds, such as Staré Město, Uherské Hradiště, and Mikulčice, where the remains of some of the earliest churches have been found by archaeologists. There is nonetheless no one-to-one relationship between the missionary activity from Passau and the church architecture associated with the beginnings of Christianity in Moravia. For example, the rotundas (round churches) discovered in Mikulčice have analogies in Dalmatia, the region of Salzburg, and the Balkans. The Frankish mission made some limited use of the vernacular (i.e., the Slavic language spoken in Moravia) for practical purposes – formal renunciation of pagan beliefs, confession, and a few fundamental prayers. Particularly illustrative in that respect are the so-called Freising Manuscripts. Although used in Carinthia, not Moravia, those texts written in a Slavic dialect shortly before 1000 contain translations done in the ninth century to assist the Frankish mission.

In the context of his conflict with Louis the German, Rastislav (Mojmir's nephew, for whom see chapter 7) sent envoys to Constantinople to request "a teacher who would explain to us in our language the true Christian faith."[1] In response, Emperor Michael III

1 Florin Curta, ed., "St. Cyril, Old Church Slavonic, and the Creation of the Glagolitic Alphabet," in *Medieval Eastern Europe, 500–1300: A Reader* (Toronto: University of Toronto Press, 2024), 31.

sent Constantine and Methodius, because they were "both Thessalonians and all Thessalonians speak pure Slavic."[2] Although younger than his brother, Constantine seems to have played a key role in the enterprise. Much of what is known about him comes from the *Life of Constantine*, a work written in Old Church Slavonic at some point between his death in 869 and December 885 (when the text is used in Rome), perhaps in 879 or 880. Constantine was born in 826 or 827 in Thessaloniki in the family of a Byzantine officer. A child of sensitive personality, he was drawn to study and religious devotion. For that, he was brought to Constantinople at a young age and attended the imperial academy at Magnaura. There he studied "Homer and geometry with Leo [the Mathematician, a great Byzantine scholar, who was archbishop of Thessaloniki between 840 and 843], and dialectics and all philosophical studies with Photius [the future patriarch of Constantinople, 858–67 and 876–86]; and in addition to that, rhetoric and arithmetic, astronomy, and music, and all the other Hellenic arts."[3] Constantine quickly turned into a serious intellectual, was tonsured as a priest, and was appointed librarian to the patriarch in the Cathedral of St. Sophia. He was in his twenties when sent on an embassy to Caliph al-Mutawwakil, probably to negotiate an exchange of prisoners between the Arabs and the Byzantines. While in Samarra, he engaged in a disputation (religious debate) with Muslim ulamas, in which he distinguished himself by citing from the Quran in support of his defense of the Holy Trinity. Upon his return to Constantinople, however, he decided to join his older brother Methodius in a monastery on Mount Olympus in Bithynia (in the northwestern part of present-day Turkey). Without taking the vows, he remained there until recalled by Patriarch Photius in 860 for another diplomatic mission. Together with his brother Methodius, Constantine embarked on a trip to the Khazar court in Itil, perhaps to negotiate an alliance against the Rus'. On their way there, the two brothers stopped in the Crimea, where Constantine discovered the relics of St. Clement, the second pope of Rome, who had died in Chersonesus in the year 99. In Itil, he engaged in yet another disputation with both Muslim ulamas and Jewish rabbis. Back in Constantinople, the two brothers were then sent to Rastislav in Moravia. The main task of this trip was to educate (i.e., to consolidate and rectify the orthodox faith of) those who had already accepted Christianity from the Frankish mission. In contrast to that mission, Constantine and Methodius focused on teaching (i.e., explaining doctrinal issues) in the vernacular. In fact, before going to Moravia, Constantine started the translation of religious texts into Old Church Slavonic, a book language that he created based on a dialect supposedly spoken in the hinterland of his hometown, Thessaloniki. To render the sounds of that language, he also devised a new alphabet, called Glagolitic (see plate 12.1). The translation made extensive use of Greek words for concepts that Old Church Slavonic could not render. For example, pairs of synonyms were used in specific contexts, such as *angel* (for angel, from the Greek) and *posăl* (for envoy, from Slavic). Although no manuscripts have survived from this early

2 Curta, ed., "St. Cyril," in *Medieval Eastern Europe*, 31.

3 Curta, ed., "St. Cyril," in *Medieval Eastern Europe*, 30.

period of the Slavonic script, it is generally accepted that the earliest translations were excerpts from the Gospels to be used in the liturgy. Gospel translations are in fact among the oldest surviving manuscripts in Old Church Slavonic, none of which could be dated before the year 1000. In addition to liturgical texts, Constantine and Methodius translated several sermons for important holidays of the year. Their approach to conversion was Christian humanist, in that they viewed pagans as fellow human beings in need of help and prayers, and not as sinful creatures completely different from Christians. This explains why they never used force during their activities in Moravia.

Warmly received by Rastislav, the two brothers were allowed to recruit young men for instruction. In five years (863–68), Constantine and Methodius thus laid the foundations of a native clergy, using the liturgy and the texts they had translated into Old Church Slavonic. In the circumstances surrounding the Photian Schism, a dispute between the patriarch of Constantinople and the pope of Rome, they decided to go to Rome for the ordination of their disciples as priests (see insert 12.1).

On their way to Rome, the group from Moravia paid a visit to Kocel in Mosapurc (see chapter 7). In Rome, Pope Hadrian II (867–72), who was interested in bringing Moravia under papal obedience, gave a warm welcome to the two brothers and their disciples. Impressed with the relics of St. Clement, which Constantine brought to Rome all the way from Crimea, the pope formally accepted the Slavonic translation of the Gospels. The Moravian disciples were ordained, and for five consecutive days they all co-celebrated the liturgy in Slavonic in four different churches of Rome. Meanwhile, however, Constantine fell ill and died on February 14, 869, not before taking the monastic vows and changing his name to Cyril. He was buried in the Church of St. Clement, on the right side of the altar, with an icon above his grave, a sign that he had already been recognized as a saint.

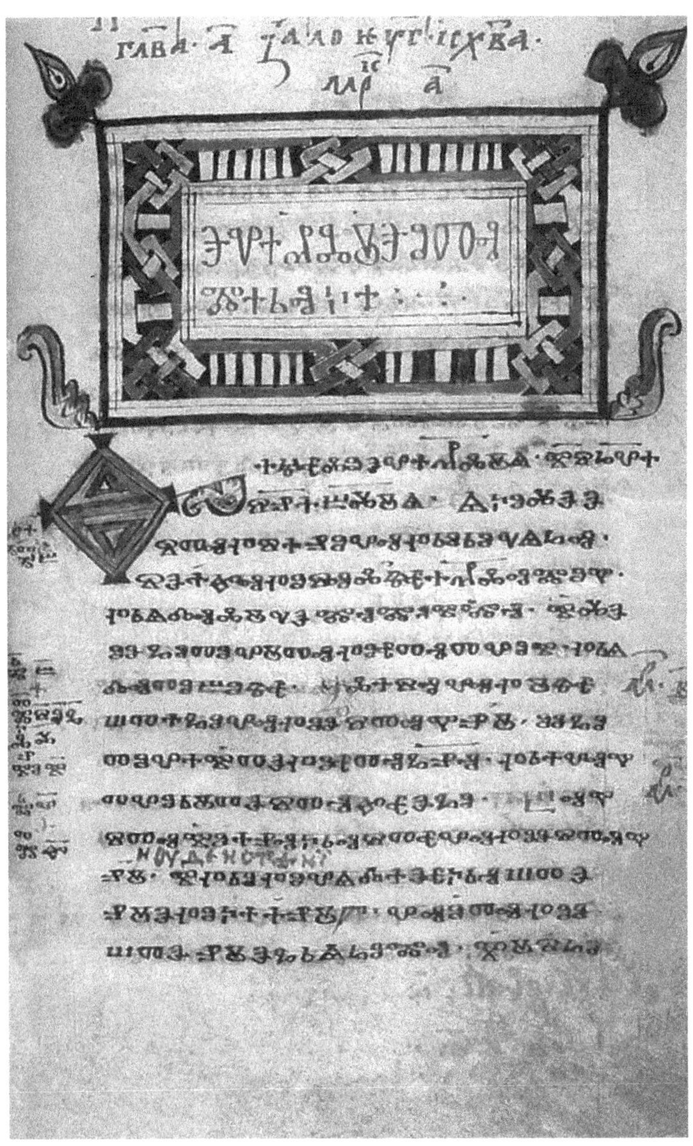

Plate 12.1. The first page of the Gospel of Mark in the Glagolitic manuscript *Codex Zographensis* (ca. 1000). Wikimedia Commons, the free media repository.

Following Constantine's death, Methodius was appointed papal legate and sent to Mosapurc to negotiate the organization of the church in Pannonia. Kocel welcomed the prospect of an archbishopric to counter the claims of the archbishop of Salzburg

INSERT 12.1. THE PHOTIAN SCHISM

Named after Patriarch Photius of Constantinople (858–67 and 877–86), the schism (split, division) was the result of growing differences between the ideas upheld in Rome and in Constantinople about the relative rank of the members of the Pentarchy (the five most important bishoprics in Christendom). Bishops of Rome, while claiming independence from any secular power, desired to occupy the first rank. Theirs would thus be the final decision in matters involving other patriarchs. By contrast, bishops of Constantinople maintained that all patriarchs were independent. Moreover, the Fourth Ecumenical Council (451) and the Council in Trullo (692) had placed Constantinople second in rank after Rome. The schism was aggravated by the competition between Rome and Constantinople for control over Bulgaria, the ruler of which had just converted to Christianity (see chapter 13). There were also serious differences in doctrine, liturgy, and discipline.

In 858, Patriarch Ignatius I (847–58 and 867–77) was deposed by Emperor Michael III (842–67). Photius, who had been a layman, was rushed through the orders to be consecrated patriarch on Christmas 858. Supporters of Ignatius appealed to Pope Nicholas I (858–67), claiming that the deposition had been illegal. The pope sent his legates to Constantinople to investigate the matter, but the legates found that Photius was the lawful patriarch. Nonetheless, Pope Nicholas convened a synod (small gathering of bishops) in Rome in 863. The synod demanded the restoration of Ignatius as patriarch and declared deposed all those members of the clergy who had been ordained by Photius. Photius retaliated by summoning another synod in Constantinople in 867, in which he declared the pope a heretic and criticized the Latin mission in Bulgaria. Because the pope and the patriarch refused to recognize each other, a schism formally came into being between Rome and Constantinople. However, the year 867 was not yet over when a palace coup in Constantinople brought to power Basil I, the founder of the Macedonian dynasty. The new emperor deposed Photius and reinstated Ignatius. The new patriarch re-established relations with the papacy (now under Hadrian II, 867–72), thus ending the schism. Ignatius died in 877 and Photius regained the imperial favor, being reappointed as patriarch. Unlike his predecessors, Pope John VIII (872–82) had no objections, and his legates recognized Photius as patriarch at a synod held in Constantinople between 879 and 880.

to jurisdiction over his realm. It is in fact under those circumstances that an unknown author wrote the *Conversion of the Bavarians and the Carantanians*, a tract meant to support the claims of the archbishop of Salzburg against Methodius's nomination as archbishop of Pannonia. Methodius was accused of disregard for the Roman doctrine and for the Latin books, both actions linked to the invention of the Slavic script (the Glagolitic alphabet), now attributed to him rather than to his brother Constantine.

In the meantime, important political changes had already taken place in Moravia, with the defeat and capture of Rastislav. He was turned over to Louis the German, who promptly ordered his blinding and imprisonment in a Bavarian monastery. The land of Kocel was also invaded, and Methodius was arrested to stand trial in the imperial court at Regensburg, along with Rastislav. He was accused of having usurped the ecclesiastical authority of the archbishop of Salzburg, and Bishop Ermenrich of Passau tried to strike him with his riding whip during the trial. Condemned by his accusers and the king, Methodius was banished to Reichenau, an abbey located on an island in the middle of Lake Constance (in what is now southwestern Germany, at the border with Switzerland). Archbishop Adalwin of Salzburg (859–73) reclaimed Pannonia, and the disciples of Methodius, including those who had been ordained priests in Rome in 868, fled, probably to northern Dalmatia. There was, however, no apparent impact of those political developments on the Christianization of Moravia, which advanced at a rapid pace during the last quarter of the ninth century. This, in fact, is when most churches in the region were erected, both large basilicas, like church 3 in Mikulčice and the so-called episcopal church in Uherské Hradiště, and rotundas, such as found in Mikulčice, Staré Město and, more recently, Pohansko.

When Svatopluk seized power in Moravia, Kocel was restored to his position in Pannonia as well. In 873, Svatopluk's envoys arrived in Rome to inform Pope John VIII (872–82) about Methodius's fate and to request him as archbishop of Moravia. A papal legate was rushed to Louis the German to obtain the immediate release of Methodius, as well as the punishment of those who had conspired against him. Methodius was appointed archbishop of Pannonia, an ecclesiastical province without defined borders, but with its see at the court of Svatopluk. The influence of Methodius may in fact have reached far beyond the area under Svatopluk's direct control. A later source claims that the duke of Bohemia, Bořivoj, was baptized by Methodius, and he continued his brother's program of translations. Perhaps to make himself useful to Svatopluk, he translated a portion of a Byzantine collection of ecclesiastical laws and used an adaptation of the Byzantine law code known as *Ekloga* for a body of civil law titled *Court Law for the People*. The law code compiled by Methodius spells out the idea of Christian faith as divine law and deals with a variety of transgressions of both penal and civil law, from marriage practices to rape, arson, bigamy, grave and church robbery, as well as pagan practices. For example, article 21 proclaims that "a soldier who has [been captured and has] abandoned our Christian faith [while in captivity] and returns to his land should be given to the church," no doubt as a slave.[4] Most interesting is the article on war spoils, which mentions that "the prince takes the sixth part, all of the people take the rest."[5]

Whether because of the *Court Law for the People* or because of Christian moral standards, Methodius seems to have challenged Svatopluk's authority. The Moravian ruler sent an embassy to Rome in 879 to complain about his archbishop. In addition to deviating from the Roman doctrine, Methodius was now accused of using the Creed without *filioque*, an accusation concocted by the Frankish clergy (see insert 12.2). Summoned to Rome, Methodius had to travel to defend himself against those accusations. He convinced Pope John VIII, who renewed the permission given by his predecessor, Hadrian II, for the celebration of the liturgy in Old Church Slavonic. In Rome, Methodius devoted himself

4 Curta, ed., "First Lawcode in Eastern Europe," in *Medieval Eastern Europe*, 266.

5 Curta, ed., "First Lawcode in Eastern Europe," in *Medieval Eastern Europe*, 265.

INSERT 12.2. *FILIOQUE* – THE MAIN DOCTRINAL DIFFERENCE BETWEEN THE WESTERN AND THE EASTERN CHURCH

The Creed adopted at the First Ecumenical Council in Nicaea (325) and confirmed at the Second Ecumenical Council in Constantinople (381) contains an affirmation of faith in the Holy Spirit, "who proceeds from the Father." To that, the participants in the Third Council of Toledo, which took place in 589 in Visigothic Spain, added "and the Son" (in Latin, *filioque*, hence the name given to the issue). The change was meant to counter Arianism, a heresy that was powerful in the kingdom at that time. From Visigothic Spain, the idea spread to Frankish Gaul, where it provoked immediate reaction. In 767, the *filioque* was condemned at the synod in Gentilly and prohibited at another church council that took place in 809 in Aachen in the presence of Pope Leo III and Charlemagne's officials. The original version of the Creed (without the *filioque*) was engraved on silver tablets to be displayed in the Church of St. Peter in Rome. During the Photian Schism, *filioque* was the main accusation that Photius directed against Rome and its initiative to convert the Bulgars to Christianity. To prove the contrary, at the Eighth Ecumenical Council in 879–80, which restored Photius to the patriarchal throne, Pope John VIII's delegates condemned the use of the *filioque*. However, Rome repudiated that decision in the eleventh century. In 1014, Henry II came to Rome to be crowned emperor and demanded that the *filioque* be added to the Creed. The issue subsequently played a key role in the Great Schism. Although the controversy has both doctrinal and canonical reasons (no additions or changes could be made to the Creed without an ecumenical church council), its impact on religious practice is what mattered most to Christians in the Middle Ages. Different interpretations of the *filioque* led to different understandings of fundamental questions, from glossolalia (speaking in tongues) to the miracle of the transubstantiation.

to promoting the cause of that language. Those are the circumstances in which the *Life of Constantine* was written by someone in his entourage. Pope John VIII confirmed Methodius as archbishop, but this time of Moravia, not Pannonia. He also appointed a suffragan in the person of Viching, the first bishop of Nitra. Relations between Methodius and his bishop rapidly deteriorated upon their return to Moravia. Profoundly disappointed, Methodius took a few disciples and went to Constantinople in 883 to gain support from Emperor Basil I (867–86) and Patriarch Photius. On his return, he is said to have translated the entire Bible in only eight months. He also wrote some of the first original hymns in Old Church Slavonic. He died on April 6, 885, not before designating as successor one of his disciples named Gorazd. However, the situation in Moravia soon deteriorated, and the new pope, Stephen V (885–91) was more inclined to listen to postmortem accusations leveled at Methodius by the Frankish clergy. In a letter to Svatopluk, Pope Stephen condemned Methodius on account of his position on such matters as the *filioque* and fasting on Saturday and prohibited the use of the Slavonic language in the liturgy. Instead of Gorazd, who was summoned to Rome, the pope appointed Viching as head of the Moravian church. However, because of the increasing hostility between Svatopluk and Arnulf (see chapter 7), Viching had to leave Moravia. A new archbishop and two suffragans were appointed by the pope by the time Mojmir II occupied the Eastern march (see chapter 7). However, none of them was a disciple of Methodius. By 900, some of those disciples had been thrown into prison, others expelled or sold into slavery, and only a few escaped to Bulgaria. In circumstances that seems to have been marked by the abandonment of churches and a return to pagan practices, at least in some of the old strongholds, the archbishopric of Moravia disappeared, soon to be followed by Moravia itself.

FURTHER READING

Betti, Maddalena. *The Making of Christian Moravia (858–882): Papal Power and Political Reality*. East Central and Eastern Europe in the Middle Ages, 450–1450, 24. Leiden: Brill, 2013.

Kosarová, Zdenka, and Jana Gryc, eds. *The Cyril and Methodius Mission and Europe: 1150 Years Since the Arrival of the Thessaloniki Brothers in Great Moravia*. Brno: Institute of Archaeology of the Academy of Sciences of the Czech Republic, 2014.

Kouřil, Pavel, ed. *Great Moravia and the Beginnings of Christianity*. Brno: Institute of Archaeology of the Academy of Sciences of the Czech Republic, 2015.

Tachiaos, Antonios-Emilios N. *Cyril and Methodius of Thessalonica: The Acculturation of the Slavs*. Crestwood, NY: St. Vladimir's Seminary Press, 2001.

Tachiaos, Antonios-Emilios N., ed. *International Scientific Conference "Cyril and Methodius: Byzantium and the World of the Slavs," Thessaloniki 2015*. Thessaloniki: Dimos, 2015.

Thessaloniki Magna Moravia. Thessaloniki: SS. Cyril and Methodios Center for Cultural Studies, 1999.

13

CONVERSION TO CHRISTIANITY: BULGARIA

Keywords in this chapter: customs, churches, Cyrillic script, translation, preaching

Only one year after Constantine and Methodius went to Moravia, Boris, the ruler of Bulgaria, favorably answered a call from the east Frankish king Louis the German for an alliance against Rastislav. He also expressed interest in converting to Christianity. In reaction to that, however, a Byzantine expeditionary corps attacked Bulgaria and occupied Mesembria (now Nesebăr, on the Black Sea coast). Under circumstances that remain unclear, Boris was forced into submission. He probably had to abandon his planned alliance with Louis the German and instead accepted baptism with Byzantine emperor Michael III as sponsor at the baptismal font (which is why his baptismal name was Michael). Several boyars were also baptized with him. Moreover, Boris's conversion to Christianity made it possible for the Byzantine clergy to come to Bulgaria and participate actively in the conversion of the country. It is not at all clear how that would have been possible with Greek-speaking clergy. Judging from a few inscriptions written with Greek characters but in a language that is not Greek, the Bulgar elites spoke a Turkic language. Inscriptions mentioning such rulers as Omurtag or Malamir were, however, written in Greek (both alphabet and language; see chapter 8), so at least someone in ninth-century Bulgaria could read and understand those texts. It is assumed that most people spoke one or several Slavic dialects but could not understand Greek. This strongly suggests that the initial conversion on which Boris was counting targeted the elites. Moreover, Boris asked Patriarch Photius to allow him control of the church in his country. Photius responded with a long letter, which contains not only religious instructions but also admonitions on kingship. More than a third of the letter is a long exposition of the seven ecumenical councils, as well as complex theological issues, the understanding of which was most likely beyond neophytes, especially those with little, if any, knowledge of Greek. Photius did not hesitate to compare Boris with Constantine the Great, but instead of answering his demand for a head of the church in Bulgaria, the patriarch recommended the Bulgar ruler build churches and give his full support to the clergy.

Boris probably received the patriarch's letter while work had just started on the earliest Christian building in medieval Bulgaria, a cross-shaped church discovered underneath the Great Basilica in Pliska. This may have been the church in which the first Bulgar boyars were baptized. Nonetheless, another group of noblemen rebelled against Boris and his adoption of Christianity. The Bulgar ruler responded with unusual harshness: all leaders were executed together with their families. To counter the impression that he was bringing Bulgaria under Byzantine control, Boris turned to Rome. On August 29, 866, he sent an embassy to Pope Nicholas I (858–67) headed by his own kinsman, Peter. The Bulgar envoys brought several questions about church practices and requested liturgical books and a civil code. Boris sent a separate embassy to Louis the German to announce the conversion of his country and to request missionaries. Louis was preparing a Frankish mission headed by Ermenrich, who had just been elected bishop of Passau, when Pope Nicholas, in a move meant to outflank him, dispatched his own mission. Led by Bishop Formosus of Porto, the Roman envoys arrived in Bulgaria in November 866.

Bishop Formosus brought Pope Nicholas's response to Boris's questions in the form of a long letter addressed not to Boris, but to all Bulgars. The 106 chapters of the letter deal with a variety of topics, from baptism to marriage, bathing, fasting, and the distinction between sin and crime. Boris is scolded for his harsh punishment of his boyars: "At least one aspect of this affair is tainted with sin, nor could you have done it without being at fault, inasmuch as innocent offspring, who were not in league with their parents and were not convicted of having taken up arms against you, were slaughtered along with the guilty. [...] You acted without weighing this matter more seriously."[1] Like Photius, Pope Nicholas compared Boris with Constantine the Great. He encouraged him to "convert all things into the battle gear of a spiritual preparation." Just as Boris had previously prepared carefully his arms and horses before the battle, he was now to ready himself for spiritual warfare. A few answers to questions regarding bride wealth, ritual sacrifice without the shedding of blood, the use of a stone with curative properties, and amulets, sexual taboos, and burial of suicides offer unique glimpses into the pre-Christian beliefs of the Bulgars. There were specific ritual practices in Bulgaria, which apparently had great political significance. When the ruler sat "down to eat his meals, it is your custom for no one, not even his wife, to dine with him." Boris had requested that all his subjects "eat at a distance, seated in chairs on the ground level."[2] Military concerns were on the Bulgar ruler's mind, as the pope writes about Bulgar sentries posted on the borders "to keep watch," who are promptly put to death if found guilty of negligence.[3] A few questions regarding such topics as marriage of priests or the position of hands during prayer indicate that Boris had already become

1 Florin Curta, ed., "Pope Nicholas I Answers the Questions of Boris of Bulgaria," in *Medieval Eastern Europe, 500–1300: A Reader* (Toronto: University of Toronto Press, 2024), 43.
2 Curta, ed., "Pope Nicholas I Answers the Questions," in *Medieval Eastern Europe*, 43.
3 Curta, ed., "Pope Nicholas I Answers the Questions," in *Medieval Eastern Europe*, 43.

aware of the differences in ritual between Western and Eastern Christians. However, the pope did not fulfill Boris's request for a patriarch. Instead, he promised that an archbishop under Roman jurisdiction may in time be appointed for Bulgaria. Meanwhile, the pope allowed the continuation of some of the old customs and adopted a generally cautious approach to the conversion of Bulgaria.

Within just one year, the Roman mission under Bishop Formosus managed to expel the Byzantine churchmen and to confirm those who had been baptized by them. Formosus began to ordain priests from among the natives and to consecrate newly built churches. His activity may have been interpreted by Boris as episcopal actions, for he tasked the pope to appoint Formosus as head of his church. However, instead of appointing him bishop of Bulgaria, Pope Nicholas I recalled Formosus. Nicholas's successor, Hadrian II, dispatched two other bishops instead.

Another papal embassy crossed Bulgaria in 869 on its way to Constantinople to attend a synod summoned by Emperor Basil I and the restored patriarch Ignatius to settle the schism with Rome. Upon returning to Rome, however, the papal envoys did not go through Bulgaria anymore, because in the meantime, the envoys that Boris had sent to the synod asked for clarification on the matter of the ecclesiastical jurisdiction over Bulgaria – Rome or Constantinople? Tired of waiting for four years for an archbishop to be appointed for Bulgaria, Boris had decided to break with Rome. In 870, Patriarch Ignatius appointed an archbishop of Bulgaria, who was promised considerable autonomy. Expelling the two bishops dispatched to Bulgaria by Hadrian II and all other members of the Roman mission who were still in the country, the archbishop established his see in Pliska, and the Great Basilica became his cathedral. Archaeologists have found a small cemetery near that church. Some of the graves had sarcophagi, an indication that aristocrats residing in the vicinity may have been buried there. The conversion had an immediate and visible impact on burial practices elsewhere in Bulgaria. Cremation burials disappeared to make room for inhumations. Burial assemblages that can be dated shortly before 900 produced a significantly larger number of dress accessories, such as finger-rings, beads, and earrings, but no grave goods such as pottery or tools, which were now abandoned in favor of Christian burial practices.

Five other churches are known from Pliska, while a large basilica has been found in Drăstăr (Dristra, now Silistra, in northern Bulgaria). This was most likely a cathedral as well, for the town became the see of the first suffragan of the archbishop in Pliska. Shortly after that, new bishoprics were established both in the interior (Philippopolis, now Plovdiv) and in the borderlands (Belgrade and Ohrid). During the first half of the tenth century, there were already thirteen bishoprics in Bulgaria. Moreover, several monasteries were established near the power center in Pliska. The church of the monastery in Ravna (between Pliska and Varna), which was established in 889, had a plan very similar to that of the basilica in Drăstăr.

Pilgrims are known to have traveled from Bulgaria to Rome, using the valley of the river Danube as the main axis of communication with Central and Southern Europe. Along that same river, but in the opposite direction, came the disciples of Methodius who had escaped from Moravia in 885. At least three of them – Clement, Naum, and Angelarius – crossed the Danube at Belgrade, where the local commander of the Bulgar garrison met and treated them with great respect. They were sent to Boris in Pliska, where they were received with even greater enthusiasm. After spending some time with the ruler, however, Clement was sent to the frontier in what is now southern Macedonia, northern Greece, and eastern Albania. In that borderland of Bulgaria, Clement was supposed to be a "teacher," much in the same way as Constantine and Methodius had been in Moravia. Much like Rastislav had supported the Byzantine mission, Boris aided Clement by means of land grants in the area. Clement began preaching in Slavic to commoners, as indicated by his surviving works, many of which are sermons. Penance and confession are the main themes of those sermons, an indication that Clement's audience was made up of newly converted Christians. Besides sermons, Clement also wrote eulogies, which he delivered as sermons on specific feast days associated with important saints. He wrote one such eulogy for St. Cyril, the first work to consecrate the image of "the shepherd and teacher of the Slavic people."[4] While the "Slavic people" appear as a unified group, Clement also describes them as linguistically fragmented and (re)united only through Cyril's introduction of Old Church Slavonic. Cyril is described as Christ-like, and even the Church as the body of Christ is attributed to him: "Blessed is your most honorable church, in which your wisest and God-exuding body reposes."[5] The eulogy was written for the feast day of St. Cyril (February 14). The word for "bless(ed)" is repeatedly used in this eulogy to draw attention to the saint as a member of the community of apostles and teachers of the Church: "Lord bless! Lovers of Christ! Here shines for us the resplendent memory of our most blessed father Cyril, the new apostle and teacher of all the lands."[6]

Clement's activity also included instruction of numerous disciples. Some of them became readers and deacons, others were later ordained priests, but most were simply his aides. Within seven years, Clement also established a monastery in Ohrid, the remains of which have been found by archaeologists underneath the former Imaret Mosque in that city. Clement eventually became bishop of the region, a position he held until his death in 916. Replacing him in Ohrid, Naum (another disciple of Methodius) continued his work for another seven years. Naum built another monastery on the shore of Lake Ohrid, to which he retired shortly before his death in 910. Within less than three decades, through the continuous efforts of Clement and Naum, Ohrid turned into a major center of Old Church Slavonic culture, deeply influenced by the tradition of Cyril and Methodius. Some of the earliest manuscripts written in Glagolitic script were most likely produced in Ohrid. At Naum's death, Clement initiated a process of canonization, whereby his friend became the first "native" saint of Bulgaria.

4 Curta, ed., "St. Clement of Ohrid on St. Cyril," in *Medieval Eastern Europe*, 283.

5 Curta, ed., "St. Clement of Ohrid," in *Medieval Eastern Europe*, 284.

6 Curta, ed., "St. Clement of Ohrid," in *Medieval Eastern Europe*, 283.

In 889, Boris abdicated in favor of his eldest son, Vladimir, and retired to a monastery in or around Pliska. With no sympathy for Christianity, Vladimir encouraged a rebellion meant to restore the old ways, including pre-Christian beliefs. Large-scale massacres, one victim of which was the archbishop in Pliska, have been associated with the mass burials discovered by archaeologists on several sites in northeastern Bulgaria. The violence of the revolt prompted Boris to leave his monastery to lead a coup against his son. Vladimir was deposed, blinded, and thrown into prison. At a general assembly that followed those events, Boris proclaimed as successor his younger son, Symeon, who had spent some time in Constantinople, perhaps in preparation for an ecclesiastical career. Boris's choice was therefore based on his firm conviction that Symeon would continue the work of conversion.

The Bulgars had been a thorn in the side of the Byzantine emperors ever since their settlement in the Balkans in the late seventh century (see chapter 8).[7] Symeon (893–927) and Peter I (927–69) went so far as to claim the title of emperor. Symeon had been educated in Constantinople, apparently for an ecclesiastical career. He came back to Bulgaria with books he had collected in Constantinople and retained a passion for learning throughout his life. He moved his main residence from Pliska to Preslav, which he turned into a booming cultural center. It is in Preslav that learned men under his patronage engaged in a monumental task of establishing solid foundations for the Christian religion and the Old Church Slavonic culture in Bulgaria. Dependent upon Byzantine models, their work was largely one of translating from Greek into Old Church Slavonic a great number of works, some of religious, others of purely secular use (such as chronicles). They abandoned the Glagolitic alphabet in favor of an adaptation of the Greek script to the needs of Slavonic. The result is what is now known as the Cyrillic alphabet, a much simpler and more flexible instrument that was used for the numerous manuscripts produced at Symeon's court or in monasteries associated with it.

Despite his affinities with the Byzantine world, Symeon proved no friend to the emperors in Constantinople. He attacked Byzantine territories throughout his reign – he ravaged Macedonia and Thrace and encroached onto Byzantine lands near Dyrrachion (now Durrës, in Albania) and Thessaloniki. The peace treaty of 897 not only confirmed the independence of the Bulgarian church, but Symeon even secured the payment of an annual tribute. He besieged Constantinople in 913 when Emperor Alexander refused to pay. After meeting with Patriarch Nicholas Mystikos, Symeon was apparently given a diadem and his daughter was promised in marriage to the young emperor Constantine VII – an arrangement that was later rescinded. Symeon began using a seal styling himself *basileus*, which made him an equal in rank to the Byzantine emperor. He attacked Constantinople again repeatedly between 920 and 924, after which he introduced a seal with the title of

7 In order to avoid confusion, historians commonly use "Bulgars" for the period before the conversion to Christianity, but "Bulgarians" after that. This terminological convention is also used in respect to the distinction between "Bulgars" (in the Balkans) and "Bulghars" (on the Volga). People who live today in Bulgaria call themselves "Bulgarians" in their own language, while "Bulgars" is the English translation of the name employed by Late Antique and medieval sources.

"emperor (*basileus*) of the Bulgarians and Romans" – probably referring to the "Romans" who lived in Bulgaria. The leading churchman of Bulgaria was now called a patriarch, mimicking the Byzantine hierarchy.

Peter I, who succeeded his father Symeon in May 927, not only called himself "emperor of the Bulgarians" but was also recognized as such by the Byzantines from the first year of his reign. This was unheard of: until then, the emperors had otherwise only, reluctantly, recognized an imperial title for the Carolingians in the West – a title that had ceased to be used with the death of Berengar of Italy in 924 and would not be renewed until Otto I's coronation in Rome in 962. Emperor Romanus I Lekapenos (920–44) also agreed to resume payment of the tribute to the Bulgarian ruler. Following plans that had been instigated by Symeon, in November 972 Peter married Maria Lekapena, the granddaughter of Romanus I, who took the new name of Irene ("peace" in Greek). Empress Maria was consistently depicted at the side of her husband on imperial seals, both holding the scepter together, in imitation of Byzantine practices but in sharp contrast to Peter's predecessors Boris and Symeon, who had always been portrayed alone. Maria regularly visited her father and grandfather in Constantinople, thus securing regular contact between the Byzantine and Bulgarian courts. The long reign of Peter was characterized by growth and stability, in continuation of the policies of Symeon.

Struggles with Byzantium resumed in the last years of Peter's reign, shortly after the death of Emperor Romanus II. The new emperor, Nicephorus II Phocas (963–69), refused to pay tribute to Peter anymore. In anticipation of war, he bribed Prince Sviatoslav of Kiev into attacking Bulgaria (see chapter 16). The Rus' arrived at the Danube in the summer of 968 and managed to conquer the country, which they refused to leave to the Byzantines. In the meantime, Peter died and was succeeded by his son, Boris II (969–71). At this moment, having contained the Arab expansion in the south, the Byzantines turned to war against Sviatoslav and managed to conquer eastern Bulgaria up to the Danube, including Preslav. Boris II was captured by Emperor John Tzimiskes (969–76), who formally deprived him of his imperial insignia in a public ceremony in Constantinople.

The western part of Symeon's Bulgaria was not affected by the war. In those parts now covering North Macedonia and northern Greece, power was taken by Samuel, the son of a military commander, who organized a successful rebellion against the Byzantine authorities. Although initially able to extend his control into eastern Bulgaria (where he took Preslav in 986) and Greece (where he took Larissa in 985[8]), Samuel simply linked his power to that of the Bulgarian emperors before him. He transferred the Bulgarian patriarch first to Triadica (now Sofia), then to Ohrid. Correctly assessing the threat, the new emperor Basil II (976–1025) had first to deal with the rebellion of two of his own generals. After squashing the latter with military assistance from Vladimir of Kiev (see chapter 16), he was bent on eliminating Bulgaria. After a long and exhausting war in the central Balkans, the Bulgarian forces were defeated in 1014 at Kleidion (in the Belasica Mountains at the

8 Curta, ed., "Scylitzes Continuatus on the Bulgarian-Byzantine War," in *Medieval Eastern Europe*, 65.

border between Macedonia, Greece, and Bulgaria). As Samuel died shortly thereafter, Bulgaria was incorporated into Byzantium along with all the regions in the central and northern parts of the Balkan Peninsula. After more than four centuries, the Byzantine Empire re-established its northern frontier on the Lower Danube.

FURTHER READING

Brzozowska, Zofia, and Mirosław Jerzy Leszka. *Maria Lekapene, Empress of the Bulgarians: Neither a Saint, nor a Malefactress.* Byzantine Lodziensia 36. Łódź: Wydawnictwo Uniwersytetu Łódzkiego, 2018.

Hupchick, Dennis P. *The Bulgarian-Byzantine Wars for Early Medieval Balkan Hegemony: Silver-Lined Skulls and Blinded Armies.* Cham: Palgrave Macmillan, 2017.

Katsovska-Malingoudi, G. *The Slavs of the Balkans: Introduction to Their History and Civilization.* Athens: Gutenberg, 2004.

Leszka, Mirosław Jerzy, and Kirił Marinow, eds. *The Bulgarian State in 927–969: The Epoch of Tsar Peter I.* Byzantina Lodziensia 34. Łódź: Wydawnictwo Uniwersytetu Łódzkiego, 2018.

Mayr-Harting, Henry. *Two Conversions to Christianity: The Bulgarians and the Anglo-Saxons.* Reading: University of Reading, 1994.

Minaeva, Oksana. *From Paganism to Christianity: Formation of Medieval Bulgarian Art.* Frankfurt a.M.: Peter Lang, 1996.

Nikolov, Angel. "The Bulgarian Church in the 9th-10th Century." In *Autocéphalies: L'exercice de l'indépendance dans les Églises slaves orientales (IXe–XXIe siècle)*, edited by Marie-Hélène Blanchet, Frédéric Gabriel, and Laurent Tatarenko, 103–8. Collection de l'École française de Rome 572. Rome: École française de Rome, 2021.

Simeonova, Liliana. *Diplomacy of the Letter and the Cross: Photios, Bulgaria, and the Papacy, 860s–880s.* Amsterdam: Hakkert, 1998.

14

CONVERSION TO JUDAISM: KHAZARIA

Keywords in this chapter: *shahadah*, coin imitation, disputation

Although sent to Itil, the capital of Khazaria, probably to negotiate an alliance against the Rus', Constantine and his brother Methodius used the opportunity to engage in a "competition of faiths" organized there by the khagan. According to the *Life of Constantine*, some 200 people were baptized on that occasion (in 861 or 862). However, the khagan was not convinced, largely because he had already opted for Judaism. A disputation ("competition of faiths") is also mentioned in the short version of the reply written by a king of the Khazars named Joseph to Hasdai ibn Shaprut (ca. 915–ca. 970), the Jewish minister of the Umayyad caliph of Córdoba, Abd al Rahman III (929–61). The reply was supposedly to Hasdai's inquiry about the existence of a Jewish kingdom in Khazaria. According to this letter, many generations before King Joseph, one of the first Khazar kings named Bulan was visited in a dream by an angel who led him, and later his deputy, to recognize the true God. Bulan organized a disputation involving Christians, Muslims, and Jews to determine which was the true religion. When the debate reached a stalemate, Bulan turned to Christians and Muslims and asked them about Judaism:

> The next day, he invited them all together and said to them in the presence of all his magnates and his people: "I ask you to choose the best and truest religion for me." They set to speaking but did not establish their words to the ground. Then the king said to the priest: "Is the Israelite, or the Mohammedan religion the best?" And the priest said: "The Israelite belief is the best." Then he asked the *kadi* [Muslim judge]: "Is the Israelite or the Roman [Christian] faith the best?" The *kadi* answered: "The Israelite is the best." The king answered: "You have now confessed with your own mouth that the Israelite religion is the best and truest. I have chosen it, as it is the

> religion of Abraham. May the Almighty be in my help. The silver and gold which you promised me, He can give without trouble. You go in peace to your country."[1]

Upon choosing Judaism as the winner, both Bulan's deputy and the people accepted the new religion. Bulan then sent for Jewish scholars from abroad to come to Khazaria and teach him and his people the Torah "with all its commandments."[2] Furthermore, Bulan's successor Obadiah "built temples [synagogues] and houses of study, gathered many learned Israelites, and gave them much silver and gold. They interpreted for him the Bible, the Mishnah [a collection of Jewish oral traditions], and Talmud [the book of Jewish law] and the whole prayerbook."[3]

In the first part of his letter to Hasdai ibn Shaprut, King Joseph claims to be a descendant of Togarmah, the son of Japheth, and mentions Khazar (from whom his people derived their name) as one of the ten sons of Togarmah.[4] This is most likely meant symbolically, for Togarmah is mentioned four times in the Bible, most special being the mentions in Ezekiel 27:14 ("The house of Togarmah furnished your marketplace with horses and horsemen") and Ezekiel 38:6 ("the house of Togarmah from the far north"). Indeed, in Jewish tradition, Togarmah was viewed as the ancestor of people on horseback, that is, of nomads. A tenth-century version of the *History* of Flavius Josephus titled *Josippon*, which was probably written in Italy, has Kozar (Khazar) as son of Togarmah, along with Pacinag (Pecheneg), Bulgar, Turq, and Ugr (Ogur). Similarly, the sons of Togarmah in King Joseph's reply to Hasdai ibn Shaprut are "Igor [Ujur, possibly Uyghur], Tiros [possibly Tauris, in reference to the Crimea], Avar, Uauz [Oghuz], Bizal, Tarna, Khazar, Zanor [Janur], Bulgar and Sarir [Sawir or Sabir]."[5] However, the idea that Togarmah was the son (not grandson) of Japheth is close to the notion of some Arabo-Persian authors, who linked Togarmah to the peoples in the Caucasus and the Caspian region. Be that as it may, it is important that the word "conversion" is nowhere in the reply of King Joseph. Instead, Bulan and his servants are circumcised, while Obadiah "reinvigorates" the kingdom and "establishes" the religion.

Another, somewhat different story appears in the so-called Cambridge Document, the name conventionally given to two loose sheets written in Hebrew and found in Cairo (Egypt). They may have once belonged to a manuscript written in the eleventh century somewhere in southern France, but the story of how the Khazars converted to Judaism was most likely written by a Jew in Egypt. According to his account, the leaders of the Khazar society were descendants of Jews fleeing from or via Armenia, who had come to Khazaria and intermarried with locals, learned their customs, participated in their wars

1 Florin Curta, ed., "King Joseph on the Conversion of the Khazars to Judaism," in *Medieval Eastern Europe, 500–1300: A Reader* (Toronto: University of Toronto Press, 2024), 39.

2 Curta, ed., "King Joseph on the Conversion," in *Medieval Eastern Europe*, 39.

3 Curta, ed., "King Joseph on the Conversion," in *Medieval Eastern Europe*, 39.

4 According to Genesis 10:3, Togarmah was the grandson, not the son, of Japheth.

5 Curta, ed., "King Joseph on the Conversion," in *Medieval Eastern Europe*, 37.

and "became one people." Since the Khazars at that time had no king, they granted their power to any successful warlord. One such warlord, who was a non-observant Jew, was convinced through divine guidance and the encouragement of his observant wife, Serah, to "return" to his ancestral faith. This supposedly aroused the anger of the Byzantine emperor and of the Abbasid caliph, whose fury could be placated only by organizing a religious disputation between Christians, Muslims, and Jews. In the aftermath of the debate, the "officers of Khazaria" brought forth from a cave the books of the Torah, following which all people in the country "returned" to Judaism. The number of Jews in Khazaria further increased with immigrants from Baghdad, Khorasan, and Byzantium. The Khazars appointed over them one of the sages as judge, calling him khagan in their language, and the warlord took the Jewish name Sabriel, the name of an angel. Similarly, the name of his wife is also symbolic, for in the Jewish literature, Serah is the daughter of Asher who reputedly lived for one hundred years and revealed the burial place of Joseph to the Israelites in Egypt.

How trustworthy are those accounts? They both highlight the disputation, which also appears in the *Life of Constantine*, albeit with Christianity, and not Judaism, as the winner. Both accounts also highlight the initiative of a Khazar leader named Bulan (in King Joseph's reply) or renamed Sabriel (in the Cambridge Document). In both narratives, following the conversion to Judaism, Jewish scholars come to Khazaria from elsewhere. Perhaps more importantly, both accounts lack any historical precision, with no indication of years. Historians have therefore long debated both the exact date and the significance of those events. Three possible scenarios have been advanced. The first is based largely on the *Meadows of Gold and Mines of Gem*, a work written in Arabic between 943 and 947 by al-Masudi. According to him, the king of the Khazars and his men were Jews, for the Khazars had converted to Judaism in the days of Caliph Harun al-Rashid (756–809). This has led some to the idea that the conversion took place during the second half of, or the late eighth century. Others have used the *Life of Constantine* to argue that the conversion must have taken place at a much later date, after 861. Finally, a third group of historians have advanced the idea that the conversion took place during the first half or the first two thirds of the ninth century. Their main argument is numismatic. Because of the diminishing number of dirhams coming to Khazaria in the 820s, the Khazars struck imitations to facilitate trade (those were not counterfeits, as they had the same content of silver as the dirhams struck inside the Muslim world). One such imitation was found in a hoard of silver (both coins and jewels) discovered in 1999 on a farm on the northeastern side of the island of Gotland in the Baltic Sea. Instead of the *shahadah* (Muslim profession of faith) – "Muhammad is the servant and messenger of Allah" – the coin has a different statement, in Arabic: "Moses is the messenger of Allah." The coin is precisely dated to 837/8 (AH 223) and has thus been interpreted as marking the official conversion to Judaism. However, this is the only issue with that message, and the number of specimens struck in this manner seems to have been quite small. If this was a message of political identity, it made no sense to make it in Arabic and not in Hebrew. Moreover, the coin with an altered *shahadah* had a good chance to anger Muslims, both those living in Khazaria at that time and those who were merchants coming to Khazaria from elsewhere for trade. The coin was most likely struck at the initiative of a Jewish minter, and the addressees of its message were Arabic-speaking (and -reading) Jews, most likely merchants coming from the Abbasid Caliphate to trade in Khazaria. With the 837/8 coin taken off the list of material proofs of the conversion, there is nothing left for the archaeology of Judaism in Khazaria. To this day, no tombstones (with or without menorah), no synagogues, no inscriptions in Hebrew, and no ritual vessels have been found anywhere within the vast territory in Eastern Europe which was controlled by the Khazars for some 300 years. The absence of material traces of Judaism in Khazaria stands in contrast to the adoption of Islam in Volga Bulgharia (see chapter 15).

In his *Redundant Treasures*, an encyclopedic work on geography written ca. 910, a Persian scholar named ibn Rusta noted that the "supreme chief" of the Khazars professed the religion of the Jews, and so did his deputy, as well as other leaders and members of the aristocracy. However, the rest of the population practiced "the religion of the Turks [nomads]." A couple of decades later, another Persian author named al-Istakhri wrote another work of geography, titled *Road of the Kingdoms*, in which he noted that the king of the Khazars was a Jew, but that Muslims, Christians, and Jews, as well as "idolaters," lived side by side in Khazaria, with Jews being the smallest group of all. Such testimonies point therefore to a conclusion that could explain the lack of any material culture related to Khazar Judaism. While the precise date of the conversion remains a matter of debate exclusively based on written sources, the conversion was most likely a gradual process involving a small number of members of the Khazar elite. Because of that, it was largely inconsequential.

FURTHER READING

Dunlop, Douglas Morton. *The History of the Jewish Khazars*. Princeton Oriental Studies 16. Princeton: Princeton University Press 1954.

Feldmann, Alex M. *The Monotheisation of Pontic-Caspian Eurasia: From the Eighth to the Thirteenth Century*. Edinburgh: Edinburgh University Press, 2022.

Golden, Peter B. *Turks and Khazars: Origins, Institutions, and Interactions in Pre-Mongol Eurasia*. Variorum CS952. Farnham/Burlington: Ashgate, 2010.

15

CONVERSION TO ISLAM: VOLGA BULGHARIA

Keywords in this chapter: mosque, *hutba*, burial customs

Trade is ultimately responsible for the religious changes taking place in the Middle Volga region shortly before 900. Contacts with Central Asia, particularly with Khwarazm, exposed the local elites to the tenets of Islam, the religion of most merchants that came to visit the markets of the Volga Bulghars in Bolgar, Biliar, and Kazan' (see insert 15.1). Archaeologists have identified mosques inside the commercial quarters of all three centers of Volga Bulgharia, and their dates coincide with the golden age of trade in the Middle Volga region – the early tenth century. Moreover, historians treat the embassy of Caliph al-Muqtadir to Almysh in 922 (see chapter 9) as the official date for the conversion to Islam. The main envoy of the caliph, ibn Fadlan, regarded Volga Bulgharia and its ruler as essentially barbarous, and treated them with a mixture of curiosity, awe, and disgust. But he also noted that "before our arrival [in Volga Bulgharia], the *hutba* [the Friday or feast sermon] was proclaimed from the minbar as following: 'God, grant wellbeing to the king, the Yiltawar and king of the Bulghars!'"[1] Ibn Fadlan mentions himself correcting Almysh, who henceforth had the *hutba* "proclaimed for him in this way: 'O my God, grant wellbeing to your servant Ja'far ibn Abdallah, the prince of the Bulghars, and the client of the commander of the faithful.'"[2] This story implies that Islam had been already adopted, albeit in incorrect forms (at least from the perspective of ibn Fadlan), prior to the embassy of 922. Ibn Fadlan is also critical of the conversion to Islam of a Bulgar clan named Baranjar, which, according to him, had no less than 5,000 members.

1 Florin Curta, ed., "The Conversion of the Volga Bulghars to Islam," in *Medieval Eastern Europe, 500–1300: A Reader* (Toronto: University of Toronto Press, 2024), 41.
2 Curta, ed., "The Conversion of the Volga Bulghars to Islam," in *Medieval Eastern Europe*, 41.

INSERT 15.1. KHWARAZM UNDER THE MUSLIM AFRIGHIDS

An oasis located just south of the Aral Sea in what is now Karakalpakstan (an autonomous republic of Uzbekistan), Khwarazm was inhabited by people speaking an Iranian language. They were ruled by the native dynasty of the Afrighids (so called after the half-legendary Afrig) between 305 and 995. In 712, the oasis was conquered by the Arabs, but the first ruler to convert to Islam was Azkajwar-Abdallah (late eighth and early ninth centuries). Even after conversion to Islam, rulers continued to call themselves Khwarazmshahs, following the Iranian tradition. In the early tenth century, the Afrighids were vassals of the Samanid emirs who ruled in Transoxiana and Khorasan. During the ninth century, Khwarazmian merchants played a major role in connecting Eastern Europe, particularly the Lower and Middle Volga region, to Central Asia along the Silk Road. The Afrighids were overthrown by a rival family, the Ma'munids of Gurganj (now Urgench, in southern Uzbekistan), a town that became prosperous in the tenth century because of its location on the main trade routes from central Asia to the Middle Volga region and beyond it, to Rus'. In 995, the Ma'munids attacked and captured Kath, the center of the Afrighids, and killed the last ruler of that dynasty. Adopting the same title of Khwarazmshah, Ma'mun I (995–97) moved the capital of the state to Gurganj, which became a great center of learning. The Ma'munids ruled until 1017, when they were defeated by the Ghaznavid sultan Mahmud, who turned Khwarazm into a province of his state.

> They [the Bulghars] had a timber mosque built for them [the Baranjar] made so that they could pray. But they did know how to recite the Quran [while praying], so I taught some of them what they needed [to do] when praying. And through me, a man [in that place] who was called Talut converted to Islam, so I wanted to give him a new name, "Abdallah." But he said, "I would like you to give me your name, Muhammad" [ibn Fadlan's name, however, was Ahmad]. And I did [as he wished]. His wife, his mother, and his children converted to Islam after that. All his sons took the name Muhammad. And I taught him [Talut] the surahs [Quranic verses] "Praise be to God" [Quran 1, opening of the *Surah al-Fatihah*] and "Say, He is God, One" [Quran 112, *Surat al-Ikhlas*]. And upon learning those two surahs, his joy was greater than if he had become king of the Saqaliba.[3]

That a timber mosque pre-dated the arrival of the Abbasid embassy to Volga Bulgharia is a clear indication that the conversion to Islam was not the result of ibn Fadlan's presence there but must have been a process that started some time before that. Timber mosques are mentioned also in ibn Rusta's *Redundant Treasures*, written ca. 910. The earliest part of the mosque discovered by archaeologists in Biliar was a timber construction, to which a stone building was added in the eleventh century, in addition to a brick minaret. According to Muslim canons, the axis of the mosque in Biliar was to the southwest, the direction of

3 Curta, ed., "The Conversion of the Volga Bulghars to Islam," in *Medieval Eastern Europe*, 41–42.

Mecca. The remains of twenty-four columns in six rows were found within the prayer hall. This is the oldest mosque known from Eastern Europe.

The time it took for the tenets and practices of Islam to be generally adopted was gradual and slow. If burial customs are any indication of thorough conversion, then Muslim practices were not universally accepted in Volga Bulgharia before 1100. Conversely, tenth-century cemeteries show no signs of drastic change from the pre-Islamic burial practices.

Almysh and his family may have adopted Islam for personal reasons, one of which seems to have been to obtain the protection, albeit from the distance, of the caliph in Baghdad. If so, it is important to note that Almysh did not subscribe to the Shafi'i school of Islamic jurisprudence, which was preferred in Baghdad. Instead, the Bulgar elite adopted Sunni Islam according to the Hanafi school, which was prevalent in Khazarazm and the Samanid emirate. That much results from the difference between the Islamic practices of Volga Bulgharia and ibn Fadlan's own understanding of Muslim canons. While according to him the Bulghar Muslims were ignorant, their practices passed for acceptable in the Hanafi school. This substantiates the idea that the conversion of Volga Bulgharia was largely the result of proselytism by merchants and not of the Abbasid caliph. Islam may have also served as an excellent ideological platform for Almysh to impose himself upon other tribal leaders in the region, especially those of the Suwar and the Askal (see chapter 9). If so, that could explain why, despite the conversion of the Bulghar elite between 920 and 940, the adoption of Islam by the entire population of Volga Bulgharia took a much longer time. In the absence of any written sources, archaeology remains the only way to gauge that process. The increasing number of burials without any grave goods, which were found in cemeteries that had been in operation before 900, may indicate an acceleration of Islamicization taking place during the second half of the tenth century. Similarly, judging from assemblages of animal bones found on settlement sites, the consumption of pork (which is *haram*, a food prohibited by the dietary laws of Islam) became minimal in Volga Bulgharia only in the eleventh century.

During the subsequent centuries, cemeteries for the nobility opened around mosques, and sometimes mausolea in the form of brick vaults were built there as well, as in Biliar. In those cemeteries, the dead were buried with the head to the west, but the torso turned to the right side, in order for the head to face Mecca (located to the southwest, on the right side of the body). Some bodies, especially in cemeteries around mosques, were placed inside timber coffins fastened with nails. No grave goods were deposited in those graves, but dress accessories, such as lock rings, have occasionally been found in burials of children. Bracelets, pendants, and beads are also known from female graves in some of the earliest Muslim-only cemeteries dated between the eleventh and the thirteenth centuries. Tombstones with epitaphs (funerary inscriptions) appear only in the thirteenth century, and only in the cemeteries of the nobility.

Arabic sources repeatedly mention the Bulghars as devoted Muslims, even if they shared ibn Fadlan's concerns that being in the north where the daylight was shorter, one could not hold five daily prayers according to the rule of Islam and could not fast properly during the holy month of Ramadan. At least one Bulghar prince is known to have gone on the *hajj* (pilgrimage to Mecca). The Bulghars produced their own literature, but nothing survives. The twelfth-century Andalusi traveler and merchant Abū Hāmid al-Gharnati, who lived for a while in the Volga region and visited several times the city of Bolgar (before going to Hungary; see chapter 63), mentions the work of a local *kadi* (Muslim judge) named Yakub ibn Numan. His book was in fact a history of the city of Bolgar, in which the *kadi* explained that the Volga Bulghars had been converted to Islam by a wise merchant and *faqih* (Islamic jurist) from Bukhara.

FURTHER READING

Abdullin, Yahya G. "Islam in the History of the Volga-Kama Bulgars and Tatars." *Central Asian Survey* 9, no. 2 (1990): 1–11.

Makó, Gerald. "The Islamization of the Volga Bulghars: A Question Reconsidered." *Archivum Eurasiae Medii Aevi* 18 (2011): 199–224.

Rudenko, Konstantin. *The Archaeology of Volga Bulgaria in the 10th–Early 13th Centuries*. East Central and Eastern Europe in the Middle Ages, 450–1450, 92. Leiden: Brill, 2023.

Zimonyi, István. "Volga Bulghars and Islam." In *Bamberger Zentralasienstudien. Konferenzakten ESCAS IV, Bamberg 8-12 Oktober 1991*, edited by Ingeborg Baldauf and Michael Friederich, 235–40. Berlin: K. Schwarz, 1994.

16

CHOICES OF CONVERSION: RUS'

Keywords in this chapter: sanctuary, coins, bishopric

As Rus' commercial networks expanded, travelers to Scandinavia or Byzantium encountered Christianity. The archaeological evidence, such as the deposition of cross-pendants or wax candles (the latter a custom of Danish origin) in graves suggests the presence of Christians in and around Kiev in the tenth century. One of the stipulations of the treaty of 944 mentions that "if any inhabitant of the land of Rus' thinks to violate this amity, may such of these transgressors as have adopted the Christian faith incur well-deserved punishment from Almighty God in the shape of damnation and destruction forevermore."[1] There were clearly Christians in the land of Rus' before the middle of the tenth century. However, it took some time for the Riurikids to accept the Christian religion.

Princess Olga, widow of Igor and regent for the young Sviatoslav (see chapter 11), was the first Rus' ruler to convert to Christianity. The *Primary Chronicle* claims that she was baptized during her trip to Constantinople and took the baptismal name Helena. Western sources recall that Olga requested a bishop and priests from King Otto I of the Eastern Franks, who in 961 sent to her court Adalbert, the future archbishop of Magdeburg. Adalbert, however, quickly left. Some of his companions had apparently been killed on the return journey, and he said it was unsafe for Christian missionaries to go to Kiev. Be that as it may, there is no evidence that Olga pushed for conversion in Rus'; her baptism was likely a personal affair.

Olga's personal baptism therefore had no direct political consequences. Her son, Sviatoslav, who came of age and succeeded her in 964, not only refused to be baptized but also remained staunchly pagan. Far from being attracted to Byzantine culture, he is said to have shaved his head while keeping a long strain of hair at the top of his skull, following

1 Florin Curta, ed., "A Trade Agreement between the Rus' and Byzantium," in *Medieval Eastern Europe, 500–1300: A Reader* (Toronto: University of Toronto Press, 2024), 73.

the fashion of the nomadic aristocracy, and to have slept with his saddle as a pillow, like the horsemen of the steppes. Olga died in 969 and Sviatoslav now ruled entirely on his own. He attacked the Khazars, the Volga Bulghars, and, at the invitation of the Byzantine emperor Nicephorus II Phokas, raided Bulgaria, aiming at controlling the main trade routes and riverways connecting Byzantium with Central Europe. His short reign came to an end in 972, when he was killed in an ambush by the Pechenegs, who allegedly turned his skull into a drinking cup.

Sviatoslav's son Vladimir, originally assigned to Novgorod, took over the succession in Kiev after having killed his two brothers, Iaropolk and Oleg. Prince Vladimir spent the first years of his reign asserting his authority, collecting tributes from the various regions of his realm – which included East Slavic, Iranian, Baltic, and Finnic populations – and gaining the support of his warriors. The *Primary Chronicle* states that he reformed the pagan cult and built an open-air sanctuary with wooden sculptures of the gods in front of his residence in Kiev. To unite spiritually the diverse populations of his realm, Vladimir promoted a pantheon combining gods and goddesses worshipped in various parts of the lands of Rus'. To the present day, however, no structure has so far been discovered in Kiev that could match the open-air sanctuary and the setup of idols described in the chronicle. Vladimir is further said to have sponsored religious ceremonies and festivals to foster a sense of belonging. This made room for some persecution of Christians that lived at that time in Rus'. When the son of a Christian Varangian was chosen by lot to be sacrificed to the gods, his father, refusing to give up his son, was killed.

Later in his reign, however, Vladimir acquired an interest in alternative religious systems. His failure at conquering the Volga Bulghars might have led to doubts regarding the efficacy of his religious innovations. The *Primary Chronicle* recounts that Vladimir sent envoys to gather information about the three monotheist faiths of his day. In 986, he welcomed in Kiev preachers of the Christian Greek rite from Byzantium, preachers of the Christian Latin rite from the German lands, Muslim envoys from Khwarazm, and believers of Judaism from the Khazar Empire. Having heard the arguments from each delegation and reflected on them, and considering that his envoys had been strongly impressed by the sophisticated rituals of the Byzantines, Vladimir opted for Greek Christianity. The chronicler furthermore claims that Vladimir was turned off by the prospect of refraining from eating pork and drinking alcohol. Parts of the story might seem far-fetched, as there was no Khazar empire any more at that time, since Itil had been conquered and sacked by Vladimir's father, Sviatoslav. However, an eleventh-century Persian source confirms that a deputation was sent to Kiev from Khwarazm, apparently in response to a request from Vladimir for information about Islam.

Meanwhile, Emperor Basil II fought against rebels near Constantinople while having to deal with an anti-Byzantine uprising in Bulgaria. While what exactly happened is not fully clear, it seems that in 988 the emperor turned to Vladimir for military assistance, promising the hand of his sister Anna Porphyrogenita in exchange. The prince of Kiev obliged and sent an army that provided crucial support to the emperor. Following these events, Vladimir was baptized in 989 in Cherson – which he might have just conquered from the Byzantines – and took the baptismal name of Basil. He came home to Kiev with his new wife Anna and many priests.

It was highly unusual for a newly converted ruler like Vladimir to marry an imperial princess. In fact, the Byzantines had long had a policy of refusing marriage alliances between imperial families and peoples whom they considered barbarians. The Rus' had been regarded as such ever since the ninth century. By the later tenth century, however, the Byzantine emperors were under increasing pressure to relax their stance and to agree to marriage alliances with rulers of the rising powers in various parts of Europe. Otto I, the king of Saxony who had been crowned emperor in Rome in 962, was insistent in his requests for a Byzantine bride for his son Otto II. He himself had been considered as potential husband for Anna but was, in the end, denied. His diplomatic endeavors resulted in the 972 marriage of Otto II with Theophano Skleraina, who might not have been "purple-born" but was the niece (by marriage) of Emperor John Tzimiskes. Otto III sent multiple embassies to Constantinople seeking a wife for himself; a daughter of Constantine VIII was to marry him when the young Otto passed away in 1002. Hugh Capet, the rising star of post-Carolingian France, also inquired to Basil II for an imperial bride for his son Robert. Basil and Constantine themselves had been approached to marry Bulgarian princesses in 969.

According to the *Primary Chronicle*, Vladimir's baptism was followed by the destruction of the Kiev sanctuary, the statues of which were thrown into the Dnieper. The inhabitants of Kiev were then invited to a mass baptism in the river, and churches were built, including that dedicated to St. Basil on the site of the former sanctuary. This was most likely a timber church, soon to be replaced by a grandiose stone-and-brick building, dedicated to the Mother of God but called the Tithe Church, because Vladimir granted a tenth of his revenue to the clergy associated with that church (see chapter 41). Baptisms are said to have taken place around the country and priests to have been sent to the major towns. Even though the extent of the effective conversions brought about by Vladimir might be exaggerated, there is no doubt that the newly converted prince was, with the help of priests from Cherson, an active promoter of Christianity. The official introduction of Christianity was not followed by pagan reactions as in Poland or Hungary.

Anna Porphyrogenita's presence contributed to improving Vladimir's status by connecting him to the emperors and bringing something of Byzantine culture to Kiev. Anna is said to have pursued a tradition of palace feasts every Sunday and might have sponsored the building of churches. She might have inspired the granting of Greek names to Vladimir's children – Boris-Romanus, Gleb-David, and Theophano. Vladimir also followed Byzantine practices when striking both gold and silver coins, on which one side shows the portrait of Christ the Almighty, while the other has him seated on a throne with a crown on his head and a scepter in his hand. He built several forts and earthworks (now known as the "Serpent Ramparts") along the main rivers on both sides of the Dnieper to protect Kiev from the attacks of the Pechenegs who had killed his father.

Christian traditions in Rus' were shaped by those of Byzantium. The leader of the new ecclesiastical province of Constantinople was based in Kiev and may well have had the rank

INSERT 16.1. THE SCHISM OF 1054

Since the Early Middle Ages, various divergences and conflicts erupted periodically between the churches of Greek and Latin rites over the leadership of the pope of Rome, doctrinal matters, iconoclasm, and rivalry in the missions to convert the pagans of Central and Eastern Europe (see insert 12.1 on the Photian schism). Efforts were made to bring the churches closer together but negotiations to that effect broke down, with dramatic consequences, in 1054: unable to come to an agreement, Humbert of Silva Candida, the envoy of Pope Leo IX, excommunicated the patriarch of Constantinople Michael I Keroularios, who responded by laying the anathema on Humbert. The reciprocal estrangement between Catholics (Christians of Latin rite) and Orthodox (Christians of Greek or Slavonic rite) has never been formally resolved. The events of 1054, however, had limited immediate impact outside of Rome and Constantinople. The hostility between Catholics and Orthodox was significantly aggravated with the establishment of the Latin Empire of Constantinople (1204–61) that created profound resentment among the Orthodox population of Byzantium. Feelings of alienation gradually spread to the rest of Europe as Catholics and Orthodox considered each other to be schismatics.

of metropolitan (equivalent to archbishop) from the very beginning. It is also possible that four more suffragan (subordinated) bishoprics were simultaneously created in Novgorod, Belgorod (now Bilohorodka, near Kiev), Chernigov (now Chernihiv, in Ukraine), and Polotsk (now Polatsk, in Belarus). Initially, Greek was the liturgical language, but after the mid-eleventh century, Christians in Rus' adopted Old Church Slavonic. That language had been in use in the church in Bulgaria since the late ninth century, and before that in Moravia through the work of the missionaries Constantine and Methodius. Constantine (St. Cyril) is said to have created the Glagolitic alphabet for writing down that language (see chapter 12). In the early tenth century in Bulgaria, another alphabet was created named Cyrillic after him and in his honor. This was a simplified writing system, derived from Greek and Glagolitic (see chapter 17). Beginning in the late eleventh century, Old Church Slavonic written in the Cyrillic script, gradually taking on East Slavic dialectical traits, became the literary language used throughout the Middle Ages in the lands of Rus'.

The schism of 1054 eventually drew a few doctrinal and customary distinctions between Roman and Orthodox Christianity (see chapter 64 and insert 16.1). However, no formal separation occurred, and there was no such division in the early period of Rus' history. Christians of Europe might have used liturgy in Latin, and those of Byzantium in Greek, but they all considered themselves to be equally part of the same Christian community. The Riurikids of the tenth to twelfth centuries entertained close connections – for example, through marriage alliances – with both Latin Europe and Byzantium; Christianity in Rus' was shaped by both, as can be seen in the veneration of saints. Rus' was not, at that time, fundamentally different from Poland or Bohemia (see chapter 66).

FURTHER READING

Featherstone, Michael. "Olga's Visit to Constantinople in *De ceremoniis*." *Revue des études byzantines* 61 (2003): 241–51.

Musin, Aleksandr E. "The Christianisation of Eastern Europe in the Archaeological Perspective." In *Christianisierung Europas: Entstehung, Entwicklung und Konsolidierung im archäologischen Befund. Internationale Tagung im Dezember 2010 in Bergisch-Gladbach*, edited by Orsolya Heinrich-Tamáska, Niklot Krohn, and Sebastian Ristow, 497–520. Regensburg: Schnell & Steiner, 2012.

Raffensperger, Christian. *Reimagining Europe: Kievan Rus' in the Medieval World, 988–1146*. Harvard Historical Studies 177. Cambridge, MA: Harvard University Press, 2012.

Shepard, Jonathan. "The Coming of Christianity to Rus': Authorized and Unauthorized Versions." In *Conversion to Christianity from Late Antiquity to the Modern Age: Considering the Process in Europe, Asia, and the Americas*, edited by Calvin B. Kendall, 185–222. Minneapolis: University of Minnesota, Center for Early Modern History, 2009.

Shepard, Jonathan. "Marriages towards the Millennium." In *Byzantium in the Year 1000*, edited by Paul Magdalino, 1–33. The Medieval Mediterranean 45. Leiden: Brill, 2003.

Tolochko, Oleksyi P. "Christians and Pagans in Kiev during the 10th C." In *The Dawning of Christianity in Poland and across Central and Eastern Europe: History and the Politics of Memory*, edited by Igor Kąkolewski, Przemysław Urbańczyk, and Christian Lübke, 11–32. Polish Studies. Transdisciplinary Perspectives 26. Berlin/Bern: Peter Lang, 2020.

17

NEW POWERS: BOHEMIA, POLAND, AND THE ABODRITES

Keywords in this chapter: monastery, native saints, strongholds

The tenth century was a period of important developments in Central Europe, at the time when Symeon's Bulgaria challenged the Byzantine hegemony in the Balkans and John Tzimiskes defeated the Rus' and occupied Bulgaria (see chapter 13). New political structures emerged in Bohemia and Poland, two countries in which the local dynasties (Přemyslids and Piasts, respectively) adopted Christianity and took position in a political landscape increasingly dominated by the Ottonians of Saxony. The Abodrites, meanwhile, were a mounting power in the Slavic Northwest between Saxony and Denmark (see map 17.1).

Dramatic transformations took place in the Bohemian Basin in the ninth century, where Slavs were organized in a variety of tribal groups. The ethnic name of the Czechs is first attested in much later Slavonic sources, but *Boemi* is a name of bookish origin used early on by authors writing in Latin. The very name of the country (Bohemia) derives from that of the ancient Celtic tribe of the Boii; as the "home of the Boii," the name retained its current geographic meaning throughout the Early Middle Ages. Repeatedly in the ninth century, the Carolingians managed to force various Bohemian leaders to pay them tribute, following a strategy that was not different from that applied to the Slavic tribes on the Elbe frontier (see chapter 6). Frankish sources record that in 845, fourteen dukes of Bohemia were baptized at the court of Louis the German in Regensburg. Christianity, however, came to Bohemia in the later ninth century, both from the southwest (Bavaria) and from the east (Moravia). It was the decisive support of the bishop of Regensburg that solidified the new religion in the early tenth century. A native source written towards the end of that century and known as *Legenda Christiani* claims that the first ruler of Bohemia known by name, Duke Bořivoj (d. before 890), and his wife Ludmila were baptized by St. Methodius in Moravia. The son of Bořivoj and Ludmila, Spytihněv I (d. 915), relied on the support of the East Frankish king Arnulf of Carinthia and of the bishop of Regensburg, who had

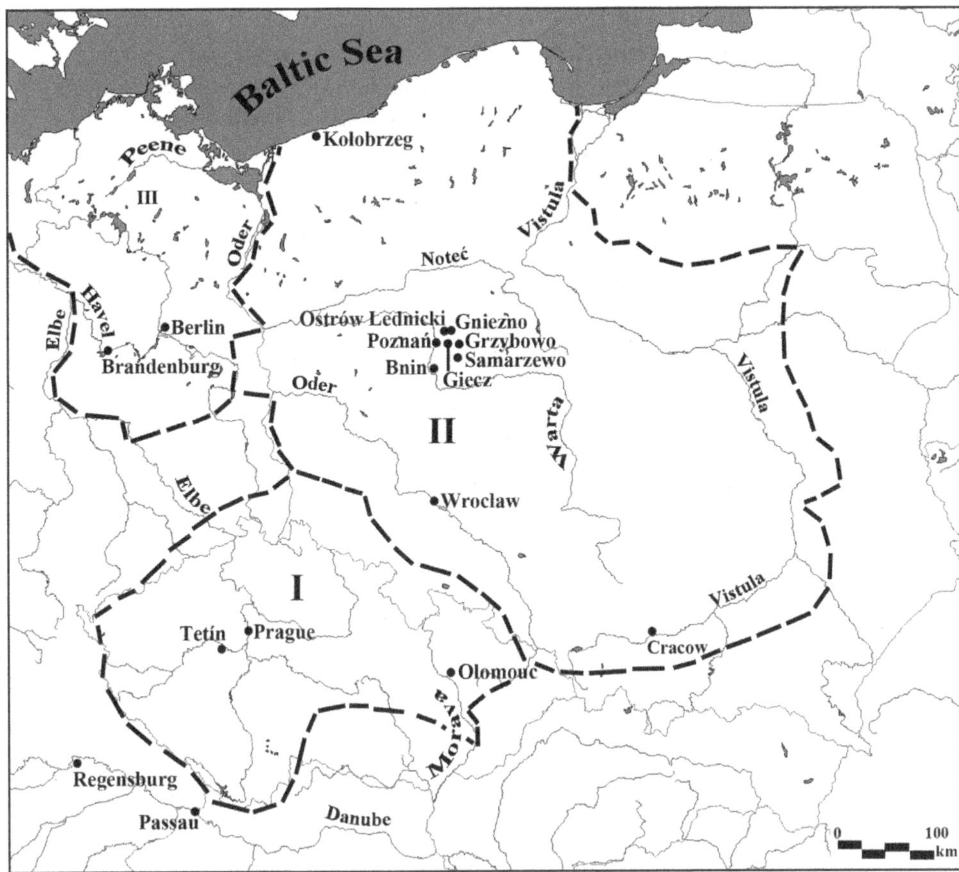

Map 17.1. East Central Europe, ca. 1000: I – Bohemia; II – Poland; III – the territory controlled by Liuticians.

taken over responsibility for Christianization from the bishop of Passau. As a counterbalance to the East Frankish power, however, Spytihněv instigated the marriage of his brother Vratislav I (915–21) with Drahomira, a princess of the Stodorans, a Slavic people that lived along the river Havel (in the region of modern-day Germany to the west of Berlin) and therefore known as Hevellians to the Franks. The Stodorans were opposed at that time to Saxon encroachment from across the river Elbe. Under Vratislav, Bohemia profited from the demise of Great Moravia to become the dominating power in the region.

After Vratislav's death, Drahomira became regent for her son Wenceslas I (921–35). The young ruler's grandmother, Ludmila, was still influential at the court, however, and later legends describe her as involved in Wenceslas's Christian education. By contrast, later sources also present Drahomira as a pagan who opposed Christianity. This is unlikely, for a Christian duke of Bohemia could have hardly married a woman who remained pagan after that. It is much more probable that the two women had different opinions on the politics of Bohemia. Ludmila was keener on maintaining close connections to the bishops of Regensburg and the dukes of Bavaria, despite Henry I of Saxony becoming the new strongman in the region, whereas Drahomira was more concerned with restricting the Saxon influence, especially after Henry conquered her family's seat of power at Brandenburg in 928. Hagiographic legends recount that Drahomira ordered the assassination of Ludmila in the castle of Tetín (near Prague) and expelled German priests from the country.

When he began to rule on his own in 925, Wenceslas had a strained relationship with his mother. The young duke reinforced church organization and instituted a repressive policy towards pagan practices. He also brought the relics of Ludmila to the Prague Castle, where he built a church dedicated to the patron of the Saxon royal family, St. Vitus. He obtained support from Regensburg in his plans for a bishopric. He also submitted to King Henry I of Saxony and paid him tribute, which seems to have made him many enemies among aristocrats in Bohemia. Drahomira, alarmed about the lingering influence of Ludmila's pro-German agenda on Wenceslas, then pushed her younger son, Boleslav, to murder his brother. Wenceslas was killed on September 28, 935, in the castle Stará Boleslav (to the northeast of Prague). In hagiographic sources, Boleslav is accused of having killed Wenceslas with his own hand, while shouting to him that "this is how a brother serves a brother!"[1] However, immediately after the assassination, he buried his brother in the Church of St. Vitus in Prague and began promoting his cult as a saint.

As a duke, Boleslav I (935–67/972) gained power over the entirety of the Bohemian Basin and his ruthlessness gained him the nickname "the Cruel." Only Duke Slavník, who ruled around Libice and was the father of Vojtěch-Adalbert (see chapter 38), longer resisted the pressure of the Přemyslids and maintained a semi-autonomous status. Despite their efforts, the Přemyslids could not prevent growing German influence throughout the tenth century. Under Boleslav I and his son, Boleslav II (967/972–99), Bohemia continued to pay tribute to the German kings and, after 962, emperors. Nonetheless, the Přemyslids managed to keep some degree of autonomy by balancing alliances with the Ottonian kings and their rivals, the dukes of Bavaria.

Boleslav II's sister Mlada traveled to Rome in 967 and obtained permission from Pope John XIII for two bishoprics, one in Prague, the other in Olomouc (in Moravia). The bishopric of Prague was created in 976 as a suffragan of the archbishopric of Mainz. Although the elites of Bohemia were fully Christian by that time, ancient beliefs and practices were slow to be eradicated in the broader population. Writing in the early twelfth century, Cosmas of Prague recounts that Duke Břetislav II (1092–1100) introduced harsh punishments against those who worked on Sundays and "those who dare to bury their dead in the fields or in the woods."[2]

Ducal authority was consolidated under Břetislav I (1034–55), who followed an aggressive foreign policy. In 1038–39 he invaded Poland, incorporated Silesia into his realm, and

1 Florin Curta, ed., "The Assassination of Duke Wenceslas," in *Medieval Eastern Europe, 500–1300: A Reader* (Toronto: University of Toronto Press, 2024), 117.

2 Curta, ed., "The Decrees of Břestislav," in *Medieval Eastern Europe*, 129.

brought the relics of Saint Adalbert from Gniezno to Prague. However, Bohemia was soon in turn invaded by the German king Henry III when Břestislav refused to pay him the tribute. Defeated, Břestislav resumed payment but retained Silesia. Břestislav made Bohemia a respected player in Central European politics, which comforted his position at home.

The earliest history of Poland was shaped by warlords whose expanding power can be traced only through archaeology. A series of strongholds was built in the second quarter of the tenth century in Greater Poland, all of them according to a similar model – Gniezno, Bnin, Giecz, Grzybowo, Ostrów Lednicki, Poznań, and Samarzewo. In the middle of that same century, older strongholds at the periphery of the territory were destroyed and burned to the ground; they were then replaced by a network of new strongholds that all looked the same. This is interpreted as the visible result of the conquest of the region by a new power that brutally replaced older elites. The first known representative of the emerging Piast dynasty was Mieszko I (d. 992), probably the successor of the anonymous warlord who had seized power in the region. The Saxon chronicler Widukind of Corvey described Mieszko as an ally of Emperor Otto I and as the "king" of the *Lisikavici*. Nothing is known about the significance of that name, for the names *Poloni* (for the people) and *Polonia* (for the realm) did not appear before Mieszko's son and successor, Bolesław I Chrobry (the Brave; 992–1025).

According to the earliest Polish annals, in 965 Mieszko married the Bohemian princess Dobrawa, the sister of Boleslav II and of Abbess Mlada, who had obtained in Rome permission to establish the first female monastic community of Bohemia at St. George in Prague. Mieszko was baptized in 966, and a bishop named Jordan arrived in Poland in 968. Moreover, Dobrawa arrived at the court of Mieszko with clerics from Bohemia, most of whom were originally from Bavaria and Swabia.

The Piasts were much more successful than the Přemyslids in keeping their distance from the imperial church. Mieszko and his second wife Oda of Haldensleben, together with their children, following the example of the Danish and Anglo-Saxon kings, placed under the special protection of the pope of Rome "an entire city called Schinesghe, with all that belongs to it inside the following boundaries."[3] *Schinesghe* was most likely Gniezno, the main see in Poland; the whole Piast realm was under papal protection. Gniezno was also the site of an unusual summit in March 1000, when Mieszko's son Bolesław Chrobry met with Emperor Otto III. According to a later chronicler, the emperor granted Bolesław and "his successors authority over whatever ecclesiastical honors belonged to the empire in any part of the kingdom of Poland or other territories he had conquered or might conquer among the barbarians, and a decree about this arrangement was confirmed by Pope Sylvester [II, 999–1003] in a privilege of the holy Church of Rome."[4] Moreover, a new ecclesiastical province was founded in Gniezno. The first archbishop, Radim-Gaudentius,

3 Curta, ed., "Dagome Iudex," in *Medieval Eastern Europe*, 113.

4 Curta, ed., "The Gniezno Summit" and "Thietmar of Merseburg on Bolesław Chrobry," in *Medieval Eastern Europe*, 120.

was Czech. Suffragan bishops were placed in Kołobrzeg, Wrocław, and Cracow. Despite protestations from the archbishop of Magdeburg, Gniezno was to be independent from the imperial church. Bolesław did not get along with Otto III's successor, Henry II, with whom he was for a long time in military conflict, but the ecclesiastical arrangement established in 1000 remained the same. Towards the end of his life, Bolesław was finally anointed as king, but without papal endorsement.

Nonetheless, the political and ecclesiastical structures put in place by Mieszko and Bolesław were fragile. Troubles emerged during the reign of Mieszko II (1025–34) and were not resolved until Casimir the Restorer (1040–58) began to retake control of the land. During this period of instability, centralized authority fell apart, as did the church structure: according to a later source, people "turned aside from the Catholic faith and rose up against their bishops and the priests of God; some they deemed worthy to be put to death by the sword, some by the baser death of stoning."[5]

Farther to the (north)west, the Abodrites under their rulers, the Nakonids, played an important role alongside the Přemyslids and Piasts in Central Europe of the ninth to eleventh centuries. They lived to the east of the Elbe and their lands extended between Saxony and Denmark. Ibrāhīm ibn Ya'kūb, an Iberian Jew who travelled to the German lands and (possibly) to Prague in the tenth century, learned about Nakon, the ruler of the Abodrites (d. ca. 966), whom he portrayed as equal in status to the rulers of Bulgaria, Bohemia, and Poland. Abodrite rulers had succeeded one another since Carolingian times with the support of Frankish kings and had close links with Denmark as well. For example, Nakon's granddaughter married King Harald Bluetooth of Denmark. Christianity gained ground at the rulers' courts in the 960s, at about the same time as in Denmark and in Poland. A bishopric was established in Starigard (Oldenburg) in 968; the chieftain Billug was married to the bishop's sister. A female monastery was set up in Mecklenburg but survived for only a few decades. Both the bishopric and the convent disappeared after the great revolt of the Liuticians (983), which restored and strengthened paganism for the subsequent century (see chapter 19).

FURTHER READING

Michałowski, Roman. *The Gniezno Summit: The Religious Premises of the Founding of the Archbishopric of Gniezno*. East Central and Eastern Europe in the Middle Ages, 450–1450, 38. Leiden: Brill, 2016.

Somer, Petr, Dušan Třeštík, Josef Žemlička, and Zoë Opačić. "Bohemia and Moravia." In *Christianization and the Rise of the Christian Monarchy: Scandinavia, Central Europe and Rus' c. 900–1200*, edited by Nora Berend, 214–62. Cambridge: Cambridge University Press, 2007.

5 Curta, ed., "The Collapse of the Piast State," in *Medieval Eastern Europe*, 130.

Trzeciecki, Maciej. "The Emergence of the Territorial State." In *The Past Societies: Polish Lands from the First Evidence of Human Presence to the Early Middle Ages*. Vol. 5, *500 AD – 1000 AD*, edited by Maciej Trzeciecki, 277–341. Warsaw: Institute of Archaeology and Ethnology, Polish Academy of Sciences, 2016.

Urbańczyk, Przemysław. "The Pace of Early Christianisation of the Piast Lands." In *Studies on the Christianisation of Europe*, edited by Józef Dobosz, 105–18. Poznań: Wydawnictwo Naukowe Uniwersytetu im. Adama Mickiewicza, 2019.

Wihoda, Martin. "The Beginnings of Christianity in Bohemia." In *The Dawning of Christianity in Poland and across Central and Eastern Europe: History and the Politics of Memory*, edited by Igor Kąkolewski, Przemysław Urbańczyk, and Christian Lübke, 33–42. Polish Studies. Transdisciplinary Perspectives 26. Berlin: Peter Lang, 2020.

Wiszewski, Przemysław. "*Dagome iudex et Ote senatrix* – On the Place of the Polish Ruler in the Aristocratic Circle of the Holy Roman Empire at the Close of the Tenth Century." In *Potestas et communitas: Interdisziplinäre Beiträge zu Wesen und Darstellung von Herrschaftsverhältnissen im Mittelalter östlich der Elbe. Interdisciplinary Studies of the Constitution and Demonstration of Power Relations in the Middle Ages East of the Elbe*, edited by Aleksander Paroń, Sébastien Rossignol, Bartłomiej Sz. Szmoniewski, and Grischa Vercamer, 111–24. Wrocław-Warsaw: Polish Academy of Sciences and German Historical Institute in Warsaw, 2010.

Zaroff, Roman. "Study into Socio-political History of the Obodrites." *Collegium Medievale* 16 (2003): 5–36.

18

THE MAGYARS AND EARLY HUNGARY

Keywords in this chapter: dual rulership, laws, pagan reaction

Under the domination of the Khazars at the beginning of the ninth century, the Magyars lived in the steppe lands between the Don and Volga rivers. In the 830s, they first emerged in the lands north of the Black Sea. They were named Turks in Byzantine sources but, after they moved to the Carpathian Basin, Latin authors called them either Huns or Avars, after the earlier nomadic peoples that had lived there. The self-designation "Magyar" is attested in Arabic sources from the tenth century (possibly going back to Khazar informants) and in European sources of the twelfth century.[1] The name "Hungarians," attested in tenth-century Latin and Byzantine sources, is derived from Onogur, the name of a Turkic group that lived in the steppe lands north of the Black Sea in the late seventh century (see chapter 3).[2] The Hungarian language is Finno-Ugrian and as such is distantly related to Finnish and Estonian. The languages closest to Hungarian, however, are those spoken by the Voguls (Mansi) and Ostyaks (Khanty) of western Siberia. Hungarian has strong affinities with the Turkic family, no doubt as result of cohabitation with the Khazars. This is confirmed by archaeologists, who point to many similarities in the material culture of the early medieval Magyars and that of the Bulgars and of other steppe peoples. Harness

1 The tenth-century Persian geographer ibn Rusta described the Magyars as "a Turkic people" who lived between the Pechenegs and the Volga Bulghars. See Florin Curta, ed., "Ibn Rusta on the Magyars," in *Medieval Eastern Europe, 500–1300: A Reader* (Toronto: University of Toronto Press, 2024), 47.

2 In order to avoid confusion and simply by historiographic convention, the name Magyars is used for the period before the conversion to Christianity, and Hungarians after that. This mirrors the pair Bulgars/Bulgarians which is used similarly in relation to the conversion to Christianity in that country (see chapter 13). At the root of the confusion for which the convention serves as a solution is the fact that in English the people now living in Hungary are Hungarians, even though they call themselves Magyars in their own language.

mounts and belt fittings found in the Chelyabinsk region of Russia, to the east of the Ural Mountains, are very similar to those found in Hungary, which suggests a rapid migration of the Magyars from that region. It remains unknown, however, how these people would have identified in that early period.

As early as 862, Magyars appear in the sources as raiding the eastern Frankish kingdom, Moravia, and northern Italy. The "conquest of" (in fact, settlement in) the Carpathian Basin (the settlement of the Great Plain – called Alföld in Hungarian – and in Transylvania happened later, in the tenth century) by a Magyar tribal confederation took place between 894 and 907, after the Magyars were pushed away from Etelköz (the westernmost segment of the steppe lands in Eastern Europe) by the Pechenegs. Transdanubia, the region to the south and west of the Danube (the western part of present-day Hungary), had been part of the Frankish realm and was therefore the main target of the newcomers. The western part of the Carpathian Basin was far more populated than the lands between the Tisza and the Danube rivers. The local population did not resist the Magyar domination, or at least no signs of large-scale destruction by the Magyars are so far known from settlement sites excavated in western Hungary that could be dated to ca. 900.

The Magyars did not stop raiding after settling in the Carpathian Basin. They regularly attacked parts of Western Europe – not only the German lands, but also France up to the Atlantic coast, Burgundy, Italy as far as Apulia, and the Iberian Peninsula, not to mention the environs of Constantinople. Around 70 raids are recorded for half a century, most of them with impunity. Raids were organized by rulers, chieftains, or clans; the goal was plunder. Magyar warriors spread fear, attacking with bows and arrows, axes, sabers, and swords uncovered in cemetery sites in Hungary and the surrounding regions of Slovakia, Austria, Serbia, and Romania. They moved at rapid speed on horseback and excelled at surprise and devastating attacks. At first plundering and making captives they sold in slavery, in the tenth century they turned to extorting protection payments and ransoms. However, the famed mounted archers of the Magyars were not invincible. Facing the heavy cavalry of the East Frankish king Henry I, they were first defeated at Riade in 933. Henry's son, Otto I, inflicted a crushing, definitive defeat upon the Magyars on the battlefield at Lechfeld, near Augsburg, in 955. This effectively put an end to Magyar incursions in the West. They kept raiding Byzantine lands, however, until the Byzantines were victorious at the battle of Arcadiopolis (today Lüleburgaz, in Turkey) in 970.

Magyar society evolved after the "conquest," no doubt in contact with local forms of social organization. Whether the invaders lived an entirely nomadic lifestyle or were cognizant of some basic agricultural practices remains disputed. Be that as it may, the Carpathian Basin offered ideal conditions for animal husbandry, but less of a nomadic and more of a sedentary kind. Magyars of the steppe lands in Eastern Europe are described as living in tents, but villages attest to how quickly they adapted to a sedentary lifestyle in the Carpathian Basin during the early tenth century. By that time, Magyar society was fragmented under the leadership of various chieftains. Muslim sources suggest that the conquering Magyars had a system of dual rulership inspired by that of the Khazars.

According to ibn Rusta, who wrote in the early tenth century, they had a "king" called a *künde*, "while the name of the man who practices the royal power of them is *gyula*."[3] Árpád, from whom all kings of Hungary before 1300 were supposed to descend, was the *künde* in the tenth century. One of his successors, Géza (d. 997) transformed the position of *künde* when attempting to make his authority be recognized by all – some contemporary sources called him "king." He married Sarolta, the daughter of a Magyar chieftain in northern Transylvania (the area around the modern city of Cluj-Napoca, in Romania).

Sarolta was Christian, and the conversion to Christianity played a key role in the integration of the Magyars in their new political environment. Early Magyars who lived north of the Black Sea had met both Byzantine and Bulgarian Christians. They also encountered Christianity in Transdanubia and in Moravia after their settlement in the Carpathian Basin. In the early tenth century, they must have witnessed the growth of Christianity in Bohemia. Two chieftains named Gyula and Bulcsú were baptized in Constantinople in 948 with Emperor Constantine VII as sponsor at the baptismal font (much like he was for Olga a few years later, see chapter 16). Moreover, Gyula left Constantinople in the company of a monk named Hierotheos, who had been previously appointed bishop of "Turkia" (i.e., the land of the Magyars now in Hungary). Cordial relations with Byzantium ended in the years after Lechfeld, however, when the Magyars devastated the country around Constantinople. Taksony (Árpád's grandson and the father of Géza) sent a delegation to Rome to request a bishop, plans that were halted by an intervention of Otto I. Géza, who had ruled in western Hungary since the early 970s, changed strategy and sought Christianization under German influence. He sent envoys to the court of Otto II in Quedlinburg at Easter 973; the bishop of Passau dispatched Brunward (or Bruno), a monk from St. Gallen, to act as missionary bishop in Hungary. The early efforts at Christianization, though, had mixed results. Géza himself is said to have venerated the Christian god and pagan deities at the same time, although he seems to have later given stronger support to the Christian religion. His wife Sarolta might have been baptized by Byzantine missionaries after her father's conversion (possibly by Hierotheos himself), but she does not appear to have been a paragon of Christian virtue; she is said to have been a talented horse rider and a heavy drinker, and to have once killed a man in anger.

Connections with the German lands were intensified when the son of Géza and Sarolta, Vajk (r. 1000/1001–38) married Gisela, the daughter of Duke Henry II the Quarrelsome of Bavaria and sister of the future German king, Henry II. Succeeding Géza in 997, with the help of Bavarian troops Vajk quickly eliminated a rival Magyar leader named Koppány and defeated another, Gyula, who ruled in Transylvania. Upon baptism, Vajk took the Christian name Stephen. He was made king in 1000 or 1001, long before the royal title would be recognized in Poland or Bohemia. Stephen's inauguration ceremony was led by the archbishop of Esztergom, whose see had just been established. The main elements

3 Curta, ed., "Ibn Rusta on the Magyars," in *Medieval Eastern Europe*, 47.

were inspired by Carolingian models – the acclamation, the anointment, and the crowning. With the consent of Emperor Otto III, Pope Sylvester granted Stephen the royal title, but not the "crown of Saint Stephen," an artifact made in the twelfth century out of a late eleventh-century Byzantine crown.

Stephen pursued Géza's political goals, and it is under him that Christianization made significant progress. By the end of his reign, Hungary had seven bishoprics subordinated to Esztergom. Gisela made many gifts to religious communities and especially to the bishopric of Veszprém, a town in which she built the cathedral church. Conversion was supported by legislation, and missionary work was intensified. Under Bavarian influence, but earlier than any other recently converted ruler in Central or Northern Europe, Stephen had extensive legislation put in writing in two legal codes that are known from copies of later compilations. Traditional rituals such as sacrifices to wells and trees were forbidden and punishable by fines, penance, and flogging. Legislation affected matrimonial and sexual matters: the abduction and rape of women, adultery, and the repudiation of wives were legal offences. Christians were expected to contribute to building churches, to pay the tithe, and to observe religious festivals. Monasteries were established, the first one in Pannonhalma (near Győr, in northwestern Hungary) in 996. The connection between Christianity and monarchy found expression as an ideological foundation in the *Admonitions*, a book of advice written by an anonymous cleric for Stephen's son, Emeric: "it is proper for you [my son] to listen with devotional attention to your father's commandments, according to the admonition of the divine wisdom, which comes from the mouth of Solomon."[4] King Stephen was canonized less than half a century after his death, in 1083.

Stephen had no heirs, as his son Emeric had died before him. The king therefore designated as his successor Peter Orseolo (1038–46), who was the son of his sister Grimelda and the doge of Venice. Peter and his mother Grimelda had left Italy and moved to Hungary, where Stephen had entrusted him with the army. Peter's rule, however, was plagued by multiple revolts against him and Stephen's widow Gisela, led by his cousin Vazul, a nephew or son-in-law of Stephen named Samuel Aba, and a regional chieftain named Vata. The nobles appear to have been resentful of his centralizing agenda and his appointment of German and Italian foreigners at the court, as well as at Gisela's Bavarian connections. Later sources claim that they wanted to reestablish pagan customs, including men shaving the top of their heads and leaving three tresses; they murdered priests and at least one bishop (Gerard of Csanád), and abolished tithes. Clearly, the aggressive enforcement of Christian practices and beliefs under Stephen had created resentment among some people. Opposition to Christianity and central power went hand in hand. Although acclaimed by the rebels, Andrew I (1046–60) quickly banned all pagan practices after being crowned king. Another pagan rebellion, around 1060, was short-lived.

4 Curta, ed., "A King's Mirror: The Admonitions," in *Medieval Eastern Europe*, 121.

FURTHER READING

Berend, Nora, József Laszlovszky, and Béla Zsolt Szakács. "The Kingdom of Hungary." In *Christianization and the Rise of Christian Monarchy: Scandinavia, Central Europe and Rus' c. 900–1200*, edited by Nora Berend. Cambridge: Cambridge University Press, 2007.

Engel, Pál. *The Realm of St. Stephen: A History of Medieval Hungary, 895–1526*. Translated by Tamás Pálosfalvi. London: I.B. Tauris, 2001.

Sághy, Marianne. "The Making of the Christian Kingdom in Hungary." In *Europe around the Year 1000*, edited by Przemysław Urbańczyk, 451–64. Warsaw: Wydawnictwo DiG, 2001.

Sutt, Cameron. "The Early Árpáds (895–1095): Consolidation, Christianization, Monarchy." *History Compass* 12, no. 2 (2014): 150–59.

Takács, B. Z. "Khazars, Pechenegs, and Hungarians in the Ninth Century." In *The Turks*, edited by Hasan Celal Güzel, Cem Oğuz, and Osman Karatay, 524–32. Ankara: Yeni Türkiye, 2002.

Tóth, Endre. *The Hungarian Holy Crown and the Coronation Regalia*. Budapest: Országház Könyvkiadó, 2021.

Zimonyi, István. *Muslim Sources on the Magyars in the Second Half of the 9th Century: The Magyar Chapter of the Jayhānī Tradition*. East Central and Eastern Europe in the Middle Ages, 450–1450, 35. Leiden: Brill, 2016.

Zsoldos, Attila. *Saint Stephen and His Country. A Newborn Kingdom in Central Europe: Hungary*. Budapest: Lucidus, 2001.

19

REFUSING CONVERSION: SLAVS EAST OF THE ELBE

Keywords in this chapter: *burgwards*, mission, pagan reaction

Converting to a monotheist religion might have been the trend, but it was not the only conceivable option for the pagans of Europe in the Early Middle Ages, nor was it attractive for everyone. The top-down conversion that started at the courts of rulers, typical of the period, was often followed by resistance or pagan reactions. In Poland, for example, the introduction of Christianity was followed by destabilization in the 1030s. However, in Central Europe, Slavic peoples east of the Elbe – the Liuticians, a faction of the Abodrites, and the Pomeranians – created what appeared at the time to be a sustainable and institutionalized form of paganism that provided a credible alternative to the centralized polity cemented through monotheism at the ruler's court, which was gaining ground in the rest of Central and Eastern Europe.

Under Charlemagne, the forced Christianization of the conquered continental Saxons had been rapid and brutal but had stopped short of extending to neighboring Slavic peoples (see chapter 6). Missionary activities among these Slavs in the ninth century took place at the initiative of bishops more than of rulers. Meanwhile, in Moravia, Bulgaria, Khazaria, Volga Bulgharia, Rus', Bohemia, and Poland (similarly to Denmark or Norway), conversions to monotheist religions accompanied the formation of centralized political structures in the ninth and tenth centuries. The rulers who chose Christianity were inspired by the political model of the early medieval kingdom.

The Ottonians of Saxony became the dominant power in the realm of the Eastern Franks after the Carolingians, and they were more invested in direct intervention in the lands of their eastern neighbors, the Slavs. Henry I gained kingship in 919; in 962 his son Otto I was crowned in Rome emperor of the Romans. The Slavic frontier was very close for them, and securing that border was a clear priority. Henry I intensified Frankish presence in the region of the Sorbs and Dalamincians, between the rivers Elbe and Saale, to protect against incursions of the Hungarians. Later, Otto, who learned the Slavic language as a young man when having an affair with an (unnamed) Slavic princess, acquired the land of Brandenburg (the region of modern-day Berlin). It was surrendered to him by Tugumir, ruler of the Stodorans (a Slavic people whom the Franks named Hevellians, along the river Havel). Moreover, the marcher lord appointed by Otto, a man named Gero, is said to have invited thirty Slavic leaders to a reception only to murder them. No ruler of the Sorbs, Dalamincians, or Stodorans was ever mentioned again after these events. In their lands, Otto established in the 960s *burgwards*: administrative districts centered upon Frankish strongholds. Further to the north appeared buffer zones known as marches that were supervised by military leaders, the margraves.

Christianity arrived in the lands between the Elbe and Oder rivers primarily through foreign authority, in the context of the extension of Ottonian power on the eastern frontier. In the ideological legitimation of Ottonian rulership, the conflicts with Slavic and Magyar pagans, the establishment of missionary bishoprics in Slavic lands and the archbishopric in Magdeburg on the Slavic frontier all played a crucial role. It was Otto I who established episcopal sees in Brandenburg and Havelberg around 948, after the surrender of the lands of the Stodorans. The Slavs, who paid tribute to Otto's margraves, now also paid tithes to bishops who, in 968, became suffragans of the archbishop newly installed in Magdeburg. Another bishopric was soon added in Starigard (called Oldenburg in German), in the lands of the Abodrites who lived in the area between Saxony and Denmark.

Ever since the early ninth century, the Franks had regarded the Slavs east of the Elbe as a source of tribute, but what was happening now was quite different. While the Nakonids who ruled the Abodrites were willing to accommodate, seeking to carve for themselves an autonomous position like that of the Přemyslids and Piasts in Bohemia and Poland (see chapter 17), Ottonian rule must have appeared oppressive in the Havel area. The Stodoran leadership there had been crushed; bishops ruled hand in hand with German margraves, squeezing out tithes alongside tributes. In such a context, the new religion probably did not appear as attractive or advantageous.

The great Slavic insurrection of 983 saw the Wilces, a Slavic tribe to the northeast, invading the territories of Brandenburg and Havelberg. Opposition had come from neither the Abodrites nor the Stodorans. Unlike them, the Wilces had had their territories left out of the borders of the new dioceses. While they might have worried about being the next target, their agenda turned out to be more expansive then defensive. They captured priests and are said to have desecrated the tomb of a prelate; the bishop and the margrave, unprepared for the attack, left in disarray. Christian institutions fell apart.

Following the insurrection, the lands to the northeast and along the Havel were ruled by a group unknown until that time, the Liuticians. They had neither ruler nor hierarchical organization; decisions were taken by a group of leaders at assemblies. They rejected monotheism and venerated multiple gods. According to contemporary sources, they had pagan priests involved in various rituals and temple buildings (see chapter 34).

The Liutician model was in stark contrast to the trend in the region but was surprisingly successful. The domination of the Liuticians between the Elbe and the Oder created a durable pagan enclave in a Christian-dominated Central Europe. In the early eleventh century, Henry II, German king (1002–24) and Roman emperor (1014–24), who was engaged in a war against fellow Christian ruler Bolesław I Chrobry of Poland (992–1025), struck a military alliance with the Liuticians. A contemporary chronicler described how the pagan warriors, carrying banners with images of their deities, were fighting alongside those of the Christian ruler against a Christian prince. The alliance raised the ire of the missionary Bruno of Querfurt.

Meanwhile, the Abodrites were torn between those diverging developments. The pagan movement reached the Abodrite realm in the early 990s, when the bishop's seat in Starigard was destroyed; what followed was a long struggle between the Christian and pagan parties. One faction favored a centralized, Christian polity along the lines of those of Poland or Denmark, and another one wanted to emulate the Liuticians. Temporary stability finally returned under the rule of Gottschalk (1043–66): son of an Abodrite ruler, his mother was from Denmark and he himself was married to a Danish princess, Sigrid; baptized, he was educated in St. Michael Abbey in Lüneburg, Saxony. A fervent promoter of Christianity, Gottschalk not only supported German priests, but he himself also preached in churches, in Slavic. The pagan faction, however, was still strong and wary of a ruler who might have been seen as too close to imperial authorities for their taste (he entertained close contacts with the archbishop of Hamburg-Bremen, Adalbert). Gottschalk was murdered in another insurrection in 1066. Priests and clerics were tortured and killed; Gottschalk's wife, Sigrid, was left naked on the road to fend for herself with other Christian women; she managed to find her way back to Denmark. Christian institutions again collapsed and the Abodrite realm returned to paganism.

In retrospect, the Liuticians' chances of maintaining in the long term their idiosyncratic political, social, and religious model might appear to have been slim. This, however, was not how things looked at that time. The Ottonian policy of establishing bishoprics supported by margraves was likely perceived by those upon whom it was imposed as a predatory, invasive foreign domination leading to resentment, which did not help in maintaining it. The success of the Liuticians was exemplified by Henry II's alliance with them against Bolesław Chrobry, showing how seriously they were taken as a political and military force in the early eleventh century. Moreover, their model was clearly attractive to a part of the elites of the Abodrites until the early twelfth century. If remaining pagan was appealing to them, this must have been seen as a viable and legitimate alternative that was worth pursuing. The final blow to Slavic paganism in Liutician fashion would only come in very different circumstances, in the age of the Crusades (see chapter 44).

The case of Pomerania was different. In Pomerania, Christianity also came through foreign authority – from Poland. A bishopric was first established in the year 1000 in Kołobrzeg, in the coastal territory conquered by the Piasts, at the same time as the other suffragans, Cracow and Wrocław, of the Polish metropolis of Gniezno. The bishop of Kołobrzeg, Reinbern, was a cleric from Thuringia. He died in 1015, imprisoned by

Vladimir during a diplomatic mission in Kiev, and no one is known to have succeeded him in Kołobrzeg. Polish domination in the region did not last anyway; it was shaken off during the troubles of the 1030s. The Piasts, however, managed to reconquer Pomerania in the 1120s. The Pomeranian mission was resumed with Otto of Bamberg in 1124–25 and 1128. Otto was a German cleric who was sponsored by both Polish and German rulers and gained the confidence of Pomeranian leaders. His biographies (*vitae*), written by contemporary authors, describe in much detail the pagan rituals of the Pomeranians, as well as the roles of their pagan priests and the temple buildings that were used for cult purposes. Unlike Reinbern, Otto was successful in establishing churches and bringing Christianity permanently to Pomerania. His *vitae* describe him presiding over assemblies in which the elites of the Pomeranians decided to switch to the new religion.

FURTHER READING

Lübke, Christian. "Christianity and Paganism as Elements of Gentile Identities to the East of the Elbe and Saale Rivers." In *Franks, Northmen, and Slavs: Identities and State Formation in Early Medieval Europe*, edited by Ildar H. Garipzanov, Patrick J. Geary, and Przemysław Urbańczyk, 189–203. Cursor Mundi 5. Turnhout: Brepols, 2008.

Lübke, Christian. "Forms of Political Organization of the Polabian Slavs (until the 10th Century)." In *Origins of Central Europe*, edited by Przemysław Urbańczyk, 115–24. Warsaw: Naukowa Oficyna Wydawnictwo, 1997.

Rosik, Stanisław, ed. *Europe Reaches the Baltic: Poland and Pomerania in the Shaping of European Civilization (10th–12th Centuries)*. Scripta Historica Europaea 6. Wrocław: Uniwersytet Wrocławski, 2020.

Rosik, Stanisław. "Pomerania and Poland in the Tenth to Twelfth Centuries: The Expansion of the Piasts and Shaping Political, Social and State Relations in the Seaside Slav Communities." In *The Expansion of Central Europe in the Middle Ages*, edited by Nora Berend, 451–89. The Expansion of Latin Europe, 1000–1500, 5. Farnham: Ashgate, 2012.

Rosik, Stanisław, and Przemysław Urbańczyk. "Appendix: Polabia and Pomerania between Paganism and Christianity." In *The Rise of Christian Monarchy: Scandinavia, Central Europe and Rus' c. 900–1200*, edited by Nora Berend, 300–8. Cambridge: Cambridge University Press, 2007.

Zaroff, Roman. "Perception of Christianity by the Pagan Polabian Slavs." *Studia Mythologica Slavica* 4 (2001): 81–96.

20

EARLY CROATIA

Keywords in this chapter: charters, inscriptions, *zhupans*, Reform movement, synod

The tenth-century treatise *On the Administration of the Empire* attributed to the Byzantine emperor Constantine VII Porphyrogenitus presents the northwestern region of the Balkan Peninsula as an area disputed between the Franks and the Byzantine Empire. The Frankish encroachment into the northern Adriatic region pre-dates by a few decades the collapse of the Avar khaganate (see chapter 6). The Istrian Peninsula came under Frankish control at some point between 780 and 787; by 805 the Franks intervened in the internal disputes in Venice, to establish their authority over the entire region of the northern Adriatic. In the early ninth century, in exchange for recognizing Charlemagne (and his successors) as emperors of the Franks, the Byzantine emperor kept control over both Venice and the cities along the Dalmatian coast. Over the following few decades, Venice did not have to deal with the Franks but with pirates from the Neretva valley, whose encampments were destroyed by a Venetian fleet in 839.

In the 860s, Arab pirates from Africa attacked some of the towns in Dalmatia as well as ports on the opposite coast in Italy. In 867, Emperor Basil I responded to a call for assistance from Ragusa (present-day Dubrovnik, in Croatia), which was besieged by the Arabs. The 100-ship fleet rescued the city. In the aftermath of the victory over the Arabs, a new theme (Byzantine province) was created on the eastern shore of the Adriatic Sea (see insert 20.1). The theme of Dalmatia, created in or shortly before 870, included all coastal towns and the islands along the coast. Its military governor resided in Zadar, a clear indication of the maritime orientation of this province. Many local Slavic leaders accepted the Byzantine overlordship and even provided troops for the military operations carried out by the Byzantines in Italy. In exchange, according to Emperor Constantine VII Porphyrogenitus, Basil I allowed the towns in Dalmatia to pay a part of the tribute initially sent to Constantinople to the Slavic leaders in the mountain region behind the coast. From an ecclesiastical point of view, most towns in Dalmatia had bishops headed by the archbishop of Split, but no episcopal structures are known from the interior during the ninth century.

INSERT 20.1. THEMES, THE PROVINCES OF THE BYZANTINE EMPIRE BETWEEN THE SEVENTH AND THE ELEVENTH CENTURIES

The transformation taking place during the seventh century in the power configuration in the eastern Mediterranean region, along with the rise of Islam, led to a drastic shrinking of the territorial extent and the military forces of the Byzantine Empire. With the withdrawal of the field armies to Asia Minor in the late 630s, each one of them was billeted in a particular region. Gradually, groups of provinces came to be known collectively by the name of the army stationed there – Opsikion, Thrakesion, or Karabisianoi. As the military reforms of the seventh century turned the field forces into local militia-like troops, their respective provinces became military districts, known since the ninth century as *themata*. Each *thema* was under a general (*strategos*), who, in time, took on civilian and fiscal attributions as well. *Themata* appeared outside Asia Minor as well, first in the Balkans (Thrace, Hellas). The origin and meaning of the word *thema* have been the subject of much debate, but the term derives from the Greek word for "to place, to deposit, to assign." This is an indication of the way in which field armies were billeted in various parts of the much-diminished empire. Many more *themata* were created between the ninth and the eleventh centuries, particularly in the Balkans – Dalmatia, Dyrrachion, Peloponnesos, Thessaloniki, Macedonia. After the mid-tenth century, the new themes, especially in the eastern parts of the empire, were typically small, often consisting of little more than a city or a fortress and its hinterland. A separate civil administration emerged under officials known as theme judges. By the eleventh century, the judge in any given theme was equal in rank to the *strategos* and shared responsibility with him for administrative decisions.

Moreover, a controversial theologian of the mid-ninth century, Godescalc of Orbais, spent some time at Trpimir's court, probably at Klis, before leaving for Bulgaria, with which Croatia shared a border somewhere in present-day Bosnia. In his work, Godescalc describes Trpimir's accomplishments, especially his victory over a Byzantine army, possibly coming from Zadar. Relations between Croats and Byzantines apparently varied greatly, from hostility to cooperation. For example, when Trpimir's son Sedesclav (Zdeslav) was deposed by a local nobleman named Domagoj, he fled to Constantinople. Domagoj, on the other hand, organized a rebellion against the Frankish overlordship established after the Treaty of Verdun (843). Sedesclav returned from Constantinople with Byzantine assistance and retook power in 876, only to be replaced by another local nobleman named Branimir, whom Pope John VIII recognized as the legitimate ruler in a letter of 879. Branimir (879–92) appears in no less than five Latin inscriptions, one calling him "duke of the Slavs," while another has him as "duke of the Croats." He was succeeded by another son of Trpimir named Muncimir, who is mentioned as the founder of a local church in another inscription dated to 895.

Table 20.1. Rulers of Medieval Croatia

Name of the Ruler	Regnal Years
Trpimir I	ca. 845–64
Domagoj	864–76
Sedesclav (Zdeslav)	876–79
Branimir	879–ca. 890
Muncimir	ca. 890–910
Tomislav	910–ca. 928
Trpimir II	ca. 928–ca. 935
Krešimir I	ca. 935–ca. 945
Miroslav	ca. 945–49
Michael Krešimir II	949–69
Stephen Držislav	969–97
Krešimir III	1000–30
Stephen I	1030–58
Peter Krešimir IV	1058–74
Zvonimir	1074–89
Stephen II	1089–90

The first duke of the Croats in the interior is Trpimir (ca. 845–64), who is mentioned in both charters and inscriptions (see table 20.1). In both charters and inscriptions, the early dukes and princes are mentioned as rulers of a people, not of a country. "Croats" may indeed have been not (only) the name of an ethnic group, but that of an elite. The "Croats" over whom Duke Branimir ruled at the same time as over the Slavs were members of the emerging noble class, members of which appear in charters with such titles as *zhupans*. This is clearly reflected in the archaeological evidence, which reveals the affirmation ca. 800 of a powerful elite in the political and military context of the Frankish encroachment into the northwestern region of the Balkan Peninsula. The most conspicuous material evidence of that elite status is the deposition of weapons and spurs in graves of high-status males. The rise of this social group coincided with the spread of Christianity and the gradual conversion of the Croat aristocracy. The exact circumstances in which the conversion took place are not known, but Christianity seems to have been regarded as just one part of the cultural "package" borrowed from Carolingian Francia. To judge by the archaeological evidence, the process of conversion was completed by the mid-ninth century, that is, under Duke Trpimir. The earliest Benedictine monks appeared in Croatia under his rule, even though the earliest churches in Croatia were built a few decades earlier. One of them is the Church of the Holy Cross in Nin, very similar to centrally planned buildings in and around Ravenna (Italy) as well as in Aachen (Germany). This suggests that the church was built at the order of a local ruler, whose name remains unknown. Elsewhere in Croatia, inscriptions show that churches had local *zhupans* as patrons. The *zhupans* headed local districts, of which, according to Emperor Constantine VII Porphyrogenitus, eleven were located south of the river Zrmanja under the direct control of the Croatian ruler. Three other districts were in Liburnia (northern Dalmatia) under the deputy of the ruler, called *ban*. *Bans* exercised considerable power, with some of them intervening in the election of the Croatian duke.

In his letters addressed to Muncimir's successor, Tomislav, Pope John X (914–28) called him "king," not "duke." All tenth-century successors of Tomislav called themselves kings in inscriptions, letters, and charters. The pope knew that Tomislav ruled over both "the province of the Croats" and the "Dalmatian regions," which may indicate that to co-opt him against Symeon of Bulgaria, Emperor Leo VI (886–912) gave the Croatian ruler full control over the cities in the Byzantine theme of Dalmatia. At any rate, when Symeon invaded Croatia, he was crushed by Tomislav. Papal legates came in 927 to mediate the peace between the two rulers. One year later, in 928, a synod was summoned in Split for all bishops in Dalmatia (see map 20.1). At an earlier synod in that same city, a dispute had emerged between the diocese of Split and that of a bishopric created at an unknown date in the interior, at Nin. In 928, Pope John X's legates approved the elevation of the bishop of Split to the rank of metropolitan, with all other bishops in Dalmatia under his jurisdiction. The bishopric of Nin was abolished, which implies that the jurisdiction of Split now extended to the entire realm of Croatia.

Byzantine support for the Croatian kings was renewed in the late tenth century, with King Stephen Držislav, who established his court in Knin, becoming governor of Dalmatia in exchange for his support against Samuel in the war with Emperor Basil II (see chapter 13). However, upon the death of King Stephen Držislav, the Byzantine emperor granted the Venetian doge the rank of proconsul and the title of imperial representative in Dalmatia. Around the year 1000, in fact, Venice dominated the entire coast of the Adriatic Sea. Attempts to curb the increasing power of Venice were unsuccessful. Svestoslav, one of Stephen Držislav's sons, recognized Venetian overlordship in Dalmatia. As a reward, his son Stephen received in marriage the daughter of the Venetian doge Peter II Orseolo (1008–26). In 1019, Emperor Basil II acknowledged the doge as his representative in Dalmatia, and Stephen's uncle, Krešimir III, submitted to Byzantine power. Trade links with Constantinople were quite strong in the early eleventh century, as indicated by cargoes of Byzantine amphorae found on shipwrecks at the entrance into the harbor of Nin. In the 1030s, a local leader from Zadar named Dobronas traveled to Constantinople, where he was very well received by the emperor, who showered him with gifts and honors. Dobronas's brother Gregory was meanwhile governor of Dalmatia, a province restored under Emperor Romanus III (1028–34).

King Peter Krešimir IV, the son born to Stephen from his marriage to the daughter of the Venetian doge, proclaimed himself "ruler of Croatia and Dalmatia" in a charter of 1069

Map 20.1. Southeastern Europe, ca. 1050: 1- Croatia; 2 – Dioclea (Zeta); 3 – Byzantine Empire. Medieval place names are in italics. Dalmatia designates the eastern coast of the Adriatic Sea in Croatia and Dioclea. Istria is the peninsula in the northern Adriatic region shown in the upper left corner of the map.

in favor of the Abbey of St. Chrysogonus in Zadar.[1] One of the witnesses in that charter appears as "Lord Leo, imperial *protospatharios* and *katepan* of all of Dalmatia," which indicates that despite King Peter Krešimir IV's title, some kind of authority was still exercised by Byzantine officials in Zadar and the city's hinterland.[2] Nonetheless, Croatia was clearly regarded as being under papal jurisdiction. At yet another council in Split, which took place in the presence of the legate of Pope Nicholas II (1059–61), measures were adopted to implement the church reform (see insert 20.2). Celibacy, simony, priestly beards, and the ordination as priests of Slavic speakers who could neither read nor speak Latin were the main points on the council's agenda.

1 Florin Curta, ed., "King Peter Krešimir IV Donates an Island," in *Medieval Eastern Europe, 500–1300: A Reader* (Toronto: University of Toronto Press, 2024), 89.
2 Curta, ed., "King Peter Krešimir IV Donates an Island," in *Medieval Eastern Europe*, 91.

INSERT 20.2. THE CHURCH (GREGORIAN) REFORM – SIMONY, CELIBACY, AND INVESTITURE

During the second half of the eleventh century, a series of reforms was implemented in the western church, primarily at the initiative of Pope Gregory VII (hence the name given to this reform movement). Many aspects of ecclesiastical organization and life were touched by those reforms, but perhaps the most important aspect from a historical perspective is the effort to free the church from secular interference. This was generally combined with a reform of the clergy, which aimed at curbing the practice of acquiring ecclesiastical dignities for money or some other material advantage (simony). The reform specifically aimed at eradicating attempts by laypeople to obtain favors from churchmen by means of material incentives. Simony was declared a heresy and played a key role in the re-establishment of ecclesiastical control over churches that had until then been controlled entirely by lay authorities. At the same time, the reform movement was preoccupied with the moral standards of the clergy. A key component of that was imposing celibacy on the clergy. At stake was more than a moral standard, even though the reformers spent much energy in forbidding priests to live in concubinage. The church authorities were concerned with curbing the practice of leaving church offices in inheritance, which was often viewed as another form of simony. By the early twelfth century, celibacy became a norm in the Catholic church and remains so to this day.

Churches under the direct control of lay lords (so-called proprietary churches) created another problem that church reformers tried to solve. Often lay lords appointed the clergy to serve in their churches, and both kings and emperors reserved the right to appoint bishops and sometimes abbots. The ecclesiastical goods at all levels – from parishes to dioceses – were thus subject to disputes and claims from secular forces, a situation compounded by hereditary transmission (in the case of married priests) and partition. The act of investing someone to a church office was thus removed from secular authority and placed squarely and entirely in the hands of the church authorities. The idea that bishops were to be selected or appointed by church authorities, primarily the pope, met with opposition from secular rulers, particularly from the German king (later emperor) Henry IV, who disputed the right of Pope Gregory VII to select candidates to the episcopate. The dispute led to one of the greatest conflicts in medieval politics, known as the Investiture Controversy, which involved not only rulers of the Holy Roman Empire but other kingdoms in Europe as well.

King Peter Krešimir IV disappears from the radar of the written sources in 1074, when he was captured by a Norman lord from Italy, who invaded Dalmatia and occupied several towns. When the Venetians intervened and pushed the Normans out, Zvonimir, the *ban* who had been in office under Peter Krešimir IV, was crowned king by Pope Gregory VII (1073–85). In exchange, he promised to implement the church (Gregorian) reform. At Zvonimir's death in 1089, his widow's brother, King Ladislas I of Hungary, laid claim to the Croatian throne (see chapter 42). He invaded Croatia, but a native ruler named Peter led the resistance in the Kapela Mountains of northern Croatia until 1097. Meanwhile, however, Ladislas opened the rest of northern Croatia (the province known as Slavonia) to colonization from Hungary and appointed his nephew Álmos to rule over the newly conquered territory as duke. A new bishopric was established in Zagreb, which was placed under the jurisdiction of the archbishop of Esztergom in Hungary. After Ladislas's other nephew, Coloman, defeated Peter in the Kapela Mountains, he was crowned king of Croatia in 1102. The title that Coloman used after 1108 ("king of Hungary, Slavonia, Croatia, and Dalmatia") remained in use until 1918. Croatia had a separate organization inside the kingdom of Hungary, with the *ban* as its ruler. The Croatian nobility retained its laws and privileges, the most important of which was that all Croatian noblemen owed service in Croatia, and not in any other parts of the kingdom.

FURTHER READING

Ančić, Mladen, Jonathan Shepard, and Trpimir Vedriš, eds. *Imperial Spheres and the Adriatic: Byzantium, the Carolingians and the Treaty of Aachen (812)*. London: Routledge, 2018.

Dzino, Danijel, Ante Milošević, and Trpimir Vedriš, eds. *Migration, Integration, and Connectivity on the Southeastern Frontier of the Carolingian Empire*. East Central and Eastern Europe in the Middle Ages, 450–1450, 50. Leiden: Brill, 2018.

Skoblar, Magdalena, ed. *Byzantium, Venice and the Medieval Adriatic: Spheres of Maritime Power and Influence, c. 700–1453*. Cambridge: Cambridge University Press, 2021.

Supičić, Ivan, ed. *Croatia in the Early Middle Ages: A Cultural Survey*. London: Philip Wilson Publishers, 1999.

21

BYZANTINE GREECE IN THE EARLY MIDDLE AGES

Keywords in this chapter: seals, Arabs, Milings, Ezerites, *theme*

The coastal regions of the Aegean and Ionian seas remained under imperial authority throughout the seventh century, but there are no signs of administrative organization before the end of that century. The creation of the theme (province) of Hellas, the second such administrative unit in the Balkan Peninsula, did not result in a gradual expansion of the imperial authority inland from the outposts on the coast. Initially, at least, Hellas was little more than a naval base. In the early ninth century, under the reign of Emperor Nicephorus I (802–11), a mixed population of settlers from other parts of the empire, "Kapheroi ['apostates,' Arab Muslims converted to Christianity], Thrakesians [inhabitants of the theme of Thrakesion in western Asia Minor], Armenians and others" moved into the lands outside the theme of Hellas, especially around the city of Patras.[1] Another province had by then emerged in southern Greece, the theme of Peloponnesos. Its purpose was less the protection of the coasts against Arab naval raids and more the protection of the outposts on the coast (particularly Corinth and Patras) against attacks from the interior. Perhaps because of those changes, especially the presence of settlers who encroached onto their lands, the locals (which were neither numerous nor uniformly distributed in the region), known as "Slavic people" in the sources, revolted in 807 or 808, attacking the "Greek" settlements and putting Patras under siege. The revolt was quelled, but more rebellions of the Slavs, both in northern Greece (near Thessaloniki) and in the Peloponnese, are mentioned under the emperors

1 Florin Curta, ed., "The Resettlement of the Peloponnese," in *Medieval Eastern Europe, 500–1300: A Reader* (Toronto: University of Toronto Press, 2024), 78.

Theophilus (829–42) and his son, Michael III (842–67). At some point during the latter's reign, the military governor of the theme of Peloponnesos launched a major expedition against the rebels, forcing them to recognize the imperial authority and to pay tribute. Two tribes, the Ezerites and the Milings, are singled out as providing troops for the Byzantine army to be included within units recruited from the theme. Not much is known about the social structure of the lands in present-day Greece during the ninth century, but the archaeological and numismatic evidence suggests that the two themes of Hellas and Peloponnesos were centers of wealth and influence. Both Empress Irene and Theophano, the wife of Staurakios (Nicephorus I's son, who ruled briefly in 811), were born into rich families from Athens.

In northern Greece, insecurity in the first half of the ninth century was caused by both Slavic bandits and Bulgar raids into Thrace. At the beginning of the reign of the Bulgar ruler Presian (836–52), one of those raids reached the Aegean coast. The military threat from Bulgaria led to the creation, shortly after 800, of three more themes in northern Greece – Macedonia, Strymon, and Thessalonike. The center of the latter was Thessaloniki, a city that had an archbishop with metropolitan status. There were several monasteries in the hinterland of the city, as well as numerous hermits in the Chalkidiki Peninsula to the southeast of Thessaloniki, especially on its easternmost part, on Mount Athos. In 883, Emperor Basil I (867–86) exempted both hermits and monasteries from any "vexations" of the imperial officials and prohibited private individuals, peasants, or shepherds from entering the area of the mountain.

The measures taken during the last three decades of the ninth century for the fortification of Thessaloniki, perhaps in response to Arab raids in the northern Aegean, as well as the conversion of Boris of Bulgaria to Christianity (see chapter 13) and the subsequent peace with the Byzantine Empire, opened a period of relative stability and prosperity in northern Greece. There is archaeological evidence of both economic growth and local elites. A male grave discovered in Spilaion (not far from the current Greek-Turkish border) contained a seal belonging to the Grand Logothete (foreign minister) Marianos, Emperor Basil I's brother. While the seal can be precisely dated to 868/9, it also reveals the high status of the man, who was apparently buried together with a letter or document bearing the seal of Marianos. The economic growth in the region is responsible for a flourishing trade across the frontier with Bulgaria, which in turn explains the presence of several *kommerkiarioi* (officials in charge of the collection of commercial taxes). Their seals have been found in Thessaloniki in considerable number. With the tacit approval of Emperor Leo VI (886–912), two of those *kommerkiarioi* named Kosmas and Staurakios moved the Constantinopolitan trade with the Bulgarians to Thessaloniki, no doubt in order to tax it to their advantage. This measure sparked a four-year long war between Symeon of Bulgaria and Emperor Leo VI (see chapter 13), but no hostilities are known to have taken place in northern Greece. There is also no sign of destruction caused by Arab pirates or raids from the emirate of Crete (see insert 21.1).

INSERT 21.1. THE ARAB EMIRATE OF CRETE

Internal strife taking place in al-Andalus in the early ninth century drove large numbers of exiles to the sea, which they crossed from west to east to attack and occupy Alexandria in Egypt at some point before 814. When the Abbasid forces drove them out in 825, the exiles fled again across the sea, but this time to the island of Crete, which was at that time under Byzantine rule. Arriving on forty ships, the Andalusians took over the island without much opposition. Byzantine troops sent against them were pushed back. Successive attempts to reconquer the island from the Arabs were equally unsuccessful, until Nicephorus Phocas (the future emperor Nicephorus II, 963–69) took Crete in 961. Between ca. 825 and 961, the emirate of Crete was one of the most advanced positions of Islam in the eastern Mediterranean. Its capital was established in Handaq (now Iraklion, on the northern coast). Crete became a launchpad for raids to Peloponnesos, the Cyclades, and the Aegean Sea. Moreover, Cretan Muslims established bases at Brindisi and Taranto in southern Italy, put Ragusa (Dubrovnik) under siege in 868, and sacked Venice in 875. The Cretans also participated in the conquest of Sicily by Aghlabid troops from Africa.

The emirs of Crete struck their own coins, a clear indication of political independence and economic prosperity. Crete participated in the trade network across the Mediterranean, primarily with exports of timber, wine, and precious metals. Muslims typically lived in cities, and several Islamic authors describe Handaq as a cultural center. However, there is no evidence of mosques or any other material correlates of the conversion to Islam of the interior regions of the island.

Comparatively more significant is the devastation of the islands in the Aegean Sea. Under Emperor Basil I, the emir of Tarsus (now in south-central Turkey) attacked the island of Evvoia (close to Athens) with a fleet of thirty ships. The military governor of Hellas gathered men from the entire theme and successfully defended the city against the attack. At that same time, all the inhabitants left Aegina, another island in the vicinity of Athens, because of Arab depredations. The Arab marauders reached the Peloponnese as well. In 879, an Arab fleet attacked the western coast of the Peloponnese, but the attackers were in turn taken by surprise by the imperial navy, the ships of which had been hauled over the Isthmus of Corinth. Another fleet from Africa attacked the western coast of Greece a year later, only to be repelled by the imperial admiral Basil Nasar, together with the military governor of the Peloponnese, John Kretikos. When at some point during the reign of Emperor Leo VI, the emir of Crete, Abdallah Uman II ibn Shuayub, attempted to raid the Peloponnese, he was defeated by the military governor Constantine Tessarakontapechys. Because of those and other attacks, a considerable number of troops were stationed at key points in southern Greece, particularly along the coast. However, no troops could stop the attack and subsequent sack of Thessaloniki on July 31, 904, by a fleet of fifty-four ships coming from Tarsus under the command of a Christian renegade named Leo of Tripoli. The attackers killed and captured almost half of the city's population, with many captives being later sent to Tarsus to be exchanged for Muslims captured by the Byzantines elsewhere. The devastation in Thessaloniki was described by John Kaminiates in his *Capture of Thessaloniki* written a few years later. However, both the city and surrounding countryside recovered rapidly and witnessed an even faster economic growth throughout the second half of the tenth and first half of the eleventh centuries. After ca. 950, the Byzantines took the initiative at sea, and in 961 the new domestic of the East (general of the eastern troops), Nicephorus Phocas (the future emperor Nicephorus II, 963–69), conquered Crete. This effectively put an end to Muslim raiding and placed the Aegean Sea firmly under Byzantine control, even though sporadic attacks from Africa continued into the first half of the eleventh century.

In northern and central Greece, the new military threat was Bulgaria, which under Symeon waged war against Byzantium. He "went about enslaving and ravaging, depriving some of life and others of freedom, forcing them to pay tribute. Some barricaded themselves in cities as if in prisons or garrisons, and others found safety" in Evvoia and in the Peloponnese.[2] Central Greece was also raided in the 940s by Magyars, who managed to kill the military governor of Thessalonike. Meanwhile, the Milings and Ezerites rose again in rebellion in the Peloponnese, only to be defeated and forced, once again, to submit to imperial authority. In the late tenth century, Bulgarian raids into Greece resumed as part of the Byzantine–Bulgarian war initiated by Emperor Nicephorus II. In 985, Larissa was conquered, and northern Greece became one of the main theaters of operation during the long war in which Samuel opposed Emperor Basil II (see chapter 13), with several forts built in the region by both sides. In 997, Samuel raided the region of Thessaloniki and then went deep into mainland Greece, reaching as far south as Corinth. The new domestic of the West, Nicephorus Ouranos, intercepted and defeated him at the river Spercheios. Under Emperor Basil II, the Byzantine army took the war to Samuel's territory in what is now Macedonia. Between 1014, the year in which Samuel died, and 1018, the Byzantines managed to take the forts in northern Greece one by one and eventually forced the surrender of the Bulgarian aristocrats. More devastation was inflicted upon central Greece in 1040 by the Bulgarian rebels led by Peter Delian.

The prolonged military conflict with Bulgaria led to dramatic changes in the administrative organization of northern Greece. Thessaloniki was put under the command of a duke, who was given units of heavy cavalry from the regiments of the field army. The neighboring theme of Strymon was split into two, and smaller themes were created around many of the forts reconquered by the Byzantines during the second decade of the eleventh century. By contrast, no changes were made to the existing administrative structures in central and southern Greece.

During the eleventh and twelfth centuries, Byzantine Greece experienced a remarkable economic growth, which attracted the interest of Venetian merchants, to whom Emperor Alexius I (1081–1118) granted rights and privileges. The wealth of many Byzantine cities in Greece was largely agricultural in origin, with Hellas supplying Constantinople with

2 Curta, ed., "St. Luke the Younger and the Bulgarian Attacks on Greece," in *Medieval Eastern Europe*, 85.

large quantities of grain in the 1030s. A fiscal document known as the Cadaster of Thebes mentions watermills in villages near Thebes, jointly owned by landlords of that area. Most of the lands around Thebes were owned by rich families residing in the city or in neighboring Chalki, Euripos, and Athens.[3] In the latter city, the cultivated fields were inside, not outside the city walls. The growth of cities brought to the forefront of political life local rulers, who were members of leading families in the region and appear as "dynasts" in contemporary sources. In the 1070s, for example, the "dynast" in Demetrias, a town in Thessaly, was a certain Noah. In Larissa, the city governor appointed by Emperor Constantine X (1059–67) was a local aristocrat named Nikulitzas Delphinas, who became the head of a revolt against a tax surcharge imposed by the imperial government. The leaders of that rebellion were, like him, prominent men of Larissa.

FURTHER READING

Armstrong, Pamela. "Greece in the Eleventh Century." In *Social Change in Town and Country in Eleventh-Century Byzantium*, edited by James D. Howard-Johnston, 133–56. Oxford: Oxford University Press, 2020.

Curta, Florin. *The Edinburgh History of the Greeks, c. 500 to 1050: The Early Middle Ages*. Edinburgh: Edinburgh University Press, 2011.

Neville, Leonora Alice. *Authority in Byzantine Provincial Society, 950–1100*. Cambridge: Cambridge University Press, 2004.

Sigalos, Eleftherios. *Housing in Medieval and Post-Medieval Greece*. Oxford: Archaeopress, 2004.

3 Curta, ed.,"The Cadaster of Thebes," in *Medieval Eastern Europe*, 99.

PART 4

Early Medieval Peripheries

22

FINNO-UGRIANS IN NORTHEASTERN EUROPE

Keywords in this chapter: bronze casts, slash-and-burn agriculture, fur trade, trade posts

According to Jordanes, who wrote his *Getica* in the mid-sixth century, Hermanaric, the legendary king of the Goths, subdued many peoples in the "North," forcing them to obey his command. Among those peoples were the Merens and the Mordens, who have been identified with the Meria and the Mordva, respectively. Known from much later sources, the Meria inhabited the central area of the forest zone of Eastern Europe between present-day Moscow and Iaroslavl', while the Mordva lived farther to the east, across the Oka River (and gave their name to modern Mordvinia). The land of the Mordva was most likely the same as that mentioned in the mid-tenth century in the treatise *On the Administration of the Empire* commissioned by the Byzantine emperor Constantine VII Porphyrogenitus. According to that source, the land of the Pechenegs was ten days' journey from "Mordia."

Both the Merian and the Mordvin languages belong to a linguistic family now known as "Finno-Ugrian." Historians therefore call "Finno-Ugrians" the medieval inhabitants of the northern part of the European continent, from the eastern shores of the Baltic Sea (in what is now Estonia) and Finland to the Ural Mountains, and even beyond them to the east. However, very little is known about the languages spoken in the Middle Ages by those peoples, as none of them produced any written records. Knowledge about them derives primarily from outside reports. Almost all of them focus on the Finno-Ugrians in the northeastern part of Europe, between the Northern Dvina and the Viatka rivers to the west and the Ural Mountains to the east. This large swathe of land (of which the largest part is now included in the Komi Republic of the Russian Federation) was densely forested and therefore rich in fur-bearing animals. Such animals also lived farther to the north in the taiga and, to a lesser extent, in the tundra next to the White, Barents, and Kara seas. The relatively milder climate of what is now Udmurtia and, across the river Kama, the northwestern part of Bashkortostan allowed for slash-and-burn agriculture,

Map 22.1. Northeastern Europe in the Early Middle Ages.

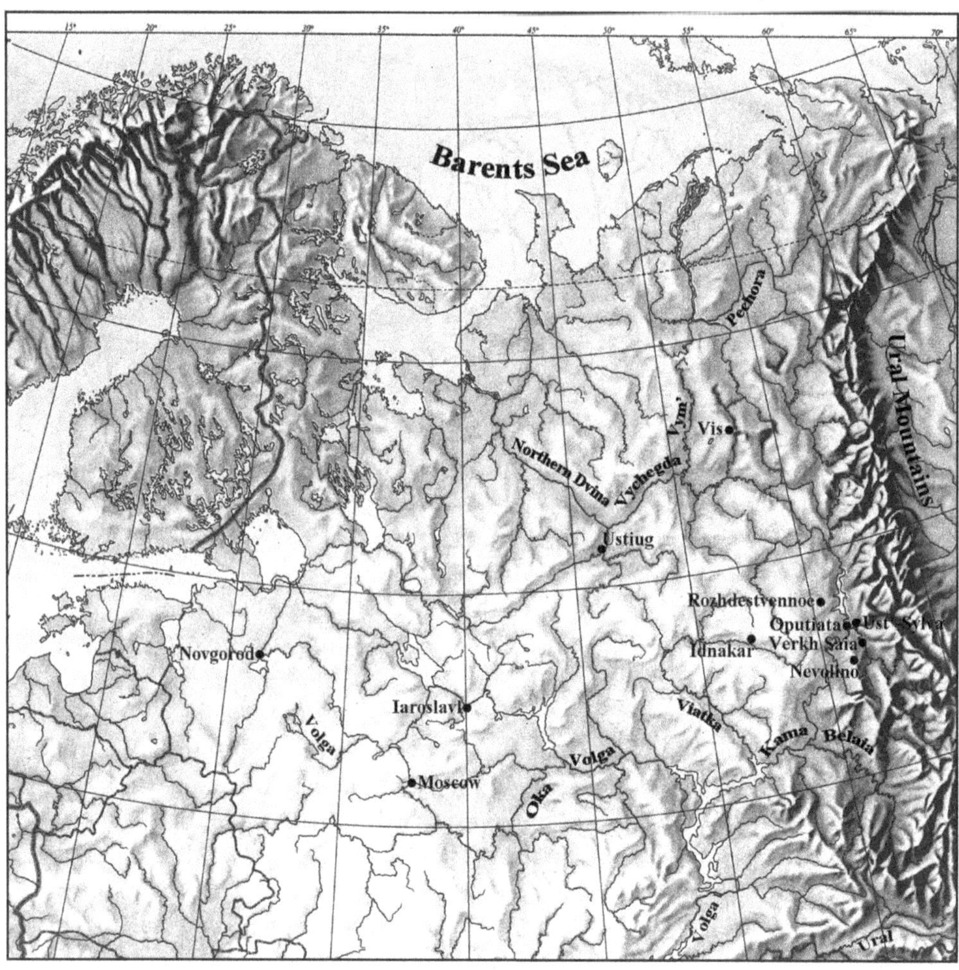

as indicated by agricultural tools found by archaeologists in settlement and burial sites. Plant seeds found on those sites show that the main crop was barley, but seeds of wheat and barley found in the Upper Kama region around the present-day city of Perm indicate grain brought by trade from elsewhere.

There is evidence of blacksmithing in the region, with smelting and ironworking facilities at Oputiata, a stronghold discovered north of Perm (see map 22.1). Moreover, northeastern Europe is famous for plaques, pendants, and idols cast in bronze in the so-called Permian animal style, as well as mortuary masks made of thin gold or silver sheet, with holes for the eyes, which were occasionally deposited in graves (see plate 22.1). Unlike ironworking, most other crafts were organized at a household level, as craftsmen had no special status. To judge from the evidence of cemeteries, such as discovered at Nevolino and Verkh Saia (both in the Perm region of Russia), the most conspicuous element of social differentiation was gender. For males, in particular, the deposition of weapons was a defining element. However, many more men were buried with bone arrowheads than with swords. While the former burials represent the group of experienced hunters, the men buried with swords may have been at the top of a developing social hierarchy. Sharp wealth differentials are deduced from the discovery of hoards of silver coins, some of them struck in Byzantium, others in Sassanian Persia. Silver (in the form of coins or ingots) has also been found on sites regarded as sanctuaries. Although next to nothing is known about the beliefs of the medieval Finno-Ugrians, the silver may have been brought to those sites as offerings from relatively affluent members of the local society. A local elite thus emerged, which was capable of controlling the collection and, probably, the commercialization of pelts.

Plate 22.1. Elk-headed man on a lizard, bronze plaque in the Permian animal style (eighth century). Wikimedia Commons, the free media repository.

The archaeological evidence of Sassanian coins and silverware, silk, and carnelian, chalcedony, and rock crystal beads suggest that merchants from Central Asia, most likely Sogdian, came to the region to procure the precious furs of the animals living in the taiga and the forest zones of Eastern Europe. They did that along the so-called "Northern Silk Road" that crossed Sogdia, Khwarazm, and the desert-steppe region of the Aral Sea and the northern coast of the Caspian Sea to reach the lands along the Middle Kama via the rivers Ural and Belaia. The hunting of fur-bearing animals to meet the demands of that trade transformed the local economic and social structures in northeastern Europe. Excavations carried out in the Vis bog, as far north as the Lower Vym' region of the Komi Republic, about 250 miles away from the Arctic Circle, have uncovered a great number of wooden artifacts, including arrows, the blunt tips of which indicate that they were used to hunt fur-bearing animals of small size. Such arrow tips did not pierce the animal and thus preserved the integrity of the fur. Runners and brush bows discovered in the nearby settlement site suggest that furs were transported by means of dog sleds to collection points farther to the south. The faunal assemblages from the Vis settlement bespeak the main occupation of its inhabitants. The most numerous are the bones of beaver, followed by marten, northern reindeer, bear, elk, sable, and otter. Beaver dominates in animal bone assemblages from the southern parts of the taiga as well. In fact, at Oputiata, the only bones of fur-bearing animals found on the site are of beaver. Hunting fur-bearing animals was an important economic activity in the south as well, and the stronghold at Oputiata was probably a collection point for pelts. To judge from the archaeological evidence in the taiga, therefore, the extraordinary prosperity of some communities, as well as the wealth of some of the locals, was the result of the intensification of the fur trade with Central Asia and, perhaps, Byzantium. Through that trade, Sassanian and Byzantine silver coins entered the region of the Sylva and Upper Kama rivers in what is now the northeastern part of the Volga Federal District of Russia. Like silver plate, gemstone beads, and silk, some of those coins were redistributed inside that region, or even father to the west, along the middle course of the Volga River. However, between local communities the main forms of exchange through which the coins circulated were non-commercial. That explains the presence of such coins not only in graves but also at sanctuary sites, such as that excavated in Ust'-Sylva, near Perm.

Furs played a key role in the trade that emerged in the ninth century between the Baltic and the Caspian seas (see chapter 33). The place of the Sogdians was now taken by Khwarazmian merchants, who came to the Middle Volga region to procure the pelts of animals hunted in the lands farther to the northeast. Islamic sources of the tenth century even list the kinds of pelts that were in the highest demand, with sable, miniver, and ermine at the top of the list. They also note that those precious furs were brought to the market by merchants from Volga Bulgharia, who went as far as the lands of the Visu and the Yugra, with whom they engaged in a dumb trade – clothes, salt, and other goods in exchange for sable and other fine furs. Both the Visu and the Yugra of the Islamic sources were Finno-Ugrians of northeastern Europe. The value of the furs that they could procure increased considerably as they traveled to the markets farther south. In Volga Bulgharia, they served as currency at an exchange rate of a pelt for two and a half dirhams. It has in fact been estimated (largely on the basis of hoards of Islamic coins) that because of the fur trade some 125 million dirhams entered Eastern Europe in the direction of Scandinavia. The Bulghar merchants extended the fur-collecting area to the northwest, including territories along the Middle Volga inhabited by Finno-Ugrians, such as those now within the Republic of Mari El. However, the territories richest in furs remained those in the northeast. It is through the Bulghar intermediary that dirhams first reached native sites in that region, much like the Sassanian and the Byzantine coins of the earlier period. Many archaeological sites in the Upper Kama region have produced remains of fur-bearing animals, particularly those of the genus *Martens*, which includes both the marten and the sable. Shortly before and after the year 1000, sable furs were entering the Bulghar trade either from the Kama region or from farther afield, in western Siberia, across the Ural Mountains. The Bulghar trade brought very large quantities of silver (sometimes gilded silver) in the form of jewelry to the region of the river Vychegda and beyond it, on sanctuary sites in the Pechora region of the subarctic tundra. Wheel-made pottery produced in Volga Bulgharia has been found at many of those same sites on which the silver jewelry was found, but at least some of those wheel-made pots brought to the northeast were produced locally, for example in the Bulghar trade center excavated at Rozhdestvennoe, to the northwest from Perm, next to a late tenth- and early eleventh-century Muslim cemetery.

The intensification of the fur trade between the ninth and the eleventh centuries had a considerable impact on local societies. Many tribal or, at least, regional centers emerged which played the same role as Oputiata, but now at a larger scale. For example, Idnakar near Glazov (in the northern part of present-day Udmurtia) played a key role as a collection point and trade post, but also as a major ironworking center for the entire region. Finds of locks and keys on many settlement sites bespeak the social transformations brought by the fur trade, particularly the articulation of notions of private property.

During the eleventh century, the Volga Bulghar merchants reaching the Visu and the Yugra in the north(east) began competing with both merchants and raiders from Novgorod. Various boyar families in that city extended their power far to the east, organizing raids and expeditions, the purpose of which was to impose the payment of tribute upon the inhabitants of the fur region. In addition, Novgorodians established fortified trading posts, from which they entered into commercial transactions with the Finno-Ugrians. It is through Novgorodian intermediaries that pennies struck in Bohemia, Denmark, and the German lands reached the native settlements. The Novgorodians did not eliminate the Bulghar competition, but during the twelfth century they used their strongholds in Yugran territory to resist other competitors, especially merchants and freebooters from the principality of Vladimir-Suzdal'. The violence caused by such rivalry, as well as the intensification of the Novgorodian raids, which coincided with the increased demands on tribute, led some of the local Yugra to migrate to the north and to the east, across the Ural Mountains. The number of Novgorodian collection points and trade posts increased considerably after 1200, and in response, the grand prince of Vladimir, Vsevolod III the Big Nest (1176–1212) established the town of Ustyug south of the confluence of the rivers Vychegda and Northern Dvina, at the point of entrance into the land of the Yugra. Because of their location at the periphery of three medieval states – Volga Bulgharia and the Rus' principalities of Novgorod and Vladimir-Suzdal' – the subsequent history of the Finno-Ugrians of northeastern Europe was shaped largely by their interactions.

FURTHER READING

Goldina, Rimma D., Igor Iu. Pastushenko, and Elizaveta M. Chernykh. "The Nevolino Culture in the Context of the 7th-Century East-West Trade: The Finds from Bartym." In *Constructing the Seventh Century*, edited by Constantin Zuckerman, 865–930. Travaux et mémoires du Centre de recherches d'histoire et civilisation byzantines 17. Paris: Association des Amis du Centre d'histoire et civilisation de Byzance, 2013.

Howard-Johnston, James D. "The Fur Trade in the Early Middle Ages." In *Viking-Age Trade: Silver, Slaves and Gotland*, edited by Jacek Gruszczyński, Marek Jankowiak, and Jonathan Shepard, 57–74. London: Routledge, 2021.

Noonan, Thomas S. "The Fur Road and the Silk Road: The Relations between Central Asia and Northern Russia in the Early Middle Ages." In *Kontakte zwischen Iran, Byzanz und der Steppe im 6.-7. Jahrhundert*, edited by Csanád Bálint, 285–302. Varia Archaeologica Hungarica 10. Budapest: Institut für Archäologie der Ungarischen Akademie der Wissenschaften, 2000.

23

THE EASTERN AND SOUTHEASTERN BALTIC REGION

Keywords in this chapter: Yotvingians, Curonians, "ash fields"

Sometime in the ninth century, a man named Wulfstan, possibly a West Saxon in the service of King Alfred the Great (869–89) traveled from Hedeby (now Haithabu, near Schleswig, in northern Germany) to Truso (now Janów Pomorski, near Elbląg, in northern Poland) in "a very large" country on the southeastern shore of the Baltic Sea that he called "Estland"[1] (see map 23.1). In his account, written in Old English, he described the customs of the inhabitants of that land, the Ests. Runestones erected in the eleventh century in southwestern Sweden also mention "Estland." Prussians, people who lived in the area by the time of Wulfstan's visit, are mentioned in the *Life of Saint Adalbert, Bishop of Prague and Martyr*, which was written in the eleventh century, probably in Rome. According to its unknown author, the land of "Prussia" was "closer and better known to the said duke" of Poland, Bolesław Chrobry (see chapter 17).[2] More ethnic or tribal names appear in the written sources of the following centuries. The eastern neighbors of the Prussians, the Yotvingians, are first mentioned in the earliest annals of Rus', the *Tale of Bygone Years*, written in the early twelfth century. Both Estonians (called *Chud* in the *Tale*) and Curonians, who lived in what is now western Lithuania and Latvia, appear in the *History of the Danes* written by Saxo Grammaticus shortly after 1216. Prussians, Yotvingians, and Curonians spoke languages now classified as Baltic, while Estonian belongs to the family of Finno-Ugrian languages, along with Finnish. Despite linguistic diversity, the peoples inhabiting the eastern and southeastern Baltic region in the Early Middle Ages had similar

1 Florin Curta, ed., "Wulfstan Travels to Truso," in *Medieval Eastern Europe, 500–1300: A Reader* (Toronto: University of Toronto Press, 2024), 57.

2 Curta, ed., "The Martyrdom of St. Adalbert," in *Medieval Eastern Europe*, 184.

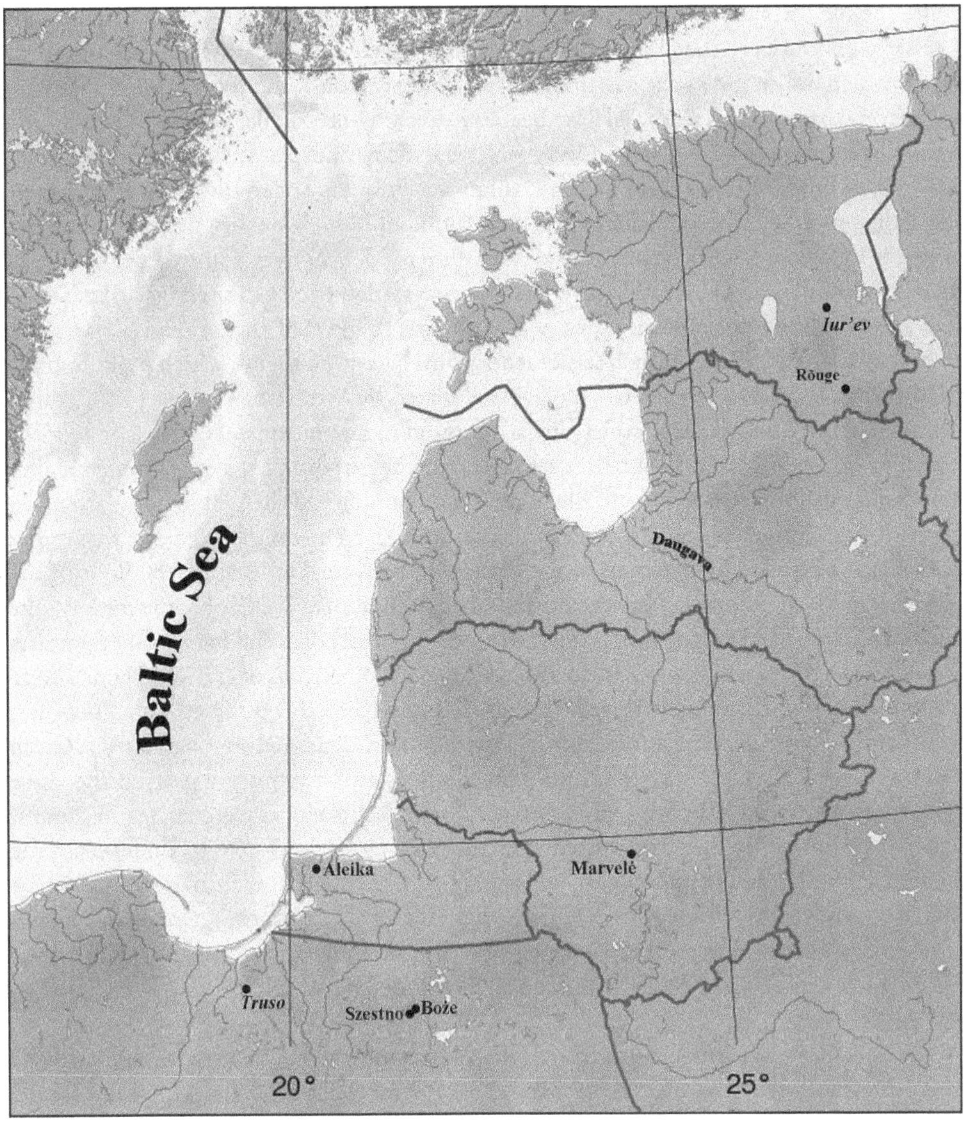

Map 23.1. The Baltic region in the Early Middle Ages. Medieval place names are in italics.

experiences resulting from a peripheral position in relation to the Viking world and, later, to the early medieval states in the region, Rus' and Poland.

The Prussians emerged in what is now northeastern Poland and the territory of the Kaliningrad region of Russia squeezed between Poland and Lithuania. That swathe of the North European lowlands was densely forested and dotted with many lakes. In the absence of written sources, much of what is known about this region in the Early Middle Ages derives from archaeological excavations. Shortly after 700, many strongholds appeared, while the old settlement sites – small hamlets with a few dwellings – were abandoned. The strongholds were themselves relatively small. Inside that excavated at Szestno (near Mrągowo, in the region of the Masurian Lakes), there was only one aboveground structure with several rooms. This may well have been the dwelling of a single, possibly elite, family. At any rate, no more than thirty individuals lived at any one time inside that stronghold. At Boże, only a few miles from Szestno, there was only a wooden tower built on top of an earthen mound. Since archaeologists have found only high-quality pottery inside the tower, it must also have been a tenth-century elite residence. Even some of the open settlements produced evidence of local elites. In open settlements inhabited by commoners, aboveground buildings typically grouped under one single roof the residential parts, the workshops, and the barns. In such settlements, coins have been found, which point to trade relations, most likely with the town of Truso visited by Wulfstan. Further proof comes from hoards of Muslim silver coins (dirhams) found in northeastern Poland.

According to Wulfstan, "that is the custom among the Ests that people of every nationality must be cremated there; and if a single bone is found unburned there, they must atone for it greatly."[3] However, no early medieval cemeteries with cremations have so far been found in the lands inhabited by Prussians in the Early Middle Ages. Underneath the floor of the dwelling in Szestno, archaeologists have found charred human bones of some twenty-one individuals, especially fragments of skulls mixed with animal bones and fragments of pottery. Moreover, on several sites outside strongholds like Szestno, remains of cremated bodies were scattered in the fields, along with grave goods, all placed directly on the ground. Such "ash fields" are known from Sambia, the lands now within the Kaliningrad region of Russia. Given that, in most cases, the grave goods found on ash fields are weapons and parts of the horse tack, those were the final resting places of warriors. That warriors were buried in groups, separately, shows that they constituted a distinct social group. Moreover, underneath the ash field at Aleika (near Kaliningrad), archaeologists have discovered burials of horses (not cremated), all arranged in a regular pattern. Sacrificial sites are also known, where the remains of dozens of horses were buried over a period of time as long as two centuries. The role of horses in the burial customs of the Ests is also mentioned by Wulfstan:

> there is among the Ests a custom that, when a man dies, he lies indoors un-cremated with his kinsmen and friends for a month, or sometimes two, and kings and the other high-ranking men as much longer as they have more wealth. Sometimes they lie un-cremated for half a year, above ground in their houses. And all the time that the body is indoors, there has to be drinking and entertainment, until the day that they cremate him. On the day that they intend to carry him to the funeral pyre, they divide up what is left of his property after the drinking and entertainment into five or six parts, and sometimes more, depending on the amount of the property. Then they lay it down, the largest portion about a mile from the

3 Curta, ed., "Wulfstan Travels to Truso," in *Medieval Eastern Europe*, 58.

> *tun* [probably homestead], then the second, then the third, until it is all laid out within that single mile. And the smallest portion must be closest to the *tun* where the dead man is lying. Then all the men with the swiftest horses in the land have to be assembled about five or six miles from the property. Then they all gallop towards the property. The man who has the fastest horse comes to the first and largest portion, and so each after the other, until everything is taken. The smallest portion goes to the man who gallops closest to the *tun* to get it. Each man then rides on his way with the property; they may have it all, and that is why fast horses are excessively expensive there.[4]

Warriors played a key role in Curonian society as well. Judging from the archaeological evidence, beginning with the ninth century, Curonians, who initially lived in the region of present-day Klaipėda, in western Lithuania, began to expand to the north, along the coast, apparently in an attempt to reach the Gulf of Riga and seize control over the maritime trade routes heading to the mouth of the river Daugava. Just like in Prussia, trade created opportunities for enrichment and sharp social differences. There is more silver in ninth-to-eleventh-century burials in western Lithuania than anywhere else in the Baltic region. Moreover, the deposition of scales and weights in the graves signals the role that men in Curonian society played in that trade. Those men were often of an elevated social status, and upon death their bodies were cremated, with the ashes deposited in graves along with weapons. The presence of locks and keys in those burials bespeak the development of notions of private property. Further afield in central Lithuania, inhumations are the rule, with most grave goods being dress accessories made of bronze, not silver. However, central Lithuania is also the area in the Baltic region with the largest number of early medieval horse burials. No less than 250 such burials have been found in Marvelė (a western suburb of Kaunas, Lithuania), grouped together in separate sections of the cemetery, away from the human burials. Those were most likely ritual sacrifices for individuals buried nearby, mostly men. That such sacrifices were linked to the status of those men in the local society is deduced not only from the deposition of weapons in their graves, but also from the fact that horse burials coincide in time with the building of strongholds in central Lithuania and the rise of a distinct group of warriors. Such developments did not reach northeastern and eastern Lithuania, where burial in barrows (burial mounds) was the rule. Each cemetery had between four and twenty barrows, but some of the burials were planted into pre-existing (often ancient) barrows. In eastern Lithuania, burial in barrows was abandoned only in the eleventh and twelfth centuries, with the latest graves dug into old barrows.

Farther to the north, in southeastern Estonia, there are no burial sites at all, despite the presence of many settlements, especially strongholds. This has been interpreted as an indication that the dead in that region were disposed of in ways that did not leave any

4 Curta, ed., "Wulfstan Travels to Truso," in *Medieval Eastern Europe*, 57–58.

archaeological traces. In northern Estonia, inhumations began in the ninth century, but entire cemeteries did not appear before the eleventh century. Moreover, in some cases, the inhumations cut through the older cremations on that same site. Such variations in burial customs are mirrored by equally dramatic transformations in the settlement pattern, which are undoubtedly linked to social changes. During the ninth and tenth centuries, most strongholds were surrounded by "satellite" settlements, but this complex arrangement disappeared after the year 1000, to be replaced by strongholds alone, and fewer of them. This is the case of Iur'ev (now Tartu) established by Iaroslav the Wise, prince of Kiev (1019–54), after an expedition against the Chud (1030). Many of the new strongholds were economic and trade centers. For example, in addition to evidence of crafts, the stronghold at Rõuge (near Võru, in southeastern Estonia) also produced evidence of fur trade, with beaver as the most important species in assemblages of bone animals from the site.

Very little is known about the religious beliefs of the people inhabiting the southeastern and eastern Baltic region. Sacred woods seem to have been located at borders between tribal or ethnic groups, but the nature of the rituals performed there remains unknown (see chapter 62). Sometimes, borders were also marked with stone statues of warriors. Each one of them shows a man holding a horn or a sword and are the only depictions of humans left behind by the medieval Prussians. Priests existed, but their role is poorly understood. The man who killed St. Adalbert is said to have been "a priest of the idols."[5] Following the death of St. Adalbert, the Prussians "cut off his noble head from the body," impaled it, and "all returned to their dwellings" carrying the head with them but leaving the body behind.[6] The gruesome yet special "treatment" of St. Adalbert's head may well be a manifestation of a cult of the head, as the seat of the soul and spiritual potency, much like the human skulls deposited underneath the dwelling at Szestno. The head is also highlighted in the choice of artifacts for ritual deposition in bogs in so-called "bridal offerings" – exclusively female dress accessories such as diadems, pins, neck rings, bracelets, and brooches. The meaning behind such bog deposits remains unknown, but it may have something to do with special requests, perhaps related to fertility cults.

FURTHER READING

Bliujienė, Audronė. "The Bog Offerings of the Balts: 'I Give in Order to Get Back'." *Archaeologia Baltica* 14 (2010): 136–65.

Kulakov, Vladimir I. *The Prussians, Scalvians and Curonians in the Viking Age.* Moscow: Editus, 2020.

5 Curta, ed., "The Martyrdom of St. Adalbert," in *Medieval Eastern Europe*, 185.

6 Curta, ed., "The Martyrdom of St. Adalbert," in *Medieval Eastern Europe*, 186.

Lang, Valter. "Riding to the Afterworld: Burying with Horses and Riding Equipment in Estonia and the Baltic Rim." In *Identity Formation and Diversity in the Early Medieval Baltic and Beyond*, edited by Johan Callmer, Ingrid Gustin, and Mats Roslund, 48–75. The Northern World 75. Leiden: Brill, 2017.

Nowakiewicz, Tomasz. "Baltic Communities Present in Today's Polish Territory between 700 and 1000 AD." In *The Past Societies: Polish Lands from the First Evidence of Human Presence to the Early Middle Ages*. Vol. 5, *500 AD – 1000 AD*, edited by Maciej Trzeciecki, 169–222. Warsaw: Institute of Archaeology and Ethnology, Polish Academy of Sciences, 2016.

Shiroukhov, Roman A. "Prussian Graves in the Sambian Peninsula with Imports, Arms, and Horse Harnesses from the Tenth to the 13th Century: The Question of Warrior Elite." *Archaeologia Baltica* 18 (2012): 224–55.

Tvauri, Andres. *The Migration Period, Pre-Viking Age, and Viking Age in Estonia*. Tartu: Tartu University Press, 2012.

Žulkus, Vladas. *Palanga in the Middle Ages: Ancient Settlements*. Vilnius: Versus Aureus, 2007.

24

INNER PERIPHERY: VLACHS AND ALBANIANS IN THE BALKANS

Keywords in this chapter: transhumant pastoralism, *cătune*, inscriptions

The Byzantine reconquest of the entire Balkan Peninsula in the early eleventh century (see chapter 13) brought into the spotlight groups of population, the origins and earlier history of which are obscured by the lack of sources. Two of them are particularly significant for the history of the peninsula during the subsequent centuries – Albanians and Vlachs. To this day, both groups speak distinct languages of considerable age: the Vlach dialects derive, like Romanian, from Latin, while the Albanian language, though clearly Indo-European, has no close affinity to any other language in that family, being the only descendant of its own linguistic group. However, neither Vlachs nor Albanians are known from any source written before the year 1000. Moreover, in the eleventh century, when they are first mentioned, both Vlachs and Albanians were on the periphery of the Byzantine society. To German participants in the Third Crusade, who were attacked by Vlachs while crossing the Balkans, they were "semi-barbarian."[1] The Vlachs had a prominent political role in the late twelfth and early thirteenth centuries (see chapter 45) but moved back to historical obscurity after that. The Albanians came to the center of the political stage of the Balkans only after 1300.

However, both the Vlachs and the Albanians first appeared in the written sources as recruits in the Byzantine army. The annals of the city of Bari in Italy, which were written in the mid-eleventh century, mention Vlachs in the Byzantine army that was sent in 1027 to conquer Sicily. Vlach recruits appear also in the Byzantine armies that fought against the Pechenegs in 1091 and against Hungary in 1166. Similarly, the Byzantine historian Michael

1 Florin Curta, ed., "The Army of Frederick Barbarossa Crosses the Balkans," in *Medieval Eastern Europe, 500–1300: A Reader* (Toronto: University of Toronto Press, 2024), 242.

Attaleiates, who wrote in the 1080s, knew of Albanian soldiers in the army with which the Byzantine general appointed to lead the Byzantine troops in Sicily marched against the imperial troops in the Balkans, after proclaiming himself emperor. In 1078, another rebel named Nicephorus Basilakes, the governor of Dyrrachion (now Durrës, in Albania), marched on Constantinople with an army of Bulgarians and Albanians (see map 24.1). While Albanians sided with rebels, the Vlachs were themselves rebels. According to Kekaumenos, a Byzantine author who wrote during the reign of Michael VII Dukas (1071–78), his grandfather Nikulitzas had been appointed leader of the Vlachs in Hellas by Emperor Basil II. However, in 1066, the Vlachs were at the center of the rebellion of Larissa, two leaders of which are specifically mentioned as being of Vlach origin – Slavota Karmalakis and a certain Beriboes (Berivoi), in whose house the conspirators used to gather to discuss their plans. In addition, the rebellion appears to have drawn large numbers of Vlachs living in the hinterland of the city. In anticipation of serious military turbulence, they had sent their wives and children to the mountains, which may suggest that they had more or less permanent settlements there. This is commonly interpreted as proof that they practiced transhumant pastoralism, moving seasonally together with their herds between the mountain pastures and the grazing fields in the lowlands. Kekaumenos placed the blame for the rebellion of 1066 entirely on the Vlachs, regarding them as "entirely untrustworthy and perfidious, with no faith in God, the emperor, a relative or a friend, striving to cheat everyone."[2] He nonetheless was aware of their ancient origins, for he traced their lack of loyalty back to Antiquity, as he identified the Vlachs with the Dacians defeated by Emperor Trajan (98–117):

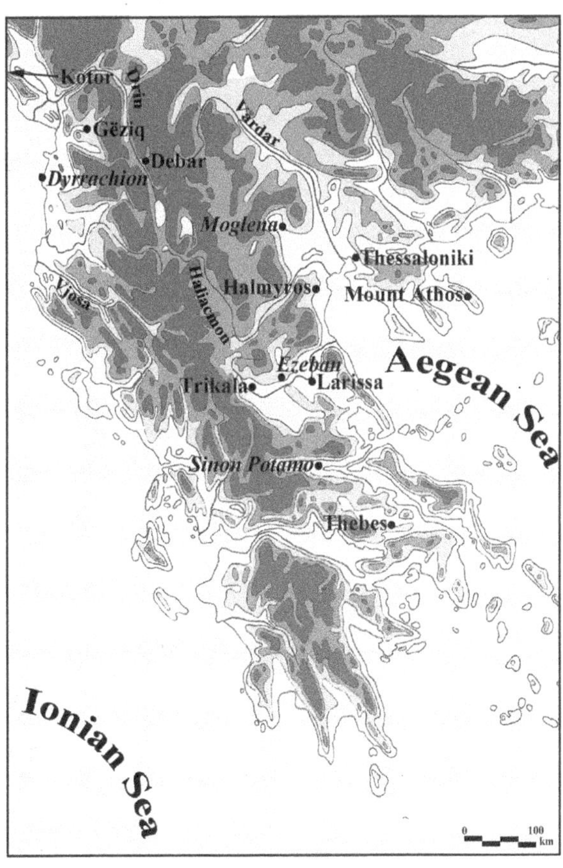

Map 24.1. Sites associated with Vlachs and Albanians, ca. 1000 to ca. 1200. Medieval place names are in italics. Shown in the upper right corner of the map are the Rhodope Mountains, while the range in the middle of the map (from north to south) is the Pindus.

> They have not kept faith with anyone, not even with the old Roman emperors (confronted by Emperor Trajan, they were completely destroyed and conquered; their king named Decebalus was killed and his head placed on a pike in the middle of the city of Rome). In fact, those are the people called Dacians and Bessi. They first lived close to the rivers Danube and Saos, which is now called Sava, where the Serbs have recently moved, and [the inhabited] places that were well fortified and difficult to reach. Relying on that [advantage], they feigned being friendly and ready to submit to the old Roman emperors, [but instead] came out of their strongholds, and devastated the Roman territory. So, the Romans, being annoyed

2 Curta, ed., "Kekaumenos on the Vlachs," in *Medieval Eastern Europe*, 88.

> with their deeds, destroyed them, as I have already said. Once they left those places, they scattered throughout Epirus and Macedonia, but the majority went to leave in Hellas [the Byzantine theme by that name, located in central Greece].[3]

By contrast, the Byzantine historian John Kinnamos, who finished his *History* a century after Kekaumenos, in the 1180s, believed the Vlachs to be descendants of Roman settlers from Italy.

Other authors were interested less in the origin of the Vlachs and more in their image as rebels. Anna Comnena, who in 1148 finished the biography of her father, Emperor Alexius I (1081–1118), relates that when the Cumans crossed the Danube in 1094, they were shown the route through the mountain passes by local Vlachs. This is remarkably like what she has to say about Bohemond of Taranto, who in 1107 invaded the Byzantine lands in what is now Albania. The Norman prince won over to his side several Albanian leaders who were familiar with the mountain passes. In fact, the Albanians helped the Normans conquer Debar, a fort at the confluence of the Radika and Drin Rivers, on the present-day Albanian-Macedonian border. Anna Comnena regarded the Vlachs as "nomads," probably referring to their transhumant pastoralism. Similarly, the twelfth-century continuation of the chronicle of John Skylitzes mentions "some 'travelling' Vlachs" in relation to events in the late tenth century.[4] However, Anna Comnena also knew of a Vlach village called Ezeban located between Larissa and Trikala, in Thessaly. A little more than fifty years after her biography of Alexius I, the monks on Mount Athos appealed to Patriarch Nicholas III of Constantinople (1084–1111) in a case involving 300 families of Vlachs, who at some point between 1100 and 1104 had moved onto the peninsula, thus causing much concern because of the presence of their wives and daughters. The Vlachs were organized in units called *cătune* (hamlets), each of ten to fifty families. At the end of that same century, a number of Vlach *cătune* in the environs of Moglena (close to Chrysi, near the Greek-Macedonian border) were donated to the Great Lavra monastery on Mount Athos. This strongly suggests that the Vlachs near Moglena were not free, since they had to fulfill obligations imposed upon them by the monks of the Great Lavra. A similar situation appears in the charter that the Serbian ruler Stephen Nemanja (see chapter 45) gave in 1198 to his and his son's foundation, the Hilandar monastery on Mount Athos. Among the goods granted to the new foundation, the Serbian ruler lists "170 Vlachs" from the "jurisdictions of Rad and Djuradj" in Serbia.[5] As with the Vlachs from Moglena, there can be no doubt about the unfree status of the Vlachs of Serbia mentioned in this source. However, it is unlikely that the Hilandar monastery received the actual people (the 170 Vlachs); rather, the Serbian ruler donated the services, most likely in kind, that had until then been rendered to him on his family estates in the above-mentioned jurisdictions.

---

3 Curta, ed., "Kekaumenos on the Vlachs," in *Medieval Eastern Europe*, 88.

4 Curta, ed., "*Skylitzes Continuatus* on the Bulgarian-Byzantine War," in *Medieval Eastern Europe*, 65.

5 Curta, ed., "Stephen Nemanja Establishes the Monastery of Hilandar," in *Medieval Eastern Europe*, 220.

Almost twenty years later, the Byzantine historian Niketas Choniates finished his *History*, in which he associated the Vlachs and their rulers with mountains. According to him, they occupied "the rough ground and inaccessible places."[6] Instead of villages, like that mentioned by Anna Comnena, they now had fortresses, which were "situated directly above sheer cliffs."[7] The Vlachs descended from Mount Haimos (Stara Planina), falling unexpectedly upon the Byzantine towns, killing many and carrying away a great number of prisoners and goods. They thus left the heights on which they moved like deer to gather in the lowlands for war and plunder. The comparison of the Vlachs with deer in the high mountains also appears in the travelogue of Benjamin of Tudela, a rabbi who journeyed from his native Navarre, in modern Spain, all the way to Baghdad and back between 1160 and 1171 or 1172. He crossed Greece from Corfu to Thebes, Halmyros, and Thessaloniki in 1161. One of his stops was in Sinon Potamo, near present-day Lamia, in Phthiotis. There were about fifty Jews in that town at that time, led by two rabbis named Shelomoh and Ya'aqov. A digression on the Vlachs follows:

> This [place] is at the foot of the mountains [of] Vlachia [Mount Othrys, in central Greece], on which mountains dwell the people called Vlachs, and they are as swift as deer and descending from the mountains to plunder and loot the country of Greece. And no man can climb up to them to fight, and no king can rule over them, and they do not hold fast to the faith of the Nazarenes [Christians] but call themselves Jewish names. And it is said that they were Jews and call the Jews "our brothers," [and that] when they meet them, they steal from them, but do not kill them the way they kill the Greeks, and they do not accept any religion.[8]

Leaving aside the transparent attempt to make the Vlachs look like allies of the Jews persecuted in the Byzantine Empire, the idea that the Vlachs were rebels that nobody, especially not the Byzantines, could defeat is a mirror of what Niketas Choniates related on the Vlachs in the context of their rebellion of 1185, which was headed by Peter and Asen (see chapter 45). To him, the Vlachs were a serious enemy, demon-inspired barbarians who rejoiced in rising in rebellion against the emperor.

Albanian lords were also independently minded, albeit in less rebellious ways. Under Emperor Manuel I (1143–80), Albania was included into a single Byzantine province in the western Balkans, together with Dalmatia and Croatia. An Albanian lord called "prior" and named Andrew appears in a document concerning the consecration in 1166 of a church in Kotor, along with an Albanian bishop named Lazarus, to whom Pope Alexander III (1159–81) later sent a letter. Another local leader named Progon, together with his sons Demetrius and Gjin, appears in an inscription from the Monastery of St. Mary in

6 Curta, ed., "The Vlach Rebels in Bulgaria," in *Medieval Eastern Europe*, 306.

7 Curta, ed., "The Vlach Rebels in Bulgaria," in *Medieval Eastern Europe*, 305.

8 Curta, ed., "Benjamin of Tudela on the Vlachs," in *Medieval Eastern Europe*, 304.

Trifandina in Gëziq (near Gjegjan, in northern Albania). Demetrius also appears in early thirteenth-century sources as the son-in-law of the Serbian ruler Stephen Nemanja. He may have welcomed the Serbian rule, much like other local leaders in northern and eastern Albania. Nonetheless, throughout the thirteenth century, local elites in the hinterland of Dyrrachion, who were descendants of the two sons of Progon, sported lofty Byzantine titles, as if any of the Byzantine administrative structures were still in place. While the Vlachs who established the Second Bulgarian Empire modelled their political actions after the Christian rulers of early medieval Bulgaria, the only political models available to the Albanian elites were Byzantine.

FURTHER READING

Curta, Florin. "Constantinople and the Echo Chamber: The Vlachs in the French Crusade Chronicles." *Medieval Encounters* 22 (2016): 427–62.

Madgearu, Alexandru. "Vlach Military Units in the Byzantine Army." In *Samuel's State and Byzantium: History, Legend, Tradition, Heritage. Proceedings of the International Symposium "Days of Justinian I," Skopje, October 17–18, 2014*, edited by Mitko B. Panov, 47–55. Skopje: "Euro-Balkan" University, 2015.

Winnifrith, Tom. *The Vlachs: The History of a Balkan People.* New York: St. Martin's Press, 1987.

25

THE BYZANTINES AND THE KHAZARS IN THE CRIMEA

Keywords in this chapter: *tudun*, agriculture, trade

Shortly after establishing their control over the steppe lands around the Sea of Azov, the Khazars made their appearance in eastern Crimea at some point during the late seventh century (see chapter 5). They do not seem to have been interested in occupying any territory, only in extracting tribute from the local communities. They also took the opportunity to intervene in Byzantine politics. After being ousted and partially mutilated in 695 by his rival and successor Leontius, the former emperor Justinian II was sent into exile to Cherson, the main city in Crimea. The inhabitants of that city, however, disliked him and allegedly planned his assassination. To escape, Justinian fled to a fort named Doros beyond the mountain district to the east (the exact location is not known). Once there, he asked the khagan of the Khazars for assistance. In response, the khagan offered the hand of his own sister, Theodora, in marriage. Exactly where the khagan and his sister resided at that time remains unclear, but upon marrying the Khazar princess, Justinian moved across the Kerch Strait, at Phanagoria, together with his wife. Learning about those developments and worried about a potential rival, the new emperor in Constantinople, Tiberius III Apsimar (698–705), asked the same khagan of the Khazars to eliminate Justinian, now that he was within his reach. Phanagoria must have indeed been under Khazar control, for the khagan had a local deputy there named Papatzys, probably the commander of the local garrison. Working together with Balgitzis, the Khazar "lord" (possibly governor) of the hinterland of Bosporus in the Kerch Peninsula (see map 25.1), he was charged to take out Justinian. A slave of the khagan revealed the plan to Theodora and she, in turn, warned her husband. Both Papatzys and Balgitzis were promptly killed, and Justinian, sending his wife back to her brother, fled from Phanagoria on a ship that took him to the western shore of the Black Sea.

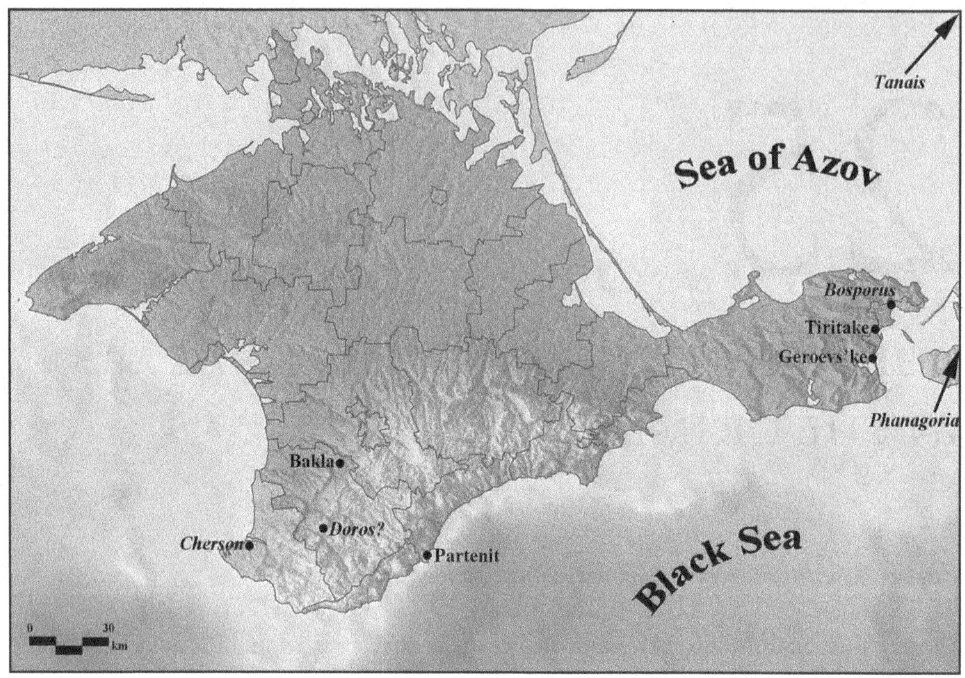

Map 25.1. Crimea in the Early Middle Ages. Medieval place names are in italics. The Kerch Peninsula is on the right side of the map (where Bosporus, now Kerch, is located), separated from the Taman Peninsula (where Phanagoria is located) by the Kerch Strait between the Sea of Azov and the Black Sea.

After obtaining the military assistance of the Bulgar ruler Tervel (see chapter 8), in 705, Justinian was able to regain the throne in Constantinople. Shortly after that, his Khazar wife and newly born son joined him in Constantinople as well. To punish Cherson for his persecution, Emperor Justinian II sent a fleet against the city. Among those captured by the punitive expedition was the *tudun*, the representative ("consul") of the khagan in Cherson, who was promptly brought to Constantinople together with other members of the city elite. The *tudun* was later released but died on this way back to Khazaria. Papatzys, Balgitzis, and the *tudun* bespeak the presence of the Khazars in the Crimean Peninsula and their involvement in the power struggle in Constantinople in the early eighth century. That the Khazar-Byzantine connection was not limited to that period results from developments in the reign of Leo III (717–41). In the early 730s, Leo married his son (future emperor Constantine V, 741–75) to the daughter of the khagan of the Khazars, Tzitzak (Irene), the second matrimonial alliance between the ruling houses of Byzantium and the khaganate.

The Khazar presence in the Crimean Peninsula was not restricted to garrisons and khaganal deputies in the main cities. Archaeologists have identified over 250 new settlement sites dated to the eighth and ninth centuries in the peninsula, 85 percent of which are located in the Kerch Peninsula – the hinterland of Bosporus. The new population consisted of immigrants from the core areas of the khaganate, who were agriculturists, not nomadic pastoralists. Typical for those new settlements are silos, each of about 660 gallons, located next to dwellings. A very large silo – 3.7 m deep and 3.5 m in diameter – was found at Tiritake, on the southern side of modern Kerch. That such silos were for storing grain is deduced from the seeds of barley, rye, and wheat found on another settlement site farther to the south, at Geroevs'ke. That the crops in question were locally produced and not brought from elsewhere is concluded from the find of a hoe on that same site, a tool dated to the eighth or ninth century. There is also good evidence of agricultural production in the hinterland of Cherson. Seeds of rye and soft wheat have been found on several eighth- and ninth-century settlement sites, including strongholds. The wheat from Bakla (near Skalyste, in the district of Bakhchesarai) has been identified as of three kinds – durum, common, and club wheat. The local production of those cereals is attested by such finds as plowshares and sickles, in addition to mattocks and hoes.

To judge from the archaeological evidence, the population increase, followed by considerable economic growth, took place especially during the second half of the eighth century, perhaps as the result of more immigrants fleeing Khazaria after the Arab defeat of the khagan (see chapter 5). The immigrants did not displace the old inhabitants, but lived peacefully side by side with them. There is clear evidence that instead of disrupting the ecclesiastical structures in the peninsula, this period witnessed their expansion, even beyond Crimea. Shortly after the marriage of Leo III's son Constantine with the Khazar princess, a bishopric was planned for eastern Crimea and another for Itil, both to be placed under the jurisdiction of a metropolitan residing in the mountain region under Byzantine control. Many churches were established in eastern Crimea during the eighth century, and one of them, dedicated to St. John the Baptist, is still standing in Kerch (ancient Bosporus). Two inscriptions record the foundation of a church somewhere in the mountain region by people with Khazar names – Ilikh and Ghapr (who is also called "the Khazar").

However, the expansion of Khazar political authority over southwestern Crimea did not go unchallenged. The biography (*vita*) of a local saint named John of Gotthia (the name of the mountain region in the interior) has details about political and military unrest. According to this text written in Greek in the early ninth century, John was from a family of recent immigrants from Asia Minor, who established themselves at Partenit on the southeastern coast, where John was born. From an early age, he chose a career in the church and later established a monastery dedicated to Sts. Peter and Paul. In 754, he was elected bishop by the "people" when the previous bishop, an iconoclast, was promoted to metropolitan of Herakleа in Thrace (see insert 25.1). Before taking his episcopal office, however, John traveled to Jerusalem and Iberia (present-day Georgia). He also went to Constantinople at some point between 780 and 784 at the invitation of Empress Irene, who appreciated his iconodule views. John may have even garnered her support for the political actions that he was determined to take upon assuming his episcopal position in the Crimea. Relations between the Khazars and the Byzantine Empire had meanwhile become tense. Under suspicion of receiving orders from Constantinople, John was thrown into prison by the khagan, and, while there, he cured the child of a "lord of Phoulai" (the location of which is much disputed), possibly the deputy of the khagan, a man who was obviously Christian. Together with the "lord of Gotthia," this time a local ruler in the mountain region of the interior, Bishop John led a rebellion of the population against

INSERT 25.1. ICONOCLASM

The word "iconoclasm" means "image breaking." An icon is a sacred image representing Christ, the Mother of God, or a saint. Icons were commonly paintings on wooden panels, but they could also be crafted in marble, ivory, ceramic, precious metals, or mosaic, or painted on church walls. Iconoclasm refers to a major theological dispute involving both the Byzantine state and the church, which spanned more than a century, from 726 to 843, with an interruption between 787 and 815. Besides the intellectual debate about the admissibility of depicting God and the holiness of icons representing Christ, the Mother of God, or the saints, the controversy was also an important phase in the reassertion of imperial power in the state after a period of decline. In certain parts of the empire, particularly in Constantinople, icons were systematically destroyed or plastered over. Very few icons survived the Iconoclastic Controversy, and those that did were kept in remote locations, such as the Monastery of St. Catherine on Mount Sinai. Emperor Leo III (717–41) issued an imperial edict in 726 (or 730), which banned the use of icons. His son, Constantine V (741–75) summoned a church council in the palace at Hieria in Chalcedon in 754, which condemned as idolatry not only the veneration but also the production of icons. Iconodules (those who wanted to venerate icons) were persecuted and some killed, which turned them into martyrs and saints, such as St. Stephen the Younger (d. 764). The decisions of the council of Hieria were overturned by the second council of Nicaea (787), but iconoclasm was revived as state policy under Leo V (813–20), until a synod under Patriarch Methodius I summoned by Empress Theodora in 843 reaffirmed religious images and declared the Triumph of Orthodoxy (which is celebrated to this day, every year, on the first Sunday of Lent).

Iconoclasm was largely a reaction to the military victories and political hegemony of Islam, but the policies introduced by the early iconoclastic emperors also targeted monasteries and their large properties. That is why the Triumph of Orthodoxy meant not only a restoration of icons but also a substantial revival of Orthodox monasticism. During the first phase of Iconoclasm (726–87), the legitimacy of icon veneration led to the refinement of a theory of images, the main advocates of which were St. John of Damascus (675–749), St. Theodore of Studios (759–826), and Patriarch Nicephorus I (758–828). The former drew the fundamental distinction between worship and veneration, which made room for the use of icons in teaching the truths of Christianity, as well as in devotional practice.

the Khazars. They expelled the Khazar garrison from Doros and occupied the passes across the mountains. The response of the khagan was swift and merciless. The "lord of Gotthia" was spared, probably out of political expediency, but seventeen Christians were executed. Fearing for his life, John fled across the Black Sea to Amastris (modern Amasra, in northwestern Turkey), where he died in 792.

The anti-Khazar revolt of 786 or 787 announced the weakening of the Khazar control over Crimea in the ninth century. To be sure, a Byzantine theme was established in 841, centered upon Cherson. In the mid-ninth century, the economy of Crimea was flourishing, and there is clear evidence of cash crops, such as vineyards. The wine industry stimulated pottery production, particularly of transportation jars. As a matter of fact, most centers of pottery production in ninth-century Crimea produced amphorae and no other types of vessels. The conspicuous standardization of production was clearly designed to meet the demands of the growing production of wine. Wine in large quantities was brought to Cherson and then sold in the markets on the southern coast of the Black Sea in exchange for grain. However, judging from finds of amphorae in which the Crimean wine was transported, large shipments moved in the opposite direction, across the Sea of Azov and beyond it, deep into Khazaria. That much results from the episode of the late 830s, when a Byzantine official named Petronas Kamateros, who was sent by Emperor Theophilus (829–42) to Khazaria to build the fortress of Sarkel together with a team of Byzantine engineers. Once in Cherson, Petronas and his men moved from the imperial ship to local round boats, with which they crossed over to Tanais, in the Don delta, that is, within Khazar territory. Crimeans used the round boats more or less regularly to go to Tanais, as indicated by Crimean amphorae found there, as well as farther into the steppe, to the east and to the southeast. Cultural influences in the opposite direction, from Khazaria to Crimea, have also been documented archaeologically, for example through finds of a special kind of pottery, the so-called Grey Ware with burnished ornament that is typical for settlement and burial sites in Khazaria. Through Khazaria, Islamic coins and their imitations produced in Eastern Europe reached Crimea, as attested by hoards of dirhams discovered in several strongholds of the mountain region. A key role in the trade with Khazaria must have been that of the Jewish community in Bosporus, which is attested archaeologically by tombstones inscribed with menorahs and found in Kerch, as well as on the other side of the strait, near ancient Phanagoria. Moreover, Anthony, the archbishop of Bosporus, received a congratulatory letter from Patriarch Photius at some point between 859 and 867 for having converted the local Jews to Christianity.

Crimea was peripheral to both the Byzantine Empire and Khazaria, and the way in which the two states interacted in the peninsula may be best described as a condominium, not unlike that between Byzantium and the Arab Caliphate on the island of Cyprus. When, shortly before 900, Bosporus and many of the settlements in its hinterland of eastern Crimea were sacked by Magyars and Pechenegs, the Khazar control over the area ceased completely. The sack of Itil by the Rus' of Sviatoslav, prince of Kiev, removed all Khazar presence in the region of the Sea of Azov. But the memory of the Byzantine-Khazar condominium persisted. In 1016, Emperor Basil II sent a fleet against "Chazaria" under the command of Mongos, the son of Sviatoslav and the brother of Vladimir, the emperor's brother-in-law. The expedition squashed the rebellion in "Chazaria" and took prisoner its "governor," a man named George Tzoulos. His name is that of a family of great prominence in Crimean politics during the tenth and eleventh centuries, as attested by lead seals found on many sites in the peninsula. Sporting imperial titles and often acting as imperial officials, the Tzoulos were in fact a local elite who aspired to become autonomous. That their aspirations were associated with the Khazars in the minds of those in Constantinople who knew about them is simply an indication that they were trying to establish with the imperial government the same kind of relation that had existed in the past between Byzantium and the Khazars.

FURTHER READING

Noonan, Thomas S. "The Khazar-Byzantine World of the Crimea in the Early Middle Ages: The Religious Dimension." *Archivum Eurasiae Medii Aevi* 10 (1998): 207–30.

Zuckerman, Constantin. "Byzantium's Pontic Policy in the *Notitiae Episcopatuum*." In *La Crimée entre Byzance et le khaganat khazar*, edited by Constantin Zuckerman, 201–30. Paris: Association des Amis du Centre d'Histoire et Civilisation de Byzance, 2006.

PART 5

Societies and Cultures in the Early Middle Ages

26

POPULATION STRUCTURES

Keywords in this chapter: demography, life expectancy, migration, diet, diseases

With no census data collected for any of the countries in the region before the modern age, there is no direct information about the size of the population in Central or Eastern Europe at any moment during its medieval history. Written sources, particularly those pertaining to newcomers, such as nomads raiding the Balkan provinces of the Byzantine Empire, are unreliable. For example, Byzantine authors exaggerated the number of Pechenegs invading the Balkans in the eleventh century (see chapter 10), with figures as high as 800,000. Considering the number of horses the nomads needed and the total grazing area available in the Balkan Peninsula, estimates are much more conservative – no more than 50,000 Pecheneg warriors may have been involved in those events, most likely less than that. Moreover, medieval chroniclers sometimes used numbers symbolically, with no concern for accuracy. To counter these problems, historians must rely on proxy data or on retrogressive estimates. The latter refer to tentative projections back in time from a moment where at least some reliable information is available. In the early thirteenth century, King Valdemar II of Denmark (1202–41) ordered a land registration across the kingdom in order to collect information about the sources of royal income and the royal estates. The result was the *Danish Census Book*, which contains valuable information about the arable (therefore taxable) lands in northern Estonia, which was at that time under Danish rule. The number of plowlands (units of measurement) recorded in the *Book* implies a population between 100,000 and 200,000 people. The number must have been smaller for earlier centuries, but it is unclear how much. As an example of proxy data, a population of 200,000 was also estimated for the late medieval principality of Moldavia (see chapter 52), covering an area now divided between Romania, the Republic of Moldova, and Ukraine. Based on the floor area of sunken-feature buildings discovered by archaeologists in several settlement sites in Moldavia, the population of that area for the sixth and seventh centuries has been estimated at between 30,000 and 45,000, with a slight increase (between 40,000 and 50,000 people) for the eighth and ninth centuries.

For Estonia, such estimates are not possible. Instead, data from forty-nine cremation barrows in the southeastern part of the country, combined with the observation that between four and six individuals were buried in each barrow, have led to the conclusion that between 5,462 and 6,827 people were buried in those barrows between the sixth and the tenth centuries. In each century, between 273 and 344 people were buried in the barrow cemeteries. The whole area of southeastern Estonia is less than 1,000 square miles (about 2,600 square kilometers), which implies a population density as low as 28.5 to 36.2 persons for every 100 square miles (260 square kilometers). In the northeastern part of the country, the anthropological analysis of human bones from a stone grave excavated in Maidla (near Kohtla-Järve, not far from the southern shore of the Gulf of Finland) suggests that each one of the families that lived there between the tenth and the thirteenth centuries was no larger than eight to nine individuals, including three or four children (see map 26.1). In other words, northeastern Estonia was sparsely populated on the eve of the Baltic Crusades (see chapter 44). Even though Estonia is almost seven times smaller than Poland, the population density was most likely the same in the lands included after the year 1000 into the realm of the Piasts. Poland had some 1.25 million inhabitants by that time, but 2.5 million by 1300. In 1000, there may have been half a million people in Hungary, including the population that the Magyar immigrants found in place. Three centuries later, the population of Hungary was between 1.8 and 2 million people.

When no absolute numbers may be estimated, the relative growth or decline of the population can be gauged by the number of settlement sites in existence in an area at any given time. For example, at the time of the great strongholds in ninth-century Moravia, each one of them was surrounded by several satellite settlements, which were abandoned, although not destroyed, when occupation of the strongholds ceased shortly after the year 900. Conversely, a great number of settlement sites appeared in northwestern Russia during the eighth and ninth centuries, which has been interpreted as a demographic explosion. The sudden increase was at least partly the result of immigration. A population surge in Thrace during that same time is undoubtedly the result of migration, as confirmed by the written sources mentioning Syrians and Armenians moving to the region in the mid-eighth century, then again in 778, with more settlers from different parts of the Byzantine Empire coming in 809 and 810.

The results of the anthropological study of excavated cemeteries, especially the sexing and ageing of the skeletal material, has produced abundant evidence for basic demographic indicators, such as life expectancy, child population, sex and age ratios, as well as the death rate. For example, children and teenagers represent almost a third of all individuals buried in the large, sixth-century cemetery excavated in Holubice (Moravia, Czech Republic). Most adults in that cemetery died between forty and fifty years of age, but there is a considerable difference between the life expectancy of men and of women. The largest proportion of children (55 percent) is that of the late eighth- to mid-eleventh-century cemetery excavated in Dolní Věstonice-Na Piskách (southern Moravia, Czech Republic), one of the largest cemeteries of early medieval East Central Europe. Given that a large

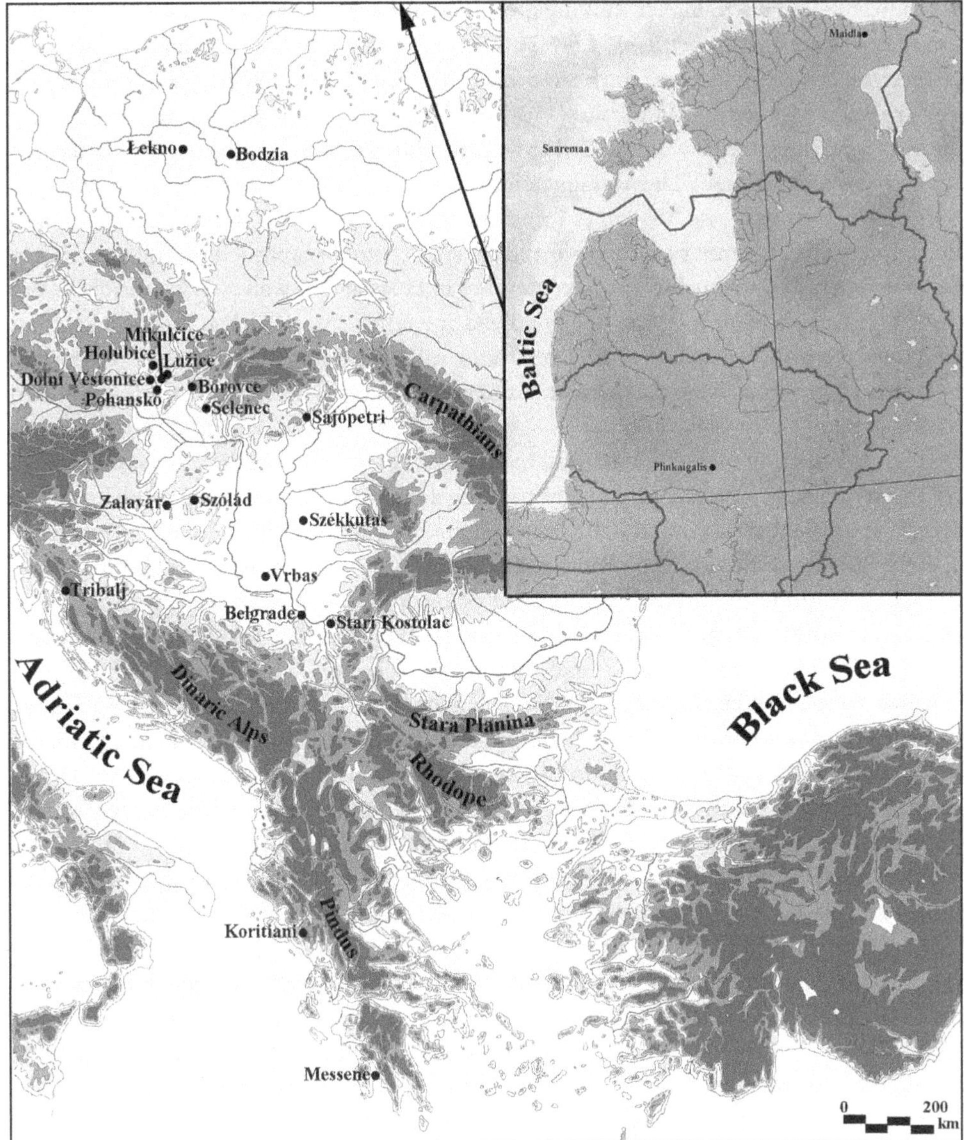

Map 26.1. Principal archaeological sites dated to the Middle Ages and containing information about population structures. Thrace is the lowland region between the Stara Planina and the Rhodope Mountains.

proportion of children is typical for all ninth- to early tenth-century cemeteries in the area, early medieval Moravia appears to have had a lower life expectancy at birth and a greater child mortality rate than any other region of Europe during the Carolingian age. In early medieval Croatia, the average life span during that age was about forty years, with men living approximately two years longer than women, and as much as 20 percent of the population dying before the age of fifteen. Despite clear evidence of social disparity, individuals belonging to higher-ranking groups do not seem to have enjoyed a better health and they did not live longer lives. This is also true for the populations burying their dead in Messene (southern Greece, sixth to seventh centuries), Vrbas (northern Serbia, eighth century), and Mikulčice-Klášteřisko (Moravia, Czech Republic, ninth century). During the Avar age, high-status women died at a much younger age than both high-status men and lower-status women. The average height of the individuals buried in three Avar-age cemeteries in Austria was 168 cm (5 feet 6 inches) for men and 159 cm (5 feet 2 inches) for women. This is similar to the male and female statures established on the basis of the skeletal material from tenth-century cemeteries in Hungary, as well as from eleventh- and twelfth-century cemeteries excavated in Poland and northeastern Serbia. By contrast, most men from the fifth-to-sixth-century cemeteries in Belgrade and Stari Kostolac (to the east of Belgrade, in Serbia) were much taller. Tall people, especially men, were typically buried with more and richer grave goods.

The introduction of biogeochemical techniques has greatly changed the study of population structures. Such techniques compare the dental and skeletal elements that formed at different times over an individual's lifetime. Enamel (on the permanent teeth) is formed in early childhood and does not change through life. During an individual's life, strontium replaces calcium in the mineral component of both enamel and bone. The ratio of the radiogenic isotope of strontium (^{87}Sr) and one stable isotope of strontium (^{86}Sr), found in the teeth and bones of skeletons excavated by archaeologists reflect the $^{87}Sr/^{86}Sr$ found in plants, animals, and water that the individual in question consumed during their lifetime. If the isotopic ratios of the place of burial are different from those of the enamel, then the individual in question must be an immigrant. Through strontium isotope analysis, it has become clear that the forty-one male skeletons buried in the mid-eighth century in two ships on the southwestern coast of the island of Saaremaa (Estonia) were all of Scandinavian origin. A similar conclusion was drawn from the same kind of analysis applied to skeletons from the Viking-age cemetery in Bodzia (near Włocławek, in northern Poland). The analysis showed that most people buried there were from Kievan Rus' (see chapter 11), perhaps Varangians in local retinues of warriors, with their wives and children. Similar conclusions have resulted from the analysis of tooth enamel from skeletons in the sixth-century cemeteries of Lužice and Holubice (Czech Republic). There were many immigrants among those buried in those cemeteries, each one in use over three successive generations. An integrative study of the skeletons from the sixth-century cemetery excavated in Szólád (on the southern shore of Lake Balaton, in Hungary), which employed anthropological, molecular genetic, and biogeochemical techniques, has shown that after just one generation, the settlement of the small community, as well as its associated cemetery, were abandoned, most likely because of emigration.

Biogeochemical and trace element analysis of skeletal remains has also been employed for reconstructing the daily diet of medieval populations. For example, trace element analysis (particularly the presence of calcium, zinc, copper, manganese, iron, lead, and strontium, as well as the ratios of zinc to calcium and strontium to calcium) was employed for the study of skeletons from the fifth-to-sixth-century cemetery excavated in Plinkaigalis (near Kaunas, in Lithuania). The analysis showed that men of high social status ate more food rich in animal protein than women of high social status, whose diet was based mostly on plant products. By contrast, no diet differences between men and women have been noticed in the analysis of the skeletons from the tenth-to-eleventh-century cemetery in Koritiani (near Igoumenitsa, northwestern Greece). This was the cemetery of an agricultural population, with a diet low in protein and based primarily on cereals and vegetables. The isotope analysis of skeletons from ninth-century cemeteries excavated in Mikulčice and Pohansko (Moravia, Czech Republic) indicates a relatively high proportion of cereals, especially millet, in the diet. Millet was also an important component of the diet for the Avar-age population in Sajópetri (near Miskolc, Hungary).

The use of more traditional bioarcheological studies of human bones has shed much light on diseases. The results are spectacular, for there is now enough evidence to observe general trends. For example, the high incidence of porotic hyperostosis (excessive growth of bone) on the roof of the orbits has been linked to iron-deficiency anemia and is believed to indicate high parasite loads and high frequency of acute and chronic infections. Increased porosity visible on infant bones from the ninth-to-eleventh-century cemetery near the Church of St. Mary in Tribalj (near Rijeka, Croatia) points to scurvy. Skeletal dysplasia (abnormal growth) of an adult male from the ninth-to-eleventh-century cemetery in Łekno (near Wągrowiec, Poland) indicates dwarfism. There are now many cases of spondylosis (a degenerative disorder of the spine associated with age) from seventh-to-eighth-century cemeteries excavated in southern and southwestern Slovakia. Tuberculosis is now documented in sixth- as well as twelfth-century cemeteries in Hungary and Poland, respectively. Metastatic carcinoma (cancer) was most likely what caused the death of two men buried in the eighth-century cemetery in Székkutas-Kápolnadűlő (near Szeged, Hungary) and in the ninth-century cemetery of Borovce (near Trnava, Slovakia), respectively. Hypertrophic pulmonary osteoarthropathy identified on the skeleton of a young individual buried in the eleventh century in Selenec (near Nitra, Slovakia) has been interpreted as a sign of pulmonary tuberculosis, which may have been associated with lung cancer. Some of the most interesting results of bioarcheological research refer to the spread of leprosy (Hansen's disease). DNA studies dealing with single-nucleotide polymorphisms have revealed that cases in seventh- and tenth-century Hungary as well as ninth-to-tenth-century Bohemia were all associated with the same strain of *Mycobacterium leprae*. The disease was probably introduced to medieval Europe by the Avars through contact with the Byzantines in the Balkans. By the ninth century, leprosy is documented in Moravia, Croatia, and Austria. Later, the disease appeared in Poland as well. A 22-to-32-old male buried in the eleventh-to-twelfth-century cemetery in Zalavár (near the western end of Lake Balaton, in Hungary) may have suffered simultaneously from tuberculosis and leprosy, for the two diseases coexisted in medieval Europe.

FURTHER READING

Bourbou, Chryssi. *The People of Early Byzantine Eleutherna and Messene (6th–7th Centuries A.D.): A Bioarchaeological Approach*. Athens: University of Crete, 2004.

Buko, Andrzej, ed. *Bodzia: A Late Viking-Age Elite Cemetery in Central Poland*. East Central and Eastern Europe in the Middle Ages, 450–1450, 27. Leiden: Brill, 2015.

Sládek, Vladimír, and Jiří Machácek, eds. *At the End of Great Moravia: Skeletons from the Second Church Cemetery at Pohansko-Břeclav (9th–10th Century A.D.)*. BAR International Series 2836. Oxford: BAR Publishing, 2017.

Šlaus, Mario. *The Bioarchaeology of Continental Croatia: An Analysis of Human Skeletal Remains from the Prehistoric to Post-medieval Periods*. BAR International Series 1021. Oxford: Archaeopress, 2002.

27

RULERS AND DYNASTIES

Keywords in this chapter: chieftain, khagan, dynasty

Writing in the mid-sixth century, Procopius of Caesarea knew that the Slavs were "not ruled by one man, but they have lived from old under a democracy, and consequently everything which involves their welfare, whether for good or for ill, is referred to the people."[1] Half a century later, the author of a military treatise titled *Strategikon* explained that, since the Slavs had many kings, Roman generals campaigning against them should win over some by persuasion or gifts, to create dissension and prevent them from coming together against the Romans under the temporary leadership of a single man. Those two apparently contradictory statements reflect very well the difficulties that both Roman authorities and Roman authors had when attempting to understand the way in which political power was organized beyond the Danube frontier of the empire. Slavic chiefs were killed by their own fellow tribesmen at feasts or on travels, which points to the ephemeral nature of political power, as well as to some of the most important tools for acquiring it. There can be no doubt that at any one time there were many leaders among the early Slavs and that they had not the same kind of power.

Although more detailed information exists about the early Slavs, similar forms of political organization likely existed elsewhere as well. Wulfstan, for example, knew that the Prussians (whom he called "Ests") had many kings, none of them known by name. By contrast, Musocius, one of the Slavic kings mentioned in the sources, was a late sixth-century chief, whose powers were largely ascribed and coincided with the privileged control of wealth. He had subjects whom he could send to reconnoiter or to give assistance to refugees from neighboring territories. He also had a territory over which he exercised his authority. Another king named Perbundos lived in the seventh century. He is described as

1 Florin Curta, ed., "Procopius on the Slavs," in *Medieval Eastern Europe, 500–1300: A Reader* (Toronto: University of Toronto Press, 2024), 3.

wearing the dress of the Roman aristocracy and speaking fluent Greek. His power relied on a special relationship with the imperial authority. A third king, Samo, also lived in the seventh century. According to a contemporary source, he won the admiration of his future subjects by military feats and proved his skills as commander in battle, his prudence and courage always bringing victory. "Becoming aware of Samo's valor, the Wends chose him to be their king. He ruled them well for thirty-five years."[2] A self-made leader, Samo forged alliances with several families, whose daughters he married. He was also involved in long-distance trade, and his economic and political influence produced not only wealth and high status but also strong alliances, especially after defeating a Frankish army led by King Dagobert (see chapters 2 and 6). Peiragast, another Slavic leader mentioned in the sources, was also a warrior leader in the late sixth century, but he had no territory. Ardagastus (see chapter 2) had a territory but not subjects, for he used that territory to gather warriors from elsewhere for raids into Roman territory. Finally, Dauritas, who appears in the late 570s, is specifically mentioned together with (other) "chiefs of his people." In the presence of Avar envoys sent to request tribute from the Slavs, he boasted that "others do not conquer our land, we conquer theirs. And so it shall always be for us, as long as there are wars and weapons."[3] Dauritas talked the talk, but did not walk the walk, for he appears not as a military leader, only as the spokesman of his group.

Conspicuously missing from the description of all those leaders is any hint at the transmission of their power from one generation to the other, or the roles of their wives. This is also true for nomadic leaders of the eleventh to thirteenth centuries. Some Pecheneg chieftains exercised more power than others, and that power was rooted in the different rankings of their respective clans. For example, Tyrach, the leader of all Pechenegs, was "highly distinguished by birth," while his rival, Kegen, was "a nobody by birth and practically nameless."[4] At the death of a chieftain like Tyrach, power typically passed to his cousin or the cousin's son, a sign that the power of the clan was about to turn that family into a dynasty. However, in the end none of those families or clans rose to a prominent position, and political power remained ephemeral, especially in the context of the Pecheneg invasion of the Balkans. Similarly, the Cuman khan was typically the leader of a clan, but his position was one of achieved, not ascribed power – more akin to Ardagastus than to Musocius. In all known cases, power was achieved by military deeds. Kutesk led a raid into Hungary in 1085–86. The 40,000 Cumans who participated in the battle of Levunion (1091) against the Pechenegs were led by Tugorkan and Boniak, while another Cuman party under Kopulch was raiding Transylvania and Hungary. When Tugorkan invaded the Balkans, Itlar and Kitan went to Pereiaslavl' in Rus' to mediate an agreement with Vladimir II Monomakh. The lack of coordination and the separate, independent actions of each one of those khans betrays a highly decentralized organization of political power.

2 Curta, ed., "Slavs, Avars, and Franks," in *Medieval Eastern Europe*, 9.

3 Curta, ed., "Avars and Slavs," in *Medieval Eastern Europe*, 7.

4 Curta, ed., "John Skylitzes on the Pechenegs," in *Medieval Eastern Europe*, 52.

Only in the early thirteenth century could one particular clan, the Sharukanid Jurgi, rise above all other Cuman clans, but its further ascension to supreme power was cut short by the Mongol conquest (see chapters 10 and 46). Following the battle of Kalka (1223), Bortz, who was known as the fourth among all Cuman chiefs, decided to send his son, along with his retinue, to Hungary to embrace Christianity. There was clearly no room for dynastic succession in the steppe lands now occupied by the Mongols.

In sharp contrast to the early Slavs, the Avars appear in the sources as always under the rule of one man, the khagan. Baian is the only khagan known by name, but in 583, he was replaced by his elder son, whose successor in 602 was his younger brother. This was clearly a dynasty of rulers, discontinued only by the defeat of the Avars under the walls of Constantinople in 626 (see chapter 2). Baian and his sons were first and foremost military leaders, who led their armies in person. The title of khagan is not attested in Bulgaria, but Omurtag was *kana sybigi*, most likely an imperial title (see chapter 8). He also called himself "ruler from God" in several inscriptions and bragged about his building projects, on which he put his people to work. More than a century before him, Tervel also had power over skilled workers, whom he ordered to carve a huge image (2.6 m high, 3.1 m wide, or more than 8 and 10 feet, respectively) of himself on horseback – at 23 m from the foot of a rock cliff in Madara (northeastern Bulgaria). Known as the "Madara Horseman," the relief is a representation of power with no parallel anywhere in Europe. Between the reigns of Tervel and Omurtag, during the Byzantine-Bulgar war, there was a change in dynasty when the Bulgars rose in rebellion and killed their "hereditary lords," replacing them with Telec. He, in turn, was ousted and killed. Omurtag's father, Krum, belonged to an entirely different line, with no ascendants in the eighth century. Boris, his son Symeon, and his grandson Peter belonged to that same dynasty. The latter two adopted the title of emperor on their seals and, at least in Peter's case, that title was recognized by the imperial government in Constantinople. To outsiders like Ademar of Chabannes, a monk in southwestern France, Samuel was only a king of the Bulgarians, but he adopted the title of emperor in the tradition of Symeon and Peter (see chapter 13).[5] All three were emperors of (Bulgarian) people, not of a country (Bulgaria).

The title of khagan is also attested among the Khazars, in reference to one of two coexisting kinds of power. The tenth-century Muslim sources describe the dual kingship in Khazaria as the simultaneous rule of a greater (the khagan) and a lesser king (the beg). Although the khagan was a ceremonial ruler, according to the letter of King Joseph to Hasdai ibn Shaprut, Obadiah was a descendant of Bulan, which most likely indicates a dynasty.[6] The khagan rarely appeared in public and had the exclusive privilege of polygamy, with up to twenty-five wives, each one being the daughter of one of the chieftains subject to him. He was also perceived as an intermediary between his people and the

5 Curta, ed., "The Echo of the Bulgarian-Byzantine War," in *Medieval Eastern Europe*, 67.

6 Curta, ed., "King Joseph on the Conversion of the Khazars to Judaism," in *Medieval Eastern Europe*, 39.

divine, and because of that he was treated like a talisman for their good fortune. Military command and political decisions, however, were in the hands of the beg (see chapters 5 and 14). This is remarkably like the power configuration among the Magyars. According to ibn Rusta, who wrote in the tenth century (when the Magyars had already occupied the Middle Danube region in what is now Hungary), there were two leaders among them, the king (called *künde*) and the *gyula*, a chieftain who commanded "in making war, invasions, and the like."[7] A third position of power emerged in the early tenth century, known as *harka* (see chapter 18), which was also associated with military command. Beginning with the mid-tenth century, the chief prince of the Magyars was a member of the family of Árpád, who was probably the *künde* elected in the 880s. Árpád had four sons, one of whom became *künde* in his stead. The last *künde* may have been Vajk (baptized as Stephen), who was crowned king in 1000 or 1001. The Arpadian dynasty ruled the kingdom of Hungary until 1300, despite the forty-year-long crisis that opened when Stephen I died heirless in 1038 (his only son, Emeric, had been killed in 1031 in a hunting accident). Stephen therefore designated a non-Arpadian, Peter Orseolo, as his successor. When his family was ousted from Venice in 1026, Peter came to Hungary together with his mother, and Stephen put him in charge of the army. Peter married Stephen's younger sister, and that was sufficient for him to become king in 1038. Those who opposed him also chose a non-Arpadian as successor, Samuel Aba, another brother-in-law of Stephen. Only the conspirators under Peter's second reign (1044–46) reverted to three members of the Arpadian line – Levente, Béla, and Andrew – with the latter becoming king in 1046.

Unlike Hungary, the dynasties of Poland, Bohemia, and Rus' are named after legendary characters. Although not unique in Europe at the time, the idea of the dynasty's humble origins played a key role in the earliest narrative sources of East Central Europe – Gallus Anonymus and Cosmas of Prague. Piast, after whom the dynasty was named that ruled in Poland until the late fourteenth century, was just a poor plowman, whose wife, Rzepka, has a name derived from the Polish word for "turnip."[8] Similarly, Přemysl, the mythical founder of the dynasty that ruled Bohemia until 1300, was a plowman who "thrust the prod he was holding in his hand into the ground and dismissing the oxen" before agreeing to become duke.[9] Both legends were likely meant to mask the violent means by which those two dynasties actually came to power. Little is known about the Piasts, but that name may in fact refer to a group of warriors from Greater Poland, who in the late tenth and early eleventh centuries began expanding to the southeast, in the direction of Lesser Poland, in the process incorporating new territories into the newly created state. All was done by violence, as illustrated archaeologically by the systematic destruction of the old regional centers and, possibly, the physical elimination of the old tribal aristocracy (see chapter 17). Mieszko allied himself with the duke of Bohemia, Boleslav I, and married Boleslav's

7 Curta, ed., "Ibn Rusta on the Magyars," in *Medieval Eastern Europe*, 47.

8 Curta, ed., "The Origins of the Piast Dynasty," in *Medieval Eastern Europe*, 110.

9 Curta, ed., "The Origins of the Přemyslid Dynasty," in *Medieval Eastern Europe*, 109.

daughter, Dobrawa, in 966, thus converting to Christianity. Their son Bolesław Chrobry drove his half-brothers out of Poland to secure succession in his own line. He appears as "duke of the Poles," but in the early eleventh century struck coins with the legend "prince of Poland," the earliest attestation of the name of the country. He proclaimed himself king in 1025, and his son, Mieszko II, who succeeded him, also assumed the royal title. Following Mieszko's death in 1034, a widespread rebellion, combined with a devastating invasion of the Bohemian armies led by Břetislav I, led to a quick collapse of the state. The "restorer" was Casimir I, Mieszko's son, who secured the continuing grip on power of the Piast dynasty.

In Bohemia, the Přemyslids also employed violence to solidify their position. Duke Wenceslas was assassinated at the order of his younger brother Boleslav, who destroyed the strongholds of all other Bohemian princes, although he allowed his relative Slavník to rule in eastern Bohemia. Under Boleslav's elder son, Boleslav II, and with his connivance, almost all members of the rival family of the Slavnikids were massacred in 995 in Libice. Boleslav II's son, Boleslav III, was in permanent conflict with his brothers Jaromír (whom he castrated) and Oldřich (whom he tried to kill). Briefly ousted, he returned to power with support from Bolesław Chrobry in Poland and took revenge on his political adversaries. Several members of a prominent family – the Vršovic – were massacred, before Boleslav III was captured, blinded, and imprisoned. Nonetheless, under Břetislav I the power of the Přemyslids had no contender, as the duke introduced the seniority principle requiring that the eldest male in the family be designated successor.

In sharp contrast to the foundation myths of the Polish and Czech dynasties, Riurik appears in the *Primary Chronicle* as one of three Varangian brothers who came to Rus'. He established himself in Novgorod before assuming "the sole authority" at the death of his brothers and exercising "dominion over all these districts."[10] The Riurikid family is not mentioned in any contemporary source before the fifteenth century. Moreover, descent from Riurik did not provide any political legitimacy. Instead, a ruler (*kniaz'*) was recognized in Rus' if ruling where his father had ruled before, if recognized as ruler by the other rulers, and if townspeople accepted him as their ruler. Much like with the early Slavs, there were many princes in Rus' at any one time, but they were all members of the same family. Each one of them ruled over a particular territory and resided in the main town or city in that territory. Each prince had his own retinue of warriors, but the ruler of Kiev could call on other members of the family to help him in some common expedition. For example, Iziaslav, the son of Iaroslav the Wise, called on his brothers Sviatoslav and Vsevolod in 1060 to go against the Oghuz and again, in 1067, to go against Vseslav of Polotsk. All princes, however, collected taxes or tribute. Moreover, like Samo and many Viking-age kings in northwestern Europe, they were involved in long-distance trade.

A dynasty also existed among the Abodrites, a Slavic tribe in what is now northern Germany at the border with Denmark (see chapter 17). Nakon and his brother Stoignev

10 Curta, ed., "Varangians in Rus'," in *Medieval Eastern Europe*, 69.

appear in the mid-tenth century as their rulers. In 983, Nakon's son Mstivoi allied himself with the duke of Saxony against the pagan reaction in Starigard (Oldenburg), and his daughter Tofa married King Harald Bluetooth of Denmark. The Nakonid dynasty remained in power until the death of Henry of Old-Lübeck in 1127. The rulers of Mecklenburg, the state that emerged out of the realm of the Abodrites, were descendants of the Slavic prince Niklot (d. 1160), who was not related to the Nakonids.

FURTHER READING

Curta, Florin. "Qagan, Khan or King? Power in Early Medieval Bulgaria (Seventh to Ninth Century)." *Viator* 37 (2006): 1–31.

Golden, Peter B. "The Khazar Sacral Kingship." In *Pre-Modern Russia and Its World: Essays in Honor of Thomas S. Noonan*, edited by Kathryn L. Reyerson, Theofanis G. Stavrou, and James D. Tracy, 79–102. Wiesbaden: Otto Harrassowitz, 2006.

Hanak, Walter K. *The Nature and the Image of Princely Power in Kievan Rus', 980–1054*. East Central and Eastern Europe in the Middle Ages, 450–1450, 25. Leiden: Brill, 2014.

Lajoye, Patrice. "Sovereigns and Sovereignty among Pagan Slavs." In *New Researches on the Religion and Mythology of the Pagan Slavs*, edited by Patrice Lajoye, 165–81. Lisieux: Lingva, 2018.

Mařík, Jan. "The Slavníks and Their Remote Neighbors." In *My Things Changed Things: Social Development and Cultural Exchange in Prehistory, Antiquity and the Middle Ages*, edited by Petra Maříková Vlčková, Jana Mynářová, and Martin Tomášek, 179–87. Prague: Charles University in Prague, Faculty of Arts/Institute of Archaeology of the Academy of Sciences of the Czech Republic, 2009.

Moździoch, Sławomir. "Consensus or Violence? Archaeology and the Beginnings of the Piast State." In *Consensus or Violence? Cohesive Forces in Early and High Medieval Societies (9th–14th C.)*, edited by Sławomir Moździoch and Przemysław Wiszewski, 299–314. Interdisciplinary Medieval Studies 1. Wrocław: Institute of History at the University of Wrocław, 2013.

Raffensperger, Christian. *Rulers and Rulership in the Arc of Medieval Europe, 1000–1200*. London: Routledge, 2023.

Sutt, Cameron. "The Early Árpáds (895–1095): Consolidation, Christianization, Monarchy." *History Compass* 12, no. 2 (2014): 150–59.

28

SOCIAL ORGANIZATION

Keywords in this chapter: family, warrior status, craftspeople, slavery, serfs

Although property relations and social structures could hardly be delineated based on archaeological excavations of settlement sites, much can be derived, at least in terms of elements of social organization, from cemetery sites. Some of the settlement sites known from East Central Europe and dated to the Early Middle Ages are quite large, although each house is similar in all respects to any other. In some of those dated to the seventh or eighth century, there is evidence of ditches, which cannot however be associated with property demarcations. At Bajč, an eighth-to-tenth-century settlement in Slovakia, dwellings were separated spatially from both silos and open-air clay ovens (see map 28.1). This has been interpreted as a functional division of the settlement area, with an "industrial" sector separated from the habitation units. However, there is no indication of social differentiation. Several sixth-to-seventh-century settlement sites excavated in Romania, the Republic of Moldova, and Ukraine display a peculiar distribution of artifacts, particularly of such "exotic" items as amphorae, dress accessories, and tools. In each case, the distribution reveals settlement nuclei, which may well represent elite residences. However, at the same time, the analysis of those settlements and the distribution of artifacts has brought to light areas of communal activities that are not separated physically from the presumed elite residences, an indication that social differentiation inside those settlements may have been quite fluid, with no distinctions firmly marked in material culture.

Mortuary archaeology (that is, the archaeology of cemetery sites) provides some context for understanding the absence of clearly cut social distinctions. Family affiliation was the principle behind the layout of many a cemetery excavated in East Central Europe. For example, at Szólád, on the southern shore of Lake Balaton (Hungary), four kin groups were buried within a relatively short period of time during the sixth century. One of them spanned three generations and included ten individuals buried next to each other in elaborate ledge graves and with many grave goods. Six males of that kin group were

Map 28.1. Principal archaeological sites dated to the Early Middle Ages and containing information about social structures and change.

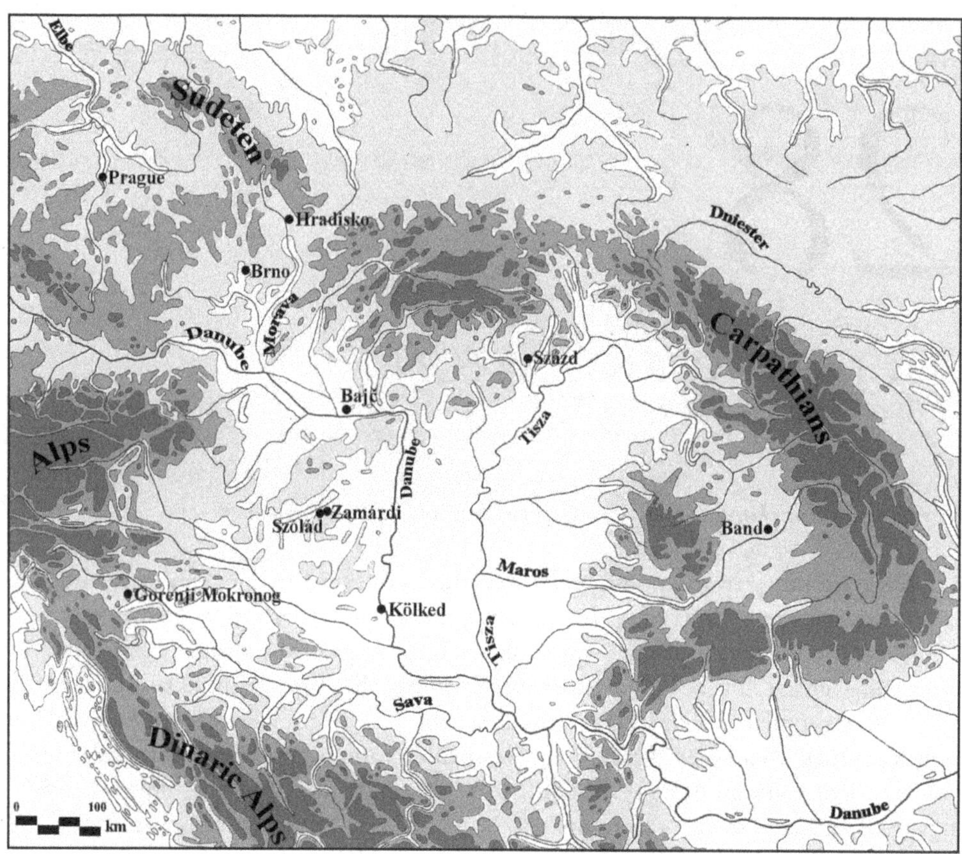

given swords, despite three of them being teenagers at the time of their death. Unlike most other people buried in the Szólád cemetery, the adult males in that group had access to a diet particularly rich in animal protein, as indicated by the analysis of strontium and oxygen isotopes of their teeth. One of those males was buried in the deepest pit of the cemetery, together with a horse, a clear indication of special status. Surrounding that tomb were the graves of the man's father, sister, child, and distant relatives, as revealed by the DNA analysis of the skeletal remains. That this was the most prominent kin group of the community is concluded from the fact that most other graves in Szólád have fewer or no grave goods at all. Even poorer cemeteries were organized based on family affiliation. The analysis of epigenetic traits (i.e., traits inherited without any change in the DNA sequence) of the twenty skeletons excavated in Gorenji Mokronog, at the foot of the Trebelno Mountain in central Slovenia, has shown that all were members of the same kin group. Besides fragments of two glass beakers found in the grave of a two-year-old child, there were no markers of social distinction. The oldest man in the cemetery (41 to 60 years at the time of death) was buried with no grave goods whatsoever.

While position in society was determined by family or clan affiliation, the deposition of weapons in (primarily) male graves shows a dramatic change taking place simultaneously in the sixth and seventh centuries in various parts of East Central and Eastern Europe. Mortuary houses and stone circles with multiple people buried in the same place were abandoned in the mid-sixth century in coastal Lithuania (Curonia) in favor of individual graves (see chapter 23). At the same time as family burials disappeared, social stratification became apparent in both male and female burials. In the central part of the forest region of Eastern Europe (modern Russia), a great number of artifacts originating in Central Europe and the Caucasus region appear in the late fifth and during the sixth century. This was the period of the greatest display of martial qualities through the deposition of weapons in male burials. Moreover, during the sixth and seventh centuries, sets of female dress accessories began to appear in male burials, apparently as "gifts" from the bereaved wives or other female relatives.

The move away from family burials and the stronger emphasis on personal achievements, particularly on the role of men as community or military leaders, is a characteristic of the whole of the European continent in the Early Middle Ages. In East Central Europe, this is also the context in which gold- and blacksmithing tools were deposited in graves, such as those found in Brno (Czech Republic) or Band (Romania). The presence of weapons, along with tools and trading implements (scales and weights) strongly suggests elevated social status, as do forms of elaborate burials that appear with such graves, such as funerary timber constructions on top of the grave pits. Whether or not those buried in Brno and Band were themselves gold- or blacksmiths, high status was associated at the time with craft production in reference to one and the same individuals. In other words, some members of the elite were producers of special artifacts. During the Avar age (particularly during the first half of the seventh century), the combination of black- and goldsmithing tools (some of which may have also been used in carpentry) deposited in one and the same grave shows that every craftsman was expected to be a jack-of-all-trades. The prominent role of male craftsmen in the Avar-age society is not the only sign of change. Burials of females highlight the role that women played as mirrors of the wealth and status of their husbands and families. The most lavishly furnished burials in western Hungary during the first half of the seventh century are of women. That rich female burials were not set apart but found in large cemeteries such as those excavated in Kölked or Zamárdi (Hungary) is an indication that the status of those women depended upon affiliation to prominent families. When such burials disappear, ca. 630, all traces of elites disappear from the region as well, and no swords or any other weapons were buried with men anymore.

The role of the family in structuring society transpires from the earliest written sources as well. In birchbark letters from northwestern Russia, the earliest of which are dated to the eleventh century, patronymics (names derived from the names of fathers or other male ancestors) were in use almost exclusively by Rus' elites. According to the laws attributed to King Stephen I and Coloman, in eleventh-century Hungary, only close kin could inherit. The importance of the social status of men is also revealed in the contemporary legislation, for example in articles pertaining to facial hair, which was regarded as a mark of social distinction. According to the statute of Iaroslav the Wise, "if someone cuts off the hair on the head or beard [of some other man], [the perpetrator will have to pay] the metropolitan twelve *grivny*, and the prince will prescribe [to that person] an additional punishment."[1] The provisions in the short version of the *Ruskaia Pravda* are exclusively about males with facial hair, weapons, and horses. Such men owned slaves:

> If a slave is [taken and] hidden either by a Varangian or a Kolbiag, and neither brings [the slave] back for three days [after the loss of the slave was announced by the owner], and [the owner] finds out [where the slave is hidden], then on the third day [the slave owner] gets back his slave, in addition to three *grivny* for the offense.[2]

Slaves were indeed the main commodity transported over long-distance trade routes across East Central and Eastern Europe (see chapter 33). The late ninth-century Moravian *Court Law for the People* is quite explicit: "If someone buys a prisoner of war with all his chattels from foreigners and the former can pay his price, let him be set free. If he cannot ransom himself let him work as a slave until he ransoms himself."[3] In the tenth century, Prague was one of the largest slave markets in Europe, and the great importance of slaves in the Rus' trade with Byzantium is confirmed by the treaties of 911 and 944 preserved in the *Primary Chronicle*. Slaves are also mentioned in the laws of Kings Stephen and Ladislas of Hungary, as well as in charters of the second half of the eleventh century. In the laws of Coloman, native slaves are singled out: "No one should dare to sell or convey outside Hungary a male or female slave of Hungarian origin or anyone born in Hungary, even one of foreign parentage, except for slaves of other languages who were brought in from other regions."[4] That slaves played a significant economic role in Hungary results from a number of charters, such as that confirming a donation to the abbey of Százd (near Miskolc, in northeastern Hungary) in 1067. The document mentions that those who intended to maintain their freedom had to move off the land of the monastery, implying that anyone remaining would lose his or her freedom. Moreover, while the laws of King Coloman prohibit Jews from buying or selling Christian slaves, they also allowed Jews who had agricultural land to farm it "with pagan slaves."[5] Indeed, most slaves seem to have worked on the private estates of lay lords, not on those of the king or the church. Elsewhere, the situation may have been quite different. According to *Legenda Christiani*, Duke Wenceslas of Bohemia purchased young pagan slaves on the market in Prague (see chapter 38). However, he did so in order to turn them into Christians, not laborers for the ducal estates.

---

1 Florin Curta, ed., "Church and Secular Law in the Statute of Yaroslav," in *Medieval Eastern Europe, 500–1300: A Reader* (Toronto: University of Toronto Press, 2024), 269.

2 Curta, ed., "Ruskaia Pravda," in *Medieval Eastern Europe*, 273.

3 Curta, ed., "First Law Code in Eastern Europe," in *Medieval Eastern Europe*, 266.

4 Curta, ed., "The Laws of King Coloman," in *Medieval Eastern Europe*, 271.

5 Curta, ed., "The Laws of King Coloman," in *Medieval Eastern Europe*, 271.

Those working on estates such as those of the duke of Bohemia were not slaves but serfs, that is, people in permanent personal dependence upon another person or institution. Serfs could be sold or donated, even treated as property, but unlike slaves, they retained some limited legal recourse. However, in Bohemia, unlike in most of Western Europe, the status of serf was not based on restricted mobility (the serf was "tied" to the land), but on the personal bond between landlord and serf, which was often hereditary. Given that the emphasis in that relation was the serf's ability to produce benefits for the lord, he or she could be not only donated to other owners but also allowed to leave the service. In Bohemia, serfs appear primarily on ducal estates. For example, in 1078, Otto I the Fair (1061–87), duke of Moravia, and his wife, Euphemia of Hungary, made a generous donation to the Benedictine abbey of Hradisko (near Olomouc, Czech Republic). The donation contains items from the duke's property and his wife's dowry, with plowmen listed along with fields, pastures, and cattle. However, the same charter lists people who, if wishing to leave their condition of dependency, had to pay (back) the money spent to purchase them. In the late eleventh century, the social categories of slavery and serfdom existed side by side.

FURTHER READING

Amorim, Carlos Eduardo G., Stefania Vai, Cosimo Posth, Alessandro Modi, István Koncz, Susanne E. Hakenbeck, Cristina La Rocca, et al. "Understanding 6th-Century Barbarian Social Organization and Migration through Paleogenomics." *Nature Communications* 9, no. 1 (2018): 1–11.

Curta, Florin. "A Social History of the Avars: Historical and Archaeological Perspectives." *History Compass* 19, no. 12 (2021): 1–19.

Ježek, Martin. "The Disappearance of European Smiths' Burials." *Cambridge Archaeological Journal* 25, no. 1 (2015): 121–43.

Látková, Michaela. "Food and Drink – a Reflection of Social Stratification." In *Great Moravian Elites from Mikulčice*, edited by Lumír Poláček, 191–95. Brno: Institute of Archaeology, 2020.

Petráček, Tomáš. *Power and Exploitation in the Czech Lands in the 10th–12th Centuries*. East Central and Eastern Europe in the Middle Ages, 40. Leiden: Brill, 2017.

Sutt, Cameron. *Slavery in Árpád-Era Hungary in a Comparative Context*. East Central and Eastern Europe in the Middle Ages, 450–1450, 31. Leiden: Brill, 2015.

29

THE EARLY MEDIEVAL ARISTOCRACY

Keywords in this chapter: elite, burial in the church, *zhupans*, service nobility

"Elite" is a term that describes collectively the members of social groups exercising control and power in their society. In other words, elites are minority groups that in any society enjoy prestige and recognition, having authority over other groups. As such, this is an umbrella term for a variety of other, more specific terms that historians employ, such as "aristocracy" or "nobility." The former refers to a ruling class (for the word actually means "the power of the best"), while the latter implies high birth and, often, especially in later times, specific legal prerogatives. In fact, several criteria may be used for the identification of early medieval elites: distinguished origin ("nobility"); landed wealth; position in the administration or hierarchy of the state ("office"); knowledge and education; royal or imperial favor (the degree of closeness to the center of power); recognition by peers (membership credentials); and lifestyle.

By contrast, archaeologists assume the existence of social stratification and elites whenever and wherever rich, unusually furnished, or specially constructed burials are found. Of all criteria employed by historians, lifestyle is the one favored by archaeologists, especially when they insist that elites were socially marked by means of, for example, luxury belt sets for men such as found in graves or strongholds. The use of specific styles for the decoration of those belt sets has also been interpreted as social strategies for setting apart groups of privileged people. Another assumption is that elites are visible archaeologically through the deposition in graves of weapons (especially swords), knouts, or spurs. In some cases, the elite status of men may be communicated vicariously through their womenfolk – wives, mothers, sisters, or daughters. In large cemeteries, such as those excavated in Hungary (for the sixth and seventh centuries), central Russia (for the eighth and ninth centuries), and Bohemia and Poland (for the ninth and tenth centuries), lavishly furnished graves of women are indeed surrounded by male burials with weapons. Burial of either males or females together with one or many horses has also been systematically used for the archaeological identification of elites. However, numerous rich graves of the late Avar age (ca. 700 to ca. 800) are not associated with horse burials, while at the same time horses were sacrificed and buried next to individuals together with few, if any, grave goods. Sometimes, even coffins are treated as sufficient evidence of high social status, for example in ninth-century Moravia.

Particularly important in that region, as well as in Croatia at that same time, in Bulgaria and Bohemia in the tenth, and Rus', Poland, and Hungary in the eleventh century are privileged burials, especially burials in churches. For example, at the western end of the Church of St. Mary in Crkvina, Biskupija (near Knin, Croatia), which was built in the first third of the ninth century, there were three sarcophagi (stone coffins) and four vaulted tombs (see map 29.1). One of them may have been that of Duke Branimir (see chapter 20). At any rate, the presence of weapons and spurs indicates elite burials. A sword and spurs have also been found in the male grave discovered in the nave of the basilica at Mikulčice (southern Moravia, Czech Republic). The grave of a 60-to-65-year-old male buried in the middle of the nave of the Basilica of St. George in Prague was that of Duke Boleslav I (who died in 967). Two graves in the middle of the nave inside the cathedral of St. Peter in Poznań (Poland) are believed to be the tombs of the first Piast rulers, Mieszko (who died in 992) and his son, Bolesław Chrobry (who died in 1025). An inscription on a sarcophagus from the Church of St. Stephen in Otok (near Solin, Croatia) mentions that the "famous Helena," said to be the wife of a king named Michael Krešimir (949–69) and the mother of another king named Stephen Držislav (969–99) (see chapter 39). She was most likely buried together with other members of her family in a dynastic mausoleum.

Not all burials found in and immediately near churches can be interpreted as the tombs of known kings. However, most "princely graves" of earlier centuries pose similar problems of interpretation. What princess or queen was buried ca. 500 in Moravia under the Žuráň (near Brno, Czech Republic) from the top of which Napoleon would later watch the battle at Austerlitz? What kind of power did the "amber coast masters" of the Sambian Peninsula (now within the Kaliningrad region of Russia) have during their lifetime, before being buried in the early sixth century in rich cremation burials? Who exactly were the aristocrats buried in the seventh century in Maglód (near Budapest) and Petőfiszállás (near Szentes, Hungary) together with gold and gilded belt sets, swords, and

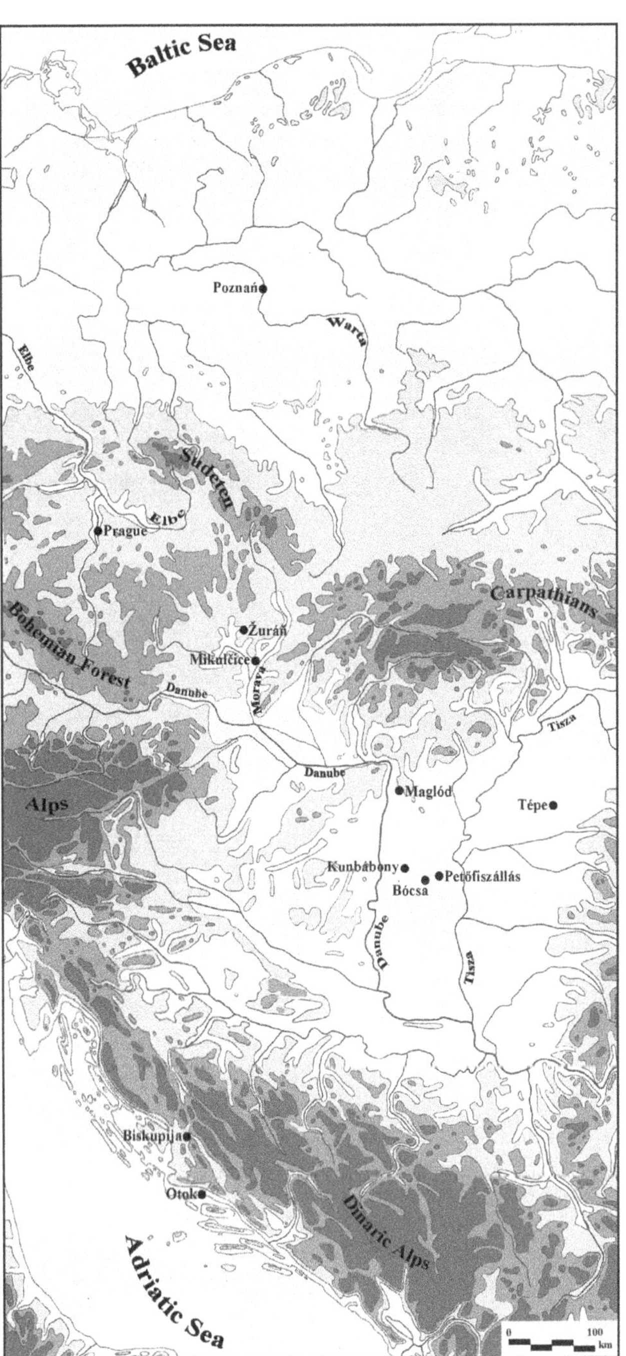

Map 29.1. Principal archaeological sites dated to the Early Middle Ages and containing information about elites.

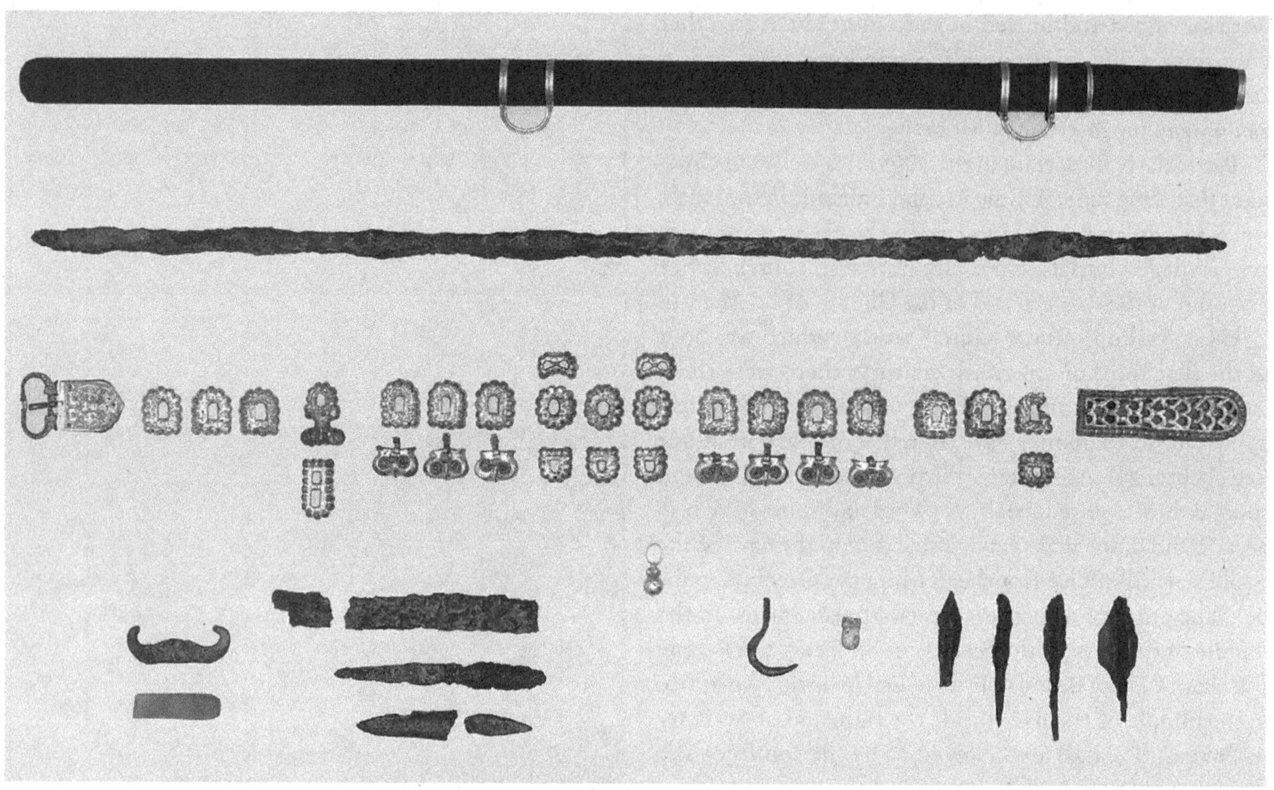

Plate 29.1. The Avar-age elite burial in Maglód (Hungary). Photo by József Rosta. © Hungarian National Museum.

quivers full of arrows? (See plate 29.1.) Was Kunbábony (in Kunszentmiklós, Hungary) the resting place of an Avar khagan? Could the old man buried underneath a large barrow at Chynhul (near Melitopol', in southern Ukraine; see plate 10.1) be one of the Cuman chieftains who fought on Johannitsa Kaloyan's side at the battle of Adrianople in 1205? There is no satisfactory answer to any of those and many other similar questions. However, the evidence of burials cannot always be interpreted in terms of the real power of the elites.

Shortly before and after the middle of the seventh century, most rich burials in what is now Hungary were in the northern part of the region between the Danube and Tisza rivers. Those were all graves of men, with the richest in Kunbábony. That burial contained a large amount of gold (for a total weight of about 5 lbs. or a little more than 2 kg), in the form of belt fittings, earrings, finger-rings, bracelets, ring-shaped sword pommels, bow trimmings, a jug, a bugle, mounts for wooden vessels, and foil ornaments. This is all a remarkable display of wealth, but the presence among the gold foil ornaments of a lunula-shaped piece with a trapezoidal bottom, originally sewn onto a textile, strongly suggests that those who buried the 60-to-65-year-old man in Kunbábony wanted to depict him (and themselves) as heirs of equestrian herdsmen coming from afar, for analogies for the lunula-shaped piece are known from as far east as Mongolia. The belt mounts in the form of buckles which decorated the belt set found in Kunbábony have good analogies in the forest-steppe region of Eastern Europe, particularly around the confluence of the Volga and Kama rivers. However, there are also clear references to Byzantium both in Kunbábony and in other contemporaneous assemblages, such as Bócsa (near Kiskunhalas, in central Hungary) and Tépe (near Debrecen, eastern Hungary). The blending of traditions in those "princely graves" of the mid-seventh century is likely to have been a reaction to the political situation of that time, marked by the serious defeat of the Avars under the walls of Constantinople and the ensuing civil war. In other words, Kunbábony represented not only the Avar elites of the mid-seventh century, but also a situation of deep crisis. Those lavishly furnished burials were a desperate attempt by local elites to project the fiction of power during troubled times. Indeed, no similarly well-furnished graves are known from the subsequent century of Avar history, which suggests that the "princely graves" were more a symptom of crisis than a long-term change leading to the establishment of social classes.

It remains unclear how elites of the Early Middle Ages developed into the aristocracy (the highest stratum of a society, whose members have inherited their positions) from the tenth century onwards. There is no direct evidence that the later nobility directly derived from the retinue of warriors as a separate, special group in early medieval society, let alone that developments were alike throughout Central and Eastern Europe. "Knights" (*milites* in Latin) were those members of social groups that could otherwise be regarded as privileged, and for whom the sources use several other, equally ill-defined terms such as "counts" or "lords." Land grants as rewards for military service are also a relatively late phenomenon in East Central Europe. Rulers in the region used a variety of gifts to reward or to entice cooperation. A true nobility, in the sense of elites linked to service provided to the ruler, is not documented before the eleventh century.

Some of the earliest texts written in Old Church Slavonic, such as the *Life of Methodius* and the *Court Law for the People*, describe elites both in general as "great" or "old" and using special terms, such as *zhupan*: "The *zhupans* [noblemen] should be content with [what is given to them from] the prince's share."[1] A differentiation of the nobility is clearly documented in ninth-century Bulgaria, where it was most certainly linked to state office. However, *boyars*, a word of uncertain origin, do not appear in the earliest texts in Old Church Slavonic, while in Rus' the word is more often employed after ca. 1100 (see chapter 56). On the other hand, in Hungary, the laws of King Stephen refer to people upon whom the king granted the right to be the masters of their own "goods, warriors, and servants." Compensation fines for various crimes varied by social categories, with the highest to be paid by perpetrators of crimes against counts or warriors of rich men. Conversely, fines paid by counts found guilty of crimes are usually twenty times higher than those paid by commoners, and ten times higher than those for warriors. This is true also for "those

1 Florin Curta, ed., "First Law Code in Eastern Europe," in *Medieval Eastern Europe, 500–1300: A Reader* (Toronto: University of Toronto Press, 2024), 265.

who kill their wives": a count murdering his wife must pay a compensation of 50 steers to her family, but a commoner pays only 5 steers for the same crime. A married woman committing theft could be redeemed by her husband, but sold as a slave if caught for the third time doing it. Moreover, the laws seem to hint at criteria for distinguishing elites in eleventh-century Hungary, such as noble birth and wealth. According to the *Admonitions* written for King Stephen's son, Emeric, "the fourth ornament of [good] rule is the loyalty, the strength, the modesty, the favor, and the trust of princes, counts, and knights." The young prince and would-be king is advised to make counts and knights his soldiers, not servants, and to rule over them "without anger, arrogance, or hatred." For if the king raises his "head above counts and princes in anger, haughtiness, hatred, and strife," he will have his royal dignity obscured by "the power of the knights," who will eventually replace him.[2] By the late eleventh century, nobles in Hungary were distinguished by their right to bring cases to the royal court and the right to judge their dependents.

Landed property is attested in Hungary in a few eleventh-century charters of donation. They show quite extensive possessions of villages, mills, manors ("courtyards"), vineyards, and fishponds, as well as people (labor force). The property of the elite in contemporaneous Bohemia was comparatively smaller, and appears only in the twelfth century, with a few villages or parts of villages, often dispersed. Most landholdings granted in eleventh-century Poland were small, and true landholding nobles do not appear before the twelfth century. By that time, "noble" was someone who made donations to the saints, participated in war and peacemaking, and provided services for the Piasts. Service nobility, therefore, was not linked to landed wealth before the High Middle Ages. Elites in the *Chronicle of the Czechs* written by Cosmas of Prague in the early twelfth century may be wealthy, but the nature of their wealth is never explained. Cosmas mentions a certain Mztis as "count" of the castle in Bílina (near Ústí nad Labem, Czech Republic). By the mid-twelfth century, the terms "count" and "castellan" were in fact interchangeable. Similarly, in both Bulgaria and Hungary the aristocracy used strongholds, which were often centers of royal power, to build regional networks and not only to acquire land.

FURTHER READING

Jovaiša, Eugenijus. "Military Aristocracy in Lower Nemunas." In *A Hundred Years of Archaeological Discoveries in Lithuania*, edited by Gintautas Zabiela, Zenonas Baubonis, and Eglė Marcinkevičiutė, 236–47. Vilnius: Lietuvos Archeologijos Draugija, 2016.

Popa-Gorjanu, Cosmin. "The Rise of the Early Medieval Aristocracy." In *The Routledge Handbook of East Central and Eastern Europe in the Middle Ages, 500–1300*, edited by Florin Curta, 155–73. Abingdon: Routledge, 2022.

2 Curta, ed., "A King's Mirror: The Admonitions," in *Medieval Eastern Europe*, 122.

Profantová, Naďa. "Power Elites in 9th–10th Century Bohemia." In *Great Moravia and the Beginnings of Christianity*, edited by Pavel Kouřil, 66–73. Brno: Institute of Archaeology of the Academy of Sciences of the Czech Republic, 2015.

Vida, Tivadar. "Prestige Burials in Pannonia and the Carpathian Basin: Elites between Mediterranean, Germanic and Steppe Traditions." In *Sepolture di prestigio nel bacino mediterraneo (secoli IV-IX): Definizioni, immagini, utilizzo. 1. Saggi. Atti del convegno Pella (NO), 28–30 giugno 2017*, edited by Paolo de Vingo, Yuri A. Marano, and Joan Pinar Gil, 441–54. Florence: All'Insegna del Giglio, 2021.

30

RURAL ECONOMY AND SETTLEMENTS

Keywords in this chapter: itinerant agriculture, paleobotany, zooarchaeology, asymmetrical plowshare

In the northern and northeastern parts of Europe, foraging (hunting and gathering) was the most important, if not the main subsistence strategy. In most of the other parts of early medieval East Central and Eastern Europe, however, agriculture was the basis of the economy. In the eastern Baltic region of present-day Estonia, the palynological (pollen) evidence from several archaeological sites indicates slash-and-burn cultivation, which was based on clearing by fire and cultivation with the hoe. The agricultural techniques employed in most other regions of East Central and Eastern Europe were typical for extensive, not intensive, agriculture. The system in place in those regions was a flexible form of fallow sequence in which arable lands were periodically allowed to regenerate naturally for a varying number of years, sometimes for as long as needed to turn old fields into waste lands. At Dulceanca (near Roşiorii de Vede, in southern Romania), four settlements have been excavated and dated to between the sixth and the seventh centuries (see map 30.1). They were no more than two miles (or a little more than 3 km) from each other, an indication of "itinerant agriculture," a form of subsistence practiced by a community moving periodically over more than a century, in order to allow old fields to regenerate naturally and clear the land for cultivation elsewhere. How far the fields were from any of those settlements is not known. The small plowshare discovered at Gropşani (near Craiova, in southern Romania), another sixth-to-seventh-century settlement, suggests that the field on which it was used was also small. The field work must have been done by a few people, probably the members of one family. Indeed, in Dulceanca, each hamlet had a relatively small number of dwellings. Nonetheless, the agriculture practiced in the region of southern Romania during the sixth and seventh centuries was the source of relative prosperity. The author of the military treatise known as the *Strategikon*, written ca. 600, knew that the Slavs had an abundance of produce, which they stored in heaps or buried (most likely in silos).

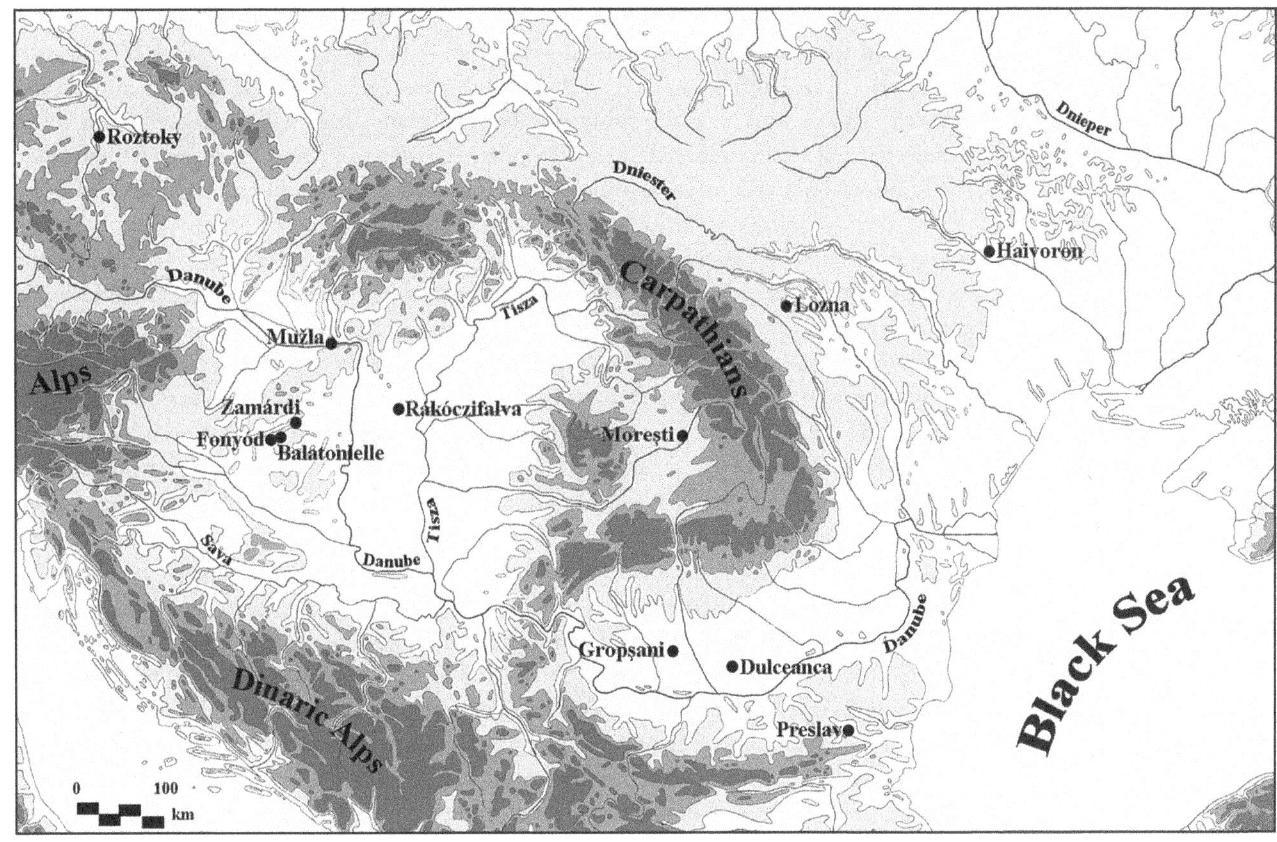

Map 30.1. Principal archaeological sites dated to the Early Middle Ages and containing information about the rural economy.

The same author also knew that they had all sorts of livestock, and the zooarchaeological evidence from excavated settlement sites confirms that cattle were raised for dairy. Procopius of Caesarea mentions that the Slavs in what is now southern Romania sacrificed cattle to "one god, the maker of lightning," implying that there the livestock supply was sufficiently large.[1] While cattle may have been used for sacrificial rituals, the inhabitants of the sixth-to-seventh-century settlements in southern Romania did not eat much beef, for they procured their meat from poultry as well as game. In contemporaneous settlements from Bohemia, neither cattle nor sheep were the main source of meat, but pigs. Unlike the small hamlets of Dulceanca, the settlement discovered in Roztoky (to the west of Prague, Czech Republic) was very large, even though the site was not in the best location possible for either extensive or intensive agriculture.

1 Florin Curta, ed., "Procopius on the Slavs," in *Medieval Eastern Europe, 500–1300: A Reader* (Toronto: University of Toronto Press, 2024), 3.

No outbuildings are known from early medieval settlements, but refuse pits, silos, and wells are documented on several sites. Silos were in fact pits of varying shapes, dug into the soil between 1 and 3.5 m deep. The volume of an early medieval silo varied between 132 and 1,057 gallons (0.5 to 4 cubic meters), and many a silo still contained plant seeds (some charred) when explored. The paleobotanical study of those seeds shows that millet predominated in the cereal diet of most people in East Central and Eastern Europe during the sixth and seventh centuries. Millet is also mentioned in the early tenth century by ibn Rusta in relation to the Slavs of Eastern Europe. In East Central Europe, the cereal diet changed significantly during the ninth and in the tenth centuries. By 800, the dominant crop was barley, followed by wheat and rye. The latter became the dominant crop between the tenth and the twelfth centuries. At Fonyód, a seventh-to-ninth-century settlement on the southern shore of Lake Balaton (Hungary), most important among all cultivated species were barley, wheat, and rye. A similar picture results from the analysis of plant seeds discovered at Gnezdovo (near Smolensk, Russia), where barley dominated in the tenth century, followed by two kinds of wheat. After the year 1000, however, the percentage of rye increased, which suggests that the lands left fallow in the hinterland of Gnezdovo were used to grow winter rye. The presence of spring and winter crops is betrayed by specific field weeds, some germinating in spring, others in fall. The evidence from the ninth-century village at Mužla (southern Slovakia) and the contemporaneous stronghold at Mikulčice point to the sowing of barley, oats, millet, and legumes in spring, as well as wheat and rye as winter crops. There is clear evidence on many eighth-to-eleventh-century sites in the region of the Don River of present-day Russia of two-, even three-field rotation.

Changes in subsistence strategies have also been detected through the analysis of faunal remains. For example, following the abandonment of the large strongholds in Moravia shortly after 900, there was not only a remarkable reduction in the cultivation of crops on sites in the region but also a greater reliance on hunted instead of domestic animals. Game represented a significant part of the meat available on both open and fortified settlements in early medieval Poland. However, the establishment of the Piast power, ca. 1000, seems to coincide with a change in stock-breeding profiles of many villages in Poland – from a predominantly cattle to a predominantly pig model. By contrast, a century earlier, pork was the preferred meat in strongholds in Moravia, while cattle dominated in villages. People living in villages did not eat more beef than pork, for the proportion of sheep and goats on such settlements is also quite large. In other words, cattle most likely represented the main draught animals, while farmers procured their meat from sheep and goats. Further changes are visible in the following two centuries, during which the proportion of horse bones increases. This points to the consumption of horse meat, which is otherwise well documented for this period in other areas of Eastern and Southeastern Europe.

Faunal remains strongly suggest that the cattle in East Central and Eastern Europe were animals both shorter and sturdier than those in existence at that same time in other parts of Europe. The sturdy character of these species was without any doubt a form of adaptation to the harsh winters of the continental climate. No structures have been found on any rural settlement in East Central or Eastern Europe that could have been used for stockbreeding. Stabling or livery, as known in many parts of Western Europe, was not practiced in the eastern half of Europe during the Early Middle Ages. In fact, implements directly associated with stockbreeding, such as cattle bells, branding irons, or shears, are quite rare. If present at all, they appear in hoards of agricultural implements and weapons. Such collections are characteristic for the Early Middle Ages in several regions of Central and Eastern Europe, especially Moravia, northeastern Bulgaria, and eastern Ukraine. Many of them include one or several plowshares, which are typically asymmetrical, an early medieval innovation. In addition, those implements are accompanied by coulters, knife-like components of the plow that were designed to cut the turf, which the asymmetrical plowshare (attached to the plow right behind the coulter) then turned to the left or to the right (depending upon which side of the plowshare was wider than the other). The purpose of this specific design of the plow was to create a turf "cushion" for the seeds, in order to protect them against the freezing temperature in the winter. However, since both coulters and plowshares in ninth- and tenth-century hoards are relatively small implements (no larger than the Gropşani plowshare), deep plowing was definitely not practiced in the Early Middle Ages.

Some of the earliest agricultural tool kits appear on eighth-to-ninth-century settlements in the lands of Eastern Europe that were at that time under Khazar rule. It is from the northern edge of the chernozem belt of Eastern Europe that asymmetrical plowshares and coulters, two essential elements of advanced plowing technique, were most likely adopted in areas of Central and Western Europe. However, the exact ways in which such innovations were transmitted (perhaps through the intermediary of the Avars) remain unknown. Advanced plowing techniques also spread to the north (into the forest belt of Eastern Europe) and to the east, across the Volga River. Besides plowshares, coulters, hoes, and sickles, several hoards of agricultural implements and weapons also include scythes with shortened "half handles." Such tools were activated by oblique slashes to left and right, which means that a part of the grass above the ground remained uncut. The short-handled scythes were best suited for wood clearings, stony soils, and all other spots where grass grew in abundance at a sufficient height. Those tools are therefore an indirect confirmation of the fact that stockbreeding in early medieval Eastern Europe involved neither high-quality meadow cultivation nor regular fodder production.

Besides agriculture and stockbreeding, the rural settlement sites of the Early Middle Ages excavated in East Central, Eastern, or Southeastern Europe have produced abundant evidence of crafts – bone and antler processing, jewelry, and dress accessory manufacture, as well as ceramic production. During the sixth and seventh centuries, all those activities were organized at household level. This was clearly small-scale, independent production for local consumption. During the ninth century, goldsmiths in the central part of the forest belt of present-day Russia were female, not male members of the community, as indicated by smelting and casting implements deposited in their burials. By contrast, in Hungary and western Romania during the seventh century, such implements were typically deposited in men's graves. The weaving sheds found in Moreşti (near Târgu Mureş, Romania), Balatonlelle (on the southern

Plate 30.1. Moreşti, plan of the weaving shed in house 13, together with selected artifacts found therein (a clay lump with textile imprint, loom weights, wheel-made pottery, and spindle whorls). Drawing by Florin Curta.

shore of Lake Balaton, in Hungary), and Rákóczifalva (near Szolnok, Hungary) are certainly evidence of part- or full-time artisans working in special-purpose facilities, most likely for elite consumption. In Moreşti, over fifty loom weights have been found in one such facility, in addition to timber remains of the upward poles and the bar of a warp-weighted loom (see plate 30.1).

Several sixth-to-seventh-century rural settlements in southern Romania and Belarus have produced evidence of smelting furnaces. They were located in the proximity of domestic spaces, which suggests a part-time activity and small-scale, independent production. Advanced metallographic studies of iron and steel artifacts (tools and weapons) found in rural settlements have revealed sophisticated techniques employed by rural blacksmiths in ninth-century Moravia, as well as tenth-to-eleventh-century Bohemia, Bulgaria, Rus', and Poland for the production of both tools and weapons. In eighth- and ninth-century Hungary and Romania, as well as in tenth-century Bulgaria, several rural settlements appear to have specialized in craft activities, particularly blacksmithing and non-ferrous metallurgy. The inhabitants of the settlement site in Lozna (near Dorohoi, in northeastern Romania) were apparently not involved at all in agricultural activities. They were most likely supplied with food from the outside, probably under the control of local political authorities. Industrial centers in the hinterland of Preslav (Bulgaria) specialized in the production of dress accessories, particularly belt buckles and mounts. The connection between political organization and appearance of rural settlements of specialists is confirmed by the large smelting sites in Zamárdi (southern shore of Lake Balaton, Hungary) and Haivoron (near Uman', Ukraine), both dated to the late seventh century. The former was linked to the reorganization of the Avar khaganate, while the latter emerged in the political circumstances surrounding the rise of the Khazar khaganate.

FURTHER READING

Alsleben, Almuth. "The Plant Economy of Northern Medieval Russia." In *The Archaeology of Medieval Novgorod in Context: Studies in Centre/Periphery Relations*, edited by Mark Brisbane, Nikolai A. Makarov, and Evgenii N. Nosov, 321–50. Oxford: Oxbow Books, 2012.

Curta, Florin. *The Long Sixth Century in Eastern Europe*. East Central and Eastern Europe in the Middle Ages, 450–1450, 72. Leiden: Brill, 2021.

Doncheva, Stela. "Workshops in the Production Centers in the Vicinity of the Capital Preslav." In *Exploring Dwellings and Manufacturing Spaces in Medieval Context (7th–14th Centuries). Proceedings of the International Conference "Exploring Dwellings and Manufacturing Spaces in Medieval Context (7th–14th Centuries)," Târgu Mureș, October 27–30, 2020*, edited by Keve László, Dan Băcueț Crișan, Ioan Stanciu, and Florin Mărginean, 177–90. *Orbis mediaevalis* 3. Cluj-Napoca: Mega, 2021.

Gömöri, János. "The Legacy of 9th Century Craftsmen in the Carpathian Basin." In *The History of Handicraft in Hungary*, edited by János Szulovszky, 15–22. Budapest: Hungarian Chamber of Commerce and Industry, 2012.

Hladík, Marek. "Rural Economy." In *The Routledge Handbook of East Central and Eastern Europe in the Middle Ages, 500–1300*, edited by Florin Curta, 204–26. Abingdon: Routledge, 2022.

Koloda, Vladimir V., and Sergei A. Gorbanenko. *Agriculture in the Forest-Steppe Region of Khazaria*. East Central and Eastern Europe in the Middle Ages, 450–1450, 66. Leiden: Brill, 2020.

Tănase, Daniela. *Craftsmen and Jewelers in the Middle and Lower Danube Region (Sixth to Seventh Centuries)*. East Central and Eastern Europe in the Middle Ages, 450–1450, 67. Leiden: Brill, 2020.

31

URBANIZATION

Keywords in this chapter: palace, court, stronghold

What makes the question of early medieval urbanization complicated is that it is not at all clear what could or should be considered a town in that historical context. Early medieval societies were fundamentally rural, with most of the population involved in an agrarian economy or some hunting and gathering (see chapter 30). Many Roman towns on the eastern Adriatic (Zadar or Ragusa, the modern Dubrovnik) or on the western Black Sea coast (Mesembria, Debeltos) survived and even grew in importance throughout the Middle Ages, while others continued to flourish in northern Greece (Thessaloniki) and Crimea (Cherson). Outside the former Roman provinces, however, in Northern and Central Europe, forms of settlement were very different, and the ancient Latin and Greek vocabulary of the sources described a changed reality. For example, *urbs* and *civitas* – traditionally a Roman town and its district – acquired new meanings as both words were typically used to denote strongholds of various sizes and shapes. *Civitas* was also the preferred term in the sources for the see of a bishop. New forms of agglomerations with urban characteristics – in size, population, or diversity of functions – nonetheless appeared in various contexts.

In Dalmatia, Roman towns continued well into the Middle Ages. Trogir was originally a Greek colony; Zadar (Iader) was established as a Roman colony in the first century BCE. Both Split and Ragusium or Ragusa, by contrast, came into being during Late Antiquity. In Trogir and Zadar, the Roman street pattern in the form of a grid was maintained in the Early Middle Ages. Trogir preserved from the classical period the design of its streets and public spaces; walls and towers remained intact. Zadar, as a typical Roman colonial town, had an orthogonal topography that is still visible today. Split developed as a town with perpendicular axes (*cardo* and *decumanus*) around the palace that Emperor Diocletian built in the late third century; an archbishopric and municipal administration were established sometime in the seventh or eighth century and Diocletian's Mausoleum was turned into a cathedral church.

Most Roman towns, however, disappeared by the seventh century in the interior of the Balkans. As their size shrank in the fifth and especially the sixth centuries, they often refocused upon fortified citadels on well-protected higher ground. Settlement transformation started earlier in the north. Sirmium (now Sremska Mitrovica, Serbia) lost its urban character in the fifth century as fortifications and public buildings were removed or abandoned and the population was dispersed in small hamlets. Public spaces disappeared in Philippopolis (now Plovdiv, Bulgaria) and Zikideva (Veliko Tărnovo, Bulgaria), where churches, buildings, and streets were reorganized with no attention to the regular street pattern that was typical of Roman towns. The most important buildings in the Late Antique towns of the Balkans and the Crimean Peninsula were generally churches.

Early medieval strongholds appeared in the northern and central Balkans as well. The exact circumstances in which Serdica (now Sofia) and Philippopolis were revived are obscure, but there is clear continuity of occupation at Durostorum, known as Drăstăr in the Middle Ages (now Silistra, in Bulgaria). Elsewhere, new settlements appeared next to the abandoned old towns. For example, Odessos, a major city on the Black Sea coast, was completely abandoned in the early seventh century, but the town of Varna emerged next to it at few decades later, at the end of that century. A major port town, Varna did not become important economically before the late tenth century, when it passed into Byzantine authority. An urban renewal occurred also in the ninth and tenth centuries in western Thrace and Macedonia.

Byzantine authorities were keen on maintaining a foothold in the Crimea to monitor developments in the steppe world. Although they insisted on maintaining Greek municipal authorities in Cherson (now Sevastopil', Ukraine) and protecting it from Khazar encroachments, they struggled to maintain control over this important outpost. In the early 830s, Emperor Theophilus appointed a military governor to lead both military and civic administration. In the later ninth century, the Byzantines relied on an alliance with the Pechenegs to keep Cherson under their control and secure safe conditions for trade in the Black Sea zone. Treaties between the Rus' and the Byzantines in the tenth century testify to anxieties in Constantinople about keeping Cherson; the struggles over the city between Vladimir of Kiev and Basil II demonstrate that Byzantine fears were not unfounded.

A new fortified settlement of unusual size appeared in Bulgaria at Pliska (near Shumen in northeastern Bulgaria). Initially a simple residence of the mobile Bulgar rulers, Pliska was surrounded by the ramparts of what would become the Inner Town in the early ninth century, when it became the main residence. A fortified camp on a plain, it lacked, however, connections to trade or river routes. Omurtag (r. 815–31) built a rectangular stone residence, the "Throne Palace," that replaced an earlier timber building and was surrounded by the stone fortifications of the Inner Town that had four gates and encompassed two square miles (or five square kilometers). The "Court Basilica," located ca. 165 feet (50 m) to the west of the palace, has been interpreted as either a pagan temple or a church. North from there was the Palatial Compound, an ensemble of various buildings surrounded by a brick wall. Omurtag's palace, with a large throne room and a thermal bath, was clearly made to impress.

Omurtag's successor Boris built a small church next to the palace that was replaced by a larger one in 870–75: the Great Basilica, a three-aisle building of early Byzantine style attached to an episcopal palace (see chapter 41). The settlement complex of the Outer Town encompassed no less than 21.8 square kilometers (2,180 ha or over 5,400 acres), which was larger than Constantinople. Recent archaeological discoveries suggest that the area inside the Outer Town was built in a planned manner in the later ninth century, with sunken houses and rural estates. Its large earthen ramparts could hardly have been built as military protection, for they had no forts and no garrisons. It is more likely that their role was to delineate the space of the central area that was under the direct authority of the ruler.

Early in his reign, Symeon moved his court from Pliska to Preslav, which earlier had probably been a minor military and administrative center. He then undertook major building projects. Preslav, although much smaller, had a concentric circular plan like that of Pliska, with an Inner Town surrounded by an Outer Town. The Inner Town was on an elevated terrace near the Ticha River and encompassed the palace complex. There were various manors in the Outer Town, each typically having a church, houses, storage buildings, and workshops. Craft activities concentrated in a specific area, trade matters in another. No fewer than twenty-five churches were built in the tenth century in Preslav, the most impressive of them being the Golden or Round Church (see chapter 41). During the tenth century, Preslav shone as a cultural center through intellectual creativity. The numerous sacral buildings and the large number of clergymen gave Preslav an atmosphere that set it apart, which was expressed in the admiration of John the Exarch, a leading scholar of the age of Symeon, for the beauty of the city. John described "towering buildings on both sides, adorned with stone and embellished with wood and other things" and "palaces and the churches, richly decorated with stone, wood, and paint, and on the inside with marble, copper, silver, and gold."[1]

Meanwhile, in East Central and Eastern Europe, the largest agglomerations the region had ever seen were the fortified settlements of Moravia. In fact, with the exceptions of Pliska and Preslav, their imposing dimensions, topographical complexity, and absence of Roman antecedents made them unique in Europe as a whole. Frankish annals mention Dowina and Neutra (Devín and Nitra, in Slovakia) as exceptionally large. Moreover, several sites studied by archaeologists in Moravia (Mikulčice, Staré Město, and Pohansko near Břeclav), close to the border between modern Czech Republic, Austria, and Slovakia, are of the same age, even though their ninth-century names remain unknown.

Pohansko, in the fluvial plain of the Dyje, a tributary of the Morava River, began in the eighth century as an agglomeration with sunken and aboveground buildings organized in an irregular manner that suggests an unstratified society involved primarily in agricultural production. Significant growth and change in settlement patterns occurred after 800, as the agglomeration became structured around a cult enclosure and a ruler's residence, the

1 Florin Curta, ed., "John the Exarch on Symeon the Great," in *Medieval Eastern Europe, 500–1300: A Reader* (Toronto: University of Toronto Press, 2024), 61.

Magnate Court – a quadrangular area surrounded by a palisade that comprised a church, a cemetery, an assembly hall, and a secular residence with stone foundations. In its later phase, the settlement had 6 m (20 feet) high fortifications with an earthen rampart and palisade, encompassing an area of 28 ha (about 70 acres); half of the 60 ha (148 acres) of inhabited space was surrounded by the fortifications. The settled areas had regular rectangular plots that suggest planned spatial organization through some sort of centralized authority; the enclosed units combined residential and production functions. A section of the enclosed settlement appears to have been inhabited by warriors, while in another part, blacksmiths, jewelry makers, and other craftspeople were clustered. Pohansko combined princely residence, military protection, and a concentration of craft and commercial activities.

Mikulčice, in the floodplain of the Morava River, was located on several islands in the middle of that river. The agglomeration was built in an area only scarcely inhabited initially, but it became a central place of strategic economic, political, and military importance at the time of Great Moravia. The ninth-century fortification system comprised a main fortress and a fortified bailey; to the north was an open settlement with several churches, buildings, and cemeteries. The main fortress encompassed other churches and a palace, whereas the bailey had mainly residential buildings. The entire area of settlement covered 50 ha (over 123 acres). The fortified agglomeration depended upon the rural estates of the surroundings where the increased density of population responded to its needs. The rural settlement network became more diversified in functions and social differentiation as it evolved to sustain the inhabitants of Mikulčice.

The Moravian fortified agglomerations were of unusual dimensions, comparable to sites discovered in Austria (Gars-Thunau) and Slovakia (Pobedim, Bojná). Power holders resided in palaces that have been compared to those of Frankish kings. The palace buildings in Mikulčice and Staré Město had stone foundations, perhaps with stone walls in the latter case; artifacts attributed to a military elite, such as Frankish swords and garter belts, have also been found on both sites. These agglomerations included churches, often in clusters, whose architecture was more impressive than that of the secular buildings. Mikulčice had at least ten sacral buildings, including a large basilica, and Staré Město had four. Artifacts indicative of trade are less characteristic of the Great Moravian centers than of the Baltic Sea *emporia* (see chapter 32) but do point out commercial contacts. For example, glass vessels from the Rhineland were uncovered in Mikulčice. Frankish swords, spears, and stirrups on all three sites likely arrived through trade networks, despite Frankish attempts to impose a weapon embargo on the Slavs. All settlements in the valley of the Morava River, however, were abandoned in the early tenth century. They remained deserted places even when new towns grew in the vicinity, as in the case of Břeclav, established shortly after the year 1000 near Pohansko.

Prague has its origins around a bend on the middle course of the Vltava River, where two strongholds were built: Prague Castle, on an elevation on the western shore, and Vyšehrad, upstream on the eastern side. The location was central in Bohemia and perfect to connect trade routes; it was also close to deposits of iron ore where metalworking occurred early on. These factors contributed to making Prague a growing political and economic center by the tenth century. Settlements of craftspeople and markets developed on both sides of the river.

The connection between early urbanization and strongholds has been especially well studied in the context of early medieval Poland. Archaeology has unveiled how strongholds of the tenth and eleventh centuries were part of settlement developments that, in some cases, had an urban character expressed by the diversity of occupation of the inhabitants and the complexity of the social and economic structures. However, strongholds were clearly not towns, even though they fulfilled both military and administrative functions. With the satellite settlements in their hinterland that had a population involved in crafts and agriculture, they did sometimes form ensembles that can be characterized as urban, or early urban. Some of these settlements became larger and more socially complex in the eleventh and twelfth centuries, but they typically lacked topographical consistency.

FURTHER READING

Buko, Andrzej. "Fortified Medieval Sites in Central Europe: Construction, Techniques, Functions, Regional Differentiations." In *Mura di legno, mura di terra, mura di pietra: fortificazioni nel Mediterraneo antico. Atti del Convegno internazionale, Sapienza Università di Roma, 7–9 maggio 2012*, edited by Gilda Bartoloni and Laura Maria Michetti, 651–67. Scienze dell'Antichità 19. Rome: Quasar, 2013.

Dall'Aglio, Francesco. "Shifting Capitals and Shifting Identities: Pliska, Preslav, Tărnovo and the Self-perception of a Medieval Nation." *Bulgaria Mediaevalis* 2 (2011): 587–602.

Fiedler, Uwe. "Bulgars in the Lower Danube Region: A Survey of the Archaeological Evidence and of the State of Current Research." In *The Other Europe in the Middle Ages: Avars, Bulgars, Khazars and Cumans*, edited by Florin Curta, 151–236. East Central and Eastern Europe in the Middle Ages, 450–1450, 2. Leiden: Brill, 2008.

Henning, Joachim. "The Metropolis of Pliska Or, How Large Does an Early Medieval Settlement Have to Be in Order to Be Called a City?" In *Post-Roman Towns, Trade and Settlement in Europe and Byzantium*, Vol. 2, *Byzantium, Pliska, and the Balkans*, edited by Joachim Henning, 209–40. Millennium-Studien 5/2. Berlin: De Gruyter, 2007.

Hladík, Marek. *Mikulčice and Its Hinterland: An Archaeological Model for Medieval Settlement Patterns on the Middle Course of the Morava River (7th to Mid-13th Centuries)*. East Central and Eastern Europe in the Middle Ages, 450–1450, 61. Leiden: Brill, 2020.

Jovič Gazič, Vedrana. "Urban Development from Late Antiquity to the Middle Ages: Dubrovnik, Split, Trogir, Zadar – the State of Research." *Archaeologia Adriatica* 5 (2011): 151–96.

Macháček, Jiří. "Great Moravian Central Places and Their Practical Function, Social Significance and Symbolic Meaning." In *Zentrale Orte und zentrale Räume des Frühmittelalters in Süddeutschland*, edited by Peter Ettel and Lukas Werther, 235–48. Mainz: Verlag des Römisch-Germanischen Zentralmuseums, 2013.

Macháček, Jiří. *The Rise of Medieval Towns and States in East Central Europe: Early Medieval Centres as Social and Economic Systems*. East Central and Eastern Europe in the Middle Ages, 450–1450, 10. Leiden: Brill, 2010.
Moździoch, Sławomir. "The Origins of the Medieval Polish Towns." *Archaeologia Polona* 32 (1994): 129–53.

32

EMPORIA AND CENTERS OF TRADE

Keywords in this chapter: trade, harbor, Vikings

In early medieval Northern Europe, urbanization developed along a path that was very different from that in the ancient Roman world, where towns typically evolved out of political and administrative centers. Around the North and Baltic Seas, early urbanization was driven primarily by long-distance trade that led to the development of port settlements called *portus* or *emporia* in Frankish sources. They were in strategic locations near the coasts or along rivers to facilitate transport that was done primarily by ship. The port settlements concentrated activities related to trade and crafts and connected their hinterlands with trade routes. Despite their modest size, their relative density of population, the diversity of economic activities, and the mobility of their inhabitants gave these settlements an early urban character that made them distinct both from rural settlements and the strongholds established elsewhere at the same time (see chapter 31). Contacts between Frisian merchants and Scandinavians had been instrumental in the development of many of these sites in the seventh and eighth centuries in Denmark and Sweden – the most well known being Hedeby and Birka; in the eighth and ninth centuries, contacts with Scandinavian merchants led to the establishment of similar sites in Slavic and Baltic territories on the southern and eastern shores of the Baltic Sea. The trade network of the Baltic Sea was thus connected with the North Sea and Western Europe, and through the East European river routes with the Black Sea area and thus with Byzantium and the Islamic world.

These coastal sites had several common features. They were typically in protected bays or along rivers that allowed easy access to the sea, and often on the borders of political territories. Many of them had regular plots and streets running parallel to the waterfront, which suggests some planning. Inhabitants were typically involved in industrial activities, primarily metalworking, processing of bone, antler, and amber, glass making, and textile production, as well as in long-distance trade with furs, salt, honey, slaves, and various luxuries. Rulers offered inhabitants protection and support; they had agents residing in the *emporia* who supervised trade activities and defense. With no ecclesiastical institutions (bishoprics), those settlements, however, had a high level of instability and were often abandoned after a while or moved to a better location over time.

The *Royal Frankish Annals* recount that in 808 the Danish king Godfred attacked the *emporium Reric* that was under the jurisdiction of Thrasco, the ruler of the Abodrites. Godfred extracted a ransom from the merchants who lived there and then forced them to relocate on Danish territory to a place named Sliesthorp. The following year, envoys of Godfred murdered Thrasco in Reric. The port settlements had a multilingual character: the annals state that *Reric* was a name in the Danish language, even though the site was located on Slavic territory. Adam of Bremen, in the late eleventh century, explained that *Sliaswich* was a Saxon name, whereas *Heidiba* was its Danish counterpart. The political competition outlined in the annals makes clear that Reric, likely a source of wealth, was important for Godfred and Thrasco. The Reric of the Frankish annals has been identified with an early medieval site on the Bay of Wismar, Groß Strömkendorf, the dendrochronological dating of which fits perfectly the chronology of events known from the annals. This was a center of trade and craft production; the artifacts suggest contacts with both Scandinavia and the Slavic hinterland. Sliesthorp is the town of Hedeby (today in Schleswig-Holstein, Germany), which was strategically located between Saxony, Denmark, and the land of the Abodrites. Hedeby boomed in the tenth century.

Other port settlements appeared in the ninth and tenth centuries on the southern shore of the Baltic Sea. They included Menzlin in the Bay of Wismar, Ralswiek on Rügen Island, and Wolin on the Dziwna River, at the mouth of the Oder that connected the coast with the hinterland. Adam of Bremen described Wolin, or *Iumne*, as the "greatest city in Europe," inhabited by "Slavs," "barbarians," and "Greeks" (Christians of Eastern rite) while visited by Saxons. In a land of pagans, Christians were tolerated if not publicly professing their religion. To be sure, no tenth-century church is known from the rather extensive excavations that took place in Wolin. The site, comprising a harbor, a hillfort, and a fortified early town extending on both shores of the Dziwna, was strategically located in terms of its long-distance trade connections.

Farther to the east, along the southern shore of the Baltic Sea, the port-town Truso was mentioned in the late ninth-century travel account of Wulfstan, who located it in Estland, on the shore of a lake from which the Elbląg river originated.[1] The site has been identified with Janów Pomorski, a ninth-to-tenth-century settlement surrounded by a moat and probably a rampart to the east from Lake Drużno, near the later town of Elbląg in northern Poland. Lake Drużno was indeed connected to the river Elbląg, which flows into the Vistula Lagoon. Ships appear to have landed on the shore sand, without the need for harbor infrastructure. Houses in Scandinavian tradition were placed in regular plan along the streets. The inhabitants occupied themselves with trade and craft production, especially the making of amber artifacts.

1 Florin Curta, ed., "Wulfstan Travels to Truso," in *Medieval Eastern Europe, 500–1300: A Reader* (Toronto: University of Toronto Press, 2024), 57.

Port settlements with a focus on trade with Scandinavia were also established in Curonia, on the eastern coast of the Baltic Sea. Grobiņa (near Liepāja, in Latvia) existed from the mid-seventh to the ninth century and had connections with Gotland and Sweden. Trade gave Palanga (near Klaipėda, in Lithuania) an early urban character in the tenth to twelfth centuries. Wiskiauten (now Mokhovoe, in the Kaliningrad region of the Russian enclave on the Baltic Sea shore) was on the spit that separates the Baltic Sea from the Curonian Lagoon, on the Sambian Peninsula, an area rich in amber. Graves in Scandinavian tradition suggest the existence of a trading place between the ninth and the eleventh centuries that prospered primarily in the tenth century. The concentration of finds of Scandinavian tradition in these sites suggests compact Norse colonies whose material culture had limited impact except in the immediate surroundings.

Towns in the lands of Rus' had their origins in settlements focused on trade and crafts located on the river routes through which the Norse traveled from the Baltic to the Black Sea. They were places of interactions between the Norse, East Slavs, and Finno-Ugrian and Baltic populations. Staraia Ladoga was an early trade center with connections to Scandinavia that played an influential role on future developments. Later sources suggest that the settlement, which was located on the river Volkhov, to the east of where St. Petersburg (Russia) now is, was the residence of Riurik. Archaeology shows that the site – a cluster of settlements on both sides of the river – was occupied since the mid-eighth century, probably with Norse craftspeople in a country dominated by Finno-Ugrians. Long-distance trade connections (such as indicated, for example, by pitchers of Tatinger type produced in northwestern Europe) were intensified at the beginning of the ninth century; Sassanian and Umayyad coins testify to contacts with the Khazar Empire. The area south of Lake Ladoga was perfect to connect with the river routes of Eastern Europe and to foster trade with northern furs and Islamic silver. Crafts, by contrast, were relatively less developed. Artifacts that were discovered indicate contacts with Scandinavia and the presence of Norse people, not least through runic inscriptions. Staraia Ladoga had a culture with diverse influences – Norse, Baltic, Finnic, and, after 800, East Slavic. At the beginning of the tenth century, Staraia Ladoga was a trade center with an early urban character comparable to Birka (Sweden) or Hedeby. In the eleventh century, Iaroslav the Wise of Kiev gave the town to his wife, Ingegerd Olofsdottir of Sweden; after her death, it became part of the land of Novgorod.

The settlement called by archaeologists "Riurik's Stronghold" (*Riurikovo Gorodishche*) was located on a hill upstreams on the Volkhov River, on the shore of Lake Il'men'. The site came into being in the late ninth century. It was a fortified agglomeration with commercial activities that connected west and east and that displayed strong features of Scandinavian material culture. The settlement was gradually replaced by Novgorod, located 3 km (less than two miles) away. That town turned into a major trade center at the beginning of the eleventh century. After that, Novgorod became an archbishopric, a princely residence, and one of the main towns of Rus'.

In the late ninth century, Rus' political development shifted to the south. The borderland between the wooded steppes and the forest zone was strategic to connect the trade routes of the Volga and the Baltic Sea. Small settlements developed in the ninth century on the edge of a high plateau on the shores of the Middle Dnieper, on the site of what would become Kiev. Around 900, the settlement had grown to 30 ha (ca. 75 acres) and included two, perhaps three fortifications; it had a stable pattern of plots and streets. It comprised sunken wooden buildings and houses with horizontal timber construction. By the end of the tenth century, Kiev was a town covering 80 ha (almost 200 acres) that had two palace buildings and a church in stone, and a population evaluated at 10,000 people.

Towns in the Khazar Empire – the residence of the khagan Itil and towns on the western coast of the Caspian Sea and in the Crimea – declined in the late ninth century. New fortified urban centers emerged, however, with the rise of Volga-Bulgharia in the tenth and eleventh centuries – the most important ones were Biliar and Suwar, located on the shores of the Cheremshan, a tributary of the Volga, and Bolgar, at the confluence of the Volga and the Kama. The development of these new towns was rapid and responded to the needs of long-distance trade in the Volga region (see chapter 9). The Volga Bulghars followed the example of the Khazars in establishing centers for the collection of tribute and favoring trade between Eastern Europe and Byzantium. Mosques and baths were built in these towns after conversion to Islam.

FURTHER READING

Bogucki, Mateusz. "On Wulfstan's Right Hand – the Viking Age *Emporia* in West Slav Lands." In *From One Sea to Another: Trading Places in the European and Mediterranean Early Middle Ages. Proceedings of the International Conference, Comacchio March 27–29, 2009*, edited by S. Gelichi and Richard Hodges, 81–109. Seminari del Centro Interuniversitario per la Storia e l'Archeologia dell'Alto Medioevo 3. Turnhout: Brepols, 2012.

Callmer, Johan. "Urbanisation in Northern and Eastern Europe, ca. AD 700–1100." In *Post-Roman Towns, Trade and Settlement in Europe and Byzantium*. Vol. 1, *The Heirs of the Roman West*, edited by Joachim Henning, 233–70. Millenium-Studien 5/1. Berlin: De Gruyter, 2007.

Englert, Anton, and Athena Trakadas, eds. *Wulfstan's Voyage: The Baltic Sea Region in the Early Viking Age as Seen from Shipboard*. Maritime Culture of the North 2. Roskilde: Viking Ship Museum, 2009.

Grigoreva, Natalja V. "Archaeological Evidence for Staraya Ladoga as an Early Scandinavian Emporium of the Global North." In *The Global North: Spaces, Connections, and Networks Before 1600*, edited by Carol Symes, 37–52. Medieval Globe. Leeds: Arc Humanities Press, 2021.

Mägi, Marika. *The Viking Eastern Baltic*. Translated by Piret Ruustal. Past Imperfect. Leeds: Arc Humanities Press, 2019.

Murasheva, Veronika V. "Vikings Abroad: The Case of Gnezdovo." In *Viking Encounters: Proceedings of the Eighteenth Viking Congress, Denmark, August 6–12, 2017*, edited by Anne Pedersen and Søren M. Sindbæk, 71–80. Aarhus: Aarhus University Press, 2020.

33

EURASIAN TRADE ROUTES IN THE EARLY MIDDLE AGES

Keywords in this chapter: trade, beads, furs, coin hoards

In Late Antiquity, only a few regions in East Central and Eastern Europe were involved in inter-regional or inter-continental long-distance trade. The Balkan and Crimean peninsulas were included in the Roman Empire during the sixth and early seventh centuries; as such, they participated in the commercial exchanges of the Mediterranean region. That explains, for example, the presence in the southern and northeastern Balkans of coins struck in the mints of Alexandria (Egypt) or Carthage. Small amphorae (called *spatheia*) for the transportation of olive oil or wine, which have been found in the eastern and northern Adriatic region (present-day Croatia and Slovenia), mark the capillaries of a commercial network based in northern Africa, where those amphorae were in fact produced. Similarly, beginning with the mid-sixth century, amphorae from Crete are most common on sites in the northern Black Sea region. Whether wine, oil, or dry substances, goods in bulk packed in those amphorae moved from the eastern Mediterranean to Crimea. A large quantity of beads made of semiprecious gemstones (agate, alabaster, amethyst, aragonite, carnelian, chalcedony, and rock crystal) and coral have been found in cemeteries excavated in the Crimean Peninsula. All of them must have been procured by means of exchange, for Crimea was connected to the long-distance trade routes inside the empire. While carnelian exists in many places in Europe (Germany, Bohemia, Poland, as well as in the Crimea), all other gemstones, as well as the coral, originated in lands much farther to the south and southeast, some of them as far as the Arabian Peninsula or India.

Long-distance trade routes made exotic goods available even for people who lived outside but not too far from the empire. For example, beads made of semiprecious gemstones or coral have also been found on archaeological sites excavated in Hungary, Slovakia, and the Czech Republic. None of those regions was directly connected to the commercial networks inside the empire, and the beads must have been purchased inside the empire or obtained by non-commercial means, such as gift exchange. In the late sixth century, Avar envoys purchased goods from the market in Constantinople. East Central Europe during the Middle Ages was connected commercially to Western, not Eastern, Europe. According to the chronicle of Fredegar, "a Frankish man" named Samo "joined some merchants and went to the Slavs called Wends, to trade with them" (see chapter 6).[1] Exactly what was traded by Samo and his fellow traders is not known, but weapons produced in the Frankish realm begin to appear in the northwestern parts of the Avar khaganate after the mid-seventh century.

Gemstone beads have also been found in the easternmost part of the forest and taiga belts of Eastern Europe, where they arrived by means of trade along the Northern Silk Road originating in Central Asia. The main commodities brought to Eastern Europe by that route were silver and silk, a clear indication of elite consumption. They were exchanged for furs collected at key points by local elites (see chapter 22). The main agents of this long-distance trade in luxury, not bulk, goods were the Sogdian merchants from Bukhara and Samarkand, in what is now Uzbekistan, who reached as far west as the northern coast of the Black Sea. According to Jordanes, who wrote in the mid-sixth century, Crimea was indeed the terminal of commercial routes by which traders brought goods from Asia. The town of Sogdaia (now Sudak; see map 33.1) on the southeastern coast of the Crimean Peninsula was established by Sogdian merchants in the mid-seventh century to become a major trade center in the region over the following two centuries (see map 33.1).

A major transformation of the Eurasian trade routes took place after the mid-eighth century. It is at that point that the desire to own and wear furs began to spread rapidly inside the Abbasid Caliphate. The fashion originated in Central Asia, where Muslims were in direct contact with the nomadic world. Early Arab settlers in Khorasan (a region now divided between Iran, Turkmenistan, and Afghanistan) were among the first to imitate the nomads in taking to furs for clothing and bedding. By the late eighth century, a fur-clad man coming to Baghdad and asking to be received in audience by Caliph al-Mahdi (775–85) was still an exotic appearance. Nonetheless, at the death of Caliph Harun al-Rashid in 809, an inventory of his treasury listed a great number of outer garments, many of which were of silk, but lined with fur. Throughout the ninth century, the fur fashion exploded and spread quickly from the capital of the Caliphate to provincial centers and farther afield, in the process creating an enormous demand. As early as the second half of the eighth century, therefore, a north-south axis of trade was established, which was based primarily on furs and only secondarily on slaves. Since the furs were of animals that lived in the forest and taiga belts of Eastern Europe, the trade dramatically transformed those regions and linked them to transcontinental trade routes, through which goods originating elsewhere in Asia and Africa reached the north. The greatest indicator of those massive transfers of commodities from one continent to the other is the silver coin struck in the Muslim world,

1 Florin Curta, ed., "Slavs, Avars, and Franks," in *Medieval Eastern Europe, 500–1300: A Reader* (Toronto: University of Toronto Press, 2024), 9.

Map 33.1. Principal archaeological sites dated to the Early Middle Ages and containing information about trade routes. Medieval place names are in italics. Shown in the lower left corner are the Carpathian Mountains, while the range on the right side of the map (from north to south) is the Ural Mountains. The Caucasus Mountains are at the bottom of the map, between the Black and the Caspian seas.

the dirham. The quantity of coined silver, largely of Central Asian origin, that entered Eastern Europe between ca. 800 and ca. 1000 was enormous and has been estimated at 300 to 600 tons (or 100 to 200 million dirhams). More than three quarters of all those coins were struck for the Samanid rulers, which indicates that the golden age of that trade was the tenth century. The Samanids, who ruled from Bukhara in Khorasan, controlled all the important silver mines in Central Asia, particularly those in the Panjshir valley of the Hindu Kush Mountains (now at the border between Pakistan and Afghanistan). While in the ninth century, furs were procured by the Abbasids through trade routes passing through Khazaria, after 900 the Samanids organized caravan trade routes going directly to Volga Bulgharia and bypassing Khazaria. By the late ninth century, at the earliest, a commercial route linked the Middle Volga region to Khwarazm (an oasis region south of the Aral Sea) across the Ustyurt Plateau (northwestern Uzbekistan and southwestern Kazakhstan), as well as the rivers Emba and Ural, north of the Caspian Sea. Throughout the tenth century, dirhams reached Volga Bulgharia by that route. Because of the commercial realignment away from Khazaria, terrestrial routes opened as well, which linked Volga Bulgharia to Rus'.

The tenth-century fur trade network certainly reached the interior of Eastern Europe, far beyond Khazaria and Volga Bulgharia, as attested by the presence of dirhams in settlement and cemetery sites discovered in northwestern Russia, Ukraine, and Belarus. In addition, camel bones found on two sites in the Middle Don region just south of present-day Voronezh show that the caravan route reached the valleys of the Don and the Donets rivers. A trading post was established at Supruty (near Tula, in Russia), between the Don and the Oka regions. A small hoard of dirhams was found on that site, in addition to five fragments of commercial scales and 23 weights. Dirhams reached the Middle Dnieper region either via the Khazar forts along the Don or from Volga Bulgharia along the Oka. Two dirham hoards are known from Kiev, in which the last coins are from 905/906 and 906/907, respectively. One of those hoards has 529, the other 2,930 dirhams. This is clear evidence that the agents of the trade in the north and the west were the Rus', who obtained the dirhams from the markets in Volga Bulgharia or farther afield inside the Muslim world. However, they did not reuse the coins monetarily, but employed them as badges of social prestige and as bullion for jewelry.

A cluster of dirham hoards appears shortly after the middle of the tenth century in the region of the modern city of Kursk (western Russia), at a time when new trade posts were established farther to the north. At Gnezdovo, near modern-day Smolensk, 400 single finds of dirhams have been found in the settlement and in the barrow cemetery nearby. Moreover, the oldest hoards of dirhams from the hinterland of that site are dated to the 920s and 930s. Dirhams appear also on the Upper Volga, at Timerevo and Shekshovo, east of Moscow. However, the most impressive of all is the mammoth hoard discovered in Murom (in the Vladimir region of Russia), with over 11,000 dirhams (for a total of 88 lbs. of silver), the latest of which is from 939/40. In the area of Novgorod, hoards are dated between 930 and 970, but dirhams appear even farther to the north, for example on the southern shore of Lake Beloe (in the Vologda region of Russia). Although the tenth-century hoards in northern and northwestern Russia post-date by a few decades those in Volga Bulgharia, the earliest hoard of dirhams found in Eastern Europe is that of Staraia Ladoga, with thirty-one coins, the latest of which was struck in 786/787. This shows that by the end of the eighth century, Viking traders based in that emporium (see chapter 32) had already responded to the explosion of the fur fashion inside the Abbasid Caliphate. A change in the axis of trade from the Abbasids to the Samanids as the main consumers of furs explains why most dirhams that entered Eastern Europe after 900 were struck in Samarkand (now in Uzbekistan) and al-Shash (now Tashkent, the capital of Uzbekistan) in the names of the Samanid rulers Ismail I (892–907), Ahmad ibn Ismail (907–14), and Nasr ibn Ahmad (914–43).

Hoards of dirhams have been found in western Ukraine as well. The one from Krylos near Halych has 1,100 coins, the latest of which was struck in 935/936.The hoard found at Khust on the Upper Tisza (near the present-day border between Ukraine, Hungary, and Romania) contains 371 dirhams (with the latest from 934/935), but a third of them are imitations struck in Volga Bulgharia and Khazaria. The western distribution of dirham hoards points to an early linkage between the north-south axis of the fur trade and other commercial routes, such as that ending in Prague. Another secondary artery linked the Middle Dnieper region to the southeast with the Lower Vistula region to the northwest, along the Bug River (in what are now western Belarus and eastern Poland). Along that artery, dirhams reached the southern shore of the Baltic Sea in western Pomerania, and from there they moved farther to the west to the Danes and the Elbe Slavs. By contrast, the dirhams that appear in hoards from Greater Poland dated to the late tenth or early eleventh century seem to have been imported from Scandinavia and were most likely not procured by trade. As indicated by their fragmentary state, they probably served as payments for (military) services.

Shortly before the year 1000, the north-south axis of the fur trade came to an end. Because of political troubles in the Samanid realm, the flow of Muslim silver dried up, and by 990 very few if any dirhams entered Eastern Europe anymore. Around 1000, the Rus' had already realigned their commercial interests with Byzantium. Another shift took place, which moved the axis of trade westward from the Volga to the Dnieper River, in the direction of the Black Sea and of Constantinople (see insert 33.1). Around that same time, German deniers and Anglo-Saxon pennies began to appear in hoards discovered in Ukraine, along with Byzantine silver coins. The Bavarian deniers, as well as the pennies struck in the name of Otto III and Adelaide, used silver from the Harz Mountains in the region of present-day Germany around Goslar. Millions of cross-deniers (called so because they had a cross on one side) were struck in the German lands specifically for long-distance trade with the Slavs. Meanwhile, Anglo-Saxon pennies, which were part of the tribute paid to the Danish and Norwegian kings, appeared as far east as Latvia and Estonia. They also were found in hoards discovered in Ukraine and in Russia and dated shortly after 1000. The flow of German and Anglo-Saxon coins came to an end in the 1020s but was renewed during the last third of the eleventh century. While the configuration of the commercial network by that time was radically different from the Eurasian trade routes of the Early Middle Ages, the demand for furs did not vanish. Moreover, old arteries linking

INSERT 33.1. THE ROUTE FROM THE VARANGIANS TO THE GREEKS

Varangians was the name given in Byzantine sources to the Norse or Rus' mercenaries employed as palace guards in Constantinople. Rus' sources made a distinction between the Rus', who were of Scandinavian heritage but were partly assimilated to East Slavic culture, and Varangians, who were the newcomers from Scandinavia who joined them. "The route from the Varangians to the Greeks" designates the river connections that were used for trade since the ninth century and linked Scandinavia with Byzantium; the phrase is derived from a passage of the *Primary Chronicle* where the route from Lake Ladoga through Novgorod and Kiev to Constantinople is described. Travelers from Sweden would cross the Baltic Sea and sail along the coast of Estonia, and crossed to Lake Ladoga through the Neva River (where St. Petersburg now is). The river route started at the mouth of the Volkhov River in Lake Ladoga, going past Staraia Ladoga; Lake Ilmen was then reached, to the south of which Novgorod was established in the eleventh century. From Lake Ilmen, one could travel east through several rivers and reach the Volga that led to the Caspian Sea. The other option was to travel south along various rivers and watersheds to reach the Daugava, near what is now Vitebsk (today in Belarus). The Daugava had several impassable rapids in its lower parts, so it was difficult to travel directly from the Baltic Sea along that river. Although not described in the *Primary Chronicle*, it is believed that an alternate route ran along the river Narva (today the border between Estonia and Russia), Lake Peipus, and the Velikaya River to reach through a watershed the Daugava around Polotsk (today Polatsk, in Belarus). From around Vitebsk or Polotsk, travelers took routes across watersheds to leave the Daugava and reach the Dnieper, along which one would travel south, pass Kiev, and reach the Black Sea. From there, Constantinople was in easy reach.

the north-south axis of fur trade to other parts of East Central Europe were put to new use, as key commercial centers emerged, such as Cracow along the trade route from Kiev to Prague, Drohiczyn along the trade route from Kiev to the Baltic region, and Iaroslavl along the route from Volga Bulgharia to Novgorod.

FURTHER READING

Asadov, Farda. "Khazaria, Byzantium and the Arab Caliphate: Struggle for Control over the Eurasian Trade Routes in the 9th–10th Centuries." *The Caucasus & Globalization* 6, no. 4 (2012): 140–50.

Grigoreva, Natalia. "The Ladoga Fortress (Staraya Ladoga) on the Trade Route 'from the Varangians to the Greeks.'" In *Fortifications in Their Natural and Cultural Landscape: From Organising Space to the Creation of Power*, edited by Timo Ibsen, Kristin Ilves, Birgit Maixner, Sebastian Messal, and Jens Schneeweiß, 167–80. Schriften des Museums für Archäologie Schloss Gottorf. Ergänzungsreihe 15. Bonn: Habelt, 2022.

Howard-Johnston, James D. "The Fur Trade in the Early Middle Ages." In *Viking-Age Trade: Silver, Slaves and Gotland*, edited by Jacek Gruszczyński, Marek Jankowiak, and Jonathan Shepard, 57–74. London/New York: Routledge, 2021.

Noonan, Thomas S. "Volga Bulghāria's Tenth-Century Trade with Samanid Central Asia." *Archivum Eurasiae Medii Aevi* 11 (2000): 140–218.

Skrzyńska, Katarzyna. "Middle Bug Area as a Part of Medieval Watertrade System." In *Siedlung, Kommunikation und Wirtschaft im westslawischen Raum. Beiträge der Sektion zur slawischen Frühgeschichte des 5. Deutschen Archäologenkongresses in Frankfurt an der Oder, 4. bis 7. April 2005*, edited by Felix Biermann and Thomas Kersting, 79–90. Beiträge zur Ur- und Frühgeschichte Mitteleuropas 46. Langenweissbach: Beier & Beran, 2007.

PART 6

Religion in the Early Middle Ages

34

PRE-CHRISTIAN RELIGIONS OF THE SLAVS AND STEPPE PEOPLES

Keywords in this chapter: temples, priests, sacrifice

The early Slavs who appeared in the Balkans in the sixth century are described by Byzantine authors as non-Christians. According to Procopius of Caesarea, they worshipped rivers, nymphs, and "some other spirits":

> They believe that one god, the maker of lightning, is alone lord of all things, and they sacrifice to him cattle and all other victims; but as for fate, they neither know it nor do they in any way admit that it has power over men. Whenever they face death, either stricken with sickness or at the start of a war, they promise that they will immediately make a sacrifice to the god in exchange for their life; and if they escape, they sacrifice just what they have promised and consider that their safety has been bought with these sacrifices.[1]

More details about the pre-Christian beliefs and practices of the Slavs appear in the sources only much later. While the *Primary Chronicle* was written more than a century after the conversion of the Rus', information about the religion of the Western Slavs of the eleventh and twelfth centuries is much more abundant and, crucially, contemporary, even though written from the perspective of antagonistically minded Christian propagandists.

Pagan temples are regularly mentioned for the Western Slavs between the eleventh and twelfth centuries (see chapter 19). The fortified temple of the Liuticians, dedicated to Svarožic, was called Riedegost by Thietmar of Merseburg and Rethra by Adam of Bremen; it was destroyed in 1068 and its exact location remains unknown. After that, the Rans of

1 Florin Curta, ed., "Procopius on the Slavs," in *Medieval Eastern Europe, 500–1300: A Reader* (Toronto: University of Toronto Press, 2024), 3.

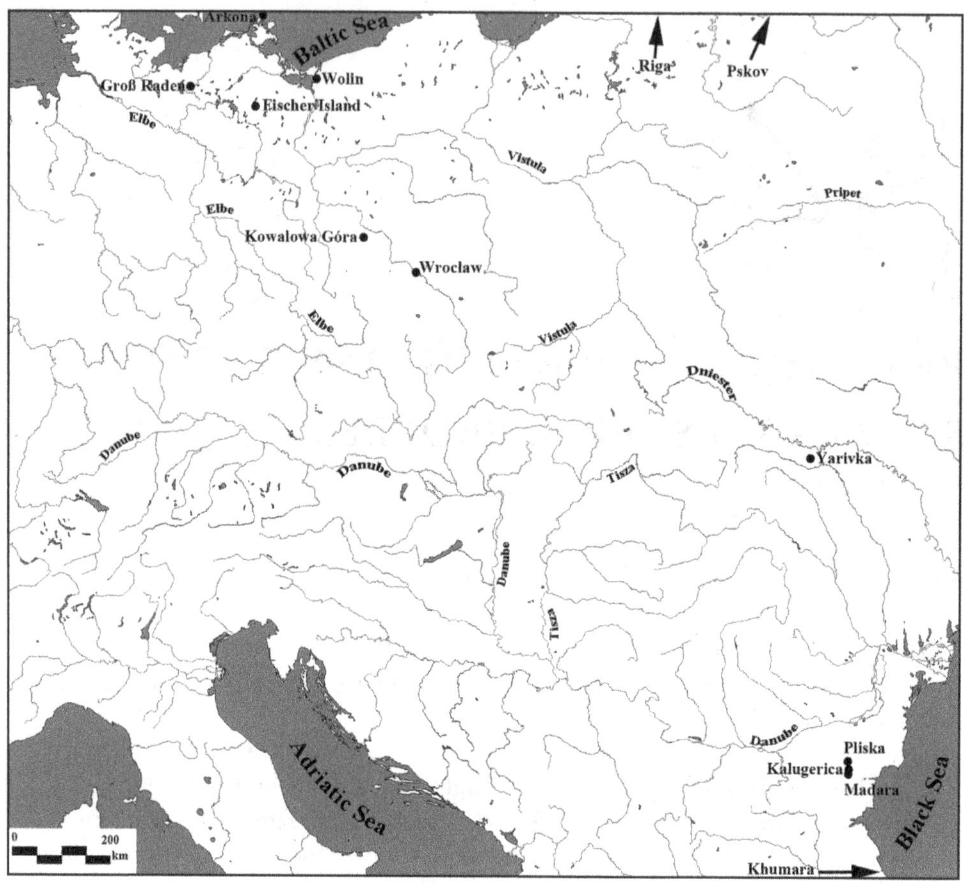

Map 34.1. Principal archaeological sites dated to the Early Middle Ages and containing information about pre-Christian beliefs.

the island of Rügen (near Stralsund, in northeastern Germany) overtook the leading role in pagan opposition to Christian expansion (see map 34.1). Their main temple in Arkona (on the northernmost tip of the island, on a cliff believed to have been lost through erosion), which was described by Helmold of Bosau and by Saxo Grammaticus and where priests led the cult of a god named Svantevit, was destroyed by Danish crusaders in 1167/1168 (see chapter 44 and plate 34.1).

Elsewhere, archaeologists have uncovered buildings that they suspect of being temples. The best known of them, dated to the tenth century, was found within the fortified settlement at Groß Raden (near Sternberg, in northeastern Germany). Both the size and the shape of the building were different from all others on the site. The place believed to have served for worship was surrounded by a row of planks ending with effigies, presumably representing divine beings (see plate 34.2). This reminds one of Thietmar of Merseburg's description of Riedegost. Another building was discovered in Wrocław and, based on the similarity of a plank with effigy to those of Groß Raden, has been interpreted as a temple. The animal bones found inside suggest sacrificial offerings; crucially, the construction has

Plate 34.1. Cape Arkona, island of Rügen (Germany). A small part of the town of the Rans may still be seen at the tip of the peninsula, together with a portion of the earthen rampart. However, the temple of Svantevit was most likely washed into the sea after its destruction by the Danish crusaders. Wikimedia Commons, the free media repository.

been dated through dendrochronology to the time of the pagan reaction of the 1030s (see chapter 17). This interpretation, however, is uncertain; the shape and size of the building could also be understood as a princely residence. Other sites, such as Kowalowa Góra in Silesia (southwestern Poland), attest to the cult of the dead: the fortified site, on a hill, was in a remote place away from any settlement and appears to have been used for ritual purposes.

Temple buildings are also mentioned for the Pomeranians, but not for the Eastern Slavs. Among the latter, archaeology has uncovered possible open-air cult sites, for example in Pskov, where a statue was surrounded by a ditch and other statues, in the context of a field of barrows. Although similar sites might correspond to descriptions in Rus' sources and in the *vitae* of the missionary to Pomerania, Otto of Bamberg, the identification of material remains in these places as religious sites is difficult to ascertain.

The existence of pagan priests is attested by many contemporary sources for the Western Slavs in the eleventh and twelfth centuries. Oracles under the guidance of specialists appear to have had a central importance in Slavic religious practices: divination was

Plate 34.2. Reconstruction of the tenth-century temple at Groß Raden (Germany). Wikimedia Commons, the free media repository.

already mentioned by Procopius and is abundantly recorded for the Western Slavs and occasionally for the Eastern Slavs. Ritual oracles involving horses or an alcoholic beverage in the horn of a god's statue, all under the guidance of priests, are described by Thietmar, Saxo Grammaticus, and Herbord, the biographer of Otto of Bamberg (see chapter 36). These practices are explained as being connected to political decision-making, for example regarding war or peace. An early thirteenth-century chronicle written in Poland also mentions a seeress accompanying the Polish army on campaign. The *Primary Chronicle* mentions sorcerers (*volkhvy*) who played a role like that of priests; they were diviners said to have magical powers and knowledge of the future. Slavic priests had various other leadership roles. Thietmar of Merseburg describes how Liutician priests looked after banners with images of gods and goddesses that were carried on military expeditions. Moreover, according to Helmold and Saxo, the priest of Svantevit and the secular ruler competed for political leadership among the Rans. The priests of both Rans and Pomeranians are portrayed as political leaders who were taking active part in assemblies and in negotiations with foreign rulers.

Slavic beliefs in the afterlife are reflected in some burial practices. Latin, Greek, and Arabic sources attest to the practice in various parts of the Slavic world of sacrificing the wife after her husband's death. The pagan Slavs practiced cremation of the dead. Grave goods were either burned with the body or deposited with the cremated remains in an urn or simply in a pit dug into the ground. Socially important individuals were buried under barrows (burial mounds). Although generally accompanying the conversion, the shift from cremation to inhumation pre-dated the adoption of Christianity in some regions. For example, in Moravia, inhumation was occasionally practiced before conversion, presumably under influence from the neighboring Avars or Franks. Conversely, in parts of Poland, cremation persisted for some time after conversion. Multiple Latin and Greek sources refer to human sacrifices to divine beings, often upon the burial of elite members, but no archaeological confirmation has so far been found. Thietmar of Merseburg and Adam of Bremen, though, independently describe Liuticians sacrificing people to their gods and placing a special ritual significance upon the beheading of their victims.

Some Slavic gods are described as having multiple heads or faces, a feature that is otherwise unknown in Norse or Baltic mythology. The name of the god Triglav (said to have been worshipped in Szczecin) means "three heads"; Svantovit, the main god venerated in Arkona, had four; Porevit and Rugevit, both from the island of Rügen, had as many as five and seven faces respectively. Wooden figurines with two or four heads, presumably of cultic role, have been discovered during excavations on Fischer Island (Tollense Lake near Neubrandenburg, in northeastern Germany), Wolin (Poland), and Yarivka (near Chernivtsi, Ukraine). The four-headed Svantevit was particularly popular, as indicated by miniature figures found in Wolin (ninth century), Denmark and Sweden (tenth to twelfth centuries), and Riga (thirteenth century) (see plate 34.3). In his *vita* of Otto of Bamberg, Ebo describes miniature figures of gods that in Pomerania were kept in private houses and displayed in public celebrations.

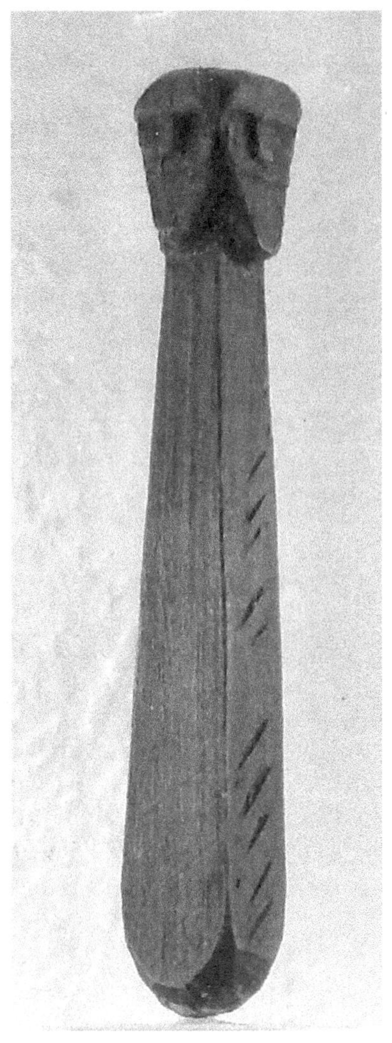

Plate 34.3. A miniature wooden figurine with four faces (possibly representing Svantevit) found in 1974 in Wolin (Poland). Wikimedia Commons, the free media repository.

Several names of Slavic gods and goddesses are known, but no deity is known that was common to all Slavs. The thunder-god Perun might be well attested among the Rus', but he was unknown either in the Balkans or to the Western Slavs. Svarog might have been the sun-god of the Eastern Slavs but is poorly attested in the sources; the Western Slavs only knew Svarožic, whose name is interpreted as "Svarog's son." Other gods and goddesses seem to have had limited regional recognition. Several names of heroic characters, however, although known only from sources written after Christianization, appear in the dynastic or ethnogenetic legends of several traditions, particularly in Bohemia, Poland, and Rus' – for example, Čech, Krok, and Libuše – and might go back to common myths.

Comparatively less is known about the religion of the Bulgars, the Khazars, the Magyars, the Pechenegs, the Oghuz, and the Cumans before their conversions to monotheistic religions. On the basis of analogies with Central Asia, scholars believe that all those steppe nomads shared beliefs in the powers of celestial bodies, as well as in shamanism. Theophylakt Simocatta mentions a "magician" or "priest" (possibly, a shaman) of the Avars named Bookolabras. A ninth-century inscription from Bulgaria mentions that Omurtag (for whom see chapter 8) made sacrifices to a god named Tengri, who appears also in the description of the religious beliefs of the Oghuz contained in ibn Fadlan's account of his travel to Volga Bulgharia: "When one of them objects to something wrong or (else) something happens to him, to which he does not agree, he raises his head to the heavens and says, '*bir tengri*,' which in Turkic means 'by one god,' for *bir* in Turkic is 'one' and *tengri* 'God,' in the language of the Turks."[2] A number of rectangular buildings found in Kalugerica, Madara, Pliska (all in northeastern Bulgaria), and Khumara (in the northern Caucasus region of Russia) have been interpreted as temples of a pre-Christian religion, possibly centered upon Tengri. Nothing is known about priests in pre-Christian Bulgaria, but Bulgar rulers exercised priestly and sacral authority. For example, Krum is said to have performed "demonic sacrifices" in front of Constantinople in 813; Omurtag, to have tried to convince a Byzantine captive of the divine power of the sun and moon. In his lengthy response to the question of Boris, Pope Nicholas I mentions local beliefs in "a certain stone":

> If someone took this stone for an illness, it would sometimes furnish healing for his body; but sometimes it would have no effect. Now why is it never certain what will happen to those taking this stone daily, so that some receive a remedy for the healing of their affliction, and others languish in their infirmity? Wherefore to your question, so to speak, of whether you ought to use it or do without it, we reply and decree that no one should be allowed to take that stone at all, and that [he] should disavow it in every way and [not] place the hope of all human salvation only in that stone.[3]

In fact, several Muslim authors of that time mention weather magic with special stones as a practice of the Uyghurs, Oghuz, or Turks.

Bulgars practiced both inhumation and cremation, and some cemeteries excavated in northeastern Bulgaria and dated to the ninth century, right before the conversion to Christianity, contain graves in both rites. Burials with horses are documented for the seventh to ninth centuries among the Avars, the Bulgars, and the Khazars.

Far less is known about the beliefs of the pagan Magyars. Shamanist cosmogony centered around a Tree of Life might be reflected in Magyar art. Shamanist beliefs typically imply the existence of a double soul: a body soul that disappears with the death of the body, expressed in Hungarian by the word *lélek*, derived from the verb "to breathe," and a shadow soul that can leave the body in dreams or after death, expressed by the Hungarian word *is* or *iz*, related to similar vocabulary in Finno-Ugric languages. The circular depression at the top of the skull of some skeletons found in tenth-century cemeteries (a so-called symbolic trepanation) is believed to have helped the shadow soul return to the body. Mortuary masks made of silver sheets with holes cut for the eyes are known both from eastern Russia and from Hungary and were presumably meant to keep the shadow

2 Curta, ed., "Ibn Fadlan on the Oghuz," in *Medieval Eastern Europe*, 49.

3 Curta, ed., "Pope Nicholas I Answers the Questions of Boris of Bulgaria," in *Medieval Eastern Europe*, 44.

soul inside and protect it from evil spirits. A tenth-century source narrating the siege of Cambrai mentions the importance that the Magyars placed on bringing back the head of their dead, presumably because that was where the shadow soul resided.

"Magicians, seers, and diviners" are mentioned in the *Legend of Saint Gerard* as being active at the court of Janus, son of Vata, an eleventh-century pagan chieftain. It has long been assumed that the Hungarian *táltos* was a shaman in Eurasian tradition. There is no medieval evidence, however, of a *táltos* connecting through trance to the world of the spirits. Judging by the legislation of the Hungarian kings, from Stephen I to Ladislas I, pagan practices persisted long after Christianization. There were witches in eleventh-century Hungary, and the royal law codes prescribe flogging as punishment for divination. Some people still made offerings "in pagan fashion" near wells, trees, springs, and stones.

FURTHER READING

Álvarez-Pedrosa, Juan Antonio. *Sources of Slavic Pre-Christian Religion*. Numen 169. Leiden: Brill, 2021.

Chobanov, Todor. "Medieval Temples of a Pre-Christian Religion and Their Priests." In *Von den Hunnen zu den Türken – Reiterkrieger in Europa und Zentralasien: Internationale Konferenz am Römisch-Germanischen Zentralmuseum – Leibniz Forschungsinstitut für Archäologie in Kooperation mit dem Institut für Mittelalterforschung der Österreichischen Akademie der Wissenschaften und dem Landesmuseum für Vorgeschichte Halle. Mainz, 25.-26. April 2018*, edited by Falko Daim, Harald Meller, and Walter Pohl, 247–70. Halle: Landesdenkmalamt für Denkmalpflege und Archäologie Sachsen-Anhalt, 2021.

Csiky, Gergely. "The Religion of Steppe Nomads." In *Saint Martin and Pannonia: Christianity on the Frontiers of the Roman World*, edited by Endre Tóth, Tivadar Vida, and Imre Takács, 152–60. Pannonhalma: Abbey Museum, 2016.

Kajkowski, Kamil. "Idols of the Western Slavs in the Early Medieval Period: The Example of Pomerania (Northern Poland)." In *New Researches on the Religion and Mythology of the Pagan Slavs*, edited by Patrice Lajoye, 47–67. Lisieux: Lingva, 2019.

Kalik, Judith, and Alexander Uchitel. *Slavic Gods and Heroes*. New York: Routledge, 2019.

Lang, Valter. "Riding to the Afterworld: Burying with Horses and Riding Equipment in Estonia and the Baltic Rim." In *Identity Formation and Diversity in the Early Medieval Baltic and Beyond*, edited by Johan Callmer, Ingrid Gustin, and Mats Roslund, 48–75. The Northern World 75. Leiden: Brill, 2017.

Rosik, Stanisław. *The Slavic Religion in the Light of 11th- and 12th-Century German Chronicles (Thietmar of Merseburg, Adam of Bremen, Helmold of Bosau): Studies on the Christian Interpretation of Pre-Christian Cults and Beliefs in the Middle Ages*. East Central and Eastern Europe in the Middle Ages, 450–1450, 60. Leiden: Brill, 2020.

Słupecki, Leszek Paweł. "The Temple in Rethra-Riedegost: West Slavic Pagan Rituals as Described at the Beginning of Eleventh Century." In *Old Norse Religion in Long-Term Perspective: Origins, Changes, and Interactions. An International Conference in Lund, Sweden, June 3–7, 2004*, edited by Anders Andrén, Kristina Jennbert, and Catharina Raudvere, 224–28. Vägar till Midgård 8. Lund: Nordic Academic Press, 2006.

35

JEWS, ARMENIANS, AND MUSLIMS

Keywords in this chapter: genizah, *hamlatsa*, Athinganoi, Mardaites, *hadiths*

Jewish presence in the eastern part of Europe can be traced back to Roman times. There were Jewish communities in Philippi, Thessalonica, Beroia, Athens, and Corinth, all mentioned in the *Acts of the Apostles*. While no synagogue was found in Corinth, its existence is documented by an inscription. By contrast, synagogues have been discovered by archaeologists in Thessalonica and in Philippopolis (now Plovdiv), the latter built in the third century, destroyed in the middle of that century, and rebuilt in the early fourth century. An inscription found in Thessalonica and dated to the fourth or sixth century contains a dedicatory text for a Samaritan synagogue. The inscription, written in both Greek and Samaritan Hebrew, mentions Neapolis (now Nablus, in Palestine) as the sacred center of the Samaritans. Another synagogue existed in the fourth century in Chersonesus (Crimea) and remained in operation until the late fifth century, when it was turned into a church. Several graffiti on plaster from the building's walls bear inscriptions in Hebrew, one of which mentions Jerusalem. Another inscription from Kerch (eastern Crimea) mentions the local governor building a Jewish prayer house for the local community. No information exists to date about conflicts between Jews and Christians in Late Antiquity, either in the Balkans or in the Crimea.

There were still Jews in the Balkans during the sixth century, for a Midrashic homilist (the author of a sermon based on the interpretation of the Hebrew Bible) complains about the havoc brought to Jewish communities by Berbers (in Africa) and Antes (in the Balkans). However, no evidence exists that any of the Jewish communities in the Balkans survived into the Early Middle Ages. Even in Thessalonica, any trace of Jews disappears after ca. 600. The same is true for the Jewish community in Chersonesus. However, in the ninth century, the Jewish community in that city had its own leader named Zoilus, who dealt directly with the deputy of the Khazar khagan. Writing in the early ninth century, the Byzantine author Theophanes Confessor knew that there were Jews in Phanagoria (on the eastern side of the Strait of Kerch, near present-day Sennoi in the Krasnodar district of Russia).[1] More than sixty tombstones are known from that site, each decorated with a menorah (seven-branch candelabrum). Some may be dated to the fourth and fifth centuries; others are later, perhaps as late as the eighth or ninth century. More tombstones have recently been found not far from Phanagoria, on the Taman Peninsula, near a rural settlement. In one of the graves from the associated cemetery, the pit was lined up with stones bonded with clay. One of the stones on the eastern side was a slab marked with a menorah. On his way to the Khazar capital in Itil, in 860, Constantine (St. Cyril) stopped in Cherson, where he learned Hebrew, presumably from local Jews. He also obtained books in Hebrew from a local Samaritan. At about the same time, Constantine's patron, Patriarch Photius, wrote a letter to the archbishop of Bosporus (Kerch) to congratulate him for having converted the local Jews to Christianity. The presence of Jewish communities on the northern shore of the Black Sea may have been instrumental in the conversion of the Khazar elite to Judaism (see chapter 14), although some sources give credit for that to a population of Jews coming from Armenia.

A document written on parchment in Hebrew and found in the genizah (repository for sacred manuscripts and ritual objects) of the synagogue in Cairo (Egypt) is an endorsement letter (*hamlatsa*) for a member of the Jewish community in a city believed to be Kiev. The man in question, named Jacob b. Hanukka, is described as generous and of good family. The "Kiev letter" encourages Jacob to raise funds from different Jewish communities in the German lands in order to redeem himself from non-Jewish creditors. The letter has nine signatures of witnesses, one of whom has a Slavic name (Gostiata) and bears the dignity of *cohen* (priest). An inscription in runes was added by a different hand, perhaps a Khazar official. Written in a Turkic language, this was a permit for Jacob to cross lands under Khazar rule. The letter may therefore be dated to the early 960s at the latest. If a Jewish community existed in Kiev at that time, it is not mentioned at all in the subsequent centuries. Another letter from the Cairo Genizah, perhaps of an eleventh-century date, mentions a Jew from Rus' who hoped to reach the land of Israel. The letter comes from the Jewish community in Thessaloniki and requests financial assistance for the man from other Jewish communities. The Jew from Rus' is said to be ignorant of Hebrew and able to speak only Slavic.

In the Balkans, the earliest mention of medieval Jewish communities appears in the *Life of St. Nikon*, written in the early eleventh century. According to its unknown author, when St. Nikon arrived in Sparta, ca. 970, he requested that the Jews be expelled in exchange for his working to take the plague out of town. A local aristocrat named John Aratos opposed him and brought a Jew back, apparently for his own interest, for the man knew how to finish garments. This is an indication that at least some members of the Jewish communities in the Balkans were already involved in the textile industry. The status of the Jew in relation to John Aratos may not have been very different from that of fifteen

1 Florin Curta, ed., "Theophanes on the Bulgar Migration," in *Medieval Eastern Europe, 500–1300: A Reader* (Toronto: University of Toronto Press, 2024), 15.

Jewish families on the island of Chios, who, according to an imperial charter of 1049, were dependents of the local monastery of Nea Mone. The Jews of Chios were most likely refugees from Fatimid Egypt. They were not the only population group that moved to Southeastern Europe in the Early Middle Ages. Many others came as willing immigrants, while others were settled more or less by force.

According to Armenian sources, Emperor Maurice (582–602) intended to settle 30,000 Armenians in Thrace, before being overthrown by Phocas. Both Armenians and Syrians were settled in Thrace after the first major victories that Emperor Constantine V (741–75) obtained against the Arabs in the mid-eighth century. More Syrians of Jacobite faith (Syrian Christians who did not agree with the decisions of the fourth Ecumenical Council in Chalcedon) were moved to Thrace in 778, under Constantine V's son, Leo IV (775–80). According to the *Chronicle of Monemvasia*, written in 900 or 901, following his campaign against the Slavs of the Peloponnese, a Byzantine general who was "native of Lesser Armenia [the territory of historic Armenia located to the west and northwest from the Euphrates River] and from the family of the so-called Skleroi [prominent family of the Byzantine military aristocracy in the ninth century]" made room for settlers from other parts of the empire to come to Greece, with Armenians among them.[2] The victorious general was most likely Leo Skleros, who became *strategos* of Peloponnesos in 811.

The admission of Armenians, especially noblemen, into the Byzantine army intensified during the Macedonian dynasty, itself of Armenian origin, and especially from the early tenth century onwards, as attested by the evidence of seals. More Armenians were transferred to Thrace under Basil II to fight against the Bulgarians of Emperor Samuel (see chapter 13). Like Leo Skleros before him, one of the generals of the Armenian troops in Byzantine service, a man named Thedorakanos, became governor of Philippopolis (modern Plovdiv, in Bulgaria) in 1000 and 1001. The name of Peter I Getadarz, the Armenian *catholicos* ("patriarch") between 1019 and 1058, appears in a graffito from a cave near Drama (northeastern Greece). It may have been scribbled by a fellow Armenian established in the region after Basil II's conquest of Bulgaria. In the Byzantine sources, the Armenians of Thrace are often mentioned together with, and commonly mistaken for, heretics such as Manichaeans and Paulicians. Following the Byzantine expeditions against them, Paulician heretics from Armenia were forcefully moved to Thrace during the first half of the eighth century, with many more settling in the environs of Philippopolis under Emperor John Tzimiskes (969–76), who was himself of Armenian origin. Under Emperor Michael I (811–13), the Athinganoi, adherents of a sect that stressed purity but indulged in astrological and magical pursuits, were removed from their abodes in Phrygia and Lycaonia (the central parts of present-day Turkey) and settled on the island of Aegina (off the coast, south of Athens) in Greece. At about the same time, if not earlier, 12,000 Mardaites, a Christian population of northern Syria, were moved to the Peloponnese and the island of Corfu (Kerkyra, off the western coast of Greece). They were to serve as reinforcements for the

2 Curta, ed., "The Resettlement of the Peloponnese," in *Medieval Eastern Europe*, 78.

local naval forces because of their excellent reputation as sailors. In 880, they were indeed recruited for the Byzantine fleet operating on the western coast of the Peloponnese against Arab pirates from Africa.

The earliest Muslims of Eastern Europe are those of Volga Bulgharia. Ibn Rusta, who wrote in 912, knew that they had timber mosques, while several other sources in Arabic mention the Bulghars as devoted Muslims. Ibn Fadlan, who visited Volga Bulgharia in 922, knew that a clan named Baranjar had a timber mosque (see chapter 15). However, according to him, the members of the clan "did not know how to recite the Quran [while praying]," so he had to teach them that.[3] The only mosques known archaeologically from early medieval Eastern Europe are indeed those excavated in several towns of Volga Bulgharia (Bolgar, Biliar, and Kazan'), but next to nothing is known about the ritual practices of the local Muslims between the tenth and the fourteenth centuries. According to ibn Fadlan, the northerly location of Volga Bulgharia posed some problems for religious practice. The days were shorter in winter, and that made it difficult to have five daily prayers as required by Islamic practice. Nor was it possible to keep the fast properly during the holy month of Ramadan. Because they adopted Islam from Central Asia (most likely from Khwarazm), the Volga Bulghars followed the Hanafi school of jurisprudence, which is the most flexible and liberal in Islamic law, particularly in matters of criminal and property law, individual freedoms, the treatment of non-Muslims, as well as marriage and guardianship. Because of that, ibn Fadlan, who was most likely an adherent of the Shafi'i school of religious law, was critical of the practices of the Bulghar Muslims. When the *hutba* (the Friday sermon) was proclaimed incorrectly from the *minbar*, ibn Fadlan explained to the ruler of Bulghars that "even the Prophet (may God bless and cherish him!) said, 'Do not exaggerate my status as the Christians have done with Jesus, the son of Mary. Verily, I am only a servant of Allah and His Messenger' [*hadith* in Shahih al-Bukhari 3345]." The rigorist approach adopted by the Arab envoy results from his reliance on the *hadiths* as primary sources of law and the simultaneous rejection of local traditions. The implication is that the religious practices of the Bulghar Muslims were different from his own. Even though the Bulghars produced their own literature, which is mentioned in various sources, nothing survives, so it is impossible to describe the life of Muslims in early medieval Eastern Europe in any detail.

FURTHER READINGS

Kulik, Aleksandr. "The Jews of Slavia Graeca: The Northern Frontier of Byzantine Jewry?" In *Jews of Byzantium: Dialectics of Minority and Majority Cultures*, edited by Robert Bonfil, Oded Irshai, Guy G. Stroumsa, and Rina Talgam, 297–314. Jerusalem Studies in Religion and Culture 14. Leiden: Brill, 2012.

3 Curta, ed., "The Conversion of the Volga Bulghars to Islam," in *Medieval Eastern Europe*, 41.

Oikonomides, Nicholas. "The Jews of Chios (1049): A Group of *Excusati*." *Mediterranean Historical Review* 10, no. 1–2 (1995): 218–25.

Ovadiah, Asher. "Ancient Jewish Communities in Macedonia, Thrace and Upper Epirus." *Gerión* 33 (2015): 211–27.

Papathanassiou, Evangelos. "The Armenian Presence in and around the Rhodope Mountain in 11th C.: Rethinking over Some New Archaeological Finds." *Peri Thrakes* 7 (2010–2015): 59–97.

Zimonyi, István. "Islam and Medieval Eastern Europe." In *Proceedings of the Ninth Conference of the European Society for Central Asian Studies*, edited by Tomasz Gacek and Jadwiga Pstrusińska, 420–27. Cambridge: Cambridge Scholars Publishing, 2009.

Zuckerman, Constantin. "On the Kievan Letter from the Genizah of Cairo." *Ruthenica* 10 (2011): 7–56.

36

RELIGIOUS PRACTICES, POPULAR RELIGION, AND HERESY

Keywords in this chapter: amulet, heresy, dualism, liturgy

Procopius of Caesarea claims that in the mid-sixth century the Slavs sacrificed cattle "and all other victims" to their god, "the maker of lightning, who is alone lord of all things" (see chapter 34). They also made sacrifices to that god if escaping death or sickness, or when victorious in war. Sacrifices were also made to "rivers and nymphs and some other spirits."[1] However, Procopius never visited the Slavs. If his informants were mercenaries in the Roman armies in Italy (where Procopius may have met them, as he was the secretary of their general, Belisarius), he clearly adapted the information to the expectations of his audience. Indeed, both the idea that the god of the Slavs was "the maker of lightning" and the mention of cattle as the sacrificial animals remind one of Zeus and religious practices of ancient Greece. Similarly, in his *Chronicle of the Czechs*, written in the early twelfth century, Cosmas of Prague claimed that before their conversion to Christianity, the Czechs worshipped Jupiter, Venus, and Mars, for his audience may have been more familiar with Roman than with local gods, if anybody still remembered the latter's names.

Pope Nicholas I (858–67) wrote a lengthy response to a letter from Boris, the ruler of Bulgaria, in which he referred to Bulgars as commonly performing incantations, jests, verses, and prophecies before battle. He also mentioned "a certain stone in your land," which could cure some, but not others, upon touching it.[2] Both practices were condemned. Similarly, when dealing with the religious practices of their Slavic neighbors to the east, tenth-to-twelfth-century German chroniclers did not hesitate to provide details about the

1 Florin Curta, ed., "Procopius on the Slavs," in *Medieval Eastern Europe, 500–1300: A Reader* (Toronto: University of Toronto Press, 2024), 3.
2 Curta, ed., "Pope Nicholas I Answers the Questions," in *Medieval Eastern Europe*, 44.

pagan beliefs of those responsible for the insurrection of 983 (see chapter 19). According to Thietmar of Merseburg, who wrote during the second decade of the eleventh century, there was a fort in the land of the Redarians (who were part of the confederation of Liuticians after 983), called Riedegost. The fort was surrounded by a large forest, which was believed by locals to be holy. Inside it was a timber building, the walls of which were adorned with images of gods and goddesses. Inside the building were their statues, foremost among them being that of Zuarasici (Svarožic). The temple had priests whose job was to dig into the ground, while shaking and murmuring (probably incantations) as they cast lots to predict the future. The Liuticians sacrificed both humans and animals to Svarožic and other gods. There were temples in other places as well, each with statues of specific gods. In the twelfth century, Helmold of Bosau knew the names of some of them: Prove, the main god in the "Oldenburg [Starigard] land," Siva, the goddess of the Slavs on the banks of the river Elbe, and Radigast, the god of the Abodrites (see chapter 34).

Archaeology cannot confirm any of those stories, whether the cattle sacrificed to the "maker of lightning" mentioned by Procopius or the fort of Riedegost. Moreover, most remains of buildings and sculptures that have been found through archaeological excavations and interpreted in association with the pre-Christian beliefs (especially in the region between the Elbe and the Oder, now in eastern Germany) provide no information about the actual religious practices. Conversely, the archaeological remains of such practices cannot be explained in the absence of written information. For example, small clay vessels were placed in the walls of clay ovens inside sunken-floored buildings, such as found in the ninth-century stronghold at Shestovytsia (near Chernihiv, in Ukraine). The very clay out of which the oven was made was mixed with seeds of rye, as in the early medieval stronghold in Poltava (Ukraine). The exact meaning of such presumably ritual practices remains unknown.

The conversion to Christianity did not dislodge pre-Christian practices, as many of them survived in altered forms or with a different meaning. Cosmas of Prague praised Břetislav II of Bohemia (1092–1100) for eradicating "half-pagan" customs, such as offerings and sacrifices next to holy springs, burial in forests, plays at crossroads, the wearing of masks at certain ceremonies, or jests over the dead. However, as late as the twelfth century, some people in Bohemia were still buried in prehistoric mounds that were probably regarded as the tombs of (pre-Christian) ancestors. Such a mixture of beliefs may be best described as "popular religion" and often encompassed magical behavior. When he came to Argos in 968 or 969, St. Nikon Metanoiete visited the house of a man who, together with his daughter, was suffering from the wiles and spells of a sorcerer. Nikon's remedy was to find the very spot where the sorcerer had buried his spell – images or objects fashioned in the likeness of his victims – near the roots of a tree on the very property of those people. Those who could not afford to hire holy men against black magic had to make do with finger-ring amulets carrying images and inscriptions to ward off the evil eye. Prayers against evil spirits were written on lead amulets, such as found in Bulgaria and dated to the tenth and eleventh centuries.

To popular religion may also be attributed beliefs about the devil with no basis in the Bible. In a collection of themes concerning the Old and the New Testament, as well as the organization of the church, which was compiled in Bulgaria in the eleventh or twelfth century under the title *Razumnik* ("clever," "smart"), the topic was approached by means of questions and answers:

Q: How did God make the devil?
A: When God made heaven and earth, God saw his shadow in the waters and said: come out, brother, and be with me. And it came out like a man and God gave it the name Samael.
Q: How did it fall from God?
A: When God was planting Paradise, and commanded it to be planted, Samael kept stealing everything. Then he went out, secretly, and heaped it all at another place. The Lord said: You steal from me; you are banished![3]

The somewhat elevated position of the devil in such stories about the creation of the world comes very close to the heretical views condemned by a priest named Cosmas, who wrote a *Sermon Against the Bogomils* in the 960s or 970s: "Because of their ignorance some call him a fallen angel; others count him as a venial manager. Nonetheless, they [the heretics] esteem him so much as to name him the creator of God's creatures, and God's glory is for them Satan's glory."[4] That Cosmas insisted upon ignorance is particularly interesting, for a few decades before him, in his *Instructions to Bishops and Priests*, St. Clement of Ohrid explained heresy as the direct result of the ignorance of bishops and priests.

The only heresy of the eastern part of Europe before 1300, Bogomilism is known primarily from Cosmas's sermon. He is the only source to mention that the founder of the heresy was a priest named Bogomil, who lived in Bulgaria during the reign of Emperor Peter (927–69). That emperor received in ca. 940 a letter from Patriarch Theophylact of Constantinople (933–56), which pointed to dualism (belief in two gods) as the basic tenet of Bogomil beliefs, although that heresy is not explicitly mentioned as such. Like other dualist sects, particularly the Manichaeans and Paulicians, Bogomils believed that God had two sons – Christ and Satan, both being entirely spiritual beings. Satan rebelled against his father and created matter. He was therefore the creator of the world and everything on it, including humans. He may have received assistance from his father, whom Satan tricked to create life, either by having God breathing on the clay or by imprisoning a captured angel into the clay. Since they believed that Satan, not God, was the creator, the Bogomils rejected the Old Testament. In their view, Christ was sent by God on earth with a message for the imprisoned human souls, to explain to them how to escape from matter and how

3 Curta, ed., "Razumnik, a Study Guide," in *Medieval Eastern Europe*, 212.

4 Curta, ed., "The Bogomils," in *Medieval Eastern Europe*, 178.

to return to the spiritual kingdom. Given that Christ was a purely spiritual being, the Bogomils denied all his earthly experiences, such as Incarnation, Passion, or Crucifixion. The Gospels were regarded as containing a (secret) message about how to escape the material world. Christ, according to the Bogomils, taught abstinence from sexual intercourse because sexual reproduction perpetuated the prison of the soul: instead of joining Christ in the spiritual kingdom, the soul was reborn in an earthly body. Moreover, Christ taught humans to avoid contact with anything born from sexual intercourse: their diet was to be exclusively vegetarian. Besides ascetic life, Christ also encouraged humans to practice only spiritual sacraments.

The Bogomils therefore rejected baptism and any material objects of cult (such as crosses, icons, or church buildings). They also rejected the hierarchy of the church and regarded priests in general as sinful. According to Cosmas, the Bogomils opposed the social order: they "slander the rich and teach theirs not to obey their lords; they hate the emperor and disparage the elders; they think that all who work for the emperor are hateful in the eyes of God and order all servants to stop working for their masters."[5] Bogomil teachers did no manual work, but just went preaching from one house to the other. The regular believers hid their beliefs and passed for regular Christians, living normal lives and receiving a spiritual initiation on their deathbeds from the teachers.

The fact that Bogomilism was popular enough in tenth-century Bulgaria to become a threat may be regarded as indirect proof of the success of that country's evangelization. The contrast between the old and the new worldviews resulting from the conversion was expressed through heresy, but within the general framework of Christianity. Indeed, "many [heretics] do not even know what kind of heresy is theirs, and think that they are suffering for the truth and God will reward them for the chains and the jail."[6] This suggests persecution, but little is known about how Emperor Peter, who first contacted the patriarch of Constantinople for advice, ultimately dealt with the heretics. Patriarch Theophylact recommended very harsh measures against them: their punishment was death. However, it remains unknown whether those measures were ever implemented in Bulgaria. The use of violence for the reinforcement of religious practices is nonetheless attested in late tenth-century Poland. According to Thietmar of Merseburg, under Bolesław Chrobry, those who consumed meat during Lent had their teeth knocked out, with even greater threats against adulterers – death or castration. Under King Stephen of Hungary, those of lesser rank who disturbed the mass by talking during the service and not paying attention were to be bound in the vestibule of the church and beaten, with their hair shaved off. Duke Břetislav I of Bohemia (1034–55) was equally firm on the matter, although he preferred confiscation and fines to physical punishment: "He who is found doing servile work on a Sunday or on feast days that have been designated for public celebration in the

5 Curta, ed., "The Bogomils," in *Medieval Eastern Europe*, 178.

6 Curta, ed., "The Bogomils," in *Medieval Eastern Europe*, 177.

church, the fruits of his labor and the team of beasts found working shall be taken away by the archpriest and three hundred coins paid to the duke's treasury."[7]

It is nonetheless difficult, if not impossible, to gauge the sincerity and depth of religious feelings among Christians after conversion. Beyond conformity with social expectations or with royal decrees, there is very little evidence to explore the way in which salvation was perceived and understood in East Central, Southeastern, or Eastern Europe in the Early Middle Ages. Collections of sermons survive from Bulgaria, but there is no way to tell what impact, if any, they had on the congregations in front of which they were delivered.

The main source for understanding liturgical practices are the liturgical books. While already in Moravia, Constantine (St. Cyril) is said to have translated into Old Church Slavonic "the Matins and the Hours, Vespers and the Compline, and the Liturgy."[8] An eleventh-century manuscript discovered in 1975 in the library of the Monastery of Saint Catherine in Sinai shows that the text translated by Constantine was a combination of the sung liturgy in use in the ninth century in the church of Constantinople and the Jerusalem rite most typical for the monastic practice in Palestine. To that, Constantine added several Latin prayers to accommodate the needs of those who had been converted by missionaries from Bavaria (see chapter 7). In fact, the earliest Old Church Slavonic manuscript, the so-called Kiev Fragments (called so because they are kept in the library of the Ukrainian Academy of Sciences in Kiev), dated to the late tenth century, contains a translation of a Latin sacramentary (service book) to be used for traveling and missionary purposes. The liturgy celebrated in Slavonic was formally approved by Pope Hadrian II (867–72) but condemned by Pope Stephen V (885–91).

There is comparatively less information about liturgical practices in other parts of East Central, Southeastern, or Eastern Europe, as no liturgical books have survived from tenth-century Bulgaria and Croatia, or from early eleventh-century Poland, Hungary, or Rus'. When the metropolitan of Corinth, on his way to Constantinople, paid a visit to St. Luke the Younger on Mount Ioannitza (near Delphi, in central Greece) in 927, the hermit asked him for advice on how to take communion in the absence of a priest. The metropolitan explained that St. Luke could use eucharistic bread previously sanctified somewhere else by an ordained priest. He also advised him to use ordinary instead of eucharistic wine, and to sing "the psalms of the *typika* (offices) or the Trisagion (Thrice Holy Prayer) along with the Creed," instead of the Communion hymn.[9] At about the same time in Bohemia, Duke Wenceslas (who died in 935) was taking things into his own hands. According to Gumpold of Mantua, who wrote Wenceslas's biography sixty years later, the duke went out in secret during the night to harvest wheat, which he then threshed, sifted, and milled to make flour for the eucharistic bread. He worked that bread with his own hands using unleavened dough. He also squashed grapes in a jar and strained the

7 Curta, ed., "The Decrees of Břetislav," in *Medieval Eastern Europe*, 129.

8 Curta, ed., "Saint Cyril, Old Church Slavonic, and the Creation of the Glagolitic Alphabet," in *Medieval Eastern Europe*, 32.

9 Curta, ed. "Instruction in Liturgical Practices," in *Medieval Eastern Europe*, 182.

liquid through a linen cloth to obtain eucharistic wine. That is the closest one can come to the description of liturgical practices in Southeastern and East Central Europe during the Early Middle Ages.

FURTHER READING

Álvarez-Pedrosa, Juan Antonio. *Sources of Slavic Pre-Christian Religion*. Numen 169. Leiden: Brill, 2021.

Kalik, Judith, and Alexander Uchitel. *Slavic Gods and Heroes*. New York: Routledge, 2018.

Marinow, Kirił, and Jan M. Wolski. "Heresy and Popular Religion." In *The Routledge Handbook of East Central and Eastern Europe in the Middle Ages, 500–1300*, edited by Florin Curta, 354–73. Abingdon: Routledge, 2022.

Michałowski, Roman. "The Nine-Week Lent in Boleslaus the Brave's Poland: A Study of the First Piasts' Religious Policy." *Acta Poloniae Historica* 89, no. 1 (2004): 5–50.

Rosik, Stanisław. *The Slavic Religion in the Light of 11th- and 12th-Century German Chronicles (Thietmar of Merseburg, Adam of Bremen, Helmold of Bosau): Studies on the Christian Interpretation of Pre-Christian Cults and Beliefs in the Middle Ages*. East Central and Eastern Europe in the Middle Ages, 450–1450, 600. Leiden: Brill, 2020.

37

ECCLESIASTICAL ORGANIZATION AND MONASTICISM

Keywords in this chapter: bishopric, archbishopric, metropolis, monastery, cenobitism

The establishment of the dioceses with precise boundaries was a major component of the process of Christianization in those parts of Central, Southeastern, and Eastern Europe that were under Roman rule in Late Antiquity. More than twenty episcopal sees are known on the northern frontier of the empire before 400. Of those, only a third remained in use in the sixth century. The creation of an archbishopric in the central Balkans at Iustiniana Prima (now Caričin Grad, near Lebane, in Serbia) brought about a regrouping of jurisdictions and the implementation of new hierarchical structures. The archbishop of Iustiniana Prima was expected to extend his authority over the entire western half of the Balkan Peninsula, as well as over territories beyond the northern frontier of the empire.

Most Roman cities in the central and southern Balkans were episcopal sees as well – Thessalonica, Salona, Serdica, Iustiniana Prima, Nikopolis, Athens, and Corinth (see map 37.1). However, there were also bishops in much smaller towns, where archaeological excavations have revealed large basilicas that served as cathedrals. For example, the large, three-aisled basilica discovered at Plaošnik in Ohrid (Republic of North Macedonia) was most likely the cathedral of the bishop of Lychnidos, who appears in the written sources in the early sixth century. The *cathedra* (bishop's throne) is preserved to this day in the basilica of Bishop Euphrasius, now the Cathedral of the Assumption of Mary in Poreč (Croatia). The *cathedra* is in the altar and has a mosaic behind it showing a gold cross on a hillock. Bishop Euphrasius is mentioned in an inscription carved into the altar table as consecrating the church in the mid-sixth century. Similarly, the donors most commonly acknowledged by mosaic inscriptions are local bishops, such as in Sandanski (Bulgaria), Nikopolis, Thebes, and Sparta (Greece).

Little is known about the exact boundaries of the sixth-century dioceses. Some were of a considerable size. For example, during the first half of the sixth century, Tomis (now

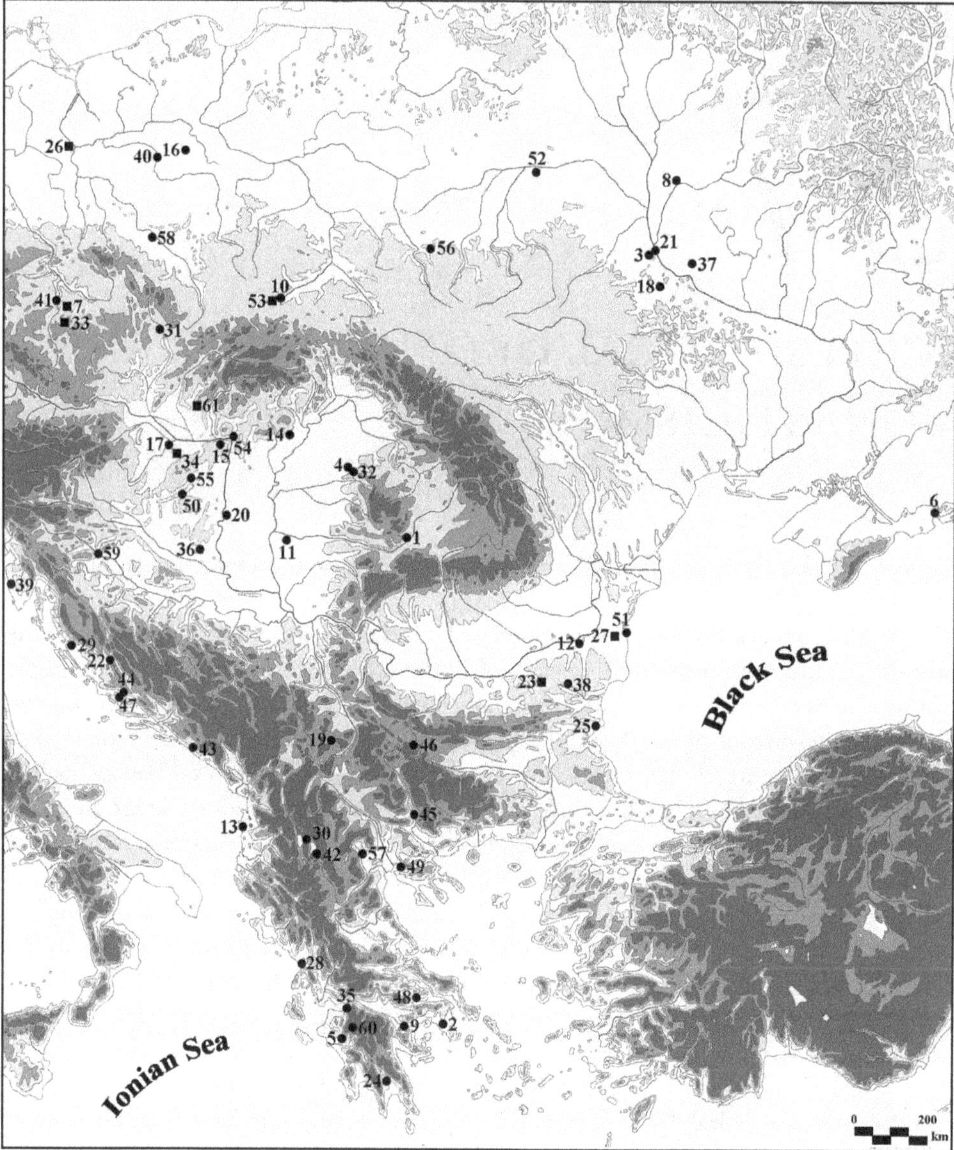

Map 37.1. Episcopal sees (circles) and monasteries (squares) in Eastern Europe, ca. 500 to ca. 1000. The location of the following sites is indicated: 1 – Alba Iulia; 2 – Athens; 3 – Belgorod; 4 – Bihar; 5 – Bolaina; 6 – Bosporus; 7 – Břevnov; 8 – Chernigov; 9 – Corinth; 10 – Cracow; 11 – Csanád; 12 – Dristra; 13 – Dyrrachion; 14 – Eger; 15 – Ezstergom; 16 – Gniezno; 17 – Győr; 18 – Iur'ev; 19 – Iustiniana Prima; 20 – Kalocsa; 21 – Kiev; 22 – Knin; 23 – Krepcha; 24 – Lakedaimon (Sparta); 25 – Mesembria; 26 – Międzyrzecz; 27 – Murfatlar; 28 – Nikopolis; 29 – Nin; 30 – Ohrid; 31 – Olomouc; 32 – Oradea; 33 – Ostrov; 34 – Pannonhalma; 35 – Patras; 36 – Pécs; 37 – Pereislavl'; 38 – Pliska; 39 – Poreč; 40 – Poznań; 41 – Prague; 42 – Prespa; 43 – Ragusa; 44 – Salona; 45 – Sandanski; 46 – Serdica (Sredec); 47 – Split; 48 – Thebes; 49 – Thessalonica (Thessaloniki); 50 – Tihany; 51 – Tomis; 52 – Turov; 53 – Tyniec; 54 – Vác; 55 – Veszprém; 56 – Vladimir-in-Volhynia; 57 – Vodena; 58 – Wrocław; 59 – Zagreb; 60 – Zemaina; 61 – Zobor.

Constanța, in Romania) was the seat of a metropolitan (archbishop) with jurisdiction over a vast area stretching from the Black Sea shore in present-day southeastern Romania and northeastern Bulgaria across that sea into the Crimean Peninsula as far to the northeast as Bosporus (now Kerch, Ukraine). Except for coastal cities, such as Mesembria (now Nesebăr, in Bulgaria), Thessaloniki, Athens, Corinth, Patras, Dyrrachion (now Durrës, in Albania), Ragusa (now Dubrovnik, in Croatia), and Zadar, none of the bishoprics in existence before ca. 620 continued into the Early Middle Ages. New bishoprics were established where none had existed in Late Antiquity. For example, the bishoprics of Bolaina (a suffragan of Patras) and Zemaina (a suffragan of Corinth), both in southern Greece, are mentioned in a list of bishoprics subject to the patriarch of Constantinople drafted in the early tenth century. Neither Bolaina (present-day Oleni, near Olympia), nor Zemaina (now Zemeno, near Corinth) existed in Late Antiquity. The oldest dedicatory inscription of medieval Greece is that found in Pallandion (Arkadia), which mentions that the Church of St. Christopher was consecrated on May 15, 903, by Nicholas, bishop of Lakedaimon.

Elsewhere in East Central and Southeastern Europe, the ecclesiastical organization served initially a small group of people, primarily rulers and the elites. The origin and early history of Nin are obscure, but a bishopric was established there in the late ninth century, most likely because of the rise of the Croatian dukes (see chapter 20). However, the bishop of Split (about 80 miles, or 130 kilometers, away from Nin) protested what he regarded as an infringement upon his diocese. The quarrel over diocesan boundaries between the bishops of Split and Nin was discussed at a synod (small gathering of local bishops) that took place in Split (Croatia) in 925, in the presence of papal legates. Through his envoys, Pope John X (914–28) gave his approval for the elevation of the bishop of Split to the rank of metropolitan (archbishop). Three years later (928), the bishopric of Nin was abolished, and the jurisdiction of the archbishop of Split extended over the entire kingdom of Croatia. In cases such as that, the establishment of dioceses depended upon the support of the ruler. Pope Hadrian II appointed Methodius as "bishop of the church in Pannonia" at the request of Kocel (see chapter 12). Moreover, in 880, Pope John VIII bestowed upon Methodius the title (and rank) of archbishop of the Moravian church, in response to Svatopluk's strong political position. The pope asked the Moravian ruler to send to Rome a candidate for the position of bishop of Nitra. Apparently, the ordination of bishops in Moravia was not the prerogative of Methodius as archbishop of Moravia, but of the pope.

When an archbishop was appointed for Bulgaria in 870, as head of an autocephalous church, his see was established in Pliska. One of his suffragans was based in Dristra (now Silistra, Bulgaria). Symeon (893–927) appointed St. Clement as bishop of Dragvista (or Velitsa), a see located on the middle course of the river Vardar, between Thessaloniki and Ohrid. Under Peter (927–69), the metropolitan of Bulgaria effectively became a patriarch. His see then moved first to Dristra, then to Sredec (Sofia), Vodena, and Prespa, and finally, in 992, to Ohrid, the capital of Samuel (see chapter 13). After the Byzantine reconquest, the patriarchate of Bulgaria turned into an autocephalous archbishopric based in Ohrid, with jurisdiction reaching far to the northern parts of the Balkan Peninsula.

Many monasteries came into existence in tenth-century Bulgaria as royal foundations. Others were established by Bulgarian noblemen in both Pliska and Preslav. Glagolitic and Cyrillic inscriptions from Krepcha (near Tărgovishte) and Murfatlar (near Constanța, Romania) are associated with a very different form of monasticism. Murfatlar was a community of anchorites, but hermits are attested also in western Bulgaria, the most famous of whom is St. John of Rila (see chapter 38). Rock-cut monasteries and hermitages dated between the tenth and the sixteenth centuries have been found in the Republic of North

Macedonia, Serbia, Bulgaria, southeastern Romania, the Republic of Moldova, eastern Ukraine, as well as in the Crimea and the Lower Don region of southern Russia. Hermits were already present in great numbers in Greece in the tenth century. St. Luke the Younger (see chapter 38) began his solitary life on Mount Ioannitza (near Delphi, central Greece). The hermits on Mount Athos developed at a very early stage a loose organization to deal with the ecclesiastical and civilian authorities. St. Athanasius introduced the cenobitic form of life in 959 on the basis of the rule (*typikon*) for the monastery of the Great Lavra of Mount Athos. Monks were to eat and pray together, do charity as a group, and welcome guests as a community. Even the end of the (Biblical) reading at meals is announced symbolically by a common gesture: "the sound of the spoons at the last serving when all together toss them in their dishes."[1] In spite of its name (which refers to a community of ascetics), the Great Lavra of St. Athanasius was much closer to the ideals of cenobitic life that were popular at that time in Constantinople, especially in the Monastery of St. John of Stoudios. When in 979 or 980, the Monastery of St. Clement was granted by Emperor Basil II as a base for a group of Georgian noblemen, Iviron became the Georgian monastery on Mount Athos, soon to be the richest of all monasteries there. At some point before 985, three other noblemen from Thrace established Vatopedi, which quickly became the second most important community after the Great Lavra. In the 980s, an Italian nobleman (the brother of Pandulf II, the Lombard duke of Benevento) established the monastery of the Amalfitans, soon followed by a Bulgarian foundation at Zographou. New monasteries were established after 1000 for the Rus' at St. Panteleimon's and for the Serbs at Hilandar. Before the mid-eleventh century, there were some 3,000 monks on Mount Athos, with 700 in the Great Lavra alone.

During the tenth century, cenobitic monasticism made its appearance in East Central Europe as well. The abbot of the Benedictine monastery of St. Chrysogonus in Zadar (Croatia) is first mentioned in 918, but the monastery had a new beginning in 986, when a monk from Monte Cassino (an abbey in central Italy established by St. Benedict in 529) was appointed abbot. The Benedictine abbey of St. Bartholomew was established in the tenth century on the Kapitul Hill near Knin. A third abbey came into being at St. Stephen Under the Pines in Split. The Benedictine monks came to Bohemia under Boleslav II (972–99). They established first the abbey at Břevnov (now a district on the western side of Prague), then that at Ostrov (south of Prague). Duke Boleslav, however, had no say in the creation of a bishopric of Prague (972), a decision taken by Emperor Otto I, who may have also been behind the creation of a second bishopric in Olomouc (Moravia). Both bishoprics were placed under the jurisdiction of the archbishop of Mainz, as compensation for losses inflicted through the creation of the archbishopric of Magdeburg in 968.

In Poland, the first bishopric was established in Poznań shortly after the baptism of Mieszko (see chapter 17), although it remains unclear whether the first bishop of Poznań

---

1 Florin Curta, ed., "Rule of the Lavra Monastery on Mount Athos," in *Medieval Eastern Europe, 500–1300: A Reader* (Toronto: University of Toronto Press, 2024), 194.

was a suffragan of the archbishop of Magdeburg or a "court bishop" subordinated directly to the pope. If the latter, the pope in question was John XV to whom Mieszko donated "an entire city called Schinesghe, with all that belongs to it."[2] Mieszko's son, Bolesław Chrobry (992–1025) invited two Italian hermits to Poland and they settled near Poznań at Międzyrzecz. During his visit to Gniezno in 1000, Emperor Otto III and Bolesław Chrobry decided to create the archbishopric of Gniezno. The first archbishop was Radim (Gaudentius), the brother of St. Adalbert (see chapter 38). The archbishop of Gniezno had four suffragans based in Poznań, Wrocław, Cracow, and Kołobrzeg. While the latter ceased to exist only a decade later, the archbishopric of Gniezno vanished for a few decades because of the social and political turbulence in the late 1030s. The ecclesiastical organization in Poland was restored under Bolesław II (1058–79), when Cracow was elevated to the rank of archbishopric. Despite the early beginning at Międzyrzecz, the earliest Benedictine abbey in Poland was established only in 1044 at Tyniec, near Cracow.

In both Poland and Rus', dioceses were very large, especially when compared to those in Italy and Greece, respectively. The area covered by the metropolis of Kiev created in the late tenth century was as large as that under the direct jurisdiction of the patriarch of Constantinople – about 541,000 square miles (or 1.4 million square kilometers). However, the two stood in sharp contrast – fifteen dioceses in Rus' and 750 in Byzantium. Before 1000, there were already ten metropolitan sees in Greece, with a great number of suffragan sees. By contrast, the only metropolitan in Rus' was that of Kiev, with only four suffragans based in Belgorod, Novgorod, Chernigov (now Chernihiv, Ukraine), and Polotsk (now Polatsk, Belarus). Two other bishoprics were established in Pereiaslavl' (now Pereiaslav, Ukraine) and Iur'ev (now Bila Tserkva, Ukraine) after 1036, with two more before the end of the century in Vladimir-in-Volhynia (now Volodymyr, Ukraine) and Turov (now Turau, Belarus). In the 1070s, the hermits in the vicinity of Kiev formed the cenobitic community of the Monastery of the Caves under Abbot Feodosii, who introduced the Stoudite principles to Rus' monasticism.

The ecclesiastical organization in Hungary came into being in three stages. Veszprém, Esztergom (as archbishoprics), and the bishoprics of Transylvania and Győr as suffragans, came into being shortly before and after the conversion to Christianity and the proclamation of Stephen as king, in 1000 (see chapter 18). The sees of Kalocsa, Pécs, and Eger were all established in 1009, followed by Csanád (now Cenad in Romania) in 1030, Vác between 1038 and 1041, and Bihar (now Biharea in Romania) between 1046 and 1060. King Ladislas I (1077–95) moved the see of Bihar to Oradea and that of Transylvania to Alba Iulia, while establishing a new bishopric in Zagreb, after the incorporation of Croatia into the Hungarian kingdom (see chapters 18 and 42). In early medieval Hungary, Benedictine houses were typically established by rulers, either Géza in the case of Pannonhalma (established in 996), or Andrew I in the case of Tihany (established in 1055). Royal patronage extended to monasteries of (possibly Greek) monks and nuns following the rule of St. Basil the

2 Curta, ed., "Dagome Iudex," in *Medieval Eastern Europe*, 113.

Great associated with eastern, not western, Christianity. Moreover, eremitic monasticism in Hungary began in the distinct tradition of Eastern Christianity. At some point during the reign of King Stephen (1001–38), a monk named Andrew (Zoerard) from the abbey of St. Hyppolitus in Zobor (near Nitra, in Slovakia) decided to withdraw from the cenobitic community. Together with a disciple named Benedict, he settled in a cave above the river Váh near present-day Trenčin (Slovakia). He "always observed the practice of fasting until he achieved great exhaustion of the body, but also fortification of the life of the spirit."[3] St. Andrew-Zoerard's ascetic practices were directly inspired by Syro-Palestinian hermits of the Late Antiquity.

FURTHER READING

Dincă, Adinel, and Mihai Kovács. "Latin Bishoprics in the 'Age of Iron' and the Diocese of Transylvania." In *Christianization in Early Medieval Transylvania: The Oldest Church in Transylvania and Its Interpretation*, edited by Daniela Marcu Istrate, Dan Ioan Mureşan, and Gabriel Tiberiu Rustoiu, 316–54. East Central and Eastern Europe in the Middle Ages, 450–1450, 83. Leiden: Brill, 2022.

Nikolov, Angel. "The Bulgarian Church in the 9th–10th Century." In *Autocéphalies: L'exercice de l'indépendance dans les Églises slaves orientales (IXe–XXIe siècle)*, edited by Marie-Hélène Blanchet, Frédéric Gabriel, and Laurent Tatarenko, 103–8. Collection de l'École française de Rome 572. Rome: École française de Rome, 2021.

Sikorski, Dariusz Andrzej. "Church Organization." In *The Routledge Handbook of East Central and Eastern Europe in the Middle Ages, 500–1300*, edited by Florin Curta, 316–37. Abingdon: Routledge, 2022.

Ware, Kallistos. "St. Athanasios the Athonite: Traditionalist or Innovator?" In *Mount Athos and Byzantine Monasticism: Papers from the Twenty-Eighth Spring Symposium of Byzantine Studies, Birmingham, March 1994*, edited by Anthony Bryer and Mary Cunningham, 4–16. Aldershot: Variorum, 1996.

3 Curta, ed., "A Hermit's Portrait: Saint Andrew-Zoerard," in *Medieval Eastern Europe*, 196.

38

SAINTS, RELICS, AND PILGRIMAGE

Keywords in this chapter: relics, translation, icons, miracles, martyrs

The cult of the saints was a fundamental component of Christian life in the sixth century. One of the most important saints from the Balkans was St. Demetrius. A native of Macedonia, he was martyred under Emperor Diocletian in Sirmium (now Sremska Mitrovica, in Serbia). During the fourth century, however, his cult moved to Thessalonica, although his remains most likely stayed in Sirmium (see map 38.1). In the absence of any relics, the visible cult center in Thessalonica was a silver-plated, timber *ciborium* (canopy-like structure), which stood in the middle of the church dedicated to St. Demetrius. Several miracles associated with St. Demetrius were used as material for sermons by the archbishop of Thessalonica, John (603–10), the author of the first book of the *Miracles of St. Demetrius*. Archbishop John shows the saint as working for the city, interceding on behalf of all its citizens in times of plague, famine, civil war, and war with external enemies. The second book of the collection was written by another, unknown author between seventy and eighty years later. Like Archbishop John, the anonymous author depicted St. Demetrius as defending his city against all enemies. However, unlike him, he showed St. Demetrius miraculously participating in battle. For example, St. Demetrius slapped in the face a dexterous Slavic craftsman who had built a siege tower, driving him out of his mind and thus causing the failure of a dangerous attack on the city walls. Three centuries later, however, the city was sacked by Muslims led by Leo of Tripoli (see chapter 21). According to John Kaminiates, the main source for the events of 904, St. Demetrius did not intervene like before, because of the terrible sins of the citizens of Thessaloniki. Shortly after the year 1000, the cult of St. Demetrius changed dramatically. In 1040, the Byzantine emperor Michael IV (1034–41) came to the shrine of St. Demetrius in Thessaloniki, hoping to obtain cure from an advanced illness, probably an acute form of epilepsy. What he wanted to obtain was myrrh, a sweet-smelling oil flowing from the *ciborium*. The appearance of that miraculous substance turned St. Demetrius into the "Myrrh-Streamer" venerated to this day, but it also transformed him from a warrior saint into a healer. Little is known

Map 38.1. Sites associated with the cult of the saints, ca. 500 to ca. 1000. Late antique or medieval place names are in italics.

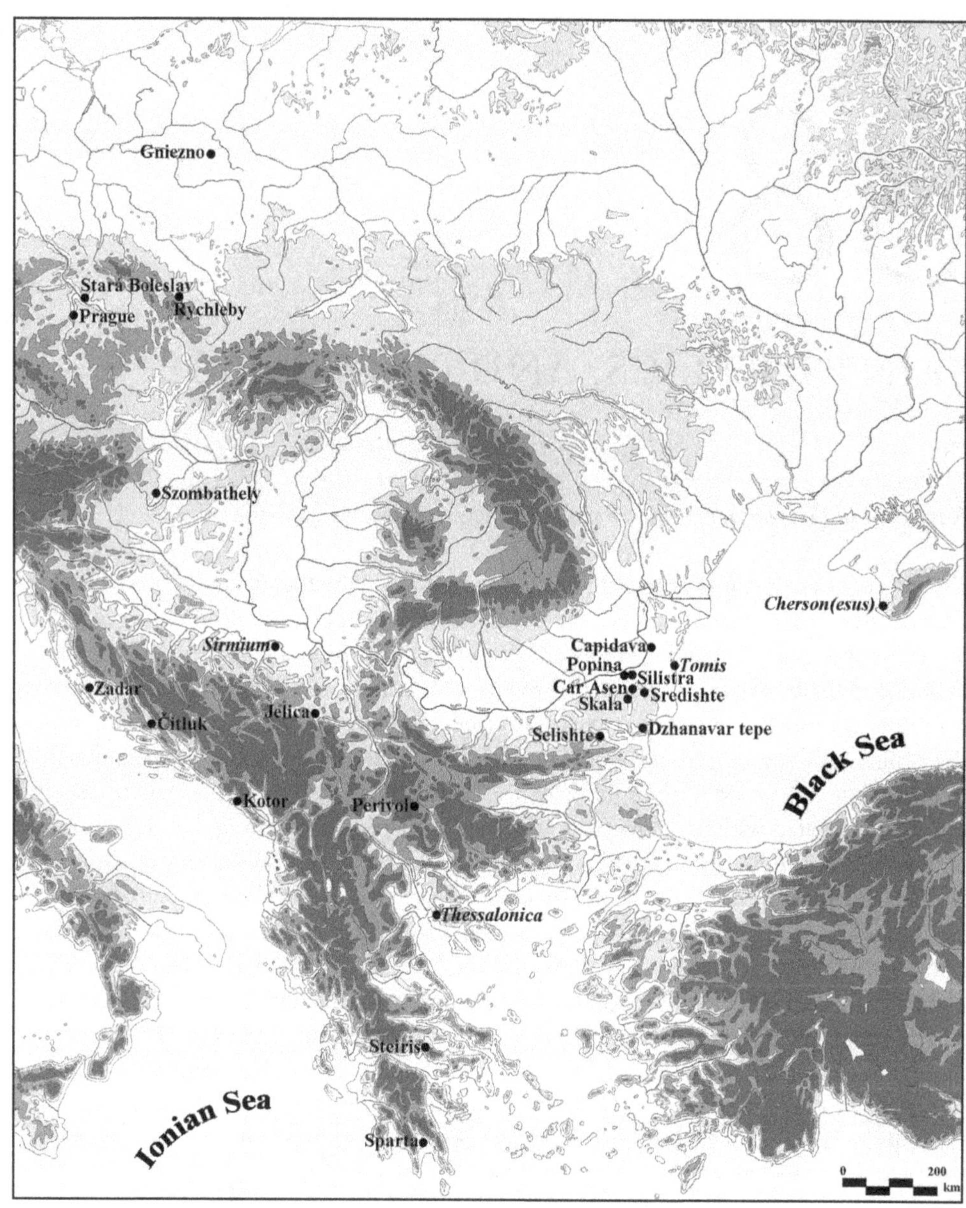

about how the feast day of St. Demetrius (October 26) was celebrated in the Early Middle Ages. In Chersonesus, a procession to the tomb of St. Clement (who had been exiled to the Crimea and was martyred there under Emperor Trajan) took place on his feast day (November 25), according to Theodosius, a pilgrim who in ca. 530 went all the way from Frankish Gaul to Jerusalem. At that time, the feast day of St. Martin of Tours (November

11) must have been celebrated in several churches in Dalmatia (the coastal region of present-day Croatia), dedicated to him. The cult of that saint was most likely introduced from Ravenna as part of the anti-Arian agenda of the war that Justinian's armies waged against the Ostrogoths in Italy.

Several other saints were venerated during the sixth century, as indicated by reliquaries. Such containers for relics were typically placed into recesses under the altar tables in the apses of churches. Some were made of gold and richly decorated with gemstones, like that found at Dzhanavar tepe, near Varna (Bulgaria). Others were of silver, like that discovered at Jelica (near Čačak, Serbia), bearing the names of Sts. Peter, Paul, and John. There may have been relics of those saints in that silver box, much like in that found in Chersonesus (Sevastopil', Crimea), which was decorated with the portrait of Christ between Sts. Peter and Paul. The inscription on a ceramic reliquary found in Perivol (near Kiustendil, Bulgaria) indicates that the relics therein were of the Apostle Thomas and of St. Babylas (bishop of Antioch under Emperor Decius, 201–51), as well as of the three children martyred together with the latter. Other saints were venerated without any relics. Terracotta icons of three military saints – St. Theodore, St. Christopher, and St. George – have been found on the sixth-century hillfort at Vinica (near Kočani, Republic of North Macedonia). Theodore is depicted on horseback, while Christopher and George are standing and holding lances. As he was believed to have been one of the Cynocephali from India, St. Christopher is depicted with a dog head. St. Phocas (a gardener) and St. Longinus (the centurion who pierced the side of Christ hanging on the Cross) appear on stamps for the manufacture of clay discs, which have been found in Chersonesus. The accompanying inscriptions refer to an almshouse in the city, and the clay discs may have been tokens offered in exchange for donations to that institution of charity. Several clay flasks for the transportation of holy water from the shrine of St. Menas at Abu Mina (Egypt) have been in found in Chersonesus, Tomis (now Constanța, Romania), Capidava (near Constanța), and Čitluk (near Sinj, Croatia), but also farther afield, at Szombathely in Hungary and at Rychleby (near Javorník) in the Czech Republic. The flasks bearing the image of St. Menas testify to pilgrims returning home from Egypt.

Conversion to Christianity often implied the rediscovery and translation (moving from one place to another) of relics. In the early ninth century, the relics of Sts. Anastasia and Chrysogonus came to Zadar (Croatia), most likely from Aquileia, while those of St. Tryphon moved from Constantinople to Kotor (Montenegro). The most famous case in that respect is that of St. Clement and his relics in Cherson. In 860, Constantine and his brother Methodius went on a diplomatic mission to the Khazars (see chapter 12). They made a stop in Cherson, where Constantine, together with the governor and the bishop of the city, launched a search for the relics of St. Clement. The expedition, which took place on January 30, 861, miraculously found on an island, not far from the shore, not only the remains of Clement's body, but also the anchor which had been attached to his body when thrown into the sea. The body of the saint, accompanied by "a procession of all the people ... jubilant and tearful in exultation of mind, spirit, and body," was then moved to the cathedral in Cherson, with only a portion taken by Constantine.[1] He carried the relics with him on the Khazar mission and then back to Constantinople. He then took them with him to Moravia, and from there to Rome, where he donated them to Pope Hadrian II in 867. Relics were also donated as gifts to a Bulgarian ruler, most likely Emperor Peter, in the tenth century. Each had a label written on tile fragments in Cyrillic, which have been discovered in the church of a small monastery at Selishte, just outside Preslav. The names on the labels were of important saints, whose remains were translated from Constantinople. Some were bishops, like St. Polycarp, martyred in 155. Others were physicians who healed people for free, like Sts. Cyrus and John, who died in the early fourth century. Labels were attached to relics of both female (St. Barbara, martyred in 290; St. Marina of Antioch, martyred in 304) and male martyrs (St. Jonas, a Persian martyr who died in 327; St. Eustatius, one of the forty Martyrs of Sebaste). That those relics were kept in a single location next to the capital indicates that the monastery in Selishte was endowed, if not also founded, by the ruler.

Several icons made of lead show St. George as foot-soldier and dragon-fighter. Those were small, portable objects, made of cheap materials, most likely imitations of larger and more expensive icons. They were found in tenth-century strongholds in northern Bulgaria, at Silistra, Popina, Skala, Car Asen, and Sredishte. St. George was the saint to whom many of the soldiers in the garrisons of those forts were praying. In fact, a tenth-century story about the "miracle of St. George with the Bulgarian" draws precisely that connection. The story is about a Bulgarian named George, who fought in Symeon's wars against the Magyars (see chapters 13 and 18). At one time, seeing that they were pursuing and about to kill him, he "turned to St. George and said: 'St. George, when I took the holy baptism, the priest gave me your name. I am your servant, save me now from the pagans!'"[2] Through the intercession of St. George, the Bulgarian warrior escaped unscathed from the encounter. Subsequent miracles of St. George, who showed himself to the Bulgarian man in a vision, saved him from danger while on another one of Symeon's campaigns and even restored the health of his wife, Maria. As the story puts it at the end, in tenth-century Bulgaria prayers to the great and holy martyr George "help the lame and in wars."[3]

The therapeutic aspect was an essential part of the cult of saints in the Early Middle Ages. All fifteen posthumous miracles reported at the end of the *vita* (saint's life) of St. Luke the Younger, which was written in the late tenth century, are about the healing of a wide variety of afflictions, from demonic possession to cancer and blindness. People from as far as Thermopylae and the island of Evvoia, many of them women, came to the tomb of St. Luke the Younger, hoping to obtain a cure from physical and spiritual diseases. St. Luke's favorite remedy for any kind of disease was olive oil from the lamp hanging above his tomb, which was in his former cell at Steiris (near Livadia, in central Greece),

---

1 Florin Curta, ed., "The Invention of the Relics of Saint Clement," in *Medieval Eastern Europe, 500–1300: A Reader* (Toronto: University of Toronto Press, 2024), 176.

2 Curta, ed., "George the Bulgarian and the Magyars," in *Medieval Eastern Europe*, 59.

3 Curta, ed., "George the Bulgarian and the Magyars," in *Medieval Eastern Europe*, 60.

where he died in 953 at the age of fifty-seven. He had long lived a solitary life on Mount Ioannitza, in constant search of an ascetic life. He preferred the wilderness to the company of men and women and talked to deer and vipers. By contrast, after coming to Greece from Crete in 968, St. Nikon the Metanoiete visited Athens, Thebes, Corinth, Argos, Naupaktos, and many other places in the Peloponnese, before settling in Sparta, ca. 970. He died there shortly before or after the year 1000. His *vita*, written in the mid-eleventh century by an abbot of the monastery Nikon had established, described him in strong colors: an unflinching, yet compassionate man with an incredible energy and an obsessive concern with repentance (hence his nickname, which means "repent!" in Greek). He was also eager to reproach both brigands and demons. Nikon did not avoid society, and, despite his ascetic habits, he gladly took the leading role in the community, a manager and an arbiter at the same time. For example, to persuade the rich men in the community to contribute money for the building of a church, he asked "that a chain be put about him and that like a slave he be dragged through the whole city by the neck."[4] The staged enslavement worked, as the rich opened their purses. After Nikon's death, the chain became a precious relic, for it was "revealed as capable of setting people free from disease and weakness."[5] At the end of his term as judge in eleventh-century Peloponnesos, a man named Basil Apokaukos traveled to Sparta to pay homage at the tomb of St. Nikon Metanoiete. His was not just a visit to the saint's tomb but a pilgrimage, since he expected healing through the myrrh pouring from the saint's tomb. Basil's intention was to take some of that home with him to treat any future diseases afflicting him or his family.

Some native saints were martyrs, like St. Adalbert. Born Vojtěch into the Slavnikid family, the main rivals of the Přemyslid dukes of Bohemia (see chapter 17), he became bishop of Prague in 982. He left his see to go to Rome and was there when Duke Boleslav II ordered the massacre of the Slavnikids in their stronghold at Libice (now Libice nad Cidlinou, Czech Republic). With no possibility of return to Bohemia, Adalbert decided to go on a mission to the northeastern borderlands of Poland, in Prussia. He was killed by the locals "on the ninth day before the Kalends of May [April 23, 997], when the emperor was lord Otto III, the faithful and most glorious Caesar, on a Friday."[6] Duke Bolesław Chrobry of Poland bought the remains of Adalbert from the Prussians and buried them in the cathedral of Gniezno, where Otto III came in 1000 as a pilgrim to the saint's tomb. The first liturgical texts were composed after that, with a sequence to the saint coinciding in time with the translation of the saint's arm to a church in Rome. Moreover, during the Czech invasion of 1039, all remains were taken from Gniezno and brought to Prague by Duke Břetislav I.

A different kind of native saints appeared in the Early Middle Ages in East Central Europe. Instead of holy men, those were typically members of the local dynasties. Some

4 Curta, ed., "Demons, Wine and Relics for a Church in Sparta," in *Medieval Eastern Europe*, 192.

5 Curta, ed., "Demons, Wine and Relics," in *Medieval Eastern Europe*, 192.

6 Curta, ed., "The Martyrdom of Saint Adalbert," in *Medieval Eastern Europe*, 186.

of them died as victims of intradynastic struggles. For example, Duke Wenceslas of Bohemia was assassinated in Stará Boleslav in 935 at the orders of his younger brother Boleslav (see chapter 17). According to the *vita* written in the late tenth century by a Czech named Christian, before being slain by Boleslav's men, Wenceslas addressed his brother: "I could crush you in my hand like a little whelp, but far be it from the hand of a servant of God to be stained with a brother's blood."[7] Boleslav, upon seizing power, buried Wenceslas in the Church of St. Vitus in Prague (which Wenceslas had built) and immediately began promoting his cult as a saint. The cult conferred an aura to the dynasty, which subsequent generations of Přemyslid dukes (and, later, kings) managed to enhance to their own advantage.

FURTHER READING

Bakirtzis, Charalambos. "Pilgrimage to Thessalonike: The Tomb of St. Demetrius." *Dumbarton Oaks Papers* 56 (2002): 175–92.

Curta, Florin, and Ethan Williamson. "Anchor of Faith: The Cult of St. Clement in Eastern Europe (ca. 500 to ca. 1050)." In *Proceedings of the International Scientific Conference "History and Theology," Constanța (Romania), November 17–18, 2020*, edited by Ionuț Holubeanu, 16–54. Bucharest: Editura Universitară, 2021.

Dimitrova, Elizabeta. *The Vinica Mystery: The Ceramic Treasuries of a Late Antique Fortress*. Vinica: Muzej "Terakota," 2012.

Minchev, Aleksandăr. *Early Christian Reliquaries from Bulgaria (4th–6th Century A.D.)*. Varna: Stalker, 2003.

Skedros, James Constantine. *Saint Demetrios of Thessaloniki: Civic Patron and Divine Protector, 4th–7th Centuries CE*. Harvard Theological Studies 47. Harrisburg: Trinity Press International, 1999.

Słupecki, Leszek P. "Where Did St. Adalbert (Wojciech) Go to Preach the Gospel and Where Did He Die?" In *Conversions: Looking for Ideological Change in the Early Middle Ages*, edited by Leszek P. Słupecki and Rudolf Simek, 343–56. Studia Medievalia Septentrionalia 23. Vienna: Fassbaender, 2013.

Vedriš, Trpimir. "'Frankish' or 'Byzantine' Saint? The Origins of the Cult of St. Martin in Dalmatia." In *Sailing to Byzantium: Papers from the First and Second Postgraduate Forums in Byzantine Studies*, edited by S. Neocleous, 221–49. Cambridge: Cambridge University Press, 2009.

7 Curta, ed., "The Assassination of Duke Wenceslas," in *Medieval Eastern Europe*, 118.

PART 7

Literacy and Art in the Early Middle Ages

39

PRACTICAL, POLITICAL, AND LEGAL LITERACY

Keywords in this chapter: runes, inscriptions, law codes

Few people living in early medieval East Central or Eastern Europe had access to book learning and literature; slightly more common, however, was the use of writing for practical needs. Unlike most of Western, Southern, Northern, and Central Europe where Latin clearly dominated written culture in the Early Middle Ages, there was a diversity of scripts and written languages in the eastern parts of the continent. Inscriptions on a variety of objects served practical purposes. For the most part, however, the development of writing responded to political and legal imperatives.

One of the oldest forms of writing available in Central and Eastern Europe in the Middle Ages were runes, which are letters designed to be inscribed on hard materials. Germanic runes scratched on a bone fragment were discovered in a seventh-century settlement excavated in South Moravia, at Lány. The inscription is not a text, properly speaking, but consists of six of the last runes of the *fuþark* (the oldest runic alphabet) in its variant known from South Germany. In other words, this may have simply been a "writing exercise," not a true message. Younger *fuþark* runes are known from inscriptions discovered in Russia and Ukraine. The oldest is that on a wooden stick found in Staraia Ladoga. Dated to the eighth or ninth century, the inscription was written in a script similar to contemporary Swedish inscriptions. The text is a fragment of Old Norse poetry, but the object was clearly of a personal nature. An eleventh-century runestone not unlike those from Sweden was found on the island of Berezan in the Black Sea, near Ochakiv (Ukraine) (see plate 39.1). The text reads: "Grani made this vault in memory of Karl, his partner." The two men (Grani and Karl) were members of a *félag*, a joint financial venture most typical for Viking-age society. In this case, the runes were used for the commemoration of a merchant in a manner similar to Roman epitaphs (inscriptions on tombstones).

Plate 39.1. Runestone discovered on the Island of Berezan' (near Mykolaiv, Ukraine) in 1905 and dated to the eleventh century. Carved in limestone, the inscription reads, "Grani made this tomb in memory of Karl, his partner." Archaeological Museum in Odessa; Wikimedia Commons, the free media repository.

Runes of a different nature, used typically to write Old Turkic, first appeared in East Central Europe with the Avars, ca. 600. The Avar runic inscriptions are typically short and appear on objects of daily use that were made of various materials (bone, clay, or metal). Most of those objects were inscribed with runes to mark them as personal property, which means that the runes themselves rendered the names of the owners. Others contain sayings, which may have operated as good wishes or greetings for the owner.

Monumental inscriptions, by contrast, were meant to be visible by as many people as possible and were used to disseminate messages of public relevance. Such inscriptions were particularly common in early medieval Croatia. They were written in Latin and used the capital and uncial scripts of Roman Antiquity. Benedictine monks probably brought epigraphic practices to Croatia in the early ninth century, inspired by the enthusiasm of Carolingian reformers for ancient modes of expression. Most inscriptions were displayed inside churches; they included dedications and epitaphs (commemorative inscriptions) and often mentioned the motives of the benefactors and the names of those who commissioned the inscriptions. Many of them indicate the reign of the ruler during which they were made. One of the oldest of these was made by a priest during the reign of Duke Višeslav sometime in the ninth century on a baptismal font in the church of Nin. Duke Branimir (879–92) is mentioned in five dedicatory inscriptions from various parts of Croatia. Other inscriptions commemorated rulers and other individuals. In the epitaph inscribed on her sarcophagus in Otok near Solin, Queen Helena (d. 976) is said to have "ruled the kingdom" and cared for widows and orphans. Helena was the wife of Michael Krešimir II (949–69) and the mother of Stephen Držislav (969–97) (see chapter 29). Craftspeople also inscribed their names on what they made or built. For example, the builder of a belfry in Baščanska Draga on the island of Krk had the words "Master Andrew made me" inscribed at the base of the tower.

Monumental inscriptions celebrating the accomplishments of rulers, commemorating their followers, or even scolding their enemies are also known from early medieval Bulgaria. Out of 100 Bulgar inscriptions, about thirty contain historical information. Malamir (831–36) declares that he was "made ruler by God" and reminds everyone that he "gave to the Bulgars to eat and drink many times." His father, Omurtag (814–31) describes himself as "ruler from God," who "made sacrifice to God Tangra." In an inscription commemorating an expedition against the Slavs on the southern slopes of the Rhodope Mountains, Presian (836–52) pontificates against "Christians," that is, the Byzantines. Some inscriptions employ biting sarcasm for the same purpose. For example, an inscription on behalf of Tervel (ca. 700–21) calls Emperor Justinian II "the emperor with cut-off nose," while another of Krum (ca. 803–14) refers to Emperor Nicephorus I as "the old bald emperor."

The Bulgar inscriptions are unlike any inscriptions known from Byzantium. The language employed, although Greek, is not that of the Homeric poems and there are no hexameters. The ruler "speaks" in them in the first-person singular. With no parallel in early medieval Europe, the Bulgar inscriptions are therefore declarations of intent, cast in a Byzantine mode for a Byzantine audience (people who could read Greek). They are not just statements of power, but politically motivated, almost sarcastic reinterpretations of the representation of power in Byzantium. Nowhere else in Europe at that time or later was the language of the enemy employed for "turning the tables" on him and making use of the written word in such a witty and personal way.

The earliest charters issued by local rulers and written on parchment are those of Croatia. No less than twenty-nine charters written in Latin are known (although preserved in later copies) for the ninth to eleventh centuries. One of the earliest charters surviving in the original form is a record of a donation that King Peter Krešimir (1058–74) made for the Benedictine abbey of St. John of Rogovo. The king "speaks" of himself in the first person singular: "while dining in my inn at Nin, together with our *župans*, counts, and *bans*, and even with chaplains of our royal court, I began to think how to make the Almighty God preserve the government of my hereditary kingdom, that was given to me, and how to give eternal peace to the souls of my predecessors."[1] Charters appeared much later in Hungary. The earliest is also the record of a royal donation for a Benedictine monastery, namely Pannonhalma Abbey; it is dated to 1001. In Bohemia, no charters of local rulers for monasteries are known before the mid-eleventh century.

1 Florin Curta, ed., "King Peter Krešimir IV Donates an Island," in *Medieval Eastern Europe, 500–1300: A Reader* (Toronto: University of Toronto Press, 2024), 90.

The Rus' who traded in Byzantium in the tenth century were already familiar with documents by that time. Copies of the 907 and 944 trade agreements were kept in Rus'; their texts were included in the *Primary Chronicle*. Rus' merchants carried with them gold and silver seals that certified their legitimate status and later boasted of written documents. In fact, the 944 agreement claims that Prince Igor "has now made known that he will forward a certificate to [the Byzantine] government, and any agents or merchants thus sent by the Rus' shall be provided with such a certificate to the effect that a given number of ships has been dispatched."[2] Once in Constantinople, Rus' merchants dealt with Byzantine bureaucrats who recorded their names before handing them the allowance to which they were entitled by the terms of the trade agreements.

In the absence of documents, public assemblies were important vectors of communication in orally dominated societies. Assemblies summoned by rulers served to discuss political and legal matters as well as to exchange and disseminate information. Royal assemblies summoned for legal purposes are mentioned in the eleventh-century law codes of Hungary and Bohemia. Cosmas of Prague claims not only that assemblies had facilitated consensual decisions on the leadership of Libuše and Přemysl in mythical times, but also that dukes and bishops were elected by assemblies in his own lifetime (early twelfth century). Participants in such assemblies were typically important men. Decrees were sometimes promulgated in churches. Distinctions between festive, political, and religious assemblies were, however, not always strict. Group consultations are also credibly attested for the pagan Slavs by Thietmar of Merseburg, Helmold of Bosau, and Ebo. According to Bruno of Querfurt, the Pechenegs summoned an assembly by sending envoys around the country.

The administration of justice provided incentives for the compilation of legal texts in book collections. Old Slavonic law codes, attested in later manuscripts from Rus', were likely already produced by Constantine and Methodius in Great Moravia (see chapter 12). Two of them were particularly popular. The *Nomocanon* was a translation of the *Collection of 50 Canons* of a sixth-century Byzantine jurist and patriarch, John Scholasticos. That Methodius translated that text is mentioned in his *Life*. The *Court Law for the People* was adapted from Title XVII – which discusses penal matters, judicial trials, and marriage – of the *Ekloga*, an eighth-century adaptation of Justinian's code. These law codes might have responded to the political agendas of missionaries and rulers more than to the needs of practically administering justice. The texts, however, include Slavic terminology that reflected legal concepts that existed in Moravia at the time of the mission. When it comes to canon law, the text that became the most popular in the Orthodox world is the *Nomocanon of Methodius*. Translated by Methodius in Moravia, the text was copied in the Balkans and then in Rus', from where numerous manuscripts are known.

Old Slavonic adaptations of legal texts were also made in early medieval Bulgaria and Serbia. Nothing is known, however, of their practical application. Although no Bulgarian manuscript has been preserved, it is likely by Preslav scholars that the Byzantine

2 Curta, ed., "A Trade Agreement Between the Rus' and Byzantium," in *Medieval Eastern Europe*, 73.

Ekloga was translated. The *Farmer's Law*, another Byzantine text often copied alongside the *Ekloga*, was probably translated under Symeon; manuscripts from Bulgaria and Serbia are extant. The *Mosaic Law*, a Byzantine penal compilation inspired by the Old Testament, was translated in Serbia, from where copies were disseminated to Bulgaria. The *Syntagma* of Patriarch Photius, a text of canon law, was presumably translated under Symeon in Bulgaria, whence it spread to Rus'.

Old Slavonic penitentials (books with instructions for confessors) were also produced in the Early Middle Ages, such as the *Commandments of the Holy Fathers* that originated in Great Moravia. Parts of the earliest copies are preserved in both Glagolitic and Cyrillic versions, the second probably made in Bulgaria under Symeon. The *Penitential of Saint John the Faster* was based on a text attributed to Patriarch John IV (582–95); its Old Slavonic version was likely done in early tenth-century Preslav.

Original law codes were written down earlier in Hungary and Rus' than in any other country of East Central and Eastern Europe. Although the earliest manuscripts are from the later twelfth century, the first Hungarian law code goes back to King Stephen I. Stephen's laws were inspired by the imperatives of Christianization. They forbade pagan rituals, magic, and the actions of witches, promoted Christian practices, and regulated marriage, sexual behavior, and even hairstyle. Legislative work is also recorded for kings Ladislaus I and Coloman, although the extant versions are probably later revisions. The *Ruskaia Pravda* is a collection of princely law from the lands of Rus'. The earliest version was probably recorded in the early eleventh century, under Iaroslav the Wise; it was expanded under his successors. Unlike Stephen's code, it is entirely secular in content; it also shows no direct influence of Roman or Byzantine legislation. The *Pravda* deals primarily with matters such as homicide, personal injury, and theft. In Bohemia, the earliest legislative action is attributed to Břestislav (1034–55), whose decrees are recorded in Cosmas of Prague's chronicle. They emphasize Christian behavior and moral values, for the duke was concerned with repairing the transgressions of his people and turning their minds from their evil deeds.[3]

FURTHER READING

Biliarsky, Ivan Alexandrov. "Law." In *The Routledge Handbook of East Central and Eastern Europe in the Middle Ages, 500–1300*, edited by Florin Curta, 425–42. London: Routledge, 2022.

Delonga, Vedrana. *The Latin Epigraphic Monuments of Early Medieval Croatia*. Monumenta medii aevi Croatiae, 1. Split: Museum of Croatian Archeological Monuments, 1996.

Feldbrugge, Ferdinand. *Law in Medieval Russia*. Law in Eastern Europe 59. Leiden: Brill, 2008.

3 Curta, ed., "The Decrees of Břetislav," in *Medieval Eastern Europe*, 128.

Granberg, Antoaneta. "On Deciphering Mediaeval Runic Scripts from the Balkans." In *Kulturnite tekstove na minaloto. Nositeli, simvoli, idei. Materiali ot iubileinata nauchna konferenciia v chest na 60-godishninata na prof. d.i.n. Kazimir Popkonstantinov. Veliko Tărnovo, 29–31 oktomvri 2003*, edited by Vasil Giuzelev, 128–39. Sofia: Universitetsko izdatelstvo "Sv. Kliment Okhridski," 2005.

Macháček, Jiří, et al. "Runes from Lány (Czech Republic) – the Oldest Inscription Among Slavs: A New Standard for Multidisciplinary Analysis of Runic Bones." *Journal of Archaeological Science* 127 (2021): 1–8.

Stipišić, Jakov. "Croatia in Diplomatic Sources Up to the End of the 11th Century." In *Croatia in the Early Middle Ages: A Cultural Survey*, edited by Ivan Supičić, 285–318. London: Philip Wilson Publishers, 1999.

40

LITERATURE AND HISTORY WRITING

Keywords in this chapter: alphabet, sermons, *vitae*

No Venantius Fortunatus came to the Balkans or to the Crimea in the sixth century, and no local bishop like Gregory of Tours decided to write history while in office. However, judging from a few inscriptions, local bishops had both literary taste and close friends who appreciated good literature, whether Greek or Latin. The Greek inscription of Bishop John on the mosaic floor of the basilica in Sandanski (near Goce Delchev, in southwestern Bulgaria) is in dactyls (three-syllable metrical patterns in poetry, with a stressed syllable followed by two unstressed syllables). The text employs Homeric words to address the viewer who supposedly desires to know "who built this splendid edifice, which delights the eye with its beauty." Similarly, the Latin inscription within the dome apse of the Euphrasius Basilica in Poreč (Croatia) has thirteen hexameters (lines of poetry with six metrical feet).

The earliest evidence of historical writing in Southeastern and Eastern Europe is linked to major episcopal sees – Chersonesus and Thessalonica. The collection known as the *Miracles of St. Demetrius* began as a didactic work written by Archbishop John of Thessalonica in the first decade of the reign of Heraclius (610–41). Book I contains fifteen sermons, each centered upon a miracle that St. Demetrius performed for the benefit of his city and its inhabitants. Although most stories took place during the episcopate of Eusebius, John's predecessor otherwise known from letters addressed to him by Pope Gregory the Great between 597 and 603, the structure of the narrative is not chronological. Archbishop John used history to educate his fellow citizens and to glorify the city's most revered saint. Unlike him, the unknown author of Book II, who wrote between 70 and 80 years later, arranged events in chronological order and used facts to support his arguments, often referring to contemporary events known from other sources. Similarly, the *Lives of the Holy Bishops of Cherson* is a work of hagiography (saints' lives) composed in Chersonesus in the eighth or ninth century. It contains original narratives about local historical events, particularly the spread of Christianity on the northern coast of the Black Sea between the reigns of Diocletian and Theodosius, with an emphasis on church leaders, political figures, and members of the local urban community. The original texts were most likely written in Greek, but they have survived in different other versions – Latin, Old Church Slavonic, Georgian, and Armenian.

Apart from their monumental inscriptions (see chapter 39), the only insight into how the Bulgars may have seen their own history is offered by a text known as the *List of Bulgar Khans*. The *List* survives only in late Russian manuscripts but was most likely composed in the eighth or ninth century. This is a list of Bulgar rulers with the duration of their reigns or lives, as well as the names of Bulgar lineages and Turkic calendar terms. There are twelve rulers listed, beginning with the legendary Avitokhol and Irnik, who are said to have reigned 300 and 150 years, respectively. The *List* is therefore made up of disparate genealogical myths, as well as historical facts. For example, while Asparukh and Tervel appear in other sources as well, Umor of the Vokil clan is known only from the *List*.

The conversion to Christianity altered but did not fundamentally change such a political use of writing. After conversion, writing in Bulgaria employed either the Glagolitic or the Cyrillic alphabet. The invention of Glagolitic is explicitly attributed to St. Constantine (Cyril) by the monk Khrabr in a treatise titled *On the Letters*: God "took mercy on humanity and sent down St. Constantine the Philosopher, called Cyril," and he "invented 38 letters" for writing Old Church Slavonic. Khrabr mentions "the Greek Tsar Michael [III] and the Bulgarian Prince Boris, and Rastitsa, the Moravian prince, and Kotsel, the prince of Blaten" to place the invention of Glagolitic in a historical context (see chapter 12).[1] One of Khrabr's contemporaries, Constantine of Preslav, shared his interest in Glagolitic and the historical depth of the burgeoning Slavonic culture. Constantine was a disciple of Methodius and began his career as priest in Pliska, before becoming bishop of Preslav. He is the author of a 36-line poem titled *Alphabet Prayer*, in which each verse begins with a letter of the Glagolitic alphabet in consecutive order. According to Khrabr, Constantine/Cyril modelled the Glagolitic characters "after the Greek letters," but the alphabet may in fact have been invented from scratch based on a system of reference signs designating biblical commentaries in manuscripts. Glagolitic was therefore a tool for writing an artificial language created for the translation of liturgical texts. The knowledge of that alphabet was restricted to a few churchmen.

The situation changed dramatically with the adoption in the early tenth century of the Cyrillic alphabet, an adaptation of the Greek uncial (majuscule script) to the needs of Slavonic. Such needs were associated with the remarkable program of translation implemented during the first years of Symeon's reign (893–927). A group of gifted churchmen, some of whom may have been Symeon's companions in Constantinople, undertook the formidable task of establishing solid foundations for the Christian religion and the Old Church Slavonic culture in Bulgaria. With no precedent in the history of East Central and Eastern Europe, this cultural project came to be associated primarily with Preslav

1 Florin Curta, ed., "Khrabr Defends the Slavonic Letters," in *Medieval Eastern Europe, 500–1300: A Reader* (Toronto: University of Toronto Press, 2024), 282.

and with Symeon's court. The learned men of Preslav had a profound sense of history, as indicated by compilations of historical works translated from Greek into Old Church Slavonic. Such compilations served a clear purpose, namely to place the newly converted Bulgarians and their kingdom in the history of the world, and in that way to justify their claims to power as successors of ancient nations, much in the same way in which that was done for Byzantium.

Besides translations, this period of cultural effervescence rightly called the "Golden Age" of medieval Bulgaria witnessed the production of a great variety of original works – sermons, hymns, and apocrypha (works outside the accepted canon of the Scriptures). The latter are particularly important for understanding the formation of historical traditions and philosophy of history. The greatest homilist (author of sermons) writing in Old Church Slavonic in tenth-century Bulgaria was St. Clement of Ohrid. His sermons have a simple, tripartite structure with an introduction addressing the congregation, a detailed description of the celebrated events, and a moralistic part asking the members of the audience to purge their wickedness and live their lives piously. The *Sermon on Palm Sunday*, the *Sermon on the Dormition of the Blessed Virgin Mary*, and the *Sermon for Sts. Peter and Paul* share a preoccupation with penance and confession, an indication that Clement's audience was made up of recently converted Christians. Clement also wrote eulogies (speeches in praise of a person), which have a more elaborate structure, with a middle narrative part dedicated to the life of the eulogized saint. The prose of the narrative, however, is combined with poetic passages in a literary effect that employs anaphora (a figure of speech based on the repetition of words at the beginning of successive clauses). The best example in that respect is the *Eulogy of Cyril the Philosopher*, written for the feast day of St. Cyril (February 14). Here, anaphora is used in a very subtle way. The word for "bless(ed)" appears throughout the text, beginning with the first lines: "Lord, bless! Lovers of Christ! Here shines for us the resplendent memory of our most blessed father Cyril, the new apostle and teacher of all the lands."[2] In the last part of the eulogy, the phrase "blessed is/are" is used twelve times, each time at the beginning of a sentence. Each sentence is addressed to St. Cyril, as if on behalf of (or together with) Clement's audience: "Blessed is your tongue of many languages, through which the dawn of the eternal Trinity without beginning shone forth for my people and dispersed the sinful darkness."[3] In addition, this part of the text is full of rhythm and syntactic parallels that are typical for poetry. Such an elaborate text structure was meant to make the message memorable.

During the tenth century, writing was also introduced to East Central Europe. The earliest evidence of writing in Latin consists of coins, not inscriptions. The first literary works appeared in Bohemia and were all hagiographical in nature. However, the earliest *vitae* were written in Old Church Slavonic instead of Latin. The *First Old Church Slavonic Legend of St. Wenceslas*, probably written in the 960s, was quickly followed by several other

2 Curta, ed., "Saint Clement of Ohrid on Saint Cyril," in *Medieval Eastern Europe*, 283.

3 Curta, ed., "Saint Clement of Ohrid," in *Medieval Eastern Europe*, 284.

vitae in Latin, of which the earliest, titled *Crescente fide* (after the first words in the text), was probably written in Bohemia ca. 970. That *vita* was in turn the basis for the "legend" written by Christian in 992–94 at the request of the bishop of Prague, St. Adalbert (see chapter 38). *Legenda Christiani* (as the text is now known) deals with the history of Christianity in Moravia, with the activity of Constantine and Methodius (who is said to have baptized Duke Bořivoj), the paganism of the Czechs, the foundation of Prague, and the beginnings of the Přemyslid dynasty. *Legenda Christiani* is thus the first attempt in East Central Europe to write history and the first attestation of Přemysl, the mythical founder of the first dynasty in Bohemia. It is possible that the earliest hymn in vernacular known from that country, *Hospodine pomiluj ny* ("Lord, have mercy on us"), was also composed in the tenth century. Like the *List of Bulgar Khans*, however, it survived only in much later manuscripts.

FURTHER READING

Kalhous, David. *Legenda Christiani and Modern Historiography.* East Central and Eastern Europe in the Middle Ages, 450–1450, 34. Leiden: Brill, 2015.

Kolarik, Ruth. "Sixth-Century Bishops as Patrons of Floor Mosaics in the Balkan Peninsula." In *La mosaïque gréco-romaine IX. Actes du IXe Colloque internationale pour l'étude de la mosaïque antique et médiévale à Rome, 5–10 novembre 2001*, edited by H. Morlier, 1255–67. Collection de l'Ecole Française de Rome 352. Rome: Ecole Française de Rome, 2005.

Miklas, Heinz. "The Glagolica During the Time of Clement of Ochrid." In *Sv. Kliment Okhridski v kulturata na Evropa*, edited by Svetlana Kuiumdzhieva, 160–95. Sofia: Izdatelstvo na Bălgarskata Akademiia na Naukite, 2018.

Nikolov, Angel. "The Perception of the Bulgarian Past in the Court of Preslav around 900." In *State and Church: Studies in Medieval Bulgaria and Byzantium*, edited by Vasil Giuzelev and Kiril Petkov, 157–71. Sofia: American Research Center, 2011.

Veder, William R. *Utrum in Alterum Abiturum Erat? A Study of the Beginnings of Text Transmission in Church Slavic. The "Prologue" to the "Gospel Homiliary" by Constantine of Preslav, the Text "On the Script" and the Treatise "On the Letters" by Anonymous Authors.* Bloomington: Slavica, 1999.

41

MONUMENTAL ART AND ARCHITECTURE

Keywords in this chapter: basilica, pastophories, opus sectile, cross-in-square plan, westwork, rotunda

During Late Antiquity, the most prominent building in any settlement in the Balkans and in the Crimea – whether a town or a fort – was the church. The variety of architectural types is remarkable and does not seem to depend much on location. Some churches are single-, others three-aisled buildings. The latter is represented primarily by basilicas with one or three apses at the eastern end and a vestibule (called "narthex") at the western end. In cities and towns, single- and three-aisled churches coexisted. Similar churches appear also on the eastern Adriatic coast, often inside forts built during the sixth century on islands. In the Crimea, three-aisled basilicas appear not only in urban centers (Chersonesus and Bosporus) but also in forts in the mountains or on the coast (for example, at Tiritake, south of present-day Kerch) (see map 41.1). A three-aisled basilica was even found at the western end of Lake Balaton in Hungary, in Keszthely, very far from the nearest point on the sixth-century frontier of the Roman Empire. In the Balkans, such basilicas were sometimes associated with episcopal palaces and must therefore have been cathedrals. The largest Late Antique basilica in the eastern part of Europe is that discovered by archaeologists in Lechaion (now Lechaio, near Corinth). Built in 525, this was a building 171.7 meters long (about 565 feet) and served as the model for several other basilicas in northwestern Greece.

The oldest still-standing church in the Balkans (and one of the oldest in Europe) is the Church of St. Demetrius in Thessaloniki. Built in the fifth century, this was a three-aisled basilica with one apse, a plan used for the slightly later Church of the Virgin Acheiropoietos in that same city. Both churches were richly decorated with marble as well as mosaics. The mosaics in the Church of St. Demetrius were restored in the seventh century, after a fire destroyed the initial building. The new building was a five-aisled basilica with a transept

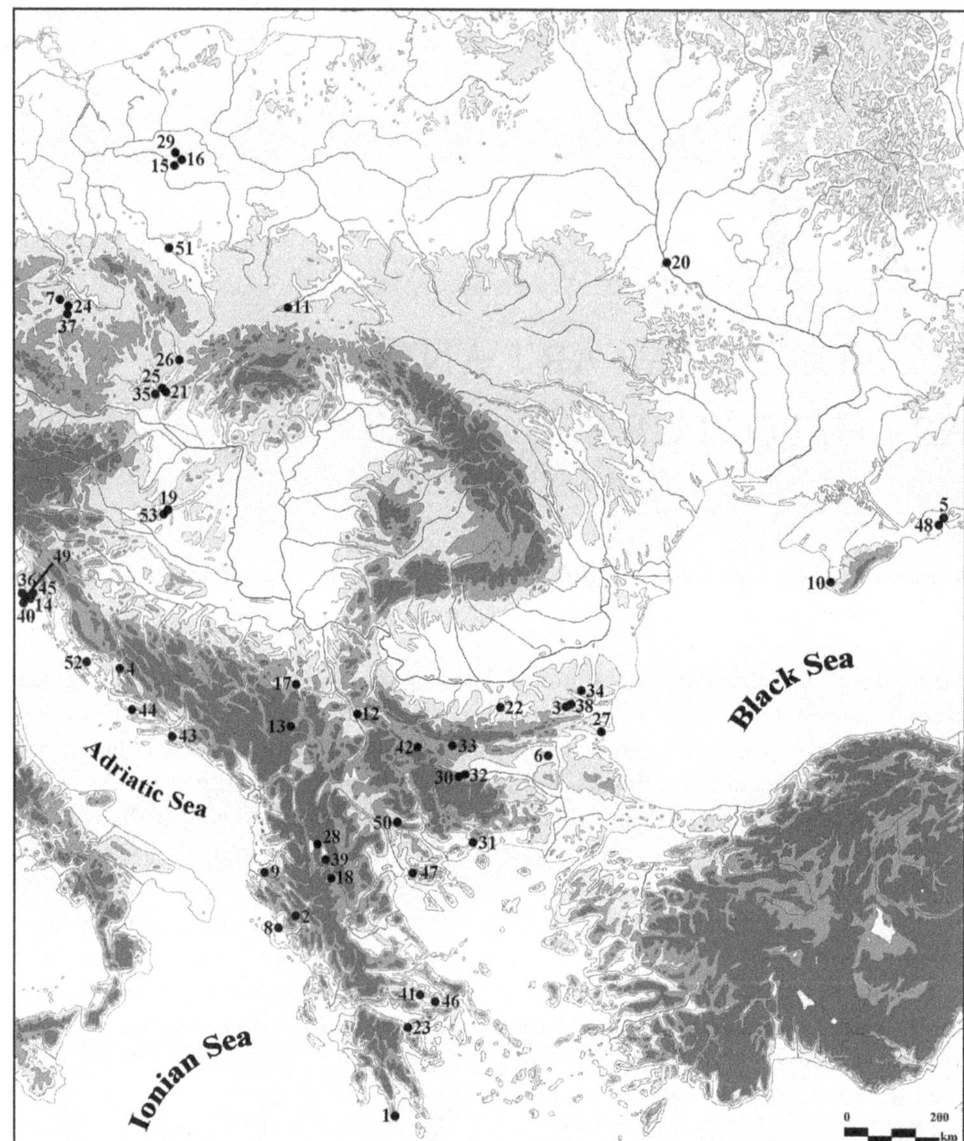

Map 41.1. Sites with monumental art, ca. 500 to ca. 1000. The location of the following sites is indicated: 1 – Ano Boularioi; 2 – Antigoneia; 3 – Avradaka; 4 – Biskupija; 5 – Bosporus; 6 – Botevo; 7 – Budeč; 8 – Butrint; 9 – Byllis; 10 – Cherson(esus); 11 – Cracow; 12 – Ćurlina; 13 – Doljani; 14 – Dvigrad; 15 – Giecz; 16 – Gniezno; 17 – Jelica; 18 – Kastoria; 19 – Keszthely; 20 – Kiev; 21 – Kopčany; 22 – Kramolin; 23 – Lechaion; 24 – Levý Hradec; 25 – Mikulčice; 26 – Modrá; 27 – Nesebăr; 28 – Ohrid; 29 – Ostrów Lednicki; 30 – Perushtica; 31 – Philippi; 32 – Philippopolis; 33 – Pirdop; 34 – Pliska; 35 – Pohansko; 36 – Poreč; 37 – Prague; 38 – Preslav; 39 – Prespa; 40 – Rovinj; 41 – Skripou; 42 – Sofia; 43 – Ston; 44 – Sutivan; 45 – Sveti Lovreč; 46 – Thebes; 47 – Thessalonica (Thessaloniki); 48 – Tiritake; 49 – Velika Gospa; 50 – Vodoča; 51 – Wrocław; 52 – Zadar; 53 – Zalavár.

(a rectangular area cutting across the main axis of the basilica and extending beyond it). One of the mosaic panels created in the seventh century shows St. Demetrius with a bishop and an imperial official. The saint has his hands on the shoulders of the two individuals, a protective gesture meant to indicate the founder (the fourth-century prefect of the city) and the restorer of the church (an unknown, seventh-century bishop). Founder portraits also appear in the mosaics of the Euphrasiana Cathedral in Poreč (Istria, Croatia). Bishop Euphrasius (543–53) holds a model of the church (another symbolic representation of the

founder) in the semidome of the apse, on the right side of the Virgin Mary holding the Christ Child. In both Thessalonica and Philippopolis (now Plovdiv, in Bulgaria), mosaic pavements appear not only in churches but in private residences as well. Some of the most elaborate mosaic pavements are known from baptisteries, such as those of Butrint (Albania) and Ohrid (see plate 41.1). Remains of frescoes have been identified in the episcopal church in Byllis (Albania), as well as in one of the basilicas excavated in Jelica near Čačak (Serbia). Frescoes also decorated the walls of burial vaults erected for local elite families.

Plate 41.1. Mosaic pavement in the baptistery of the five-aisled basilica at Plaoshnik, Ohrid (Macedonia). Photo by Florin Curta.

In the western Balkans, a particularly popular type of church is the tri- or tetraconch ("four shells"), with three or four apses, respectively. Such churches were found at Sutivan (on the island of Brač, off the eastern coast of the Adriatic Sea, in Croatia), Doljani (near Jablanica, Bosnia-Herzegovina), and Antigoneia (now Saraqinisht, near Gjirokastër, Albania). The so-called "Kruse" basilica in Chersonesus is also a triconch. The most famous tetraconch in the Balkans is the Red Church in Perushtica (near Plovdiv, Bulgaria), so called because of the large amount of brick that was used for its construction. Since graves have been found both inside and outside some of those churches, they probably had a commemorative function. It is possible that at least some of them were linked to the cults of local martyrs. The same is true for cross-shaped churches, such as that found in Botevo (near Yambol, Bulgaria), which may well have been a memorial chapel.

Although most basilicas had flat timber roofs, some had capped domes, as in the case of churches discovered in Philippi (near Kavala, in Greece), Kramolin (near Pleven, Bulgaria), and Sofia and Ćurlina (near Niš, Serbia). The so-called Stag Church near Pirdop (Bulgaria) may have even had two domes. However, the most famous, still-standing example of a cross-domed church is Hagia Sophia in Thessaloniki. Built on the site of a late fifth-century basilica, the church was rebuilt after an earthquake in 620. Much smaller in size than its predecessor, the new church incorporated many building materials from the earlier structure but replaced the three-aisled plan with pier clusters in the nave supporting a dome, as well as with a barrel-vaulted "cross." The entire inner chamber of the church (called "naos") was thus covered by the dome. The apse at the eastern end of the church is flanked by two subsidiary rooms (called "pastophories"). The façade shows alternating bands of brick and stone. Although an innovation in the architecture of the early medieval Balkans, the church is decorated with mosaics in the Late Antique tradition. The earliest have been dated between 780 and 788 and are primarily non-figurative, decorated with crosses (with a large one in the apse) and leaves. A second phase of mosaic setting is dated to the second half of the ninth century. This is when the scene of the Ascension of Christ was added in the dome. Christ is shown at the center of an almond-shaped aureola (called "mandorla") upheld by two flying angels. He is surrounded by the apostles and the Virgin Mary, flanked by two archangels.

In Cherson, Zadar, and Thessaloniki, basilicas built in the fifth or sixth century continued in use throughout the Middle Ages, with changes and additions. Moreover, the basilica became the preferred form of architecture in countries newly converted to Christianity. For example, the earliest church built in Bulgaria during the Middle Ages is the Great Basilica in Pliska, which was erected under Boris (see chapter 13). Almost 30 m (98 feet) wide and 100 m (328 feet) long, this was the largest church in the eastern part of Europe during the ninth century. Judging by the size of the pillars separating the nave from the aisles, the church had galleries above the aisles. The interior was richly decorated, as indicated by fragments of columns and capitals, some of them with carved crosses and inscriptions. More basilicas were built during the tenth century in and around Preslav, some of them with floors decorated with thin sections of colored stone cut in various sizes to form a pattern (a technique known as "opus sectile"). Basilicas were associated with centers of power, as indicated by the basilica of St. Achilleus in Prespa (on an island in the Small Prespa Lake, now in northern Greece), which was built by Samuel in the late tenth century (see chapter 13).

After 800, domed cross-in-square churches appeared in the Balkans. Such buildings typically had two longitudinal walls with narrow openings supporting the dome, and

Plate 41.2. The Church of the Dormition of the Holy Virgin, Skripou (Orchomenos, Greece), view from the northeast. Wikimedia Commons, the free media repository.

the eastern arm of the cross forming the sanctuary together with the pastophories. Some twenty-five churches of this type are known from Greece, but the most famous is the Church of the Virgin in Skripou (Orchomenos, Boeotia), built in 873/4 (see plate 41.2). Its founder was an imperial official from Constantinople, who was probably the steward of the imperial domain. His name (Leo) is mentioned in four inscriptions, one of which is in iambic trimeters (a form of rhythmic poetry consisting of three units per line, each made up of an unstressed syllable followed by a longer stressed syllable). The walls of the church incorporate abundant material taken from the ancient site at Orchomenos, but Skripou is the earliest example of the use of large blocks of stone for the façade, a feature most typical of the architecture of tenth-century churches in Greece. The style of the architectural sculpture in the interior is an outstanding example of Constantinopolitan standards, but local carvers must have been responsible for its execution. They most likely also worked for the much smaller Church of St. Gregory the Theologian in Thebes, which was built in 872.

Farther to the south, rural churches form a cluster in the Deep Mani (the southernmost part of the Peloponnese), at a short distance from each other. Those were simple, single-naved churches, founded by local churchmen. For example, the church in Ano Boularioi has a dedicatory inscription that bears the date 991/2 and mentions a priest-monk as a founder. The walls of the Church of St. Panteleimon in Ano Boularioi are covered in frescoes, which are related stylistically to those in the neighboring churches in Palaiochora Keria, which suggests the existence of itinerant painters working on commission in the region.

Over thirty domed cross-in-square churches are known from Preslav, some of them with more than one dome. For example, one of the churches discovered in Avradaka, near Preslav, was a quincunx (five-domed) built in the early tenth century. A few buildings of that same type are still standing – St. John the Baptist in Nesebăr (on the shore of the Black Sea) and St. Leontius in Vodoča (near Strumica, in Macedonia). Despite the evident popularity of the domed cross-in-square church, the iconic building of tenth-century Bulgaria is the Round Church in Preslav. This is a rotunda combining a centrally planned main space with a large vestibule flanked by turrets with spiral staircases inside and a large courtyard with slender columns and niches. The Round Church was most likely built during the reign of Symeon (893–927), and the excavations produced abundant evidence of architectural sculpture – marble reliefs and inlay – as well as of mosaic decoration and painted tiles.

In those parts of the Balkans that were outside the Byzantine Empire, church architecture continued to imitate Late Antique architectural formulas, particularly basilicas with three apses. The churches built shortly before or after 800 in Dvigrad and Velika Gospa (both near Rovinj, on the western coast of the Istrian Peninsula, in Croatia) are halls with no internal division into aisles. Hall churches remained the dominant form of church architecture in Istria well into the eleventh century. The decorative sculpture of the church in Velika Gospa is stylistically related to that of the Church of St. Thomas in Rovinj, which has a transept with three apses. Most analogies for that church are from northern Italy and southern Switzerland, and a burial discovered next to the western wall of the church suggests that St. Thomas in Rovinj was the proprietary church of a member of the Carolingian elite. In central Dalmatia (southern Croatia), the preferred form of church inspired by the Late Antique architecture was the hexaconch ("six-shells"). Away from the Adriatic coast, the earliest churches are dated to the first quarter of the ninth century and are similar to Carolingian buildings in northern Italy. The Church of St. Mary in Biskupija (near Knin, Croatia) had a monumental entrance, which is the earliest example of westwork in Croatia (see insert 41.1). The first floor served as a mausoleum for the ninth-century rulers of Croatia and members of their families. Responsible for the earliest stone carvings in the church was a team of carvers who worked at several other sites in the first half of the ninth century. The influence of the Carolingian architecture reached as far south along the Adriatic coast as Ston (near Dubrovnik), where a massive tower was added as westwork to a domed, single-naved church built by the prince of Zahumlje, Michael Višević (910–30). Dalmatia also has one of the largest rotundas in Europe, the Church of St. Donatus in Zadar. Built in the early ninth century, this building had two

INSERT 41.1. WESTWORK – A FEATURE OF THE CAROLINGIAN AND POST-CAROLINGIAN ARCHITECTURE

Beginning with the ninth century, the western façade of most churches built as basilicas received a monumental treatment in the form of towers flanking the main entrance. As large, vertical structures, those towers rose above the roofline and thus dominated the surroundings. The upper levels of one or both towers were accessed by spiral stairs and commonly contained chapels flanked by aisles – small upper churches available for parish services (while the main floor was reserved for the clergy). This feature of Carolingian architecture is known as "westwork," because it is typically located at the western end of the church.

The oldest example is the façade of the main entrance into the Benedictine abbey church at Corvey (near Höxter, in northern Germany). The structure was built at the same time as the church in 885. At Corvey, the westwork was used to accommodate the king or the emperor during visits. The feature was adopted and amplified by the post-Carolingian (Ottonian) architecture in the German lands. The churches of the abbeys of Saint Pantaleon in Cologne (built between 966 and 980) and St. Michael in Hildesheim (built between 1001 and 1031) show the continuation on a much larger scale of the Carolingian models.

horseshoe-shaped apses on the eastern side. At a later date within that same century, a second floor was added with a gallery.

The variety of architectural forms is also typical for Moravia. Rectangular churches with right-angle chancels are known from Mikulčice (near Hodonín, Czech Republic) and Modrá (near Velehrad). The Church of St. Margaret of Antioch in Kopčany (near Skalica, in western Slovakia) is the only still-standing building of that type, and the oldest church in East Central Europe (see plate 41.3). The vaulting with triangular stones of the original windows of the church was meant to match aesthetically the unplastered façade – a feature of the Carolingian architecture in Germany – and to hint symbolically at the parable of the stone rejected by masons that becomes the cornerstone (Psalm 118:22; Matthew 21:42). By contrast, one of the two churches discovered in Pohansko (near Břeclav, Czech Republic) was built of quarry stone bound with mortar, but its walls were plastered and whitewashed to make room for murals, as indicated by remains of color paintings discovered by archaeologists. Three-aisled basilicas were also in existence in ninth-century Moravia, with either one or three apses. There are also examples of rotundas. The one recently found in Pohansko was probably a proprietary church of a local lord of lower status.

In the neighboring Frankish territories now in western Hungary, three churches were found inside the stronghold at Zalavár, believed to have been Pribina's seat of power (see chapters 7 and 12). One of them was a three-aisled basilica with clear political associations, much like in Bulgaria. However, unlike all other three-aisled basilicas in Europe at that time, this building had an ambulatory (an annular corridor around the apse, which was divided into rooms). The Carolingian influence was also felt in Bohemia. The Church of the Virgin Mary in Prague was built in the ninth century as a rectangular building with

Plate 41.3. Church of St. Margaret of Antioch in Kopčany (Slovakia), view from the west. Wikimedia Commons, the free media repository.

a right-angle chancel. During the tenth century, more architectural forms made their appearance – three-aisled basilicas (the Church of St. George in Prague) as well as rotundas (Levý Hradec, St. Peter in Budeč, and St. Vitus in Prague). Rotundas are also among the first examples of church architecture in Poland. Those in Gniezno and Cracow, both built in the late tenth century, co-existed with cross-shaped churches (Ostrów Lednicki) and single-naved churches with transepts (Wrocław) built after 1000.

Why were different architectural types used concomitantly? Early Přemyslid and Piast rulers underscored their status by making careful choices of architectural forms. The evident preference for rotundas in Bohemia and Poland, more than in any other area of East Central and Eastern Europe during the Early Middle Ages, is a mirror of how circular spaces of representation were used in secular architecture. The palaces excavated in Giecz and Ostrów Lednicki, both erected during the last decades of the tenth century, were rectangular buildings, very similar to each other, and each with attached rotundas. Whether private chapels or ceremonial rooms, such buildings illustrate the political motivations behind the stylistic decisions of rulers of countries recently converted to Christianity.

The architectural forms adopted in Rus' after the conversion to Christianity are very different from those in use during the tenth century anywhere else in the Balkans or in East Central Europe. Byzantine architects and masons erected the large Tithe Church in Kiev during the last decade of that century. This was a basilica with transept, a large dome on eight pillars, and a very large vestibule with galleries. The obvious model for this brick building was the Church of the Holy Apostles in Constantinople. Fragments of a mosaic made of pieces of marble of different colors suggest that the source of inspiration for the decorative patterns of the floor in the Tithe Church was also Constantinopolitan. Fragments of the altar screen and of a frieze with Greek inscription substantiate that idea. The walls of the church were covered with murals, as indicated by fragments of frescoes.

Well-preserved tenth-century frescoes are known from Greece. The so-called "historic wall painting" on the southern wall of the Church of St. Demetrius in Thessaloniki consists of two panels, one showing a man on horseback, most likely an emperor, being received by people in a city. The other panel shows the interior of a church and frightened people fleeing inside from invading barbarians who pursue them. The paintings have been dated to the early tenth century and interpreted as referring to the sack of Thessaloniki by Leo of Tripoli in 904 (see chapter 21). Of the same age is the scene of the Last Judgment in the Church of St. Stephen in Kastoria (northern Greece). The Church of the Holy Unmercenaries in that same town contains the earliest founder portrait of the eastern part of Europe, painted ca. 1000. Shortly before or after that year, the walls of the three-aisled basilica in Sveti Lovreč (Istria, Croatia) were painted. Surviving in relatively good shape are the Deisis (a scene with Jesus Christ flanked by the Virgin Mary and St. John the Baptist) and four unidentifiable saints in the southern apse. The oval eyes with large eyebrows and round pupils, as well as the small, expressive mouths, bring those paintings very close to contemporary murals in Kastoria and the Deep Mani.

FURTHER READING

Bouras, Charalambos. *Byzantine and Post-Byzantine Architecture in Greece.* Athens: Melissa, 2006.

Ćurčić, Slobodan. *Architecture in the Balkans: From Diocletian to Süleyman the Magnificent.* New Haven: Yale University Press, 2010.

Marašović, Tomislav. *Dalmatia Praeromanica: Early Medieval Architecture in Dalmatia. 1st Synthesis.* Knjiga Mediterana, 80. Split: Književni krug Split/Muzej Hrvatskih Arheoloških Spomenika, 2017.

Mavropoulou-Tsioumi, Chrysanthi. *Hagia Sophia: The Great Church of Thessaloniki.* Athens: Kapon, 2014.

Terry, Ann Bennett, and Henry Maguire. *Dynamic Splendor: The Wall Mosaics in the Cathedral of Euphrasius in Poreč.* University Park: Pennsylvania State University Press, 2007.

Totev, Totiu. *Great Preslav.* Sofia: Professor Marin Drinov Academic Publishing House, 2001.

PART 8

The High Middle Ages

42

EAST CENTRAL EUROPE: HUNGARY, BOHEMIA, AND POLAND

Keywords in this chapter: coronation, regency, Mongols

Between the eleventh and the thirteenth centuries, the Arpadians in Hungary and the Přemyslids in Bohemia consolidated their authority in overcoming internal conflicts. The realm of the Piasts, meanwhile, was partitioned into autonomous provinces. While Bohemia became a constitutive part of the Holy Roman Empire, Hungary and Poland remained independent entities (see map 42.1 and insert 42.1).

INSERT 42.1. THE HOLY ROMAN, OR WEST ROMAN, EMPIRE

The title of Roman emperor was reinstated in the West when a Frankish king, Charlemagne, was crowned emperor in Rome by Pope Leo III in 800. Under the Ottonian dynasty that originated in tenth-century Saxony, imperial power shifted towards the German lands. Under Charles IV, imperial power shifted again, this time towards the Czech lands. Charles, who was both king of Bohemia and Holy Roman emperor, made Prague a capital city of European importance. Moreover, since the Golden Bull of 1356, the king of Bohemia was officially one of the seven prince-electors who chose the new emperors. The Carolingian and Ottonian polity was known as the "Empire of the Romans"; in the twelfth century, the adjective "Holy" was added. Only since the end of the fifteenth century, however, was it officially called Holy Roman Empire of the German Nation, the name it would preserve until its final dissolution in 1806. In fact, the empire had always been multilingual and multicultural, encompassing German, Romance, and Slavic populations.

Map 42.1. East Central Europe, ca. 1100: I – Bohemia; II – Hungary; III – Poland.

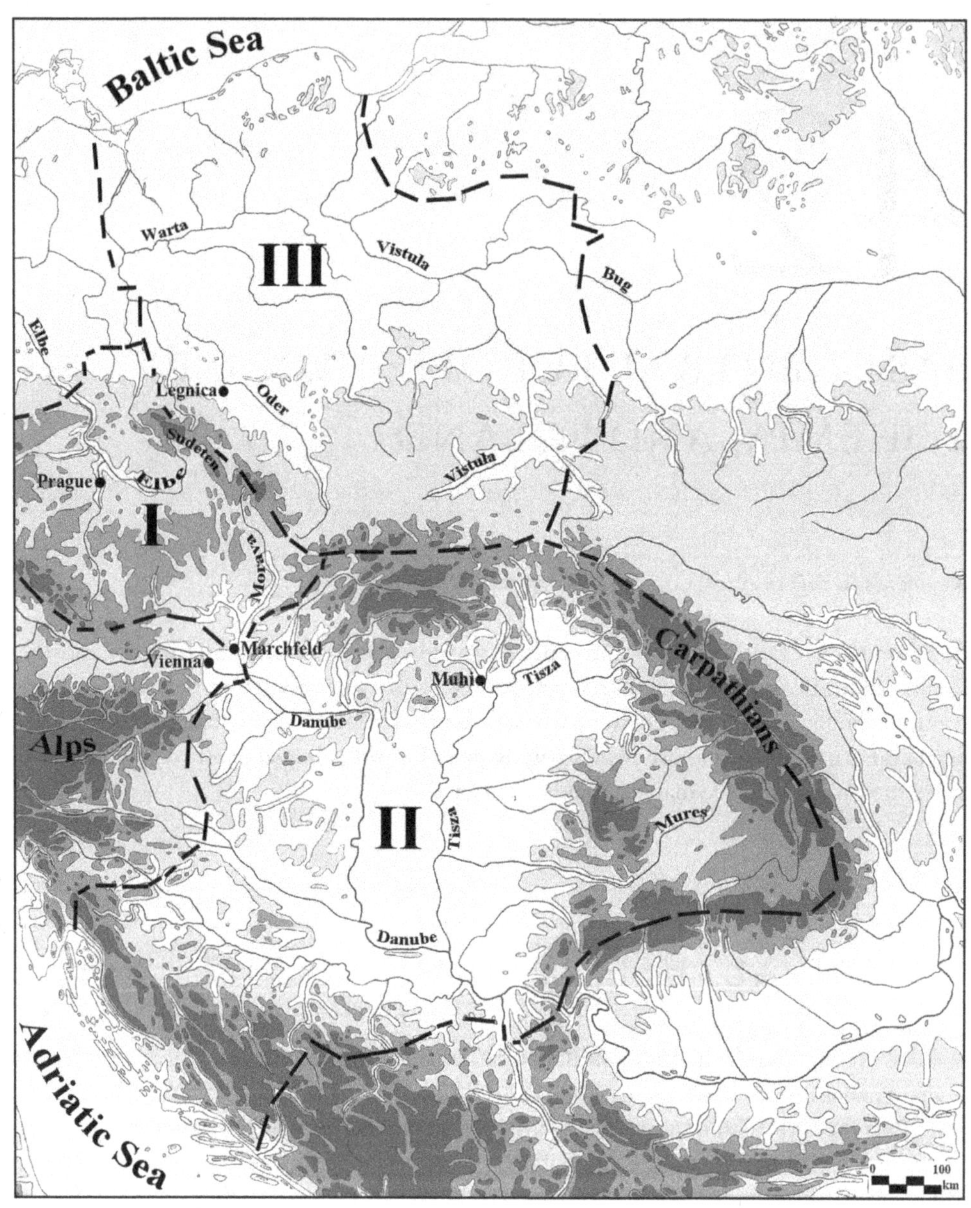

Since Stephen I, Hungary had a king who not only was anointed by the archbishop of Esztergom but also had full recognition from both the pope and the Holy Roman emperor. The kingdom remained united under the Arpadian dynasty, although the rules of succession were not fully clear, which often led to contestations (see table 42.1). For example, Andrew I designated his son Solomon as his successor and had him crowned as

Table 42.1. Rulers of Hungary between 1000 and 1300

Name of the Ruler	Regnal Years
Stephen I	997–1038
Peter Orseolo	1038–41; 1044–46
Samuel Aba	1041–44
Andrew I	1046–60
Béla I	1060–63
Solomon	1063–74
Géza I	1074–77
Ladislas I	1077–95
Coloman	1095–1116
Stephen II	1116–31
Béla II	1131–41
Géza I	1141–62
Stephen III	1162–72
Béla III	1172–96
Emeric	1196–1204
Ladislas III	1204–05
Andrew II	1205–35
Béla IV	1235–70
Stephen V	1270–72
Ladislas IV	1272–90
Andrew III	1290–1301

a child, but his brother Béla sought support in Poland to oust him. When Andrew died after being injured in a battle, he was succeeded by Béla; Solomon, however, returned after the death of Béla and fought against the latter's sons. Similar scenarios became common as competing contenders fought for succession with internal and external support. Solutions devised to bring stability included giving the heir governance of a duchy or giving the successor a territory recently conquered, such as the kingdom of Croatia. When it comes to Transylvania, its situation is not fully clear for the eleventh and twelfth centuries, but since 1263 the region was governed separately by a voivode who combined military and administrative tasks on behalf of the king. Sometimes, candidates to the throne invoked the principle of idoneity (suitability), even though they were members of the Arpadian dynasty.

Some members of the Arpadian dynasty left a particularly memorable imprint on the history of Hungary in this period. King Ladislas I (1077–95), a generous patron of the church, was canonized in 1192 but was mostly remembered as a gallant knight. Legend tells that he defeated in duel a Cuman warrior to free a captive Hungarian girl; the story became a common motive as Ladislas became the popular figure of an ideal knight embodying Christian virtues. He was succeeded by his nephew Coloman (1096–1116), although he had designated Coloman's younger brother Álmos. Coloman, who is said to have been of frail appearance, had a solid education and was originally foreseen for an ecclesiastical career; the breadth of his knowledge earned him the nickname "the Learned." He intensified the use of written documentation in administration, issued legislation, and protected the autonomy of Hungary against the centralizing agenda of the reform papacy. Queen Gertrude, a German noblewoman from the house of Andechs-Merania and sister of Hedwig of Silesia and of Queen Agnes of France, was the wife of Andrew II (1205–35). Gertrude took an influential role at the court and facilitated the awarding of offices and grants to relatives and various foreigners. Her brother Berthold, for example, was appointed archbishop of Kalocsa, ban of Croatia, and voivode of Transylvania despite being poorly skilled for these positions. Gertrude was so unpopular at the court that she was murdered by Hungarian nobles in 1213 during the king's absence.

The Arpadian kings generally had good relations with the Holy Roman emperors. Marriage alliances between Hungary and the German lands were common: for instance, Solomon married Judith, sister of Emperor Henry IV. Relations with the Byzantine emperors, meanwhile, alternated between cooperation and conflict, the latter in relation to influence in the Balkans – in Serbia, Croatia, or Dalmatia. Some claimants to the throne sought refuge in the Byzantine Empire or obtained support from the emperors. Moreover, Géza II, his son Prince Géza, and Stephen IV all married Byzantine princesses.

Ladislas I invaded Croatia in 1091 after his sister Helena, wife of King Zvonimir, had become a widow and requested support. With few interruptions, the kings of Hungary ruled as kings of Croatia from that time. Coloman also invaded Dalmatia in 1105. The Dalmatian cities, however, were accustomed to a high degree of autonomy, and Dalmatia remained the subject of disputes between Hungary, Venice, and Byzantium. From the eleventh century onwards, Hungarian kings also encroached into the borderlands of Serbia.

The Pechenegs, the Oghuz, and the Cumans often raided border territories of the Hungarian kingdom. Hungarian kings fought them but also employed them as auxiliary troops. Stephen V (1270–72) married a Cuman princess, Elizabeth. Their son, Ladislas IV (1272–90), was nicknamed the Cuman king; he was ten years old when his father died and the regency was taken over by Elizabeth. When the papal legate Philip of Fermo tried to enforce the conversion of the king's pagan Cuman allies who lived in Hungary in 1279, Ladislas opposed him. He abandoned the court, leaving the government of the kingdom to the barons and bishops, and went to live with the Cumans on the Great Plain, following their fashions and customs. Amongst multiple controversies, he was murdered by Cuman opponents in 1290.

Dynastic dominance was also characteristic of the history of Bohemia during this period: the Přemyslids reigned with no interruption over Bohemia and the margraviate of Moravia from the eleventh to the early fourteenth century. The Přemyslids originally expected that the most senior male relative of the ruler would succeed him and be accepted by the magnates (see table 42.2). As in Hungary, however, several relatives

Table 42.2. Rulers of Bohemia between 1000 and 1300

Name of the Ruler	Regnal Years
Dukes	
Boleslav III	999–1002; 1003
Vladivoj	1002–3
Jaromír	1003; 1004–12; 1033–34
Boleslav IV (Bolesław Chrobry)	1003–4
Oldřich	1012–33; 1034
Břetislav I	1034–55
Spytihněv II	1055–61
Vratislav II	1061–92
Conrad I	1092
Břetislav II	1092–1100
Bořivoj II	1100–7; 1117–20
Svatopluk	1107–09
Vladislav I	1110–17; 1120–25
Soběslav I	1125–40
Vladislav II	1140–72
Henry	1173; 1178–89
Soběslav II	1173–78
Conrad II Ota	1189–91
Wenceslas II	1191
Henry Břetislav	1193–97
Vladislav Jindřich	1197
Kings	
Přemysl Ottokar I	1197–1230 (king in 1198)
Wenceslas I	1230–53
Přemysl Ottokar II	1253–78
Wenceslas II	1278–1305
Wenceslas III	1305–6

often had competing claims leading to conflicts. Moravia was divided by Břestislav I; the Moravian territories became hereditary, appanage principalities ruled by descendants of his sons, while the ruler of Prague was the senior duke with authority over his relatives. Dissatisfaction with the existing system, however, led to several conflicts throughout the twelfth century.

Přemyslid rulers accepted the authority of the German kings or emperors. The emperor, though, did not rule directly in Bohemia or Moravia and did not own land there; he was mostly symbolically recognized as the leading secular authority in western Christendom. The Přemyslids often relied on the German rulers; they offered them military service in expectation of support for their causes. Vladislav II, for example, sent troops to support Frederick Barbarossa in his campaigns in Poland and Italy. According to the twelfth-century chronicler Vincent of Prague, Vladislav decided to help the emperor in Italy out of his own will "and in answer to the honors bestowed" upon him by Frederick.[1] Vladislav was indeed rewarded with the royal title and in 1169 the right for the rulers of Bohemia to take part in the election of the king of the Romans.

Unlike the rulers of Hungary, the Přemyslids were late in acquiring the royal title. The ruler traditionally styled himself a duke; he was elected by the nobles and invested on the old stone throne in Prague Castle. Vratislav II and Vladislav II were granted the royal title by Holy Roman emperors in reward for their service, but that title was not hereditary. Přemysl Ottokar I, put in place by Frederick Barbarossa in 1192, obtained a royal crown in 1198 from Otto IV of Brunswick, whose imperial claim he had supported. His royal position gained wider recognition, including from the papacy, and was recognized as hereditary by Frederick II in the 1212 Golden Bull of Sicily, a foundational document for the kingdom. Bohemia was an autonomous entity as part of the empire, and the king was an imperial prince. From 1228 onward, the king was crowned in St. Vitus Cathedral in a ceremony led by the archbishop of Mainz; the traditional electoral diet lost significance and the stone throne ceased to be used. Moravia, meanwhile, was ruled as a margraviate subordinated to Prague.

The authority that the rulers of Bohemia gained in the thirteenth century can be gauged by examining the conflict that opposed Přemysl Ottokar II to Rudolf of Habsburg. Rudolf, formerly count of Swabia, who wanted to strengthen imperial authority after the long interregnum, disputed Přemysl Ottokar II's control of properties outside Bohemia. Military confrontation led to a peace agreement in Vienna in 1276 and renewed conflict in the battle of Marchfeld in 1278 in which the king of Bohemia died. His successor Wenceslas II aimed at imposing Přemyslid power in Central Europe: he was crowned king of Poland in Gniezno in 1300, and his son, Wenceslas III, became king of Hungary in 1301, after the heirless death of Andrew III. He gave up Hungary after his father's death, however, to focus his efforts on Bohemia and Poland, but was murdered in 1306.

In Poland, rulers alternated between the ducal and the royal titles, although the latter had limited recognition outside the country (see table 42.3). Bolesław Chrobry was crowned in 1025 in unclear circumstances and died the same year; Mieszko II was king from 1025 to 1031; Bolesław II the Bold was crowned in 1076 with approval of the pope but was expelled from the kingdom in 1079. No king was crowned until the end of the thirteenth century, and Bolesław II's crown was kept in Cracow.

1 Florin Curta, ed., "Vincent of Prague on King Vladislav II," in *Medieval Eastern Europe, 500–1300: A Reader* (Toronto: University of Toronto Press, 2024), 136.

Table 42.3. Rulers of Poland between 1000 and 1100

Name of the Ruler	Regnal Years
Bolesław I Chrobry	992–1025
Mieszko II Lambert	1025–31; 1032–34
Bezprym	1031–32
Casimir I	1039–58
Bolesław II	1058–79
Władysław I Herman	1079–1102
Zbigniew	1097–1107

The Polish realm remained united in the eleventh century, but that did not last. At the death of Władysław Herman in 1102, the kingdom was divided between his sons Zbigniew, who took Greater Poland, Kuyavia, and Mazovia, and Bolesław III the Wrymouth, who obtained Silesia and Lesser Poland. The two brothers fought, however, and Bolesław managed to get rid of Zbigniew, despite the latter having the support of Henry V. To prevent further conflict, Bolesław introduced the principle of seniority: all legitimate heirs would receive a province to govern, but they would accept the leadership of the older one, the senior duke who would reside in Cracow. Following this plan, the kingdom became divided after his death in 1138. The provinces, however, quickly became *de facto* independent, and the position of senior duke fell in disuse after the 1202 death of Mieszko III the Old.

Numerous attempts were made at reuniting the kingdom. Duke Henry IV Probus of Wrocław would likely have been crowned after his capture of Cracow if he had not died of poisoning in 1290. Przemysł II was crowned in 1295 in Gniezno but was murdered the following year. He was succeeded by the kings of Bohemia Wenceslas II and Wenceslas III, after which the throne again remained vacant until Władysław the Short (Łokietek), the Piast duke of Kuyavia, managed to unite Polish provinces – except Silesia and Mazovia – and be crowned king in Cracow in 1320.

Piast rulers were sometimes allies of Holy Roman emperors. Many of them married women of the high German nobility, or even imperial families. Władysław Herman, for example, married Judith, sister of Emperor Henry IV and widow of King Solomon of Hungary. Henry I the Bearded, duke of Silesia, married Hedwig of Andechs, sister of the queens of Hungary and France. Such connections proved useful: Władysław II the Exile owed to his wife Agnes of Babenberg the support he got from her half-brother King Conrad III and the latter's nephew, Emperor Frederick Barbarossa, in regaining Silesia for his sons. The Piasts also secured marriage alliances with rulers of Rus' and of Sweden.

Pomerania was briefly incorporated into the Polish kingdom in the late eleventh century and a bishopric subordinated to Gniezno was established in 1000 in Kołobrzeg, but all those developments came to an end with the crisis of the 1030s. Regaining Pomerania became a priority under Władysław Herman, who subjugated the region in 1090. Bolesław III the Wrymouth resumed incursions into Pomerania as he wanted to incorporate the region into the kingdom. Pomeranians were pagan, and the war against them was imagined as a religious conflict for the defense of Christendom. After the conquest, Bishop Otto of Bamberg was sent in 1124 by Bolesław to convert the pagans to Christianity, which he achieved with great success.

The Mongol invasion of 1241–42 (which followed upon the conquest of Rus' – see chapter 46) was a major disruption in East Central Europe (see map 42.2). Although short-lived, the invasion resulted in significant death and destruction in Hungary and parts of Poland. According to Roger of Torre Maggiore, who described the devastation in Hungary as an eyewitness, the "slaughter was repeated day after day."[2] The extraordinary success of the Mongol expedition of 1241 in Hungary and Poland was largely based on coordinated, simultaneous attacks. The nomad warriors, moving at rapid speed as mounted archers and employing the most modern siege technology of the time, conquered and destroyed with great efficacy, and the brutality of their attacks sent shockwaves of fear across the continent. The Mongols were in Lesser Poland in March 1241; on April 9 at Legnica, in Silesia, they faced a Polish army that was decimated, with Duke Henry II the Pious left dead on the battlefield. Many villages and towns were destroyed, including Cracow and probably Wrocław. Memories of the devastation were still alive generations later, although the extent of the destruction and mortality is difficult to assess. The Mongols made a few incursions into Moravia, but the Czech lands were left mostly untouched.

Hungary was the most affected. The royal army was annihilated at the battle of Muhi on April 11, 1241. According to Archdeacon Thomas of Spalato, a contemporary of those events, seeing that "all hope of saving their lives was spent, and death, as it were, passed through the camp gazing in their faces, the king [Béla IV] and the leading men, abandoning their standards, turned to seek refuge in flight."[3] Béla fled to Dalmatia and even embarked on a ship in the Adriatic Sea, having the intention to go to Rome, if the Mongols would pursue him any further. The Mongols stayed in Hungary until March 1242, when they unexpectedly withdrew, for reasons that remain unclear. Contemporary sources describe them inflicting serious destruction, and archaeologists have found remains of villages with unburied bodies and many hidden treasures that were never recovered. The greatest destruction happened in the eastern and central parts of the kingdom, while the more populated western regions were spared. The death toll is difficult to assess: while some estimates are as high as 50 percent of the overall population of Hungary, it is generally believed to have been somewhere around 15 to 20 percent (see chapter 53).

2 Curta, ed., "The Mongol Sack of Oradea," in *Medieval Eastern Europe*, 336.

3 Curta, ed., "The Battle of Muhi," in *Medieval Eastern Europe*, 334.

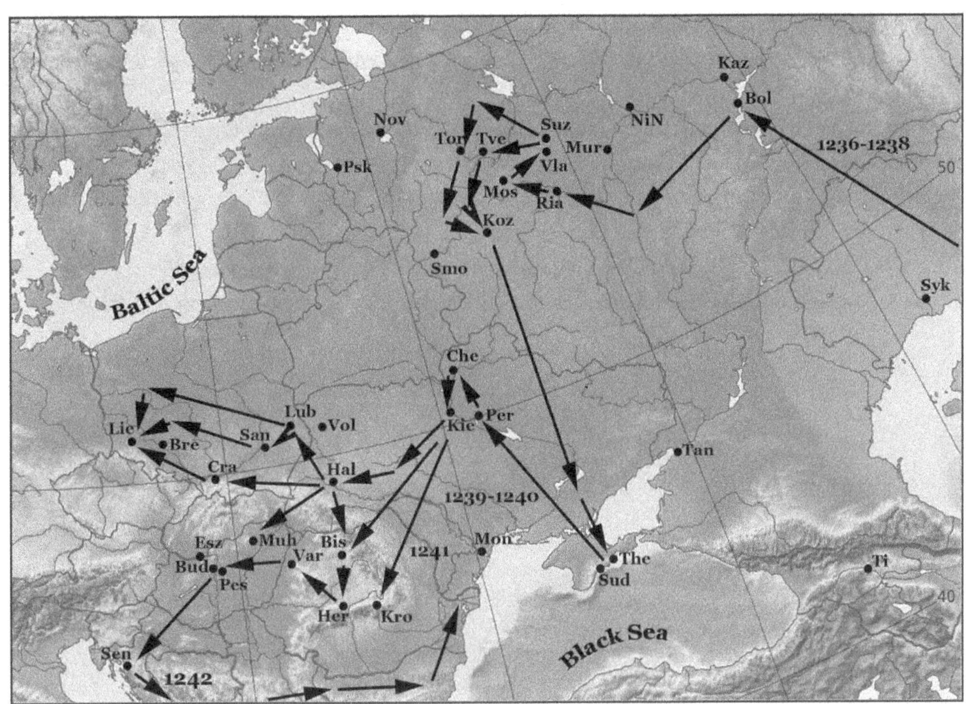

Map 42.2. The Mongol invasion of Eastern Europe, 1236–42. The location of the following sites is indicated: Bis – Bistritz (Bistrița); Bol – Bolgar; Bre – Breslau (Wrocław); Bud – Buda; Che – Chernigov (Chernihiv); Cra-Cracow; Esz – Esztergom; Hal – Halych; Her – Hermannstadt (Sibiu); Kaz – Kazan; Kie – Kiev; Koz – Kozelsk; Kro – Kronstadt (Brașov); Lie – Liegnitz (Legnica); Lub – Lublin; Mon – Moncastro (Bilhorod Dnistrovs'kyi); Mos – Moscow; Muh – Muhi; Mur – Murom; NiN – Nizhnii Novgorod; Nov – Novgorod; Per – Pereiaslavl' (Pereiaslav); Pes – Pest; Psk – Pskov; Ria – Riazan'; San – Sandomierz; Sen – Senj; Smo – Smolensk; Sud – Sudak; Suz – Suzdal'; Syk – Sarayjuk; Tan – Tana (Azov); The – Theodosia (Caffa, Feodosiia); Ti – Tiflis (Tbilisi); Tor – Torzhok; Tve – Tver; Var – Várad (Oradea); Vla – Vladimir; Vol – Volodymyr.

FURTHER READING

Bagi, Dániel. *Divisio regni: The Territorial Divisions, Power Struggles, and Dynastic Historiography of the Árpáds of 11th- and Early 12th-Century Hungary, with Comparative Studies of the Piasts of Poland and the Přemyslids of Bohemia.* Arpadiana 2. Budapest: Research Centre for the Humanities, 2020.

Burkhardt, Julia. "Assemblies in the Holy Roman Empire and the East Central European Kingdoms: A Comparative Essay on Political Participation and Representation." In *Rulership in Medieval East Central Europe: Power, Ritual and Legitimacy in Bohemia, Hungary, and Poland*, edited by Grischa Vercamer and Dušan Zupka, 198–216. East Central and Eastern Europe in the Middle Ages, 450–1450, 78. Leiden: Brill, 2022.

Font, Márta F. *Koloman the Learned, King of Hungary.* Szeged: Szegedi középkorász műhely, 2001.

Gál, Judit. *Dalmatia and the Exercise of Royal Authority in the Árpád-era Kingdom of Hungary.* Series Arpadiana 3. Budapest: Bölcsészettudományi Kutatóközpont, 2020.

Maiorov, Aleksandr V., and Roman Hautala, eds. *The Routledge Handbook of the Mongols and Central-Eastern Europe.* London: Routledge, 2021.

Rosik, Stanisław. "Pomerania and Poland in the 10th to 12th Centuries: The Expansion of the Piasts and Shaping Political, Social and State Relations in the Seaside Slav Communities." In *The Expansion of Central Europe in the Middle Ages*, edited by Nora Berend, 451–90. Burlington: Ashgate, 2012.

Wiszewski, Przemysław. *Domus Bolezlai: Values and Social Identity in Dynastic Traditions of Medieval Poland (c. 966–1138)*. East Central and Eastern Europe in the Middle Ages, 450–1450, 9. Leiden: Brill, 2010.

Wolverton, Lisa Ann. *Hastening toward Prague: Power and Society in the Medieval Czech Lands.* Philadelphia: University of Pennsylvania Press, 2001.

Zsoldos, Attila. *The Árpáds and Their People: An Introduction to the History of Hungary from ca. 900 to 1301.* Budapest: Research Centre for the Humanities, 2020.

Zupka, Dušan. *Ritual and Symbolic Communication in Medieval Hungary under the Árpád Dynasty (1000–1301)*. East Central and Eastern Europe in the Middle Ages, 450–1450, 39. Leiden: Brill, 2016.

43

THE CRUSADES IN CENTRAL EUROPE AND THE BALKANS

Keywords in this chapter: indulgence, Wendish Crusade, conversion

The First Crusade was launched at the instigation of Pope Urban II after his speech in Clermont in November 1095. The Crusade was an armed pilgrimage to the Holy Land in the eastern Mediterranean, the purpose of which was said to be protecting Christians from Muslims. The pope promised that participants would obtain full remission of sins, and his appeal resonated with European Christians, who had long been fascinated with the Biblical lands, and with young knights in search of adventure. The Muslim powers at that time were divided between the Seljuk Turks, who controlled Baghdad, Syria, and Anatolia, and the Fatimids of Egypt, the latter having control over Jerusalem. The conquest of that city by Europeans in July 1099 was violent and brutal but a full success. Following that, crusaders established new states in the conquered lands of the Near East.

Crusading in the eastern Mediterranean had limited appeal in East Central Europe. Nothing is known of Polish participation in the First Crusade, although the crusading ideology might have resonated in the wars of Bolesław the Wrymouth against the pagan Pomeranians (see chapter 42). Some Polish participants, though, are mentioned in the sources for the Second and Third Crusades. Bernard of Clairvaux wrote to Duke Vladislav II of Bohemia and asked him "to put this business of Christ before anything else and not to neglect it for what can be done at other times."[1] The first king from East Central Europe to take the crusading vows was Béla III of Hungary, but he died before fulfilling them. His son, Andrew II, was the first Hungarian king to join crusaders fighting in the

1 Florin Curta, ed., "Bernard of Clairvaux Calls the Czechs to Take the Cross," in *Medieval Eastern Europe, 500–1300: A Reader* (Toronto: University of Toronto Press, 2024), 235.

Near East. According to a contemporary chronicler, "fearing to expose himself and his kingdom to such risks and believing his vow to the Lord to be fully satisfied," he returned home in 1218 after less than a year in the Holy Land.[2]

While few people from East Central Europe joined the Crusades to the Near East, the region was affected by the movement in other ways. West European crusaders typically traveled by land through East Central and Southeastern Europe to reach Constantinople, and from there marched towards the Near East. Hungary was on the route of pilgrims to Jerusalem and, since 1018, these pilgrims had been under royal protection; the crusaders who followed the call of Pope Urban II in 1096 took the same route when heading for the eastern Mediterranean. The army led by Peter the Hermit might have comprised as many as 20,000 people, including noncombatants. Bands of participants plundered the country on their way through Hungary, which led to retaliation against them by King Coloman, and further groups of crusaders were prevented from entering the kingdom. When Godfrey of Bouillon arrived, Coloman only allowed him through under escort, while holding his brother Baldwin as hostage. "So it was," a German chronicler tells, "that the duke and the people crossed the kingdom of Hungary, every day in peace and quiet, buying in fair and just measure."[3] Few crusaders crossed Bohemia on their way, but a group of German armed pilgrims did, arriving from Saxony; they prompted anti-Jewish actions while in Prague. Crusader troops regularly pillaged towns and villages in the Balkans when they ran out of supplies. Just like the Hungarian kings, the Byzantine authorities insisted on striking deals with the crusaders when they reached the border. They gave them supplies and escorts in exchange for the promise that they would abstain from foraging in the country.

Tension was high in 1147, and King Géza II of Hungary paid protection money to the German crusaders – "no less than three thousand pounds of silver," according to Otto of Freising.[4] Despite crusader promises to Byzantine Emperor Manuel I to avoid trouble, violent incidents occurred on the way through Byzantine Thrace, as the armed pilgrims helped themselves to food and wine. In 1189, the only crusading army that reached the Near East by land was that of Holy Roman Emperor Frederick Barbarossa, who followed the usual route through Hungary. Careful negotiations between him and King Béla III made it possible for the well-planned passage to unfold peacefully. However, crossing the Byzantine provinces of the Balkans proved more difficult. Emperor Isaac II had a weak hold over those territories, distrusted Frederick, and was a poor negotiator. The crusaders were harassed by hostile local populations in Serbia, Bulgaria, and Thrace. Promised supplies went missing and fortifications were erected against them. Cornered in Adrianople, Frederick undertook to occupy Thrace, threatened to attack Constantinople, and negotiated with Serbs and Vlachs who promised "to come to the assistance of this expedition,

2 Curta, ed., "The Crusade of King Andrew," in *Medieval Eastern Europe*, 253.

3 Curta, ed., "The Army of the First Crusade in Hungary," in *Medieval Eastern Europe*, 232.

4 Curta, ed., "Hungary at the Time of the Second Crusade," in *Medieval Eastern Europe*, 236.

especially against the emperor of Greece."[5] In the end, Emperor Isaac was forced to secure free passage for all crusaders.

This was not the only instance of tensions between Catholics and Orthodox in the Balkans in the context of the Crusades: in 1225, Pope Honorius III encouraged crusaders to wage war on heretics in Bosnia; this appeal was repeated under Gregory IX in 1234. Moreover, in 1238, Gregory IX launched a crusade against the Bulgarian emperor John Asen II, who had ceased to recognize the authority of the papacy. These initiatives were halted, though, when the Mongol invasion forced Christian armies to face much more pressing dangers (see chapters 42 and 46).

During the eleventh and early twelfth centuries, the German kings and emperors were too busy dealing with internal conflicts in the imperial lands and with the contest with the papacy to bother fighting the Slavic pagans on their eastern frontier. Regaining the lands and re-establishing the ecclesiastical structures that had been lost with the 983 Slavic insurrection (see chapter 19) were not priorities on the imperial agenda. Bishops organized occasional military campaigns into the lands of the Liuticians, as in 1068 when Bishop Burchard of Halberstadt succeeded in destroying the Rethra temple. Furthermore, archbishops in border areas, such as Magdeburg and Bremen, supported missions to convince Slavic rulers and their retinues of the benefits of Christianity, as in the 1120s, when Vicelin was sent to the court of the Abodrite Henry. However, the real push came in the early twelfth century from German margraves who made inroads into Slavic territories, grabbing border lands in power struggles with Slavic lords.

In 1146, when Pope Eugenius III began organizing a renewed expedition to support the Crusader states, he enrolled one of the great churchmen of that time, Bernard of Clairvaux, to help him recruit crusaders. Bernard was well connected throughout Europe and was also a respected theologian and prolific writer. Bernard wrote letters to rulers and decision-makers and went on a lecture tour in an effort to convince them of the good cause of launching a new Crusade. He won over the French and German kings, Louis VII and Conrad III, as well as many knights from France and southern Germany.

However, while Conrad III had a solid grasp over the lands of southern Germany, that was not the case in the northern regions that were governed by powerful territorial lords. In March 1147, Bernard attended an imperial assembly in Frankfurt-am-Main and intervened to convince the German lords to participate in the Crusade to the Levant. The lords from Saxony and northern Germany replied that if the expedition was about protecting Christendom by fighting its enemies, they could do just as well by fighting the pagan Slavs on their doorstep. Bernard knew that in the Iberian Peninsula, Christians were fighting Muslims and had received the same privileges from the pope as those fighting Muslims in the Near East. Bernard forwarded the request of the north German lords to the pope, and in April Eugenius III issued the bull *Divina dispensatione* by which Christians fighting

5 Curta, ed., "The Army of Frederick Barbarossa Crosses the Balkans," in *Medieval Eastern Europe*, 242.

pagans in northern Europe and defending Christendom in those lands benefitted from the very same privileges and indulgences that applied to Christians fighting Muslims in the Near East. The pope entrusted the fight against pagans to the leadership of Bishop Anselm of Havelberg.

In Bernard's view, the objective of the wars Christians were expected to launch on pagans was conversion. In the tradition of Augustine, Christian thinkers had always been opposed to forced conversion; pagans had to be converted through persuasion, not coercion. However, Bernard argued that for preachers to persuade pagans, they had to be in a position to preach to them, and military victory would allow them to do just that. The first step was to destroy temples and cult places and to demonstrate how the pagan gods were powerless and pagan priests could not do anything at all. The second step was to start preaching to explain why the Christian god was much better. From the point of view of many German clerics, war was also justified by the fact that the Slavs between the Elbe and Oder rivers had been collectively Christian in the past before the insurrection of 983. In theological understanding, to have been Christian and to have relapsed into paganism was worse than being pagan, since paganism was equated with ignorance (pagans knew nothing better). Much like in the Iberian Peninsula, the aim was to win back territories that had once been Christian. What the Saxon and German lords wanted, however, was to pursue their aggressive agenda towards Slavs – to gain land and obtain the payment of tributes – with the blessing of the pope. To his credit, Bernard insisted that since the aim of the conflict was conversion, Christians were to refrain from taking tribute and booty.

In the late summer of 1147, an army of Saxons and Danes moved against the pagan Slavs in what has become known as the Wendish Crusade. Anselm of Havelberg was their leader; several other bishops at the head of their troops and German margraves joined him. The crusaders obtained a few successes, strengthened their positions towards Slavic rulers, and baptized a few Slavic warriors. More spectacularly, they destroyed a pagan temple in Malchow (between the Plau and Kölpin lakes in northeastern Germany). As they advanced into Slavic territory, the margraves Conrad and Albert the Bear convinced their companions to march towards Szczecin. When they laid siege to the town, the inhabitants appeared on the walls with the bishop of Pomerania, Adalbert, displaying crosses. They explained that they were already Christian. The confused crusaders gave up the siege and went back home.

There was no formal Crusade in the north in the decades after 1147. No pope repeated the privileges that had made fighting northern pagans the equivalent of fighting Muslims in the Near East. With the fall of Jerusalem in 1187, however, renewed appeals to crusade were sent by the popes throughout Europe, but they requested an expedition to the Near East, not to northern Europe. Fighting against pagans, however, did not stop in the north, and the spirit of the 1147 Wendish Crusade lived on without papal intervention. The Liuticians and Abodrites were now attacked on all fronts by Germans, Danes, and Pomeranians. The German margraves resumed their drawn-out struggle to gain more land and defeat their Slavic neighbors. The territory of the Abodrites was partitioned between German lords; only the land of Mecklenburg remained under Christian Slavic lords, Niklot and his descendants. The lordship of Brandenburg, meanwhile, was shaped by the marcher lord Albert the Bear, who had gained lands from the Slavs and had obtained the stronghold of Brandenburg bequeathed to him by the Stodoran lord Pribislav-Henry.

Denmark was a prosperous Christian kingdom in the twelfth century. The Danish islands, however, were exposed to raids from Slavic pirates that were a thorn in the side of Danish kings. Absalon, bishop of Roskilde (1158–92) and later archbishop of Lund (1178–1202), was a close ally of King Valdemar I (1157–82) and tireless campaigner against paganism. He spent most of his life on military expeditions and was receptive to the crusade ideas that had been propagated by Bernard of Clairvaux.

Absalon and Valdemar dealt a major blow to the last bulwark of Slavic paganism with the invasion of Rügen in 1168/69. After ten years of repeated attacks, they destroyed the last temple of the pagan Slavs and subjugated the island. The Slavic prince of the Rugians, Jaromar, converted to Christianity and became a vassal of the Danish king. When Pope Alexander III heard of the invasion and the destruction of the temple, he congratulated Valdemar for being such a great crusader. However, the invasion of the island of Rügen had not formally been a crusade, as no remission of sins had been proclaimed by the pope.

The last Liutician territories, meanwhile, were conquered by the dukes of Pomerania who incorporated them into their principality. By the end of the twelfth century, there were no more independent pagan Slavic territories in Central Europe. The process that had begun under the Ottonians in the tenth century was finally completed and the "anomaly" of the pagan Slavs surrounded by Christian kingdoms on all sides had been removed. At a time when Denmark, Poland, and Bohemia were being shaped into Christian kingdoms, the Liuticians had provided a pagan alternative to centralized Christian polities and had succeeded for a surprisingly long time. The Liuticians, however, had been restricted in their networks of alliances because of their religion and absence of centralized rulership. As the dominant position of the Liuticians waned in the later eleventh century, the pagan option ceased to be seen as attractive to Slavic rulers such as the princes of Rügen and some of the lords of the Abodrites.

FURTHER READING

Dall'Aglio, Francesco. "Crusading in a Nearer East: The Balkan Politics of Honorius III and Gregory IX (1221–1241)." In *La papauté et les croisades. Actes du VIIe Congrès de la Society for the Study of the Crusades and the Latin East, Avignon, 27–31 août 2008*, edited by Michel Balard, 173–84. Crusades Subsidia 3. Farnham: Ashgate, 2011.

Dragnea, Mihai. *The Wendish Crusade, 1147: The Development of Crusading Ideology in the Twelfth Century.* London: Routledge, 2020.

Gładysz, Mikołaj. *The Forgotten Crusaders: Poland and the Crusader Movement in the Twelfth and Thirteenth Centuries.* The Northern World 56. Leiden: Brill, 2012.

Güttner-Sporzyński, Darius von. "The Archetypal Crusader: Henry of Sandomierz, the Second Youngest Son of Bolesław III." In *Rome, Constantinople and Newly-Converted Europe: Archaeological and Historical Evidence*, edited by Maciej Salamon, Marcin Wołoszyn, Aleksandr E. Musin, and Perica Špehar, 215–32. Cracow: Instytut Archeologii i Etnologii PAN, 2012.

Hunyadi, Zsolt. "Hungary and the Second Crusade." In *The Second Crusade: Holy War on the Periphery of Latin Christendom*, edited by Jason T. Roche and Janus Møller Jensen, 55–65. Outremer: Studies in the Crusades and the Latin East 2. Turnhout: Brepols, 2008.

Tyerman, Christopher. *God's War: A New History of the Crusades*. Harvard, MA: Belknap Press, 2006.

Veszprémy, László. "The Crusade of Andrew II, King of Hungary, 1217–1218." *Iacobus* 13–14 (2002): 87–110.

44

THE BALTIC CRUSADES

Keywords in this chapter: Sword-Brothers, Teutonic Knights, Knights of Dobrzyń

During the twelfth and thirteenth centuries, Baltic and Finnish peoples from Northeastern Europe were still pagan and living like they had for hundreds of years. They sustained themselves through agriculture and animal husbandry, with elites living in small forts. In the North, Finnish tribes lived as hunters and gatherers. Trade contacts with Scandinavia had been established in the Early Middle Ages, and Rus' princes extracted tribute from some territories. Beyond that, Balts and Finns had only limited contact with Christian Europe (see chapters 22, 23, and 32).

Attempts at conversion began in the late twelfth century. Meinhard, a canon from the Augustinian abbey of Segeberg (today in Bad Segeberg, near Lübeck, in northern Germany), joined a group of merchants from Gotland going to the region of the Lower Daugava River in what is now Latvia. There, in the land of the Livs, he began his mission. The area was said to be "in Rus'" and Meinhard obtained the support of Vladimir, the prince of Polotsk who collected tribute there. Shortly after that, Archbishop Hartwig II of Bremen named him bishop for the new converts. Meinhard built a church and stone fortifications in Üxküll (now Ikšķile, near Riga), but his success in converting Livs was modest (see plate 44.1). In 1195, upon the request of one of Meinhard's companions, Pope Celestine III (1191–98) granted full crusading privileges to those who would go to fight the pagans in the eastern Baltic, following the example of the Wendish Crusade (see chapter 43). Three years later, the privileges were renewed by Innocent III (1198–1216). According to their understanding, every time that newly baptized natives reverted to their ancient ways, it was legitimate to fight them as apostates.

After Meinhard's death (1196), Albert of Buxhövden, a canon from the Augustinian abbey of Neumünster (not far from Segeberg) and nephew of Archbishop Hartwig, was appointed as missionary bishop in the Daugava area. Accompanied by an army of crusaders and with the support of the Danish king, he found a place more promising than Üxküll and in 1201 established the town of Riga at the mouth of the river

Plate 44.1. The ruins of the church built in 1185 by Bishop Meinhard in Ikšķile (Latvia). View from the west. Wikimedia Commons, the free media repository.

Daugava (see map 44.1). Because the area was within the lands of the Livs, the surrounding country came to be known as Livonia. Albert created a new order of warrior monks, the Brothers of the Knighthood of Christ in Livonia: they were nicknamed the Sword-Brothers because of their coat of arms that showed a red sword below a cross. According to the German chronicler Henry of Livonia, "Pope Innocent gave them the rule of the Templars [to follow]" and "placed them under the jurisdiction of the bishop [Albert of Riga]."[1] The goal of this monastic-military order was to fight pagans and

1 Florin Curta, ed., "The Sword Brothers," in *Medieval Eastern Europe, 500–1300: A Reader* (Toronto: University of Toronto Press, 2024), 245.

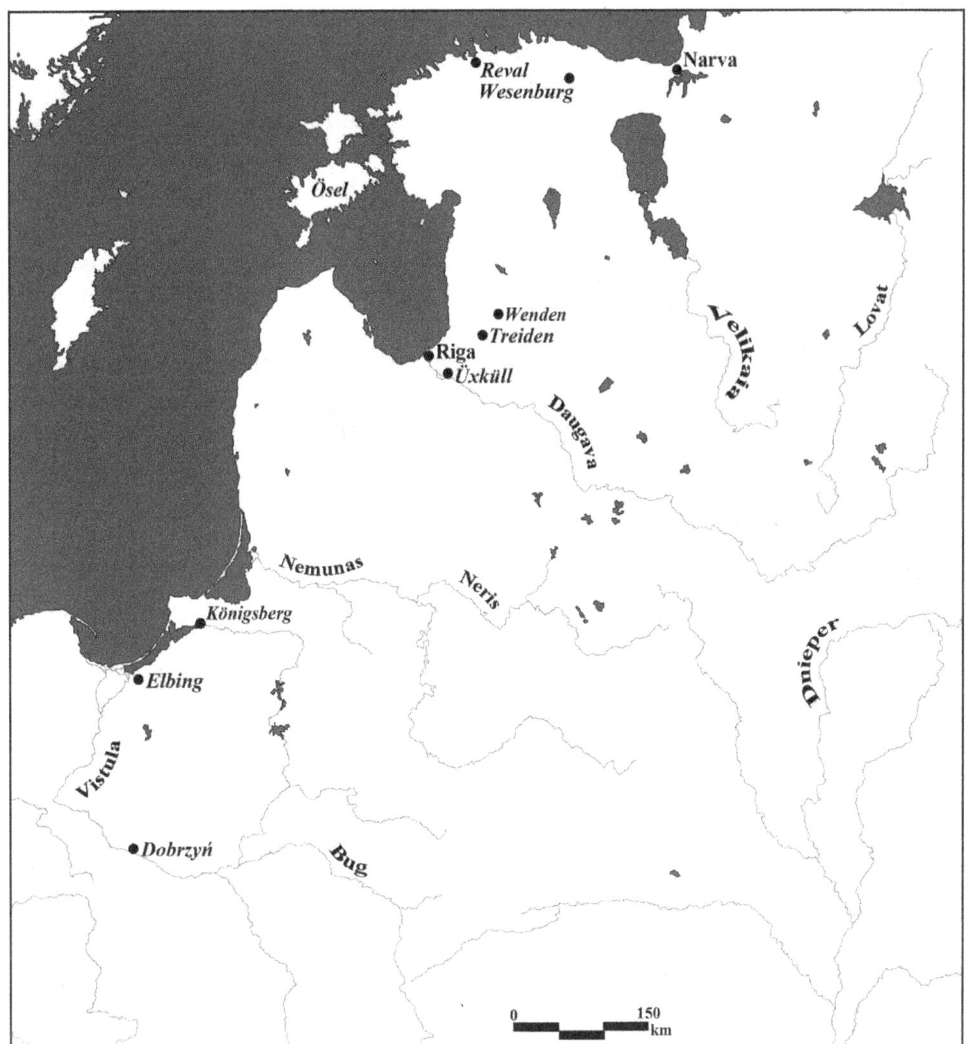

Map 44.1. The crusading lands in the Baltic region. Shaded area represents the Baltic Sea. Medieval names are in italics.

help Bishop Albert in subjugating the land. Unlike the military orders in the Iberian Peninsula and the Near East, the Sword-Brothers did not rely on extensive properties of their own but were dependent upon their bishop and on revenues from lands they conquered. Albert and the Sword-Brothers invaded the lands of the Letts, north and east of the Daugava, of the Semigallians to the south, and of the Curonians in the coastal area; they were successful in quelling revolts and defending the land against incursions from the Rus' and Lithuanians. Henry of Livonia explains how, defeated at Treiden (now Turaida, half-way between Riga and Rubene, in Latvia), the local Letts "humbly besought [Albert] to spare them and promised that they would immediately accept the neglected faith of Christ, that they would henceforth observe the sacraments faithfully, and that they would never again call to mind pagan rites."[2]

The result of those efforts was the creation of a new territorial power in Livonia, which was governed by the bishop of Riga (archbishop since 1253) with the assistance of the Sword-Brothers. They had under their power various local tribes under their own leaders. Henry of Livonia says that Albert "consecrated the cathedral [in Riga] and dedicated it, as well as the entire land of Livonia, to Mary, the blessed Mother of God."[3] The Virgin Mary was depicted on banners and Livonia was called "the land of the mother" (as opposed to "the land of the Son," the Holy Land), which turned it into a legitimate destination for pilgrims.

Meanwhile, things were not going well for crusaders in the Near East. The Kurdish general Saladin conquered Jerusalem in 1187, which ushered in a period of disarray for Christians. Preparations for a new Crusade were soon under way and the combined armies of the French (led by King Philip II) and the English (with King Richard I) descended upon Acre. A third army of German crusaders, commanded by Frederick Barbarossa, returned home after the emperor drowned while crossing a river in what is now Turkey, on the way to the Holy Land. However, a small number of German crusaders made it to Acre and there, during the siege of the city, a new military-monastic order was formed – the Teutonic Order. The order was named after the Hospital of Saint Mary, which was established for pilgrims by the German knights. Like the Sword-Brothers and all other similar orders, the Teutonic Knights were at the same time monks and warriors; their mission was to protect Christian pilgrims. The Order gained importance under Grand Master Hermann of Salza (1209–39), who was a clever manager and obtained active support from both pope and Holy Roman emperor. The Order had its headquarters in the Crusader states where the knights built Montfort Castle (near Eilon, northern Israel). Moreover, they cumulated estates granted to them by pious donors across Europe.

As his order was growing more prosperous, Hermann of Salza was offered new opportunities for expansion. In 1211, he responded to a call from King Andrew II of Hungary, who needed assistance in fighting the pagan Cumans across the eastern Carpathian Mountains. In his 1211 charter, the king explains that he "sent the crusaders of the hospital of St. Mary," which was at that time based in Acre, "to the land called Borza [now Ţara Bârsei, the region around the city of Braşov, in central Romania], which is beyond the forest in the parts toward the Cumans."[4] The Teutonic knights were granted permission to settle in the Burzenland and to use the resources available to them in eastern Transylvania. As they grew ever more independent of royal power and began to erect castles without permission of the king, however, Andrew expelled the knights from his kingdom in 1225. That same year, Duke Conrad of Mazovia requested the help of Teutonic Knights to fight

2 Curta, ed., "The Crusades Against Lettgallians," in *Medieval Eastern Europe*, 240.

3 Curta, ed., "The Sword Brothers," in *Medieval Eastern Europe*, 245.

4 Curta, ed., "The Teutonic Knights in Transylvania," in *Medieval Eastern Europe*, 255.

pagan Prussians on the northern border of his duchy. The Prussians were threatening the mission of the duke's protégé, Bishop Christian of Prussia, despite his efforts to defend him and the new converts by means of yet another military monastic order. However, a letter from Hermann of Salza reveals that the order of the Knights of Dobrzyń (named so after the castle near Włocławek, in Poland, that Duke Conrad donated to them) comprised "no more than 15 men"; they proved to be unreliable and ended up amalgamated with the Teutonic Knights in 1235.[5]

Before accepting Conrad's offer, Hermann sought the support and protection of both the emperor and the pope. In 1226, he obtained from Frederick II the Bull of Rimini, which recognized the grand master of the Teutonic Order as an imperial prince for the lands he would conquer. In 1234, Hermann received from Pope Gregory IX a special privilege: the territories that the knights would conquer were to be integrated into the Patrimony of Peter and thus placed directly under papal authority and protection. As they were under his direct jurisdiction, the pope granted those territories to the Order as a fief to administer in his name, which turned the grand master into a papal vassal. Those arrangements were meant to eliminate interference in the domestic affairs of the Order by any ruler of the neighboring regions. Hermann had ambitious plans.

Armed with those privileges, the Teutonic Knights began their conquest of Prussia in 1230. In a few decades they took vast territories, and at the end of the thirteenth century their control was solid and definitive. What had taken shape in Prussia was a political entity ruled by an order of monk warriors that was declared a papal fief. Four bishoprics were created in Prussia that, along with the four bishoprics of Livonia, were suffragans of the archbishop of Riga. In the newly conquered territories, the Teutonic Knights were headed by the master of Prussia who resided in Elbing (today Elbląg, in northern Poland). Despite multiple Prussian revolts, the Teutonic Knights were there to stay. Moreover, in 1237 the Sword-Brothers were incorporated into the Teutonic Order as a separate branch, the Livonian Order.

Meanwhile, the situation in the Near East deteriorated further, and the Teutonic Order lost Montfort Castle in 1271. When Europeans were expelled from Acre, the last standing crusader state, in 1291, Grand Master Conrad of Feuchtwangen (1290–97) moved the Order's headquarters to Venice. However, given that the crusader conquests in the north were such a resounding success, in 1309 his successor Siegfried of Feuchtwangen (1303–11) finally moved the main convent of the Order and his residence to Marienburg ("Mary's Fortress," today Malbork, Poland) in Prussia (see plate 44.2).

The Teutonic state in Prussia had one of the most modern and efficient administrative systems for its time. It relied on brothers who had made vows of obedience to the grand master. Since the brothers were celibate, hereditary control by influential families was not the problem that it was everywhere else. This facilitated the establishment of stable and long-standing structures. Bishops and warrior monks competed for political control. In

5 Curta, ed., "The Conquest of Prussia and St. Barbara," in *Medieval Eastern Europe*, 257.

Plate 44.2. Panoramic view of the castle built by the Teutonic Knights at Malbork (Poland), ca. 1280. The castle was completely rebuilt when the headquarters of the Order moved here in 1309. Wikimedia Commons, the free media repository.

Livonia, the power struggle dragged on between the bishop and the knights. In Prussia, however, the power of the grand masters and their knights was uncontested. All of them were subordinated to the papacy. Both Prussia and Livonia were theocratic states that can be seen as the ultimate achievement of the reform papacy. Beginning with Gregory VII in the eleventh century, popes had wanted to impose their will as both spiritual and political leaders of Christendom. In Prussia and Livonia, they achieved that goal at a level unseen any time before and anywhere else. Prussia and Livonia had no kings; they were ruled by religious men. Any distinction between secular and religious authority was absent. The struggle between emperors and popes as secular and spiritual leaders of the Christian world had come to an end.

The Danish kings, at the instigation of Albert of Buxhövden, also wanted to get involved in the eastern Baltic. Valdemar II (1202–41) had the backing of the pope, who gave him permission to conquer as much land as he could if it was with the aim of converting the pagans. Sent by Valdemar, Archbishop Anders Sunesen (1201–28) first attacked the Estonians of Ösel Island (now Saaremaa, in western Estonia) in 1206 without much success. Valdemar, however, himself led a large fleet in 1219 and conquered northern Estonia.

The land became a dependency of the kingdom of Denmark, and the king's son Knut was given the title of duke of Estonia. The Danes founded a city they named "the Danish Fortress" (Danskeborgen), which German inhabitants renamed Reval (today Tallinn). The newly established bishop of Reval was not a suffragan of the archbishopric of Riga, but of that of Lund in Denmark (today in Sweden). Castles were built in Reval and Wesenberg (now Rakvere, in northeastern Estonia), later in Narva, and the duchy was administered by a royal governor. From 1266 to 1282, the duchy belonged to Queen Dowager Margaret Sambiria, and from 1303 it was ruled by the brother of King Eric VI Menved, who became king as Christopher II in 1319. A period of dynastic trouble followed his death, and Estonia was sold to the Teutonic Order in 1346 after 127 years of Danish rule.

The Crusades also extended to pagan Finland where the Swedish kings sent expeditions with the backing of the pope, under the pretense of protecting Swedish settlers in coastal areas against pagans. By the late thirteenth century, Finland had been conquered, a bishopric had been established in Turku (Åbo in Swedish), and the "Eastland" was incorporated into the kingdom of Sweden.

FURTHER READING

Bysted, Ane L., Carsten Selch Jensen, Kurt Villads Jensen, and John H. Lind. *Jerusalem in the North: Denmark and the Baltic Crusade, 1100–1522*. Outremer: Studies in the Crusades and the Latin East 1. Turnhout: Brepols, 2012.

Fonnesberg-Schmidt, Iben. *The Popes and the Baltic Crusades, 1147–1254*. The Northern World 26. Leiden: Brill, 2007.

Hunyadi, Zsolt. "The Teutonic Order in Burzenland (1211–1225): Recent Reconsiderations." In *L'Ordine teutonico tra Mediterraneo e Baltico. Incontri e scontri tra religioni, popoli e cultura*, edited by Hubert Houben and Kristjan Toomaspoeg, 151–72. Acta Theutonica 5. Galatina: M. Congedo, 2008.

Leighton, Gregory. "The Baltic Crusades (1147–1300)." In *The Routledge Handbook of East Central and Eastern Europe in the Middle Ages, 500–1300*, edited by Florin Curta, 393–408. London: Routledge, 2022.

Pluskowski, Aleksander. *The Archaeology of the Prussian Crusade: Holy War and Colonisation*. London: Routledge, 2013.

Sclart, Anti. *Livonia, Rus' and the Baltic Crusades in the Thirteenth Century*. Translated by Fiona Robb. East Central and Eastern Europe in the Middle Ages, 450–1450, 29. Leiden: Brill, 2015.

Starnawska, Maria. "Military Orders and the Beginning of Crusades in Prussia." In *The Crusades and the Military Orders: Expanding Frontiers of Medieval Latin Christianity*, edited by Zsolt Hunyadi and József Laszlovszky, 417–28. Budapest: Department of Medieval Studies, Central European University, 2001.

Urban, William L. *The Livonian Crusade*. Chicago: Lithuanian Research and Studies Center, 2004.

Urban, William L. *The Teutonic Knights: A Military History*. London: Greenhill, 2003.

45

THE BALKANS: NEMANJID SERBIA AND THE SECOND BULGARIAN EMPIRE

Keywords in this chapter: *zhupans*, Vlachs, Cumans, inscriptions

During the twelfth century, two new powers emerged in the Balkan Peninsula: Serbia under the Nemanjid dynasty and the Second Bulgarian Empire. Before that, during the eleventh century, the Byzantine rule over the Balkans was challenged by several rebellions (in 1040, 1043, 1073, 1078, and 1083), Pecheneg and Norman attacks, the passage of crusading armies (in 1096/7, 1147, and 1189), and a long military conflict with Hungary (under Emperor Manuel I). Despite such turbulence, no part of the Byzantine possessions broke away and no native rulers declared independence. Things changed, however, with the onset of the political crisis following the death of Emperor Manuel I in 1180, a crisis which culminated with the catastrophe inflicted by the Fourth Crusade – the conquest and sack of Constantinople in 1204.

In Serbia, the Nemanjids were a family of local leaders (called *zhupans*) who had already begun to distance themselves from Byzantium when they sought the alliance of the kings of Hungary. Helena, the daughter of a zhupan named Uroš (ca. 1113–ca. 1131), even became queen of Hungary in 1131, when the crown passed to her husband, Béla II (1131–41). In 1165, Emperor Manuel I (1143–80) intervened in local affairs and appointed a man named Tihomir to rule over the Serbian lands together with his brothers Srcimir, Miroslav, and Nemanja. Each brother was assigned a specific region, with Nemanja ruling over the eastern parts of Serbia, closer to the lands under direct Byzantine rule. He managed to expand westwards, in the direction of the Adriatic coast, where he took over Kotor (in what is now Montenegro) (see map 45.1). In the conflict that erupted between the four brothers, Nemanja – who gave his name to the dynasty – managed to defeat and kill Tihomir, and his surviving siblings duly acknowledged him as grand zhupan. However, when attacked by Emperor Manuel in 1172, Nemanja promptly surrendered without a battle, employing a theatrical display of obedience: according to the contemporary Byzantine historian John

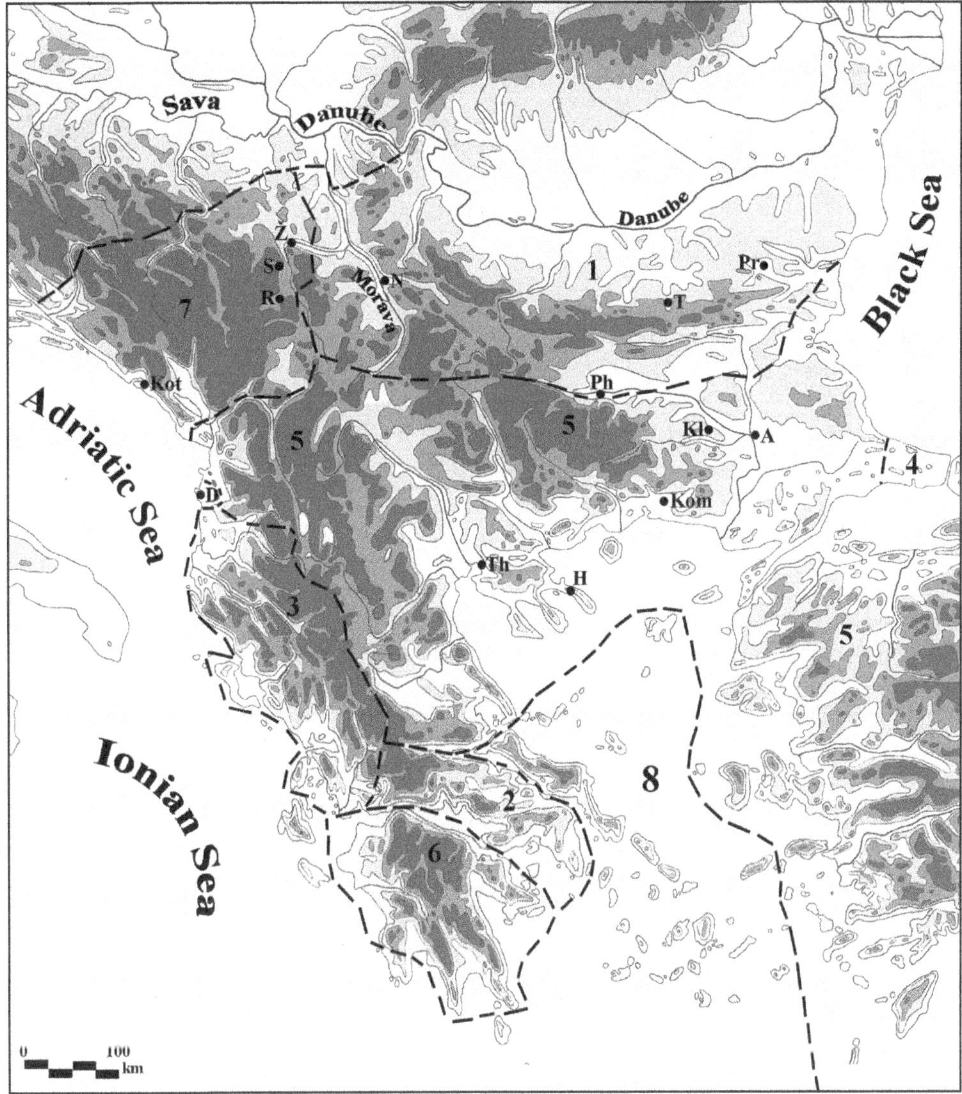

Map 45.1. The Balkans in the mid-thirteenth century: 1 – Bulgaria; 2 – Duchy of Athens; 3 – Epirus; 4 – Latin Empire of Constantinople; 5 – Nicene Empire; 6 – Principality of Achaea; 7 – Serbia; 8 – Venetian possessions. The location of the following sites is indicated: A – Adrianople (Edirne); D – Drach/Dyrrachium (Durrës); H – Hilandar; Kl – Klokotnica; Kom – Komotini; Kot – Kotor; N – Niš; Ph – Philippopolis (Plovdiv); Pr – Preslav; R – Ras; S- Studenica; T – Tărnovo; Th – Thessaloniki; Ž – Žiča. Thrace is the region at the southern border of Bulgaria, where Philippopolis and Adrianople are located.

Kinnamos, "he arrived in front of the imperial authority with his head uncovered and his arms bare to the elbow, his feet unshod, and a rope around his neck. He gave to the emperor the sword that he was holding in his hand, so that the emperor could do with him what he wished to do."[1] Although paraded as prisoner of war in the triumphal procession

1 Florin Curta, ed., "Stephen Nemanja Submits to Emperor Manuel I," in *Medieval Eastern Europe, 500–1300: A Reader* (Toronto: University of Toronto Press, 2024), 308.

Table 45.1. Rulers of Serbia between 1100 and 1400

Name of the Ruler	Regnal Years
Zhupans	
Uroš I	ca. 1113–ca. 1131
Uroš II	ca. 1131–ca. 1153; 1155–61
Desa	ca. 1153–55; 1161–62; ca. 1165–ca. 1168
Tihomir	ca. 1168–ca. 1170
Stephen Nemanja	ca. 1170–96
Kings	
Stephen Prvovenčani	1196–1202; 1203–27
Vukan	1202–03
Radoslav	1227–34
Vladislav	1234–43
Uroš I	1243–76
Dragutin	1276–82
Milutin	1282–1321
Stephen Dečanski	1321–31
Stephen Dušan	1331–55; emperor in 1345
Stephen Uroš V	1355–71 (emperor)

that the emperor organized on his return to Constantinople, Nemanja was soon released and returned to his homeland.

After Manuel's death in 1180, Nemanja openly rejected his affected Byzantine allegiance and sided with the king of Hungary, Béla III (1172–96). In the process, he was able to snatch more territories to the southwest (between his domain and the Adriatic coast) and to annex Niš and parts of Macedonia. Although defeated in battle by the new emperor, Isaac II Angelos (1185–95, 1203–4), Nemanja sealed an alliance with the victor by marrying his son Stephen to the emperor's niece, Evdokia. Since Evdokia was the daughter of Alexius III Angelos, who in 1195 overthrew his brother Isaac to assume the crown in Constantinople, Nemanja's son, now an imperial son-in-law, was bestowed the title of *sebastokrator*, which placed him in the immediate family circle of the emperor.

To smooth his son's ascension to power, Nemanja abdicated in his favor at an assembly specially summoned in Ras (now Novi Pazar in southern Serbia) in 1196 (see table 45.1). He put Stephen in power instead of himself but bestowed the title of grand zhupan on his other son, Vukan. After that, according to the *vita* written by his son, Sava, Nemanja "took leave of his dominion, his children and his God-given wife of the first marriage (for he did not marry twice)" and withdrew to the monastery of Studenica (near Ušće, in the Middle Ibar region of central Serbia), his own foundation of ca. 1183.[2] Having taken the monastic vows, Nemanja (now rebaptized Simeon) moved to Mount Athos in 1198, where his third son Ratko had already become a monk under the name Sava. The son and the father established Hilandar Monastery, which Emperor Alexius III Angelos granted in perpetuity to the Serbian monks. The charter that Simeon issued for the occasion, as if he were still the grand zhupan Nemanja, insists upon the divine origin of the power of the Byzantine emperor, the Hungarian king, and the grand zhupan.[3] In Nemanja's eyes, the zhupan of the Serbs was clearly not inferior in status to the ruler of any neighboring country. Nemanja-Simeon died a few months later (in 1199) and was buried initially at Hilandar. Seven years later, however, Sava translated (transferred) the remains to Studenica, where Simeon was proclaimed a saint.

The canonization of Nemanja-Simeon was the result of a complicated political process. In 1202, his younger son Vukan attacked his brother Stephen, and while Nemanja was still alive, he adopted the title of king. Vukan even wrote to Pope Innocent III (1198–1216) to ask for a crown. Not to be outdone, Stephen wrote with the same request to the pope but, like his brother, to no avail. While Vukan was initially successful in the ensuing civil war, Stephen eventually regained power. To ease tensions between his brothers, Sava decided to bring the remains of their father to Serbia. The cult of St. Simeon became a major component in the establishment of the Nemanjid dynasty. Stephen promoted the cult of his father by writing his *vita*, followed by Sava who drafted another in 1208. Both texts established the cult of the Serbian ruler, now regarded as the founder of a dynasty with sacred roots.

Meanwhile in Bulgaria, which had been under Byzantine rule since the late tenth century (see chapter 13), events that would lead to the formation of the Second Bulgarian Empire were unfolding. In the civil war against his brother Vukan, Stephen had won the upper hand because of the military assistance he received from Bulgaria. Although trouble may have been brewing for a while in the region, a revolt broke out in 1185 in the lands between the Danube and the Stara Planina Mountains now in northern Bulgaria. The uprising was led by two Vlach brothers, named Peter (whose initial name was Theodore) and Asen (whose Christian name was John). According to the testimony of a late twelfth-century chronicle of the Third Crusade, "over a large part of Bulgaria, as well as along the Danube up to where it flows into the sea, Kalopeter [Peter] the Vlach and his brother Assanius [Asen] ruled as tyrants together with their Vlach followers."[4] Peter and Asen were most likely members of Vlach troops in the Byzantine service stationed in a number of fortresses in the mountains. Indeed, in the words of another historian of that

2 Curta, ed., "Saint Sava on Stephen Nemanja's Abdication," in *Medieval Eastern Europe*, 310.

3 Curta, ed., "Stephen Nemanja Established the Monastery of Hilandar," in *Medieval Eastern Europe*, 218.

4 Curta, ed., "The Army of Frederick Barbarossa Crosses the Balkans," in *Medieval Eastern Europe*, 243.

time, the rebels occupied "the rough ground and inaccessible places," while their fortresses were "built on sheer cliffs and cloud-capped peaks."[5]

The spark that ignited the Bulgarian revolt was a tax that Emperor Isaac II Angelos introduced to cover the expenses of his wedding to the daughter of the Hungarian king Béla III. Their initial claims rejected, the Vlach brothers Peter and Asen descended from the mountains with an army of rebels and fell unexpectedly upon the Byzantine towns in Thrace, killing many and carrying away a great number of prisoners and goods. The mobilization for the rebellion skillfully capitalized on the cult of St. Demetrius, the patron saint of Thessaloniki. As that city had just been conquered and sacked by the Normans, the saint was believed to have left it in favor of a "house of prayer" built by the two brothers in their main fortress of Tărnovo (now Veliko Tărnovo, in Bulgaria). Peter had meanwhile begun sporting a gold chaplet on his head and scarlet buskins on his feet, thus pushing imperial claims reminiscent of the Bulgarian past. Moreover, the first town that the rebels attacked was Preslav, the old capital of Bulgaria, which they apparently wanted to restore. Nonetheless, the rebels were defeated in the first encounter with the Byzantine troops, and Peter and Asen fled across the river Danube, where they found trustworthy allies among the Cumans, with whom they may have already been in contact. Nonetheless, in 1188 Emperor Isaac managed to capture Asen's wife and to obtain his brother John (later known as Johannitsa, or "little John") as a hostage. It is at this point that Peter ("Kalopeter") offered his military assistance to the western emperor Frederick Barbarossa. During the 1190 campaign against the rebels, Isaac and his army were ambushed in a mountain defile (probably near the modern city of Gabrovo) and Isaac barely escaped alive. Taking advantage of the Byzantine setback, the rebels and their Cuman allies took cities on the Black Sea coast as well as in the interior. However, the troops did not cross the Morava River into Serbia, and no Serbian intervention in the region east of that river is known to have taken place before 1200.

Defeated by the rebels in Bulgaria, Isaac II Angelos was nonetheless victorious over Nemanja in Serbia, and the valley of the river Morava remained in Byzantine hands. Asen was murdered in 1196 by a nobleman named Ivanko, who seized Tărnovo and immediately called for Byzantine assistance against Peter, who was already moving against him from Preslav. With no Byzantine army coming to his rescue, Ivanko fled to Constantinople, and Peter took over Tărnovo, only to be murdered a few months later. His younger brother Johannitsa succeeded to the throne (see table 45.2). A charismatic figure, he was immediately recognized as emperor.

With Johannitsa (nicknamed "Kaloyan" or "Fair John"), the Vlach revolt turned into the Second Bulgarian Empire. When the Vlach and Cuman troops reached the outskirts of Constantinople in 1200 or 1201, the Vlach leader Johannitsa had already entered negotiations with Pope Innocent III to secure for himself a crown and recognition of the imperial title. In his letters to the pope, Johannitsa referred to the Bulgarian emperors

5 Curta, ed., "The Vlach Rebels in Bulgaria," in *Medieval Eastern Europe*, 306.

Table 45.2. Rulers of the Second Bulgarian Empire between 1185 and 1400

Name of the Ruler	Regnal Years
Peter	1185–97, with
John Asen I	1187–96
Johannitsa Kaloyan	1196–1207
Boril	1207–18
John Asen II	1218–41
Coloman Asen I	1241–46
Michael Asen I	1246–56
Coloman Asen II	1256
Mico Asen	1256–57
Constantine Asen	1257–77
Michael Asen II	1277–79
Ivailo	1278–79
John Asen III	1279–80
George Terter	1280–92
Smilec	1292–98
John II	1298–99
Theodore Svetoslav	1299–1321
George Terter II	1321–22
Michael Shishman	1322–30
John Stephen	1330–31
John Alexander	1331–71
John Shishman	1371–93

Peter (927–69) and Samuel (997–1014) as his ancestors, and soon began to call himself "emperor of the Bulgarians." This he was doing while the rapid and formidable growth of the new state caused a Hungarian reaction. Under King Emeric (1196–1204), Hungarian troops invaded the northwestern parts of Bulgaria. Those are the circumstances in which Johannitsa offered his support to Stephen of Serbia in his conflict with Vukan, who had King Emeric as an ally.

A papal legate eventually came to Tărnovo and crowned Johannitsa as emperor on November 8, 1204, almost six months after the coronation of Count Baldwin of Flanders as emperor of Constantinople, in the wake of the conquest of the Byzantine capital by the forces of the Fourth Crusade (see insert 45.1). Johannitsa tried to establish good relations with the crusaders, but he was met with haughty rejection. The deteriorating relations between Bulgaria and the Latin Empire of Constantinople (as the new empire is known) quickly led to military conflict. On April 14, 1205, the allied Bulgarian and Cuman forces obtained a major victory against the crusaders at Adrianople, with Emperor Baldwin himself being taken captive (he subsequently died in captivity in Tărnovo). Crusader chronicler

INSERT 45.1. FRANKISH MOREA

The conquest of continental Greece, including the Peloponnese, was a direct consequence of the Fourth Crusade. Acting on behalf of Boniface of Montferrat, king of Thessalonica, two "Frankish" knights – William of Champlitte and Geoffrey of Villehardouin (the nephew of the chronicler by the same name) – invaded southern Greece with only 100 knights and 500 infantrymen. They defeated the local Greeks in 1205 at the Battle of Koundouros (in Messenia), and Champlitte became the first ruler of the Principality of Achaea (later known also as Morea). However, he left for France three years later, to settle an inheritance, and died on his way there. Geoffrey of Villehardouin became ruler for the following decade. He established his residence at Andravida (northwestern Peloponnese) and divided the principality into twelve baronies. The owners of those baronies owed military service to the prince but otherwise had considerable power and autonomy. The barons and the ecclesiastic hierarchy formed a High Court, which was an advisory body to the prince, but also operated as the highest court for all matters pertaining to disputes. Frankish Morea had its own set of laws, the Assizes of Romania, in which elements of Byzantine law were combined with French customary law. The golden age of the principality of Achaea came with the reign of William II of Villehardouin, a crusader (who participated in the Seventh Crusade led by King Louis IX of France) and a troubadour, who moved his court to Glarentza (near modern-day Kyllini, western Peloponnese). Allied with Michael II, despot of Epirus, William was defeated by a Byzantine army at Pelagonia in 1259. Taken prisoner, he was released upon relinquishing large parts of the territory and swearing an oath of allegiance to Emperor Michael VIII Palaiologos. He broke his oath and managed to defeat two Byzantine armies sent against him and recognized the suzerainty of Charles of Anjou (who had just conquered Sicily) in exchange for military aid. His daughter, Isabelle, married Charles's son Philip, but when the latter died without male heirs (1277), and after William's own death a year later, Charles became prince of Achaea. He never set foot in Morea, which was governed in his name by deputies (*baillis*). That arrangement continued under his son, Charles II, but in 1289, William's widow, Isabella of Villehardouin, took over until 1307. For much of the fourteenth century, Frankish Morea was disputed by various successors, many of whom did not set foot in Greece but exercised power through baillis. From 1377 to 1381, Frankish Morea was even ruled by the Hospitallers, a monastic-military order based at that time in Rhodes. After that, a company of mercenaries from Navarre and Gascony, known as the Navarrese Company, ruled the principality in the name of James of Baux (1381–83). By 1430, much of Frankish Morea was in Byzantine hands, but the Byzantine reconquest was short-lived, as Peloponnese was taken in 1460 by the Ottoman Turks.

Robert de Clari explains that "those who escaped came fleeing to Constantinople, and the doge of Venice came fleeing and many people with him, and they left their tents and their harness just as they were when they were encamped before this city, because they never dared turn that way, so great was the rout."[6]

6 Curta, ed., "Robert de Clari on the Battle of Adrianople," in *Medieval Eastern Europe*, 314.

Although Emperor Johannitsa plundered the hinterland of Constantinople, he was not interested in taking the city. Instead, he turned against Thessaloniki, whose king, Boniface of Montferrat, was ambushed by a Vlach-Cuman raiding party in September 1207, somewhere near present-day Komotini, in northern Greece. A month later, Johannitsa was murdered as he laid siege to Thessaloniki. Although he was most likely killed by his own men, his death was later attributed to St. Demetrius: the saint had deserted the Bulgarians to return to his city and defend it against them.

A major political crisis erupted after the death of Johannitsa. His brother Asen's first-born, also called John, fled to Rus', while power was taken by a relative named Boril, who married Johannitsa Kaloyan's widow, a Cuman princess of unknown name. Boril was defeated by the troops of the Latin Empire of Constantinople in the battle of Philippopolis (now Plovdiv) in 1208. To distract attention from his military failure, three years later Boril summoned a church synod in Tărnovo, the main purpose of which was to condemn the Bogomil heresy (see chapter 36). He also allied himself with the Latin Empire of Constantinople by marrying his stepdaughter to Emperor Henry. This enabled him to patch up relations with Hungary, whose new king, Andrew II (1205–35), offered him assistance against an uprising in the town of Vidin.

When Emperor Henry died in 1216 and King Andrew departed for the Fifth Crusade (see chapter 43), Boril was left without allies. Seizing the opportunity, John (Asen's son) returned from Rus', took Tărnovo, and was proclaimed emperor of Bulgaria in 1218 as John Asen II (John Asen I being his father). He took King Andrew's daughter, Maria, as his first wife. His victory at Klokotnica (1230) over the forces of the newly proclaimed Empire of Thessaloniki turned Bulgaria into a major power of the thirteenth-century Balkans (see insert 45.2). In an inscription on a stone column in the Church of the Forty Martyrs in Tărnovo, John Asen II bragged about ruling from "Adrianople [present-day Edirne, in the European part of Turkey] to Drach [Durrës, in Albania], the Greek [part], as well as the Serbian and Albanian parts."[7] In 1235, he obtained the recognition of the autocephaly (ecclesiastical autonomy) of the Bulgarian Church from Patriarch Germanos II, and the archbishop of Tărnovo (until then subordinated to the pope) now became Patriarch of Bulgaria. His rejection of papal primacy and his alliance with the Nicene Empire that was challenging the Latin Empire of Constantinople prompted Pope Gregory IX to call a crusade against John Asen II (see chapter 43). Only diplomatic maneuvers prevented that from happening.

Meanwhile, Stephen of Serbia finally received a royal crown from Pope Honorius III in 1217, and his brother Sava obtained from Patriarch Germanos II of Nicaea the recognition of the autocephaly of the Serbian Church with him as archbishop. Sava summoned a synod in 1221 at the newly established monastery of Žiča (near Kraljevo, on the Western Morava River), the see of the archbishopric. Like that summoned in Tărnovo a decade earlier, the synod of Žiča dealt with heretics, but Sava took the opportunity to present his *Nomokanon* (a compilation of canon law in Slavonic translation, also known as *Zakonopravilo*), which

7 Curta, ed., "John Asen II Boasts of His Victory at Klokotnica," in *Medieval Eastern Europe*, 319.

INSERT 45.2. THE DESPOTATE OF EPIRUS AND THE EMPIRE OF THESSALONIKI

Following the fall of Constantinople to the Fourth Crusade (1204), several successor states emerged in the formerly Byzantine territories. One of them was Epirus. Its beginnings are linked to a cousin of Emperor Alexius III Angelos (1195–1203) named Michael Dukas. He took refuge in the mountains of northwestern Greece and southern Albania and established his capital at Arta. He recognized the papal primacy of Innocent III and the suzerainty of Emperor Henry I, as he wanted to use the Latins against the rival Nicene Empire, another successor state. However, he also wanted to occupy the neighboring kingdom of Thessaloniki established in 1204 by Boniface of Montferrat. When attacked by Emperor Henry, Michael Dukas switched his allegiance to the Venetians, but to no avail. Forced to recognize himself a vassal of Emperor Henry, he then turned against the Venetians, from whom he took Dyrrachion and the island of Corfu. He was assassinated in 1215 and succeeded by his half-brother, Theodore Dukas. Theodore began by attacking Bulgaria to take Ohrid, and then managed to ambush and kill Peter of Courtenay, Emperor Henry's successor to the throne of Constantinople. Using the opportunity, he occupied Thessaly and pushed into the kingdom of Thessaloniki. He put that city under siege and eventually took it in 1224. Three years later, he was proclaimed emperor by the metropolitan of Ohrid. Emboldened by his success, he invaded Bulgaria in 1230 but was defeated by John Asen II at Klokotnica and taken prisoner. Epirus broke away from the kingdom of Thessaloniki (now overrun by Bulgarians) under an illegitimate son of Michael Dukas – Michael II Dukas. In Bulgaria, Theodore Dukas was blinded, but under his brother Manuel, the kingdom of Thessaloniki effectively became a Bulgarian client.

In 1248, Michael II Dukas acknowledged John III Dukas Vatatzes (1221–54) as emperor in exchange for the title of despot for himself. The despotate of Epirus gradually took a back seat in Balkan politics as the star of the Nicene Empire began to rise. Allied with the troops of Manfred of Sicily, the illegitimate son of Frederick II, as well as with William of Villehardhouin, the prince of Achaia, Michael II Dukas saw the Nicene troops defeat the alliance and occupy much of Epirus. By 1263, he had to acknowledge the suzerainty of Emperor Michael VIII Palaiologos (1261–82). At Michael II Dukas's death in 1271, the despotate of Epirus was divided between his two sons – John, who took Thessaly, and Nicephorus, who took Epirus proper. The territory of the despotate was occupied by the Byzantine troops in 1337 and included into the empire in 1340.

became the legal foundation of the Serbian church. Six years later, at Stephen Prvovenčani's death, Sava crowned his son Radoslav as king of all the Serbian lands and left for a pilgrimage to the Holy Land. Radoslav married the daughter of Theodore Dukas, the emperor of Thessaloniki, but after the battle of Klokotnica, his position became precarious at best. With John Asen II's star rising, Radoslav was removed from power by a conspiracy of disgruntled noblemen, who replaced him with his brother Vladislav (1234–43).

During King Vladislav's reign, Serbia was devastated in 1242 by the Mongols on their way back from Dalmatia (see chapters 42 and 46). Following the Mongol invasion,

Hungarian King Béla IV renewed his father's aggressive policies towards Serbia, after establishing a firm control over Bosnia. The march of Mačva, which stretched from the Sava to the Ub rivers, was directed against Serbia. War between Hungary and Serbia broke in the 1260s, during the reign of King Uroš I (1243–76). Bulgaria was also devastated by the Mongols in 1242, under the same circumstances. Tărnovo was sacked, and during the subsequent decades the Mongols instituted a tribute to be paid to the Golden Horde. Much like with Serbia, conflict with Hungary followed the Mongol invasion. Hungarian troops occupied the northwestern parts of the country, which were promptly included into the march of Mačva. Under King Stephen V (1270–72), a Hungarian army invaded Bulgaria and sacked Tărnovo. The ruler of a region in western Bulgaria centered upon Vidin recognized Hungarian lordship and effectively declared his independence from Tărnovo. However, unlike in Serbia, the last decades of the thirteenth century witnessed an increasing Mongol influence, especially from an independent warlord named Nogai who controlled the western lands of the Golden Horde.

FURTHER READING

Aglio, Francesco dall'. "New Powers – Serbia and Bulgaria." In *The Routledge Handbook of East Central and Eastern Europe in the Middle Ages, 500–1300*, edited by Florin Curta, 530–46. Abingdon: Routledge, 2022.

Madgearu, Alexandru. *The Asanids: The Political and Military History of the Second Bulgarian Empire (1185–1280)*. East Central and Eastern Europe in the Middle Ages, 450–1450, 41. Leiden: Brill, 2016.

Papageorgiou, Angeliki. "Serbia 1196–1282: From a Vassal State to an Empire." In *Politichka istorija Slovena između mita i stvarnosti. Zbornik radova sa međunarodne nauchne konferencije odrzhane 15. novembra 2019. godine*, edited by Sanja Suljagić, 140–69. Belgrade: Institut za političke studije, 2019.

Simpson, Alicia. "Byzantium's Retreating Balkan Frontier during the Reign of the Angeloi (1185–1203): A Reconsideration." In *The Balkans and the Byzantine World Before and After the Captures of Constantinople, 1204 and 1453*, edited by Vlada Stanković, 3–22. Lanham: Lexington Books, 2016.

Stanković, Vlada. "John II Asen (1218–1241), the Importance of Being Roman, and the Battle for Dominance Over Southeast Europe." In *Car Ivan Asen II (1218–1241). Sbornik po sluchai 800-godishninata ot negovoto văzshestvie na bălgarskiia prestol*, edited by Vasil Giuzelev, Iliia G. Iliev, and Kiril Nenov, 49–54. Plovdiv: Fondaciia "Bălgarsko istorichesko nasledstvo," 2019.

Stanković, Vlada. "Stronger Than It Appears? Byzantium and Its European Hinterland after the Death of Manuel I Komnenos." In *Byzantium, 1180–1204: "The Sad Quarter of a Century"?*, edited by Alicia Simpson, 39–47. Athens: National Hellenic Research Foundation, 2015.

Stephenson, Paul. *Byzantium's Balkan Frontier: A Political Study of the Northern Balkans, 900–1204*. Cambridge: Cambridge University Press, 2000.

46

THE MONGOL CONQUEST OF EASTERN EUROPE

Keywords in this chapter: Golden Horde, *ulus*, *basqaqs*

The events that unfolded in Central Asia in the early thirteenth century with the Mongol conquests rapidly extended their reach to Eastern Europe. Beginning his campaigns in 1211, Genghis Khan secured the Jin Empire of northern China and quickly conquered the kingdom of Kara Khitay, the empire of Khwarazm, and a large part of Iran. Generals of his army then marched towards Georgia and the plains north of the Caucasus range. In 1222, Mongols attacked the Crimea and the Cumans in the steppe, and by 1223 they were at the doorstep of the lands of Rus'. Two princes named Mstislav – Mstislav the Bold of Halych (1219–27) and Mstislav III of Kiev (1212–23) – led an army of Rus' and allied Cumans to counter the invaders, but they were utterly defeated at the battle of the Kalka River, where several Rus' princes were killed or captured. Despite the major defeat of the Rus', the Mongols retreated – but would soon come back.

Rus' in the eleventh and twelfth centuries had been ruled by the descendants of Vladimir I of Kiev, who had derived their legitimacy from their assumed common ancestor, Riurik (see chapters 11 and 16). Succession went vertically from father to son, or laterally to brothers and cousins. Conflicts were common. Upon Vladimir's death, for example, three of his sons were murdered, and the other three fought with one another. Twenty years later, the only survivor was Iaroslav.[1] At his death in 1054, Iaroslav the Wise divided the land between his sons, who were to recognize the senior status of the elder brother residing in Kiev. Gradually the system of seniority gained acceptance: a deceased prince

1 Florin Curta, ed., "The Passion of the Holy Martyrs Boris and Gleb," in *Medieval Eastern Europe, 500–1300: A Reader* (Toronto: University of Toronto Press, 2024), 202.

was succeeded by his eldest brother. When no brother was alive, succession went to the eldest nephew.

The prince of Kiev might have had a senior position, but the regional princes followed their own political interests. Joint actions relied on the goodwill of participants, and collective diplomacy with external powers became difficult. Marriage alliances with European ruling houses were nonetheless common. Iaroslav the Wise, for example, married Ingigerd, daughter of the king of Sweden, and their daughter Anna married Henry I of France. Other princes had English, German, Polish, or Byzantine wives. Ecclesiastical and cultural connections with Byzantium were maintained: the metropolitans of Kiev, subordinated to Constantinople, were mostly Greek men. Bishops, however, tended to be monks from Rus' monasteries. Political, diplomatic, and economic contacts between Rus' and Byzantium continued but were far from exclusive. Already by the early twelfth century, the lands of Rus' had become partitioned into principalities that were practically autonomous. They were dominated by three main branches of the Riurikids: those ruling in Chernigov, Volhynia-Smolensk (the Mstislavichi), and Suzdalia – the latter two descending from Vladimir Monomakh. Suzdalia, in the basins of the upper Volga and the Oka rivers in northeastern Rus', was the most stable of all.

In the thirteenth century, however, on the eve of the Mongol invasion, three principalities competed for power in the southern part of Rus'. The Rostislavichi ruled in the land of Smolensk that was connected to the southern principalities through the Dnieper River and to the Baltic region through the Daugava. The Ol'govichi were based in Chernigov, strategically located between Smolensk and Kiev, connected to both by waterways. The Mstislavichi maintained their hold on the southwestern lands of Volhynia and Halych. Rich from agriculture and trade, those lands bordered on Hungary and Poland, Volhynia being connected to the latter via the river Bug, a tributary of the Vistula, while Halych was connected to the Black Sea through the Dniester River. Senior princes in Kiev alternated between the branches of Smolensk and Chernigov, while the princes of Suzdalia in the northeast retained a stronger degree of independence.

Disputes among the Riurikids were typically won by the princes who had the most powerful armies or who could forge the strongest alliances. Despite all internal divisions, however, the lands of Rus' maintained cohesion by being ruled by the Riurikids and belonging to the same ecclesiastical province, the metropolitan see of Kiev. In foreign affairs, early thirteenth-century princes of Rus' emphasized connections to their immediate neighbors. Marriage alliances, for example, took place with Poland and Hungary, while political and diplomatic contacts with Byzantium dwindled. The plight of Constantinople during the Fourth Crusade left the Rus' princes unconcerned.

When the Mongols arrived, the Rus' had long cohabited with a variety of nomadic or semi-nomadic steppe peoples – beginning with the Khazars during the formative period of early Rus'. In the eleventh and twelfth centuries, Rus' princes regularly interacted with the "Black Hoods" and with the Cumans. These peoples were sometimes enemies, sometimes allies of the Rus' princes, especially those of Chernigov and Suzdalia. These contacts had made the Rus' familiar with the steppe, its peoples, and its geography and environment.

INSERT 46.1. MONGOLS AND TATARS

The Mongols were generally called Tatars in Rus' and European sources during the Middle Ages; in Rus' sources, the ethnonym was used for all steppe peoples. In Latin sources, the name was often spelled Tartars in conflation with Tartarus, the hellish underworld of ancient mythology from which the Mongols were thought to have come. In fact, the Tatars appear to have originally been a tribe on the border of China that was rivals with the Mongols. The Mongols of the mid-thirteenth century are said to have disliked being called Tatars, since it was people from that tribe who had killed the father of Genghis Khan; the Mongols were said to have annihilated them. It is unclear why Mongols and Tatars were confused with one another by outsiders. Be that as it may, the Tatar name was retained in Europe and eventually became a self-identification, for example for the Lithuanian Tatars, the Volga Tatars (in today's Republic of Tatarstan, in Russia), and the Crimean Tatars.

Diplomatic missions resulted especially in personal connections between the Rus' elite and the Cumans that necessitated familiarity with customs and sufficient language proficiency to communicate. Marriage alliances took place as well, usually involving a Cuman princess marrying a Rus' prince and converting to Christianity.

Despite such precedents, the Rus' princes were utterly unprepared for what was about to happen in the early thirteenth century. At his death in 1227, four years after the battle on the Kalka, Genghis Khan was succeeded by his son Ögedei. The Mongols returned to the steppe in 1237 and, this time, subjugated the Cumans. The Rus' princes must have been aware of the defeat of the Volga Bulghars and of the refugees it had sent into their lands. The Ol'govichi and Mstislavichi, however, were exhausted by years of internal conflicts, while the prince of Suzdalia was estranged from his southern relatives. The Mongols assaulted Riazan' in eastern Rus', and from there moved on Suzdalia.[2] In the second phase starting in 1239, the Mongols attacked Rus' from Pereiaslavl' in the south, and from there conquered Chernigov, Kiev, and Halych-Volhynia. The invasion left Riazan', Vladimir, and Kiev devastated. By 1240 the Mongols had taken control of all the lands of Rus' except those in the northwest (around Novgorod); the following year, they moved towards Central Europe (see chapter 42).

The Rus' might have known steppe nomadic warfare before, but they had never experienced it on such a scale (see insert 46.1). The Mongols not only had an enormous army of well-organized mounted archers; they also had quickly learned to use Chinese and Islamic siege weaponry and employed it to destroy towns and strongholds. While earlier nomads had pillaged and gone home, the Mongols intended to kill, spread terror, and permanently conquer the land. As the Rus' princes considered their options, they soon

2 Curta, ed., "Mongols in Northeastern Rus'," in *Medieval Eastern Europe*, 327–30.

INSERT 46.2. HORDE AND *ULUS*

The word "horde" derives from the Mongolian term *orda*. The *orda* was the khan's court and his military headquarters; the word referred at the same time to an army, a place of power, the people subjected to the ruler, and the camp where the ruler resided. An *orda* did not have to be connected to a specific place; in fact, the court regularly migrated and could be dispersed and reassembled; what was crucial was the power it represented. Variations of the word "horde" have entered Persian and Arabic as well as multiple Slavic and other European languages following the Mongol conquests, especially in the lands that were under Mongol domination.

The Mongolian word *ulus*, by contrast, designated the peoples under domination of the four sons of Genghis Khan and his main wife, Börte – Jochi, Chatagay, Ögedei, and Tolui – and their successors. The people of an *ulus* included the Mongol warriors and their families as well as the peasants, merchants, and craftspeople in the lands under Mongol domination. An *ulus* was understood not as a territorial unit but as a political community. The *ulus* of Jochi, for example, encompassed the populations of Eastern Europe that were governed by the successors of Jochi; descent from Jochi (and thus Genghis Khan) gave the khans of the Golden Horde their legitimacy. The *ulus* was ruled by the khan alongside the *beg*, as *begs* were the heads of the dominant Mongol clans.

The name Golden Horde is not recorded in the Middle Ages; it was first mentioned in seventeenth-century Russia, long after the *ulus* of Jochi had ceased to exist. In the Middle Ages, the Mongols referred to it as either the *ulus* of Jochi or as the Kipchaq khanate (in reference to the Cumans, the Turkic-speaking people of the steppes whose language was dominant in the Volga area). The name Golden Horde, however, has been used for so long in scholarship that it has become the accepted convention.

realized that there was little hope in opposing the Mongols: attempts at resistance typically resulted in failure and the miserable deaths of leaders. Many chose the more reasonable course of cooperation, especially as it turned out that Mongols were more lenient to those who submitted readily. For example, the prince of Novgorod, Alexander Nevsky, was a successful military leader who had gained fame in defeating Swedish invaders and the Livonian Order (see chapter 44). Alexander, however, was willing to cooperate right away with the Mongols. He offered his submission and pleaded for leniency as soon as they arrived.

Mongol overlordship of the lands of Rus', or parts of it, lasted from 1240 to 1480. During that time, the lands of Rus' belonged to the Golden Horde, the inheritance of Genghis Khan's son Jochi, who predeceased him, and of his grandson Batu (see insert 46.2). Batu secured permanent possession of the lands of Eastern Europe and built his capital city, Sarai, on the Lower Volga. The Golden Horde reached from the Danube to Khwarazm and included the Crimea, the North Caucasus, and the lands of Rus'. The Golden Horde was part of a Mongol empire that stretched from Eastern Europe and Persia to China (Song China was conquered in 1279) and Korea (see map 46.1). Within that empire, when compared to China and Persia, Eastern Europe was little more than an impoverished and underdeveloped periphery. The imperial center and the residence of the Great Khan was

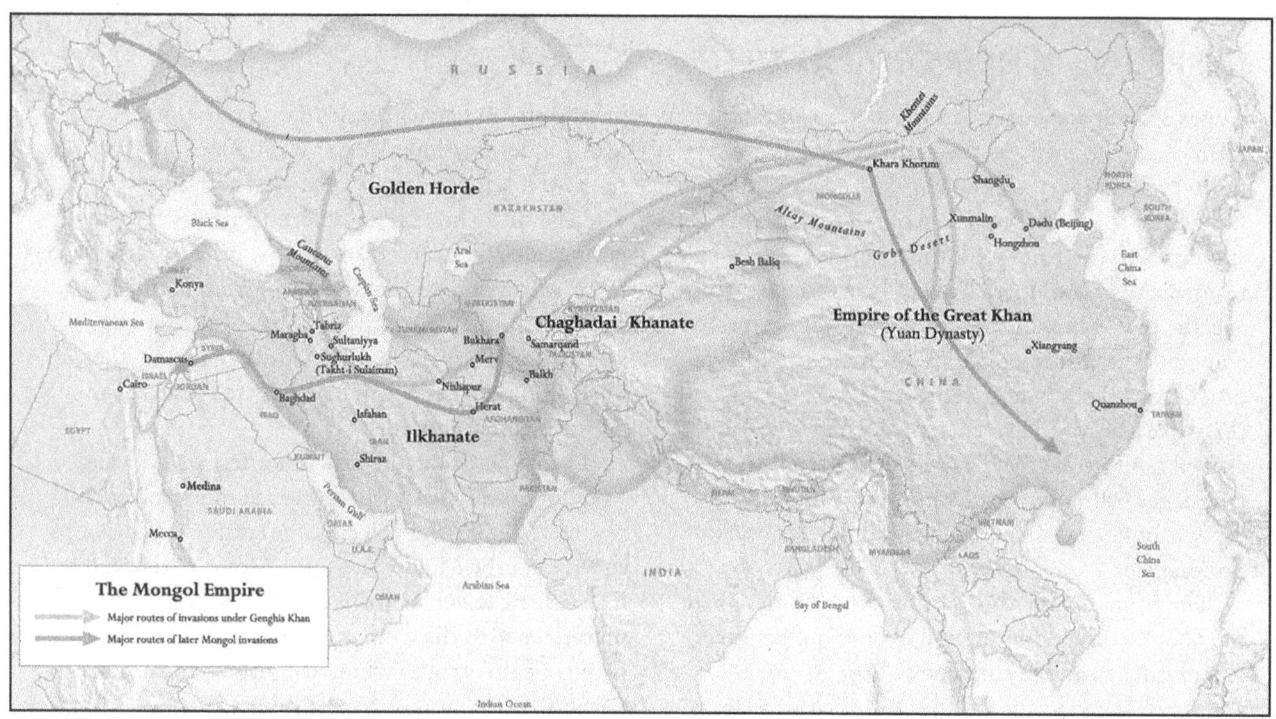

Map 46.1. The Mongol Empire and the Golden Horde, ca. 1300. Wikimedia Commons, the free media repository.

nowhere near Eastern Europe but in Khara Khorum (Karakorum) (near Kharkhorin, in Mongolia). Under Mongol domination, Rus' remained culturally European: a Christian country with social structures that were not fundamentally different from those elsewhere in Europe. However, within the Mongol Empire, the elites of Rus' had their closest political ties with the Mongols. Rus' princes regularly "went to the Horde," that is, traveled to Sarai to obtain confirmation of their titles from the khans and make tribute payments; Rus' and Mongol leaders eagerly cooperated.

The Golden Horde took on some specific features as part of the Mongol Empire. The Mongols and the Cumans they had conquered spoke different languages – the first Mongolian, the second Turkic – but they shared some cultural traditions. As they cohabited in the steppe, the Turkic language of the Cumans became the dominating language; when the khans in Sarai adopted Islam in the fourteenth century, Mongols and Cumans were united through a common religion. Although the Mongols retained the nomadic way of life that was necessary to uphold the military training that made them so powerful, governing their vast empire necessitated a complex administrative system. They built effective governance structures and even an urban society: Sarai became an important city with mosques, palaces, and imposing buildings.

The khans of the Golden Horde did not occupy the lands of Rus' directly. While local elites were replaced with Mongol officials in the Crimea and in the Volga area, that did not happen in Rus'. The khans expected the Rus' to pay tributes and relied on the princes to collect and deliver them. Rus' might have been ruled indirectly through Mongol administrators, the *baskaks* (see chapter 54), but the Mongol presence was real in many ways. The princes, as representatives of the khans, regularly traveled to Sarai: from 1242 to 1252, Suzdalian princes visited Sarai no less than nineteen times, and princes of Rostov three times. Andrei of Vladimir and his brother Alexander Nevsky even made their way to Karakorum; Alexander became a close partner of Khan Sartak, Batu's successor in Sarai. Rus' princes occasionally requested Mongol military support when fighting against each other. For example, Vasily of Suzdal' had Mongol troops with him in his war against Novgorod (1272–73). While stationed in Vasily's land, however, those troops ignored their Rus' commanders and ravaged the country, going on a raid against the Lithuanians. Rus' princes sent supporting troops to their Mongol masters during the 1277 Caucasian campaign and to quell an uprising in Bulgaria in 1278. Mongols returned the favor, and during their conflict in the 1280s, the brothers Andrei and Dmitri of Vladimir were each supported by Mongol battalions. Alliances were reinforced as Rus' princes married Mongol princesses. Prince Fedor of Iaroslavl' and Smolensk, for example, married the khan's daughter after having spent several years at the court in Sarai, where he served in high posts.

The Lower Volga was not far, and the Rus' princes knew that if they did not do what was expected of them, it would not take long for the Mongols to send punitive forces. Notwithstanding political and military pressure, under the Mongols the princes of Rus' ruled their country following traditional Riurikid traditions of succession. Their overlord was now, however, the Mongol khan whom they called the tsar, the Slavonic title formerly reserved for Byzantine emperors. The Mongol tribute was a heavy exaction on the Rus' population. The taxes were collected for the sole benefit of the Mongols, and princes suspected of embezzlement were severely punished. Church institutions, however, were from the beginning exempted from the Mongol taxes (see chapters 64 and 65).

FURTHER READING

Fennell, John. *The Crisis of Medieval Russia, 1200–1304*. Longman History of Russia. London: Longman, 1983.

Halperin, Charles J. *Russia and the Mongols: Slavs and the Steppe in Medieval and Early Modern Russia*. Florilegium magistrorum historiae archaeologiaeque Antiquitatis et Medii Aevi 1. Bucharest: Editura Academiei Române, 2007.

Halperin, Charles J. "'No One Knew Who They Were': Rus' Interaction with the Mongols." In *The Steppe Lands and the World Beyond Them: Studies in Honor of Victor Spinei on His 70th Birthday*, edited by Florin Curta and Bogdan-Petru Maleon, 377–87. Iași: Editura Universității "Alexandru Ioan Cuza," 2013.

Hautala, Roman. "The Mongols in Eastern Europe." In *The Routledge Handbook of East Central and Eastern Europe in the Middle Ages, 500–1300*, edited by Florin Curta, 547–59. Abingdon: Routledge, 2022.

Maiorov, Aleksandr V. "The Mongol Conquest of Rus'." In *The Mongol World*, edited by Timothy May and Michael Hope, 164–82. London: Routledge, 2022.

PART 9

The Late Middle Ages

47

THE GREAT FAMINE AND THE BLACK DEATH

Keywords in this chapter: famine, plague, Mongols

The early fourteenth century was a challenging period for parts of Northern and Central Europe. A panzootic disease of cattle, probably rinderpest, spread from Eastern Europe towards the West; it seems to have arrived from Mongolia, where it was attested in 1288. Rus' chroniclers noticed it in 1298 and 1309; an annalistic compilation noted a great mortality of cattle that affected "all of Poland" in 1298. In Bohemia, the death of cattle, sheep, and horses was noticed in 1314 and 1316. From East Central Europe, the disease moved to Alsace, Bavaria, and Denmark, and then to the Low Countries, France, and the British Isles. British sources report that the disease killed an average of 60 percent of the livestock. Should it have been as devastating in Eastern and Central Europe as it was in England, the panzootic must have had a strong negative impact on agriculture. The demise of cattle depleted fields of manure and deprived farmers of access to draught animals.

The Great Famine was a hunger catastrophe that, between 1315 and 1322, affected parts of England, northern France, southern Scandinavia, and most of the German lands, but also parts of Poland, Bohemia, and the Baltic area. The crisis began when torrential rain caused large-scale crop failures. Bad weather continued in the following years; food reserves were quickly depleted, and the geographical extent of the problem made importing grain from faraway places nearly impossible. Hunger was compounded by epidemics that soon struck human and animal populations weakened by multiple years of malnourishment.

The famine reached Poland and was reported in Silesia in 1317. In Bohemia, the death of Wenceslas III in 1306 led to political turmoil that did not fully end with John of Luxembourg's coronation in 1310 (see chapter 48). In a context of social unrest, the Elbe flooded in 1315, which was followed by heavy rain and again floods in 1316; the loss of crops and death of livestock resulted in famine. Then came an unusually cold winter and the Vltava froze over. The combination of warfare and famine led to high casualties. The peace of

Domažlice in April 1318 finally brought a return to political stability, and reports of hunger ceased after that; normal harvests and lower prices for grain resumed. In Hungary, hunger was already noted in 1312, likely related to the incessant warfare that had plagued the country since the coronation of Charles of Anjou in 1301 (see chapter 48). As in Bohemia, the problems caused by political and military disruptions were made worse by the great floods and excessive rain that lasted from 1316 to 1321.

The consequences of the Great Famine were multifaceted, but hunger affected urban populations the most. Food scarcity challenged municipal governments in finding ways to distribute the available food fairly and prevent price gouging. Urban records noted cases of cannibalism in Livonia in 1315, and in Poland and Silesia in 1317. While these allegations might have been rhetorical exaggerations inspired by Biblical models, they are a striking evocation of how dire the situation was experienced at that time. Moreover, contemporary evidence suggests that the famine forced countrypeople from western Germany to leave their villages, which were abandoned by all inhabitants. Beggars from the west German lands were asking for bread in the towns along the southern coast of the Baltic Sea; they were in Lübeck, for example, in 1317. Some of them moved to eastern Poland: new rural estates multiplied in the areas of Cracow and Warsaw in the years after 1315, presumably because of an influx of people migrating east to escape the famine.

However, the worst catastrophe to affect Europe in the Middle Ages was the Black Death, the deadly pandemic that struck the continent in the mid-fourteenth century. The disease, identified as the plague caused by the bacterium *Yersinia pestis*, arrived at the worst possible time, on the heels of decades of challenges. The economic and demographic expansion of the High Middle Ages was reaching its limits; on top of that, unstable weather had had ripple effects on various sectors of the economy. Some estimates of the death toll of the Black Death are as high as 60 percent of the overall European population. While it is undisputed that mortality was extremely high in some affected areas, especially around the Mediterranean during the first wave, the extent to which the disease impacted populations, however, varied significantly from region to region. Central Europe was, in fact, among the least affected parts of Europe.

The Black Death was first mentioned in Caffa, a merchant town in Crimea with colonies of Genoese and Venetian merchants who, during the Pax Mongolica, had taken advantage of the increased trade connections with China along the Silk Roads (see chapters 59 and 60). In the early fourteenth century, however, trade between Europe and China declined, and it came to a stop in 1341. The unity of the Mongol Empire collapsed amidst conflicts between the regional khans. More importantly, the khans of the Golden Horde increasingly came into conflict with Christian merchants. In this context, beginning in 1343, Khan Janibek (1342–57) repeatedly attacked Caffa as he sought to diminish trade with Europe.

According to contemporary sources from Rus' and Byzantium, the Black Death appeared in the spring of 1346 in the lands of the Golden Horde between the areas of the estuary of the Don in the Black Sea and of the Volga in the Caspian Sea. From there the plague reached the Crimea; merchants from besieged Caffa carried it to Constantinople and

Italy. A notary from Piacenza, Gabriele de Mussis, famously attributed the spread of the plague to events during the siege of Caffa in the autumn of 1346. The Mongols allegedly used catapults to throw infected corpses into the besieged city to infect the population there. This episode, however, is likely spurious. De Mussis was not present at the siege of Caffa and probably invented the story to boost his claim that the Muslim Mongols were barbaric degenerates. Be that as it may, the Mongols retreated at the end of the autumn. The Genoese and Venetian merchants left Caffa and returned to Italy for the winter. The disease struck in Sicily, Sardinia, and Provence in 1347. Typically, the disease raged for a few months upon arrival, leading to massive mortality, and then retreated.

In 1348, the Black Death reached the British Isles and northern France, whence it spread to Scandinavia and the Low Countries in 1349. The German lands were affected unevenly, with the plague probably traveling along the Rhine. The first wave, which lasted until 1352, was the most destructive. A second wave spread across Europe along similar lines in 1359–62, and a third one in 1372. The disease then became endemic; in the following centuries, it reappeared occasionally in local or regional contexts. For the most part, Hanseatic and other German towns were struck only in the later waves, when the disease had become less lethal.

Sources attesting to the dissemination of the Black Death along the Baltic coast during the first wave are few and uncertain. In Prussia, the plague might have arrived in 1349 in Elbing and Königsberg, before then expanding east and west. It is certainly attested in Gdańsk (eastern Pomerania) and in Toruń (Prussia), both in the territories of the Teutonic Order, in 1351 and 1352.

The question of the dissemination of the Black Death in Bohemia and Poland, by contrast, has been the subject of much scholarly debate. Sources suggesting that it arrived in these regions during the first wave, in 1349–50, are either questionable or late and thus less reliable. In fact, most scholars believe that the plague reached the Baltic Sea coast during the first wave but arrived in Poland and Bohemia only later, when it was not as lethal as during the first wave. The plague is attested in Silesia in 1356; it spread more widely in Bohemia during the second wave in 1359–60. The Black Death did reach Hungary during the first wave, coming from heavily affected Dalmatia; villages around Oradea and Sopron were depopulated, and Queen Margaret died of the disease. The spread of the plague, however, was limited. Just like Bohemia, Hungary appears to have been struck mostly in the subsequent waves.

Bohemia, Poland, and Hungary (along with remote Finland) were among the few regions of Europe in which the Black Death had a moderate impact, without the high levels of mortality that had been witnessed elsewhere. This was perhaps due, at least partially, to the less urbanized character of Central Europe and to more limited connections with infected regions. Whatever the reason, the available evidence for Poland clearly shows that there was no significant decrease in population, as one would expect had the Black Death raged there as it did elsewhere. The registers of Peter's Pence, a head tax paid to the papacy, do not indicate any drastic decrease of population for the kingdom of Poland in the 1340s and 1350s, in sharp contrast to Sweden and Norway, where a considerable drop in revenue is visible in the same records, suggesting a significant decline in population due to the plague.

The policies of the Golden Horde khan Janibek to curtail commercial contacts with Christian merchants resulted in a decline of trade between Eastern Europe and the Black Sea region. Commercial contacts between Rus' and Western Europe through Hanseatic merchants, however, were in full expansion (see chapter 60). This likely explains why the plague did not travel directly from the Crimea to Rus' but only arrived in Rus' from the Baltic area, after moving into the rest of Europe. The plague, having reached Livonia through Hanseatic merchants, arrived in Pskov in 1352, at the tail end of the first wave. From Pskov the disease spread to Novgorod, Suzdal', Chernigov, and Kiev. It was in Moscow in 1353. In formulations that echo those of Western Europe, contemporary records attest to the extremely high mortality. Rus' sources ceased to mention the Black Death, however, after these events.

FURTHER READING

Benedictow, Ole J. *The Complete History of the Black Death*, 2nd ed. Woodbridge: Boydell, 2021.

Guzowski, Piotr. "Did the Black Death Reach the Kingdom of Poland in the Mid-Fourteenth Century?" *Journal of Interdisciplinary History* 103, no. 2 (2022): 193–223.

Jordan, William Chester. *The Great Famine: Northern Europe in the Early Fourteenth Century*. Princeton: Princeton University Press, 1996.

Newfield, Timothy P. "A Cattle Panzootic in Early Fourteenth-Century Europe." *Agricultural History Review* 57, no. 2 (2009): 155–90.

48

EAST CENTRAL EUROPE: POLAND, HUNGARY, AND BOHEMIA

Keywords in this chapter: Golden Bull, last crusades, Hussitism

In all three kingdoms of East Central Europe, the fourteenth century marked the return of strong royal power after periods of trouble. Moreover, Bohemia and Hungary became more involved than ever in European politics under Charles IV and Sigismund respectively, as both rulers held the title of Holy Roman emperor. Dynastic ties connected the three kingdoms throughout the period (see map 48.1). The crisis that erupted in Bohemia during the Hussite Wars also affected all three countries.

Monarchy returned to Poland with the short reigns of Przemysł II (1295–96), Wenceslas I (1300–5), and Wenceslas II (1305–6) (see chapter 42), then disappeared again (see table 48.1). Władysław the Short (the Elbow-High, Łokietek), Piast duke of Kuyavia, had long had royal ambitions. Having gained control of both Lesser and Greater Poland, he obtained the reluctant support of Pope John XXII and was crowned king in Cracow in January 1320. Truncated from Mazovia and Silesia – most of the independent Silesian Piasts would pay homage to John of Luxembourg in 1327 and 1329 – the kingdom of Poland was reunited, and this time for good.

Władysław the Short died in 1333 and was succeeded by the last Piast king – Casimir III the Great, who strengthened and expanded the kingdom. Casimir gave up on Silesia while John of Luxembourg abandoned pretentions to the Polish throne. Mazovia, however, joined the kingdom in 1355 when Duke Semovit III recognized Casimir as king. Meanwhile, trouble erupted in the Rus' kingdom of Halych (Galicia) and Volhynia (Lodomeria). The Riurikid Daniel had received a royal crown from Pope Innocent IV in 1253. His successor, Bolesław-Iurii II, who was of Riurikid and Mazovian Piast descent and married to Euphemia, a daughter of the Lithuanian grand duke Gediminas, was murdered by boyars in 1340. He died childless. Casimir, whom Bolesław-Iurii had earlier asked for help, invaded the country with Hungarian assistance in 1340 and again in 1349.

Map 48.1. East Central Europe, ca. 1500: I – Bohemia; II – Hungary; III – Lithuania; IV – Poland; V – Teutonic Order. Medieval names are in italics.

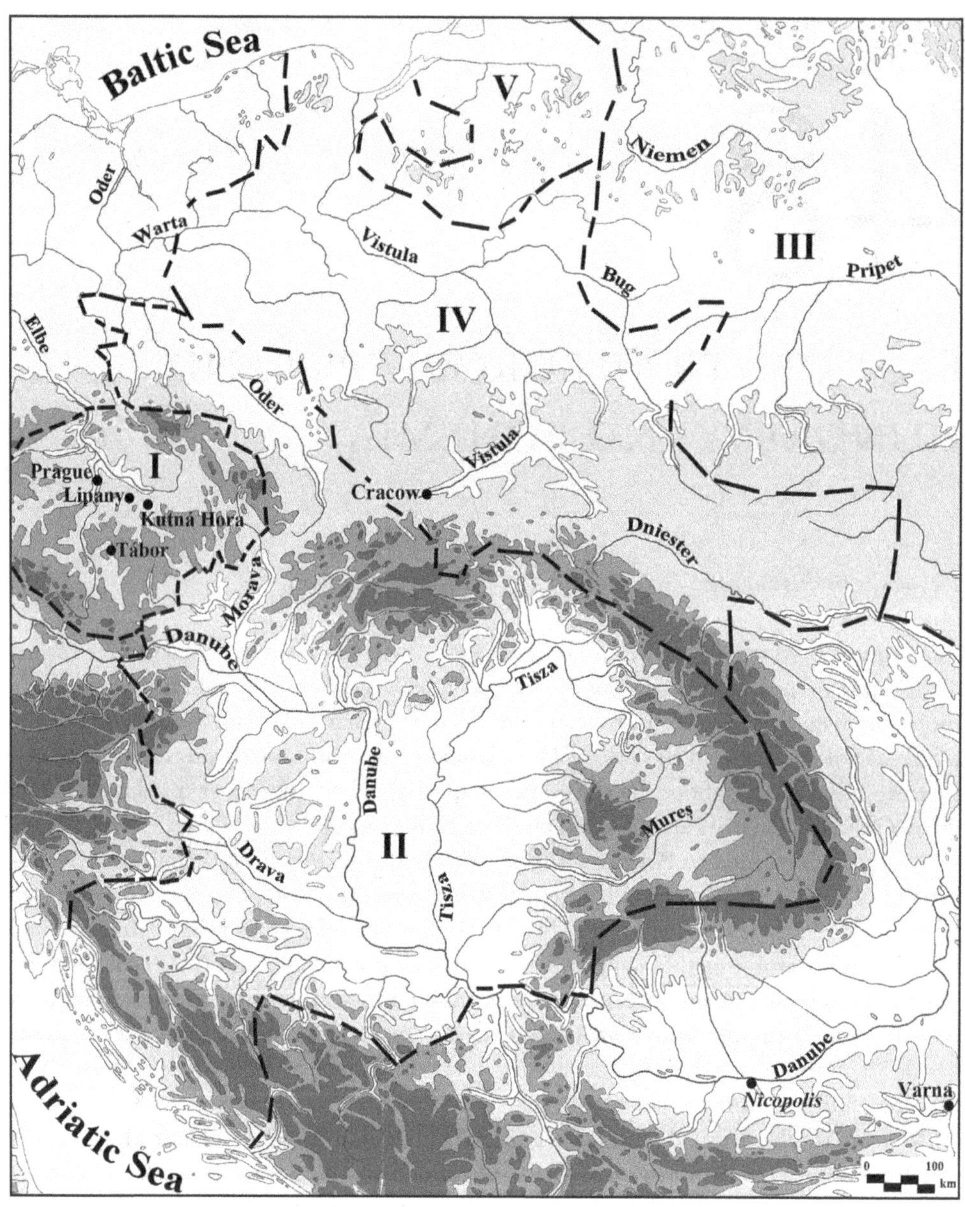

Although most of Volhynia was taken by the Gediminids of Lithuania (see chapter 49), Red Ruthenia, as it became known, was joined to the Polish kingdom. Western Podolia, to the east of Halych, would become a dependence of the Polish kingdom sometime after Casimir's reign. Casimir's hold on the region was strengthened when, in 1346, the Black Death ravaged the land of the Golden Horde but spared Poland. For Red Ruthenia, Casimir nonetheless remained tributary to the khan. All the while Casimir reinforced royal

Table 48.1. Rulers of Poland in the Late Middle Ages

Name of the Ruler	Regnal Years
Przemysł II	1295–96
Wenceslas I	1300–5
Wenceslas II	1305–6
Władysław I Łokietek	1320–33
Casimir III	1333–70
Louis of Anjou	1370–82
Jadwiga	1384–86
Władysław II Jagiełło	1386–1434
Władysław III	1434–44
Casimir IV	1444–92
John I Albert	1492–1501

government and established a university in Cracow to train the jurists he needed for the administration of his growing kingdom (see chapter 69).

The death of King Andrew III in 1301 marked the end of the Arpadian dynasty as a period of Hungarian history. The country was briefly headed by Wenceslas III of Bohemia and Otto Wittelsbach of Bavaria, but in reality, it was ruled by fifteen great lords or oligarchs. While nominally acknowledging royal authority, they governed their territories independently. Relying on the warriors of their castles, they exploited the country for their own needs and failed to provide security.

Stability returned under Charles of Anjou. Charles (or Charles Robert) was the son of King Charles II of Naples and Mary, daughter of the Hungarian king Stephen IV; he grew up at the Angevin court in Naples. As the son of an Arpadian woman, he had ambitions for the Hungarian throne ever since the death of Andrew III. His claims were supported by popes Boniface VIII and Clement V. Although later regarded as the first king of the Hungarian "Angevin" dynasty, Charles always insisted on being the legitimate heir of the Arpadians (see table 48.2). He was crowned in August 1310; nobles, the ecclesiastic leaders, and towns rallied behind him. King Charles I began his reign involved in a long conflict with the oligarchs as he endeavored to curtail their power; he succeeded and reinforced royal government. Charles of Anjou was on good terms with the Habsburgs, the Piasts, and the Luxembourgs. He gained borderlands from Serbia while his power in Croatia was diminished and Dalmatian cities placed themselves under Venetian protection. None of his first three wives bore children, but his fourth one, Elizabeth, daughter of Władysław the Short, gave him three sons. Charles died in 1342 and was succeeded by his sixteen-year-old son Louis.

Louis the Great, as he became known, was a bellicose ruler fixated on wars of expansion. His mother, Elizabeth of Poland, had an influential role at court for most of his career;

Table 48.2 Rulers of Hungary in the Late Middle Ages

Name of the Ruler	Regnal Years
Andrew III	1290–1301
Wenceslas I	1301–5
Otto of Wittelsbach	1305–7
Charles I Robert of Anjou	1308–42
Louis I of Anjou	1342–82
Mary	1382–85, 1386–95
Charles II	1385–86
Sigismund of Luxembourg	1387–1437
Albert of Habsburg	1437–39
Władysław I Jagiełło	1440–44
Ladislas V	1444–57
Matthias Corvinus	1458–90
Vladislav II Jagiełło	1490–1516

feared by the barons, she acted as unofficial co-regent. Conflict emerged in 1343 with the death of King Robert of Naples. Robert had designated his daughter Joan as sole heiress; her husband Andrew, Louis's brother, was refused a royal title and was assassinated in 1345. Louis went to war in Italy to avenge him. Joan having fled, Louis marched on Naples, took the city, and assumed the royal title. As soon as he returned to Hungary, however, Joan retook Naples, and Louis's further efforts failed. He was more successful in the Balkans: his authority was fully recognized in Croatia, he regained the Dalmatian cities from Venice, and he extended his authority in Serbia and Wallachia.

Meanwhile, Bohemia took center stage in European politics under a new dynasty (see table 48.3). The murder of Wenceslas III in 1306 was followed by short reigns. Henry of Carinthia was driven out by Albert of Habsburg, who placed his son Rudolf on the throne but was himself murdered in 1308. Rudolf died in 1307, Henry returned, but was expelled in 1310. John of Luxembourg, son of Emperor Henry VII, was sent to Bohemia in September 1310 to marry Elizabeth, daughter of Wenceslas II; the wedding was followed by John's royal coronation. The Luxembourgs, who were well connected with the French royal court, were counts in a region of the former Lotharingia that belonged to the Holy Roman Empire but had a French-speaking culture. In Bohemia, John was a foreigner and mostly an absentee ruler. He surrounded himself with courtiers from Luxembourg, the German lands, France, and Italy. The Czech nobility, however, used John's weakness to gain various privileges. On the international scene, John remained a steadfast ally of Louis IV the Bavarian, king of the Romans since 1314, and of the Capetians; his sister Marie married King Charles IV the Fair in 1322. Affected by blindness in his later years, John died a chivalric hero at the 1346 battle of Crécy, fighting on behalf of the French king against the English army.

Table 48.3. Rulers of Bohemia in the Late Middle Ages

Name of the Ruler	Regnal Years
Wenceslas II	1278–1305
Wenceslas III	1305–6
Henry I	1306, 1307–10
Rudolf of Habsburg	1306–7
John of Luxembourg	1310–46
Charles IV	1346–78
Wenceslas IV	1378–1419
Sigismund of Luxembourg	1419–21, 1436–37
Albert I	1437–39
Ladislas I	1453–57
George of Poděbrady	1458–71
Vladislav II	1471–1516

John of Luxembourg's son Wenceslas (the future Charles IV) was born in 1316. Living in Paris from the age of seven, he was socialized in French and at his confirmation took the name of his royal godfather, Charles. In 1329 he married Blanche of Valois, the king's cousin. He spent time in Luxembourg and Italy before returning to Prague in 1333. His father made him margrave of Moravia, and he governed the kingdom during the king's absences. In 1346, shortly before Crécy, he was elected king of the Romans as Charles IV; in 1347, he was crowned king of Bohemia. An imperial coronation in Rome would follow in 1355.

Under Charles IV, Bohemia rose to prominence in Europe. After the death of Blanche, Charles married in succession Anne of the Palatinate, Anne of Świdnica, and Elizabeth of Pomerania; his marriages secured him alliances in Nuremberg, Silesia, and Brandenburg. His children married into ruling houses across Europe, including England, where his daughter Anne became the wife of Richard II. The multilingual and well-connected Charles IV turned the Czech lands into the political center of the Holy Roman Empire, shifting power towards the eastern regions. He invested massively in Prague, which he made a capital city, cultural center, and residence of European reputation. He built a new royal palace, established the New Town, and founded a university in 1348 (see chapter 69). In Frankfurt-am-Main in 1356, Charles IV promulgated a foundational document, the Golden Bull, that formalized the procedures for the election and coronation of emperors. The Golden Bull gave permanent position to the king of Bohemia in the college of prince-electors and made it mandatory for them to learn the Czech language. Never had the Czech lands been so important.

The late fourteenth century witnessed a rapprochement between Poland and Hungary. Casimir III, lacking a son, designated as heir his long-time ally Louis of Anjou, the son of his sister Elizabeth. When Casimir died in 1370, Louis elected to stay in Hungary and to entrust the government of Poland to his Polish mother Elizabeth. Following an earlier arrangement, he attached Red Ruthenia to Hungary. When the queen-mother died in 1380, the regency of Poland turned to Louis's wife Elizabeth of Bosnia.

Like Casimir before him, Louis, who passed away in 1382, had daughters but no son. Louis and his wife Elizabeth of Bosnia, married since 1353, had long remained childless, until three daughters were born – Catherine in 1370 (she died in 1378), Mary in 1371, and Jadwiga in 1374. Mary was betrothed to Sigismund of Luxemburg, the son of Charles IV, who was at that time margrave of Brandenburg; she was crowned "king" of Hungary at the age of eleven. Regency for the young Queen Mary was entrusted to her mother Elizabeth of Bosnia. Mary's rule, however, was challenged by her father's only male relative, his nephew, who ruled Naples as King Charles III after having assassinated Joan. In 1385, Charles marched on Buda and found enough support to be crowned there as Charles II. He was wounded while being besieged in Buda by his enemies, however, and died in February 1386. Mary and Elizabeth then made a comeback. After further troubles with the Neapolitan party that led to Elizabeth's assassination, stability returned to Hungary when Sigismund of Luxembourg, Mary's husband since October 1386, was crowned king (thus formally co-ruler) in March 1387.

Mary, while being granted formal prerogatives and lands, does not seem to have intervened much in royal government after her wedding. She died in 1395. Sigismund's reign marked a high point for the place of Hungary in European politics. At the beginning of his reign, though, the new king faced many problems. As he was crowned without hereditary legitimacy, the nobility forced him to make concessions. He nonetheless managed to improve royal administration and to restrict the power of the barons. Sigismund also spent many years keeping the Neapolitan Angevins at bay and defending Hungary against the Ottomans. He barely escaped from the battle of Nikopolis in 1396, where European troops were crushed by the army of Sultan Bayezid I. Hungary then retreated to a defensive position towards the Ottomans.

The Hussite movement that engulfed Central Europe in the fifteenth century had its origins in Bohemia during the unstable and unpopular rule of the son of Charles IV, Wenceslas IV (1378–1419). The teachings of the Oxford theologian John Wycliffe (ca. 1330–84), who criticized corruption and advocated a stronger focus on the Bible, resonated in Bohemia, along with the *devotio moderna* that emphasized personal piety. Translations of the Bible into Czech and German began to circulate. John Hus, a professor of theology at the University of Prague, was inspired by the writings of Wycliffe and agitated for church reform. The reform movement scored a success when Wenceslas IV, with the 1409 decree of Kutná Hora, amalgamated all foreign nations represented at the University of Prague into one German nation; the reform-minded Czech nation was given three out of four votes (see chapter 69). The result was a massive exodus of foreign masters and students, many of whom went to the newly established University of Leipzig. Wenceslas IV, however, soon earned the ire of the reformers with his support of Pope John XXIII's sale of indulgences.

Meanwhile, Wenceslas IV's brother Sigismund was elected king of the Romans in 1411; his imperial coronation in Aachen followed in 1414, but a coronation in Rome would not happen until 1433. Sigismund summoned the Council of Constance in 1414. For four years, the council sought to put an end to the papal schism and unite Christendom. John Hus was invited to explain his controversial views at the council, but when he did, he was seen as stubborn and inflexible. He was condemned for heresy and was burned at the stake on July 6, 1415. The execution of John Hus caused uproar among the Czech-speaking nobility of Bohemia and Moravia: a letter of protest was sent to the council with the seals of 452 nobles.

In Prague, Hus's companion Jakoubek of Stříbro (Jakobellus von Mies) introduced the practice of communion in both species (bread and wine) for laypeople. This became a powerful symbol for the religious reformers who came to be known as Hussites, or followers of John Hus – even though Hus himself had been ambivalent on that matter. Communion in both species reduced the difference between clerics and laypeople and symbolized opposition to clerical privileges.

When Wenceslas IV died of a stroke shortly after a major protest action in Prague in 1419, his brother Sigismund was the obvious successor. However, Sigismund was unable to take control of Prague, although he managed to get there long enough to be crowned in 1420; he established residence in Silesia – Wrocław was the second largest city of the lands of the crown of Bohemia. This was the beginning of the Hussite revolution, a period of transformational change led by religious reformers who ruled the land until 1436 in the absence of a king. The revolution began in violence with the plunder of convents and monasteries. The reformers formulated their demands in the Four Articles of Prague: complete freedom of preaching, communion in both kinds for all believers (*sub utraque specie*, the Utraquist position), poverty for the church, and punishment of mortal sins by a selected body. The most radical of reformers assembled around the newly established town of Tábor (southern Bohemia) and were led by the military commander John Žižka; more moderate reformers rallied behind theologians in Prague. Church properties were confiscated throughout the Czech lands by the revolutionary reformers. Although some German-Bohemians joined the movement, it was clearly dominated by speakers of Czech.

German crusaders sent against the Hussites suffered defeats. In 1427, the Hussites launched raids into neighboring countries – Hungary, Silesia, Lusatia, Austria, Franconia, the land of Meissen. The Hussite Wars had become a European conflict that sent shock-waves across the continent. The tide finally turned when the Táborites were crushed by moderates and Catholics at the battle of Lipany in May 1434, leaving the more moderate Prague reformers to negotiate a peaceful outcome. At the Council of Basel, they obtained recognition of the Compacts, an arrangement that included communion in both species. The Compacts were formally promulgated in Latin, Czech, and German in Jihlava in July 1436. However, they were never recognized by the papacy.

Sigismund entered Prague in August 1436 and was acknowledged as king; he promised to respect the Compacts of Basel but died the following year. The revolution had made Bohemia a different country. Relations between speakers of German and Czech had changed. The influence of the German-speaking minority declined while the Hussite movement had resulted in broader social acceptance of Czech as a literary language (see chapter 68). The confiscated church properties – around 90 percent in Bohemia – were not returned, which resulted in massive ecclesiastical impoverishment; the personnel of religious institutions was also dramatically reduced. The wars and destruction had a heavy toll: Bohemia might have lost as much as 40 percent of its population. Prague, which had 40,000 inhabitants before the revolution, is estimated to have been reduced to 30,000. Trade relations were disrupted by years of embargo and the reputation of Bohemia in Europe was damaged.

In Hungary, Sigismund was followed by three short-reigned kings – Albert of Habsburg (1437–39), who was also king of the Romans and king of Bohemia; the king of Poland Władysław (Vladislav) III Jagiełło (1440–44); and Albert's son Ladislav (Vladislas) V the Posthumous (1444–57), who was also king of Bohemia. At the center of political life in Hungary was John Hunyadi, a Wallachian knight in royal service who, as reward for his military success, was named voivode of Transylvania. The Hungarians suffered a major defeat at the hands of the Ottomans in 1444 at the battle of Varna, where Władysław, king of Poland and Hungary, was killed. John Hunyadi became regent. After the childless death of Ladislas V in 1457, John Hunyadi's 15-year-old son Matthias was elected king with the support of the nobility and of leading ecclesiastics; he would be crowned in 1464. Matthias Hunyadi, better known by his nickname Corvinus (hinting at his coat of arms, a raven), turned out to be an energetic ruler who made Hungary a leading European power (see chapter 71). As the Ottomans advanced into the Balkans, Matthias, mindful of the defeats suffered by his predecessors, avoided direct confrontation; his prudent policies were more defensive and focused on consolidating his position in Central Europe.

In Bohemia, Sigismund was briefly succeeded by Albert of Habsburg (1437–39). A nobleman named George of Poděbrady used the uncertainty of the time to gain influence; he was named regent for the young Ladislas the Posthumous, crowned in 1453. When Ladislas died in 1457, George of Poděbrady was elected king. The Utraquist movement, far from disappearing at the end of the Hussite Wars, found a champion in King George, who went out of his way to secure papal recognition for the Compacts. Pope Paul II, however, agitated against him, and opponents of the Utraquists rallied behind Matthias Corvinus.

The Hungarian king invaded Moravia and most of Silesia in 1468. In 1469, supporters elected him king of Bohemia while he was in Brno. George of Poděbrady died in 1471. Years of struggle ensued that ended with the arrangements of 1479. Władysław (Vladislav) II Jagiełło, son of the Polish king Casimir IV, was given the kingdom of Bohemia, while Matthias Corvinus kept hold of Moravia, Silesia, and Lusatia; Bohemia and the lands of the crown would be reunited after the death of one of the rulers. Matthias Corvinus died in 1490; the kingdom of Hungary, along with the crown lands of Bohemia, went to Vladislav II Jagiełło.

FURTHER READING

Bartoš, František Michálek. *The Hussite Revolution, 1424–1437*. East European Monographs. New York: Columbia University Press, 1986.

Fudge, Thomas A. *Jerome of Prague and the Foundation of the Hussite Movement*. Oxford: Oxford University Press, 2016.

Kaminsky, Howard. *A History of the Hussite Revolution*. Berkeley: University of California Press, 1967.

Knoll, Paul W. *The Rise of the Polish Monarchy: Piast Poland in East Central Europe*. Chicago: University of Chicago Press, 1972.

Lahey, Stephen E. *The Hussites*. Past Imperfect. Leeds: Arc Humanities Press, 2019.

Polívka, Miroslav. "The Expansion of the Czech State During the Era of the Luxemburgs (1306–1419)." In *A History of the Czech Lands*, edited by Jaroslav Pánek, Oldřich Tůma, et al., 117–46. Prague: Karolinum Press, 2009.

Van Dussen, Michael, and Pavel Soukup, eds. *A Companion to the Hussites*. Leiden: Brill, 2019.

Vardy, Steven B., Géza Grosschmid, and Leslie S. Domonkos, eds. *Louis the Great, King of Hungary and Poland*. East European Monographs 185. New York: Columbia University Press, 1986.

49

EASTERN EUROPE: LITHUANIA, MUSCOVY, AND THE GOLDEN HORDE

Keywords in this chapter: *Reisen*, *veche*, Ottoman Turks

Two emerging powers competed for overlordship in the lands of Rus' in the later Middle Ages: Lithuania and Moscow (see insert 49.1). Lithuania became a major European power despite its rulers remaining pagan (see chapter 62): their religion did not prevent them from being involved in marriage alliances with ruling houses in Poland and Rus', to great success. The Muscovite princes became their main rivals. The Golden Horde, while still collecting tribute from the princes of Rus', struggled to maintain its dominating position in Eastern Europe after the internal troubles of the late fourteenth century (see map 49.1).

INSERT 49.1. RUS', RUTHENIA, AND RUSSIA

The modern states of Belarus, Ukraine, and Russia all have distant origins connected with the lands of Rus' of the Kievan period. The eastern and western parts of Rus', however, have evolved in different directions since the early fourteenth century. In the east, Muscovy became the dominant principality and, in the fifteenth century, expanded to the east and to the west. Mongol domination impacted Rus' society in various ways: some Muscovite governance practices were likely inspired by those of the Mongols; the Rus' church garnered authority and wealth thanks to Mongol privileges and tax exemptions. In the Ruthenian lands of the grand duchy of Lithuania and the kingdom of Poland, connections with Central and Western Europe were more important: Ruthenian towns were granted the privileges of Magdeburg law; Latin documentary practices and west European literature influenced Ruthenian written culture (see chapters 67 and 68); ecclesiastical leaders were more receptive to the unionist movement (see chapter 64).

The name Rus' reflects usage in medieval Slavonic sources (it originally designated the Norse who settled in Eastern Europe, and eventually the East Slavic population over which they ruled), while the name Ruthenia reflects usage in late medieval writings in Latin. Variations of the Latin name Russia, while also used in medieval European sources to designate Rus', Ruthenia, or Muscovy, have led to the adoption of that name in the early modern period for the state that emerged out of late medieval Muscovy (under rulers called grand princes and, since Ivan IV, czars or emperors). The modern designation of Russia in the Russian language (Россия, *Rossiya*) is derived from the Greek form of the name.

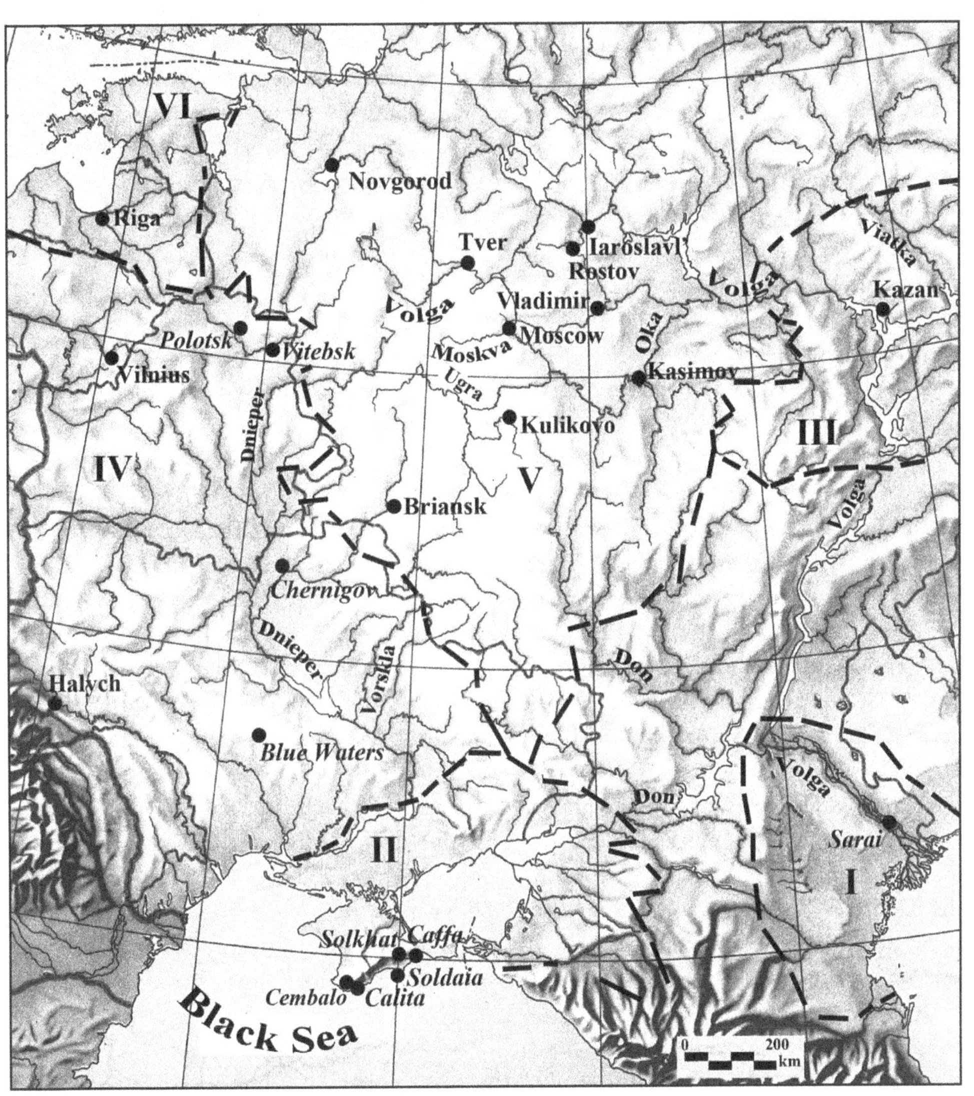

Map 49.1. Eastern Europe, ca. 1500: I – Khanate of Astrakhan; II – Khanate of Crimea; III – Khanate of Kazan; IV – Lithuania; V – Muscovy; VI – Teutonic Order. Medieval names are in italics.

Only fighting pagans allowed the Teutonic Knights to justify their continued existence as a political force: with the conquest of Prussia completed, they turned to Lithuania. In the fourteenth century, it became popular for European knights to go to Lithuania and fight the pagans alongside the Teutonic Knights. Kings of Bohemia and Hungary, high nobles and knights from Germany, France, England, and Scandinavia took part in the *Reisen* ("expeditions") against those whom they called the "Saracens of the North." Not everybody, however, agreed with the policies of the Order: the merchants of Riga, for example, who had support from the archbishop, opposed them as detrimental to their commercial interests. Pagan Lithuanian troops were briefly garrisoned in Riga to defend the city against the Teutonic Knights.

Lithuania was a land very different from Livonia or Prussia. Instead of small tribes, the Teutonic Order faced strong regional leaders by the thirteenth century. In 1219 a peace agreement was reached between the Romanovichi of Halych-Volhynia and twenty-one Lithuanian leaders – among them one woman, probably a widow. Mindaugas centralized authority in the Lithuanian lands and reached out to Pope Innocent IV; he was baptized in 1251 and crowned king in 1253, subordinating Lithuania to the Patrimony of Peter, after which a bishop named Christian arrived in the country. Mindaugas, however, confronted fierce resistance and was assassinated in 1263 by his opponents. While Christianization efforts fell apart, a tradition of centralized rulership was maintained. In the remainder of the thirteenth century, Mindaugas's relatives expanded their influence in the lands of Rus'. For example, his Catholic nephew Tautvilas supported his sister's husband Daniel of Halych (Galicia), who had also received a royal crown from the pope. Daniel rewarded him with the land of Polotsk (now Polatsk, in Belarus).

Lithuanian expansion was accelerated in the early fourteenth century with the Gediminids who ruled Upper Lithuania (Aukštaitija). Staunchly pagan, Gediminas (1316–41) and his son Algirdas (1341–77) navigated alliances between Catholics, Orthodox, and Muslims. They were masters at making ambiguous promises to both Catholic and Orthodox rulers while remaining noncommittal about a possible conversion. Gediminas positioned himself on the international scene through diplomatic correspondence – he sent Latin letters, written by friars in his service, to Pope John XXII, towns of northern Germany, and chapters of mendicant orders. He styled himself "king of the Lithuanians and of the Ruthenians," occasionally adding "prince and duke of Semigallia" – a region coveted by the Teutonic Order. On his seal, Gediminas was depicted as holding in his hands a crown (presumably the one that had been sent to Mindaugas by the pope). He welcomed Polish and Ruthenian Christians and gave them freedom to practice their rites according to their customs, stating that, just like pagan Lithuanians, they all "have one God." He denounced the policies of the Teutonic Order and alluded to his possible baptism. Peace treaties confirmed with Latin documents were made with the Livonian Order, the Teutonic Order, Muscovy, and Mazovia. Algirdas ruled in Vilnius and held senior authority over his six brothers.

Algirdas introduced the Slavonic title *velikii kniaz'*, rendered in Latin as *magnus rex* and usually translated as "grand duke." According to a German chronicle, he stated that "all Rus' should belong to the Lithuanians." Gediminas and Algirdas implemented a bold agenda of marriage alliances: they let their daughters convert to Catholicism to marry Piasts, while some of their sons became Orthodox Christians to marry Riurikid princesses. Algirdas remained pagan despite being married twice to Rus' princesses. His first wife, Maria, whom he married in 1318, was the daughter of the prince of Vitebsk (today in Belarus); when she inherited her father's land, Algirdas took it for himself. His second wife was Iuliana, a princess from Tver.

The alliances orchestrated by Gediminas and Algirdas targeted their main competitors, the princes of Moscow and the kings of Poland: Gediminid women, as wives and widows, played important political roles in supporting Lithuanian expansion. The Muscovite heir Simeon was married to Aigusta-Anastasia, sister of Algirdas, and later to Maria of Tver, sister of Algirdas's wife Iuliana. While their connections with the princes of Moscow proved short-lived, the grand dukes of Lithuania developed a strong alliance with the latter's rivals, the princes of Tver. For example, a daughter of Gediminas, Maria, married Prince Dmitri Mikhailovich in 1320. Maria lived for twenty-four years after Dmitri's death in 1325. As a wealthy dowager princess who stayed in the land of Tver, she is believed to have played a role in the close relationship that that land maintained with Lithuania.

King Casimir III of Poland was bound to Lithuania through two of his wives. In 1325, he married a daughter of Gediminas, Aldona-Anna, which ushered in a cessation of Lithuanian raids that lasted until her death in 1339. Casimir's later wife, Jadwiga, was a great-granddaughter of Gediminas. Casimir married his grandson and expected heir, Kaźko of Słupsk, to a daughter of Algirdas, Kenna (Joanna). Lithuanian alliances with the rivals of the Polish kings, the dukes of Mazovia, however, were older, dating back to 1279 when Gaudemantė-Zofia, daughter of the successor of Mindaugas, Traidenis (ca. 1270–82), married Bolesław II of Mazovia (1251–1313). The daughter of Gediminas and sister of Casimir's wife Aldona-Anna, Elizabeth, married Wenceslas of Mazovia around 1316. When Wenceslas died twenty years later, Elizabeth became a wealthy dowager who ruled over the castellany of Wyszogród in Mazovia. She actively supported her pagan brothers Kęstutis and Vytautas until her death in 1364.

Gediminas and Algirdas did not refrain from using military means. Going to war in 1356, Algirdas took Briansk and probably Chernigov. He fought Mongol troops to take control of Podolia (now in western Ukraine and northeastern Moldova), a region with river ports giving access to the Black Sea that was secured after the battle of Blue Water in 1362. Fedor, who had ruled Kiev since the 1320s, might have been put in place after an attack by Gediminas; his successor was Vladimir, a son of Algirdas. Lithuanian control over the lands south of Podolia was extended under Vytautas in the later fourteenth century, all the way to the Black Sea coast. Gediminid rule had advantages for the Rus': Lithuanian power protected trade routes that connected the lands of Rus' with the Hanse and provided an alternative to the growing influence of Muscovy.

The dependence of Rus' princes upon their Mongol overlords did not change significantly under the Gediminids, who entertained constructive relationships with the khans. Gediminas signed a treaty with Khan Özbek in 1324, and the Rus' princes continued paying the tribute and requesting approval from the khans to rule. The grand dukes occasionally

Table 49.1. Rulers of Muscovy in the Fourteenth and Fifteenth Centuries

Name of the Ruler	Regnal Years
Ivan I Kalita	1328–40
Simeon	1340–53
Ivan II	1353–59
Dmitri I	1359–61
Dmitri II	1361–89
Vasily I	1389–1425
Vasily II	1425–33, 1434–46, 1447–62
Iurii IV	1433–34
Dmitri III	1446–47
Ivan III	1462–1505

obtained Mongol military support in fighting Poland or the Teutonic Order. Lithuanian rulers implemented the Mongol trade policies and collected the tribute for the khan like the Rus' prince of Kiev had done earlier; they still sent the tribute to the Horde in the fifteenth century.

After the disruption of the conquest and despite the Black Death, the Mongol trade policies facilitated growing economic prosperity in Suzdalia (northeastern Rus'), especially in Tver and Moscow. Moscow had an easy connection to Sarai through the Moskva River, a tributary of the Volga, and trade with Novgorod and the Baltic Sea network was intensified. Riurikid succession led to the partition of Suzdalia until, in the early fourteenth century, the princes of Moscow gained ascendancy in competing for the title of grand prince of Vladimir. The Daniilovichi – named after their forebear Prince Daniel of Moscow (1263–1303) – imposed their hegemony in the region; key to their success was how they bent the Riurikid succession rules with the support of their Mongol overlords. While the khans generally respected Riurikid traditions, they favored the most reliable princes. Ivan I Kalita ("the Moneybag"; 1331–40) especially gained the trust of the khan by being an effective tax collector (hence his nickname). By the mid-fourteenth century, the Daniilovichi had prevailed over their main rivals, the princes of Tver, and monopolized the throne of Vladimir (see table 49.1).

Dmitri II Donskoi ("of the Don"; 1359–89) was recognized as grand prince of Vladimir in 1362 by Mamai, a military leader who controlled the politics of the Golden Horde at the time. When Dmitri ceased paying the tribute in 1373, Mamai transferred the title of grand prince to Dmitri's rival, Mikhail of Tver. Dmitri, however, defeated in battle both Mikhail and, soon thereafter, Mamai himself at the 1380 battle of Kulikovo Field, in the Upper Don area (whence his nickname). He nonetheless resumed paying the tribute to the new khan, Tokhtamysh, and sent his son Vasily as hostage to Sarai.

While collecting the tribute of other Rus' princes on behalf of the khans, the grand princes of the late fourteenth century kept enriching themselves by raising other taxes. The death of Prince Vasily I (1389–1425), however, was followed by a civil war in Muscovy, from which Vasily II (1425–62) emerged as the dominant leader by the mid-century. The coins he issued styled him "sovereign of all Rus'." Primogeniture had now fully replaced the Riurikid principle of lateral succession. Moreover, Vasily II was the last grand prince to rule with authorization of the khan; when he designated his son Ivan III as heir in 1448, he did not ask permission. Khan Ulu-Muhammed attacked Vasily and made him prisoner, but he was released for a ransom and only agreed to increased tribute payments.

Ivan III (1462–1505) succeeded as grand prince while his brothers accepted subordinated positions. Under his rule, Muscovy, now a dynastic state, expanded dramatically. Between 1471 and 1489, Ivan gained control of Iaroslavl', Perm, Rostov, Viatka, and the long-time rival Tver (see chapter 50). A major gain was Novgorod, the merchant town that ruled a territory reaching north up to the White Sea (see chapter 51). Novgorod had traditionally chosen its own prince until, in 1456, the municipal authorities agreed to seek approval of the prince of Moscow for external policies. In 1478, Ivan III abolished the municipal assembly (*veche*) and, in a powerful symbolic gesture, removed the bell used to call the meetings. His main rival in the Rus' land was now clearly the Lithuanian grand duke. In 1495, Ivan's daughter Helena married Grand Duke Alexander; the wedding took place in a Catholic church, but Ivan insisted that Helena be allowed to remain Orthodox. Under the pretext of supposed persecution of Orthodox believers, he attacked Lithuania in 1500. Although he failed to take Smolensk, he captured Chernigov and large swathes of land – about one third of the territory of the grand duchy.

The death of the unpopular Khan Berdibek in 1359, and the subsequent murder in 1360 of his grandmother Taidula, who had dominated Horde politics for 20 years, sparked a civil war in the Golden Horde. Berdibek and Taidula were the last direct descendants of Batu. The Black Death had devastated the country, and the Ottoman advance disturbed ship transport in the Black Sea. At the same time, the Mongol Empire was dismantled as the Ilkhanate in Persia was partitioned and the Ming took over China in 1368. In Sarai, the begs dominated Horde politics in the absence of a consensual khan. The beg and military commander Mamai and his wife Tulunbek, daughter of Berdibek, called the shots from the 1360s. They were challenged by Tokhtamysh, who was of Chinggisid and Jochid descent, albeit not of the line of Batu. Stability returned when Tokhtamysh was recognized as khan in 1378 with support of the begs. Mamai, returning from his defeat by Dmitri Donskoi, was beaten by Tokhtamysh and soon thereafter murdered in Caffa, while the new khan forced Dmitri to resume payment of the tribute.

Tokhtamysh, however, faced relentless attacks by his former ally Timur Lenk (Tamerlane), a military leader married to a Chinggisid princess who was building a new empire around Samarkand (now in Uzbekistan). Tokhtamysh, who had long entertained friendly relations with the Lithuanian grand dukes, found an ally in Vytautas, as well as refuge at his court in 1399 when a beg named Edigei, an ally of Tamerlane, took control of Sarai.

Edigei's hold on power was weak, however: not being of Chinggisid descent, he could only rule through puppet rulers. Vytautas sent Lithuanian troops in support of Tokhtamysh; they ventured on the steppe and met the army of Edigei and Khan Timur-Kutlug on the Vorskla River, a left-hand tributary of the Dnieper. They were defeated, however, and Vytautas gave up attempts at taking on the Horde. Thousands of Mongol warriors and their families followed Tokhtamysh to Lithuania and, unable to return to Sarai, settled there permanently at the invitation of Vytautas. Their descendants eventually became known as the "Lipka Tatars" ("Lithuanian Tatars," see chapter 63). Tokhtamysh – who died in 1405 in western Siberia – and his son, Jalal al-Din, remained staunch allies of Vytautas. Jalal al-Din's Mongol troops fought alongside those of Poland and Lithuania at the battle of Grunwald (see chapter 50) before his return to Sarai where he briefly reigned as khan (1411–12).

The Golden Horde did not survive intact this period of trouble: it was partitioned during the second quarter of the fifteenth century. A separate khanate was formed in the Middle Volga region around Kazan' (now the capital city of the Republic of Tatarstan in the Russian Federation), and another in the Crimea, while the remaining territories were under the control of the Great Horde. The khanate of Kazan' was established in 1445 after Ulu-Muhammed, a Chinggisid who ruled in Sarai, moved his court there, before being murdered by his own son Mamutek. Mamutek's brother Kasim was chased from Kazan' and established yet another khanate, that of Kasimov, under the protection of the princes of Moscow.

The Crimea was administered by governors appointed by the khans of Sarai who resided in Solkhat (now Staryi Krym, in eastern Crimea). The peninsula had a diverse population. The merchant towns Caffa (now Feodosia), Soldaia (now Sudak), Calita (now Yalta), and Cembalo (now Balaklava), all on the southern coast, had populations of Greeks, Armenians, and Jews, along with Italian merchants (see chapter 59). The rest of the population in the peninsula had, since the late thirteenth century, been mostly Muslim and Turkic-speaking, because of the khans' immigration policies. The governors of Solkhat became more assertive after the crisis that unfolded in the late fourteenth century. The Chinggisid Haci Giray, who was born and lived in Lithuania, challenged his cousin, the khan of Sarai Sayyid Ahmed II. His first attempt at a takeover of the Crimea in 1428 failed, but he succeeded the second time, in 1443. Haci Giray established a new khanate that attracted Mongols dissatisfied with the khans of Sarai. He sought allies among the enemies of the Great Horde – Poland-Lithuania and Muscovy. In 1454, the Ottomans of Mehmed II (1444–46 and 1451–81) helped him in forcing Caffa to acknowledge his authority.

Having conquered Constantinople in 1453 (see chapter 52), Mehmed II was seeking hegemony in the Black Sea area. His son Bayezid II took Caffa in 1475, taking advantage of the instability that followed the death of Haci Giray. The southern coast of Crimea became a separate Ottoman province. The newly appointed khan, Mengli Giray, submitted to Bayezid in 1478 and ruled from the mountain interior until 1514, as vassal of the sultan. The Crimean khans were now selected by the clan leaders but had their positions approved by Ottoman authorities. The Crimean khans remained allies of the Ottomans while following independent policies. They offered the sultan military service, for example in the 1484 expedition to Moldavia. They inherited from the Golden Horde the tribute from the lands of Rus' that was collected by the grand dukes of Lithuania and the grand princes of Muscovy. The khans entertained diplomatic relations with Poland-Lithuania and Muscovy that were independent of Ottoman policies. They had permanent envoys in Moscow, for example, who resided in a building called the Crimean Court.

The Chinggisid khan Ahmed (1465–81) attempted to revive the Great Horde, which encompassed the territory of the lower Volga, Sarai, and the central steppe region, the successor of the Golden Horde. Ahmed sought to restore his authority and marched towards Moscow in 1480. His army and that of Ivan III made a stand on opposite sides of the river Ugra; they exchanged arrow and arquebus shots. Hoping for support from Casimir IV of Poland-Lithuania that never came, Ahmed decided to leave after two weeks without a proper battle. The encounter did not change much, but it was the last open confrontation between Muscovy and the Horde. Ivan III had probably already stopped paying the tribute some time before these events. Nonetheless, he maintained friendly relations with the rival khan of the Crimea. The Great Horde was finally conquered in 1502 by Mengli Giray, who incorporated its territory into the Crimean khanate.

FURTHER READING

Crummey, Robert O. *The Formation of Muscovy 1304–1613*. Longman History of Russia. London: Longman, 1987.

Favereau, Marie. *The Horde: How the Mongols Changed the World*. Cambridge: Belknap Press, 2021.

Fisher, Alan. *The Crimean Tatars*. Stanford: Hoover Institution Press, 1978.

Gulevych, Vladyslav. "Expansion of the Grand Duchy of Lithuania in the Middle and the Second Half of the Fourteenth Century and Its Relations with the Horde." In *The Routledge Handbook of the Mongols and Central-Eastern Europe: Political, Economic and Cultural Relations*, edited by Alexander V. Maiorov, 340–67. London: Routledge, 2021.

Gulevych, Vladyslav. "The Grand Duchy of Lithuania, the Kingdom of Poland, and the Tatar World in the Fifteenth Century." In *The Routledge Handbook of the Mongols and Central-Eastern Europe: Political, Economic and Cultural Relations*, edited by Alexander V. Maiorov, 368–88. London: Routledge, 2021.

Kiaupa, Zigmantas, Jūratė Kiaupienė, and Albinas Kuncevičius. *The History of Lithuania Before 1795*. Vilnius: Lithuanian Institute of History, 2000.

Kołodziejczyk, Dariusz. *The Crimean Khanate and Poland-Lithuania: International Diplomacy on the European Periphery (15th–18th Century). A Study of Peace Treaties Followed by Annotated Documents*. The Ottoman Empire and Its Heritage 47. Leiden: Brill, 2011.

Mažeikas, Rasa. "Bargaining for Baptism: Lithuanian Negotiations for Conversion, 1250–1258." In *Varieties of Religious Conversion in the Middle Ages*, edited by James Muldoon, 131–45. Gainesville: University Press of Florida, 1997.

Rowell, S. C. *Lithuania Ascending: A Pagan Empire Within East-Central Europe, 1295–1345*. Cambridge Studies in Medieval Life and Thought. Cambridge: Cambridge University Press, 1994.

50

THE POLISH-LITHUANIAN UNION

Keywords in this chapter: conversion, Christianity, Teutonic Knights

At the death of Louis of Anjou, at that time king of Hungary and Poland, in 1382 (see chapter 48), his daughter Jadwiga, who had spent her childhood in Vienna and Buda, moved to Cracow. In October 1384, at the age of ten, she was crowned "king" of Poland. She had been expected to marry William of Habsburg, but the arrangement was rescinded when the pagan ruler of Lithuania, Jogaila, proposed to convert to Christianity and espouse her. Jogaila, whose mother Iuliana of Tver was Christian Orthodox, was solemnly baptized in the cathedral of Cracow on February 15, 1386, taking the Christian name Władysław. Three days later, on her twelfth birthday, Jadwiga was married to the man, then in his mid-thirties. Władysław II Jogaila (Jagiełło in Polish) was crowned king on March 4, which made him co-ruler with Jadwiga. Shortly after the coronation, Red Ruthenia, which had passed to the kingdom of Hungary, was returned to Poland through the personal intervention of Queen Jadwiga, who traveled to Lviv while her husband was in Lithuania.

Jogaila had taken the title of grand duke of Lithuania and Ruthenia after the murder of his uncle, Kestutis. The latter's son, Vytautas (Witold in Polish), competed for power with him. At the time of Jogaila's wedding, the grand duchy encompassed many more territories than those inhabited by Lithuanians, including the lands of western Rus' (known as Ruthenia in western sources) up to the upper Volga (those territories are now in Belarus and in parts of Ukraine; see map 50.1). The Ruthenian lands of the grand duchy were typically governed by Slavicized Gediminids who had converted to Orthodox Christianity. In Jogaila's grand duchy, pagan Lithuanians were outnumbered three to one by Orthodox Christian Ruthenians.

The union with Poland and his Catholic baptism presented several advantages to Jogaila. Conversion to Catholicism, much more than a conversion to Orthodox Christianity, deprived the Teutonic Order of its reason to wage war on Lithuanians. Catholics might

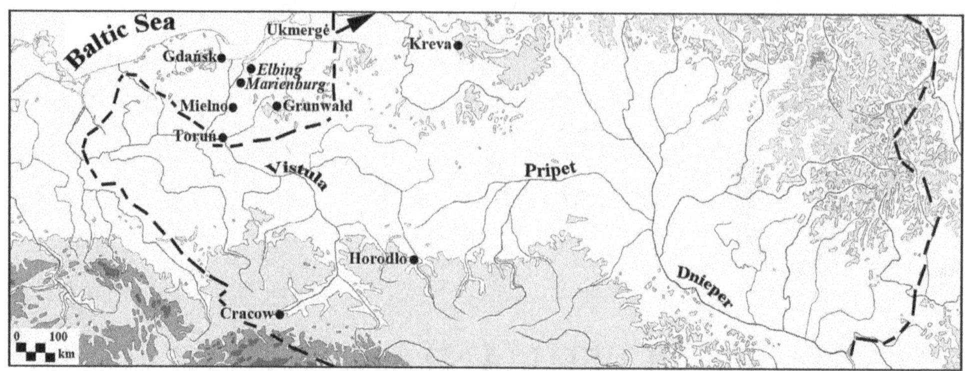

Map 50.1. The Polish-Lithuanian union, ca. 1400. Medieval names are in italics. Shown at the bottom are the Carpathian Mountains.

have regarded the Orthodox as schismatics, but the Teutonic Knights had no reason at all to wage war on Catholics on religious grounds. Moreover, Catholicism allowed Lithuanians, in following Jogaila's example, an option to preserve a separate identity that distinguished them from their Orthodox subjects. On the political level, Poland promised Lithuanians a solid alliance against the Teutonic Order. The Polish barons who selected Jogaila as the new co-ruler also hoped for some advantages coming from the union. They expected support in retaking lands conquered by the Teutonic Order, and they wanted assurances that the Polish crown would keep Red Ruthenia, which was coveted by both Lithuania and Hungary.

Jogaila's cousin Vytautas was already Christian at the time of the wedding with Jadwiga. He had converted to Catholicism in 1382, turned to Orthodoxy a few years later – when he took the baptismal name Alexander, which he retained to the end of his life – before returning to Catholicism. Vytautas, however, was less keen than Jogaila on the alliance with Poland and wanted to preserve the grand duchy's distinct institutions and autonomy. Upon his royal coronation, Jogaila named his brother Skirgaila regent in the grand duchy while he himself dealt with Polish affairs. Vytautas, unhappy with this arrangement, lobbied for the position. In 1392 Jogaila recognized Vytautas as grand duke of Lithuania and Ruthenia; in exchange, Vytautas formally acknowledged the overlordship of Jogaila and Jadwiga. In practice, though, he was allowed to administer the grand duchy independently.

The formal relationship between kingdom and grand duchy remained ambiguous. In 1385 Jogaila had promised, through the act of Kreva, to "join perpetually" his lands in Lithuania and Ruthenia to the kingdom of Poland; what this meant was not specified. Jogaila became sole ruler in Poland when Jadwiga passed away in 1399. With the 1401 treaty of Vilnius, Jogaila, Vytautas, and the assemblies of noblemen from both countries confirmed the titles of "duke" for Vytautas and "supreme duke" for Jogaila. The expectation seems to have been that, at the death of Vytautas, the grand duchy would return to the authority of the king and the royal council of Poland. The document of the 1413 treaty of Horodło stated the incorporation of Poland and Lithuania in its preamble but otherwise treated kingdom and grand duchy as separate entities with their own rulers – the king and the grand duke, respectively. The various treaties that followed upon one another maintained an ambiguity that well suited Jogaila and the nobility of the grand duchy but frustrated the nobility of Poland. Sigismund of Luxembourg suggested at the 1429 conference in Lutsk that Vytautas be crowned king. Jogaila was not opposed; however, the nobles of Poland were vehemently against the proposition. The project came to nothing, and in 1430 Vytautas died.

During his tenure as grand duke, Vytautas strove to rein in the autonomous tendencies of the Gediminids who ruled through hereditary right in Ruthenia and to replace them with Catholic Lithuanian office holders. However, Vytautas had limited success in expanding into Rus' or in helping his ally Tokhtamysh against his rivals in the Golden Horde; retaking Samogitia (Lower Lithuania) from the Teutonic Knights proved challenging.

Both Poland and Lithuania had long been at loggerheads with the Teutonic Order. The kings of Poland had never accepted the Order's 1308 conquest of Eastern Pomerania, and the Order had never ceased to wage war on the pagan Lithuanians. Since Jogaila's Christianization efforts without their help deprived them of a good reason to pose as protectors of Christendom, the Knights refused to recognize Lithuania as a Christian country. To justify their position, the grand masters went out of their way to smear Lithuanians on the international scene as false Christians.

To improve relations, Queen Jadwiga met with Grand Master Conrad of Jungingen in the company of her sister Mary, whose husband Sigismund of Luxembourg was an ally of the Order, but to no avail. The Order went to war with Lithuania over Samogitia in 1401–4 and came out victorious. The conflict between the Order and Poland-Lithuania came to a head at the 1410 battle of Grunwald (German: Tannenberg; Lithuanian: Žalgiris) in what is now northeastern Poland. The battle was a crushing defeat for the Order, and the Knights never really recovered from that blow. The Polish-Lithuanian forces, however, failed to take Marienburg and administer the final strike. Victory in Grunwald placed Lithuania in an enviable position. Samogitia was temporarily returned to Lithuania until, at the 1422 peace of Mielno, the arrangement was made permanent. The conflict with the Teutonic Order also drew Jogaila and Vytautas into the Hussite Wars (see chapter 48). The two cousins sought allies in Bohemia against Sigismund of Luxembourg when he partnered with the Teutonic Order. To annoy the Luxembourg ruler, Vytautas supported the claim to the throne of Bohemia of a Lithuanian lord named Sigismund Korybut, who went to fight with the Hussites. Jogaila, Vytautas, and Sigismund of Luxembourg reconciled after the battle of Lake Mielno in 1422, where the Teutonic Order was defeated.

With the 1385 agreement of Kreva, Jogaila had promised that all his subjects in the grand duchy would convert to Christianity. Catholic dioceses and parish churches were established rapidly, and he himself became a zealous propagator of the new religion: he is said to have translated the Lord's Prayer and the *Acts of the Apostles* into Lithuanian. He rewarded with privileges the nobles who accepted conversion. Countering any pretension of the Teutonic Order, Polish and Lithuanian clergy together undertook the Christianization of Samogitia.

Władysław II Jogaila was succeeded as king of Poland by his sons Władysław III (1434–44) and Casimir IV (1447–92). Władysław III died in 1444 on the battlefield at Varna while fighting against the Ottomans. Casimir IV ruled as both king of Poland and grand duke of Lithuania; his son Władysław became king of Bohemia and, after the death of Matthias Corvinus, king of Hungary as well (as Vladislav II) (see chapter 48).

The neighbor of Jagiellonian Poland, the state of the Teutonic Order, was in dire straits in the fifteenth century. The heavy taxes that the Knights imposed to fund their endless wars made them unpopular. In 1454, the Prussian league of towns sent a delegation to the king of Poland, asking him to free them from Teutonic rule. Casimir IV named a Polish governor in Eastern Pomerania, which sparked the Thirteen Years' War that ended through the mediation of the pope at the 1466 peace of Toruń. Poland kept Eastern Pomerania, including Gdańsk along with parts of Prussia that comprised Marienburg and Elbląg. The grand master, humiliated, was relegated to Königsberg and was forced to pay homage to the king of Poland. Royal Prussia, as it was known, remained part of Poland as Gdańsk, Toruń, and Elbląg received generous privileges and thrived.

The separation between kingdom and grand duchy was maintained in the fifteenth century, although the Lithuanian nobility was polarized on this question. At the death of Vytautas in 1430, two rival claimants vied for his position: Švitrigaila, brother of Jogaila, and Sigismund, brother of Vytautas. Švitrigaila rejected the union with Poland and sought the help of the Teutonic Order and Sigismund of Luxembourg. Vytautas's brother, meanwhile, counted on the support of Poland to maintain the union. The Lithuanian nobility was divided between the two parties. The Lithuanian Sigismund managed to beat his rival in 1435 at the battle of Ukmergė, and Švitrigaila surrendered in 1437; Sigismund did not, however, manage to quell opposition and was murdered in 1440.

To prevent further uncertainty, the Lithuanian nobility acclaimed Jogaila's son Casimir as grand duke in 1440. Casimir IV was elected king of Poland in 1446 after the death of Władysław at the battle of Varna, and crowned in 1447. The Lithuanian Council of Lords obtained guarantees for the autonomy of the grand duchy. Since King Casimir resided in Poland, government of the grand duchy was effectively entrusted to the Council of Lords. After Casimir IV's death in 1492, the Lithuanian Council of Lords elected his son John Albert as grand duke, while his other son, Alexander, was elected king of Poland. The 1499 treaty of Vilnius foresaw a union of two autonomous states, equal in rights but with a common ruler. The two countries were reunited under one ruler when John Albert passed away in 1501 and Alexander became king of Poland.

FURTHER READING

Baronas, Darius, and S. C. Rowell. *The Conversion of Lithuania: From Pagan Barbarians to Late Medieval Christians*. Vilnius: Institute of Lithuanian Literature and Folklore, 2015.

Frost, Robert. *The Oxford History of Poland-Lithuania*. Vol. 1, *The Making of the Polish-Lithuanian Union, 1385–1569*. Oxford: Oxford University Press, 2015.

Halecki, Oscar. *Jadwiga of Anjou and the Rise of East Central Europe*. East European Monographs 308. Boulder: Columbia University Press, 1991.

Mickūnaitė, Giedrė. *Making a Great Ruler: Grand Duke Vytautas of Lithuania*. Budapest: Central European University Press, 2006.

51

THE TAIGA PERIPHERY OF EUROPE IN THE LATE MIDDLE AGES

Keywords in this chapter: furs, forts, conversion, Christianity

The modern city of Perm is located on the southern border of the taiga, the wooded area of the cold, subarctic region of Northern Europe. However, the city took its name from the language of the Veps (a Finnic people that lived along the river Onega, just south of the White Sea) (see map 51.1). In that language (as well as in modern Finnish), *perämaa* means "far-away country." Perm referred initially to the vast swathe of land between the river Onega to the west and the Ural Mountains in the east. The word was used in that sense in charters issued in Novgorod between 1264 and 1371 in reference to a district from which tribute was collected in the form of furs. The speakers of East Slavic dialects who adopted the word in that sense were therefore Novgorodians, who learned it from Veps guides assisting them to penetrate the taiga region to the northeast. As early as 1096, a Novgorodian nobleman named Goniata Rogovich led a raid against the Yugra, a population living east of the river Pechora. The number and frequency of the Novgorodian raids against the Yugra increased during the twelfth century. From the 1080s to the late fifteenth century, the Yugra (perhaps the same people designated as Vis in earlier sources written in Arabic) appear in charters along with Pechora, the territory controlled from Novgorod which they inhabited. Shortly after 1150, Novgorod secured access to the Sukhona River (a left-hand tributary of the Northern Dvina), then to the Vychegda (a right-hand tributary of the Northern Dvina), in the process subjugating the local population, forced to pay tribute in furs.

However, shortly after the mid-twelfth century, Suzdalia under Andrei Bogoliubskii began to challenge the Novgorodian claims to "Perm." Under Grand Prince Vsevolod III the Big Nest (1176–1212), two major forts were built in the region – Gleden on the river Yug (1178) and Ustyug on the Sukhona (1212). To the south from that region, Rus' settlers from Suzdalia began to appear in the lands along the river Viatka inhabited by Cheremis

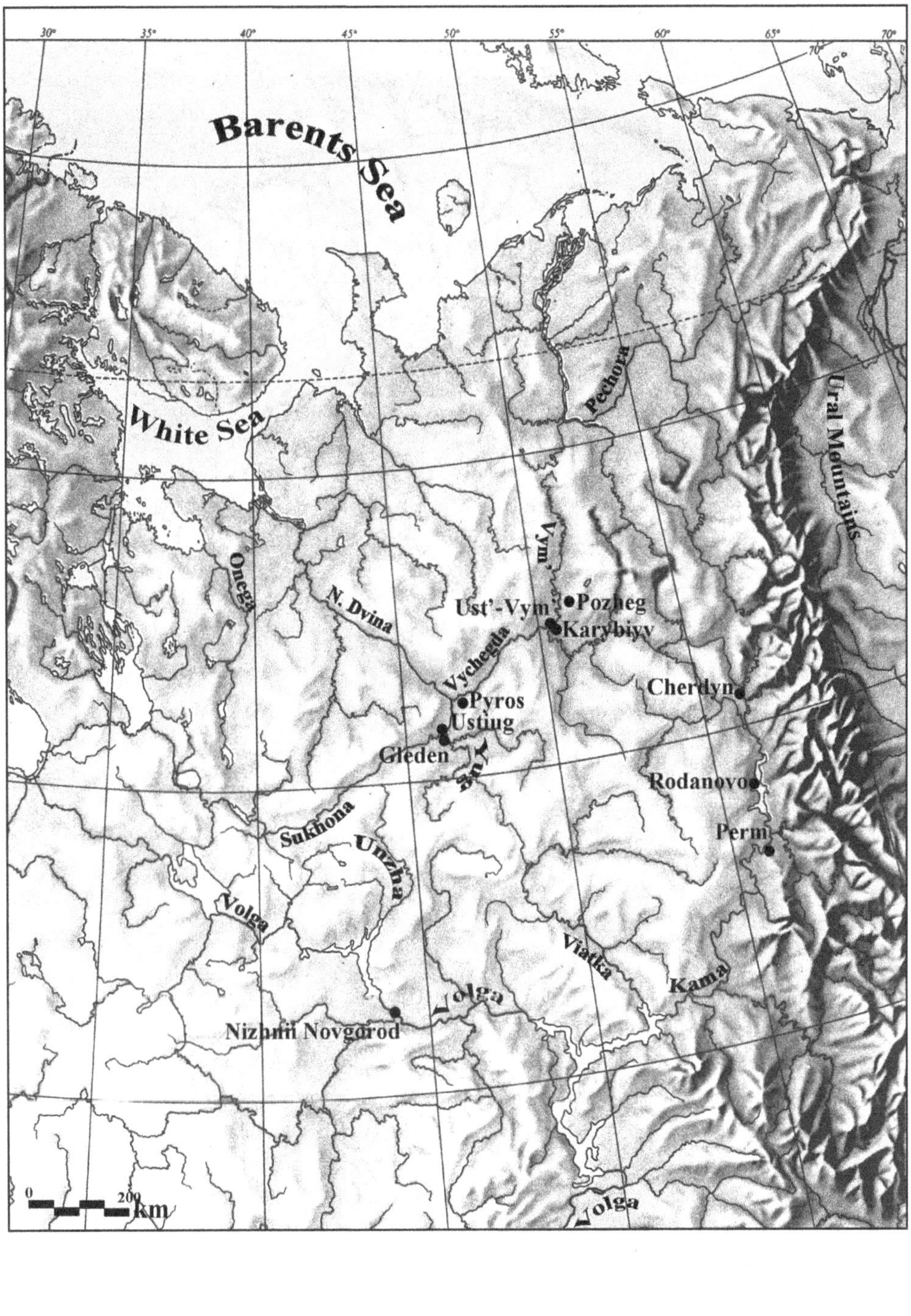

Map 51.1. The taiga region of northeastern Europe during the Late Middle Ages.

(Mari) and Votyaks (Udmurts). They were most likely intruders into a catchment area claimed by merchants from Volga Bulgharia, who moved upstream along the Volga, then along the Unzha to the headwaters of the Yug. When the town of Nizhnii Novgorod was established on the Volga in 1221, Suzdalia effectively eliminated the Bulghar competition in the area. Fifteen years later, the Mongols sacked and destroyed the main urban centers of Volga Bulgharia (see chapter 46). The Mongol conquest, however, created a new demand, as both the Bulghars and the Rus' were forced to pay tribute, at least initially, in furs. To meet the demand, Bulghar merchants moved farther up the Kama River to reach the Yugra at the headwaters of the Pechora. Traveling by dogsled in the winter along the Kama River through the lands of the Udmurts, their northern neighbors, the Bulghar merchants exchanged the luxury fur pelts for iron tools, clothing, salt, and trinkets.

Finds of Baltic amber in the stronghold at Rodanovo near Pozhva (on the right bank of the Kama, north of Perm) confirm that Novgorodians were the main competitors of the Bulghar merchants in the Upper Kama region. By 1200, however, their influence in that region was also challenged by Suzdalians. The Suzdalians moved even deeper into the taiga region, as documented by several fortified settlements. The fort at Karybiyv (near Ust'-Vym', in the Komi Republic) produced evidence of smelting and blacksmithing, but also an abundance of pottery of Suzdalian type, if not manufacture. Pozheg (near Emva, Komi Republic) was in existence between the twelfth and fourteenth centuries, built most likely by Novgorodians to monitor, if not to curb, the Suzdalian (and, later, Muscovite) encroachment in the area. Christian artifacts found at Pozheg and its hinterland bespeak the spread of Christianity in the taiga shortly after 1200.

By the late twelfth century, Novgorod was part of a vast commercial network across the Baltic Sea, exchanging goods with trading partners in Scandinavia and northern Germany. The most important commodity that German merchants sought in Novgorod was furs, which had meanwhile become a key element of aristocratic clothing in Western Europe. The sables and ermines that King Richard I of England and King Philip II of France promised to renounce while embarking on the Third Crusade in 1189 had undoubtedly been procured by means of trade from the Novgorod markets. In response to demand in England, France, and other parts of Western Europe, therefore, Novgorod extended its realm farther into the taiga. While the northern population in the valley of the Northern Dvina supplied squirrel pelts, sable and ermine were procured from farther afield. Shortly before 1200, Novgorod made two attempts to subjugate the Perm and the Yugra of the northeast, without success. During the thirteenth and fourteenth centuries, however, changes in Western European fashions changed the nature of demand on the Novgorod market. Fine woolen clothes dyed in brilliant colors were lined with northern squirrel, known as vair or miniver for its soft and silky texture, as well as its gray or white color. It was the northern (gray) squirrel that was traded in large quantities between Novgorod and the German Hanse (see chapter 60). Squirrel pelts were exchanged for salt, cloth, sweet wine, herring, metal products, and, occasionally, grain in Peterhof, the Hanseatic quarter of Novgorod. The furs were then taken by ship to Livonia and resold in Gdańsk, Lübeck, and Bruges for further distribution in Flanders and England.

After 1300, the squirrel supply system in Novgorod was based on large estates owned by boyars. They were typically located in the lands between the Onega and the Northern Dvina. The boyars collected rents in the form of squirrel fur from peasants who engaged in hunting as a supplementary occupation, given that the growing season in northern Europe is relatively short. The boyars then sold the furs to the Novgorodian merchants, who resold the pelts to the German merchants at Peterhof. Some peasants provided furs to the merchants directly. Shortly before 1400, the Novgorod supply network involved almost all social groups in the city and its hinterland and brought a regular flow of northern gray squirrel to the market. The deterioration of relations with the Hanse, which blockaded Novgorod in the 1440s, as well as another change in fur consumption patterns in Western Europe, led to a rapid decline of the Novgorodian fur trade network during the second half of the fifteenth century. This coincided with the conflict with Muscovy and the annexation of Novgorod by Ivan III in 1478 (see chapter 49).

The Rus' influence from either Novgorod or Suzdalia explains the earliest forms of agriculture that appeared in the Vychegda region. One of the first pieces of evidence in that respect is the twelfth-century plowshare found at Karybiyv together with wheel-made pottery of Rus' manufacture. Both archaeological and written sources confirm that after 1300, the population in the Middle Vychegda region practiced slash-and-burn agriculture, in which the woodland was burned and cleared for planting such crops as barley, rye, and oats (see chapter 58). Quern stones for handmills first appear in the fourteenth century. Farther to the north and northeast, hunting, particularly for fur pelts, remained the dominant economic activity.

Shortly after 1300, the growing principality of Moscow began to show interest in the supply routes north of the Severnye Uvaly hill, particularly the Sukhona-Vychegda corridor. In 1328, Ivan I Kalita (1325–41) incorporated Ustyug into his principality of Moscow. While the initial impetus for encroachment may have been the increasing tribute for the Mongols (see chapter 49), after the mid-fourteenth century the tribute collected in the taiga became the basis for a fur trade network centered upon Moscow. In 1380, a monk from Rostov named Stephen, moving upstream along the Vychegda, reached its confluence with the river Vym'. He had the support of both Pimen, the metropolitan of Moscow (1380–84), and Grand Prince Dmitri Donskoi (1359–89). Having lived for a while in Ustyug, Stephen learned the language of the Zyriane (Komi), the local population in the Upper Vychegda region. Following in the footsteps of St. Cyril and Methodius (see chapter 12), he created an alphabet (known as Old Permian script) to render the sounds of that language for his translation of several liturgical books. In 1379 he moved to the confluence of the Vychegda and Northern Dvina rivers and began converting to Christianity the people of the native settlement at Pyros (now Pyrskii, near Kotlas, in the Arkhangel'sk region of Russia). One year later he worked his way up to the confluence of the Vychegda and Vym' rivers, where he built a church. In 1383, he was appointed bishop of a newly created eparchy (diocese) of Perm but had to face attacks from both Voguls in the Upper Pechora region and Novgorodian "private armies." In 1386, Stephen went to Novgorod to discuss with Archbishop Aleksei (1359–88) the conditions for a lasting peace. The see of his bishopric was in Ust'-Vym' (near Syktyvkar, Komi Republic), which became the main center of Muscovite power in the region. Stephen died in 1396 and was recognized as a saint shortly after 1400. He was succeeded as bishop of Perm by Isaac (1398–1416), Gerasim (1416–43), Pitirim (1444–55), Jonah (1456–70), and Filofei (1471–1501).

Under Pitirim, the Muscovite hegemony extended into the Upper Kama region as well. Its local representative was a prince named Michael Ermolich, who converted to Christianity in 1462. He resided in Cherdyn (near Solikamsk, in the modern Perm region of Russia), where local chieftains paid the tribute that he forwarded to Moscow. Under Bishop Jonah, a monastery dedicated to St. John Chrysostom was established in Cherdyn in 1462. Nine years later, the archbishop of Novgorod conceded to Moscow the lands along the Upper Kama, which were taken over by an army sent by Grand Prince Ivan III (1462–1505) in 1472.

To secure its control over the taiga, in 1465 another Muscovite army invaded the lands along the Pechora inhabited by the Yugra. Two princes named Kalpak and Techik were brought to Grand Prince Ivan III in Moscow. They were released when promising that they would pay tribute in furs. Twenty years later, the Muscovite armies crossed the Ural Mountains against the local Voguls, whom they defeated. By 1500, Moscow had brought all the fur-producing populations in the taiga to tributary status. All of them made payments in sable furs.

The Udmurts, known as Votyaks in Russian, are first mentioned in Muscovite sources in 1469, but not as tributaries. They inhabited the southern parts of present-day Udmurtia (north of the confluence of the Kama and the Viatka) and were one of the most important suppliers of furs for the khanate of Kazan', which rose as a political unit in the Middle Volga region in the mid-fifteenth century (see chapter 49). During the second half of the fifteenth century, Moscow and Kazan' were the main rivals in the fur trade, with Kazan' controlling the routes extending from the Upper Kama across the Urals to western Siberia. The encroachment of the Muscovite power and economic interests in the Upper Kama region was perceived as a direct attack on the Mongol fur supply routes from Siberia. In 1462, the Mongols of Kazan', accompanied by Cheremis (Mari) allies, attacked Ustyug, only to be repelled by local forces. The Mongols returned in 1468, without much success. The Muscovite campaign of 1472, which established Ivan III's control over the Upper Kama region, effectively secured Muscovite access to the fur-producing region of western Siberia. Pressure increased when Moscow replaced the line of native princes with appointed governors in 1505. The Udmurts and their lands became subjects of Muscovy after the annexation of Kazan' in 1552.

FURTHER READING

Chekin, Leonid S. *Northern Eurasia in Medieval Cartography: Inventory, Texts, Translation, and Commentary.* Terrarum Orbis 4. Turnhout: Brepols, 2006.

Kovalev, Roman K. "The Infrastructure of the Northern Part of the 'Fur Road' Between the Middle Volga and the East During the Middle Ages." *Archivum Eurasiae Medii Aevi* 11 (2000): 25–64.

Kuznetsova, Anna. "Saint Stephen of Perm: Missionary and Popular Saint." In *The Man of Many Devices: Who Wandered Full Many Ways. Festschrift for János M. Bak*, edited by Balázs Nagy and Marcell Sebők, 222–29. Budapest: Central European University Press, 1999.

Martin, Janet. *Treasure of the Land of Darkness: The Fur Trade and Its Significance for Medieval Russia*. Cambridge: Cambridge University Press, 1986.

Vásáry, István. "The 'Yugria' Problem." In *Chuvash Studies*, edited by András Róna-Tas, 247–57. Wiesbaden: Otto Harrassowitz, 1982.

52

SOUTHEASTERN EUROPE IN THE LATE MIDDLE AGES

Keywords in this chapter: civil war, Ottoman Turks, *sipahis*

When the Mongol ruler Nogai (see chapter 45) died in 1299, the Bulgarian Empire recovered its independence. By 1300, the Mongol hegemony in the Lower Danube was fading away. Under Emperor Theodore Svetoslav (1300–21), Bulgarians re-established control over the valley of the Lower Danube and the lands between the river's delta and the mouth of the river Dniester. Theodore Svetoslav reached the Black Sea in 1305, taking the main ports of Mesembria (now Nesebăr) and Anchialos (now Pomorie), as well as Yambol in the interior (see map 52.1). His son and successor, Emperor George II Terter (1321–23), got involved in the first Byzantine civil war that lasted from 1321 to 1328; he opposed his uncle (the future emperor Andronicus III) and sided with Andronicus II. When George Terter died, the Bulgarian noblemen elected the son of the ruler of Vidin (see chapter 45), Michael Shishman, to be their emperor (1323–30). Much like his predecessor, Shishman intervened in the Byzantine civil war on the side of Andronicus II. However, he ended up making peace with Andronicus III in 1328. The new alliance between the empires of Byzantium and Bulgaria was directed against Serbia. Together with Wallachian and Mongol allies, Shishman invaded Serbia, but was defeated at Velbăzhd (now Kyustendil) on July 28, 1330. The battle opened the path for the Serbian hegemony in the Balkans.

The Wallachian allies of Michael Shishman were from the lands north of the river Danube, where the withdrawal of the Mongol power had made room for new political configurations. The rise of Wallachia began within the framework of the control that the Golden Horde had exercised in the region since 1291 and which operated as a shield against the Hungarian encroachment from the north. The process seems to have been complete by 1320, when two centers of power emerged in the foothills of the Transylvanian Alps, one at Câmpulung, the other at (Curtea de) Argeş. The latter is specifically associated with a local ruler named Basarab (ca. 1310–52) in a charter issued in 1324 by the

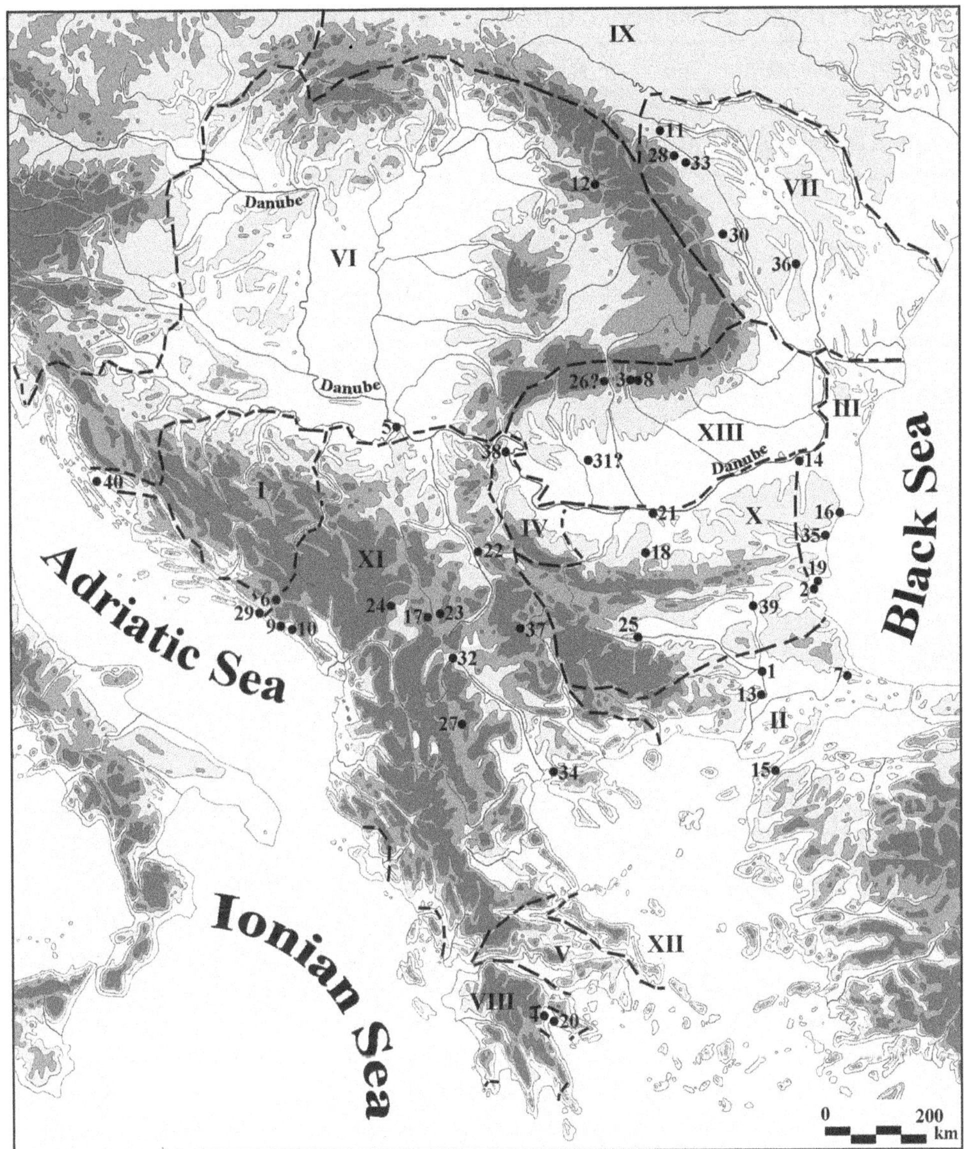

Map 52.1. Southeastern Europe between 1300 and 1500: I – Bosnia; II – Byzantine Empire; III – Despotate of Dobrudja; IV – Despotate of Vidin; V – Duchy of Athens; VI – Hungary; VII – Moldavia; VIII – Morea; IX – Poland; X – Second Bulgarian Empire; XI – Serbia; XII – Venetian possessions; XIII – Wallachia. The location of the following sites is indicated: 1 – Adrianople; 2 – Anchialos; 3 – (Curtea de) Argeş; 4 – Argos; 5 – Belgrade; 6 – Bileća; 7 – Bizye; 8 – Câmpulung; 9 – Castelnuovo; 10 – Cattaro; 11 – Codrii Cosminului; 12 – Cuhea; 13 – Didymoteichon; 14 – Drăstăr; 15 – Gallipoli; 16 – Karvuna; 17 – Kosovo Polje; 18 – Lovech; 19 – Mesembria; 20 – Nauplia; 21 – Nicopolis; 22 – Niš; 23 – Novo Brdo; 24 – Peć; 25 – Philippopolis; 26 – Posada; 27 – Prilep; 28 – Rădăuţi; 29 – Ragusa; 30 – Războieni; 31 – Rovine; 32 – Skopje; 33 – Suceava; 34 – Thessaloniki; 35 – Varna; 36 – Vaslui; 37 – Velbăzhd; 38 – Vidin; 39 – Yambol; 40 – Zadar.

king of Hungary, Charles I. One year later, Basarab, the "voivode of the lands beyond the mountains," was noted for disloyalty towards Charles. Relations between Basarab and King Charles deteriorated rapidly and, in 1330, the Hungarian king crossed the mountains against the seditious voivode. Charles was utterly defeated in a mountain pass at Posada (location unknown today) on November 9, 1330. Under Basarab, Wallachia expanded in the following years from the foothills of the mountains to the lowlands by the river Danube.

Table 52.1. Rulers of Wallachia in the Fourteenth and Fifteenth Centuries

Name of the Ruler	Regnal Years
Basarab I	ca. 1310–52
Nicholas Alexander	1352–64
Vladislav I (Vlaicu)	1364–ca. 1377
Radu I	ca. 1377–ca. 1383
Dan I	ca. 1383–86
Mircea I the Elder	1386–1418
Vlad I	1394–97
Michael I	1418–20
Dan II	1420–21; 1421–23; 1423–24; 1426–27; 1427–31
Radu II Prasnaglava	1421; 1423; 1424–26; 1427
Alexander I Aldea	1431–36
Vlad II Dracul	1436–42; 1443–47
Mircea II	1442
Basarab II	1442–43
Vladislav II	1447–48; 1448–56
Vlad III the Impaler	1448; 1456–62; 1476
Radu III the Fair	1462–73; 1473–74; 1474–75
Basarab III Laiotă	1473; 1474; 1475–76; 1476–77
Basarab IV the Younger	1477–81; 1481–82
Mircea III	1481
Vlad IV the Monk	1481; 1482–95
Radu IV the Great	1495–1508

Although Basarab was of Catholic faith, his son Alexander leaned towards Orthodoxy. Upon conversion, he took the name Nicholas. He ruled as Nicholas Alexander between 1352 and 1364 and established the Orthodox metropolitan of his country appointed from Constantinople, with a see at Argeş (1359) (see table 52.1).

The victor at Velbăzhd, where Emperor Michael Shishman of Bulgaria had been defeated, was the king of Serbia, Stephen III Dečanski (1321–31). He was the son of King Milutin (1282–1321), who had attacked and seized the Byzantine possessions in Macedonia, including the city of Skopje. Married to Elizabeth, the sister of the Hungarian king Ladislas IV, Milutin recovered the territories by the Danube and imposed his suzerainty upon Vidin, the center of a separate Bulgarian principality (see chapter 45). Milutin's daughter Anna (Stephen Dečanski's sister) had married Michael Shishman in 1292. Milutin's own marriage (his fifth) with Simonis, the daughter of the Byzantine emperor Andronicus II, led to the recognition of his territorial acquisitions in Macedonia at the expense of the Byzantines. Since at that point in time his older son, Stephen, was a hostage at the court of the Mongol ruler Nogai, Milutin shared power with his brother Dragutin, who ruled over the Adriatic coastland around Lake Skadar (at the present-day border between Montenegro and Albania). To isolate his brother, Milutin allied himself in 1304 with the strongman of Dalmatia, Ban Paul I Šubić of Bribir and divided Bosnia with his family. A decade later, the Adriatic coastland was in the hands of Milutin's son Stephen, who had returned from Mongol captivity. A conflict broke out between Milutin and Stephen, who was defeated and blinded at Milutin's order. He was then banished to Constantinople, together with his own son (future Serbian king and emperor Stephen Dušan).

Meanwhile, Milutin lost Belgrade to the Hungarians and, in 1319, the Albanian lords in the western lands rose against Serbian rule. Even before Milutin's death in 1321, therefore, his son was allowed to return from Constantinople. He was crowned Serbian king in 1322 as Stephen III Uroš Dečanski, with his son Stephen Dušan as "young king." Stephen Dečanski intervened in the first Byzantine civil war on the side of Andronicus II. He therefore married the emperor's niece, Maria, in 1324. Shortly after his victory at Velbăzhd against Michael Shishman, Stephen Dečanski found himself in conflict with his son, who managed to obtain the crown in 1331. Stephen Uroš IV Dušan promptly threw his father in jail, where he died under mysterious circumstances. Nonetheless, Stephen Dušan promoted the cult of his father, the second Nemanjid to be recognized as a saint (see chapter 45).

Both the rise of Wallachia and the growth of Serbia took place in the vacuum of power created by major political changes taking place in Hungary. When the Arpadian dynasty died out, royal power passed to Charles (or Charles Robert) of Anjou, a grandson of the king of Naples, Charles I of Anjou (1266–82; see chapter 48). Once crowned king of Hungary (with three separate coronations, in 1301, 1309, and 1310), Charles Robert turned his attention to the Croatian nobility, the power of which he wanted to break. His first victim was Mladen II, the son of Ban Paul I Šubić, Milutin's ally. The demise of Mladen, who was defeated in battle in 1322 and taken prisoner, brought to the surface an old vassal of Ban Paul, a Bosnian lord named Hrvatin. His son Stephen (II Kotromanić) became the overlord of the lands along the river Neretva, later known as Herzegovina. He established the Kotromanić dynasty of bans and (after 1377) kings of Bosnia.

Stephen II Kotromanić's rule as ban of Bosnia (1322–53) coincided in time with the creation of the Serbian Empire. Pressed by Andronicus III from the south and by Charles of Hungary from the north, King Stephen Dušan allied himself with Venice, the archenemy of Hungary. When Andronicus III died in 1341, Dušan pushed his troops all the way to the walls of Thessaloniki. He also got involved in the second civil war of Byzantium (which lasted from 1341 to 1347), initially on the side of Emperor John Cantacuzene (1347–54), then on that of the regency defending his underage rival, John V. The alliance between Dušan and John Cantacuzene's enemies was sealed by the marriage of Dušan's son Uroš with a sister of John V. Against the Serbs, John Cantacuzene called in Turkish mercenaries, who defeated the Serbian cavalry in Macedonia. However, Dušan managed to occupy parts of Epirus and much of Macedonia. He crowned himself emperor in Skopje on April 16, 1346. The archbishop of Serbia was simultaneously elevated to the rank of patriarch, with his see in Peć (now Peja, in Kosovo). It remains unclear whether Dušan's intention was to claim the title of Byzantine emperor or, in imitation of the Bulgarian emperors, just to add another empire to the two empires already existing in the Balkans. At any rate, he called himself "emperor of the Serbs and the Greeks." His conquests in the following years were greatly facilitated by the Black Death. As the plague swept through the Balkans, Dušan took over all of Epirus (1347) and Thessaly (1348). He appointed his son Uroš king over the northern (Serbian) part of the empire, while taking Skopje for his residence. During his reign, the Ottoman Turks defeated a Serbian army in 1352, but their raids in the subsequent years were directed mostly at Bulgaria. When Stephen Dušan died in 1355, his son Uroš was only seventeen years old.

Although he ruled for the next sixteen years as Serbian emperor, Stephen Uroš V's empire began to split into fragments, each one more or less independent from the central power. Two brothers named Vukašin and Uglješa, members of the Mrnjavčević clan, ruled *de facto* over the central part of the empire – the region of Prilep, Kosovo, and North Macedonia. Vukašin was even made co-emperor by Stephen Uroš V in 1365, with Vukašin's son Marko (the "Krali Marko" of the Serbian heroic epics) becoming "young king." Ruler over the northern parts, along the Morava valley, was Lazar, a member of the Hrebeljanović family controlling the silver mine region at Novo Brdo. Between Lazar's lands and those around Lake Skadar controlled by the Balšići brothers was the regional power of the Branković family.

In the Bulgarian Empire, a palace coup brought to power in 1331 the son of a local ruler from Lovech (northern Bulgaria). John Alexander (1331–71) began his long rule as Bulgarian emperor by establishing peace with the Byzantine Emperor Andronicus III, after taking back Yambol and Anchialos. His son married Andronicus's daughter Maria (renamed Irene), while his sister Helena married Dušan in 1332. During this reign, several regional lords proclaimed themselves independent – Momchilo in the Rhodope Mountains, as well as Balik, who ruled from Karvuna (now Balchik, on the Black Sea coast) together with his brothers Theodore and Dobrotich. The lands of the three brothers, organized in the despotate of Dobrudja (the name of the region between the Danube and the Black Sea was derived from that of Dobrotich) benefitted economically from a large presence of Genoese and Venetian merchants on the western coast of the Black Sea. They had been expelled in 1344 from Tana (the medieval name of ancient Tanais) on the Sea of Azov by Janibek, the khan of the Golden Horde (1342–57). When John Alexander died in 1371, the Bulgarian Empire split into three parts – what remained of the empire itself, centered upon Tărnovo, the despotate of Vidin in the northwest, and the despotate of Dobrudja on the Black Sea coast.

During the last two decades of their respective reigns, the Serbian emperor Stephen Uroš V and the Bulgarian emperor John Alexander witnessed the conquest of Thrace by the Ottoman Turks (see insert 52.1). Under Orhan and his son Suleyman, the earliest Ottoman province was created – the Paşa sancak, which turned in the 1360s into the beylerbeylik (or vilayet) of Rumelia. After Suleyman's death in 1357, his younger brother Murad used the town of Gallipoli (now Gelibolu, in Turkey) as a launchpad for raids into the Balkans. Didymoteichon (on the present-day border between Greece and Turkey) fell in 1361, while ghazi warriors such as Yakub Bey and Hacı İlbeği established

INSERT 52.1. THE EARLY OTTOMANS

The Mongol invasion caused a great upheaval in Central Asia. A large-scale migration of Turkish (Turkoman) nomads from the steppe lands reached Anatolia in the late thirteenth and early fourteenth centuries. The Seljuk sultans resettled the newcomers on their frontier with Byzantium. Within the no-man's land between the Seljuks and the Byzantines, the revival of the Muslim traditions of holy war against infidel Christians created a peculiar association between dervishes (holy men) and ghazis (warriors for the faith).

Under Emperor Andronicus II (1282–1321), a band of ghazis under emir Osman defeated the Byzantines and ravaged northwestern Asia Minor. Soon after that, a little polity (emirate) was organized under Osman, and the Turk(oman)s under his rule therefore came to be known as Ottomans. Although this was the least important of all emirates established in western Asia Minor, it was closest to the Byzantine lands. Because of that, the jihad was carried out to its ultimate consequences in Ottoman territory. Osman's son and successor, Orhan (1324–60), conquered Bursa in 1326 and turned that city into the first capital of the Ottoman state. Three years later, the Ottomans defeated the army of Andronicus III at Pelekanon (Maltepe, near present-day Izmit, in Turkey). Following that battle, Nicaea and Nicomedia, the main cities in northwestern Asia Minor, fell to the Ottomans. The empire was forced to pay annual tribute in 1333 in exchange for peace. To secure his alliance with the Ottomans, in 1346 Emperor John V Palaiologos gave his daughter in marriage to Orhan. In this way, the Ottomans became involved in internecine strife in Byzantium. In his struggle with John VI Cantacuzene, John V obtained 10,000 Ottoman horsemen from Orhan's son Suleyman for an attack on his own son's troops besieging Adrianople. Those were *sipahis* (heavily equipped horsemen) armed with lance and scimitar (saber) for hand-to-hand combat, as well as units of light cavalry for hit-and-run tactics (*akinjis*). Suleyman's infantry troops, lightly armed *azabs*, occupied several forts on the European side of the Straits and refused to leave. Taking advantage of the devastating earthquake of 1354, Suleyman settled many Turkish families in Gallipoli. With that, the Ottoman conquest of the Balkans had begun.

themselves, along with their followers, in Thracian towns. Lala Şahin, the first beylerbey of Rumelia, took Philippopolis in 1363, Bizye (now Vize, in Turkey) in 1368, and Adrianople (now Edirne, in Turkey) in 1369. However, most early conquests were done by non-Ottoman Turks.

The beginnings of Moldavia (the land between the eastern Carpathian Mountains and the river Dniester) are linked to Hungarian efforts of organizing a march-like structure beyond the mountains against the Mongols. The first ruler, Dragoş, is said to have come from Maramureş (northern Transylvania) in 1359. His historical reality, however, is disputed, even though a Hungarian march was most likely created in what is now eastern Romania at some point between 1343 and 1354. In 1363, Bogdan, a Romanian nobleman from Cuhea (now Bogdan Vodă in Maramureş, near the Romanian-Ukrainian border), rose against King Louis of Hungary and moved across the mountains to lead a rebellion

Table 52.2. Rulers of Moldavia in the Fourteenth and Fifteenth Centuries

Name of the Ruler	Regnal Years
Dragoş	ca. 1352–53
Sas	ca. 1354–ca. 1358
Balc	1359
Bogdan I	1359–ca. 1365
Laţcu	ca. 1365–ca. 1375
Peter I	ca. 1375–ca. 1391
Roman I	ca. 1391–ca. 1394
Stephen I	ca. 1394–99
Iuga	1399–1400
Alexander I the Good	1400–32
Iliaş	1432–33; 1435–42
Stephen II	1433–35; 1442–47
Peter II	1447; 1448–49
Roman II	1447–48
Alexăndrel	1449; 1452–54; 1455
Bogdan II	1449–51
Peter Aron	1451–52; 1454–55; 1455–57
Stephen III the Great	1457–1504

of the locals against the Hungarian rule. He took over the march of Moldavia and established the local dynasty of the Muşatini (see table 52.2). The family of Moldavian rulers is named after his daughter Muşata, whose son Peter I (1375–91) is buried in the Church of St. Nicholas in Rădăuţi (see chapter 70). Rădăuţi was the first center of power in Moldavia, soon to be replaced by Suceava. Muşata and her brother Laţcu, who ruled between 1368 and 1375, were Catholics, but under Peter's successors, Orthodoxy became a counterweight to Polish influence. An Orthodox metropolitan of Moldavia was appointed from Constantinople in 1401.

While Hungary lost control over the lands to the east and to the south from the Carpathian Mountains, King Louis (1342–82) focused on the Dalmatian coast, particularly on the city of Zadar (see chapter 48). The inhabitants of the city organized a rebellion in 1345, and the Venetian troops put the city under siege. The royal army was defeated under the walls of the city, so Zadar was retaken by Venice in 1346. Ten years later, Louis started another war against Venice, which ended in the Peace of Zadar (1357). This time, Venice had to give up all possessions in the Adriatic region, including Ragusa (now Dubrovnik, in Croatia) and Cattaro (now Kotor, in Montenegro). The Dalmatian cities were thus incorporated into Croatia, which had been under Hungarian rule since the early twelfth century (see chapter 42). The Hungarian king recognized the internal autonomy of Ragusa, which became an almost independent republic (*Respublica Ragusina*), in exchange for a tax paid to the royal treasury. Ragusa flourished in the second half of the fourteenth century, its territory expanding onto the neighboring peninsulas and islands. Ever since 1322, the local aristocracy had been led by a local count. Besides the large and small councils, the city government had a senate and a board council (*Consilium rogatorum*) with powers to take decisions in cases of emergency.

King Louis of Hungary also campaigned in Bosnia against Ban Stephen II Kotromanić's nephew, Tvrtko. Although a crusade was proclaimed against Bosnians, regarded as heretics by the papacy, King Louis eventually bestowed the title of ban upon Trvtko (1354–77). Allied with the Serbian prince Lazar Hrebeljanović, Tvrtko occupied the hinterland of Ragusa, before becoming king in 1377. He attempted to take the city of Cattaro, but not being able to do so, he built his own town on the Bay of Kotor – Castelnuovo (now Herceg Novi, Montenegro). He intervened in the civil war in Hungary after the death of King Louis and, with Hungarian support, by 1390 acquired all towns on the Dalmatian coast except Zadar.

Meanwhile, the Serbian and Bulgarian emperors had very different concerns. Uglješa and his brother Vukašin, who ruled in central Serbia, mounted an expedition against the Ottomans and marched towards Adrianople. On September 26, 1371, they were defeated and killed somewhere on the banks of the river Maritsa. Less than a year after the battle on the Maritsa River, the empires of Bulgaria and Byzantium, as well as what was left of Serbia (Stephen Uroš V was the last Serbian ruler to be called emperor), were all vassal states of the Ottoman Turks. However, because the Gallipoli Peninsula had been in Byzantine hands between 1366 and 1377, and communication across the Straits had thus been interrupted between the Asian and European parts of the Ottoman realm, Sultan Murad I (1360–89) came to Rumelia only in 1376. The Ottomans were pressing hard on Bulgaria as well: Yambol fell in 1373, Niš in 1386, and all towns along the Lower Danube were taken in 1388. By then, Murad had his eyes set on the northwest. Ottoman troops returning from a campaign in Albania were intercepted by Bosnian troops led by Vlatko Vuković and Radič Sanković and defeated at Bileća (now in southern Bosnia-Herzegovina) on August 27, 1388. Venice, on the other hand, taking advantage of the weakness of the last Byzantine possessions in Greece, took the island of Corfu in 1386, as well as Argos and Nauplia (now Nafplion) in 1388. In the summer of 1389, Sultan Murad therefore moved against Serbia with a large army. A coalition of Serbian princes led by Lazar Hrebeljanović met him at the Kosovo Polje (Field of Blackbirds) near Pristina. One of the most famous battles of the Balkan Middle Ages was fought there on June 15, 1389. Lazar was taken prisoner and later slain, while Sultan Murad was killed by a Christian warrior. The Bosnian ruler Tvrtko, whose troops participated in the battle, regarded the outcome as a victory for the Christians.

The days of the remaining two empires in the Balkans were numbered. After the battle of Kosovo, the Ottomans got an easier path to Bosnia, and from there they began raiding the southern parts of the kingdom of Hungary and Bulgaria. Vidin fell without a battle in 1390, followed by Tărnovo in 1393, both in Bulgaria. Following the conquest of Tărnovo, 110 Bulgarian noblemen were executed, while the population of the city was moved forcibly to Anatolia. A mosque was planted in the city, and a Greek metropolitan replaced the

Bulgarian patriarch. The Second Bulgarian Empire had now ceased to exist. The region of the Lower Danube was administered by the Ottomans from Drăstăr (now Silistra, in northern Bulgaria), which was briefly occupied by the voivode of Wallachia, Mircea the Elder (1386–1418). When the new sultan, Bayezid I (1389–1402), crossed the Danube against him in 1395, Mircea won a major victory at Rovine (unknown location). The following year, Wallachian troops participated in an anti-Ottoman crusade with Burgundian, French, English, German, Italian, and Hungarian troops. However, the crusaders were defeated at Nikopolis (Bulgaria) on September 15, 1396, by an Ottoman army supported by Serbian troops.

Shortly after the fall of the Bulgarian Empire, Wallachia came under Ottoman overlordship. Bayezid was beaten in 1402 at Ankara by Timur Lenk (Tamerlane), who took him prisoner. In the ensuing succession crisis, Mircea the Elder sided with one of Bayezid's sons named Musa, but the winner was Mehmed I (1413–21). Mircea was therefore forced to pay tribute to the Ottomans in 1415, the first Wallachian voivode to do so. Moreover, Wallachian troops had to participate in Ottoman expeditions across the Carpathian Mountains into Transylvania. In Moldavia, the tribute for the Ottomans was first paid by Petru Aron (1452–55). Neither Moldavia nor Wallachia, however, were ever occupied by the Ottomans, and they continued to exist as more or less independent states even after the complete conquest of the Balkans.

The last bastion of Serbian independence under Despot George Branković (1427–56) fell to the Ottomans in 1439. A counterattack from Hungary in the form of another anti-Ottoman crusade led by the 20-year-old Władysław III, king of Poland and of Hungary, ended with the disaster in Varna in 1444. This was the last European attempt to save Constantinople. With the fall of that city in 1453, the Byzantine Empire also came to an end. The front lines had by then moved to the Danube. John Hunyadi, the governor of Hungary appointed after King Władysław died in battle at Varna (see chapter 48), took the initiative and defeated a number of Ottoman troops in Wallachia. He successfully defended Belgrade against the Ottomans in 1456. His protégé on the throne of Wallachia, Vlad III (1456–62), known as Drăculea (the historical character behind Dracula), withstood an expedition led by Sultan Mehmet II (1444–46, 1451–81). Vlad organized a bold attack by night on the Ottoman camp, aiming at killing the sultan. Mehmet therefore withdrew.

Meanwhile, in Moldavia, Voivode Stephen III the Great (1457–1504) crushed another Ottoman army at Vaslui in 1475, before being defeated one year later at Războieni. Stephen renewed the payment of the tribute (which he had stopped in 1473) and relied on Ottoman support against Poland. When King John Albert (1492–1501) tried to force him into submission, Stephen defeated the Polish army at Codrii Cosminului in 1497.

In the Balkans, the Ottoman conquest made further progress after the fall of Constantinople: the duchy of Athens (established in 1205 by participants in the Fourth Crusade) fell between 1456 and 1458, followed by Byzantine Morea (the Byzantine territories in Greece) in 1458–60, and Bosnia in 1463 (see insert 52.2). The Albanian resistance also ended with the death of George Kastrioti, the lord of Albania otherwise known as Skanderbeg (1442–68). Venice, having regained control over the entire Dalmatian coast (except Ragusa),

INSERT 52.2. THE DUCHY OF ATHENS

Athens was conquered in 1205 by a Burgundian knight named Otto de la Roche, who became the first ruler of the duchy created after that conquest. During his reign (1205–25), the duchy also included Thebes, Argos, Nauplia, and Damala. Otto's son and successor, Guy (1225–63), was defeated by William II of Villehardouin, the prince of Achaea, who attempted to turn him into his vassal. King Louis IX of France, who was called to arbitrate the dispute, recognized Guy's title as duke. Meanwhile, William was defeated at Pelagonia and was taken prisoner by the Byzantines. In his absence, Guy became the administrator of Achaea. Under his son, John I (1263–80), the army of the duchy intervened in neighboring Thessaly. John's son, William I (1263–87), married a Thessalian princess, while his own son, Guy II (1287–1308), became the guardian of the young Thessalian ruler John II Dukas. When John attempted to break free from the tutelage of the duke of Athens, Guy II's successor, Walter of Brienne (1308–11), called in the Catalan Company, a band of professional soldiers who had fought for some years on the side of Frederick III, the Aragonese king of Sicily (1295–1337), against Charles II of Anjou, king of Naples (1285–1309), before being hired by the Byzantine emperor Andronicus II (1282–1328). Even though Walter of Brienne hired the Catalan mercenaries to bring John II to the heel, the Catalans devastated Thessaly and intended to keep it for themselves. Walter of Brienne therefore marched his army against them but was defeated and killed in the battle of Halmyros (1311). In the aftermath of their victory, the Catalans occupied the duchy of Athens, which they ruled until 1388 in the name of Frederick III of Sicily. The end of the Catalan rule in Athens came when the Florentine banking family of the Acciaioli hired the Navarrese Company, another band of mercenaries, to occupy the duchy on their behalf. Shortly after that, under Duke Nerio I Acciaioli (1388–94), Athens was first besieged by the Ottoman Turks. However, the Ottoman conquest of the duchy was postponed until 1456, and the last duke, Francesco II Acciaioli (1455–58), was killed on the order of sultan Mehmet II.

went to war against the Ottomans, who were nonetheless able to cross into Italy and establish a bridgehead, albeit briefly, at Otranto in 1480. At Mehmet II's death in 1481, the Balkan Peninsula was completely conquered. Less than fifty years later, Suleyman the Magnificent (1520–66) put Vienna under siege. By that time, the kingdom of Hungary had also ceased to exist.

FURTHER READING

Achim, Viorel. "Ecclesiastical Structures and Political Structures in 14th Century Wallachia." In *Church and Society in Central and Eastern Europe*, edited by Maria Crăciun and Ovidiu Ghitta, 123–35. Cluj-Napoca: European Studies Foundation, 1998.

Cazacu, Matei. *Dracula*. East Central and Eastern Europe in the Middle Ages, 450–1450, 46. Leiden: Brill.

Ćirković, Sima. "Between Kingdom and Empire: Dušan's State Reconsidered." In *Byzantio kai Serbia kata ton ID' aiona*, edited by Eutychia Papadopoulou and Dimitris Komini-Dialeti, 110–20. Athens: Institouto Vyzantinon Ereunon, 1996.

Fine, John V. A. *The Late Medieval Balkans: A Critical Survey from the Late Twelfth Century to the Ottoman Conquest*. Ann Arbor: University of Michigan Press, 1987.

Pilat, Liviu, and Ovidiu Cristea. *The Ottoman Threat and Crusading on the Eastern Border of Christendom during the 15th Century*. East Central and Eastern Europe in the Middle Ages, 450–1450, 48. Leiden: Brill, 2018.

Vucinich, Wayne S., and Thomas A. Emmert, eds. *Kosovo: Legacy of a Medieval Battle*. Minnesota Mediterranean and East European Monographs 1. Minneapolis: University of Minnesota Press, 1991.

PART 10

Societies and Cultures in the High and Late Middle Ages

53

POPULATION STRUCTURES

Keywords in this chapter: demography, life expectancy, age categories

Some of the rare statistical data that are available for pre-modern periods offer opportunities for evaluating demographic changes. In Poland, population estimates for the earlier period are based on the extent of cultivated lands, agricultural outputs, and food consumption. It is believed that in the early eleventh century Poland had around 1.25 million inhabitants spread out over 250,000 square kilometers (6,177,6345 ha), with a density of five inhabitants per square kilometer. Population calculations are more reliable for the early fourteenth century, before the arrival of the Black Death, thanks to the records of Peter's Pence (a tax paid to the papacy) that were kept at the papal court. After the 1318 reform, all adults in Poland paid a poll tax. Jews were excepted; it is not fully clear if nobles and clergy were exempted. The records suggest that at that time the kingdom of Poland had around 2 million inhabitants. The three main provinces (Greater Poland, Lesser Poland, and Mazovia) had around 1.25 million inhabitants. Population had grown by an estimated 80 percent since the early eleventh century, and the population density now ranged between 7.9 (in Lesser Poland and Mazovia) and 9.7 (in Greater Poland) inhabitants per square kilometer. Based on various records, it is estimated that the population of the three main provinces had grown to about 3.1 million inhabitants by 1580, with a density then of 21 inhabitants per square kilometer.

No data are available from Hungary to estimate population numbers before the early fourteenth century. In view of the growing number of settlements and the arrival of foreign settlers that are well recorded in the sources, it appears that the population grew between the eleventh and the thirteenth centuries. It is impossible, however, to know the extent of that growth; nor is it possible to fully assess the population decline that resulted from the Mongol invasion. Indirect evidence suggests that the loss of population due to the invasion was between 15 and 20 percent, but that population levels rose quickly through immigration in the subsequent decades. Two sources of data exist for the early fourteenth and the late fifteenth centuries. Papal registers have been preserved from the 1330s that were compiled to record the tithe revenues from parishes. Accounting books record revenues from royal taxes in 1494 and 1495. Both censuses count household units, exclude nobles and the clergy, and are incomplete in their geographic coverage. The records suggest no significant population decline in the period of famine and plague; on the contrary, population appears to have steadily increased during the fourteenth century, as was the case in Poland. Settlement networks became denser, and previously unoccupied lands became settled. The population of Hungary at the end of the fifteenth century was around 3 million inhabitants; while it is certain that it had grown in earlier centuries, the extent to which it did is a matter of speculation.

On the territory of the Baltic states (the modern states of Estonia, Latvia, and Lithuania), population numbers have been estimated based on the thirteenth-century Danish census in Estonia and on early modern cadastral registers. Population is believed to have risen from 500,000 in 1200 to 1–1.5 million inhabitants by the mid-sixteenth century. A larger proportion of those people lived in towns in the later than in the earlier period. The population of Reval (modern Tallinn) evolved from 3,300 inhabitants in 1372 to between 7,000 and 8,000 by the mid-sixteenth century; Riga had between 6,000 and 8,000 inhabitants in the fifteenth century; Vilnius had 20,000 inhabitants in the fourteenth century.

The Mongols relied on administrative methods and trained personnel that allowed them to effectively govern their immense empire and to manage tax collection with great efficacy. From the very beginning, shortly after the invasion, it is known that the Mongol khans organized population censuses in the lands of Rus' for fiscal purposes, for example in Kiev in 1245, 1257, and 1270. Mongol administrators counted all adult males except for clerics, residents of monasteries, and dependent peasants of church and monastic properties, who were free from taxes. Unfortunately, none of the Mongol census records from the lands of Rus' has survived. The oldest population surveys that have been preserved are cadastral registers from the lordship of Novgorod that were made in the late fifteenth century, after annexation by Muscovy. The preserved records are incomplete. They nonetheless attest that villages at that time did not exceed ten households and were often smaller, sometimes even counting only one household. It is generally accepted that the Mongol invasion and the Black Death resulted in periods of serious demographic decline, but little more can be said. Preserved cadastral registers from the lands of Muscovy are more numerous and complete than for Novgorod; however, they begin only in the later sixteenth century. Various calculations (extrapolating from the fragmentary evidence and by comparison with Poland) have led to population estimates for Muscovy in the mid-sixteenth century that range from 5 million to 14 million inhabitants. Estimates of the urban population have also been made based on the archaeological record and postulated average numbers of individuals per household. By such estimates, Kiev would have had between 35,000 and 45,000 inhabitants in the twelfth century, while Novgorod would have had between 25,000 and 30,000 inhabitants in the fourteenth century.

Life expectancy in medieval Europe was between 30 and 35 years for men and slightly less for women; these low averages were due to very high levels of child mortality. Mortality was very high for children up to six years old and even higher for infants in the first two years of life. Levels of child and infant mortality in Central and Eastern Europe do not seem to have been very different from those in other parts of the continent. The low averages of life expectancy do not mean that reaching old age was exceptional. Nonetheless, the percentage of the population that reached 60 varied considerably. In prosperous societies like those of the North Italian towns of the Late Middle Ages, it could be as high as 14 to 16 percent; in Poland, at the same time, it was around 7 percent, which was close to the estimated European average of 8 percent.

Age categories were not always clearly defined for children. In Central Europe as in the Latin West, a child (*puer*) grew to a youth (*iuvenis*) and then to a man or a woman. Young boys in Poland went through a ceremony of the cutting of the hair at the age of seven. Polish sources attest to a stereotype of youths being foolhardy and irresponsible, and in need of adult advice. In the lands of Rus', the lifespan was understood as being comprised of cycles of either seven or ten years. Infancy and childhood were marked by stages. The first transition was the ceremony of *postrig* that was organized for boys at the age of three; the second was at age seven, when confession began. At that time children moved from games and toys to more formal education such as learning to read. Adulthood began at marriage.

Medieval views on when old age began varied, although human life was considered to proceed in three phases: youth, maturity, and old age. The Rus'-Byzantine treaty of 944 reflects this threefold division: it refers to young, mature, and old people. Similar categories were used in Poland. For example, according to Vincent Kadłubek, Bolesław the Curly died "in the mature age" (he was between 48 and 55 years old). Late medieval sources from Poland attest that old age typically began around 60; some authors distinguished between old age and "extreme old age," or "decrepitude," which probably referred to seniors experiencing disabilities.

FURTHER READING

Fügedi, Eric. "The Demographic Landscape of East-Central Europe." In *East-Central Europe in Transition: From the Fourteenth to the Seventeenth Century*, edited by Antoni Mączak, Henryk Samsonowicz, and Peter Burke, 47–58. Cambridge: Cambridge University Press-Éditions de la Maison des Sciences de l'Homme, 1985.

Koval, Matthew. *Childhood in Medieval Poland (1050–1300): Constructions and Realities in a European Context*. East Central and Eastern Europe in the Middle Ages, 450–1450, 73. Leiden: Brill, 2021.

Kubinyi, András, and József Laszlovszky. "Demographic Issues in Late Medieval Hungary: Population, Ethnic Groups, Economic Activity." In *The Economy of Medieval Hungary*, edited by

József Laszlovszky, Balázs Nagy, Péter Szabó, and András Vadas, 48–63. East Central and Eastern Europe in the Middle Ages, 450–1450, 49. Leiden: Brill, 2018.

Myśliwski, Grzegorz. "Old Age and Longevity in Medieval Poland Against a Comparative Background." *Acta Poloniae Historica* 86 (2002): 5–46.

Petrov, Mikhail I. "Childhood in Medieval Novgorod: From Infancy to Adolescence." In *Lübecker Kolloquium zur Stadtarchäologie im Hanseraum VIII: Kindheit und Jugend, Ausbildung und Freizeit*, edited by Manfred Gläser, 363–69. Lübeck: Schmidt-Römhild, 2012.

54

RULERS AND GOVERNMENTS

Keywords in this chapter: regents, regalian rights, *szlachta*, *duma*

In medieval Europe, the highest secular rulers were the emperors. While kings could recognize (or reject) a superior authority, emperors might occasionally acknowledge an equal power, but never one that was above them. Emperors typically ruled over multiple kingdoms or territories and were expected to provide guidance and leadership. While the Holy Roman emperors claimed leadership in western (Latin) Christendom (although that did not go unchallenged), the influence of the Byzantine emperors extended to a large part of Eastern Europe. The Bulgarian and Serbian emperors challenged them, claiming to be their equals (see chapter 52). The khans of the Golden Horde who became overlords of the princes of Rus' were called "tsars" in Slavonic sources, just like Byzantine emperors; their position was not only regarded as superior to that of the Riurikids, but also perceived as comparable to that of the rulers of Constantinople.

Kingdoms emerged in the Early Middle Ages as the dominant form of rulership in post-Roman Europe. Kings were military leaders heading groups of elite warriors; especially since the Carolingians, Christianity had adorned the monarchy with a sacral function. The royal title was typically granted through a ceremony that included anointment by a prelate (in direct imitation of the anointment of King David, as described in the First Book of Kingdoms 16:13); recognition through emperors and popes was expected. While the rulers of Croatia had been kings since the tenth century and those of Hungary since Stephen I's coronation, royal titles were only incrementally introduced to Poland and Bohemia (see chapter 42). The Riurikids styled themselves with the Slavonic title *kniaz'*, which, although translated in English as "prince," was typically rendered as *rex* ("king") in medieval Latin texts. While power usually remained within the reigning dynasties, new modes of succession had to be devised in the absence of unambiguous heirs. Charles of Anjou in Hungary and John of Luxembourg in Bohemia were thus elected, that is chosen and acknowledged, by the elites of their kingdoms in the early fourteenth century. The assent of the nobility for the succession of new rulers gained in importance throughout Central and Eastern Europe in the fourteenth century.

The roles of female rulers varied depending upon circumstances and local traditions. The designation of a son to a father, the easiest way to maintain political stability, gave added recognition to the wife of a ruler as mother of his children. In the lands of Rus', where lateral succession held sway, the wives of the Riurikids were much less prominently portrayed in the sources than in Central Europe. Apart from fulfilling ceremonial functions, the female consorts of rulers were often expected to propagate Christian values or to sponsor religious institutions. They occasionally filled in when their husbands were absent. Hedwig of Silesia, for example, negotiated with Conrad of Mazovia for the release of her husband Henry the Bearded from captivity. Queen Elizabeth acted as regent in Poland when her husband Louis I of Hungary succeeded to the kingdom after Casimir III. When they were foreigners at the courts of their husbands, queens were vulnerable. Should they be seen as being too assertive, they could run into danger – such as Queen Gertrude, wife of Andrew II of Hungary, who was murdered by nobles of the court (see chapter 42).

In Poland, it was common for widows of rulers to act as regents for their underage sons. Many regent widows were successful in maintaining political stability, especially when they obtained effective support from male relatives or external powers: for example, Grzymisława of Lesser Poland and Viola of Opole in Silesia had the backing of the archbishop of Cracow and of the pope, respectively. Women rarely held power on their own, though. The cases of Mary and Jadwiga, who were crowned "kings" of Hungary and Poland, were exceptional; once they came of age, they ruled as co-rulers with their husbands. Mary, who formally ruled the kingdom before her wedding, was described in the contemporary writings of Lorenzo Monaci as a wise virgin, a frail girl who displayed maturity and "male" virtues, in contrast to her power-hungry regent mother, Elizabeth of Bosnia. Women could, however, govern territories of various extent as dowager widows. For example, Agnes of Austria effectively ruled the duchy of Świdnica and Jawor, in Silesia, for about twenty years after the death of her husband Bolko II. Barbara of Celje, the second wife of King Sigismund of Hungary (and later, Holy Roman Emperor), energetically organized the military defense of the kingdom against the Hussites in 1431.

Medieval kings were supposed to be devoted Christians and successful military leaders; queens were expected to be pious, generous, and faithful. The power of rulers was shown through public events such as the coronation ceremony or the ruler's arrival in a town (the *adventus regis*). John of Luxembourg and Charles IV introduced to Bohemia rituals inspired by French chivalric practices that involved, for example, the public knighting of young men. Feasts and banquets where rulers appeared with their insignia also served that purpose. Special objects, such as the so-called crown of Saint Stephen in Hungary, or costly relics that were connected to the dynasty were displayed on special circumstances. Prague had always been the main residence and political center of Bohemia; in Poland, Cracow took a similar function in the fourteenth century. The kings of Hungary, by contrast, remained itinerant rulers until the end of the Middle Ages. They stayed in hunting palaces or in more centrally located residences in Esztergom, Visegrád, or, later, Buda.

Throughout the Middle Ages, marriage alliances remained a fundamental instrument of international relations. The Riurikids established themselves on the international scene through their numerous matrimonial connections; Anna of Kiev, for instance, married King Henry I of France, and the second wife of King Béla III of Hungary was Margaret, the daughter of King Louis VII of France. Despite their pagan beliefs, the Gediminids also used marriage alliances extensively to extend their authority into the lands of Rus' (see chapter 49). Princesses of prestigious origins elevated the courts where they married. This was the case with several Byzantine princesses who, in the age of the Second Bulgarian Empire (1185–1393), espoused Bulgarian emperors. Maria Palaiologina, the Byzantine wife of Emperor Constantine Tih, ended up playing an especially prominent role at the Bulgarian court. Another Byzantine princess, Sophia Palaiologina, married Ivan III in 1472 and exercised a great deal of power and influence at the court in Moscow in subsequent decades.

Medieval kings and queens had sacral authority: they were anointed by churchmen and appointed "by the grace of God." Dynasties often had some of their members recognized as saints. In Hungary, Stephen I and his son Emeric were canonized in 1083, and Ladislas I in 1192. The martyr saint of the Přemyslids, Wenceslas, enjoyed continuous reverence, and the Czech army repeatedly carried his lance into battle to secure divine support. The Piast dukes of Silesia related to Saint Hedwig as the holy patron of their family. There are many royal saints in the Nemanjid dynasty of Serbia, beginning with Stephen Nemanja (the founder), his son St. Sava, and ending with Stephen Dečanski. In Rus', the influence of the cult of Sts. Boris and Gleb, both "passion-bearers" of Riurikid stock, was considerable until the Mongol invasion but waned after that.

The main responsibilities of medieval rulers were to maintain peace, administer justice, and defend the country and its resources. Regalian rights – which were often delegated – included the control of woodlands, waters, lands, and mineral resources. Kings administered justice at regularly held assemblies – often four times a year – or delegated it through special privileges. Rulers counted on various agents to support them in their duties, help them in collecting taxes, and issue the necessary documentation. The revenues of rulers could come from their estates, or from various taxes and rents, tolls, and fines. The incomes of Central European rulers increased in the thirteenth century with the settlement of new villages and towns, where tenants paid standardized rents in cash. Special taxes, approved by the nobles, multiplied in the later Middle Ages; they were used to finance wars or to fund feasts for weddings or to celebrate the birth of children of rulers. The Polish tax on beer provided revenues that were shared by the crown and municipal governments. Jewish communities paid taxes that were a significant source of income to rulers in exchange for promises of protection (see chapter 63).

To govern effectively, rulers needed recognition. Until Přemysl Ottokar I obtained hereditary rights, Czech rulers' main source of legitimacy came from their election by nobles and warriors. Moreover, councils and assemblies were expected to support the decisions of kings. In Hungary, an assembly of the nobility sent delegates to the royal council beginning in the late thirteenth century. Louis I elevated a small group of councilors as the "true barons of the kingdom." Matthias Corvinus oversaw a smaller and a larger council and appointed to them special members as experts in law or finance.

In the later Middle Ages, Poland's governing institutions became especially strong in counterbalancing the authority of kings. Polish rulers had long governed with the advice of secular nobles and leading ecclesiastics. In the fourteenth century, the main advisory body was the King's Council in which bishops represented the clergy and castellans and palatines represented the nobility (the *szlachta*). In the later fourteenth century, the Council was supplemented by the Sejm, or parliament, that met annually. By the late fifteenth century, the Sejm had two chambers: half of the delegates were nominated by the magnates, the other half by the regional diets (*sejmiki*) that were also entrusted with a growing number of government duties. Decision-making aimed at consensus but occasionally accepted majority. The nobility of Poland, referring to the doctrine of the right to oppose tyranny, increasingly restricted royal authority. The 1501 Charter of Mielnik proclaimed the right of resistance; government officials (starosts) responded to the King's Council and not to the king. The 1505 constitution *Nihil Novi* forbade the Council to make any decision without approval of the Chamber of Deputies. Poland (and eventually Lithuania) was evolving into a republic of nobles where major decisions were made by the Sejm.

The grand princes of Muscovy ruled with the support of the council (*duma*) of the boyars, an institution that was likely inspired by the divan of *qarachi beys*, the council of clan chieftains (beys or begs) in the Golden Horde. Like the Mongol beys, the Rus' boyars had ceremonial and advisory functions. To control decision-making more efficiently, Ivan III devised a system of place-ranking (*mestnichestvo*) that combined factors such as family, status, and service to determine the position of courtiers. The grand prince appointed governors to the lands under his domination by selecting them from among his court servitors.

In Central Europe, government functions were originally in the hands of the rulers, who were supported by a warrior elite. Territorial administration developed around strongholds where office holders resided. The systems in Bohemia, Poland, and Hungary appear to have emerged out of similar circumstances. The practice of government became more complex, however, in the later Middle Ages, requiring civil servants to produce documents and manage written records. Royal and ducal chanceries were established in Bohemia, Hungary, and Poland in the later twelfth century and gained complexity in the thirteenth century. Notaries were often trained in the specialized schools of collegiate chapters set up to train them (see chapter 67). Charles IV's chancery, dominated by clerics of burgher background, inspired practices in the rest of Central Europe. Its leading figure was John of Środa (Neumarkt), a prolific author of treatises on administrative matters who refined the style and usage of notaries writing in both Latin and German.

Government practices evolved differently in Rus' under the rule of the Mongols who, to administer the world's largest empire, had developed structures of their own. The Muscovite princes sought inspiration from them. The Mongols used a dual administrative system of Chinese origin; it was devised around civil and military administrators who were called *darugas* and *baskaks*. The latter were military governors stationed in Rus' territories whose duties included collecting taxes. By contrast, the *darugas* resided mostly in Sarai and kept in touch with the Rus' princes through envoys. In the early fourteenth century, the responsibilities of the *baskaks* were entrusted to the Rus' princes themselves, who thus became direct agents of the khan. Ivan Kalita, whose brother Iuri III had spent two years in Sarai and was married to a sister of Khan Özbeg (Konchaka, baptized as Agrafa), introduced a similar approach for his own administration. The grand prince appointed *namestniki* and *volosteli* as civil and military agents, the equivalents of the Mongol *darugas* and *baskaks*.

FURTHER READING

Antonín, Robert. *The Ideal Ruler in Medieval Bohemia*. Translated by Sean Mark Miller. East Central and Eastern Europe in the Middle Ages, 450–1450, 44. Leiden: Brill, 2017.

Bak, János M., and Suzana Miljan. "Government: Central and Local Administration." In *The Oxford Handbook of Medieval Central Europe*, edited by Nada Zečević and Daniel Ziemann, 99–111. Oxford: Oxford University Press, 2022.

Dvořáková, Daniela. *Barbara of Cilli (1392–1451)*. East Central and Eastern Europe in the Middle Ages, 450–1450, 77. Leiden: Brill, 2021.

Górski, Karol. "The Origins of the Polish Sejm." In *Communitas, Princeps, Corona Regni: Selected Studies*, 57–71. Warsaw: Państwowe Wydawnictwo Naukowe, 1976.

Guzowski, Piotr, and Urszula Sowina. "Kingdom of Poland and the Grand Duchy of Lithuania." In *The Routledge Handbook of Public Taxation in Medieval Europe*, edited by Denis Menjot et al., 356–71. London: Routledge, 2023.

Mielke, Christopher. *The Archaeology and Material Culture of Queenship in Medieval Hungary, 1000–1395*. Cham: Palgrave Macmillan, 2021.

Ostrowski, Donald. *Muscovy and the Mongols: Cross-Cultural Influences on the Steppe Frontier, 1304–1589*. Cambridge: Cambridge University Press, 1998.

Vercamer, Grischa, and Dušan Zupka, eds. *Rulership in Medieval East Central Europe: Power, Rituals and Legitimacy in Bohemia, Hungary and Poland*. East Central and Eastern Europe in the Middle Ages, 450–1450, 78. Leiden: Brill, 2022.

Zupka, Dušan. "Rulers Between Ideal and Reality." In *The Routledge Handbook of East Central and Eastern Europe in the Middle Ages, 500–1300*, edited by Florin Curta, 174–90. London: Routledge, 2022.

55

SOCIAL ORGANIZATION

Keywords in this chapter: *Saxon Mirror*, *familia*, dowry, *iobagiones*

Legal status in medieval Europe provided individuals with a variety of legal personalities. Land (or territorial) laws that became more common in the later Middle Ages, by contrast, applied to all inhabitants and regulated interactions between people of various statuses. For example, the "Land Law" is a section of Eike of Repgow's *Saxon Mirror*, a popular compilation written in early thirteenth-century Thuringia that was disseminated across Central Europe in both its German version and the Latin translation of Conrad of Opole. Eike distinguished between Saxons, Swabians, Wends, and Jews, who had to be judged according to the status they obtained at birth. Illustrated manuscripts depict members of these groups with stereotypical attributes: Saxon men carry a short sword; Wendish men wear leg bands and cut their hair short; Jews have their Jewish hats. Eike's "Land Law" discusses family, inheritance, and conflicts between villagers and neighbors.

Individuals typically responded to a tribunal corresponding to their legal identity. Clerics were excepted from secular legislation; they attended separate courts where they were judged according to canon law. Burghers were judged in municipal courts by judges supported by benches of jurors (*scabini*, *Schöffen*), laymen who acted as judgment finders for their peers. Religious minorities had their own tribunals. Jews accessed either the tribunal of a "judge of the Jews" appointed by the secular ruler of their lordship, or the "Jewish tribunal" where rabbinic law was applied. Linguistic minorities could also have protected rights. During the Late Middle Ages, Wends in eastern Germany attending court had the right to an interpreter if they could express themselves only in Slavic. The procedure for requesting access to an interpreter is outlined in the *Saxon Mirror*, and municipal records attest that Wends did make use of their linguistic rights.

In addition to legal issues involving clerics, canon law covered matters of the lives of laypeople that were seen as being of religious nature; this included marriage and family law. Canon law developed in the Early Middle Ages through compilations of decisions taken at church councils as well as pronouncements of popes in the Latin West and patriarchs in the Greek East. In the West, important turning points were the Carolingian reforms of the eighth and ninth centuries, as bishops sought to influence the lives of laypeople, including secular rulers, and the twelfth-century work of Gratian, who produced the most comprehensive compilation of canon law available to date. The acts of Lateran IV (1215) were also disseminated throughout the Catholic world. In the Orthodox world, canon law was known through Old Slavonic compilations of texts of Byzantine origins (see chapter 39).

In Late Antiquity and much of the Early Middle Ages, marriage was considered a secular affair that was dealt with between families, according to local customs. The basic principle of Roman tradition was that a marriage was made valid by the consent of the two partners. The blessing of the marriage partners could be included into the wedding celebration but did not have legal significance. This changed when Byzantine Emperor Leo VI decreed in 893 that in addition to the consent of the partners, church solemnization was necessary to make a marriage valid. By the twelfth century, this rule had been accepted in the Orthodox world at large. In the Latin West, church blessings were still rare in the ninth century, but marriage was considered a sacrament by the time of Pope Gregory VII. Church solemnization was prescribed but was not considered necessary for the validity of a marriage – only the consent of the marriage partners was.

Family structures find expression in the vocabulary used to designate family members. In Late Antiquity, Roman kinship followed a parallel (lineal) model in which relatives on the side of either the mother or the father were designated by the same words. In Germanic, Slavic, Baltic, and Finno-Ugric languages, by contrast, different words were used for uncles, aunts, and other relatives on the mother's and the father's side, respectively. This reflected collateral kinship in which these relationships had different meanings. During the Middle Ages, the shift from the collateral to the parallel system happened in waves – first in the German lands, then in East Central Europe, and later in the lands of Rus' and the Baltic lands. In the Balkans, however, this shift never happened: the collateral system is still reflected today in the Bulgarian, Macedonian, Serbian, Bosnian, and Albanian languages. The Balkans are also the only region of Europe where, in various languages, an entirely different vocabulary is used for relatives by blood and by marriage. The collateral system reflects a stronger trend towards patrilineal kinship in the Balkans, whereas the parallel system that replaced it elsewhere signals equal or similar value given to the male and female lines of kinship.

Parallel kinship resulted from marriage practices that focused on the nuclear family and from inheritance favoring impartible transmission. The papal reforms of the High Middle Ages promoted a "spouses-centered" family by insisting on the consent of the marriage partners; they blurred the lines of traditional kinship systems by imposing strict prohibitions on the marriage of relatives and by equating kinship by blood, by marriage, and by godparenthood. These new concepts were adopted most successfully in regions of Europe where the papacy, with the help of supporting religious orders such as the mendicants, was best able to impose its views on the population at large. Marriage prohibitions were less respected in Eastern Europe and the Balkans (where the practice of levirate survived longer), not because the Orthodox church held fundamentally different views, but because it was less effective in changing understandings of kinship. The standardization of the manse as a unit of land meant to sustain a household, in the High Middle Ages, reinforced the trend towards a spouses-focused family: husband and wife worked together in a more gender-balanced labor unit. Cohabitation with non-relatives became common: in the countryside, these were hired workers; in the towns, journeymen and apprentices. The *familia* was defined as comprising those who lived under one roof, irrespective of their kinship connections.

Inheritance rights of sons and daughters varied greatly according to local traditions. In Bulgaria, family properties were divided equally among sons and daughters; in Rus', daughters inherited only if they had no brothers; elsewhere, a common practice was to bequeath landed properties to sons and movable goods to daughters. The 1222 Golden Bull of Andrew II (see chapter 56) clarified that Hungarian women who had brothers would inherit movable property; a woman could inherit landed property only if she had no brother. In the early fourteenth century, however, this was changed so that all landed property would go to male relatives; a married woman could not have property of her own. The king, however, had the right of "promotion to a son": if a woman had no brother, the king declared her to have the rights of a son and to inherit as such.

A woman, however, normally received a share of the family inheritance as a dowry at her wedding. The dowry, which typically comprised movable goods, was meant to support her in marriage and widowhood. The bride could also receive a dower from the family of her husband. In Magdeburg law, the wife's property was managed by the husband during marriage; in Polish tradition, the wife could manage her own property, and important transactions had to be approved by the spouse, children, and relatives. Ashkenazi Jewish women received the largest dowries: the practice of giving large dowries was meant to support the newly married couples in establishing themselves independently. These large dowries contributed to giving a high social status to Jewish women.

Divorce became more restricted with the enforcement of canon law. In the Latin West, the concept of indissolubility of marriage appeared in the eighth century and was generally enforced in the twelfth. Separation was possible in the case of adultery; annulment and remarriage were only possible for marriages in the prohibited degrees. These regulations were slower to be implemented in Central Europe. In eastern Germany, Wendish women could still obtain a divorce in the thirteenth century by paying a "heel fee." In the Orthodox world, by contrast, divorce and remarriage were considered acceptable in various circumstances. Ashkenazi Jewish women had much easier access to divorce than the Christian women of their majority societies. Polygamy had been prohibited since the eleventh century, as was unilateral divorce initiated by the husband.

In medieval societies, the main distinction in the social status of men and women was between free and unfree. In Hungary, the "golden liberty" applied to those who could choose at will their lords and their place of residence: the nobles, the burghers, and a small class of landholding peasants. Most peasants were bound to their pieces of land and could thus be best described as serfs. Only a free man, usually a warrior owing military service to a lord, had the capacity to attend a tribunal as accuser or witness. The Hungarian *iobagiones* (warriors) who owned landed estates in hereditary tenure and the castle peasants on land that belonged to the castle were all free in the sense that they could participate in lawsuits, give testimony, and had the right to bear arms. The *udvornici* (a word of Slavic origin), by contrast, formed an upper class of Hungarian peasants but, unlike the free, could not attend tribunals. By the early fourteenth century, the earlier categories were merged into the status of *iobagiones* who could leave their land under certain conditions.

In medieval Europe, social status was expressed by how people dressed. Following practices in Italian cities and the German lands, sumptuary laws were introduced to Poland in the thirteenth century. The first of such laws, promulgated at the synod of Sieradz (Greater Poland) in 1233, was for members of the clergy, who were prohibited from wearing garments with decorated sleeves or extravagant-looking shoes. Municipal authorities and craft guilds in Poland, Silesia, Red Ruthenia, and the state of the Teutonic Order issued sumptuary laws in the thirteenth and fourteenth centuries that provided guidance on appropriate clothing for burghers and on the organization of feasts for weddings, baptisms, or other occasions. The laws limited inappropriate shows of luxury, sometimes providing different limitations based on social status, profession, or wealth. They aimed at restraining the public display of wealth inequality among the communities of burghers.

FURTHER READING

Dembińska, Maria. "Women in Daily Life of Medieval Poland." In *Frau und spätmittelalterlicher Alltag: Internationaler Kongress Krems an d. Donau 2.–5. Oktober 1984*. Sitzungsberichte. Akademie der Wissenschaften in Wien, Philosophisch-historische Klasse 473, 387–407. Veröffentlichungen des Instituts für Mittelalterliche Realienkunde Österreichs 9. Vienna: Verlag der Österreichischen Akademie der Wissenschaften, 1986.

Dobozy, Maria. "From Oral Custom to Written Law: The German *Sachsenspiegel*." In *Oral History of the Middle Ages: The Spoken Word in Context*, edited by Gerhard Jaritz and Michael Richter, 154–63. Medium Aevum Quotidianum Sonderband 12. CEU Medievalia 3. Krems-Budapest: CEU Press, 2001.

Keil, Martha. "Public Roles of Jewish Women in Fourteenth and Fifteenth-Century Ashkenaz: Business, Community and Ritual." In *The Jews of Europe in the Middle Ages (Tenth to Fifteenth Centuries): Proceedings of the International Symposium Held at Speyer, 20–25 October 2002*, edited by Christoph Cluse, 317–30. Cultural Encounters in Late Antiquity and the Middle Ages 4. Turnhout: Brepols, 2004.

Mitterauer, Michael. "European Kinship Systems and Household Structures: Medieval Origins." In *Distinct Inheritances: Property, Family and Community in a Changing Europe*, edited by Hannes Grandits and Patrick Heady, 35–51. Halle Studies in the Anthropology of Eurasia 2. Münster: Lit, 2003.

Myśliwski, Grzegorz. "Medieval Sumptuary Laws in Polish Historiography: The State of the Question, and Directions of New Research." *Quaestiones Medii Aevi Novae* 22 (2017): 335–54.

Pushkareva, N. L. "Women in the Medieval Russian Family of the Tenth through Fifteenth Centuries." In *Russia's Women: Accommodation, Resistance, Transformation*, edited by Barbara Evans Clements et al., 29–43. Berkeley: University of California Press, 1991.

56

THE HIGH AND LATE MEDIEVAL ARISTOCRACY

Keywords in this chapter: boyars, allods, ministerials, *druzhina*, *knezes*

The medieval nobility was a social group typically defined by a military ethos, a status conferred through birth into a recognized family, and the consciousness of belonging to a privileged group. The origins of the nobility varied, as did the terminology used to designate nobles. The barons were usually the select few who took part in rulers' councils or the rulers' inner circles. The Slavic word *zhupan*, derived from the word *zhupa* (referring to a territorial unit), was used in Wallachia and Moldavia for members of the princely councils (*jupâni*). The Hungarian title *ispán*, the equivalent of a count, derives from *zhupa*, much like *pan* in Polish and Czech. The term *boljar (boyar)* is perhaps of pre-Slavic origin; it was used for the aristocracy and was disseminated in Old Slavonic writings throughout Eastern Europe and designated the wealthy landowners or the members of rulers' councils in Wallachia, Moldavia, Lithuania, and Rus'. In Hungary, the *iobagiones* were originally warriors and officials dependent upon the king or a lord, but in the Late Middle Ages the word came to designate serfs. In the later Middle Ages, the nobilities of Bohemia and Poland became known as *šlechta* (attested in old Czech in the fourteenth century) or *szlachta* respectively, both words derived from the German *Geschlecht* ("clan").

The nobility of eleventh- and twelfth-century Central Europe had its origins in military and administrative functions (see chapter 29). In Poland and Bohemia, the nobility emerged out of warriors and office holders in the service of dukes and lords. As they gained land, revenues, and authority, they came to be seen as a privileged group defined by birthright. The sons of these families were entrusted with important posts at the courts or given preferential treatment in ecclesiastical careers. Polish nobles and knights followed the *ius militare*, the "law of warriors" or "law of knights." Those who served as mounted warriors received lands in hereditary property that could be bequeathed to their sons and daughters.

In Hungary, the nobles emerged out of the ranks of warriors (*iobagiones*) of royal castles and the servants of the king. The castle districts were led by the *ispáns* (counts) who combined administrative and military duties. Nobles of local and foreign origins filled posts in royal administration. Hungarian nobles, when they emerged as a class in the thirteenth century, were defined as those who owned landed property (allods). The Hungarian noble status had little to do with lifestyle or chivalric culture and many nobles lived like landholding peasants. However, prominent among them were the "real nobles of the kingdom," who were the warriors owing hereditary military service. Members of the upper elite of the nobility traced their descent to illustrious ancestors such as those who had taken part in the Conquest of the Carpathian Basin. Beginning in the thirteenth century, they identified as members of the kindred (*gens*) established by a well-known ancestor.

Access to the revenues of extensive land ownership made Hungarian kings very powerful in the eleventh and twelfth centuries. However, King Andrew II was more liberal in donating land to church institutions and to nobles as reward for their support. His policies created a class of mighty barons, some of whom were German knights. The barons, seeking protections for their status, formed a league to force the king to grant them privileges. The result was the Golden Bull that Andrew II granted in 1222 and that purported to restore rights introduced by Stephen I. The bull put limits on royal authority (such as on giving away large swaths of land), restricted the influence of foreigners, and protected the rights of both lesser nobles and barons. Nobles were not to pay any tax, could not be requested to perform military service without reward, and could not be judged in the counts' tribunals. Moreover, the barons even had the right to disobey the king if he did not follow expectations. The bull was renewed, in slightly modified form, by Louis of Anjou in 1351: it remained a foundational document for the rights of the Hungarian nobility for the rest of the Middle Ages.

The Central European nobility was profoundly changed in the thirteenth century by the migration of knights from the German lands and from other parts of Western Europe, and by the adoption of their military, social, and cultural practices. At the Hungarian court, foreign warriors had had a strong presence ever since Stephen I's marriage to the Bavarian princess Gisela. In Prague, cultural influences of German-language courtly culture became obvious in the early thirteenth century. The Polish lands were affected to various degrees; Silesia attracted an especially large number of German knights, typically from families of ministerials (see chapter 57), starting in the mid-thirteenth century. At that time, the Silesian Piasts were engaged in conflicts with one another and sought the support of incoming knights. Many of the Polish and Silesian knights were attracted to the international courtly culture and fashion of the day, to which they were exposed in its German expression. The German knights who settled in Silesia typically married Polish women; Polish nobles and German knights intermingled and formed a new nobility. Through migration and acculturation, the German language came to dominate at the courts of Lower Silesia (see chapter 61). Mastering the German language could be seen as a marker of status: Duke Bolesław the Bald, a Silesian Piast, is said to have been ridiculed for his poor pronunciation of German.

In the lands of Rus', a Riurikid prince counted on the support of the warriors of his *druzhina*, or retinue. These men were their prince's main military force; they accompanied him on military expeditions and stayed with him at his main residences. They assisted him in the administration of the principality. The princes entrusted their men with administrative and judiciary tasks; they occasionally acted as governors in towns. The Rus' boyars who came out of these ranks were the property-owning secular elite and typically resided in the fortified towns with the princes or their representatives.

Rulers of the later Middle Ages sought to bind the nobility to themselves in new ways. In Hungary, Charles of Anjou struggled to trust the many nobles who had opposed his coronation. He undertook to reform the nobility by rewarding with important court posts those who supported his policies and, in this way, counterbalance the power of the territorial lords. Sigismund spent most of the early years of his reign fighting the domination of oligarchs. When Poland and Lithuania were joined in personal union by Jogaila and Jadwiga, Catholic Lithuanian and Orthodox Ruthenian nobles were formally given the same rights. However, in Lithuania – let alone in Poland – only Catholics had access to high offices, as was stated in the 1413 treaty of Horodło. Polish Catholics could aspire to offices in Lithuania. Catholic Lithuanians, however, were expected to stay away from offices in the Ruthenian lands of the grand duchy. When a Catholic official was named governor of Kiev in 1470, a show of force was needed to have the population accept him. In the lands of the grand duchy, Lithuanian and Ruthenian nobles generally kept to themselves.

In Red Ruthenia, the conquest of Casimir III was followed by the migration of nobles. Casimir and his successors claimed ownership of the land and distributed landed property to loyal followers. Properties were given to Polish noblemen who became important lords in the region. Wallachian knights who were recruited to move to the region were also given lands in similar manner. Many Ruthenian boyars became socially and culturally Polonized; captivated by the culture of the royal court, they came under the influence of the Polish nobility. The nobility of Red Ruthenia nonetheless developed a class consciousness that crossed ethnic and religious differences. Nobles were all part of one group and saw no problem in interacting with one another and cooperating to defend their common interests. An awareness of differences in religion and customs did not disappear, though. In legal affairs, Catholics swore oaths on a cross while Orthodox swore while holding the ring on a church door. The king was careful to treat Polish and Ruthenian nobles equally.

Although they were never forced to do so, some Ruthenian nobles converted to Catholicism. This might have facilitated their social advancement, although it was not a formal prerequisite for social success. For them, the Polish language and Catholicism probably represented the most fashionable court culture. Conversion to Catholicism often followed marriage to a Catholic. By contrast, there is no mention of Catholic nobles converting to Orthodoxy; however, mixed marriages in which each partner kept his or her religion were common. Other Ruthenian nobles were more conservative and stuck to their religion and culture, avoiding marrying Catholics: this did not prevent them from having the same rights and privileges as Catholic nobles. Others preferred a middle way: they remained Orthodox but became culturally and socially, to diverse degrees, Polonized. All of them had a consciousness of belonging to the same group. A very similar interaction between Catholic and Orthodox nobles existed in Transylvania under Hungarian rule. Much like in Red Ruthenia, some Romanian noblemen converted to Catholicism and thus adopted the Hungarian language, names, and customs as well. The Orthodox Romanian nobility of Transylvania (*knezes*) was nonetheless in a socially lower position than the Ruthenian nobility in relation to their Catholic counterparts.

In Muscovy, the leading families of boyars served the Daniilovichi without being attached to a particular prince: their loyalty went to the dynasty. Rus' society did not have a clear definition of who belonged to the boyars. Some of them were from clans established for generations at the service of princes; others were land-owning warriors. When the princes of Moscow annexed new territories, they expected the boyars to serve them in their army, in Moscow, or to represent them in their homeland. The practice of partitioning lands among sons and daughters made it difficult for boyar families to maintain power over generations. Women of the Muscovite boyar classes rarely participated in military or administrative matters; they lived a secluded life in separated sections of their residences. Seclusion was likely meant to highlight the importance of women who avoided direct contact with lower classes. Boyar widows nonetheless did manage family properties as noble women did in other parts of Europe.

FURTHER READING

Jurek, Tomasz. "Married to a Foreigner: Wives and Daughters of German Knights in Silesia during the Thirteenth and Fourteenth Century." *Acta Poloniae Historica* 81 (2000): 37–50.

Klápště, Jan. *The Czech Lands in Medieval Transformation*. Translated by Sean Mark Miller and Kateřina Millerová. East Central and Eastern Europe in the Middle Ages, 450–1450, 17. Leiden: Brill, 2012.

Popa-Gorjanu, Cosmin. *Medieval Nobility in Central Europe: The Himfi Family*. Cluj-Napoca: Mega, 2019.

Rady, Martyn. "Hungary and the Golden Bull of 1222." *Banatica* 24, no. 2 (2014): 87–108.

Rady, Martyn. *Nobility, Land and Service in Medieval Europe*. Studies in Russia and East Europe. New York: Palgrave, 2000.

Zazuliak, Yurij. "Rebaptism, Name-Giving and Identity among Nobles of Ruthenian Origin in Late Medieval Galicia." In *An der Grenze des lateinischen Europa: Integration und Segregation in Rotreußen, 1350–1600. On the Frontier of Latin Europe: Integration and Segregation in Red Ruthenia, 1350–1600*, edited by Thomas Wünsch and Andrzej Janeczek, 47–60. Warsaw: Institute of Archaeology and Ethnology of the Polish Academy of Sciences, 2004.

57

FEUDALISM AND CHIVALRY IN EAST CENTRAL EUROPE

Keywords in this chapter: *familiaritas*, vassalage, court culture, chivalry

The problem with "feudalism" is that the word means different things to different people. In most countries of the former Eastern Bloc, the concept of feudalism has long been understood in Marxist terms. Feudalism, in that sense, was a mode of production in which a lord owned the land (the means of production) that was tilled by serfs (the forces of production). The idea behind serfdom (workers bound to the land) was therefore the result of the attempt to secure the labor force necessary for that mode of production to work. The essential relation between landlords and serfs was vertical and of fundamental inequality. On the other hand, in Western Europe, feudalism was understood primarily as vassalage, that is referring to the relationship between a lord and his vassal. That relation was horizontal, as it involved a relationship between service (typically military) and a piece of land given as reward. That piece of land was called a fief (*feodum* in Latin, hence feudalism), and it was always in principle a conditional grant. The existence of fiefs and vassals is well attested for the High and Late Middle Ages in most of Western Europe; although they found rather limited application, these concepts were also introduced in some parts of East Central Europe in the context of the transformations of the thirteenth century, along with many other social and cultural innovations that were introduced from Western Europe and the German lands during that time. Other types of relationships, such as the *familiaritas* of medieval Hungary, might have been inspired by vassalage and applied to local circumstances.

Vassalage implies a transaction, with the fief used as a reward, because as an estate worked by serfs, it provided steady revenues. The fief was granted by the lord in exchange for military service, either before (as incentive) or afterwards (as recompense). Originally offered on a retractable basis (i.e., conditional upon loyal service), the fief often became in practice hereditary to the extent that its holder continued to provide service to the lord. In

France, England, and the German lands, the granting of a fief involved a public ceremony of homage, during which the vassal swore an oath of fealty to his lord. The ceremony concluded with a kiss on the mouth symbolizing the deeply personal relationship between the two men in a one-to-one partnership. While the partners were usually men, women (as widows or heiresses) could also participate in vassalage. A lady could give a fief to a vassal; if receiving a fief from a lord, a woman delegated military service to a man from her kin group or entourage. The result was the creation of often complex networks of social and military dependencies based on individual connections between two partners with mutual obligations.

Vassalage developed in France in the eleventh century; it appeared in the German lands in the twelfth century, where it was applied in a variety of circumstances. Unlike in France (and many of the other countries in Western Europe), those in Germany providing service to their lords and called ministerials (from the Latin word for service, *ministerium*) were typically not free. In other words, ministerials provided service because they were servants (i.e., obligated to provide service), not because they were (or wanted to be) vassals. The non-free status, however, did not prevent lords from rewarding them, often with land, and certainly did not stop ministerials from being socially and economically successful. Emperors and bishops preferred ministerials as courtiers and warriors in order to counteract the authority of the ancient noble families. On the other hand, true vassalage also existed for the purpose of regulating relations between powerful lords: the princes of the empire were vassals of the emperor, a privilege that provided them with direct access to the person of the ruler.

Despite the existence of a wide variety of forms of unfree status, in East Central Europe there is no evidence of ministerials: not in Hungary, not in Poland, not even in Bohemia, which was nonetheless a part of the Holy Roman Empire, and therefore much more exposed to the influence of its specific institutions. However, vassalage reached East Central Europe through the empire in the thirteenth century, and its primary purpose seems to have been the same – a tool of governance. In Western Pomerania, Wartislaw III (1219–64) and Barnim I (1220–78) attracted German knights to their courts and provided them with fiefs held as vassals. In Silesia, where, after the mid-thirteenth century, the Piast dukes also strove to attract German knights, vassalage was introduced in similar manner. In Silesia and in Poland, the *locatores* who supervised the settlement processes (see chapters 58 and 59) were also typically given lands as fiefs, and thus became vassals.

Irrespective of vassalage, oaths of fealty were often utilized in East Central Europe to regulate relationships between powerful lords, a practice that imitated customs in the Holy Roman Empire. Henry IV Probus, the Piast duke of Wrocław in Silesia, paid homage to Rudolf of Habsburg in Vienna in 1278, which was an unusual practice for the Piasts at that time. Henry Probus thus became an imperial prince. In 1327 and 1328, most of the Piast dukes of Silesia paid homage to the king of Bohemia, John of Luxembourg. The practice, introduced by the French-speaking duke from a region of former Lotharingia, was a novelty to them. For the Silesian dukes, homage to King John was a way to rebuke the attempts of Władysław the Short to attach the Silesian lands to the recently reunited kingdom of Poland. The relation of dependence between their Silesian lands and the kingdom of Bohemia established a personal relationship between the dukes and the king, which continued for the rest of the Middle Ages.

In Silesia and in Poland, vassalage competed with the traditional custom according to which Polish knights received landed properties as reward for their military service in perpetuity, not conditionally. By the end of the thirteenth century, the two types of personal dependence had sufficiently influenced one another to become indistinct. While the dependent men owed military service in a manner not unlike that of vassals, it does not appear that the ceremonial oaths of fealty in chivalric tradition, however, had the same importance, if they existed at all, as in the German lands or in France. Traditions of vassalage were adopted only when they matched the needs of local societies.

In Hungary, King Andrew II established a new cavalry force by giving lands to mounted warriors, a practice that might have been inspired by the granting of fiefs to knights in the Holy Roman Empire or in France but was clearly different. However, the king did not give these lands on a retractable basis (in other words, as fiefs), but in perpetuity, as allodial (hereditary) property. These men owed military service to the king not because they were holding fiefs, but because they had taken oaths of fidelity to their ruler. Nonetheless, in the later thirteenth century, a new concept appeared in Hungary that is quite like vassalage. *Familiaritas* was a personal relationship between a lord and another free man that involved fealty, service, and mutual obligations. The free man entered the service of a lord and lived under his roof, becoming part of his family (hence the name of the institution, derived from the Latin word for family). The free man fought in the army of his lord, under his banner, and was rewarded for service not with land, but with stipends or other forms of revenue. The relationship typically involved an oath of allegiance taken in a "place of authentication" – a church or monastery that produced documents with recognized validity. When the free man was rewarded with income from landed property, the land itself remained in formal possession of the lord. Although *familiaritas* was understood in Hungary as being something different from vassalage, both practices responded to similar imperatives of creating personal bonds for mutual interest.

Court culture defined the noble lifestyle. The thirteenth-century courts of Central Europe became increasingly cosmopolitan and influenced by the chivalric culture that served as a marker of class status. Under Wenceslas I and Přemysl Ottokar II, Prague became a renowned center of chivalric culture where German was adopted as the common language of the Central European nobility. Poetry and romance were symbols of secular upper-class culture; in Bohemia, this literature was first available in German (see chapter 68). While German was the language of the sophisticated fashion of the day, its dominance attracted criticism. The Czech-language *Alexandreida* and the *Chronicle of Dalimil* reveal the perspective of the traditional Czech-speaking land nobility that fantasized about a traditional order free from the centralizing tendencies of the Prague court under foreign influence.

Foreign knights were also present in noticeable numbers at the court of the Hungarian kings in the early eleventh century. Most Hungarian nobles of later centuries, though, related their ancestry to the time of the Conquest, often by inventing their ancestors (sometimes based on place names in use within Hungary). Chivalric culture gained popularity in thirteenth-century Hungary. Names from chivalric romances – Alexander, Roland, Lancelot, Tristan and Iseult – became popular. In the fourteenth century, it became common for noble families to send their sons to the royal court to be educated in courtly and chivalric manners. Serving at the court opened career opportunities.

In Poland, ceremonies of induction into knighthood are attested as early as the time of Gallus Anonymus (early twelfth century). However, it was not until the fourteenth century that dubbing young knights became a widespread practice, no doubt under German influence. Latin sources differentiated between a knight (*miles*) and a dubbed knight (*miles strenuus*). Dubbing had a prestigious character as a special distinction but did not change the formal status of a knight.

In Lithuania, Vytautas and his successors encouraged young knights to go abroad and become acquainted with the practices of knighthood. They also encouraged foreign knights to visit the grand ducal court. Lithuanian nobles were interested in the superior military equipment of European knights and in learning their manners and practices, not least because many of those European knights had joined the members of the Teutonic Order in their annual expeditions (*Reisen*) against the Lithuanians. Lithuanian knights now traveled to England and Burgundy; Dutch, Spanish, and Italian knights found their way to Vilnius. Knights from Silesia were especially numerous at Vytautas's court: many of them made successful careers in their new country. Knighting ceremonies became common. In 1429, Vytautas was inducted by Sigismund of Luxembourg, king of Hungary, into the Order of the Dragon, which had been created in 1408 by the king and his wife, Barbara of Celje.

Chivalric orders appeared in Central Europe in the fifteenth century. The Order of the Dragon was an association of noblemen dedicated to the fight against "the heathen and the schismatics" (i.e., the Ottoman Turks and the Hussites). Its symbol was a dragon vanquished by a cross. Membership in the order was a distinction granted by Sigismund and his Hungarian successors to their supporters, including foreign rulers. One of those upon whom the Hungarian king bestowed the distinction was the ruler of Wallachia, Vlad II, nicknamed Dracul precisely because of his membership in the Order (the old Romanian word for dragon was "drac"). His son was therefore known as "Drăculea" (literally, "the son of the one who was a member of the Order of the Dragon"), and that is how Vlad III (see chapter 52) came to be known as Dracula. In Silesia, Wenceslas II, duke of Legnica and bishop of Wrocław, and Louis II, duke of Legnica and Brzeg, established the Hound Collar (Rüdenband) Order in 1413. Its symbol was a hound collar in reference to dogs wearing spiked collars to prevent attacks by other dogs or wolves. The association organized tournaments that took place every year in Legnica or Görlitz as well as hunting expeditions.

The noble lifestyle included various features that bound nobles of Central Europe to their international peers. Tournaments were festivals in which knights fought one another, reenacting battles for the exclusive purpose of entertaining audiences of noble men and women. Despite vehement criticism from churchmen, tournaments gained great popularity in the thirteenth century; they were organized by rulers of Hungary, Bohemia, and Silesia and were later well attested at the court of Jogaila. Hunting was also a popular pastime with the nobility. Much like Frankish and, later, Norman-English rulers, Hungarian kings had royal forests rich in bears, bison, and even aurochs. Silesian rulers relied on monasteries located in wooded areas to organize hunting expeditions for them and their nobles.

Castles were the material embodiment of the noble lifestyle. In Hungary, the traditional earth-and-timber castles began to be replaced by stone castles after the Mongol invasion. The typical new castles were built by the kings in royal forests, for example the Spiš Castle in what is now eastern Slovakia. The castle of Visegrád, on the Danube north of Budapest, was built by Queen Mary in the forest Pilis. Nobles typically built towers, sometimes surrounded by a palace, a chapel, and a stone wall.

FURTHER READING

Bak, János M. "Feudalism in Hungary?" In *Feudalism: New Landscapes of Debate*, edited by Sverre Bagge, Michael H. Gelting, and Thomas Lindkvist, 203–16. Turnhout: Brepols, 2011.

Curta, Florin. *Eastern Europe in the Middle Ages (500–1300)*. Brill's Companions to European History 19. Leiden: Brill, 2019.

Filippov, Igor S. "The Notion of Feudalism in Russian Historiography." In *El temps i l'espai del feudalisme: Reunió científica. VI Curs d'Estiu Comtat d'Urgell (Balaguer, 11, 12 i 13 del juliol de 2001)*, edited by Flocel Sabaté and Joan Farré, 149–65. Lleida: Pagès, 2004.

Petrauskas, Rimvydas. "Knighthood in the Grand Duchy of Lithuania from the Late Fourteenth to the Early Sixteenth Centuries." *Lithuanian Historical Studies* 11 (2006): 39–66.

Szymczak, Jan. "Knightly Tournaments in Medieval Poland." *Fasciculi Archaeologiae Historice* 8 (1995): 9–28.

58

RURAL ECONOMY AND SETTLEMENTS

Keywords in this chapter: *melioratio terrae*, *locatores*, German law, Wallachian law

For much of Central, Southeastern, and Eastern Europe, a long period between the eleventh and the fourteenth centuries was marked by economic growth before various crises erupted in the fifteenth century. In Central Europe, migrant peasants moved during the twelfth and thirteenth centuries from further west into regions that were less populated and where land was readily available for cultivation. They migrated for the most part at the instigation of local rulers who wanted to grow the population and maximize the agricultural use of the land, all for the purpose of generating more revenue. Agriculture was the dominant rural activity in the region, although the raising of horses and cattle played a more important role in Hungary than elsewhere.

The land surface used for agricultural production increased with the clearing of woodlands, the draining of marshes, and the occupation of marginal areas. Lords coveted revenues from additional rents, and peasants aspired to surpluses they could sell on the markets. The expansion of agricultural land through available means reached limits in the twelfth century; it was pursued with immigrants in the thirteenth century. Settlers of mostly German, but also Flemish and French, origin moved to regions where they expected better economic conditions. To put it in the language of contemporary charters, the immigration program initiated by rulers aimed at the *melioratio terrae* ("improvement of the land"), which was understood as making better use of existing land resources to maximize productivity. This process had profound consequences. East Central Europe had integrated politically with the West European world since the tenth century; in the thirteenth century, economic integration was also pursued.

By the twelfth century, settlers were already being recruited by German margraves, bishops, and monasteries (especially of Cistercians), all of whom had a vested interest in bringing new peasants to the Slavic lands of what is now eastern Germany. In conquered territories, integrating settlers with the local population served to minimize local resistance. Ecclesiastic institutions were interested in bringing Christian settlers who would disseminate Christianity. However, first and foremost the arrival of new settlers brought economic growth as the newcomers cleared land that, until then, had brought little revenue to local lords. Rulers of East Central Europe followed suit in the thirteenth century. In Poland, Western Pomerania, Bohemia, and Hungary, local rulers sought to recruit settlers to further economic profit. In Hungary, the migration of peasants was accelerated after the Mongol invasion that had left many parts of the country devastated (see chapter 42). Royal grants aimed at facilitating a "gathering of peoples" (*congregatio populorum*) with newcomers who came either from abroad (e.g., German or Francophone lands, Italy) or from regions of Hungary that had been spared. The Teutonic Knights also actively promoted the settlement of the regions they had conquered: settlers came to Prussia from the German lands, Scandinavia, or Poland. Unlike Prussia, however, there was no peasant immigration into more remote Livonia and Estonia. On the local level, the settlement of newcomers was coordinated by agents called *locatores*. Some, usually knights, received responsibility for a territory; most others, being of more modest background, were entrusted a village or town. The *locatores* recruited settlers, prepared the sites, drew parcels of land, and allocated them to the newcomers. In return, they received economic privileges and parts of the revenues from village mills and other sources. Their descendants became the hereditary village headmen.

Moreover, increased agricultural productivity was achieved through improved technology (heavy iron plows, mills), methods (three-field crop rotation), and management (a simplified rent system incentivizing improved production), all of which were imported from the lands of Western Europe or Germany, or found wider dissemination when they already existed. The landscapes were transformed by woodland clearings and the watermills that, typically combined with fishponds, multiplied on streams and rivers. Mills used renewable energy primarily to grind grain, thus liberating the labor force to now be available for other endeavors (grinding grain by hand had been typically a domestic task performed by women). Windmills were occasionally used in Prussia.

The status of the peasants of East Central Europe varied before the transformations of the thirteenth century. Typically, serfs owed their lords combinations of rents, dues, and services. In Hungary, agriculture relied largely on the labor of slaves until the end of the thirteenth century. While peasants on royal estates and on church lands had some degree of regulated autonomy, the *servi* (slaves) working on secular landowners' properties were treated as objects and could be bought and sold separately from the lands on which they worked. Charters often mentioned the absence of limitations on the work that could be requested of them. When landowners were willing to give plots of land to any newcomer, it became tempting for slaves to flee and move to other parts of Hungary: the scale of the flight of slaves thus accelerated in the thirteenth century.

Settlers were promised opportunities that were better than the conditions they had left behind in the lands from which they came. They had no rents to pay for the period of the land-clearing process; after that, they paid fixed rents that provided incentives to produce more and make profits. The settlers in the new villages were granted the German law (*ius Teutonicum*), a legal framework devised for settlers that combined features from various parts of the German lands. Settlers had a community organization and village courts headed by their hereditary headmen. After the first wave of migration and the establishment of new villages, the German law and the accompanying communal organization were often granted to local peasants as well, making management more efficient there.

Archaeological excavations in Slavonia (eastern Croatia) illustrate the differences in village structures between the High (twelfth and thirteenth centuries) and the Late Middle Ages (late thirteenth and fourteenth centuries) in that region ruled by the kings of Hungary. During the High Middle Ages, villages comprised sunken or semi-sunken buildings placed in irregular fashion in dispersed settlements with large unbuilt areas between the buildings that served as gardens, fields, or pasturelands. By contrast, villages of the Late Middle Ages were built in more compact manner, approaching the notion of nucleated settlements. The buildings, identified by postholes, were often placed around a central open space. Those were mostly aboveground houses divided into multiple rooms. Semi-sunken buildings, probably serving as forges or smithies, were sometimes attached to the main buildings. Narrow ditches are believed to reveal plot boundaries. The excavated villages lacked churches; in fact, a royal decree stipulated that a parish church was expected to serve up to ten villages.

None of those transformations in the thirteenth century affected the lands of Rus', where agriculture dominated in the forest belt and the forest steppe. Peasants used scratch plows adapted to the soil. Climate and soil conditions limited the variety of crops: rye dominated; oats fed horses; barley and wheat were rare. Yields were very low. The slash-and-burn method was the most common: peasants burned down a piece of woodland, cultivated the soil enriched by ash, and moved to a new place when the soil was depleted. The low population density and the easy availability of land made this method convenient.

In Bohemia, Poland, and Hungary, the transformations of the thirteenth century brought prosperity and stability that lasted until the beginning of the fifteenth century. The Black Death did not cause the crisis that it did in Western Europe; population kept growing steadily (see chapter 53). In Hungary, the export of cattle to Germany and Italy for meat consumption expanded after the mid-fourteenth and reached its peak in the fifteenth century. Demand for meat rose in many towns of Germany and Italy because of higher wages that were paid to workers following labor shortages after the Black Death. The hardy cattle from Hungary that could easily withstand travel of long distances was perfectly suited to meet this demand. The animals were brought to gathering points and were driven from there to their destination where they were slaughtered.

Whereas the German and Francophone settlers of the thirteenth century had moved to countries that, except in lands conquered from pagans, had long been part of Latin Christendom despite their different cultures, Polish settlers of the fourteenth century moved into lands with an Orthodox population. Polish migration and settlement were the result of Polish expansion into the land of Rus' in the fourteenth century; whereas a large part of Ruthenia that included Kiev (modern Belarus and parts of Ukraine) was under Lithuanian overlordship, Red Ruthenia (Halych and western Podolia, corresponding to parts of modern western Ukraine) was joined to the lands of the Polish crown (see chapters 48 and 49). The two parts of the western lands of Rus' experienced different developments. Little changed in the lands under Lithuanian rule, as the pagan grand dukes and their Christian successors followed a hands-off approach. The parts of Ruthenia under Polish control, by contrast, were subjected to an increasing influence of Western and Central European economic and social models that accompanied peasant immigration from Poland. The settlement of migrants began shortly after the Polish takeover. The conflicts of these years and the punitive expeditions of the Mongols had brought instability; Casimir III and his successors sought to reform the country and intensify economic growth. Newcomer peasants were recruited to settle in new villages established with German law; most settlers were of German or Polish culture. Other villages were established for Wallachian peasants from eastern Hungary who had their own legal system, the Wallachian law (*ius Walachicum*).

In the lands of Muscovy, agricultural methods changed in the mid-fifteenth century: after the civil war (see chapter 49), population rose so that the traditional, extensive slash-and-burn method became increasingly difficult to maintain. By the end of the century, three-field crop rotation gradually replaced the traditional method in the south-central and southern parts, leading to higher production; this new method had become widespread by the mid-sixteenth century. It required more labor and the availability of draught animals, as well as better planning. The loosely scattered farmsteads were replaced by villages with fields divided in strips to allow each peasant access to an equal amount of land. To bring stability, a law code promulgated by Ivan III in 1498 limited the freedom of movement of peasants.

FURTHER READING

Górecki, Piotr. *Economy, Society, and Lordship in Medieval Poland, 1100–1250*. New York: Holmes & Meier, 1992.

Hoffmann, Richard C. *Land, Liberties, and Lordship in a Late Medieval Countryside: Agrarian Structures and Change in the Duchy of Wrocław*. Philadelphia: University of Pennsylvania Press, 1989.

Janeš, Andrej, and Ivana Hirschler Marić. "The Transformation of Rural Settlements in Slavonia in the Period from the 12th to the 15th Centuries." In *Settlement Change across Medieval Europe: Old Paradigms and New Vistas*, edited by Niall Brady and Claudia Theune, 383–94. Ruralia 12. Leiden: Sidestone Press, 2019.

Laszlovszky, József. "Agriculture in Medieval Hungary." In *The Economy of Medieval Hungary*, edited by József Laszlovszky, Balázs Nagy, Péter Szabó, and András Vadas, 81–112. East Central and Eastern Europe in the Middle Ages, 450–1450, 49. Leiden: Brill, 2018.

Martin, Janet. "Russia." In *Agrarian Change and Crisis in Europe, 1200–1500*, edited by Harry Kitsikopolous, 292–329. New York: Routledge, 2012.

Myśliwski, Gregorz. "Utilisation of Water in Central Europe (12th–16th Cents.)." In *Economia e energia, secc. XIII-XVIII: Atti della XXXIV Settimana di studi Istituto internazionale di storia económica*, edited by Simonetta Cavaciocchi, 321–33. Pubblicazioni Istituto internazionale di storia economica F. Datini, Prato 2/34. Firenze: Le Monnier, 2003.

Petráček, Tomáš. *Power and Exploitation in the Czech Lands in the 10th–12th Centuries: A Central European Perspective*. Translated by Sean Miller. East Central and Eastern Europe in the Middle Ages, 450–1450, 40. Leiden: Brill, 2017.

Rady, Martyn. "The German Settlement in Central and Eastern Europe during the High Middle Ages." In *The Expansion of Central Europe in the Middle Ages*, edited by Nora Berend, 177–213. The Expansion of Latin Europe, 1000–1500, 5. Farnham: Ashgate, 2012.

Sárosi, Edit. "Rural Land Management in Medieval Central Europe." In *The Oxford Handbook of Medieval Central Europe*, edited by Nada Zečević and Daniel Ziemann, 239–65. Oxford: Oxford University Press, 2022.

Sutt, Cameron. *Slavery in Árpád-Era Hungary in a Comparative Context*. East Central and Eastern Europe in the Middle Ages, 450–1450, 31. Leiden: Brill, 2015.

59

TOWNS AND CITIES

Keywords in this chapter: *locatio, slobody, posadnik*

Urbanization profoundly changed Europe in the twelfth and thirteenth centuries in various ways. In Central Europe and the eastern Baltic, standardized models of urbanism and legal communities were introduced with the arrival of migrants; in Southeastern Europe, urban traditions from Central Europe, Italy, and Byzantium competed with one another; in the lands of Rus', the lack of institutional transformations did not prevent towns from expanding.

While in northern Italy and the Rhineland of the eleventh and twelfth centuries, town dwellers were granted privileges after uprisings and conflicts with their lords, in the lands east of the Elbe municipal laws were established by the lords to attract merchants and craftspeople, and to intensify the market economy. The law of Lübeck was applied in Scandinavia and around the Baltic Sea. The law of Magdeburg (in the variations of Chełmno, Wrocław, or Środa) was the most popular in Poland, the land of the Teutonic Order, Bohemia, and Red Ruthenia. Relying on a hereditary advocate and a bench of jurors, in later stages it included a municipal council. In Hungary, municipal laws were modelled on those of Székesfehérvár and Buda and derived from the law of Walloon settlers. Municipal communities had an elected body made up of a judge and a bench of jurors. The South German Law, largely based on the laws of Nuremberg and Vienna, was adopted in Old Prague, as well as in many cities of the Hungarian lands (including Croatia and Transylvania).

The process of *locatio* referred, strictly speaking, to the introduction of a new legal framework, which was a regalian right. Much like with villages of German law (see chapter 58), implementation of the legal framework was entrusted to *locatores* whose descendants became the hereditary advocates. The legal changes were part of a broader process that included recruiting new townspeople, providing them with resources, and setting up the urban organism in a rational manner, commonly by drawing standard-size plots that facilitated taxation. The street grid was typically centered upon a multipurpose marketplace;

Plate 59.1. The Old Town Hall in Wrocław. Built shortly before 1300, the building expanded during the fourteenth century, but especially between 1470 and 1510, when the Burghers' Hall (a large room for public gatherings and ceremonies) was vaulted and a Treasury was added. The late fifteenth- to early sixteenth-century reconstruction is responsible for the current look of the building, a typical example of late Gothic architecture. Wikimedia Commons, the free media repository.

a regular chessboard-style street grid was common in parts of Poland, Silesia, Bohemia, and Moravia, but rare in Hungary.

Central European towns were defined by their status, not their size. Most counted a few hundreds or thousands of inhabitants, while the larger towns such as Wrocław and Gdańsk barely exceeded 10,000 inhabitants by 1300 (see plate 59.1). Towns formed networks covering their territories; in the most densely urbanized regions, such as Silesia, countrypeople now lived close enough to a town to be able to go there and back in the same day, giving them convenient access to markets, commodities, and other services. Fortifications were the visual symbols of the success of urban communities, along with churches and town halls, cloth halls, guild halls, and the ostentatious buildings that surrounded the central marketplaces.

Among the largest and most successful of these towns were Prague, Cracow, Wrocław, and Buda. Prague was a conglomerate of three municipalities (Vyšehrad, the Old Town, and the Lesser Side near the castle) to which a fourth one, the New Town, was added by Charles IV. Cracow was fully reimagined with a new, larger marketplace and a regular street pattern after the destruction inflicted by the Mongol invasion. The revitalized Wrocław replaced scattered settlements with a grid of new streets around the central marketplace. Béla IV founded (New) Buda on a hilltop after the Mongol invasion, to form an urban ensemble with Pest and Óbuda (Old Buda) on both sides of the Danube.

The new towns of East Central Europe were populated mainly by immigrants. Newcomers in Hungary of the twelfth century were mostly Romance speakers (sometimes called "Walloons," although not all of them came from Wallonia) who settled near Pécs, Eger, and Oradea, in the region of Srem, and near the royal residences Esztergom and Székesfehérvár. In the thirteenth century, however, immigrants came mostly from the German lands. In Poland and Bohemia, most newcomers were from the German lands, although Wrocław also had a neighborhood of Walloon weavers.

In Central Europe, the prosperity of the fourteenth century was disrupted in the fifteenth by the Hussite Wars, but a new wave of urbanization began in the later fifteenth century with the establishment of mining towns. Copper mining expanded in the Hungarian kingdom, in Banská Bystrica (today in Slovakia) and other towns. The mastermind of the mining agenda was John Thurzó, an entrepreneur from Cracow established in Hungary. Thurzó pioneered new technologies and, with investments from the Fuggers of Augsburg, turned enormous profit.

Central European towns were transformed in the thirteenth century through the arrival of immigrant merchants and craftspeople and the introduction of German law; similar processes occurred on the peripheries of East Central Europe in the fourteenth century. Foreign merchants and craftspeople came from Poland to Red Ruthenia after the Polish conquest (see chapter 48). Whereas the law of Magdeburg was normally granted only to Catholic Christian citizens, Casimir III, in his 1356 privilege for Lemberg (today Lviv, in western Ukraine), allowed the Armenians, Jews, Ruthenians, and Tatars (Muslim Mongols) to establish their own communities either with Magdeburg law or a legal system of their choice. In addition to the Catholic citizens, Armenians set up their own municipal community with Magdeburg law in 1378; Jews had their autonomous administration in 1367, regulated by their own law. Ruthenians would have their separate government in the sixteenth century, but the minority Mongols did not have a distinct administration. Outside of Lviv, smaller towns of Red Ruthenia were granted Magdeburg law in the later fourteenth century.

Gediminas was also invested in attracting merchants and craftspeople to Lithuania: he wrote to the councils of north German towns to recruit them. Vilnius became a major city in the fourteenth century. Merchants and artisans lived in the lower town at the foot of the castle; on the other side of the river was a pagan-dominated settlement; a "Ruthenian city" hosted newcomers from the grand duchy's eastern lands; and German inhabitants gathered around the church of St. Nicholas. Jogaila granted the citizens of Vilnius the law of Magdeburg in 1387. In the Ruthenian lands of the grand duchy, however, towns did not receive rights of municipal autonomy.

In the Romanian principalities of Wallachia and Moldavia, towns emerged on trade routes leading to the Danube and the Black Sea in the fourteenth century. Despite Byzantine influences in the region, the models for the new towns came from Central Europe. German, Hungarian, and Armenian merchants and craftspeople were attracted by political stability and economic opportunity. The municipal institutions were inspired by those of Transylvania in Wallachia and of Poland in Moldavia. Câmpulung, for example, began as a settlement of Saxon (German-speaking) colonists arriving from Transylvania. They occupied the central area of the future town, with later Romanian inhabitants moving into the outskirts, as shown by the distribution of Orthodox churches. The leader of the community was a judge (*județ*) elected by the community. At Baia, in Moldavia, a settlement was in existence in the thirteenth century; it was destroyed by the Hungarian army in 1345 or 1347. Settlers from Transylvania came to Baia, with the local Saxons being mentioned several times in the fifteenth century. The town had a leader called *șoltuz* (from the German word for the hereditary advocate, the *Schultheiss*) assisted by a council of twelve *pârgari* (from the Hungarian word for burgher, *polgár*).

Italian, Central European, and Byzantine urban institutions intersected in the Balkans. Zadar, Trogir, Split, and Ragusa (today Dubrovnik) in Dalmatia obtained privileges of municipal autonomy from the Hungarian king; they were inspired by Italian models. Stephen Uroš I emulated Central European rulers and recruited foreign settlers to populate the mining towns of Serbia and Bosnia. The "guests," mostly Germans, came from Slovakia and Transylvania. The centralized imperial administration of Byzantium, by contrast, did not allow for the development of autonomous municipal authorities in Macedonia. Byzantine towns were primarily fortified settlements that housed garrisons headed by agents of the emperor. Privileges were limited to tax exemptions in Monemvasia in 1284 and 1416, and the right to elect a representative in Ioannina in 1319 (both towns are today in Greece). These minimal rights disappeared after the Ottoman conquest.

In Bulgaria, Byzantine rule in the eleventh and twelfth centuries led to a certain revival of urbanism with administrative, religious, and military centers. New towns, however, arose primarily during the Second Bulgarian Empire along the Danube and on the coast of the Black Sea. Venetian and Genoese merchants were attracted to Bulgarian towns that strategically connected Central Europe with Byzantium; they did not, however, receive institutions of civic government. Tărnovo, the residence of the emperor, was the most important urban agglomeration.

Just like the Germanic *burg*, the East Slavic word for town, *gorod*, originally referred to a fortified settlement. Towns in the lands of Rus' typically emerged around fortified seats of power where diverse economic activities developed that included trade and crafts as well as military, administrative, and religious functions. Kiev was exceptional in that, with a population between 35,000 and 50,000 inhabitants, it was comparable in size to London or Paris and was the largest city of the eastern half of Europe after Constantinople. Kiev's cityscape was dominated by the hilltop residences of the prince and the metropolitan. Crafts that developed in Kiev and other Rus' towns were sometimes inspired by Byzantine techniques.

The eleventh and twelfth centuries were a golden age for Rus' towns. A town's kremlin was the fortified core where administrative and military functions were concentrated. Outside was the *posad*, the main commercial suburb with its marketplace that was often walled and sometimes subdivided; other suburbs could spread around. Unlike in Western and Central Europe, in Rus' it was rare to have the entire town enclosed in a common fortification. *Slobody* ("freedoms") were rural districts dependent on a town. While most urban buildings were of timber, masonry churches first appeared in Kiev, Chernigov, and Novgorod under Iaroslav the Wise. In Kiev, Iaroslav built a complex that symbolized the center of the Orthodox world in Rus': it included the Cathedral of St. Sophia and other churches along with the palaces of the prince and the metropolitan. Contrary to towns in Western and Central Europe where cathedrals were located on marketplaces or places where they were fully visible and integrated into the urban layout, in Rus' towns they were separated by walls. Monasteries were also typically built in or near urban centers. The Monastery of the Caves, for example, was built on top of caves that had served as dwellings for hermits and were located three kilometers (less than two miles) south of Kiev.

Although Rus' towns did not have municipal rights that could be compared to those of Central Europe, some of them developed original institutions of local governance. Novgorod established its autonomy as Riurikids competed with one another in the eleventh century. Political leadership rested with the bishop, the boyars (descendants of tribal leaders), and the agents of the prince (the *tysiatskie*, "thousanders"). By the mid-twelfth century, Novgorod's assembly of free citizens, the *veche*, elected the bishop, elected a boyar as governor (*posadnik*) who administered justice jointly with the prince, and selected the prince. By the end of the thirteenth century the *posadnik*, the head of the *tysiatskie*, and the archimandrite were elected annually. The Council of Lords, mentioned since the fourteenth century, was a smaller group of agents of the prince and representatives of the neighborhoods ("ends") that had a consultative function. The regime of Novgorod, although it was dominated by boyars, allowed all "free men" some degree of participation.

Pskov (today in northwestern Russia) had similar institutions. By contrast, Moscow and other towns of northeastern Rus' had no *veche*. Moscow was administered by a governor who represented the grand prince. The merchants and craftspeople, military men, clergy and monks, secular elites, and their domestic personnel had separate organizations; a sense of urban community fostered by common institutions did not develop. Towns of Rus' expanded in the fifteenth century, especially Moscow, the largest city with a population estimated at between 50,000 and 100,000. Prosperity was exemplified by major building projects in the late fifteenth century: after a devastating fire in 1476, Ivan III invited Italian architects to rebuild the churches and palaces of the Kremlin (see chapter 70).

Genoese immigrants settled in the late thirteenth century in the Crimea and established a thriving entrepôt in Caffa. In 1307–8, however, Khan Toqta forced them to leave. The Genoese soon returned, and in 1314 Khan Özbeg offered them his protection. By the late thirteenth century, Tana, at the mouth of the river Don in the Sea of Azov, was the easternmost colony of Italian (Genoese) merchants on the trade route to East Asia. In 1332, Khan Özbeg gave Venetians permission to settle in the town in a separated, fortified area under the jurisdiction of their consul. When Khan Janibek activated his anti-Christian policy in 1343, he nonetheless allowed a smaller community of Italians to remain in Tana, mostly on a temporary basis. It was still there at the time of the Ottoman conquest in 1475.

FURTHER READING

Krekić, Bariša, ed. *Urban Society of Eastern Europe in Premodern Times*. Berkeley: University of California Press, 1987.

Lück, Heiner. "Urban Law: The Law of Saxony and Magdeburg." In *The Oxford Handbook of European Legal History*, edited by Heikki Pihlajamäki, Markus D. Dubber, and Mark Godfrey, 1–40. Oxford: Oxford University Press, 2018.

Lukin, Pavel V. "The Veche and the 'Council of Lords' in Medieval Novgorod: Hanseatic and Russian Data." *Russian History* 41 (2014): 458–503.

Nagy, Balázs, Martyn Rady, Katalin Szende, and András Vadas, eds. *Medieval Buda in Context*. Brill's Companions to European History 10. Leiden: Brill, 2016.

Rădvan, Laurențiu. *At Europe's Border: Medieval Towns in the Romanian Principalities*. East Central and Eastern Europe in the Middle Ages, 450–1450, 7. Leiden: Brill, 2010.

Rădvan, Laurențiu. "Towns and Cities." In *The Routledge Handbook of East Central and Eastern Europe in the Middle Ages, 500–1300*, edited by Florin Curta, 245–64. London: Routledge, 2022.

Szende, Katalin. "*Iure Theutonico*? German Settlers and Legal Frameworks for Immigration to Hungary in an East-Central European Perspective." In *Minority Influences in Medieval Society*, edited by Nora Berend, 83–102. London: Routledge, 2021.

Szende, Katalin, and Felicitas Schmieder. "Cities and Towns in Medieval Central Europe." In *The Oxford Handbook of Medieval Central Europe*, edited by Nada Zečević and Daniel Ziemann, 267–90. Oxford: Oxford University Press, 2022.

60

GLOBAL CONNECTIONS: THE SILK ROAD AND THE GERMAN HANSE

Keywords in this chapter: Silk Road, trading posts, commercial agreements

East Central and Eastern Europe were strategically located between the Baltic Sea that linked with Northern and Western Europe and the Black Sea that gave access to Central Asia and the Near East. These two major zones of commercial networks were connected with one another through the river routes of Eastern Europe. Merchants had traveled on these routes connecting Northern Europe with Byzantium (see chapter 33) since the Viking age. The same routes gained renewed importance during the heyday of the Mongol empire and with the establishment of the German Hanse.

The phrase "Silk Road" was coined in the nineteenth century by a German explorer, Baron Ferdinand von Richthofen, to designate a series of land routes that connected Europe and China and thrived during various periods of history; one of these eras was the Pax Mongolica that followed the invasions of the thirteenth century. The Silk Road(s) formed a zone of exchange in Eurasia. The merchants themselves usually did not travel all the way from China to Europe. The objects they transported did, while the merchants connected the nodal points of that network. The main road departed from Xi'an in western China and led to Dunhuang, a major town in the northwest of the country. Roads left Dunhuang in westward directions, leading either to Lahore (today in Pakistan) or to the major trade hub that was Samarkand (today in Uzbekistan). From Samarkand, the main route to the southwest went through Baghdad and from there either to Damascus and Antioch, or to Constantinople; another route left from Samarkand in a northwesterly direction and reached the Volga and the Crimea.

Long-distance trade was expanding in the thirteenth century, and the Mongols tapped into that. Venice, initially a Byzantine enclave in Italy, had long had special connections with the East; the 1204 conquest of Constantinople by Crusaders created an integrated political zone that allowed Venetians to expand their commercial network to the Black Sea area. The Genoese followed in their footsteps after the fall of the Latin Empire, obtaining privileges from Emperor Michael VIII Palaiologos through the Treaty of Nymphaion (1261). At the time of the Mongol invasions, merchants on the Eurasian Silk Roads were predominantly Muslims and their common language was Persian. The Mongol khans were very invested in promoting trade, which, once the conquests were completed, became their most important source of income. The khans were welcoming of travelers of any religion, guaranteed freedom of movement, provided merchants with safety on the roads and with the necessary infrastructure, and the customs fees they collected were low. They made treaties with Byzantium, the Genoese, and the Venetians, as well as with the Mamluks of Egypt, to regulate and facilitate trade, creating a zone of easy transport going from the Volga to the Nile.

Silk was not the only product exchanged along the Silk Roads, although it was one of them. What medieval Europeans called spices was traded on the routes between Europe, Asia, and the Near East. Those could be actual spices (pepper, cinnamon, ginger, cloves), but also dyes for textiles, frankincense, sugar, or even precious stones – any small and costly item that was worth carrying over long distances. Transporting these products was expensive, especially on land roads. The roads of Central Asia, however, were uniquely placed to connect China, the Islamic world, and Europe; demand for these products made the profits attractive to merchants and investors despite the costs of transport.

For the first time in the thirteenth century, some merchants, ambassadors, and missionaries were able to make the entire trip from Europe to China relatively easily. Some of these travelers reported on what they had seen. William of Rubruck, for example, a Flemish Franciscan missionary, traveled through the Crimea and Sarai on the way to Karakorum in 1253–55 and left a detailed report of his experiences. Another Franciscan named John of Plano Carpini went to Karakorum in 1245–47 as papal envoy. He crossed Bohemia and Poland on the way to Kiev, whence he moved to the east to reach the Volga River. The khans gave him and his companions permission to use their highly effective post-horse service, the *yam*, to reach Mongolia at record speed. John's companions included two friars from Bohemia, Stephen and Ceslaus, as well as Benedict the Pole, a friar from Wrocław. Benedict joined them to help with his knowledge of Slavic languages as they crossed Eastern Europe. Benedict's experience was described in two accounts that were recorded upon their return from Mongolia, as the team went on a lecture tour throughout Europe.

Northern Europe did not have anything resembling the political stability of the Mongol Empire or even the short-lived political integration favored by the Latin Empire of Constantinople. Long-distance trade there was dominated by German merchants scattered through various towns and territories. Since the twelfth century, Lübeck, with its Baltic connections, became the model merchant town. The foundations of the German Hanse, an association of north German towns, were put in place between 1150 and 1250. In the context of political fragmentation and underdeveloped infrastructure, the Hanse made things easier. Hanseatic membership lowered the costs of trade in manifold ways: privileges freed merchants from these towns from fees; infrastructure reduced the costs of storage; networks provided easier access to various resources. In addition to the member towns, the Hanse counted on trading posts (*Kontore*) in London, Bergen, Bruges, and Novgorod. Contacts in the lands of Rus' allowed Hanseatic merchants, whose common language was Low German, to send their sons to learn Russian in the households of boyars to facilitate interactions in Novgorod. The Hanse even became a political force of its own that could declare embargos when rulers contradicted their interests. Hanseatic towns were regularly involved, for example, in conflicts with the Danish kings.

During the Early Middle Ages, the river routes of Eastern Europe connected Scandinavia with Byzantium. In the Late Middle Ages, they provided vital connections between the expanding commercial networks of the German Hanse and of the Mongol Empire. Both Smolensk (today in Russia) and Kiev are located on the Dnieper that flows into the Black Sea; Smolensk is near the Daugava that reaches the Baltic Sea. Lviv is on the Poltva River that flows into the Bug, a tributary of the Narew that joins the Vistula. It is also in close vicinity of the Dniester that flows into the Black Sea. The Dniester was difficult to navigate in its upper part, so merchants instead used a land route that became known as the *via Thartarica*, the "Mongol road."

While Central European merchants did not themselves travel to Central Asia, those from the lands of Rus' did. The integration of Rus' into the Mongol Empire facilitated their access to Asian markets. The territories of the Golden Horde included important trade centers – Samarkand, Astrakhan, Sarai, and Sudak in the Crimea – that were regularly visited by Rus' merchants. Merchants from Bohemia, Silesia, and Poland frequented the Fondaco dei Tedeschi in Venice, the headquarters of the German merchants in the city. Hungary was connected to those networks through the strong presence of Venetian merchants in the kingdom; Hungarian merchants had access to the Adriatic coast through Croatia. Merchants from Poland and Silesia were also present in Kiev, where they traded alongside their colleagues from Vienna, Genoa, and Venice, until Kiev began to decline in the later thirteenth century. For a while, the place of Kiev was taken by Vladimir (now Volodymyr) in Volhynia, then by Lviv.

Lviv gained importance after Casimir III's conquest: Polish merchants profited from the connection to the lands of Rus' through Red Ruthenia. Casimir sought to create a Polish monopoly of trade with Lviv; Charles IV responded by making arrangements with the Teutonic Order to allow merchants from Bohemia access to Ruthenia through Prussia and Lithuania. Hungarian merchants also maintained connections to Lviv in the later fourteenth century, and Casimir's ineffective plan was abandoned. Polish merchants, however, did not have direct contact to the Black Sea: they relied on their colleagues from Wallachia and Moldavia who connected the Black Sea trade with Lviv and Brașov (Kronstadt) in Transylvania. Further north, Vilnius, Riga, and Tallinn were fully involved in trade with the Hanse but did not have direct connections to the Black Sea either. When Vytautas settled Karaite merchants (Turkic-speaking Jews from the Crimea, see chapter 63) in Trakai, it was likely in an attempt to facilitate commercial contacts between Lithuania and the Black Sea.

The Hanse was the first European trade organization that had global dimensions. Although primarily a North European institution, it was connected with, and to some extent depended upon, trade with Asia, Africa, and the North Atlantic. The core of the Hanseatic network was in the Baltic and the North seas, from the *Kontore* in the west to that of Novgorod in the east. In fact, the first *Kontor* that came into being, ca. 1200, was in Novgorod, at Peterhof, while that of London, the Steelyard, was only established in 1282. Through the North Atlantic, the Hanseatic trade connections reached Iceland and Greenland; through the English Channel to the Middle Atlantic, and from there, to the Mediterranean and North Africa; through the eastern Baltic, to the river routes that connected with the Black Sea and thus Asia and the Near East. Some of the main commodities involved were beeswax, furs, timber, tar, flax, honey, wheat, and rye – all brought from the eastern parts of the Baltic Sea. The Hanseatic merchants traded with cloth from England and Flanders and with salt from northern Germany, France, and Portugal. Stockfish came from Norway and salted herring from Scania (southern Sweden). Furthermore, the Hanseatic merchants accessed rare items from Asia or the eastern Mediterranean such as silk, spices, or frankincense. Dyes and mordants sourced by the Hanse fulfilled the needs of European textile producers: potash, used to bleach textiles, was exported from Poland and Finland; cochineal, a red dye, also came from Poland. Trade connections boosted economic production and made local economies dependent upon these networks.

Trade on the Silk Roads declined in the later fourteenth century as the Mongol Empire became regionally fragmented and the Ming took over China. Some of the foreign products that arrived in Central and Eastern Europe through eastern connections were still mentioned in the sources, although it is often unclear if they came from Asia or from the Near East. They included spices (pepper, saffron, ginger, and others); dried fruit (figs, raisins); medicines; soap; dying products (indigo, brazilwood); luxury textiles (silk, cotton); carpets; and precious stones. Rare products that are mentioned include a parrot in Mazovia and exotic candies in Bohemia. Moreover, Rus' merchants imported horses from the lands of the Mongols and paper from China. The Hanse had a wide-ranging and well-organized distribution system that made consumer products available on the markets of Europe. Salted herring and stockfish from Scandinavia were sold in Bohemia and Central Europe, Lviv and the lands of Rus', and as far as the cities of northern Italy. Animal oil and fat from Northern Europe and beeswax from Central and Eastern Europe could be purchased across the continent.

Central and Eastern Europe, with key trade centers such as Kiev and Lviv, played a crucial role in connecting European markets with those of Asia and the Near East throughout the Middle Ages. As the merchant roads of Central Asia opened direct connections to China to clerics and diplomats during the age of the Mongol Empire, West Europeans who wanted to reach them crossed Central Europe and the lands of Rus'. When, in the later fifteenth century, Europeans expanded their travel routes across the Atlantic and around Africa, this drastically changed the game. A few merchants from Moscow and Tver are known to have traveled to Ormus and India, and a merchant from Cracow went to Alexandria in the late fifteenth century. By that time, however, the leading role of Central and Eastern European merchants in connecting Europe and Asia had come to an end.

FURTHER READING

Ciocîltan, Virgil. *The Mongols and the Black Sea Trade in the Thirteenth and Fourteenth Centuries*. East Central and Eastern Europe in the Middle Ages, 450–1450, 20. Leiden: Brill, 2012.

Dollinger, Philippe. *The German Hansa*. Stanford: Stanford University Press, 1970.

Harreld, Donald J., ed. *A Companion to the Hanseatic League*. Leiden: Brill, 2015.

Myśliwski, Grzegorz. "Central Europe." In *Agrarian Change and Crisis in Europe, 1200–1500*, edited by Harry Kitsikopoulos, 250–91. Routledge Research in Medieval Studies 1. New York: Routledge, 2011.

Wubs-Mrozewicz, Justyna, and Stuart Jenks, eds. *The Hanse in Medieval and Early Modern Europe*. The Northern World 60. Leiden: Brill, 2012.

61

MIGRATIONS AND CULTURAL CHANGE

Keywords in this chapter**:** Wends, Magdeburg law

The High and Late Middle Ages were characterized by movements of population across Central and Eastern Europe that had significant long-term consequences. The most numerous immigrants spoke German dialects. It is estimated that about 200,000 German-speaking settlers migrated to the lands of East Central Europe in the twelfth century, and another 200,000 in the thirteenth century – at a time when the population of the Holy Roman Empire was between 5 and 6 million. Germans were not the only migrants. Francophones, Wallachians, and Poles also moved to new regions where they contributed to cultural change. Jews, Armenians, and Muslims who migrated to Central and Eastern Europe created communities of religious minorities (see chapter 63).

At the end of the Middle Ages, parts of East Central Europe, formerly populated by Slavs or Balts, had been partly or completely Germanized; in others, the migrant population had been assimilated by the host society and become Slavicized. What is now eastern Germany was peopled by Slavic tribes in the Early Middle Ages. At the end of the fifteenth century, few still spoke Slavic between the Elbe and the Oder – primarily the Wends in the Hanoverian Wendland and the Sorbs in Lusatia (see insert 61.1). By 1500, Poland, Bohemia, and Hungary had towns and cities in which the dominant language was German, while the population in the surrounding countryside spoke Polish, Czech, or Hungarian. The divide was even starker in the Baltic countries between the German-speaking upper class of burghers, clergy, and nobles, and a Baltic or Finno-Ugric population in the countryside that had been little affected by cultural change.

Political and social circumstances contributed to linguistic and cultural shifts. In Brandenburg, the Slavic rural population was subjugated by German secular and religious elites. German settlers were tasked not only with cultivating the land, but also with contributing to political integration and religious conversion. Slavic peasants were occasionally taken from their land and resettled in less attractive places to make room for newcomers. The Teutonic Knights actively promoted the settlement of conquered Prussia. The migrant

INSERT 61.1. SLAVS AND WENDS

The ethnonym Wends had been associated with the Western Slavs since the Early Middle Ages. Fredegar, for example, called Wends the Slavs who were ruled by Samo (see chapter 6). The name is believed to derive from that of the Venedi, a people mentioned by Tacitus and other ancient Roman authors. Wends became the name given by Germans to the Slavs with whom they came into contact; that designation became very common in the later Middle Ages, and bilingual texts make clear that "Wend" in German was understood as being the same as "S(c)lavus" (Slav) in Latin. Following the migration of German settlers in the thirteenth century, villages in what is now eastern Germany were often prefixed with the words Wendisch (Slavic) and Deutsch (German) to flag the predominant language in the community. Hanseatic towns located in formerly Slavic territories (in what is now northeastern and eastern Germany) were also called "Wendisch" towns. Ironically, however, the Wend towns of the later Middle Ages, dominated by German citizens, implemented discriminatory policies against Wends (Slavs) who moved to these towns from the countryside, where the Slavic language was still spoken.

A tribe that lived on the territory of modern-day Latvia was also called "Wends" in German sources of the thirteenth century. These Wends had a material culture that was similar to that of the Baltic Livs. They came to live near the castle and town of Cēsis, in Livonia. The German name of that town is Wenden. Whether the Wends of Livonia had anything to do with the Slavic Wends remains unclear.

peasants settled in villages of a new type, regulated by German law and divided into equal plots. Villages under Prussian law, by contrast, had smaller plots for peasants paying higher rents. Prussian peasants were punished for their multiple uprisings against the Teutonic Order, whose regime separated newcomers from the native population, giving the latter an inferior status. Subjugated and discriminated against, forcefully converted to Christianity by German clerics, the Prussian peasants were eventually assimilated. A native Baltic aristocracy was maintained nonetheless in Curonia (western Lithuania) until well into the sixteenth century.

However, the oppressive context of Prussia and parts of Brandenburg was not representative of the population movements of the High Middle Ages. In most cases, migration was initiated not by conquerors but by local rulers and lords. Hungary had been known as an immigrant-friendly kingdom since the early eleventh century. Transylvania became the target of German and Flemish emigration in the mid-twelfth century; in the thirteenth century, migrants came from the Rhine and Mosel regions. They settled in the south and southeast of Transylvania around two towns, Sibiu (Hermannstadt) and Braşov (Kronstadt), but a strong community was also created around the silver mines of Rodna and in Byzturch (now Bistriţa), in northeastern Transylvania. The Saxons of Transylvania, as they came to be known, were given privileges by Andrew II in 1224. Immigration to town and country was considerable and turned parts of Transylvania into enclaves of

German language and culture. In the mid-thirteenth century, immigrants to the region of Spiš (now in Slovakia, then part of Hungary) came from Poland, Halych, and Silesia. The northern mountain ranges were populated by Slovak settlers who came to predominate. Many Rus' moved to Hungary in the thirteenth and fourteenth centuries, particularly from Halych-Volhynia (the western parts of present-day Ukraine), after the Mongol invasion.

Cultural shifts often had to do with the attitudes of the secular and clerical elites. Rügen might have been conquered by Valdemar I (see chapter 43), but the Slavic dynasty remained in place as Prince Jaromar and his descendants became vassals of the Danish kings. The princes of Rügen recruited peasant settlers from Denmark and the German lands. In the mainland part of the principality, Danish and German settlers were particularly numerous, and by the early fourteenth century the German language dominated. Names of noble men and women recorded in charters reveal the cosmopolitan nature of the population: many had Slavic given names and Danish patronyms. On the island, by contrast, there were fewer immigrants. Slavic peasants contributed to woodland clearings but built new villages in their traditional, more dispersed fashion. The Slavic language was maintained longer on the island; the last Slavic-speaking woman there died in the fifteenth century. Like the princes of Rügen, the Slavic dukes of Western Pomerania became strongly influenced by German court culture in the thirteenth century; Christianization was spearheaded by German clerics. Western Pomerania had been Christianized late and did not have a strong ecclesiastical organization. German newcomers intermingled with the Slavic peasants, and the German language dominated by the end of the Middle Ages.

Assimilation processes, meanwhile, proceeded in opposite directions in Lower and Upper Silesia. Settlement with foreign peasants was the most intensive in Lower Silesia, as was the immigration of German knights. In the thirteenth century the courts of the Piast dukes came under the strong influence of German aristocratic culture. The Lower Silesian countryside was, as names of peasants recorded in charters reveal, a meeting place of Germans, Francophones, and Slavs who often lived in the same villages. In the longer term, most Slavs and Francophones adopted German, which had become the majority language. In Upper Silesia, by contrast, the courts of the Piasts remained predominantly of Slavic culture. In the countryside, the descendants of German immigrants assimilated with the majority Slavic population so that, by the end of the Middle Ages, the rural population was of diverse ancestry but predominantly of Slavic language and culture.

In Red Ruthenia, the rural population of the later fourteenth century was not only ethnically diverse, but also divided between Catholic and Orthodox Christians. Assimilation mostly followed religious lines. The Wallachian settlers were eventually absorbed into the Ruthenian peasantry with whom they shared their Orthodox beliefs. In the towns where Polish outnumbered German citizens, Catholic German settlers were gradually Polonized. Wallachians and Ruthenians, Germans and Poles spoke very different languages, but that played a more limited role than the religious difference.

Cohabitation of newcomers and older populations was, overall, peaceful in East Central Europe during the period of migration. Lords were careful not to infringe on the rights and resources of those who already lived there, and the local populations profited from the arrival of settlers. Locals learned from the migrants' more effective methods and techniques, and the entire process led to economic prosperity for all (see chapters 58 and 59). Moreover, in most regions the German law was eventually granted not only to the newcomers but to the local Slavic and Hungarian population as well, which profited everyone.

In Central Europe, German was the primary language of international trade; it was also the language of the legal culture of Magdeburg law. Unsurprisingly, German became dominant in towns and cities where wealthy merchants occupied positions in the municipal governments. Arrangements could be made, however, to accommodate diverse communities. In Buda, where the twelve councilors and the judge were elected by the burghers, members of government were originally prosperous German-speaking merchants. In the early fifteenth century, under pressure from Hungarian-speaking citizens, two council seats were reserved for Hungarians. After 1439, the municipal council was evenly divided with six German and six Hungarian councilors; the position of judge alternated between the two communities. Oaths of the judges and councilors were delivered in both German and Hungarian. In the overall population, Germans and Hungarians tended to keep to themselves, having their separate guilds, markets, and churches. The population of Red Ruthenian towns included Catholic Poles, Orthodox Ruthenians, Jews, and sometimes Christian Armenians. They typically lived side by side in the same towns but had their own neighborhoods, churches, hospitals, schools, guilds, and fraternities.

Tensions between ethnic groups in Poland first emerged among churchmen. Polish churchmen jealously defended the autonomy of the Polish church and resented the growing influence of German-speaking friars and the granting of ecclesiastic posts to German-speaking clerics. Jacob Świnka, archbishop of Gniezno (d. 1314), passionately defended the rights of Polish churchmen against their German-speaking colleagues, and his anti-German rhetoric did not refrain from xenophobic tones. The 1285 synod of Łęczyca (near Łódź, in central Poland), presided over by the archbishop, forbade the appointment of priests and schoolteachers who did not speak Polish. John Muskata (d. 1320), a German-speaking Silesian who became bishop of Cracow, was accused of favoring German-speaking clerics and became the lightning rod of conservative Polish clerics.

In eastern Germany, the "paragraph on the Wends" came to be introduced in the status of guilds since the mid-fourteenth century. The clause stipulated that guild members were to be honest, born free, and not born out of wedlock; moreover, prospective guild members had to assert that they were of German descent and not Wends. At around the same time, guilds of Livonian towns forbade membership to "non-Germans." These clauses were introduced in a period of economic instability after the Black Death; guilds sought to protect their rights by limiting access to new members. They did that by distancing themselves from the lower classes and the peasant population; in the towns of East Germany and Livonia, use of the Slavic and Baltic languages signaled unwanted groups.

The populations of the Crimea, the Volga region, and the steppes underwent cultural and ethnic changes under the domination of the Golden Horde. At the time of the Mongol conquest, these regions were populated by a variety of Turkish peoples such as the Oghuz and the Cumans who, despite the similarity of the Turkic languages they spoke, were of diverse heritage and did not form any cultural or political unity. By the end of the fourteenth century, these various peoples had merged with the descendants of the immigrant Mongols. Their common language had become Turkic, they were now Muslims, but they shared a Mongol identity and related to Mongol traditions.

FURTHER READING

Donecker, Stefan. "Locals and Immigrants in Medieval Central Europe." In *The Oxford Handbook of Medieval Central Europe*, edited by Nada Zečević and Daniel Ziemann, 191–211. Oxford: Oxford University Press, 2022.

Kapral, Myron. "Legal Regulation and National (Ethnic) Differentiation in Lviv, 1350–1600." In *An der Grenze des lateinischen Europa: Integration und Segregation in Rotreußen, 1350–1600. On the Frontier of Latin Europe: Integration and Segregation in Red Ruthenia, 1350–1600*, edited by Thomas Wünsch and Andrzej Janeczek, 211–28. Warsaw: Institute of Archaeology and Ethnology of the Polish Academy of Sciences, 2004.

Lee, Joo-Yup. "Some Remarks on the Turkicisation of the Mongols in Post-Mongol Central Asia and the Qipchaqs Steppe." *Acta Orientalia Academiae Scientarum Hungaricae* 71, no. 2 (2018): 121–44.

Marek, Miloš. "The Ways of Immigration of Foreigners into the Medieval Kingdom of Hungary." *Studia Historica Tyrnaviensia* 11–12 (2011): 177–90.

Piskorski, Jan M. "Medieval Colonization in East Central Europe." In *The Germans and the East*, edited by Charles Ingrao and Franz A. J. Szabo, 27–36. Central European Studies. West Lafayette: Purdue University Press, 2008.

Zientara, Benedykt. "Foreigners in Poland in the 10th–15th Centuries: Their Role in the Opinion of Polish Medieval Community." *Acta Poloniae Historica* 29 (1974): 5–28.

Zientara, Benedykt. "Nationality Conflicts in the German-Slavic Borderland in the 13th–14th Centuries and Their Social Scope." *Acta Poloniae Historica* 22 (1970): 207–25.

PART 11

Religion in the High and Late Middle Ages

62

PAGANISM IN THE EASTERN BALTIC

Keywords in this chapter: cremation, sacrifices, sacred groves

Baltic paganism refers to the religious beliefs of the ancient Prussians, Livonians, and Lithuanians. These beliefs evolved in different contexts in the Late Middle Ages. Prussians were subjected to the aggressive conversion policies of the Teutonic Order. In Livonia, it was the bishop of Riga and the Sword-Brothers (later the Livonian Order) who were tasked with the conversion of pagans; Estonians were converted following the Danish conquest. Lithuania, by contrast, remained officially pagan until the conversion of Jogaila in 1386 (see chapter 50). His predecessor Grand Duke Vytenis (d. 1316) is said to have trampled the host in front of Christians and to have shown disrespect for Christian clergy and churches. Such an attitude, however, became rare after him. Lithuanian paganism might have been a sort of "state religion" in the sense that it had a formal status and was actively promoted by the Gediminids, but it was not meant to compete with monotheistic religions. The grand dukes never compelled anyone to subscribe to their religious beliefs. The endurance of paganism had much to do with the political circumstances: avoiding commitment to either Catholic or Orthodox Christianity provided the Gediminids with real advantages.

Cremation burial in shallow pits was practiced by the ancient Prussians, Curonians, Samogitians, and Semigallians. Among the Yotvingians, inhumation was gradually introduced between the tenth and thirteenth centuries. In Lithuania, cremation was practiced up to the time of Jogaila's conversion, as is attested by both contemporary written sources (that describe the ostentatious burning of the dead with horses, weapons, and various goods) and archaeology. Lithuanian burial traditions became more homogeneous following political unification in the thirteenth and fourteenth centuries. Mythological narratives preserved in medieval chronicles attest to the importance that was attached to the cremation of the dead with sacred fire.

Sources often referred to pagan Lithuanians sacrificing roosters, pigs, or oxen; the Livs are said to have sacrificed dogs and goats, which is confirmed by archaeological findings of dogs in burials. Humans were also sacrificed to divinities: two different chroniclers attest to cases of Christian knights who, following auguries, were burned alive while sitting on horseback in full armor. Augurs were said to be able to see the dead reaching the otherworld. Apart from soothsayers and diviners, Baltic paganism does not seem to have had a fully established cast of priests. Peter of Dusburg (a chronicler of the Teutonic Order who wrote in the early fourteenth century) mentioned a man named Krivė who lived in a place called Romow and was considered the equivalent of a "pope" for the pagans. Romow, located in Prussia, was supposedly a religious center to which all Baltic pagans related. However, this does not seem to be more than Peter's attempt to depict paganism as an inverted form of Christianity. No pan-Baltic cult center has so far been found anywhere in the region, nor is there any archaeological evidence suggesting the existence of priests as a special category of individuals.

A bull issued in 1388 by Pope Urban VI mentions a pagan sanctuary that was destroyed where the Vilnius cathedral would later be built, but archaeological investigations failed to uncover any pre-Christian structure. In fact, in his correspondence with the papacy, Jogaila had obvious reasons to exaggerate the importance of the pagan cult prior to conversion. Baltic pagans nonetheless believed in the supernatural value of certain religious sites, such as sacred groves and holy fires. Mindaugas is said to have refused to enter a sacred grove after a hare had crossed his path. The village of Romainiai, in Samogitia, was destroyed by Crusaders in 1294/1300 as it was considered a cult place; a sacred forest was mentioned there in 1398, and a sanctuary, probably in the same place, was demolished by Jogaila in 1413. According to Peter of Dusburg, Prussians believed that trees in sacred groves were not to be cut, the soil there was to be left untouched, and animals were not to be killed; only authorized persons were allowed to enter the groves. Several place names called Šventaragis ("sacred horn") might refer to cult places, typically on hills or highlands. Holy groves (*alḱos* in Lithuanian) are also alluded to in many place names.

Carved stones known as *kamienie baby* ("old women made of stone") have been found in Prussia and are strikingly similar to those associated in the thirteenth century with the Cumans in the steppe lands north of the Black and Caspian seas. Some of those carved stones represent women with large breasts, others men with weapons or drinking horns. The meaning that was attached to these statues remains mysterious. The context of the finds in the tenth-to-eleventh-century site of Poganowo (near Kętrzyn, northeastern Poland), however, suggests that the monuments had cultic functions. The carved stone belonged to a complex that comprised a mound surrounded by a circle; close by were a rectangular hearth and large numbers of animal bones hinting at rituals.

A 1249 treaty in Prussia mentioned religious leaders named *tulissones* and *ligaschones* who, among other things, presided over funerary rituals. The word *kunigas*, which today means "priest" in Lithuanian, originally designated a military leader. In fact, in the fourteenth century, the grand dukes were something like high priests. The sacrifice of oxen or other animals, typically by rulers, and the smearing of blood on participants were common practices. Pagan oath rituals were even accepted as binding in treaties with Christian partners.

For example, the 1351 treaty between Kęstutis and Louis of Hungary was confirmed by invocations of the Christian God and of Lithuanian deities, followed by an animal sacrifice by the pagans.

Baltic mythology has been reconstructed based on historical sources, some archaeology, and ethnography. Sources suggest that Prussians venerated the natural world and atmospheric phenomena. Perkūnas ("Thunder"), mentioned in sources throughout the centuries, had a central place in the pantheon of Baltic divinities. The goddess Žvorūna, another important divinity, was associated with hunting. Baltic mythology is thought to be the result of a combination of Indo-European beliefs, characterized by the dominance of male gods, and older beliefs in which feminine divinities were at the forefront. Older goddesses were associated with life and death, health, and energy (for example, Laima and Ragana); male gods were connected to vegetation, animals, the elements, weapons, and power (the main gods were Dievas, Perkūnas, and Velinas).

Unlike Prussia, Livonia and Estonia did not experience immigration of foreign peasant settlers (see chapter 58). Outside urban centers, the native population thus had more limited exposure to the dissemination of Christian beliefs and practices. As a result, Christianization there long remained formal and superficial, more than anywhere else. Parish churches were far apart even in Prussia; preachers typically relied on interpreters. In Estonia, parish and private churches appeared after the Danish conquest. The dead were then increasingly buried in churchyards, but village cemeteries continued to be used. However, innovations in burial customs, such as west-orientation and the absence of grave goods, suggest that Christian practices were disseminated early. Nonetheless, in southern Estonia cremation was practiced well into the sixteenth century. Sacred natural sites such as groves and trees long continued to be visited by country people who made offerings there. Stones with cup-marks for offerings, common since the Iron Age, continued to be used; holy springs were associated with healing. Clerics of the fifteenth century, who had a great interest in the beliefs and practices of rural populations, tended to conflate them with paganism and heresy.

Whereas Prussia, Livonia, and Estonia had originally pagan native populations ruled by newcomer Christian upper-classes, Lithuania was in the unique situation of having pagan rulers administering a largely monotheistic grand duchy. From the mid-thirteenth to the late fourteenth century, the pagan Lithuanian grand dukes ruled over vast Rus' territories with a Christian Orthodox population, not to mention minorities of Jews and Muslim Mongols (see chapters 49 and 63). Far from being antagonistically opposed to Christianity, the grand dukes were accommodating to various religious beliefs and welcomed Christians into their land. Gediminas, in particular, went out of his way – as his letters to the municipal councils and mendicant convents of German towns attest – to attract Christian settlers and merchants from the German lands. Churches probably existed in Vilnius since the early fourteenth century. Mendicants were even welcome, if their enthusiastic proselytism did not cause trouble (some were condemned to death for their trouble-making behavior). Ruthenians from the eastern parts of the grand duchy were also present in Vilnius and other towns of Lithuania.

The formal conversion of Lithuanians began under the reign of Jogaila. The conversion of Samogitia, incorporated into the grand duchy in the early fifteenth century, took place even later. Contemporary sources attest to how quickly the conversion was implemented, which suggests that by that time the population had been quite familiar with Christian practices, so that the change did not come across as a complete break with the past. Neither Lithuania nor Samogitia experienced a "pagan reaction" comparable to what had happened in the early phase of Christianization in Poland or Hungary (see chapter 42). Paganism, despite its status as "state religion," lacked a proper clergy and institutions to support its continued existence; it was more a set of traditions than an organized religion. By the time of the conversion, Lithuanians had been surrounded by Christians for centuries: not only in the neighboring countries, but also in the grand duchy itself, where pagans were outnumbered by Orthodox Rus', in addition to Catholic merchants and friars in Lithuanian towns. Without being formally baptized, it is likely that by the time of Jogaila most Lithuanians, at least in the upper classes, had been sufficiently exposed to and influenced by Christian practices that conversion was a smooth affair. In fact, many Gediminids who ruled in the Ruthenian parts of the grand duchy had long since converted to Orthodox Christianity. Jogaila's mother herself, Iuliana of Tver, was Orthodox. Gediminids in Podolia had shown sympathy for Catholicism before Jogaila's baptism.

Jerome of Prague (ca. 1369–ca. 1440) was a Camaldolese monk who preached in Lithuania in the early years of Vytautas's reign. He was later interviewed by Aeneas Silvius Piccolomini (the future Pope Pius II) during the Council of Basel about his experience in Lithuania. He told about peasants keeping grass-snakes in their dwellings; others worshipping a fire in a sacred building, tended by "priests" (probably magicians or healers); worshippers of the sun; and rituals in sacred groves. Jerome, however, never explicitly referred to these peasants as "pagans" and did not mention the necessity of baptism. These people were likely formally but superficially Christians; they had been baptized but needed instruction in Christian beliefs and customs. In fact, the women who complained about the felling of holy trees referred to the groves as places where God was worshipped. Religious beliefs at that time were a form of syncretism, rather than of paganism.

FURTHER READING

Baronas, Darius. "Christians in Late Pagan, and Pagans in Early Christian Lithuania: The Fourteenth and Fifteenth Centuries." *Lithuanian Historical Studies* 19 (2014): 51–81.

Baronas, Darius, and S. C. Rowell. *The Conversion of Lithuania: From Pagan Barbarians to Late Medieval Christians*. Vilnius: Institute of Lithuanian Literature and Folklore, 2015.

Gimbutas, Marija. "The Pre-Christian Religion of Lithuania." In *La cristianizzazione della Lituania. Atti del Colloquio internazionale di storia ecclesiastica in occasione del VI centenario della Lituania cristiana, Roma, 24–26 giugno 1987*. Pontifico Comitato di scienze storiche, 13–25. Atti e documenti 2. Città del Vaticano: Libreria editrice vaticana, 1989.

Vaitkevičius, Vykintas. “The Main Features of the State Religion in Thirteenth-Century Lithuania.” *Balto-Slavic Studies* 16 (2004): 331–56.

Valk, Heiki. “Christianisation in Estonia: A Process of Dual-Faith and Syncretism.” In *The Cross Goes North: Processes of Conversion in Northern Europe, AD 300–1300*, edited by Martin O. H. Carver, 571–79. York: York Medieval Press, 2003.

Young, Francis, ed. and trans. *Pagans in the Early Modern Baltic: Sixteenth-Century Ethnographic Accounts of Baltic Paganism*. Leeds: Arc Humanities Press, 2022.

63

JEWS, ARMENIANS, AND MUSLIMS

Keywords in this chapter: Karaites, pogroms, mosques

Jews had lived scattered in parts of Central and Eastern Europe since the Early Middle Ages (see chapter 35). Prague had a Jewish community since the tenth or eleventh century; Kiev might have had one around the same time. By that time, Jewish populations were well established in the Rhineland (especially in Worms, Mainz, and Speyer). In the High Middle Ages, communities of Jewish traders appeared in smaller towns along trade routes that connected Central with Eastern Europe, from Regensburg or Prague to Cracow and Kiev. Moreover, Jewish experts in trade and finance followed in the footsteps of German merchants and craftspeople who migrated to towns of East Central Europe in the twelfth and thirteenth centuries. Jews of Hungary, Poland, Bohemia, and the German lands shared cultural similarities; they were part of the land of Ashkenaz, named in rabbinic writings after a grandson of Noah.

The status of the Jews as a religious minority varied, but there were generally fewer restrictions on their activities in East Central than in Western Europe. Jewish communities grew when rulers and lords had an interest in attracting them and other migrants. Those rulers and lords offered Jews protection and privileges as they did for other newcomers. Prompted by the decisions of the Fourth Lateran Council, Polish churchmen at a synod that took place in 1267 in Wrocław attempted to prevent Jews and Christians from having meals together, to limit the number of synagogues to no more than one per town, and to relegate Jews to separate neighborhoods. However, there is no indication that those restrictions were ever implemented.

More consequential than ecclesiastical legislation were the privileges issued by rulers. In Poland, Bolesław the Pious's 1264 privilege of Kalisz was inspired by those of Frederick II of Austria (1244) and Přemysl Ottokar II for Bohemia (1262). In Hungary, Béla IV produced a similar document in 1251. Those privileges requested that Jews pay a special tax to their ruler but stipulated that they were, in exchange, granted special protection as "servants of the royal chamber." Jewish communities were given various guarantees. It was forbidden to extort toll fees from Jewish merchants that were higher than those paid by their Christian counterparts. A "judge of the Jews" was to solve legal disputes between Jews. Jewish communities were administered according to their own customs; the rights to observe the Sabbath and to take part in their religious rituals were protected. Moreover, unproven accusations of Jews using Christian blood in their religious practices were to be severely punished. In Poland, the rights guaranteed by the Kalisz privilege were extended under Casimir III (whose favorable attitude towards Jews led to the rumor that he had a Jewish mistress): Polish Jews could reside in any place of their choice and were allowed to rent noble estates and to visit municipal bathhouses with Christians. These rights were extended to the Jews of Lithuania in the later fourteenth century.

Plate 63.1. Bracteate (one-sided coin) with a Hebrew inscription ("good blessing") struck in Gniezno for the duke of Great Poland, Przemysław I (1242–57). Wikimedia Commons, the free media repository.

In Hungary and Poland, Jews, trusted by rulers because of being under their direct jurisdiction, were often appointed as tax collectors or mint masters, despite criticism by clergy who, ever since the Fourth Lateran Council, opposed the idea of Jews having authority over Christians. In late twelfth- to late thirteenth-century Poland, some of those mint masters even produced coins with Hebrew inscriptions. Until the thirteenth century, most Jews were involved in long-distance trade. From the thirteenth century on, however, many of them branched off into the business of moneylending, for which demand was increasing as the monetary economy was expanding. Money could be lent against pawns or promissory notes, for large amounts or for the constant needs of daily life. Small loans offered to ordinary or impoverished citizens gained in popularity in the later Middle Ages (see plate 63.1).

Opportunities for Jews to be involved in other economic activities, however, were limited. Jews in Poland and Hungary occasionally purchased or received lands or vineyards as sureties for loans; as urban dwellers, though, they were not much interested in agricultural pursuits. Jews were, as a rule, not allowed to become members of Christian guilds that did double duty as professional organizations and religious confraternities. A rare exception to that rule is known from the small town of Grodno (now Hrodna, in Belarus), where, in 1389, guilds accepted Jewish members. Jewish artisans, however, were active as tailors, shoemakers, and in other professions that responded to the specific needs of their communities. Jewish butchers who prepared kosher meat regularly faced opposition from their Christian counterparts who resented exceptions to their monopoly.

The Karaites were Jews who, not acknowledging the authority of the Talmud, focused their worship on the Torah (the first books of the Bible). Although Christians did not distinguish them from other Jews, they lived separately from rabbinic Jews, who were often hostile to them. Karaites fled the Near East after the First Crusade and found refuge in Byzantium, especially in the Crimea, where they adopted a Turkic language (Kipchak, the language of the Cumans). Some Karaites settled in Trakai, Lithuania, in the late fourteenth century, probably at the request of Vytautas; their community was granted a charter of municipal autonomy in 1441. Other Karaite communities are attested in Red Ruthenia in the early fifteenth century, particularly in Lutsk (Volhynia) and in Halych.

As anti-Jewish sentiments were disseminated in the later Middle Ages from Western Europe, the legal conditions of Jewish life deteriorated in various places. A wave of pogroms started in Austria in 1338 and spread to Bohemia and Moravia; a major pogrom shook Prague in 1389. Moreover, rulers increasingly neglected the enforcement of the protections granted to the Jews of their territories. In Bohemia, Charles IV delegated the protection of Jews to municipal governments who collected the taxes but failed to offer protection, and even strove to expel Jews from their towns. A wave of accusations and expulsions of Jews spread through Silesian towns following the preaching tour of John Capistrano in 1453.

Following the examples of the kings of England and France, Louis of Anjou expelled Jews from Hungary sometime before 1360, although he readmitted them a few years later. Grand Duke Alexander expelled them from Lithuania in 1495 but allowed them to return in 1503. In fourteenth-century Hungary, Jews lost the rights to own property and to be employed as tax collectors. Restrictions were more numerous than in earlier times, and the Jews of Central Europe were not free from experiencing pogroms, violence, and growing intolerance. Nonetheless, in the Late Middle Ages, Jews enjoyed comparatively better positions in Hungary and Poland than in Western Europe, where, by the end of the fifteenth century, they had been expelled from most countries. Royal protections given to them and other minority groups were better maintained.

Armenian Christians, who followed the Monophysite faith, had their own language, literary culture (based on their own script), and churches, and they were the largest non-Greek and non-Orthodox minority in the Byzantine Empire. In the eastern parts of the empire, Armenians had made up the majority of the population since Late Antiquity; minority groups were spread out across the Italian-Byzantine enclaves, the Balkans, and Constantinople. The last autonomous Armenian kingdoms were conquered by Byzantium in the mid-eleventh century. Many Armenians served in the Byzantine military, often in separate units. Despite the success of their integration into Byzantine society, sources attest to recurrent recriminations against their beliefs after the Fourth Ecumenical Council in Chalcedon (451). Relations between the Armenian and Orthodox churches alternated between hostility and pragmatic acceptance; reunification was never achieved.

Armenians settled in the Crimea in the eighth century, mostly as Roman administrators or soldiers (see chapter 35); Armenian merchants appeared in the High Middle Ages. Caffa had an Armenian community in the eleventh century. Armenian merchants lived in Halych in the thirteenth century: the Armenians of Lviv were given their own municipal government in 1378. Armenians had lived in Hungarian towns since at least the twelfth century where they, however, ceased to be mentioned around 1300. In the fourteenth century, Armenians were present in towns of Moldavia and Wallachia; they might have migrated from across the Black Sea and from the Balkans, respectively.

During the eleventh and twelfth centuries, Hungary was home not only to religious minorities of Jews and Armenians but also to Muslims. Of different origins, some Muslims arrived in Hungary from the Balkans, others from the steppe area or from Eastern Europe. They were organized in small groups with varied occupations. Some lived in separate villages (such as that discovered by archaeologists on the outskirts of Orosháza, in south-eastern Hungary), while others worked in towns or were warriors hired as mercenaries. Charters of privileges for Hungarian Muslims have not been preserved but presumably existed and might have been like those for Jews. A variety of sources provide indirect evidence about their legal status. Much like Jews, Muslims paid a special tax, and their right to practice their religion was protected; the king or queen had direct jurisdiction over them. When King Andrew II went on Crusade in 1218 to fight Muslims in the eastern Mediterranean, he promised his wife the revenues of the Hungarian Muslim tax if he were to die on Crusade.

An Andalusi scholar who traveled to Hungary in the mid-twelfth century, Abū Hāmid, opined that King Coloman was very benevolent towards Hungarian Muslims. Abū Hāmid described a variety of circumstances in which some Muslims "serve the kings [of Hungary] and pretend to be Christians, although they practice Islam in secret," while others "do not do any service to Christians, except in war [military service], and practice Islam in the open," with some Muslim men even having multiple wives.[1] The Muslims who had protected status were primarily warriors in the king's army. A papal letter from 1225 that was based on information provided by the archbishop of Esztergom suggests that Hungarian Christian peasants converted to Islam to obtain a more favorable legal status. In fact, there is no indication of mass conversion to Islam in Hungary, and the archbishop's concerns likely reflected his uneasiness at the king's tolerant policies. Hungarian bishops made attempts, in the late eleventh and early twelfth centuries, at obtaining royal support for the conversion of Muslims. These efforts that resulted from crusading fervor did not last long. After that, bishops insisted on restricting the rights of Muslims and on keeping Muslims and Christians apart, but not on conversion.

The Muslims of Hungary had little contact with coreligionists outside of the country; in contrast to European Jews whose communities always remained well connected with one another, the Hungarian Muslims were left to themselves. Abū Hāmid decried how ignorant Hungarian Muslims supposedly were of Islamic practices and beliefs and spent his time teaching them about religious matters. Yāqūt, an Arabic author who traveled to Hungary in the 1220s, was surprised that Hungarian Muslims dressed like ordinary Hungarians and that the men shaved their faces according to European fashion. In fact, some Muslim communities were concerned about their lack of access to Islamic learning and funded some of their members to study abroad. Hungarian Muslim students are known to have studied in Aleppo and Jerusalem. Sources for medieval Hungary do not indicate any

1 Florin Curta, ed., "Abu Hamid on Hungary," in *Medieval Eastern Europe, 500–1300: A Reader* (Toronto: University of Toronto Press, 2024), 133.

animosity between Muslims and Christians. By the fourteenth century, however, Muslim minorities ceased to be mentioned. Muslims, who had always been small, heterogeneous minority groups, appear to have been gradually assimilated.

Islam became the majority religion of the Mongols of the Golden Horde in the fourteenth century. Not only Jews but also Muslims ("Tatars") were mentioned in the charter of privilege of Casimir III for Lviv, which was confirmed throughout the fifteenth century (see chapter 59). The Lviv Muslims were likely Mongol merchants who maintained connections with Muslim lands. Unlike their Jewish and Armenian neighbors, the Lviv Muslims did not avail themselves of the possibility of forming their own municipal government; they nonetheless kept living there as a separate religious group that was fully recognized by the Polish kings.

When, in the later fourteenth century, Khan Tokhtamysh was defeated by a rival, he found an ally in Grand Duke Vytautas of Lithuania (see chapter 49). The Muslim troops of Tokhtamysh and the Christian troops of Vytautas fought together on multiple occasions and the alliance was maintained after Tokhtamysh's 1406 death: the Mongol warriors of Tokhtamysh's son Jalal al-Din provided support to Lithuanians and Poles against the Teutonic Knights at the battle of Grunwald in 1410. It is in those circumstances that Muslim Mongols settled in Lithuania and Poland. When Vytautas and Tokhtamysh returned from their joint expedition against the Golden Horde in southern Rus', they arrived in Lithuania with Mongol warriors and their families. According to the Polish chronicler John Długosz, the Mongols who settled in Poland became Christians, while those who took lands in Lithuania remained Muslims. The Mongols in Poland were probably prisoners forced to move there; those who settled in Lithuania were the companions of Tokhtamysh who had fought alongside Vytautas. These warriors and their families were given lands and became part of the land-owning upper class of the grand duchy.

According to a sixteenth-century source, some Lithuanian towns had communities of Mongols (or Tatars, as they were called) who, as Muslims, had small wooden buildings that served as mosques, albeit without minarets. These mosques had probably already existed earlier. The status of Tatar Muslims is well documented for the sixteenth century in the Polish-Lithuanian Commonwealth, where their rights to build mosques and to train imams and mullahs were protected by the Sejm. Their religious rights had been guaranteed since the period when they first settled in Lithuania.

FURTHER READING

Berend, Nora. *At the Gate of Christendom: Jews, Muslims and 'Pagans' in Medieval Hungary, c. 1000–c. 1300.* Cambridge: Cambridge University Press, 2001.

Berend, Nora. "Northeastern Europe." In *The Cambridge History of Judaism*. Vol. 6, *The Middle Ages – the Christian World*, edited by Robert Chazan, 282–304. Cambridge: Cambridge University Press, 2018.

Rózsa, Zoltán, and Csaba Tóth. "This King Likes Muslims … Traces of an Exceptional Settlement from the Árpádian Age 3." In *Hadak útján. A népvándorláskori fiatal kutatóinak XXVI. konferenciája. Gazdaság – kereskedelem – kézművesség*, edited by Zsófia Rácz, István Koncz, and Bence Gulyás, 315–24. Dissertationes Archaeologicae, Supplementum 2. Budapest: Institute of Archaeological Sciences, 2018.

Stojkovski, Boris. "Jews, Armenians and Muslims." In *The Routledge Handbook of East Central and Eastern Europe in the Middle Ages, 500–1300*, edited by Florin Curta, 298–315. London: Routledge, 2022.

Štulrajterová, Katarína. "Convivenza, Convenienza and Conversion: Islam in Medieval Hungary (1000–1400 CE)." *Journal of Islamic Studies* 24, no. 2 (2012): 175–98.

Szende, Katalin G. "Traders, 'Court Jews,' Town Jews: The Changing Roles of Hungary's Jewish Population in the Light of Royal Policy between the Eleventh and Fourteenth Centuries." In *Intricate Interfaith Networks in the Middle Age: Quotidian Jewish-Christian Contacts*, edited by Ephraim Shoham-Steiner, 119–51. Studies in the History of Daily Life (800–1600) 5. Turnhout: Brepols, 2016.

Visi, Tamás. "Jews in Medieval Europe." In *The Oxford Handbook of Medieval Central Europe*, edited by Nada Zečević and Daniel Ziemann, 483–505. Oxford: Oxford University Press, 2022.

64

CATHOLICISM AND ORTHODOXY

Keywords in this chapter: *filioque*, Council of Florence, Hussitism

Since the fourteenth century, the line dividing Catholic from Orthodox Christianity ran through the lands of Poland and of the grand duchy of Lithuania and Ruthenia. In the Early Middle Ages, Catholic and Orthodox Christians followed different liturgies but, despite their differences, were generally considered as belonging to the same Christian community. Cracks in Christian harmony had appeared in the ninth century; they became larger when, in the eleventh and twelfth centuries, the popes of Rome gained ascendancy in the world of the Latin rite and claimed to be spiritual leaders for the whole of Christendom. In the lands of the Greek or Slavonic rite, the patriarchs of Constantinople were the dominating figures, although independent, autocephalous patriarchs appeared in Bulgaria and Serbia.

In the thirteenth century, the popes built or strengthened connections to East Central and Northeastern Europe in various ways. Poland's special relationship with the papacy might have gone back to the tenth-century document *Dagome iudex*; it was concretized by Peter's Pence, a tax collected in Poland (as well as in Hungary, the Scandinavian kingdoms, and England) for the benefit of the curia (the papal court). The papal connection came in handy to Polish rulers in their territorial disputes with the Teutonic Order in the early fourteenth century. Since the conquest of Prussia, the popes were nominally the feudal lords of the country that was administered by the Teutonic grand masters as papal vassals. Livonia, headed by the archbishops of Riga, was also directly subordinated to the papacy. Popes intensified their efforts at centralizing their authority during the fourteenth century. In Poland, papal envoys (nuncios) were tasked with improving the collection of tithes; others arbitrated the conflict between Poland and the Teutonic Order over Eastern Pomerania or sorted out disputes between German settlers and Poles over practices of fasting.

The papacy experienced its greatest challenge during the Great Western Schism (beginning in 1378) that opposed the popes of Rome to those of Avignon (see insert 64.1). Poland, Bohemia, and Hungary sided with Rome. The Council of Constance (1414–18)

INSERT 64.1. THE WESTERN SCHISM (1378–1417)

In 1309, Pope Clement V moved his main residence to Avignon, a papal enclave surrounded by French territory. When Gregory XI moved back to Rome in 1377 and died the following year, cardinals in Rome elected an Italian, Clement VII, while shortly thereafter a Frenchman, Urban VI, was elected in Avignon. Neither of the two popes recognized the other; Catholic Europe was divided. The rulers of France, Scotland, and the Iberian kingdoms acknowledged the popes of Avignon, while those of England, Italy, and most of the German lands, as well as of the kingdoms of East Central Europe and Scandinavia preferred the popes of Rome. The division was not resolved until the election of Pope Martin V, in 1417, during the Council of Constance (1414–18). The Council, convened under the leadership of Sigismund of Luxembourg, had been tasked with the reunification of Western Christendom. Apart from the resolution of the schism, the council also dealt with the threat to Christian unity that was presented by John Hus and his followers in Bohemia.

was tasked with uniting Catholic Christians, and some of the matters discussed had direct implications for East Central Europe: participants in the council strove to end the wars between Poland and the Teutonic Order and confronted the perceived heretical ideas of John Hus (who was burned at stake during the council). The election of Pope Martin V (1417) returned unity to the Catholic world, but that unity was again shaken by the Hussite revolution (see chapter 48).

While the papacy rose in authority and then struggled under tests to Catholic unity, the Orthodox church in Rus' profited greatly from Mongol rule once the situation stabilized after the conquest. Mongol rulers gave clergy of all religions the same status as the Mongol shamans, as long as they prayed for the well-being of the khans. The Golden Horde remained true to that principle of religious tolerance even after conversion to Islam. An Orthodox bishopric was established in Sarai; the khans granted exemptions from taxes to churches and monasteries. As a result, Rus' ecclesiastic institutions became wealthy as never before. This put churchmen in Rus' in an awkward position. They profited significantly from the Mongol regime yet found it inconceivable to regard their submission to pagans or Muslims as legitimate. When Mongol domination began to weaken, church leaders generally supported attempts of Muscovite princes at gaining independence.

The head of the Orthodox church in Rus' was the metropolitan of Kiev and all Rus', who was under the jurisdiction of the patriarchate of Constantinople. Metropolitan Maximus (Maksim; 1283–99) first relocated to Vladimir during the last year of his term; the seat of the metropolitan was formally transferred there in 1354. Maximus was concerned that the lands of what was becoming Muscovy would drift away from his influence. He and his successors traveled constantly throughout the lands of Rus' that were under Muscovite, Lithuanian, or Polish domination, and to Sarai and Constantinople, in efforts to maintain unity in the church of Rus'.

A separate Orthodox metropolitan see was established in Halych in 1303 but was abolished five years later; another one was set up, sometime between 1315 and 1318, for the Rus' lands of the grand duchy (including Kiev since the Gediminid takeover) and was maintained despite short interruptions. To the princes of Vladimir and the metropolitans "of all Rus'" who resided there, these moves were seen as threats to Orthodox unity. On a trip to Kiev in 1358, Metropolitan Aleksei of Vladimir (1354–78) was arrested and imprisoned by Grand Duke Algirdas for interfering in the affairs of the local metropolitan. When Aleksei died in 1378, the Lithuanian metropolitan, a Bulgarian man named Cyprian, succeeded him. His suffragans (subordinated bishops) were now in both metropolitan jurisdictions of Rus'. Cyprian had a difficult relationship with Prince Dmitri but was fully recognized in both parts of Rus' after the prince's death. The princes of Moscow advocated for an Orthodox church in which the metropolitan of Moscow was to be the leader of "all Rus'." The churches of Moscow were embellished in the fifteenth century to reinforce the concept that the city was the new center of the Slavonic-Orthodox world.

Since the baptism of Władysław Jogaila and the conversion of the Lithuanian nobility to Catholicism, the grand duchy of Lithuania and Ruthenia bridged the divide between Christians of Latin (Catholic) and Slavonic (Orthodox) rites. The growing antagonism between Latin and Greek churches had origins in the schism of 1054 but took shape primarily in the aftermath of the 1204 conquest of Constantinople by Latin Crusaders. Catholic and Orthodox Christians disagreed over the primacy of the pope, the existence of purgatory, and the procession of the Holy Spirit from the Father and the Son (the question of the *filioque*), as well as matters of practice, such as the use of leavened or unleavened bread for the Holy Communion, celibacy of the priests, and rules of fasting in Lent. This tension took longer to resonate, however, in northern Europe. By the early fourteenth century, though, the Orthodox Christians of Rus', who were by then subordinated to Mongols who adopted Islam, were increasingly othered by Catholics of Western Europe who saw them not only as schismatics, but also as collaborators with Muslim powers.

The Lithuanian grand dukes might have rivaled with the Orthodox princes of Moscow for domination in the lands of Rus'; they got along quite well, by contrast, with the Muslim Mongols of the Horde. A "king of Lithuania" is even said to have fought on the Ottoman side at the battle of Nikopolis (1396). In Ruthenia, Catholic and Orthodox Christians had, formally, equal rights. This duality was also reflected in the municipal council of Vilnius that had two mayors, one Catholic and one Orthodox. Disputes, however, emerged around Orthodox baptism: Polish clergy insisted that converts had to be rebaptized in the Catholic rite. Orthodox Christians, regarded as schismatics by Catholics, were forbidden to attend mass in most Catholic churches; the mendicant orders were the only ones to let them in. Despite these disagreements, though, Catholics and Orthodox Christians generally lived peacefully with one another. Donations by Catholics to Orthodox churches and vice versa were common.

An attempt was made at the 1274 Council of Lyon, and on other occasions, to reunite the Catholic and Orthodox churches – all without any success. The idea was revived when, in 1396, Jogaila and Vytautas approached the patriarch of Constantinople to organize an ecumenical council to discuss a union of the Catholic and Orthodox churches under their leadership. Patriarch Anthony replied that fighting against the Ottomans was a more pressing priority. The two cousins promised support against the Ottomans to Sigismund of Luxembourg. Meanwhile, Cyprian, during his term as the Lithuanian-backed metropolitan of Moscow (1390–1406), spent time in the grand duchy as he strove to unite Orthodox Christians not only in Rus' but also in Bulgaria and Wallachia. Metropolitan Photius (Fotii) succeeded Cyprian in 1406 in both Muscovy and the Ruthenian lands of the grand duchy; he died in 1431. A metropolitan was appointed for Lithuania but passed away in 1435.

Meanwhile, the Byzantine emperors were desperate for help against the Ottomans and hoped for papal support in organizing a Crusade against the Turks. Church union was again brought to the fore in those circumstances. In 1437, the patriarch of Constantinople appointed Isidore, a Greek monk, as metropolitan of all Rus' in Moscow. Isidore had only arrived in Moscow when he left for the council of Ferrara (later moved to Florence), which was organized by Pope Eugenius IV and the Byzantine Emperor John VIII Palaiologos. The union of the two churches was decided there in 1439 – a controversial decision in Byzantium. The council mandated that wherever there was both a Catholic and an Orthodox bishop, the passing away of one would mean the remaining one would be the sole prelate of the united community. Most Orthodox delegates signed the union document, but many were scolded for that by their Orthodox coreligionists at home, when they returned. Similarly, upon his return to Moscow, Isidore's pro-unionist attitude was regarded as scandalous, and he was thrown into prison by Prince Vasily II (1425–62), who refused to recognize the union. Isidore was eventually allowed to leave, and in 1448 the Rus' bishops elected their own metropolitan in the person of Jonah (Iona), the bishop of Riazan'. Despite being installed without the approval of the patriarch in Constantinople, Jonah did not refrain from adopting the traditional title of "metropolitan of Kiev and all Rus'." When Constantinople fell to the Ottomans in 1453, the feeling in the Rus' church was that this was divine punishment for the union: the Muscovite churchmen were comforted in their belief that they had been right to go their separate way.

Plans, however, had begun in 1439 to implement the union in Lithuania, and the mendicant orders agitated for the Latinization of the Orthodox church. The Uniates (a name used for those who accepted the decisions of the Council of Florence), though, had little support. The Catholic bishops of Poland and Lithuania, faithful to the decisions of the Council of Basel, had not been involved in the discussions of Ferrara-Florence, and some considered Pope Eugenius IV to be illegitimate. Metropolitan Isidore, the main cheerleader of union, who had taken refuge in Poland, was regarded in Rus' as a foreigner with no local connections in either the grand duchy or Muscovy. In 1449, Casimir IV, king of Poland and grand duke of Lithuania and Ruthenia, acknowledged Jonah, who opposed the union, as Orthodox metropolitan for all lands of Rus'. Casimir, however, soon changed his mind and became a supporter of the Uniate church. In 1458, the Uniate Gregory was named metropolitan for the Orthodox eparchies in Poland and the grand duchy. Supported by Casimir who now firmly rejected Jonah's authority, Gregory was recognized by the Ruthenian bishops of the grand duchy – with the exception of the bishop of Briansk – who distrusted the prelate of Moscow. Gregory's acceptance grew when, around 1470, he obtained recognition from the patriarch of Constantinople, which was much desired in Ruthenia, while at the same time maintaining his allegiance to the pope and upholding the Slavonic liturgy. Union was now formally accepted in the Orthodox lands of the grand duchy but was rejected in Muscovy. In that context of the later fifteenth century, the concept of Jagiellonian Poland and Hungary forming a "bulwark" (*antemurale*) protecting Christendom against non-Christian invaders from the East increasingly lumped together not only Ottomans and Mongols, but also "schismatics" that included Muscovites, Moldavians, and Wallachians.

Pope Alexander VI (1492–1503) was not impressed with the ambiguous positions of the Ruthenian clergy on matters of doctrine and their preference for the patriarch residing in Constantinople (now under Ottoman rule) instead of the exiled patriarch. He nonetheless insisted that rebaptism of Orthodox Christians who converted to Catholicism (large numbers of people apparently remained Orthodox well into the sixteenth century) was unnecessary. While they kept some distance in their relationship with the papacy, the metropolitans of Kiev in the sixteenth century formally maintained the union. Ferrara-Florence would inspire the promoters of the Union of Brest (1596) that created the Ruthenian Uniate Church. In the Ruthenian lands of the Polish-Lithuanian Commonwealth (today Belarus and western Ukraine), that church maintained the Slavonic liturgy and recognized the popes of Rome but, against the decisions taken in Ferrara-Florence, broke with the patriarchs of Constantinople.

While the Catholic church strove for union with its Orthodox counterpart, it faced an existential threat in the center of Europe, in Bohemia, through the Hussite revolution. Władysław, the eldest son of King Casimir IV of Poland, became king of Bohemia as Vladislav II (1471–1516) after the death of George of Poděbrady, who had spent much of his reign seeking papal support for the Utraquist church. Under Vladislav II's reign, the Compacts that had been negotiated by Hussites at the Council of Basel were formally recognized at the 1485 diet of Kutná Hora. This meant that the liturgical practices of both Utraquists and Catholics were normalized in Bohemia, a measure recognizing confessional equality. The diet of Kutná Hora gave full freedom of religion to individual believers who could select the communion of their preference. The arrangement was renewed in 1512 and declared valid for eternity.

FURTHER READING

Alberigo, Giuseppe, ed. *Christian Unity: The Council of Ferrara-Florence 1438/39–1989*. Ephemerides Theologicae Lovanienses – Bibliotheca 97. Leuven: Uitgeverij Peeters, 1991.

Decaluwé, Michiel, Thomas M. Izbicki, and Gerald Christianson, eds. *A Companion to the Council of Basel*. Brill's Companions to the Christian Tradition 74. Leiden: Brill, 2017.

Dendrinos, Charalambos. “Reflections on the Failure of the Union of Florence.” *Annuarium historiae conciliorum* 39, no. 1–2 (2007): 135–52.

Srodecki, Paul. “‘*Universe christiane reipublice validissima propugnacula*’ – Jagiellonian Europe in Bulwark Descriptions around 1500.” In *The Jagiellonians in Europe: Dynastic Diplomacy and Foreign Relations*, edited by Attila Bárány and Balázs Antal Bacsa, 57–74. Debrecen: Lendület, 2016.

65

ECCLESIASTICAL ORGANIZATION AND RELIGIOUS ORDERS

Keywords in this chapter: autocephaly, parish, canon orders, mendicants, cave monasticism

Following conversion to Christianity in Central, Southeastern, and Eastern Europe, the structures of ecclesiastical hierarchy expanded in waves across the region. Church organization typically accompanied the development of political institutions and often followed political borders. Dioceses were established in Bohemia (tenth and eleventh centuries), Poland (eleventh century), and Hungary (eleventh century), and eparchies (Orthodox dioceses) in Bulgaria in the tenth, Rus' in the eleventh, and Serbia in the thirteenth centuries. Hungary and Poland had their archbishoprics by the early eleventh century in Esztergom and Gniezno, respectively. Bohemia, by contrast, did not have its own church province until Charles IV's establishment of the archbishopric of Prague in 1344. The church of Rus' was headed by the metropolitans of Kiev and all Rus', usually Greek men who were appointed by the patriarchs of Constantinople. The bishop of Novgorod (archbishop since the twelfth century) was a suffragan of the metropolitan like the other bishops. Bulgaria's patriarchate was abolished after the Byzantine conquest of the early eleventh century; the archbishop of Ohrid was subordinated to the patriarch of Constantinople. The Bulgarian patriarchate was restored in 1235, when it obtained recognition from the ecumenical patriarch of Constantinople (at that time residing in Nicaea), and its existence continued until the Ottoman conquest. Serbia, meanwhile, obtained an autocephalic archbishopric in 1219. The Serbian archbishop Joannicius (Joanikije) II was elevated to the rank of patriarch in 1346, when the Serbian patriarchal see was established in Peć (where it remained until 1766). In the eastern Baltic, bishops appeared only in the thirteenth century, in the age of the Crusades. Once elevated to the status of archbishop in 1255, the prelate of Riga was responsible for suffragans in both Livonia and Prussia.

The rituals of medieval church services are known through liturgical books. Manuscripts from Hungary and Poland suggest liturgical influences from German and Francophone lands; connections of church leaders were especially strong with Lotharingia, a borderland between speakers of German and Romance languages that belonged to the Holy Roman Empire. The brothers Alexander and Walter of Malonne, for example, who became bishops of Płock and Wrocław, respectively, were from that region and brought liturgical manuscripts with them.

Still in the twelfth century, churches were generally rare outside of episcopal centers; early churches were often in or near strongholds or on the estates of nobles. Networks of parish churches took shape in East Central Europe in the thirteenth century in the context of migration: newcomers expected easier access to church services. The concept of clerical celibacy was not popular among the parish clergy of Central Europe, and in the thirteenth century it was still common for priests to be married. In Hungary, a synod convened during the reign of Coloman stated that married priests should keep their wives "in consideration of human frailty"; the synod only condemned remarriage, concubinage, and bigamy. By contrast, in Orthodox lands priests were expected to be married. Everywhere, Christianization of the population long remained superficial. The Council of Lateran IV (1215) brought renewed insistence in Catholic lands on the importance of preaching, confession, and the sacraments; as a result, efforts were invested in making these more easily accessible. The mendicant orders brought new vigor to preaching and educating the population, especially in urban milieus. Complaints nonetheless continued up to the end of the Middle Ages about the inadequacies of the parish clergy's pastoral duties. By 1400, parish networks were still less dense than in most of Western Europe.

Collections of sermons provide evidence of the ways in which Christian doctrines and beliefs were disseminated. While the Catholic liturgy was in Latin, sermons were delivered in the vernacular. In towns, preachers gave their sermons either in German or in the local Slavic, Hungarian, or other language; some preachers were apt to give them in several languages. The Silesian friar Peregrine of Opole (early fourteenth century), for example, was comfortable preaching in German, Polish, and Latin. In Prussia, preachers often relied on interpreters to reach the Prussian-speaking population. Interpreters were also used when John Capistrano went on a preaching tour in East Central Europe: he spoke Latin and local friars translated his words into the local vernacular(s). Despite the growing differences between Old Church Slavonic, on one hand, and Slavic languages such as Bulgarian, Serbian, or various East Slavic dialects (that later turned into Russian, Ukrainian and Belarusian), on the other hand, there is no evidence that Orthodox priests needed interpreters. Liturgical books written in Old Church Slavonic circulated just as freely between Serbia and Rus', for example, as did those written in Latin between Hungary and Poland. Metropolitans of Kiev who were appointed by the patriarch of Constantinople from among Greek-speaking churchmen in the empire do not seem to have had problems of language in the Slavic-speaking milieu of Rus'.

The earliest monasteries were the Benedictine communities established in Croatia in the ninth century, then in Bohemia, Hungary, and Poland by the late tenth and eleventh centuries. The earliest abbeys were founded by men and women of the ruling dynasties; the nobility became involved in foundation and patronage of monastic institutions only after the mid-eleventh century. The monks and nuns typically came from the German lands. A few Orthodox male and female monasteries existed in Hungary; by the thirteenth century, however, they had transitioned to the Latin rite. Poland acquired Orthodox monasteries by virtue of incorporating Red Ruthenia. In Hungary, new monasteries were established in the later fourteenth century by Serbian immigrants and the local Wallachian nobility in Transylvania. An unusual case was Emmaus Monastery, established by Charles IV in a suburb of Prague with monks from Krk Island in Croatia: they followed the Benedictine rule but used Slavonic in their liturgy. Daughter monasteries were established in Oleśnica (Silesia) and Cracow.

Cistercian monasticism reached Central Europe in the twelfth century and competed with the Benedictines; by the thirteenth century, Cistercians of German culture clearly dominated in Poland and Bohemia. In Hungary, King Béla III established contact with Cistercian houses in Burgundy, including Clairvaux, which explains the strong French influence upon the Cistercian abbeys in Hungary. In Central Europe, Benedictine and Cistercian monks outnumbered nuns. One of the most well regarded of all convents (female monasteries) was Trzebnica, established in Silesia by Henry the Bearded and his wife Hedwig of Andechs.

The Teutonic Knights and Sword-Brothers who governed Prussia and Livonia belonged to the original religious institutions of Central and Northeastern Europe; the military orders of the Templars and Hospitallers were also established in Bohemia, Hungary, and Poland. Premonstratensian (or Norbertine) and Augustinian canons regular gained popularity in Bohemia, Poland, and Hungary in the twelfth century, as did convents of Premonstratensian canonesses. The canons of the Red Star and the Stephenites were new orders of canons regular created in Bohemia and Hungary, respectively. The Paulines, or hermits of the Order of Saint Paul, originated in Hungary of the early thirteenth century. The order became very popular in Hungary and from there spread to Poland and Silesia.

Franciscans and Dominicans already had convents in the 1220s in Central Europe; they expanded in the later thirteenth century. They were sponsored by rulers, bishops, and secular lords; townspeople became patrons only at a later stage. Observant Franciscans typically accepted sons of the nobility, while burghers were more attracted to the Dominicans and the Conventual Franciscans. The Observant Franciscan reform became popular in the region; in Poland, the Observants were known as Bernardines because of their dedication to Bernardine of Sienna. Mendicant nunneries were less common than friaries. The convents of mendicant nuns were mostly supported by the rulers, typically by female patrons. Agnes, sister of Wenceslas I of Bohemia, established a convent of Clarisses (Poor Clares) in Prague in 1234.

From the very beginning, mendicants (a general term for members of the Franciscan and Dominican orders) were active as mediators and diplomats between European rulers, the papacy, and the Mongols. When John of Plano Carpini was sent by Innocent IV to Karakorum, he was accompanied by friars from Bohemia and Silesia. Mendicant diplomats connected European rulers with the khans of the Ilkhanate in the later thirteenth century. Mendicants were sent as missionaries and preachers to the territory of the Golden Horde: Franciscans established priories in Caffa, Sarai, and Solkhat, where the friars enjoyed the active support of the khans when facing backlash from irritated Muslims. Iaylak, wife of Khan Nogai, was baptized by Franciscans, and other Mongols followed suit. The khans, however, were mostly interested in maintaining interfaith order and preventing expressions of intolerance – even Khan Özbeg, despite his zeal for promoting Islam, followed this path. Mendicant churches responded to the needs of resident merchants (a priority for the khans), which led to the establishment of a Catholic bishopric in Caffa in 1322.

Beguines appeared in Bohemia, Poland, and Hungary in the later thirteenth century. They were typically organized in communities of 12 to 15 women who kept their distance from clergy. A community was led by a mistress (*magistra*); the sisters made vows of poverty, chastity, and obedience, and confessed their sins to her. The mistress had multiple tasks: she supervised the sisters' activities and presided over weekly meetings on Fridays; she approved new women who joined the community. The sisters were not considered nuns, as they did not follow a written rule. They wore a typical dress and engaged in manual work, fasting, and various forms of body mortification.

Rus' monasticism was influenced by Byzantine traditions; it combined cenobitic and anchoritic models. Monasteries were typically placed in or near towns, close to centers of power. For example, the Monastery of the Caves was founded by an anchorite, Anthony, in a cave above the Dnieper, near Kiev. As his followers grew to a community living above the original caves, under the leadership of Feodosii (Theodosius) they adopted the cenobitic lifestyle of the great monastery of Studios in Constantinople. Monastic institutions flourished in the following centuries but were hit hard by the devastations of the Mongol invasion.

Once firmly established in Rus', though, the Mongol khans supported monastic institutions by granting them extensive tax exemptions. As a result, Rus' monasticism experienced a revival in the fourteenth century. Sergius of Radonezh (1314–92) played a leading role in that growth. He sought solitude in the wilderness, but his life as a hermit attracted followers, for whom he established a cenobitic community. The Trinity Monastery, which was located to the northeast of Moscow, became the largest monastic institution in Muscovy. Following his example, monasteries of the later Middle Ages were typically founded in wooded, isolated areas, some as far north as the shore of the White Sea. Sergius eventually was recognized as the patron saint of Muscovy.

Cave monasticism, inspired by the lifestyle of Old Testament prophets, emerged as a specific Orthodox phenomenon of the Balkans. John of Rila, who lived in a cave in the Bulgarian Rila mountains, attracted emulators such as Peter of Koriša in thirteenth-century Serbia. Rock-cut monasteries and hermitages have been found in Greece, Macedonia, Serbia, Bulgaria, Romania, Moldova, and the lower Don region – in various parts of the Orthodox world.

FURTHER READING

De Cevins, Marie-Madeleine, Marek Derwich, and Beatrix Romhány. "Monasticism in Medieval Central Europe (ca. 800–ca. 1550)." In *The Oxford Handbook of Medieval Central Europe*, edited by Nada Zečević and Daniel Ziemann, 507–29. Oxford: Oxford University Press, 2022.

Hautala, Roman. "Catholic Missions in the Golden Horde Territory." In *From Pax Mongolica to Pax Ottomanica: War, Religion and Trade in the Northwestern Black Sea Region (14th–16th Centuries)*, edited by Ovidiu Cristea and Liviu Pilat, 39–65. East Central and Eastern Europe in the Middle Ages, 450–1450, 58. Leiden: Brill, 2020.

Jamroziak, Emilia. "East-Central European Monasticism: Between East and West?" In *The Cambridge History of Medieval Monasticism in the Latin West*, edited by Alison I. Beach and Isabelle Cochelin, 882–900. Cambridge: Cambridge University Press, 2020.

Klaniczay, Gábor. "The Mendicant Orders in East-Central Europe and the Integration of Cultures." In *Hybride Kulturen im mittelalterlichen Europa: Vorträge und Workshops einer Frühlingsschule*, edited by Michael Borgolte and Bernd Schneidmüller, 245–60. Berlin: Akademie Verlag, 2010.

Sikorski, Dariusz Andrzej. "Church Organization." In *The Routledge Handbook of East Central and Eastern Europe in the Middle Ages, 500–1300*, edited by Florin Curta, 316–37. London: Routledge, 2022.

66

RELIGIOUS PRACTICES

Keywords in this chapter: dual faith, *kaliki*, Judaizers

Little is known of the religious practices of Jews in medieval East Central Europe. Rabbi Eliezer b. Isaac of Speyer complained in the twelfth century about the ignorance of Jews in Hungary, Poland, and Rus', who did not have rabbis or proper religious teachers; according to him, this was due to their poverty. By contrast, there was at that time a well-known yeshiva (a school of Talmudic higher learning) in Prague, and its teachers were familiar with the writings of Jewish scholars in northern France.

Pre-Christian elements survived after the conversion to Christianity in many parts of Europe. The *Zapusty* was a Polish carnival on the last Thursday before Lent; the fertility feast of Saint John the Baptist was widespread among the Eastern Slavs. Festivities that were perceived as not fully Christian did not always go unchallenged. When Rus' village priests approved of a festival honoring spirits helping women in childbirth, the *Rozhanicy*, and suggested adding hymns to Mary to the celebrations, they were criticized by their superiors for their leniency. In the lands of Rus', depictions of Saint Elijah riding a chariot in the sky are believed to be inspired by the figure of the god Perun; images of Saint Blasius (Vlasii) surrounded by cattle and farm animals are thought to reflect a conflation between Blasius and the ancient god Veles. This phenomenon has been called in Russian scholarship *dvoeverie* ("dual faith"), although there is no evidence of two separate faiths.

Popular religion sometimes strayed from the teachings of church leaders. Archbishop Sava of Serbia referred to sorcerers called werewolves who were thought to drive away clouds, hail, or rain. Bulgarian popular tales of the devil that deviated from Biblical teachings are recorded in various texts of the eleventh and twelfth centuries (see chapter 36).[1] Archaeological finds also suggest beliefs in the supernatural: images or artefacts with

1 Florin Curta, ed., "Razumnik, a Study Guide," in *Medieval Eastern Europe, 500–1300: A Reader* (Toronto: University of Toronto Press, 2024), 210–12.

symbols of the evangelists, for example, were sometimes buried in the corners of buildings. In Hungary, ceramic vessels containing eggs or skeletons of birds or small animals were found deposited in houses in villages and towns, sometimes in churches. The meaning of these practices remains elusive.

The Catholic clergy's teachings influenced populations in various ways; they inspired works of mercy, the foundation of hospitals, and charity. Parishioners invested efforts in implementing moral teachings in their lives. Religious confraternities, associated with mendicant priories or with craft guilds, fostered a sense of belonging while supporting the needy and contributing to the salvation of souls; members were typically buried in the same cemetery next to the parish church. In towns of late medieval Transylvania, for example, it was primarily the Dominicans who were active in promoting the establishment of confraternities. In Livonia, female members participated in the social gatherings of religious confraternities; in professional guilds, by contrast, it was only when the festivities foresaw dancing that they were invited alongside their husbands. Last wills show how burghers demonstrated their piety through charity, by founding altars, or by setting up votive masses. Rituals connected to religious feasts and festivals, processions, and pilgrimages to local saints grew in popularity in the later Middle Ages.

In the late medieval and early modern lands of Rus', popular piety found expression in the poems of the *kaliki*. These wandering singers, often crippled or blind, were found on the roads or near the gates of monasteries and churches and recited to the passersby, especially pilgrims, poetry that was in the style of heroic poems (*byliny*) but celebrated spiritual subjects. While little is known about the authors of those poems, their contents reveal familiarity with hagiographical and apocryphal writings. Favorite subjects were the celebration of poverty, ascetic ambitions, and earthly suffering.

The biggest challenge to Catholic doctrine in Central Europe came from the teachings of John Hus and his followers that set the stage for the Hussite revolution. In the end, though, the liturgical practices of the Utraquists came to be accepted (see chapter 64). Heretical threats raised concerns among church authorities on a few other occasions; papal inquisitors in Poland and Bohemia, however, relied on a much weaker organization than did their counterparts in Western Europe. Waldensians moved to Bohemia and Silesia with German settlers; led by ministers, they rejected the sacraments of the Catholic clergy. Trials in Wrocław, Nysa, and Świdnica in 1315 led to dozens of executions. Small groups of Waldensians were also found in Western Pomerania in the later fourteenth century. In 1332, a Dominican inquisitor, John of Schwenkenfeld, led an investigation of the beguines of Świdnica who were suspected of adhering to the doctrine of the Free Spirit. The procedure reflected concerns expressed at the Council of Vienne (1311–12). The religious women, who lived in communities but did not follow a monastic rule, attracted suspicion. The Świdnica beguines were accused of believing in the achievement of salvation without the sacraments offered by the clergy; meetings between senior beguines and beghards, members of male communities, led to suspicions of sexual promiscuity.

In the lands of Rus', religious dissidents attracted attention in the 1470s. First found in Novgorod, they were called "Judaizers" by their opponents. They became enthralled by a series of texts that had been translated from Hebrew into Slavonic by a Jewish scholar from Kiev, Zacharia ben Aharon ha-Cohen; the controversial books included treatises on philosophy, astronomy, and cosmography. The movement spread to Moscow and found interest at the court. Archbishop Gennadius of Novgorod, however, attacked its followers as heretics; the 1490 council convened by Metropolitan Zosimus condemned nine adherents, who were excommunicated and subjected to corporal punishments.

The cult of saints played a central role in Christian devotion. The Virgin Mary was popular in East Central and Eastern Europe since the period of conversion: many early churches were dedicated to her, for example in Poznań, Gniezno, Prague, and Kiev (the Tithe Church). Her cult was promoted by the Piasts and Arpadians, but Mary also enjoyed popularity with the clergy and the broader population. Moreover, the Teutonic Order gave special significance to Mary: the Knights carried her image on their banners; the land they conquered became "Mary's Land"; the fortified residence of the grand master in Prussia, Marienburg (Malbork), was named after her.

Some saints were popular in both Catholic and Orthodox lands. The cult of Saint Nicholas moved east from the Holy Roman Empire (where it had come from Byzantium in the late tenth century); it reached Poland through the Lotharingian connections of Richeza, wife of Mieszko II. Their daughter Gertrude married the Rus' prince Iziaslav, who introduced the veneration of Nicholas to Eastern Europe. His successor, Sviatoslav II, was an enthusiastic promoter of his cult. In the twelfth and thirteenth centuries, Nicholas had churches in towns such as Gdańsk and Novgorod and became the patron saint of sailors and merchants. The veneration of other saints spread from east to west. For example, Helena, the mother of Constantine, was very popular in Byzantium and Rus'. Her feast day, May 21, entered calendars in Poland, Hungary, and Bohemia, even though that date was not usually celebrated in Western Europe. Even more spectacular was the growing role of Saint Demetrius, the patron saint of Thessaloniki, in late medieval Hungary after the Fourth Crusade.

Canonization became, in the thirteenth century, a standardized procedure controlled by the papacy, which opened the door to giving broader legitimization to the cult of local saints. Hungary's intercessors included Bishop Gerard of Csanád (Cenad, in western Romania), who died as a martyr during a revolt against King Peter Orseolo, and two hermits, Andrew-Zoerard and Benedict, popular in what is now Slovakia (see chapter 37).[2] The royal saints of Hungary included Stephen I, his son Emeric, and Ladislas I. Stephen was honored as a fighter against pagans, ideal Christian king, and founder of bishoprics and monasteries. Late medieval frescoes in Hungarian churches show Ladislas killing a Cuman who had abducted a young woman.

Dynastic and political saints gained prominence. Bohemia had Ludmila and her grandson Wenceslas, the divine protector of Přemyslid rulership. Legends portrayed Ludmila as a promoter of Christianity in contrast to Drahomira, (wrongly) imagined as a pagan. In

2 Curta, ed., "A Hermit's Portrait: St. Andrew-Zoerard," in *Medieval Eastern Europe*, 195–98.

Rus', the martyr brothers Boris and Gleb were proclaimed saints when their remains were deposited in a church in Vyshgorod, near Kiev, in 1072. Miracle accounts reveal that their popularity bridged social classes. Princess Olga's remains were transferred to the Tithe Church in Kiev in the eleventh century, and she was recognized as a saint in 1284. In Serbia, Archbishop Sava and his father Simeon (the name that Stephen Nemanja took when he became monk) were declared saints in the thirteenth century. In Poland, Saint Stanisław symbolized opposition to secular rulers' interventions in ecclesiastical affairs. As bishop of Cracow, Stanisław was associated with a conspiracy of magnates and Bolesław II ordered him executed; this backfired when Stanisław became venerated as a saint martyr. He was canonized in 1253, and his life was the subject of a *vita* written by Vincent of Kielcze at the request of Prandota, bishop of Cracow.

In the thirteenth century, the most influential saints of Central Europe were royal women, who became role models for new forms of religious devotion. The most famous of them was Elizabeth of Hungary (also known as Elizabeth of Thuringia). Daughter of King Andrew II, Elizabeth was married at the age of 14 to Landgrave Louis IV of Thuringia; mother of three children, she became a widow at the age of twenty. She spent the rest of her life, under the guidance of her confessor Conrad of Marburg, exercising extreme asceticism and looking after lepers in the hospital she had founded in Marburg. Elizabeth died in 1231 at the age of twenty-four; she was canonized in 1235, and her cult spread like wildfire throughout Central Europe. While it had long been common for widowed princesses and noble women to retire in convents, Elizabeth's active devotion to helping the sick and needy, inspired by the mendicant orders, was a novelty that struck the imagination. Elizabeth became a model of female sanctity and especially appealed to women of ruling dynasties.

One of Elizabeth's admirers was her aunt, Hedwig of Andechs, wife of Henry the Bearded of Silesia. Hedwig was instrumental in the foundation of Trzebnica, the first Cistercian convent in the region, where she spent the last years of her life. Her *vita* describes how, in imitation of Elizabeth, Hedwig helped the poor and the needy. Her daughter, Gertrude, was abbess of Trzebnica and supported her canonization, achieved in 1267. Hedwig attracted widespread veneration, and not only among the Piasts. Inspired by his Silesian wife Anne of Świdnica, Charles IV, for example, visited St. Hedwig's shrine.

Agnes of Bohemia was the daughter of Přemysl Ottokar I; educated in Trzebnica Abbey, she refused arranged marriages proposed by her parents and, corresponding with Clare of Assisi, aspired to a religious life. In 1234, Agnes founded in Prague the first convent of Franciscan nuns in Central Europe, where she spent the rest of her days. Her sister Anne, married to Duke Henry II of Silesia, followed her example when widowed and founded a convent of Poor Clares (Clarisses) in Wrocław.

Elizabeth, Hedwig, and Agnes inspired countless other women, many of whom became venerated as saints. They provided role models for secular women who were wives and mothers (Elizabeth and Hedwig) or virgin nuns (Agnes). Their followers included Margaret of Hungary (d. 1270), daughter of Béla IV, nun in the convent of Rabbit Island, near Buda; the Polish princess Salomea (d. 1268), who, as widow of Prince Coloman and dowager queen of Halych, entered the Clarisse convent in Cracow; and two sisters of Margaret,

Kinga (Cunigond) of Cracow (d. 1292) and Yolanda (d. 1298), who both followed Salomea's example and became Poor Clares as widows. Blanche of Castile, mother of King Louis IX of France, was also directly inspired by the example of Elizabeth of Hungary.

Pilgrimages to holy shrines were a way to demonstrate veneration to saints. Some went to visit sites in the Holy Land: Daniel, an abbot from Rus', visited Jerusalem in the twelfth century, as did Bishop Henry Zdík (who brought to Olomouc a piece of the Holy Cross) and Sava of Serbia. Pilgrim badges found in archaeological sites attest that ordinary individuals had gone to Rome or Santiago de Compostela, while others traveled to Thessaloniki to venerate Saint Demetrius. The penitential of Bishop Nifont of Novgorod (1130–56), however, condemned pilgrimages to Jerusalem: Nifont advised that pilgrims were too often prompted to drinking and partying more than to religious devotion. European shrines were also popular. Bishop Gotthard was venerated in Hildesheim after his canonization in 1131. Pilgrims from Hungary, Poland, and Rus' were mentioned at his tomb shortly thereafter; they included ordinary people alongside rulers such as Duke Bolesław the Wrymouth of Poland. Dedications of churches and mentions in calendars attest to the popularity of the cult of Gotthard in Poland and Bohemia well before the migration of German settlers.

FURTHER READING

Figurski, Paweł, and Grzegorz Pac. "Saints and Relics." In *The Routledge Handbook of East Central and Eastern Europe in the Middle Ages, 500–1300*, edited by Florin Curta, 338–53. London: Routledge, 2022.

Florea, Carmen. "The Third Path: Charity and Devotion in Late Medieval Transylvanian Towns." In *Communities of Devotion: Religious Orders and Society in East Central Europe, 1450–1800*, edited by Maria Crăciun and Elaine Fulton, 91–120. London: Routledge, 2016.

Klaniczay, Gábor. *Holy Rulers and Blessed Princesses: Dynastic Cults in Medieval Central Europe*. Past & Present Publications. Cambridge: Cambridge University Press, 2000.

Kras, Paweł. "Repression of Heresy in Late Medieval Poland." In *Przestrzeń religijna Europy Środkowo-Wschodniej w średniowieczu: Religious Space of East-Central Europe in the Middle Ages*, edited by Krzysztof Bracha and Paweł Kras, 309–29. Warsaw: DiG, 2010.

Kuzmová, Stanislava. "Religious Practices (and Confessional Variants) in Medieval Central Europe." In *The Oxford Handbook of Medieval Central Europe*, edited by Nada Zečević and Daniel Ziemann, 431–56. Oxford: Oxford University Press, 2022.

Mänd, Anu. "*Memoria* and Sacral Art in Late Medieval Livonia: The Gender Perspective." In *Images and Objects in Ritual Practices in Medieval and Early Modern Northern and Central Europe*, edited by Krista Kodres and Anu Mänd, 239–73. Newcastle upon Tyne: Cambridge Scholars Publishing, 2013.

Rock, Stella. *Popular Religion in Russia: "Double Belief" and the Making of an Academic Myth*. London: Routledge, 2007.

PART 12

Literacy and Art in the High and Late Middle Ages

67

POLITICAL AND PRACTICAL LITERACY

Keywords in this chapter: charters, *gramoty*, chanceries, birchbark letters

Oral and symbolic communication continued to have a significant role in medieval Europe long after the use of written documents became more common. Judicial rituals involved a high level of formalism that never disappeared; nonverbal communication through public acts and gestures dominated political culture. Documents nonetheless obtained broader acceptance in legal matters and diplomacy, which points to shifts in mentality.

Charters – authenticated documents attesting to legal affairs – written in Latin and confirmed with seals were the dominant form of written documentation in most of Western Europe (see plate 67.1). Their format, appearance, and formularies became the standard model in East Central Europe as well. There are only a few charters produced in the region during the eleventh and twelfth centuries, typically donations by rulers and nobles to bishoprics, churches, or monasteries. The documents were made on behalf of the donors by the beneficiaries; the donors authenticated them by attaching their seals. The Cistercians, who insisted on having written documentation for their properties, played a pioneering role in the dissemination of charters. The use of rulers' charters, however, expanded exponentially during the thirteenth century. Rulers became more invested in the production of documents: they hired officials who produced charters for them, and the practice of having them prepared by beneficiaries became less common. The most popular use of charters was to attest to property rights, especially for landed property. Charters also served to document various rights for individuals and communities. Their necessity increased in the context of migration and settlement: charters described the new rights granted to burghers, villagers, and their community organization. Some charters had broad implications. For example, the Golden Bull (named so after the golden seal attached to it) issued by King Andrew II in 1222 (see chapter 56) outlines the rights and privileges of the Hungarian nobility, granted after years of unrest.[1] Sales of land, inheritance, and

1 Florin Curta, ed., "The Golden Bull of 1222," in *Medieval Eastern Europe, 500–1300: A Reader* (Toronto: University of Toronto Press, 2024), 136–39.

Plate 67.1. A charter of privileges from King Matthias Corvinus for the Thurzó family (1475). The document is now in the Princely and Comital Archive of the Fugger Family and Foundation in Dillingen. Wikimedia Commons, the free media repository.

donations could be attested through documents; eventually, written documents came to be seen as the only legal proofs accepted in tribunals. While in earlier times legal affairs were authenticated in public ceremonies attended by witnesses, by now their validity was expected to be proven not by the voices of living witnesses, but by the reading of charters and the examination of wax seals.

In Central Europe, charters were all in Latin until the late thirteenth century. The first vernacular language used in documents was German, introduced for urban and secular matters in documents that followed the model of Latin charters. Documents written in Czech have appeared since the late fourteenth century, first in urban milieus and soon thereafter at the royal court. By the end of the fifteenth century, the use of Czech, now fully normalized, spread to a few municipal chanceries in southern Silesia. In Hungary,

German was used for documents alongside Latin in the fourteenth century in towns before finding its way at the royal court; Italian and Czech were occasionally used.

Traditions of written documents in Kievan Rus' evolved independently from Western and Central European developments. Although Rus' documents were called *gramoty*, a word of Greek origin, they were composed in Church Slavonic, and their appearance and formulary resulted from internal developments, inspired by oral practices. Princely charters, which might have existed earlier, are attested in the twelfth century. Their use was fully established by the thirteenth century, but they nonetheless long remained rare. In Muscovy, princely charters only became more common in the late fourteenth century; they followed the traditional models of Kievan Rus'. Other types of documents included trial documents, known since the thirteenth century – trial records that described court proceedings and judgement charters that laid out the courts' decisions. Rare private charters, sometimes written by princely notaries, are attested in Novgorod as early as the twelfth century. Professional scribes offering their services to produce private charters, however, did not become a feature of Muscovite life until the sixteenth century.

Like other Mongol rulers, the khans of the Golden Horde used golden tablets with Mongol inscriptions in Uighur script, called *paizas*, that gave bearers access to the services of the *yam*, the horse relay system that allowed fast travel through the empire. Moreover, the khans issued written decrees called *yarlyks* that provided instructions on rights and privileges. *Yarlyks* served in communications between khans and Rus' princes: they gave legitimacy to rulers approved by the khans and attested to their tax-collecting privileges. The chancery of the Golden Horde khans quickly switched from the original Mongolian language to Khwarezmian Turkic (derived from Kipchak dialects), first written in the Uighur and then in Arabic script. The Crimean khans pursued the tradition of producing documents in Turkic with the Arabic script.

In the Ruthenian lands of the grand duchy of Lithuania, in contrast to Muscovy, late medieval charters written in the Ruthenian language were partly inspired by the models and formularies of Latin charters that had long been common in Poland; vocabulary and grammar were also often influenced by spoken Polish. In fifteenth-century Red Ruthenia, Latin documents were used alongside those in the Ruthenian language. Ruthenian is the name given to the written Slavic language that was used in the Rus' lands under Lithuanian and Polish domination (in what are now Belarus and western Ukraine). This language was different from the Old Church Slavonic that had developed in Rus' in the eleventh and twelfth centuries. Ruthenian was a composite language combining features of literary Old Church Slavonic with the spoken languages from which modern Belarusian and Ukrainian later derived. It was the chancery language used by rulers for their written documents at least since Władysław Jogaila, who issued documents in that language for the Ruthenian lands of the grand duchy. Under Vytautas, Ruthenian was fully established as the chancery medium in the grand duchy. Alexander expanded the services of the chancery, employing notaries in multiple departments. Documents were written in Ruthenian for internal affairs and in correspondence with Muscovy; German was utilized for correspondence with the

Teutonic Order; Latin served for Polish and European correspondents; and Turkic was used in written communication with the Mongol authorities.

Whereas charters and notarial documents in Latin (and later Italian) dominated in Croatia and Dalmatia (except for some Slavonic documents in Glagolitic or Cyrillic script, the latter popular among late medieval Croat nobles), documents in Slavonic were the rule in Bulgaria and Serbia. Serbian documentary production was spurred by urban development and the input of settlers from the West, especially Saxon (German) miners and merchants, but documents followed the formal expectations of Byzantine traditions. They were written, however, not in Greek, but in a language that combined Old Church Slavonic (typically in the standardized sections and the preambles) with formulations that reflected the spoken language (mostly in the sections describing the legal acts). In Serbia, it was also common to inscribe documents on the walls of churches and monasteries, painted as part of frescoes or inscribed in stone or brick. Serbian rulers maintained chanceries able to produce diplomatic written communication in Slavonic, Latin, or Greek, depending upon the addressees. While rulers' charters could sometimes be issued simultaneously in two languages, it was also common for the recipients to keep informal written translations alongside the originals to help with the practical communication of the contents.

In the Romanian principalities of Moldavia and Wallachia, the first princely charters appeared in the late fourteenth century and were written in Latin. Soon, however, the princely chanceries turned to Slavonic, which, although it was entirely unrelated to the Romance language of the majority population, was by then not only the dominating language of chanceries in the region but also the liturgical language of the Orthodox Romanians. While the language of the documents was inspired by the Slavonic employed in the chanceries of Bulgaria and Serbia, the charters combined typical formulae and clauses of Latin and Byzantine traditions. The use of Slavonic presented challenges for Romanian scribes who typically limited themselves to stereotypical formulations. Princely chanceries often relied on foreign scribes – from Ruthenia and Poland in Moldavia, or from Bulgaria and Serbia in Wallachia – for their specialized skills. Latin and German were also utilized for external correspondence.

Apart from legal documents, writing could be used to disseminate information in the form of correspondence. That the practical use of writing was widespread in the towns of Rus' is attested by the finds of birchbark letters that were uncovered in great numbers especially in Novgorod, where their use was extensive in the twelfth and thirteenth centuries. Inscriptions were made by cutting in the bark with a sharp instrument; they reproduced the East Slavic dialect spoken in the region, occasionally mixed with Old Church Slavonic. The birchbark documents deal with a variety of matters for individuals of all walks of life – men and women, nobles, clerics, merchants, artisans, peasants. Correspondence flowed between husbands and wives, business partners, or masters and apprentices. Documents include marriage certificates, titles to land, and business deals. Some attest to the ease of communication over long distance, such as the letter of a man named Giurgii to his father and mother: "After selling the farm, come [all of you] here, either to Smolensk or to Kiev. Grain is cheap. If you don't come, send me a note, so that

Plate 67.2. A birchbark letter from Novgorod, early twelfth century. The letter was written by a man named Giurgii to his parents asking them to come and stay with him. Wikimedia Commons, the free media repository.

I know that you are well."[2] Many such documents were probably not written by the persons involved but by clerks and other literate individuals on their behalf. Few might have mastered the skill to write, but many more had learned to read in urban schools (see plate 67.2).

Numerous letters of merchants from Dubrovnik and other coastal cities demonstrate how they understood the practical advantages of correspondence. Letters served to convey information to absent addressees; in the Middle Ages, they were also a literary genre of their own. The *Lives* of Simeon and Sava of Serbia attest to the practice among rulers and clerics to communicate through letters. Writing formal letters was also common practice in medieval Rus': stylized letters served to disseminate homiletic messages or take a stance in theological or political controversies. The late fifteenth-century letter collection of the monk Nil Sorski attests to the practice of writing "friendship letters" inspired by classical tradition: Sorki's missives reveal traits of his personality along with his mastery of rhetorical expression.

Minority languages were sometimes used for official purposes. For a short period of time in the twelfth century, coins were produced for Polish kings with inscriptions in Hebrew: they were designed by Jewish mint masters in royal service. Greek inscriptions could be seen in some churches of Rus'. Muscovite rulers occasionally minted coins with inscriptions in the Arabic alphabet that were inspired by the coins of their overlords, the khans of the Golden Horde.

FURTHER READING

Adamska, Anna. "The Introduction of Writing in Central Europe (Poland, Hungary and Bohemia)." In *New Approaches to Medieval Communication*, edited by Marco Mostert, 165–90. Utrecht Studies in Medieval Literacy 1. Turnhout: Brepols, 1999.

Bubalo, Đorđe. *Pragmatic Literacy in Medieval Serbia*. Utrecht Studies in Medieval Literacy 29. Turnhout: Brepols, 2014.

2 Curta, ed., "Birchbark Letters," in *Medieval Eastern Europe*, 286.

Franklin, Simon. *Writing, Society and Culture in Early Rus, c. 950–1300*. Cambridge: Cambridge University Press, 2002.

Goina, Mariana. *The Use of Pragmatic Documents in Medieval Wallachia and Moldavia (Fourteenth to Sixteenth Centuries)*. Utrecht Studies in Medieval Literacy 47. Turnhout: Brepols, 2020.

Kołodziejczyk, Dariusz. *The Crimean Khanate and Poland-Lithuania: International Diplomacy on the European Periphery (15th–18th Century): A Study of Peace Treaties Followed by Annotated Documents*. The Ottoman Empire and Its Heritage 47. Leiden: Brill, 2011.

Schaeken, Jos. *Voices on Birchbark: Everyday Communication in Medieval Russia*. Studies in Slavic and General Linguistics 43. Leiden: Brill, 2019.

Szende, Katalin. *Trust, Authority and the Written Word in the Royal Towns of Medieval Hungary*. Utrecht Studies in Medieval Literacy 41. Turnhout: Brepols, 2018.

68

LITERATURE AND BOOK CULTURE

Keywords in this chapter: courtly literature, chronicles, dictionaries, manuscripts

Courtly literature of French or German style thrived in Central Europe beginning in the High Middle Ages. The troubadours Peire Vidal and Gaucelm Fecit visited the court of King Emeric of Hungary and his wife Constance of Aragón. The romance of Troy is said to have been translated from Latin into Hungarian in the early thirteenth century. Though the text has not survived, it was translated later into Slavonic in the Balkans. The legend of Saint Ladislas, although written in Latin, was inspired by chivalric models. It was mostly Prague, though, that became a vibrant center of chivalric culture in the thirteenth century. The German poets Reinmar of Zweter, Sigeher, and Frederick of Sunburg visited the Přemyslid court. A Bohemian-German poet named Ulrich of Etzenbach wrote romances in Middle High German for the king's entourage, including one that featured Wenceslas II. Courtly literature appealed to aristocrats in other parts of East Central Europe as well. *The Crusade of Landgrave Ludwig*, a historical romance about the 1191 siege of Acre, was written in Silesia, probably for Duke Bolko I of Świdnica and Jawor. Duke Henry Probus of Wrocław and Prince Wizlaw III of Rügen were celebrated as authors of love poems in *Minnesang* tradition. In the fourteenth century, it was courtly romance in Czech that flourished: Bohemia had now a trilingual literary culture – Latin, German, and Czech – that often appeared together in one and the same manuscript. Popular romances – from the cycles of Dietrich von Bern and King Arthur, Tristan and Isolde, *Herzog Ernst*, or Alexander – were adapted into Czech verse narratives that typically had stronger didactic components. By contrast, Hungarian was used for only a few poems and other texts surviving in fragments.

In the Late Middle Ages, literary traditions evolved in different directions in Muscovy and the Ruthenian lands of Lithuania and Poland. Two Slavic literary languages were used in the grand duchy and eastern Poland: Old Church Slavonic was a liturgical and ecclesiastical book language; Ruthenian, the chancery language (see chapter 67), was also used for popular literature. Monasteries remained the main centers of a literary production that was based on synthesizing, rewriting, and elaborating on existing texts. Original literature in Ruthenian was inspired in part by Czech works. *The Vision of Tundal*, originally written in Latin in twelfth-century Regensburg, recounts the story of an Irish knight who falls dead at a feast; coming back to life, he tells of his visions of heaven and hell. By the end of the fifteenth century, this text had been translated into various languages that included Croatian and Czech – the latter being adapted in the late fifteenth century to both Ruthenian and Old Church Slavonic. The *Tale of Sibyl the Prophetess*, a story of prophecies told to King Solomon, circulated in Latin and Middle High German before being translated into Czech and Ruthenian in the fifteenth century.

While French and German models dominated in Central Europe, Bulgarian authors of the Second Empire (1185–1393) sought literary inspiration in Byzantium. Emperor John Alexander (1331–71) gathered scholars in Tărnovo who strove to improve and update Biblical and liturgical translations in Slavonic. They revised them through consulting the Greek originals. These efforts were pursued in the later fourteenth century by Euthymios (Evtimii) of Tărnovo, who standardized the Slavonic orthography. In the fifteenth century, his work inspired Constantine Kostenečki's reform of spelling that aimed at reflecting phonetic differences between Serbian and Bulgarian. New translations from Greek books on history and theology emphasized the importance of Bulgaria. Anne, the queen of Vidin and wife of John Alexander's son, commissioned a book on the lives and miracles of female saints. After the fall of the Second Bulgarian Empire, scholars such as Gregory Tsamblak and Metropolitan Cyprian brought the achievements of Bulgarian scholarship to Muscovy, where they spurred an intellectual revival. Muscovite literature – in sermons, hagiography, adaptations of stories from Troy and Alexander, ethnographic accounts of India – was characterized by an archaic, antiquarian language and a preference for an ornate style.

History writing was still popular in the Late Middle Ages. Hungarian narratives focused on rulers. John of Küküllő wrote a biography of Louis the Great, while Lorenzo Monaci produced a Latin epic recounting the attempts of Charles II – the story's villain – to take the throne from Queen Mary. The *Hungarian Chronicle*, begun under Charles of Anjou in 1332–33, was continued in 1358. One of its manuscripts is the richly decorated *Illuminated Chronicle*, most likely made at the court of Louis, who is depicted enthroned on the first page (see plate 68.1). History writing in Latin flourished in Poland with the works of Janko of Czarnków and John Długosz. In Bohemia, the early fourteenth-century *Chronicle of Dalimil*, written in Czech, gave voice to resentment towards foreigners, especially Germans. Charles IV promoted Latin chronicles; by that time, Dalimil's xenophobic sentiments had disappeared. The monk Neplach emphatically placed Bohemia in the context of world history, as did John of Marignolli (a Florentine missionary who had traveled to China and India before moving to Bohemia); the *Chronicle of the Bohemians* connected Czech, Biblical, and Roman history. Přibík Pulkava's *Bohemian Chronicle* (written in Latin and translated by the author himself into Czech) began with the Tower of Babel before moving on to the history of Bohemia, while highlighting the historical importance of Great Moravia.

Plate 68.1. The first page of the Hungarian *Illuminated Chronicle*, a manuscript copied in 1358 and illustrated between 1370 and 1373. The illumination at the top of the first page shows King Louis I sitting on the throne. The manuscript is now in the National Széchény Library in Budapest. Wikimedia Commons, the free media repository.

In contrast to religious literature, historical writing in the lands of Rus' showed limited influence of Byzantine models: the main inspiration came from the chronicles of the Kievan period – themselves continuations of Byzantine world chronicles. Chronicles from Novgorod or Muscovy combined in annual entries events of the lives of rulers, stories of churches, monasteries, and saints, and various digressions. The *Galician-Volhynian Chronicle*, recording events of the thirteenth century, is a rare historical work displaying conceptual influences of Greek histories. In Muscovy, Dmitri Donskoi's victory at Kulikovo Field in 1380 provided the subject of epic narratives. In the grand duchy, historical works included the *Genealogy of Lithuanian Princes* (ca. 1398), the *Eulogy of Vytautas* (ca. 1428), and the *Chronicle of the Grand Dukes of Lithuania*, all written in Ruthenian.

Princess Cunigond, after being married to Bolesław of Mazovia, divorced and became abbess of the Convent of St. George in Prague. She was an avid patron of devotional books. A breviary she sponsored for her personal use includes a prayer in Czech, which was new at the time. Charles IV promoted the literary use of Czech as well as Latin. The Czech-Latin dictionaries and textbooks of Bartoloměj of Chlumec (Claretus) testify to efforts to promote literary writing in Czech. Translations and new versions of the lives of local and ancient saints were made. Easter plays staged scenes from the Bible in Czech. Inspired by French examples, Biblical books were also translated; a full Czech Bible, commissioned for nuns, was available around 1360. The reform movement that led to the Hussite revolution gave renewed importance to Czech as a language of literature, theology, and polemical writing. A textbook on Czech orthography that systematized the use of diacritical signs is even attributed to John Hus himself. Czech emerged out of the revolution as a more common and more accepted literary language.

Dalmatia was located at the crossroads of the Catholic and Orthodox worlds and had a mixed population of Romance speakers and Croats. Under Venetian influence, Latin dominated in documents and history writing. However, Slavonic written culture flourished, albeit not in the Cyrillic script used in Serbia and Bulgaria but in the older Glagolitic alphabet. Old Church Slavonic was the liturgical language in many churches of the region, but Glagolitic gained in popularity for missals and breviaries, Biblical books, and moralistic or hagiographic works. Some of those books contained Cyrillo-Methodian translations, while others had more recent texts responding to the evolving needs of the Christian and learned communities. Written in Glagolitic, they were composed in a Croatian version of Old Church Slavonic. In 1248 Pope Innocent IV authorized the use of Slavonic in the liturgy (and the Glagolitic script for its writing), which made the language popular among (native) Benedictine monks and Franciscan friars. While most of the Glagolitic books had religious contents, a few preserved examples testify that the script found a wider dissemination. These include a rendering of the life of Alexander the Great – in a book that belonged to a merchant – in a Slavonic language showing Dalmatian dialectical traits, and a few documents. A Croatian legend made Jerome the inventor of the Glagolitic letters.

In Bohemia, Charles IV set up, with papal permission, a monastery in Prague that promoted Glagolitic writing. Called Emmaus Monastery (and colloquially the monastery "of the Slavs"), this was founded with Dalmatian monks (see chapter 65). Glagolitic monasteries in the Dalmatian tradition were also established in Oleśnica, Silesia, by Duke Conrad II (1380) and in Kleparz, a suburb of Cracow, at the invitation of Queen Jadwiga (1390). Jadwiga may have heard of Slavonic writing from her mother, Elizabeth of Bosnia. Meanwhile, the revived Sázava Monastery maintained Cyrillic culture in the Czech lands.

While monasteries of the Latin tradition typically had scriptoria as separate venues dedicated to the copying and binding of books, Orthodox monasteries lacked such facilities: books were copied either in the libraries or in individual cells. In Poland, illuminated books were first introduced from the German lands, France, and Italy, shaping the artistic traditions of Polish scriptoria. The art of manuscript illumination reached a peak in the age of the Jagiellons, with prelates, scholars, and members of the dynasty acting as sponsors of manuscripts. In the lands of Rus', manuscript illuminations of the eleventh to thirteenth centuries were also influenced by those of Latin Europe. Western books with full-page illustrations and decorated initials arrived through dynastic connections and merged with features of Byzantine style.

Book culture in Central Europe was also originally the preserve of monastic institutions, but books reached a wider readership in the later Middle Ages, especially in urban milieus. Those who sent their sons to universities were often burghers. These educated men – and women who attended municipal schools or were taught at home – were interested in books for professional purposes or personal interest. They read books on legal and administrative matters, theology, or didactics, but also entertaining literature, history, and geography. Manuscript books were commissioned to professional scribes. One of the earliest such books, as attested by a note at the end of the manuscript, is a missal copied in 1399 in the diocese of Wrocław for a woman named Ursula, widow of a master craftsman. The scribe, Nicholas Brevis, had studied in Cracow. He made a living copying ecclesiastical books and legal compilations. Professional scribes such as Nicholas Brevis responded to the growing needs of an educated public.

Printing presses were established in Bohemia and Moravia in the 1460s, and in Hungary in 1473. More than half of the known books that were printed in Bohemia before 1500 were in the Czech language. In Poland, Kaspar Straube set up shop in Cracow in 1473 and printed calendars and theological works in Latin. Between 1489 and 1491, Schweipolt Fiol, another printer from Cracow, designed the very first printed books in Cyrillic script. These liturgical books in Church Slavonic were intended for readers in the Ruthenian lands of the kingdom and the grand duchy. Fiol's pioneering work, however, was immediately condemned by Catholic authorities. It inspired an entrepreneur in Montenegro who, beginning in 1493, printed Cyrillic books for the Serbian and Bulgarian markets. In the Balkans, books in Glagolitic script were already circulating by then: for example, a missal was printed in Venice for Croat readers. Books in Polish, however, did not appear in print before 1503. In Muscovy, the first printing press appeared only in the mid-sixteenth century.

FURTHER READING

Thomas, Alfred. *Anne's Bohemia: Czech Literature and Society, 1310–1420*. Medieval Cultures 13. Minneapolis: University of Minnesota Press, 1998.

Verkholantsev, Julia. *Ruthenica Bohemica: Ruthenian Translations from Czech in the Grand Duchy of Lithuania and Poland*. Slavische Sprachgeschichte 3. Vienna: Lit, 2008.

Verkholantsev, Julia. *The Slavic Letters of St. Jerome: The History of the Legend and Its Legacy, or, How the Translator of the Vulgate Became an Apostle of the Slavs*. DeKalb: Northern Illinois University Press, 2014.

Wallace, David, ed. *Europe: A Literary History, 1348–1418*. Vol. 2. Oxford: Oxford University Press, 2016.

69

UNIVERSITIES, EDUCATION, AND SCHOLARSHIP

Keywords in this chapter: universities, student life, Jewish academies

The earliest universities in Italy, France, and England had their origins in the twelfth century and gradually obtained privileges protecting their autonomy. Others appeared in Italy, the Iberian Peninsula, and southern France in the thirteenth century. Dublin had one in 1311. Central European students, by that time, could either attend cathedral schools or the schools of the mendicant orders, or go abroad. They often frequented French and Italian universities but did not go to Spain and rarely to England. The first Central European city to obtain a university was Prague. After Wenceslas II's failed attempt in the late thirteenth century, Charles IV requested Pope Clement VI's approval for the foundation of a university and obtained it in 1347. The new institution, with the archbishop as chancellor, was fully operational around 1360. Soon thereafter universities appeared in Cracow (1363), Vienna (1365), Pécs (1367), and, up to the early fifteenth century, in several cities of the German lands. Prague was the only Central European university, however, that reached a truly international reputation; the others primarily served regional needs.

The universities of Bohemia, Poland, and Hungary, like that of Naples established in 1224, had their origins in acts of foundation by rulers – Charles IV, Casimir III, and Louis I, who ruled in an era of growth and expansion in their respective kingdoms. The universities of Cracow, Vienna, and Pécs focused at first on law and lacked faculties of theology altogether; they responded to the needs of territorial governments. Charles IV endowed the university of Prague and augmented funding once competing establishments had been set up in Cracow and Vienna. Despite its royal origins, the university maintained academic autonomy until the heavy-handed interventions of Wenceslas IV. Universities founded slightly later, by contrast – Heidelberg, Cologne, or Erfurt – related to the expectations of municipal councils.

It was not Italian schools but Prague that was the model for the development of German universities. The institution of the college offering professors posts with lodging and salary, which was introduced in Prague by Charles IV, was emulated at other Central European universities. While in Paris the rector was invariably chosen from the Faculty of Arts, in Prague the post of rector rotated between faculties; the shared rectorate was adopted elsewhere in Central Europe. In Paris, only the Faculty of Arts was divided into four nations; in Prague, all faculties had four nations – those of Bohemia (which included Hungarians), Poland (including students from Rus' and Lithuania), Saxony (including Scandinavians), and Bavaria (including Austrians and Rhinelanders). University nations in Vienna and Leipzig followed the model of Prague. By contrast, and to avoid the frequent disputes that had arisen in Prague, the universities in Cracow, Pécs, Heidelberg, Cologne, Erfurt, and Rostock refrained from adopting the system of nations.

The papal schism that began in 1378 positively affected Prague. Paris theologians who opposed the Avignon papacy, such as those of the English and Picard nations, were eager to move to Prague or Vienna. In that context, Wenceslas IV established a new college to accommodate professors coming in from Paris, and the Prague Faculty of Theology even began to eclipse that of Paris in European reputation. Many might have been attracted to the newly established universities of Heidelberg and Cologne and have left Prague in 1388 and 1392, but Prague nonetheless remained the leading university of the region.

The establishment, in the early 1390s, of Bethlehem Chapel, where the preaching of university scholars was entirely in Czech, strengthened the self-confidence of the Czechs in the Prague Faculty of Arts. At the same time, the writings of John Wycliffe created a wedge between conservative German scholars, who stuck to traditional nominalism, and their Czech colleagues, who were attracted to innovative ideas and felt they were treated unfairly. The most divisive disputes that erupted were those involving matters of Christian doctrine. In 1403, German nominalists enforced a ban on the teachings of the ideas of Wycliffe that they regarded as heretical. Their Czech colleagues, however, obtained support from Wenceslas IV who, with the 1409 decree of Kutná Hora, merged the three German nations (Bavarians, Saxons, and Poles) into one, giving the nation of Bohemia the remaining three votes: Czech votes thus outnumbered German votes. Outraged by this move, most of the German scholars left Prague right away. Initially, though, the decree of Kutná Hora had little effect on the Faculty of Law, which had become a separate institution in 1372. Law students were primarily men with ecclesiastic positions and were conservatives who opposed the followers of John Hus. The faculty kept attracting foreign students for a while but was finally dissolved in 1419.

Most of the academic émigrés from Prague went to Heidelberg and Leipzig. Connections were well established with Heidelberg, where many Prague graduates had already taken up posts. The university of Leipzig was in fact founded as a direct result of the departure of German scholars from Prague. Others went to teach in Cracow. Not only had Prague lost many of its scholars, but those who left smeared its reputation, portraying it as a university of heretics. The Council of Constance suspended the university's recognition. Utraquist domination of university life long after the end of Hussite disruptions acted as deterrent for the recruitment of foreign students, so that Prague did not return to its earlier reputation.

The university of Cracow was founded in 1364 by Casimir III, who followed the example of Charles IV. It had Faculties of Law, Liberal Arts, and Medicine. The institution had a rough start, however, and by the end of the 1370s had ceased to operate. The driving force behind renewed attempts around 1390 to revive the university was Queen Jadwiga: she was interested in a university that would train qualified clerics to effectively advance the Christianization of Lithuania. The reformist bishop Peter Wysz, for his part, who had been elected with strong support of Jadwiga, hoped that restoring the university would elevate the intellectual qualifications of the Polish clergy. Jadwiga and Peter Wysz teamed up to advance the project and convince Władysław Jogaila to seek a papal privilege to establish a Faculty of Theology. The request was approved by Boniface IX in 1397.

Jadwiga's charitable work also supported education early on. She wrote to Wenceslas IV to allow the establishment of a college providing accommodation and financial support to Lithuanians studying theology in Prague. When Wenceslas approved her request in 1397, she purchased a building for them near the Bethlehem Chapel. It took some time, however, for the college to be fully set up and running. A first cohort of twelve students began their studies in 1411, long after Jadwiga's death in 1399; by that time, the original goal of privileging Lithuanian students might have been forgotten, but not Jadwiga's leading role: the institution was known as the Collegium Reginae (Queen's College).

Jadwiga remained committed to the university project to the end of her life. In her will, she urged her husband to pursue her efforts and bequeathed funds for the university. In 1400 Władysław Jogaila gave the university a building in the former Jewish quarter and issued an official charter of foundation. The hiring of professors and recruitment of students began; teaching and research resumed. Although Jogaila's charter did not mention Jadwiga by name, it quoted from her document for the Lithuanian theology students in Prague, thus indirectly acknowledging her influence. Jadwiga was long remembered – alongside Casimir and Władysław Jogaila – at celebratory and commemorative events for the crucial role she had played in the revival of the university.

Unlike Bohemia and Poland, in Hungary royal attempts at founding universities had no lasting results. Pope Urban V authorized in 1367 the establishment of a university in Pécs, at the request of Bishop William of Bergzabern. However, the institution did not survive. Efforts at establishing universities in (Old) Buda and Bratislava also failed. The solid book collections that were available at some Hungarian parish schools and in private property, however, attest that university studies and book culture appealed not only to the nobility but also to burghers. The universities of Vienna and Cracow were the most popular for Hungarian students in the fifteenth century. Cracow was especially attractive to students from the towns of Upper Hungary (present-day Slovakia). Hungarian students there had their own boarding house since 1464 – the *Bursa Hungarorum*, a college that offered accommodation and scholarships; the building had been purchased with the donation of a Polish nobleman, and most of its residents were from Szeged, Pest, or Buda. University records suggest that wine drinking was a common pastime of Hungarian students and that brawls were common – especially with groups of students of other nationalities. Traditions maintained by Hungarian students included older students beating younger ones on Saint Innocents' Day (December 28) to remind them of this Biblical event – a practice that was punished in Cracow.

As elsewhere in Europe, scholars at the universities of Prague and Cracow engaged in research with Arabic authors whose works had been translated into Latin. The study of optics, based on the work of Ibn al-Haytham (Alhazen), had been pioneered in the thirteenth century by Wittelo, a Silesian scholar who made a career in Italy and Poland. His work was pursued in Cracow by various researchers in the fifteenth century. John Stobner established the first chair of astronomy in Central Europe at the university of Cracow (1405). The study of Arabic scholarship in astronomy – the works of Alī ibn Rijāl (Hali Abenragel), for example – was introduced by Matthias of Koło, who had brought books he had acquired in Prague. Research in astronomy flourished with Martin Król of Żurawica, who had studied in Prague, Vienna, and Bologna; it was fully established when Nicholas Copernicus studied in Cracow, from 1491 to 1495, and examined the works of Averroes and al-Battānī.

The Muslims of Hungary are said to have followed the Sunnite branch of Islam. Abū Hāmid, the Andalusian scholar who sojourned in Hungary in the twelfth century, decried the poor knowledge of Hungarian Muslims in religious matters. In the early thirteenth century, however, evidence suggests that communities of Hungarian Muslims cared about access to a religious education. In 1217, a Hungarian nobleman encountered Hungarian Muslims in Jerusalem who facilitated his release from captivity. They were students who had traveled to the Near East to further their education.

During the twelfth and thirteenth centuries, Prague was the most important center of Jewish scholarship in East Central Europe. Rabbi Isaac ben Moses (ca. 1180–ca. 1250), author of an influential treatise of halakhic rulings that compiled the teachings of French and German masters, *Or Zaru'a*, was probably born in Bohemia. His familiarity with Czech culture is shown by his use of Slavic words in his writings.[1] Prague retained its reputation for Jewish learning in the Late Middle Ages. Rabbi Yom Tov Lipmann Mülhausen, for example, wrote a learned defense of Judaism in the fifteenth century to help his coreligionists against the polemics of Christian theologians. Poland had rabbis in the thirteenth century who corresponded with Torah scholars from the German lands and Bohemia to obtain advice in halakhic matters. Polish scholars are regularly mentioned in the correspondence of Rabbi Judah ben Samuel he-Ḥasid (ca. 1150–1217), who acted as their mentor. He-Ḥasid, born in Speyer, moved to Regensburg to establish an academy; from there, contacts with members of the Ashkenazi diaspora were easier. His work on ethics, the *Sefer Ḥasidim*, was very influential in the region.

1 Florin Curta, ed., "Jews in Medieval East Central Europe," in *Medieval Eastern Europe, 500–1300: A Reader* (Toronto: University of Toronto Press, 2024), 210.

FURTHER READING

Klaniczay, Gábor. "Late Medieval Central European Universities: Problems of Their Comparative History." In *Universitas Budensis 1395–1995: International Conference for the History of Universities on the Occasion of the 600th Anniversary of the Foundation of the University of Buda*, edited by László Szögi and Júlia Varga, 171–81. Budapest: ELTE, 1997.

Knoll, Paul. *"A Pearl of Powerful Learning": The University of Cracow in the Fifteenth Century*. Education and Society in the Middle Ages and Renaissance, 52. Leiden: Brill, 2016.

70

MONUMENTAL ART AND ARCHITECTURE IN THE LATE MIDDLE AGES

Keywords in this chapter: *katholikon*, synagogues, "brick Gothic"

Several building traditions intersected in East Central, Southeastern, and Eastern Europe between ca. 1000 and ca. 1500. From the south, Byzantine architecture developed new forms in the eleventh century. For example, the *katholikon* (monastery church) of the Monastery of St. Luke the Younger in Steiris (Boeotia, Greece) has a wide dome resting on a shallow, polygonal drum, one of the first examples of the domed cross-in-octagon type in Greece. New solutions for the treatment of the façade appear with the Church of the Holy Theodores in Athens and the Church of Our Lady of the Coppersmiths in Thessaloniki, both of which feature relief ceramic plaques and glazed tiles (see map 70.1). The Church of Our Lady of the Coppersmiths represents another architectural innovation known as the tetrastyle cross-in-square dome, because of the four pillars inside the nave (see plate 70.1). The mural decoration of the first phase, dated to 1028, contains typically Constantinopolitan themes.

Despite its dedication to St. Sophia, the church that Iaroslav the Wise built in Kiev during the first half of the eleventh century is different from both from the cathedral in Constantinople and the church in Thessaloniki with the same dedication (see chapter 41). While still based on the idea of a domed cross-in-square plan, the church in Kiev (see map 70.2) is a building with five apses and no fewer than thirteen domes surrounded by galleries and incorporating stairwell towers. The division of the interior space into smaller units – either cubical bays or shortened aisles – has no direct parallel in the Byzantine architecture and must be treated as a feature of the Rus' architecture. Byzantine, if not altogether Constantinopolitan, is the idea of decorating the dome, the central apse, and the four arches of the central crossing with mosaics. The remaining walls were covered with frescoes with

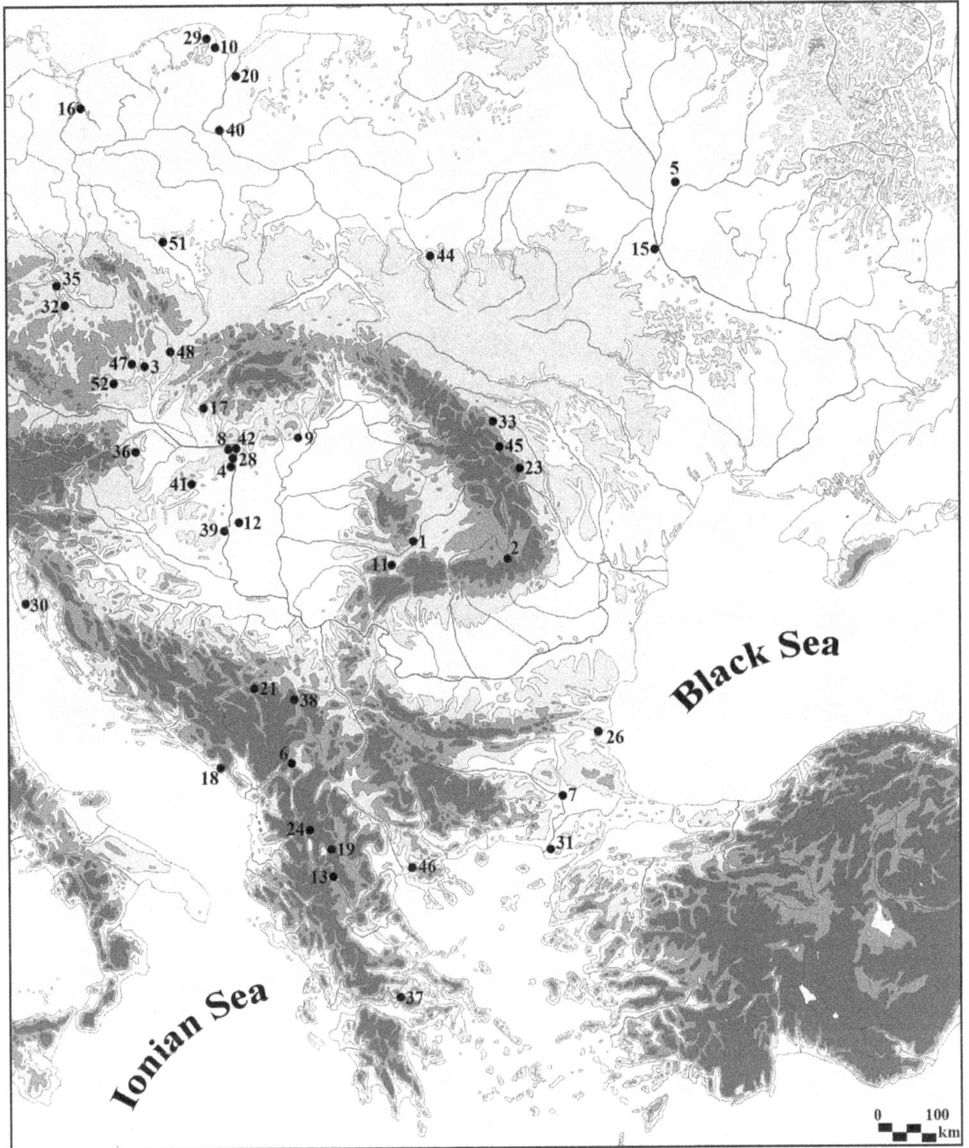

Map 70.1. Sites with monumental art, ca. 1000 to ca. 1500. The location of the following sites is indicated on Maps 70.1 and 70.2: 1 – Alba Iulia; 2 – Braşov; 3 – Brno; 4 – Buda; 5 – Chernihiv; 6 – Dečani; 7 – Edirne; 8 – Esztergom; 9 – Feldebrő; 10 – Gdańsk; 11 – Hunedoara; 12 – Kalocsa; 13 – Kastoria; 14 – Kaunas; 15 – Kiev; 16 – Kołbacz; 17 – Kostoľany pod Tribečom; 18 – Kotor; 19 – Kurbinovo; 20 – Malbork; 21 – Mileševa; 22 – Moscow; 23 – Neamţ; 24 – Nerezi; 25 – Nerl; 26 – Nesebăr; 27 – Novgorod; 28 – Nyék; 29 – Oliwa; 30 – Peroj; 31 – Pheres; 32 – Prague; 33 – Rădăuţi; 34 – Riga; 35 – Říp Mountain; 36 – Sopron; 37 – Steiris; 38 – Studenica; 39 – Szekszárd; 40 – Toruń; 41 – Veszprém; 42 – Visegrád; 43 – Vladimir; 44 – Vladimir-in-Volyhnia; 45 – Voroneţ; 46 – Thessaloniki; 47 – Tišnov; 48 – Tovačov; 49 – Üxküll; 50 – Vilnius; 51 – Wrocław; 52 – Znojmo.

extensive narrative cycles from the lives of Christ and the Virgin Mary, the apostles Peter and Paul, St. George, and other saints – all of which would become a typical feature of Rus' church decoration throughout the Late Middle Ages and even after 1500. The combination of mosaics and frescoes appears in the decoration of the Cathedral of the Dormition inside the Monastery of the Caves, which was inspired by the slightly earlier Cathedral of the Transfiguration in Chernihiv. Both churches consecrated the pyramidal, vertical emphasis

Plate 70.1. The Church of Our Lady of the Coppersmiths in Thessaloniki. Wikimedia Commons, the free media repository.

of the volumes that would become the distinctive feature of the Rus' architecture of the subsequent centuries. During the twelfth century, this architectural form appeared in the principality of Vladimir-Suzdal'. The façades of the Church of the Intercession on the Nerl (Bogoliubovo) and of the Cathedral of St. Demetrius in Vladimir, built in 1165/6 and 1197, are richly decorated with carvings betraying the influence of the Romanesque tradition discussed below. The same influence coming from Poland may be detected in the case of the churches of St. Michael (built before 1268) and St. Basil (built in 1294) in Vladimir-in-Volhynia (western Ukraine), both of which are rotundas (see chapter 41).

Irrespective of their architectural forms, twelfth-century churches in the Balkans are unique because of the number and quality of the surviving mural paintings. Constantinopolitan painters were responsible for the mural decoration of the church of the Monastery of the Mother of God *Kosmosoteira* at Pheres (northeastern Greece), painted shortly after the middle of the twelfth century; the Church of St. Panteleimon in Nerezi (near Skopje, North Macedonia), painted in 1164; and the Church of St. George in Kurbinovo (on the northeastern shore of Lake Prespa, North Macedonia), painted in 1191. Painters from Constantinople were also at work in the Cathedral of St. Sophia in Novgorod and at St. Michael of the Golden Domes in Kiev. Those working in the Church of the Savior of the Mileševa Monastery (near Užice, in southwestern Serbia), which was painted between 1222 and 1228, came from Thessaloniki (see plate 70.2). By contrast, the thirteenth-century churches in Kastoria (northern Greece), Mani (the southernmost region of continental Greece), and Bulgaria were painted by local artists, some of whom are mentioned in inscriptions.

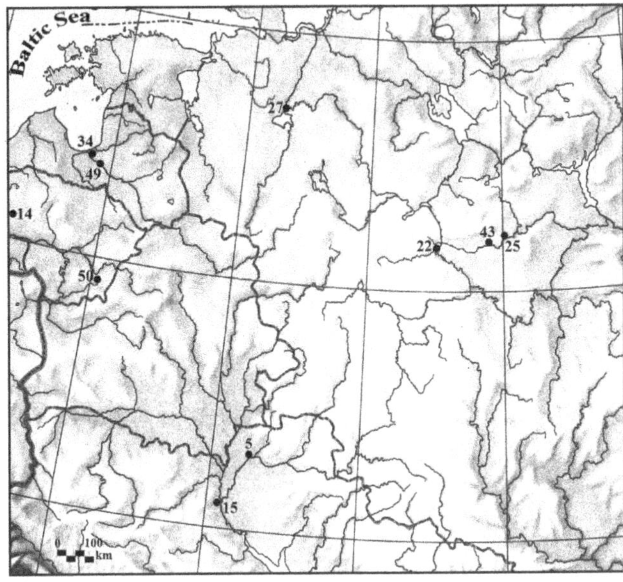

Map 70.2. Sites with monumental art, ca. 1000 to ca. 1500. For the location of sites, see map 70.1 and its caption.

The Byzantine tradition continued into the fourteenth and fifteenth centuries. The Church of the Pantokrator in Nesebăr (Bulgaria) has a cross-in-square plan and a dome decorated on the outside with bands of glazed ceramic discs. The triconch plan is a distinctive feature of a group of monuments in Serbia known as the "Morava School." They further inspired the church architecture of Wallachia from the late fourteenth to the early sixteenth centuries. Meanwhile, the Byzantine tradition also influenced the early Ottoman architecture. For example, the enormous dome of the Üç Şerefeli Cami in Edirne (Turkey), erected by Sultan Murad II between 1438 and 1447, was the largest such structure built since the sixth-century dome of Hagia Sophia in Constantinople.

Another important tradition is the Romanesque architecture, which was dominant in Western and Central Europe beginning with the mid-eleventh century. The earliest Romanesque churches in Hungary are of Italian inspiration – the church of the Benedictine abbey in Szekszárd (near Pécs, in southern Hungary), built in 1061, and the slightly later abbey church in Feldebrő (near Eger, northern Hungary). The capitals in the cathedral in Veszprém, which was built by Queen Gisela at some point before 1038, display ornaments inspired by stone carvings in Venice. Local lords in Hungary established both single-naved churches and rotundas built in the Romanesque style. Royal foundations, such as the cathedral of St. Michael in Alba Iulia (built in the eleventh century) and the cathedral in Esztergom (probably finished in the mid-twelfth century) were large, three-aisled basilicas without transept, but with two towers flanking the western façade. In Poland, the models for the earliest Romanesque churches came from the Holy Roman Empire. Most Romanesque churches may be associated with two prominent Piast founders – Casimir I and Bolesław II.

Nowhere in East Central Europe was the rotunda more popular between the eleventh and the thirteenth centuries than in Bohemia. The Church of St. George on the Říp Mountain near Mělník (central Bohemia) was built by Soběslav I after his 1126 victory at Chlumec against King Lothar III (see chapter 42). The most famous rotunda, however, is the Church of St. Catherine in Znojmo (Moravia), which was built in the late eleventh or early twelfth century. In the early twelfth century, that church received magnificent frescoes showing the Přemyslid genealogy of the local prince, Conrad (1061–92). One

Plate 70.2. The "White Angel," detail of the scene of the Myrrh-Bearing Women at the tomb of Christ, fresco on the southern wall of the Church of the Savior in the Mileševa Monastery (Serbia). Wikimedia Commons, the free media repository.

of the most significant examples of Romanesque mural decoration, the early twelfth-century frescoes in the Church of St. Fosca near Peroj (Istria, Croatia) were the work of an "itinerant" workshop from northern Italy. By contrast, a local artist working after models, possibly manuscript illuminations, was responsible for the wall paintings in the Church of St. George in Kostoľany pod Tribečom (near Nitra, Slovakia).

Cities in Bohemia and Moravia offer a glimpse into the secular use of Romanesque architecture. Particularly important in that respect is Prague, with no less than sixty-three still-standing Romanesque houses in the Old Town. Built in ashlar between the 1170s and the 1230s, each with two stories and vaults on the ground floor used for storage, those were houses of merchants involved in long-distance trade. A wealthy merchant, possibly involved with the Hanse, was responsible for the building of the so-called House of Perkūnas in Kaunas (Lithuania) in the late fifteenth century. Its Gothic architectural style had much in common with town halls such as those in Wrocław (ca. 1300), Gdańsk (1382), and Toruń (1391–1399).

The Gothic tradition, originating in France in the late twelfth century, made its first appearance in East Central Europe shortly after that. The cathedral built by Archbishop Berthold (1206–1218) in Kalocsa (Hungary) had an ambulatory with radiating chapels, a polygonal sanctuary, and a pair of towers to the west. During the second half of the thirteenth century, Gothic was also adopted in the architecture of castles, particularly that of Visegrád, built by King Béla IV and his wife. Even more significant is the adoption of that architectural style by Jewish communities, as in the case of the Old Synagogue of Sopron, built shortly before 1300. At that time, polygonal apses and Gothic vaults were also common in parish churches in western Hungary and Transylvania. The Cistercians had a major contribution to the spread of Gothic architecture to East Central Europe, for example the Cistercian abbeys of Kołbacz (1173) and Oliwa (1186), both in Eastern Pomerania. The church that Bishop Meinhard erected in Üxküll (now Ikšķile, in central Latvia) was most likely a timber building, followed by a stone, single-naved church with rib vaults. In the Baltic region, brick churches, such as those built in the thirteenth century in Riga, were large, three-aisled basilicas with westwork and conspicuously Gothic elements of decoration. The so-called "brick Gothic" was also adopted in those lands of Prussia that were conquered by the Teutonic Knights. One of the earliest examples of Gothic decorative carvings in East Central Europe is the monumental western portal of the abbey church in Tišnov, a foundation of Queen Constance, the wife of Přemysl Ottokar II (1180–1240). The apostle statues on either side of that portal are directly inspired by the Gothic art of northern France. The chapel of the Holy Virgin Mary in Brno shows, on the other hand, that by 1300, Gothic architecture had also entered the urban landscape.

Some of the most impressive monuments of the Gothic style in East Central Europe were built after 1300. The most famous is the Cathedral of St. Vitus in Prague, erected between 1367 and 1410. Its German architect, Peter Parler (1333–99), also built the Charles Bridge over the Vltava River. The east (Old Town) tower of that bridge contains a net vault, the first of its kind in Bohemia. In the south transept of the cathedral, Parler employed a triradial vault with flying ribs, an openwork spiral staircase, and blind tracery decoration for the window (see plate 70.3). A large mosaic showing the Last Judgment was later added

Plate 70.3. The Cathedral of St. Vitus in Prague (Czech Republic), view from the south. Wikimedia Commons, the free media repository.

to the façade to enhance the ceremonial role of this space, used primarily for coronations. The Black Church in Braşov (Romania), erected between 1383 and 1476, is the largest and easternmost extant Gothic church of Europe. One of the very few monuments of Gothic architecture in Lithuania is the Church of St. Anne in Vilnius, a brick building erected in 1500. Castles were also built in the Gothic style. Some were made of brick, such as the castle erected in Marienburg (Malbork, in Poland) around 1300 for the headquarters of the Teutonic Order; others were of stone, such as the castle built in 1446 in Hunedoara (Romania) by John Hunyadi, the governor of the Hungarian Kingdom (see plate 70.4).

John Hunyadi's son, King Matthias Corvinus (1458–90), together with Grand Prince Ivan III of Muscovy (1462–1505), first introduced to Central and Eastern Europe,

respectively, the fourth building tradition, that of the Italian Renaissance. In Moscow, the reconstruction of the Cathedral of the Dormition in the Kremlin (1475–79) was undertaken by an architect from Bologna named Rodolfo Fioravanti. Together with Marco Friasin, Pietro Antonio Solari (who came to Moscow in 1490) is responsible for the so-called "Faceted Palace" in the Kremlin, with its façade made of rough-surfaced masonry blocks, like that of fifteenth-century buildings in Ferrara or Bologna. The

Plate 70.4. The Hunyadi Castle in Hunedoara (Romania). Wikimedia Commons, the free media repository.

Cathedral of Archangel Michael in the Kremlin was built between 1505 and 1509 by Alevisio Lamberti da Montagnana, an architect from Venice, who used such elements of Renaissance decoration as Corinthian capitals for the pilasters and large shells for the lunettes. In Hungary, elements of Renaissance architecture were incorporated into the royal villa at Visegrád (north of Budapest), as well as the hunting lodge at Nyék (now within Budapest). In Buda, a Florentine architect named Chimenti Camicia built a courtyard for the king's palace in which he placed a statue of Athena on top of a fountain. Unfortunately, very little survives from the monumental art and architecture of the second half of the fifteenth century in Hungary (all of which was destroyed by the Ottoman occupation of the sixteenth century). The earliest examples of architecture under Italian influence cannot be dated before 1500. It is nonetheless known that several other Italian artists came to the court of King Matthias, who received, ordered, or tried to order works of art from prominent Renaissance painters. His example was quickly emulated elsewhere. A Moravian nobleman named Ctibor Továčovský z Cimburka had a portal built in 1492 for his castle in Tovačov (near Olomouc, Czech Republic) in Renaissance form, complete with an inscription in Latin. The most impressive monument of early Renaissance architecture in East Central Europe is the so-called Vladislav Hall in the Castle District of Prague. Upon succeeding Matthias Corvinus on the throne of Hungary in 1490, King Vladislav II of Bohemia (1471–1516) commissioned the German architect Benedict Ried (ca. 1450–1531) to build an addition to the Prague Castle. Between 1493 and 1502, Ried turned the upper part of the old palace built by Charles IV into the largest secular hall of late medieval Europe. This was designed for indoor tournaments, with more than a hundred riders participating at any one time. The hall's enormous vault is supported and organized by curved ribs in Late Gothic style (see plate 70.5). However, half-columns framing double windows on the southern façade, the fluted pilasters and columns on the portal leading from the Vladislav Hall into the old Parliament room, and Corinthian capitals decorating the exterior portal of the riders' staircase are all elements of Renaissance architecture.

The eastern part of Europe offers many other examples of blending architectural traditions. Some of the most impressive are from Serbia. Stephen Nemanja's most famous foundation of 1186, the Church of the Mother of God in the monastery of Studenica, is a surprising mixture of Byzantine and Romanesque architecture. The use of high-quality white marble for the façade, a portal with tympanum and lions, and an east window with scrolls and flanking figures jutting from the wall – all betray the workmanship of builders from southern Italy (see plate 70.6). At the same time, the frescoes that decorate the interior constitute a remarkable ensemble of Byzantine visual expression that can be attributed to painters from Constantinople. Similarly, the Church of the Pantokrator at Dečani Monastery was built between 1327 and 1355 for King Stephen Dečanski by Fra Vita, a Franciscan friar from Kotor (now in Montenegro). He drew inspiration from the Romanesque architecture of Italy, but the interior of the church is covered with frescoes in the Byzantine tradition. Much in the same vein, the earliest monuments of architecture

Plate 70.5. The Vladislav Hall in Prague (Czech Republic). Wikimedia Commons, the free media repository.

in Moldavia betray the influence of Romanesque architecture, as with the Church of St. Nicholas in the Bogdana Monastery in Rădăuți (northeastern Romania), built in ca. 1360. A distinctive regional style emerged in Moldavia under the reign of Prince Stephen III (1457–1504) through the blending of Gothic and Byzantine traditions. The Church of the Ascension at Neamț Monastery (near Târgu Neamț, Romania), built between 1486 and 1497, and the Church of St. George at Voroneț Monastery (near Suceava, Romania), built in 1488, are good illustrations of the Moldavian architecture. Each feature a naos surmounted by a steeple-like dome, as well as such Gothic elements of decoration as window frames and portals.

Plate 70.6. The Church of the Mother of God at the Studenica Monastery (Serbia), view from the north. Wikimedia Commons, the free media repository.

FURTHER READING

Benešovská, Klára, Petr Chotěbor, Tomáš Durdík, and Zdeněk Dragoun. *Architecture of the Romanesque*. Ten Centuries of Architecture 1. Prague: Prague Castle Administration, 2001.

Białostocki, Jan. *The Art of the Renaissance in Eastern Europe: Hungary, Bohemia, Poland*. Ithaca: Cornell University Press, 1976.

Čurčić, Slobodan. *Architecture in the Balkans: From Diocletian to Süleyman the Magnificent*. New Haven: Yale University Press, 2010.

Markus, Kersti. *Visual Culture and Politics in the Baltic Sea Region, 1100–1250*. East Central and Eastern Europe in the Middle Ages, 450–1450, 63. Leiden: Brill, 2020.

Rossi, Maria Alessia. "Monumental Art." In *The Routledge Handbook of East Central and Eastern Europe in the Middle Ages, 500–1300*, edited by Florin Curta, 506–29. Abingdon: Routledge, 2022.

Sullivan, Alice Isabella. "The Currency of the Gothic in the Carpathian Mountain Regions." In *Lateness and Modernity in Medieval Architecture*, edited by Alice Isabella Sullivan and Kyle G. Sweeney, 287–313. AVISTA Studies in Medieval Technology, Science and Art 16. Leiden: Brill, 2023.

Szakács, Béla Zsolt. "The Place of East Central Europe on the Map of Romanesque Architecture." In *Medieval East Central Europe in a Comparative Perspective: From Frontier Zones to Lands in Focus*, edited by Gerhard Jaritz and Katalin G. Szende, 205–24. London: Routledge, 2016.

Takács, Imre. "The First Century of Gothic in Hungary." In *The Art of Medieval Hungary*, edited by Xavier Barral i Altet, Pál Lővei, Vinni Lucherini, and Imre Takács. Bibliotheca Academiae Hungaricae – Roma. Studia 7. Rome: Viella, 2018.

71

HUMANISM IN EAST CENTRAL EUROPE

Keywords in this chapter: Renaissance, astronomy, library

While in late medieval Bulgaria and Muscovy, literary innovation was shaped by the study of Greek and Byzantine literature, new translations, and spelling reforms in Church Slavonic (see chapter 68), in Western Europe renewal came from the intensified study of classical Latin literature by humanists. The word "humanist," derived from Cicero's phrase *studia humanitatis*, has been used since the fifteenth century to refer to scholars of classical literature in Latin (and, to a lesser extent, Greek and Hebrew) and the values they associated with it. Humanists followed in the footsteps of the pioneer, Petrarch. While their movement started in Italy of the fourteenth century, in the later fifteenth century the passion for ancient languages and literature expanded to various parts of Europe.

Humanism arrived in Poland and Hungary through students, mostly from the lower aristocracy, who had attended Italian universities. Poland had in the late fifteenth century its *Sodalitas litteraria Vistulana*, a learned society established by John Heydecke and Conrad Pickel, who also contributed to founding its Hungarian counterpart, the *Sodalitas litteraria Danubiana*. Pickel taught in Cracow; he wrote commentaries on Plato, Horace, and Seneca and staged comedies of Plautus and Terence. Filippo Buonaccorsi, known as Callimachus, was an Italian poet and politician; he arrived in Poland in 1470 and became a leading humanist there. He taught the sons of Casimir IV and maintained connections with the court of Matthias Corvinus. Callimachus's poetry and historical works that centered on Poland and Hungary, however, found wider reception in printed form only after his death. John Długosz (1420–80), a teacher of the young Władysław Jogaila, regularly visited Italy; his historical writing was inspired by the style of Roman historians and by the text criticism of the humanists. Humanist thought, however, did not fully dominate in Poland's scholarship and court culture until the sixteenth century, when it ushered in a literary revival in both Latin and Polish.

Humanism reached Silesia in the late fifteenth century, where it appealed to bishops and members of municipal councils. John Roth was born in Bavaria; he studied in Rome (with the famous humanist Lorenzo Valla) and Bologna before serving at the royal courts of Bohemia and Hungary, and at the imperial court. He was appointed bishop of Wrocław in 1482 at the request of Matthias Corvinus. Corresponding with the most renowned Italian humanists of his time, John Roth was passionate about ancient Roman literature; he collected a large library and attracted scholars with similar interests. Lorenz Rabe, who Latinized his name as Laurentius Corvinus, was the son of a councilor in Środa in Silesia. He studied in Cracow and was appointed school rector and municipal secretary in Wrocław. Friend with the German humanists Conrad Celtis and Heinrich Bebel, he was also devoted to classical literature. He staged comedies of Terence and Plautus at the City Hall and wrote poetry. His didactic book on geography, the *Cosmographia*, extolled the historical importance of Poland and Silesia.

Humanism had a more limited impact in the Czech lands. Charles IV, who had a keen interest in languages, was attracted to humanism in its infancy. He and his wife Anne of Świdnica entertained friendly contacts with Petrarch. In the post-Hussite period, however, Bohemia did not provide much fertile ground for the reception of external cultural influences. Moravia had been exposed to early humanist thought since the time when John of Środa (Neumarkt), the chancellor of Charles IV, had occupied the post of bishop of Olomouc (from 1374 to his death in 1380). Humanist influence returned when Bishop John Filipec of Várad (Oradea) was named administrator of Olomouc from 1484 to 1490, at the request of Matthias Corvinus. Stanislav Thurzó was elected bishop of Olomouc in 1497; he was the brother of John Thurzó, who became bishop of Wrocław in 1506. The Thurzó brothers had studied in Cracow and surrounded themselves with poets and scholars while sponsoring humanist education.

Central European humanism thrived the most in Hungary where, during the reign of Matthias Corvinus and Beatrice of Aragón, it was promoted at the royal court and in the circles of the higher clergy. Matthias's father, John Hunyadi, entrusted his education to respected scholars such as his trusted advisor, the bishop of Oradea, John Vitéz. From a young age, Matthias became fluent in Latin while also learning German, Czech, and Italian. As king, he surrounded himself with scholars, artists, and poets. After a brief marriage to Catherine of Poděbrady, Matthias was married a second time, in 1476, to Beatrice, daughter of Ferdinand (Ferrante) of Aragón, king of Naples. Just like Matthias, Beatrice had enjoyed a solid education: she grew up studying Cicero and Virgil with a private tutor. Beatrice did not speak Hungarian, but at their wedding, she impressed the audience with an oration in Latin. The marriage strengthened connections between Naples and Hungary at a time when the university of Naples attracted students from Hungary who intermingled with those from Italy and Spain. Matthias and Beatrice were both fond of humanist culture and entertained cordial relationships with Lorenzo de Medici in Florence.

The court of Matthias and Beatrice, held at Buda and Visegrád, attracted international attention. The Hungarian astronomer Johann Tolhopf, after an education in Italy, became professor in Ingolstadt and Leipzig and was a regular visitor. Hungarian scribes and book illuminators studied in Italy and found employment at the royal court. Beatrice brought to Buda some of the best Italian musicians of the time, such as the lutenist Pietro Bono, who spent fifteen years in Hungary. The castle in Buda and the residence in Visegrád were restored in Renaissance style, inspired by Italian models. Matthias and Beatrice, both avid readers, were fond of learned discussion at the dinner table and regularly left their guests confounded. Humanist culture, however, had little influence outside of the royal court, perceived as an eccentric island of sophisticated culture.

The mastermind of the Hungarian renaissance was John Vitéz, archbishop of Esztergom since 1465. A man of Slavonian origin, he might have studied in Zagreb; he was briefly a student in Vienna. Trained in traditional scholasticism, he became enthralled by Italian humanism at the courts of Sigismund of Luxembourg, Albert I of Habsburg, and Frederick III. Once archbishop, Vitéz welcomed Italian humanists in Hungary and was instrumental in the foundation of a university in Bratislava. Keen to access the most accurate texts of classical authors, he collected books in Greek and Latin. Another leading Hungarian humanist was the king's nephew, John Csezmicei, known as Janus Pannonius (1434–72). Probably of Slavonian background, he studied Latin and Greek for eleven years in Ferrara before being appointed bishop of Pécs and ban of Slavonia. As an author, he wrote satirical verses and love poems with a strong dose of eroticism. Janus Pannonius and Matthias Corvinus ended up in a dispute, however, and Pannonius died in 1472 while in exile in Italy.

Matthias Corvinus was eager to attract foreign humanists: he needed talented civil servants to build a more centralized and sophisticated government. Few foreign scholars, however, were interested in a country where humanist culture was restricted to the bubble of the royal court. An exception was Johannes Müller von Königsberg (Regiomontanus), an expert in astronomy who spent a long time in Buda where he oversaw the collection of Greek books. Matthias, who was passionate about astronomy, established an observatory in Buda. The Italian humanists who stayed in Hungary tended to be scholars of second rank. Paolo Vergerio (1370–1444), a pedagogue and humanist from Florence, worked in the chancery of Sigismund of Luxembourg before moving to Buda. Taddeo Ugoleto, tutor of Matthias's son John, oversaw the royal library. Antonio Bonfini, who spent years at the court, wrote a Latin chronicle in classical style that covered the period of Matthias Corvinus and disseminated his nickname (which Matthias did not adopt himself but was used in his lifetime). Bonfini claimed that the Hunyadis, whose coat of arms depicted a raven, were descended from Valerius Corvinus of ancient Rome, himself born of the seed of Jupiter. Courtly literature written in Latin extolled the history and culture of Hungary, presenting Hungarians as defenders of Christendom against the Ottoman threat.

A major achievement of Hungarian humanism was the Biblioteca Corviniana, the royal library established by Matthias Corvinus and Beatrice of Aragón that had received massive investments since the early 1480s. Beatrice came from a family of bibliophiles. Her father Ferdinand and her brother Cardinal John – who for some time was employed by the archbishop of Esztergom – both had remarkable book collections. They were especially fond of richly decorated manuscripts that served as displays of both authority and erudition. The coat of arms of Beatrice can be found on many Corviniana codices. Scribes and artists were active in the palace scriptoria; others were hired to copy manuscripts in Italy. Taddeo Ugoletti was sent to German libraries. Despite the existence of a printing press in Buda, the library's books were primarily manuscripts, often richly decorated.

The books were held in two halls in the palace, one for Latin books, the other for books in Greek. Matthias and Beatrice wanted a library to provide scholars of the court with comprehensive knowledge of the ancient and modern worlds. At the end of Matthias's reign, it is said that the Corviniana comprised 2,000 volumes and was the largest library in Europe after that of the Vatican. The collected books concerned philosophy, history, poetry, astronomy, medicine, theology, and more. The collection included most of the scholarship and literature that were available in fifteenth-century Europe – the works of most of the authors of ancient Rome and Greece that were known to humanists alongside books of late medieval scholars in a variety of disciplines. While among the latter the works of Italian authors clearly dominated, Hungarian and German scholars were also represented – for example Regiomontanus or the Austrian Georg Peurbach in astronomy, Matthias's pet discipline. The works of scholars from France or England, however, had a lesser presence.

Despite the eccentricities of the royal court, most of the high nobles of Hungary remained, in the Late Middle Ages, illiterate and unable to sign documents with their names. The literate men were clerics or laymen engaged in chanceries; even the training of the latter was often narrowly limited to legal and practical matters. John Thuróczy, for example, was from the lesser nobility and became notary at the court of the royal judge. His *Chronicle of the Hungarians* was a collage of existing works with limited interventions from the author; the part of the narrative that he wrote himself, covering events after 1387, was based on charters and oral recollections of contemporaries. The chronicle attests to Thuróczy's restricted knowledge of classical Latin.

When Matthias Corvinus died in 1490, Beatrice of Aragón intended to succeed him. Never very popular in Hungary, however, she was regarded as a foreign queen who had not given birth to an heir. She married Vladislav II, the king of Bohemia (see chapter 48), who, once he had secured the throne, immediately attempted to annul the marriage. Despite Beatrice's protests – she lived in Esztergom, surrounded by Italians – the marriage was formally dissolved in 1500 and Beatrice returned to Naples. Vladislav II inherited the Biblioteca Corviniana. Investments in broadening the collection rapidly declined but the library was, however, maintained; at the time of the battle of Mohács (1526), it was in a similar state as at Matthias's death.

FURTHER READING

Borkowska, Urszula. "Humanism at the Court of the Jagellons." In *Christianity in East Central Europe: Late Middle Ages. La chrétienté en Europe du Centre-Est: Le bas Moyen Âge*, edited by Jerzy Kłoczowski, 147–56. Lublin: Instytut Europy Środkowo-Wschodniej, 1999.

Farbaky, Péter, Enikő Spekner, Katalin Szende, and András Végh, eds. *Matthias Corvinus, the King: Tradition and Renewal in the Hungarian Court 1458–1490*. Budapest: Történeti Múzeum, 2008.

Földesi, Ferenc, ed. *A Star in the Raven's Shadow: János Vitéz and the Beginnings of Humanism in Hungary*. Budapest: National Széchényi Library, 2008.

CONCLUSION

While there is no specific event that marked a definitive turning point between the medieval and early modern periods in East Central or Eastern Europe, the early sixteenth century witnessed several important changes and developments. The victory of Suleyman the Magnificent against Hungarian troops at the battle of Mohács in 1526 was the culmination of Ottoman advances on European soil that had begun in the fourteenth century. As a result, not only were the Balkans under the domination of an Islamic empire that encompassed European, Near Eastern, and North African territories, but the kingdom of Hungary was now also partitioned – one part Ottoman, the other under another emerging power in Europe, the Habsburgs. The Habsburgs, meanwhile, had built an empire coming out of Austria that comprised a large part of Central Europe (German lands, Bohemia, Silesia, part of Hungary) along with the Netherlands, Spain, and Spanish colonies in the Americas.

The union between the kingdom of Poland and the grand duchy of Lithuania led to the creation of the Commonwealth of the Two Nations with the treaty of Lublin in 1569. The Commonwealth, one of the largest territorial states in Europe at the time, had a unique political system in which the Sejm, the assembly of the nobility, counterbalanced the power of the monarchy. With culturally and religiously diverse populations (Catholics, Orthodox, Uniates, Jews, Tatar Muslims), the Commonwealth gained a reputation for religious tolerance in an age marked by wars along religious and confessional lines in Western Europe.

Muscovy continued its ascension as the dominating power in Eastern Europe. Ivan IV the Terrible, grand prince of Moscow, took the title of tsar of all Russia in 1547. Tsar (or emperor, derived from Caesar) had been, until then, the Old Slavonic title given to Roman (as well as Bulgarian and Serbian) emperors and to Mongol khans. The theory emerged that, after the fall of Constantinople, Muscovy (or Russia, as it was now known) was the successor of the Byzantine Empire, and Moscow, after Constantinople, was now the Third Rome. What was left of the Golden Horde, meanwhile, remained in the form of the Crimean khanate; instead of being connected to Mongolia and China, though, it was subordinated to the Ottomans based in what is now Turkey.

West European powers (France, England, Spain, Portugal, the Dutch) built world empires in the sixteenth century that stretched across the oceans to the Americas as well as to African and Asian colonies; a new world system was emerging that was quite different from the one that had existed in the Middle Ages. The connections between Europe, the Near East, and Asia that had thrived in the thirteenth and fourteenth centuries were built on the pursuit of commercial, more than political interests; while the Mongol Empire played an important role in facilitating these connections, the system was built on a balancing act as European, Near Eastern, and Asian powers profited from exchanges that connected Europe, the Islamic world, and China. The early modern world system, by contrast, was built on one-sided European hegemony and colonialism.

East Central and Eastern Europe might have lost, in the early modern age, the key strategic position the region had throughout the Middle Ages in connecting various civilizations, but it long retained cultural and religious diversity as a characteristic feature of its societies. Paganism had remained alive and well there longer than anywhere else on the continent, even peacefully coexisting with Christianity; Jewish and Muslim minorities had strong roots in the region and maintained centuries-long traditions; Catholics and Orthodox cohabited for centuries and found ways to accommodate their differences. Literary traditions continued to develop not only in multiple languages but also with various scripts – Latin, Cyrillic and Glagolitic, Hebrew and Arabic – that are fully part of European culture and history. Hopefully, this book will have shown that the history of Europe in the Middle Ages is more complex than a focus on the western parts of the continent would suggest.

INDEX

Note: Page numbers in *italics* refer to plates, maps, and tables.